Foundations for the LPC

put your knowledge into practice

@ Business Law
J. Scott Slorach and Jason G. Ellis

@ Foundations for the LPC
George Miles et al.

@ Lawyers' Skills
Julian Webb et al.

@ Criminal Litigation Handbook
Martin Hannibal and Lisa Mountford

@ Civil Litigation Handbook
Susan Cunningham-Hill and Karen Elder

@ Property Law Handbook
Robert Abbey and Mark Richards

@ A Practical Approach to Civil Procedure
Stuart Sime

@ A Practical Approach to Conveyancing
Robert Abbey and Mark Richards

@ A Practical Approach to ADR
Susan Blake et al.

@ Commercial Law
Robert Bradgate and Fidelma White

@ Employment Law
James Holland and Stuart Burnett

@ Family Law Handbook
Jane Sendall

Interactive online resources
www.oxfordinteract.com

↗ LPC Skills Online
Liz Polding and Jill Cripps

↗ LPC Accounts Online
James Catchpole

For more vocational law titles please visit www.oxfordtextbooks.co.uk

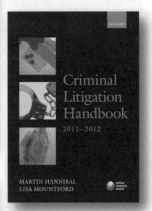

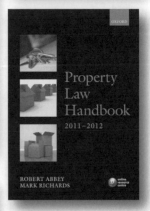

Foundations for the LPC

Professional Conduct
Kathryn Wright, LLB, Solicitor, Senior Lecturer, BPP Law School, Leeds

Financial Services and Money Laundering
Clare Firth, LLB, Solicitor (non-practising), Senior Lecturer in Legal Practice, formerly Director of Legal Practice, University of Sheffield and
Pauline Laidlaw, LLB, Solicitor (non-practising), Deputy Director of Legal Practice, University of Sheffield

Revenue Law
Clare Firth, Pauline Laidlaw

Probate and Administration of Estates
George Miles, LLB (Exon), Solicitor, sometime Associate Dean, Head of Professional Legal Studies, Faculty of Law, University of the West of England, Bristol and
Paulene Denyer, LLB (Hull), LLM (Lond), Solicitor, Senior Lecturer, Bristol Institute of Legal Practice, University of the West of England, Bristol

EU Law
Zoe Ollerenshaw, LLB, Solicitor and Senior Lecturer, University of Sheffield

Human Rights
Elizabeth Smart, Senior Academic, BPP Law School, Leeds

OXFORD
UNIVERSITY PRESS

Great Clarendon Street, Oxford OX2 6DP

Oxford University Press is a department of the University of Oxford.
It furthers the University's objective of excellence in research, scholarship,
and education by publishing worldwide in

Oxford New York

Auckland Cape Town Dar es Salaam Hong Kong Karachi
Kuala Lumpur Madrid Melbourne Mexico City Nairobi
New Delhi Shanghai Taipei Toronto

With offices in

Argentina Austria Brazil Chile Czech Republic France Greece
Guatemala Hungary Italy Japan Poland Portugal Singapore
South Korea Switzerland Thailand Turkey Ukraine Vietnam

Oxford is a registered trademark of Oxford University Press
in the UK and in certain other countries

Published in the United States
by Oxford University Press Inc., New York

© The authors hold the copyright for their respective chapters 2011

The moral rights of the authors have been asserted
Database right Oxford University Press (maker)

Contains public sector information licensed under the Open Government Licence v1.0
(http://www.nationalarchives.gov.uk/doc/open-government-licence/open-government-licence.htm)

Crown Copyright material reproduced with the permission of the Controller, HMSO (under
the terms of the Click Use licence)

Twelfth edition 2008
Thirteenth edition 2009
Fourteenth edition 2010

All rights reserved. No part of this publication may be reproduced,
stored in a retrieval system, or transmitted, in any form or by any means,
without the prior permission in writing of Oxford University Press,
or as expressly permitted by law, or under terms agreed with the appropriate
reprographics rights organization. Enquiries concerning reproduction
outside the scope of the above should be sent to the Rights Department,
Oxford University Press, at the address above

You must not circulate this book in any other binding or cover
and you must impose the same condition on any acquirer

British Library Cataloguing in Publication Data
Data available

Typeset by Laserwords Private Ltd, Chennai, India
Printed in Great Britain
on acid-free paper by
Ashford Colour Press Ltd, Gosport, Hampshire

ISBN 978–0–19–960937–6

10 9 8 7 6 5 4 3 2 1

OUTLINE CONTENTS

Preface	xv
Online resources to accompany this book	xvi
Acknowledgements	xviii
Table of Cases	xix
Table of Statutes	xxii
Table of Statutory Instruments	xxvi
Table of EU Legislation	xxvii
Table of EU Secondary Legislation	xxviii
Table of International Treaties and Conventions	xxix
Table of Codes of Conduct	xxx

Professional conduct — 1

1	Introduction	3
2	Financial services	41
3	Money laundering	59

Revenue law — 65

4	An introduction to revenue law	67
5	Income tax	73
6	Capital gains tax	93
7	Inheritance tax	109
8	Corporation tax	147
9	Value added tax	159
10	Taxation of sole proprietors and partnerships	169
11	Taxation of trusts and settlements	185

Wills and administration of estates — 197

12	Introduction to wills and administration of estates	199
13	Entitlement to the estate	201
14	Application for a grant of representation	241
15	Post-grant practice	285

EU Law — 325

16	EU Law	327

Human rights — 371

17	Human rights	373

APPENDIX 1 Answers to self-test questions	397
APPENDIX 2 Investments	399
Index	405
Taxation rates and allowances for 2011/2012	421

DETAILED CONTENTS

Preface	xv
Online resources to accompany this book	xvi
Acknowledgements	xviii
Table of Cases	xix
Table of Statutes	xxii
Table of Statutory Instruments	xxvi
Table of EU Legislation	xxvii
Table of EU Secondary Legislation	xxviii
Table of International Treaties and Conventions	xxix
Table of Codes of Conduct	xxx

Professional conduct — 1

1 Introduction — 3
1.1 An era of change — 3
1.2 A brief history of legal ethics — 4
1.3 How this chapter is divided — 6
1.4 What being a member of the profession and a good solicitor means — 6
1.5 The Handbook — 11
1.6 Practical application of the OFR Code — 16
1.7 Professional conduct and the LPC core subject areas — 27
1.8 Suggested solutions to Chapter 1 activities — 30

2 Financial services — 41
General introduction to the regulation of financial services — 41
2.1 Introduction — 41
2.2 Relevance to solicitors — 47
2.3 The regulatory regime — 48
2.4 Financial promotions — 49
Solicitors and the financial services legislation — 49
2.5 Solicitors regulated by the Solicitors Regulation Authority — 49
2.6 Conclusion: solicitors and the financial services legislation — 55
2.7 Commentary to scenarios — 56

3 Money laundering — 59
3.1 Introduction — 59
3.2 Money laundering — 59
3.3 The legislation — 60
3.4 The offences — 60
3.5 Relevance to solicitors — 61
3.6 Money laundering: checkpoints — 63

Revenue law — 65

4 An introduction to revenue law — 67
4.1 The history of taxation — 67
4.2 Changing taxes — 67
4.3 Taxes in the LPC context — 67
4.4 The main taxes — 68
4.5 The EC dimension — 68
4.6 Sources of tax law — 68
4.7 Administration of income tax, capital gains tax, and corporation tax — 69
4.8 Administration of inheritance tax — 70
4.9 Administration of value added tax — 70
4.10 Who pays tax? — 71
4.11 Tax planning — 72

5 Income tax — 73
5.1 Introduction: basic structure of income tax — 73
5.2 Calculation of income tax — 75
5.3 Rates of tax — 75
5.4 Total income — 76
5.5 Grossing up — 77
5.6 Reliefs — 80
5.7 Personal reliefs treated as income tax deductions — 82
5.8 Applying the rates of tax to statutory income — 83
5.9 Personal reliefs treated as income tax reductions — 84
5.10 Deduction of tax deducted at source — 86
5.11 Date for payment — 87
5.12 Appeals — 88
5.13 Back-duty cases — 89
5.14 Conclusion: checkpoints — 89
5.15 Income tax calculations — 89

6 Capital gains tax — 93
6.1 Introduction: basic structure of capital gains tax (CGT) — 93
6.2 Who pays CGT? — 94
6.3 The charge to CGT — 95
6.4 Chargeable assets — 96
6.5 Disposal — 96
6.6 Calculation of the gain — 97
6.7 Capital losses — 99
6.8 Exemptions and reliefs — 100
6.9 Taxation of the chargeable gain (the applicable rates of tax) — 104
6.10 Instalment option — 105
6.11 Assets held at 31 March 1982 — 105
6.12 Disposals of part — 106
6.13 Tax planning — 106
6.14 Example — 107
6.15 Conclusion: checkpoints — 107

7	**Inheritance tax**	**109**
7.1	Introduction: basic structure of inheritance tax (IHT)	109
7.2	The charge to inheritance tax	110
7.3	Potentially exempt transfers	111
7.4	The transfer of value on death	112
7.5	The occasions to tax	112
7.6	The charge to tax and a lifetime chargeable transfer	119
7.7	The charge to tax and a lifetime chargeable transfer where the transferor dies within seven years of the lifetime chargeable transfer	126
7.8	The charge to tax and a PET	130
7.9	The charge to tax and death	132
7.10	Gifts subject to a reservation	139
7.11	Liability, burden, and payment of tax	140
7.12	Tax planning	142
7.13	Conclusion: checkpoints	143
7.14	Commentary to exercises	144
8	**Corporation tax**	**147**
8.1	Introduction: basic structure of corporation tax (CT)	147
8.2	Taxable profits	147
8.3	Calculation of income profits	147
8.4	Capital allowances	149
8.5	Trading loss relief	149
8.6	Calculation of chargeable gains	150
8.7	Charges on income	151
8.8	Rates of tax	152
8.9	Distributions of profit	153
8.10	Calculating the liability	154
8.11	Payment of CT	154
8.12	Close companies	154
8.13	Steps to calculate CT, including chargeable gains	156
8.14	Example of CT calculations	157
8.15	Conclusion: checkpoints	158
9	**Value added tax**	**159**
9.1	Introduction to value added tax (VAT)	159
9.2	Sources of VAT law	159
9.3	Administration of VAT	160
9.4	Classifications of supply	160
9.5	Inputs and outputs	161
9.6	The charge to VAT	162
9.7	Registration	163
9.8	Rates of tax and tax points	164
9.9	Accounting for VAT	165
9.10	Penalties	167
9.11	Conclusion: checkpoints	168
10	**Taxation of sole proprietors and partnerships**	**169**
10.1	Introduction to the taxation of sole proprietors and partnerships	169

10.2	Income tax liability of partnerships	169
10.3	Basis of assessment: accounting basis	171
10.4	Basis of assessment: taxation basis	171
10.5	Starting a new business: the opening-year rules	172
10.6	Ceasing business: the closing-year rules	174
10.7	Overlap relief	175
10.8	Changes in the membership of a partnership	175
10.9	Capital allowances	177
10.10	Partnerships: allocation of profits/losses between partners	180
10.11	Trading loss relief	180
10.12	Statutory income	182
10.13	Taxable income	183
10.14	Conclusion: checkpoints	183
11	**Taxation of trusts and settlements**	**185**
11.1	Introduction and background	185
11.2	Inheritance tax	186
11.3	Capital gains tax	191
11.4	Income tax	193
11.5	Conclusion: checkpoints	195

Wills and administration of estates 197

12	**Introduction to wills and administration of estates**	**199**
12.1	Introduction	199
12.2	Breakdown of the task	199
13	**Entitlement to the estate**	**201**
13.1	Basic structure of entitlement to the estate	201
13.2	Wills	201
13.3	Validity of wills	202
13.4	Revocation of a will	207
13.5	Alterations in wills	210
13.6	Incorporation by reference	211
13.7	Failure of gifts by will	212
13.8	Gifts to children in wills	217
13.9	Wills: checkpoints	218
13.10	Intestacy	219
13.11	Intestacy: the basic position	220
13.12	Entitlement where there is a surviving spouse (or a surviving civil partner) of the intestate	221
13.13	Issue of the intestate	224
13.14	Other relatives of the intestate	225
13.15	The Crown	225
13.16	Inheritance tax and intestacy	225
13.17	Intestacy: checkpoints	226
13.18	Property not passing under the will or the intestacy rules	228
13.19	Property passing outside the will or intestacy rules	228
13.20	Property not forming part of the succession estate but forming part of the deceased's estate for inheritance tax purposes	230

13.21	Property not forming part of the deceased's estate for succession or inheritance tax purposes	230
13.22	Property not passing under the will or the intestacy rules: checkpoints	231
13.23	Provision for family and dependants	231
13.24	The basis of the claim for provision	232
13.25	The application	232
13.26	The applicant	233
13.27	Reasonable financial provision	234
13.28	The guidelines	235
13.29	Family provision orders	238
13.30	Property available for financial provision orders	238
13.31	Family provision: checkpoints	239
14	**Application for a grant of representation**	**241**
14.1	Introduction	241
14.2	Grants of representation	241
14.3	Responsibilities of solicitors instructed by personal representatives	242
14.4	The effect of the issue of a grant	243
14.5	Grant not necessary	244
14.6	Types of grant	245
14.7	Personal representatives: capacity	247
14.8	Personal representatives: several claimants	248
14.9	Personal representatives: number	249
14.10	Personal representatives: renunciation/power reserved	249
14.11	Grants of representation: checkpoints	250
14.12	Obtaining the grant: practice overview	251
14.13	Registering the death	253
14.14	Preparing the papers to lead the grant	254
14.15	Funds for payment of inheritance tax	254
14.16	Swearing or affirming the oath	256
14.17	Lodging the papers	256
14.18	Obtaining the grant: practice overview: checkpoints	256
14.19	The court's requirements: oaths	257
14.20	The requirements generally	258
14.21	Oath for executors	258
14.22	Oath for administrators with will annexed	265
14.23	Oath for administrators	268
14.24	Further affidavit evidence	273
14.25	The court's requirements: checkpoints	274
14.26	HMRC's requirements	275
14.27	Excepted estates	276
14.28	Form IHT 400	280
14.29	Form IHT 400 Calculation	283
14.30	Summary	283
14.31	HMRC's requirements: checkpoints	284
15	**Post-grant practice**	**285**
15.1	Introduction	285

15.2	Duties and powers of personal representatives	285
15.3	Duties of personal representatives	285
15.4	Administrative powers of personal representatives	287
15.5	Duties and powers of personal representatives: checkpoints	294
15.6	Administering the estate	294
15.7	Protection of personal representatives	295
15.8	Financial services	298
15.9	Collecting/realising the assets	299
15.10	Payment of debts (solvent estate)	301
15.11	Payment of debts (insolvent estate)	303
15.12	Post-death changes	305
15.13	Administering the estate: checkpoints	307
15.14	Distributing the estate	308
15.15	Payment of legacies	308
15.16	Ascertainment of residue	311
15.17	Estate accounts	314
15.18	Assents	317
15.19	Financial services	319
15.20	Beneficiaries' rights and remedies	319
15.21	Distributing the assets: checkpoints	321

EU law — 325

16	**EU law**	**327**
	The European Union, its institutions and sources of law	**327**
16.1	Introduction	327
16.2	The institutions	327
16.3	The sources of EU law	331
16.4	The European Union, its institutions, and sources of law: checkpoints	333
	The relationship between EU and national law	**333**
16.5	Introduction	333
16.6	The concept of direct effect	333
16.7	Supremacy	336
16.8	The relationship between EU and national law: checkpoints	337
	Remedies	**338**
16.9	Introduction	338
16.10	Article 267 reference procedure	338
16.11	Judicial review	339
16.12	Enforcement of law against Member States	340
16.13	Seeking a remedy in the national courts	340
16.14	Remedies: checkpoints	341
	Free movement of goods	**342**
16.15	Introduction	342
16.16	Treaty provisions	342
16.17	Customs duties	343
16.18	Quantitative restrictions	343
16.19	Exceptions to Article 34 TFEU	344
16.20	Free movement of goods: checkpoints	347

		Free movement of persons	**347**
	16.21	Introduction	347
	16.22	Workers	347
	16.23	Families of workers	349
	16.24	Exceptions to Article 45	349
	16.25	Free movement of persons: checkpoints	351
		Freedom of establishment and provision of services	**351**
	16.26	Introduction	351
	16.27	Freedom of establishment	352
	16.28	Freedom to provide services	352
	16.29	Limitations	352
	16.30	Freedom to receive services	354
	16.31	Freedom of establishment and provision of services: checkpoints	354
		Competition law	**355**
	16.32	Introduction	355
	16.33	Article 101 TFEU	355
	16.34	Exemptions to Article 101(1)	359
	16.35	Article 101: Flow chart	361
	16.36	Article 102 TFEU	361
	16.37	Competition law: checkpoints	365
	16.38	UK competition law	366
	16.39	The EU and fundamental rights	368
		Further information	**369**
	16.40	Bibliography and further reading	369

Human rights — 371

17		**Human rights**	**373**
	17.1	Introduction	373
	17.2	General principles	374
	17.3	European and international doctrines	375
	17.4	The Convention rights	379
	17.5	Judicial remedies	394
	17.6	Conclusion: checkpoints	395
	17.7	Bibliography	395

APPENDIX 1 Answers to self-test questions — 397

APPENDIX 2 Investments — 399

Index — 405

Taxation rates and allowances for 2011/2012 — 421

Preface

This book provides foundations for study on the Legal Practice Course, containing materials relating to the Core and Pervasive areas (other than Accounts and Skills) identified in the 'Outcomes for the course' defined by the Solicitors Regulation Authority. Accounts and Skills are each the subject of a dedicated volume in the Legal Practice Course Guide series. The principles introduced here will be further developed in the Core Practice and Elective areas of the Course.

Those familiar with previous editions will notice a number of significant changes in this volume. The content of Chapter 1 (Professional Conduct) has been rewritten to take account of the new 'outcome-focused' regulation enshrined in the Solicitors Regulation Authority Code of Conduct to be implemented in October 2011. The material relating to Financial Services and Money Laundering has been separated and now occupies Chapters 2 and 3 respectively. In Chapter 14, the decision has been taken no longer to reproduce the IHT Forms which are readily downloadable from the HMRC website. European Law and Human Rights no longer feature as 'requirements' of the latest version of the LPC but it has been suggested to us that students may find it helpful to have easy access to 'reminders' in relation to these topics; these can be found in Chapters 16 and 17 respectively. The chapters on Revenue Law generally take into account the proposals contained in the Budget introduced by the Chancellor of the Exchequer in March 2011. However, they do not reflect changes that may have been made subsequently.

The authors are, as ever, grateful for the support and assistance afforded to them by members of the Higher Education Division at Oxford University Press—and in particular by Olivia Rowland, Lalle Pursglove, Kizzy Taylor-Richelieu, and Sarah Brett.

George Miles
Bristol
May 2011

ONLINE RESOURCES TO ACCOMPANY THIS BOOK

Online Resource Centres are websites that have been developed to provide students and lecturers with ready-to-use teaching and learning resources. They are free of charge, designed to complement the textbook and offer additional materials that are suited to electronic delivery.

The Online ResourceCentre to accompany this book can be found at www.oxfordtextbooks.co.uk/orc/foundations11_12/

Student resources

Student resources are open access and free to use.

Updates

Bookmark this site and visit it regularly to find updates on changes to key legislation and procedures, including:

- Updated information from the Solicitors Regulation Authority on changes to the Handbook
- Additional updates on key legislative changes in other key areas

Useful websites and resources

Useful links and resources selected by the authors and organized by chapter to provide you with additional information on the areas covered in the book.

Lecturer resources

Password-protected to ensure only lecturers adopting this book can access these resources, each registration is personally checked to ensure the security of the site. Use these resources to complement your own teaching notes and the resources you provide for your LPC students.

Registering is easy: go to the homepage, complete a simple registration form which allows you to choose you own user name and password, and access will be granted within three working days (subject to verification).

Figures from the book

Lecturers can access figures featured in the book online in a format suitable for using in PowerPoint slides or inserting into handouts. Use these diagrams to complement your teaching and encourage your students to get the most from this book.

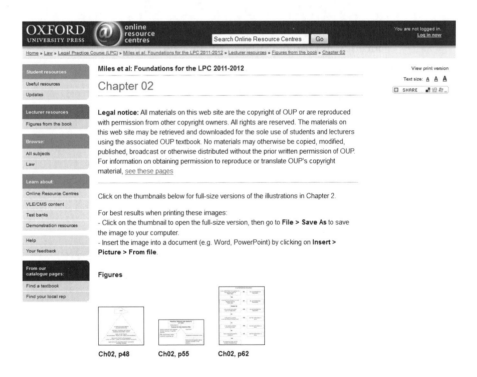

ACKNOWLEDGEMENTS

In Chapter 1, extracts from the Solicitors Regulation Authority Handbook are reproduced with kind permission of the Law Society.

In Chapter 14, the forms of Oath for Executors, for Administrators with the will annexed, and for Administrators are reproduced for educational purposes only by kind permission of Oyez Professional Services Limited.

In Chapter 1, extracts from the Law Society's Solicitors' Code of Conduct 2007 are reproduced with kind permission of the Law Society.

TABLE OF CASES

Adams (Deceased), Re [1990] Ch 601; [1990] 2 WLR 924; [1990] 2 All ER 97 (Ch D) ... 209

Adoui and Cornuaille v Belgium (Cases 115 and 116/81) [1982] ECR 1665; [1982] 3 CMLR 631 (ECJ) ... 350

Akzo Nobel NV v Commission of the European Communities (Case C- 97/08) [2009] ECR I-8237; [2009] 5 CMLR 23 (ECJ) ... 359

Allhusen v Whittell (1867) LR 4 Eq 295 (Ct Chancery) ... 287

Appleton, Re (1885) LR 29 Ch D 893 (CA) ... 313

Atlan v United Kingdom (Application 36533/97) (2002) 34 EHRR 33; [2001] Crim LR 819 (ECHR) ... 386

Attorney General's Reference (No.3 of 2000), Re [2001] UKHL 53; [2001] 1 WLR 2060; [2001] 4 All ER 897; [2002] 1 Cr App R 29 (HL) ... 387-9

Austin and Saxby v Commissioner of Police of the Metropolis [2007] EWCA Civ 989; [2008] QB 660; [2008] 2 WLR 415; [2008] 1 All ER 564; [2008] HRLR 1; [2008] UKHRR 205 (CA) ... 381

Banks v Goodfellow (1869-70) LR 5 QB 549 (QB) ... 203

Beckles v United Kingdom (Application 44652/98) (2003) 36 EHRR 13; 13 BHRC 522 (ECHR) ... 385

Benjamin, Re [1902] 1 Ch 723 (Ch D) ... 296

BMW Belgium SA v Commission of the European Communities (Case C32/78) [1979] ECR 2435; [1980] 1 CMLR 370 (ECJ) ... 355

Bonsignore v Oberstadtdirektor of the City of Cologne (Case C67/74) [1975] ECR 297; [1975] 1 CMLR 472 (ECJ) ... 350

Brodie's Will Trustees v Inland Revenue Commissioners (1933) 17 TC 432 ... 195

Callaghan (Deceased), Re [1985] Fam 1; [1984] 3 WLR 1076; [1984] 3 All ER 790; [1985] Fam Law 28 (Fam Div) ... 236

Campus Oil Ltd v Minister for Industry and Energy (Case 72/83) [1984] ECR 2727; [1984] 3 CMLR 544 (ECJ) ... 345

Centrafarm BV v Sterling Drug Inc (Case C-15/74) [1974] ECR 1147; [1974] ECR 1183; [1974] 2 CMLR 480 (ECJ) ... 345

Chalcraft, Re [1948] P. 222; [1948] 1 All ER 700; 64 TLR 246; [1948] LJR 1111 (PDAD) ... 206

Chaplin (Deceased), Re [1950] Ch 507; [1950] 2 All ER 155 (Ch D) ... 223

Charles v Fraser [2010] EWHC 2154 (Ch D) ... 207

Charman v Charman (No.4) [2007] EWCA Civ 503; [2007] 1 FLR 1246; [2007] 2 FCR 217 (CA) ... 237

CILFIT Srl v Ministero della Sanita (Case 283/81) [1982] ECR 3415; [1983] 1 CMLR 472 (ECJ) ... 338

Collins (Deceased), Re [1975] 1 WLR 309; [1975] 1 All ER 321 (Ch D) 224, ... 288

Collins (Deceased), Re [1990] Fam 56; [1990] 2 WLR 161; [1990] 2 All ER 47; [1990] 2 FLR 72 (Fam Div) ... 236

Comet BV v Produktschap Voor Siergewassen (Case 45/76) [1976] ECR 2043 (ECJ) ... 340

Commission of the European Communities v Ireland (Case C249/81) [1982] ECR 4005; [1983] ECR 4005; [1983] 2 CMLR 104 (ECJ) ... 343

Commission of the European Communities v Italy (Case 7/68) [1968] ECR 423; [1969] CMLR 1 (ECJ) ... 345

Commission of the European Communities v Luxembourg (Case 2/62) [1962] ECR 425; [1963] CMLR 199 (ECJ) ... 343

Commission of the European Communities v United Kingdom (Case C- 40/82) [1982] ECR 2793; [1982] 3 CMLR 497 (ECJ) ... 345

Commissioner of Stamp Duties (Queensland) v Livingston [1965] AC 694; [1964] 3 WLR 963; [1964] 3 All ER 692 (PC) ... 319

Condron v United Kingdom Condron v United Kingdom (Application 35718/97)(2001) 31 EHRR 1; 8 BHRC 290; [2000] Po LR 139; [2000] Crim LR 679 (ECHR) ... 385

Conegate v Customs and Excise Commissioners (Case C-121/85) [1987] QB 254; [1987] 2 WLR 39; [1986] 2 All ER 688; [1986] ECR 1007; [1986] 1 CMLR 739 (ECJ) ... 344

Cook, In the Estate of [1960] 1 WLR 353; [1960] 1 All ER 689 (PDAD) ... 206

Cooke, Re (1889) 5 TLR 407 ... 4

Coventry (Deceased), Re [1980] Ch 461; [1979] 3 WLR 802; [1979] 3 All ER 815 (CA) ... 236

Cowan v French Treasury (186/87) [1989] ECR 195 ... 354

Crispin's Will Trusts, Re [1975] Ch 245; [1974] 3 WLR 657; [1974] 3 All ER 772 (CA) ... 223

Cunard's Trustees v Inland Revenue Commissioners [1946] 1 All ER 159 (CA) ... 195

Defrenne v SA Belge de Navigation Aerienne (SABENA) (Case 43/75) [1981] 1 All ER 122; [1976] ECR 455; [1976] 2 CMLR 98 (ECJ) ... 334

Doughty v Rolls Royce Plc [1988] 1 CMLR 569; [1987] ICR 932; [1987] IRLR 447 (EAT) ... 335

Douglas v Hello! Ltd (No.1) [2001] QB 967; [2001] 2 WLR 992; [2001] 2 All ER 289; [2001] EMLR 9; [2001] 1 FLR 982; [2002] 1 FCR 289; [2001] HRLR 26; [2001] UKHRR 223 (CA) ... 378

Duce and Boots Cash Chemists (Southern) Ltd's Contract, Re [1937] Ch 642 (Ch D) ... 318

Duke v GEC Reliance Ltd [1988] AC 618; [1988] 2 WLR 359; [1988] 1 All ER 626; [1988] 1 CMLR 719 (HL) ... 337

Earl of Chesterfield's Trusts, Re (1883) LR 24 Ch D 643 (Ch D) ... 287

Etablissements Consten Sarl v Commission of the European Economic Community (Case 56/64) [1966] ECR 299; [1966] CMLR 418 (ECJ) ... 358

Evans v Westcombe [1999] 2 All ER 777 (Ch D) ... 296

Eve, Re [1956] Ch 479; [1956] 3 WLR 69; [1956] 2 All ER 321 (Ch D) ... 302

Faccini Dori v Recreb Srl (Case C-91/92) [1995] All ER (EC) 1; [1994] ECR I-3325; [1995] 1 CMLR 665 (ECJ) ... 335

Fitt v United Kingdom (Application 29777/96) (2000) 30 EHRR 480; [2000] Po LR 10 (ECHR) ... 386

Foglia v Novello (No.1) (Case 104/79) [1981] ECR 745; [1980] ECR 745; [1981] 1 CMLR 45 (ECJ) ... 339

Foglia v Novello (No.2) (Case 244/80) [1981] ECR 3045; [1982] 1 CMLR 585 (ECJ) ... 339

Foster v British Gas Plc (Case C-188/89) [1991] 1 QB 405; [1991] 2 WLR 258; [1990] 3 All ER 897; [1990] ECR I-3313; [1990] 2 CMLR 833 (ECJ) ... 335

Francovich v Italy (Case C-6 and 9/90) [1991] ECR I-5357; [1993] 2 CMLR 66 (ECJ) ... 341

Garden Cottage Foods Ltd v Milk Marketing Board [1984] AC 130; [1983] 3 WLR 143; [1983] 2 All ER 770 (HL) ... 341

Garland v British Rail Engineering Ltd (Case 12/81) [1982] 2 All ER 402; [1982] ECR 359; [1982] 1 CMLR 696 (ECJ) ... 337

Germany v Council of the European Communities (Banana Suppliers Cartel) (Case C280/93) [1994] ECR I-4973 (ECJ) ... 357

GHR Co Ltd v Inland Revenue Commissioners [1943] KB 303 (KBD) ... 317

Goodwin v United Kingdom (Application 17488/90) (1996) 22 EHRR 123; 1 BHRC 81 (ECHR) ... 392

Grad v Finanzamt Traunstein (Case 9/70) [1970] ECR 825; [1971] CMLR 1 (ECJ) ... 334

Griffin v South West Water Services Ltd [1995] IRLR 15 (Ch D) ... 335

Gül v Regierungspräsident Düsseldorf (Case 131/85) [1986] ECR 1573; [1987] 1 CMLR 501 (ECJ) ... 349

Gullung v Conseil de l'Ordre des Avocats du Barreau de Colmar (Case C292/86) [1990] 1 QB 234; [1989] 3 WLR 705; [1988] ECR 111; [1988] 2 CMLR 57 (ECJ) ... 354

Gully v Dix [2004] EWCA Civ 139; [2004] 1 WLR 1399; [2004] 1 FLR 918; [2004] 1 FCR 453 (CA) ... 233-4

Handyside v United Kingdom (1979-80) 1 EHRR 737 (ECHR) ... 377, 392

Harman v Harman (1686) 2 Show 492; 3 Mod Rep 115; Comb 35 ... 305

Höfner and Elser v Macrotron GmbH (Case C-41/90) [1991] ECR I- 1979; [1993] 4 CMLR 306 (ECJ) ... 356

Hobbs v Knight (1838)163 ER 267; (1838) 1 Curt 768 (KB) ... 209

Hoek Loos NV v Commission of the European Communities (Industrial and Medical Gases) (Case T-304/02) [2006] ECR II- 1887; [2006] 5 CMLR 8 (CFI) ... 357

Hokkanen v Finland [1996] 1 FLR 289; [1995] 2 FCR 320; (1995) 19 EHRR 139 (ECHR) ... 378

Howe v Earl of Dartmouth 32 ER 56; (1802) 7 Ves Jr 137 (Ct Chancery) ... 287

Hugin Kassaregister AB v Commission of the European Communities (Case C22/78) [1979] ECR 1869; [1979] 3 CMLR 345 (ECJ) ... 362

Intel case (IP/09/745) (Unreported) (EU Comm) ... 364

Internationale Handelsgesellschaft mbH v Einfuhr- und Vorratsstelle fur Getreide und Futtermittel (Case 11/70) [1970] ECR 1125; [1972] CMLR 255 (ECJ) ... 336, 368

Ireland v United Kingdom (1979-80) 2 EHRR 25 (ECHR) ... 380

Jasper v United Kingdom (Application 27052/95) (2000) 30 EHRR 441; [2000] Po LR 25; [2000] Crim LR 586 (ECHR) ... 386

Jemma Trust Co Ltd v Liptrott [2004] EWCA Civ 1476; [2004] 1 WLR 646; [2004] 1 All ER 510 (CA) ... 313

Kane v Radley-Kane [1999] Ch 274; [1998] 3 WLR 617; [1998] 3 All ER 753; [1998] 2 FLR 585 (Ch D) ... 288

Keck, Criminal Proceedings Against (Case C-267 and 268/91) [1993] ECR I-6097; [1995] 1 CMLR 101 (ECJ) ... 344, 346

Kempf v Staatssecretaris van Justitie (Case 139/85) [1986] ECR 1741; [1987] 1 CMLR 764 (ECJ) ... 348

Khan v United Kingdom (Application 35394/97) (2001) 31 EHRR 45; 8 BHRC 310; [2000] Po LR 156 (ECHR) ... 392

King's Will Trusts, Re [1964] Ch 542; [1964] 2 WLR 913; [1964] 1 All ER 833 (Ch D) ... 318

Knatchbull v Fearnhead (1837) 3 M & C 122; 1 Jur 687 (Ct Chancery) ... 295

Lamy v Belgium (1989) 11 EHRR 529 (ECHR) ... 381

Lawrie-Blum v Land Baden-Wurttemberg (Case 66/85) [1986] ECR 2121; [1987] 3 CMLR 389 (ECJ) ... 347

LCD Panel case (IP/10/1685) (Unreported) (EU Comm) ... 357

Levin v Staatssecretaris van Justitie (Case 53/81) [1982] ECR 1035; [1982] 2 CMLR 454 (ECJ) ... 348

Ludi v Switzerland (1993) 15 EHRR 173 (ECHR) ... 389

Luisi v Ministero del Tesoro (Case 286/82) [1984] ECR 377; [1985] 3 CMLR 52 (ECJ) ... 354

Macarthys Ltd v Smith (C-129/79) [1980] ECR 1275; [1980] 2 CMLR 205 (ECJ) ... 337

McCann v United Kingdom (1996) 21 EHRR 97 (ECHR) ... 375, 379

McVeigh, O'Neill and Evans v United Kingdom (Application 8022/77) (1983) 5 EHRR 71 (Eu Comm) ... 391

Malone v United Kingdom (1985) 7 EHRR 14 (ECHR) ... 376

Marleasing SA v La Comercial Internacional de Alimentacion SA (Case C-106/89) [1990] ECR I-4135; [1993] BCC 421; [1992] 1 CMLR 305 (ECJ) ... 336

Marshall v Southampton and South West Hampshire AHA (Case 152/84) [1986] QB 401; [1986] 2 WLR 780; [1986] 2 All ER 584; [1986] ECR 723; [1986] 1 CMLR 688 (ECJ) ... 335

McFarlane v McFarlane [2006] [2006] UKHL 24; [2006] 2 AC 618; [2006] 2 WLR 1283; [2006] 3 All ER 1; [2006] 1 FLR 1186 (HL) ... 237

Micheletti v Delegacion del Gobierno en Cantabria (Case C369/90) [1992] ECR I-4239 (ECJ) ... 347

Microsoft case (IP/04/382) (Unreported) (EU Comm) ... 365

Miller v Miller [2006] UKHL 24; [2006] 2 AC 618; [2006] 2 WLR 1283; [2006] 3 All ER 1; [2006] 1 FLR 1186 (HL) ... 237

Neumeister v Austria (1979-80) 1 EHRR 91 (ECHR) ... 378

Nold (J) KG v Commission of the European Communities (Case 4/73) [1974] ECR 491; [1975] ECR 985; [1974] 2 CMLR 338 (ECJ) ... 368

Northcote's Will Trusts, Re [1949] 1 All ER 442; [1949] WN 69 (Ch D) ... 314

Nottingham City Council v Amin [2000] 1 WLR 1071; [2000] 2 All ER 946; [2000] 1 Cr App R 426 (DC) ... 389

Observer v United Kingdom (Application 13585/88) (1992) 14 EHRR 153 (ECHR) ... 392

Omega Spielhallen- und Automatenaufstellungs GmbH v Bundesstadt Bonn (Case C-36/02) [2004] ECR I-9609; [2005] 1 CMLR 5; [2005] CEC 391 (ECJ) ... 369

Osman v United Kingdom [1999] 1 FLR 193; (2000) 29 EHRR 245 (ECHR) ... 375

Parker v Felgate (1883) 8 PD 171 (PDAD) 202-4

Pearce, Re [1909] 2 Ch 492 (CA) ... 309

PG and JH v United Kingdom (Application 44787/98) (2008) 46 EHRR 51; [2001] Po LR 325 (ECHR) ... 386

Pilkington v Inland Revenue Commissioners [1964] AC 612; [1962] 3 WLR 1051; [1962] 3 All ER 622 (HL) ... 293

Procureur du Roi v Dassonville (Case 8/74) [1974] ECR 837; [1974] 2 CMLR 436 (ECJ) ... 343

Pubblico Ministero v Ratti (Case 148/78) [1979] ECR 1629; [1980] 1 CMLR 96 (ECJ) ... 335

R. (on the application of D) v Secretary of State for the Home Department [2006] EWCA Civ 143; [2006] 3 All ER 946 (CA) ... 375

R. (on the application of O) v Harrow Crown Court [2006] UKHL 42; [2007] 1 AC 249; [2006] 3 WLR 195; [2006] 3 All ER 1157 (HL) ... 382

R. (on the application of Amin (Imtiaz)) v Secretary of State for the Home Department [2003] UKHL 51; [2004] 1 AC 653; [1998] 1 WLR 972; [2003] 3 WLR 1169; [2003] 4 All ER 1264; [2004] HRLR 3; [2004] UKHRR 75 (HL) ... 375

R. (on the application of Laporte) v Chief Constable of Gloucestershire [2006] UKHL 55; [2007] 2 AC 105; [2007] 2 WLR 46; [2007] 2 All ER 529; [2007] HRLR 13; [2007] UKHRR 400 (HL) ... 381

R. v Birtles [1969] 1 WLR 1047; [1969] 2 All ER 1131 (Note); (1969) 53 Cr App R 469 (CA) ... 391

R. v Bouchereau (Pierre Roger) (Case 30/77) [1978] QB 732; [1978] 2 WLR 250; [1981] 2 All ER 924; [1977] ECR 1999 (ECJ) ... 338, 350

R. v Cole (Konrad) and Keet (Rocky) [2007] EWCA Crim 1924; [2007] 1 WLR 2716 (CA) ... 384

R. v Director of Public Prosecutions Ex p Kebeline [2000] 2 AC 326; [1999] 3 WLR 972; [1999] 4 All ER 801 (HL) ... 383

R. v Doldur [2000] Crim LR 178 (CA) ... 385

R. v Doubtfire (Robert Henry) (No.2) [2001] 2 Cr App R 13; [2001] Crim LR 813 (CA) ... 386

R. v Henn (Maurice Donald) (Case 34/79) [1980] 2 WLR 597; [1980] 2 All ER 166; [1979] ECR 3795 (ECJ) ... 344

R. v Immigration Appeal Tribunal Ex p Antonissen (Case C- 292/89) [1991] ECR I-745; [1991] 2 CMLR 373 (ECJ) ... 348

R. v Moon (Dianna Ross) [2004] EWCA Crim 2872 (CA) ... 388

R. v Secretary of State for Transport Ex p Factortame Ltd (No.2) [1991] 1 AC 603; [1990] 3 WLR 818; [1991] 1 All ER 70 (HL) ... 337, 340, 341

R. v Smurthwaite (Keith) and Gill (Susan) [1994] 1 All ER 898; (1994) 98 Cr App R 437 (CA) ... 388

R. v Thompson (Ernest George) (Case 7/78) [1980] QB 229; [1980] 2 WLR 521; [1980] 2 All ER 102; [1978] ECR 2247; [1979] ECR 2247; (1979) 69 Cr App R 22; [1979] 1 CMLR 47 (ECJ) ... 344

Rewe-Zentral AG v Bundesmonopolverwaltung fur Branntwein (Cassis de Dijon case) (Case 120/78) [1979] ECR 649; [1979] 3 CMLR 494 (ECJ) ... 343-4

Reyners v Belgium (Case 2/74) [1974] ECR 631; [1974] 2 CMLR 305 (ECJ) ... 353

Reynolds Will Trusts, Re [1966] 1 WLR 19; [1965] 3 All ER 686 (Ch D) ... 223

Rheinmuhlen-dusseldorf v Einfuhr- und Vorratsstelle fur Getreide und Futtermittel (Case 146/73) [1974] ECR 139 (ECJ) ... 338

Rooke, Re [1933] Ch 970 (Ch D) ... 309

Rowe and David v United Kingdom (2000) 30 EHRR 1; 8 BHRC 325; [2000] Po LR 41; [2000] Crim LR 584 (ECHR) ... 385

Rutili v Ministre de l'Interieur (Case 36/75) [1975] ECR 1219; [1976] 1 CMLR 140 (ECJ) ... 350

Salabiaku v France (1991) 13 EHRR 379 (ECHR) ... 383

Simmenthal SpA v Commission of the European Communities (Case C92/78) [1979] ECR 777; [1980] 1 CMLR 25 (ECJ) ... 337

Société Technique Minière v Maschinenbau Ulm GmbH (Case 56/65) [1966] ECR 235; [1966] CMLR 357 (ECJ) ... 357

Soering v United Kingdom (1989) 11 EHRR 439 (ECHR) ... 377

Sotgiu v Deutsche Bundespost (Case 152/73) [1974] ECR 153 (ECJ) ... 347

Spracklan's Estate, Re [1938] 2 All ER 345 ... 209

Stauder v City of Ulm (Case 29/69) [1969] ECR 419; [1970] CMLR 112 (ECJ) ... 368

SW and CR v United Kingdom [1996] 1 FLR 434; (1996) 21 EHRR 363 (ECHR) ... 390

T and V v United Kingdom (Applications 24724/94 and 24888/94) [2000] 2 All ER 1024 (Note); (2000) 30 EHRR 121 (ECHR) ... 382

Teixeira de Castro v Portugal (1999) 28 EHRR 101 (ECHR) ... 387-9

Townson v Tickell 106 ER 575; (1819) 3 B & Ald 31 (KB) ... 305

United Brands Co v Commission of the European Communities (Case 27/76) [1978] ECR 207; [1978] 1 CMLR 429 (ECJ) ... 362

Van Binsbergen v Bestuur van de Bedrijfsvereniging voor de Metaalnijverheid (Case 33/74) [1974] ECR 1299; [1975] 1 CMLR 298 (ECJ) ... 353

Van Colle v Chief Constable of Hertfordshire [2008] UKHL 50; [2009] 1 AC 225; [2008] 3 WLR 593; [2008] 3 All ER 977 (HL) ... 375

Van Duyn v Home Office (Case 41/74) [1975] Ch 358; [1975] 2 WLR 760; [1975] 3 All ER 190; [1974] ECR 1337; [1975] 1 CMLR 1 (ECJ) ... 334

van Gend en Loos v Nederlandse Administratie der Belastingen (Case 26/62) [1963] ECR 1 (ECJ) ... 334, 336

Von Colson v Land Nordrhein-Westfahlen (Casse C-14/83) [1984] ECR 1891; [1986] 2 CMLR 430 (ECJ) ... 335

Webb, Criminal proceedings against (Case 279/80) [1981] ECR 3305; [1982] 1 CMLR 719 (ECJ) ... 337

Wemhoff v Germany (1979-80) 1 EHRR 55 (ECHR) 381

White v White [2003] EWCA Civ 924; [2004] 2 FLR 321; [2004] Fam Law 572 (CA) ... 237

Wood Pulp, Re [1985] 3 CMLR 474 (ECJ) ... 357

Wood v Smith [1993] Ch 90; [1992] 3 WLR 583; [1992] 3 All ER 556 (CA) ... 206

X and Y v Netherlands [1986] 8 EHRR 235 (ECHR) ... 390

TABLE OF STATUTES

Administration of Estates Act 1925 ... 287
  Pt.IV ... 220
  s.10(2) ... 305
  s.25 ... 286
  s.33(1) ... 220
  s.34(3) ... 302
  s.35 ... 301, 303
  s.36 ... 317
  s.36(2) ... 318
  s.36(4) ... 318
  s.36(5) ... 318
  s.36(6) ... 318
  s.36(7) ... 318
  s.36(10) ... 318
  s.39 ... 287
  s.41 ... 288, 310
  s.42 ... 289, 311
  s.46 ... 225
  s.47 ... 220
  s.47A ... 223
  s.55(1)(ix) ... 309
  s.55(1)(x) ... 222
  Sch.I ... 302
Administration of Estates (Small Payments) Act 1965 ... 244, 255
Administration of Justice Act ... 1932
  s.2 ... 242
Administration of Justice Act 1982 ... 207
  s.17 ... 204
  s.20 ... 298
Administration of Justice Act 1985
  s.50 ... 248, 314
Adoption Act 1976 ... 217
  s.39 ... 224
  s.45 ... 298
Anti-Terrorism, Crime and Security Act 2001 ... 60-1
Apportionment Act 1870 ... 315
  s.2 ... 287

Bail Act 1976 ... 381

Capital Allowances Act 2001 ... 177
Capital Transfer Tax Act 1984
  s.100 ... 110

Children Act 1989
  s.3 ... 289
  s.3(3) ... 289
  s.6 ... 209
Civil Evidence Act 1995
  s.1 ... 235
Civil Partnership Act 2004 ... 208, 220, 229
Competition Act 1998
  s.2 ... 367
Corporation Tax Act 2009 ... 68, 147
Corporation Tax Act 2010 ... 68, 147
  s.37 ... 149
  s.45 ... 150
Criminal Justice Act 2003 ... 383-4
  s.114 ... 384
  s.114(2) ... 384
  s.115 ... 384
Criminal Justice and Public Order Act 1994
  s.25(1) ... 382
  s.34 ... 384-5
Criminal Procedure and Investigations Act 1996 ... 383-4
Customs and Excise Management Act 1979 ... 68

Enterprise Act 2002 ... 368
Equality Act 2010 ... 22
European Communities Act 1972 ... 333
  s.2(1) ... 334

Family Law Reform Act 1987 ... 217
  s.18 ... 224
  s.18(2) ... 225
Finance Act 1984 ... 110
Finance Act 1986
  s.102 ... 139
Finance Act 1991
  s.72 ... 181
Finance Act 2006 ... 186, 188-9
Financial Services Act 1986 ... 43, 295
Financial Services and Markets Act 2000 41, 43-5, 47, 49, ... 53, 56, 298-9
  Pt.XX ... 44, 47, 53, 57-58, 298-9
  s.2 ... 43
  s.3 ... 44
  s.19 ... 44, 298

s.19(2) ... 44
s.21(1) ... 49
s.22 ... 44
s.22(1)(b) ... 45
s.22(5) ... 45
s.23 ... 44
s.26 ... 44
s.28 ... 44
s.31 ... 44
s.38 ... 44
s.197 ... 53
s.327 ... 48, 52
s.327(6) ... 48

Human Rights Act 1998 ... 369, 373, 379, 387, 394
s.2 ... 395
s.2(1) ... 374
s.6 ... 378
s.6(1) ... 374
s.6(3) ... 374
s.8(1) ... 394
Sch.1 ... 379
Sch.2 ... 395

Income and Corporation Taxes Act 1988 ... 68, 73, 76
Income Tax Act 2007 ... 68, 73
Income Tax (Earnings and Pensions) Act 2003 ... 68, 73, 76-8, 88, 155-6, 182
Income Tax (Trading and Other Income) Act 2005 ... 68, 73, 76-7, 169-70, 182
Pt.2 ... 77
Pt.3 ... 77
Pt.4 ... 77
Income Taxes Act 2007 ... 180
s.64 ... 180-2
s.72 ... 182
s.83 ... 181-2
s.86 ... 182
s.89 ... 182
Inheritance (Provision for Family and Dependants) Act 1975 ... 202, 231-2, 252, 297
s.1(1) ... 239
s.1(1)(a) ... 233
s.1(1)(b) ... 233
s.1(1)(ba) ... 233
s.1(1)(c) ... 233
s.1(1)(d) ... 234
s.1(1)(e) ... 234
s.1(2) ... 234
s.1(2)(a) ... 234
s.1(2)(b) ... 235
s.1(3) ... 234
s.2 ... 236
s.3(1) ... 235
s.3(2) ... 236
s.3(2A) ... 237
s.3(3) ... 237
s.3(4) ... 238
s.3(5) ... 235
s.9 ... 238
s.10 ... 232, 238
s.11 ... 232, 238
s.14 ... 235
s.15 ... 233
s.15A ... 233
s.19(1) ... 238
s.25(1) ... 238
Inheritance (Provision for Family and Dependents) Act 1975 ... 305
Inheritance Tax Act 1984 ... 68, 110, 116, 186
s.1 ... 110
s.1(3) ... 111
s.2 ... 110
s.3 ... 110
s.3A ... 111
s.4 ... 132-3
s.6 ... 111
s.8A ... 135
s.11 ... 111
s.18 ... 114
s.19(A) ... 144
s.20 ... 123
s.21 ... 123
s.22 ... 123
s.23 ... 114
s.24 ... 114
s.25 ... 114
s.42 ... 306
s.43(2) ... 186
s.47 ... 111
s.48 ... 111
s.49 ... 189
s.58 ... 187
s.65 ... 188
s.71A ... 188-9
s.71A-C ... 188
s.71D ... 188
s.73 ... 190
s.88 ... 190
s.125 ... 133
s.131 ... 129
s.141 ... 134
s.142 ... 307
s.144 ... 188
s.151 ... 190
s.176 ... 132
ss.178-89 ... 133
ss.190-8 ... 133
Intestates Estates Act 1952
Sch.2 ... 224

Judgments Act 1838
s.17 ... 305

Land Registration Act 2002 ... 317
Law of Property Act 1925
   s.27 ... 294
   s.184 ... 214
Law Reform (Miscellaneous Provisions) Act 1934
   s.1(1) ... 300
Legal Services Act 2007 ... 4-5
Legitimacy Act 1976 ... 217
   s.5 ... 224
   s.10 ... 224

Married Women's Property Act 1882
   s.11 ... 229, 252-3, 255
Mental Capacity Act 2005 ... 202-3
   s.1 ... 203
   s.2 ... 203
   s.3 ... 203
   s.16 ... 203
Mental Health Act 1983 ... 204
Merchant Shipping Act 1988 ... 337, 341

Obscene Publications Act 1959 ... 377

Police Act 1997
   Pt.III ... 391
Police and Criminal Evidence Act 1984
   Code C ... 388
   s.78 ... 387, 389
   s.78(1) ... 387-8
Prevention of Terrorism Act 1989
   s.16A ... 383
   s.16B ... 383
Proceeds of Crime Act 2002 ... 60-1
   s.333A ... 60
   ss.327-9 ... 60
   ss.330-2 ... 60

Regulation of Investigatory Powers Act 2000 ... 391
   Pt.II ... 391

Senior Courts Act 1981
   s.109 ... 275
   s.114 ... 248-9
   s.116 ... 248
Settled Land Act 1925 ... 263
Statute of Westminster I 1275 ... 4

Taxation of Chargeable Gains Act 1992 ... 68, 93, 191
   s.3 ... 192
   s.62 ... 306-7
   s.71 ... 192
   s.72 ... 193
   s.73 ... 193
   s.76 ... 193
   s.152 ... 103, 192

   s.155 ... 103
   s.162 ... 103
   s.165 ... 101
   s.225 ... 192
   Sch.1 ... 192
Taxes Management Act 1970 ... 68
Terrorism Act 2000 ... 60-1
Trustee Act 1925 ... 287
   s.1 ... 289
   s.15 ... 289
   s.19 ... 289
   s.20 ... 289
   s.25 ... 290
   s.27 ... 295-7, 305, 309
   s.27(2) ... 295
   s.31 ... 194-5, 292-3
   s.31(1) ... 292
   s.31(2) ... 292
   s.32 ... 293
   s.42 ... 314, 316
   s.61 ... 321
   s.63 ... 311, 316
Trustee Act 2000 ... 285, 287
   s.1 ... 286
   s.3 ... 291
   s.4 ... 292
   s.5 ... 292
   s.8 ... 292
   s.11 ... 290
   s.12 ... 290
   s.14 ... 290
   s.15 ... 290
   s.21 ... 290
   s.22 ... 290
   s.23 ... 290
   s.28 ... 314
   s.28(4)(a) ... 215-16
   s.31 ... 290
   s.34 ... 289
   s.35 ... 285
Trustee Delegation Act 1999
   s.5 ... 290
Trusts of Land and Appointment of Trustees Act 1996 ... 287, 289
   s.6(3) ... 292

Value Added Tax Act 1994 ... 68, 159
   Sch.1 ... 163
   Sch.8 ... 160
   Sch.9 ... 161

Wills Act 1837
   s.9 ... 204-5, 273
   s.13 ... 273
   s.14 ... 274

s.15 ... 206, 215-16, 246, 274, 314
s.18 ... 207
s.18(3) ... 208
s.18(4) ... 208
s.18A(1) ... 208
s.18B ... 208

s.18C ... 209
s.20 ... 209
s.21 ... 210
s.24 ... 212-13
s.33 ... 215-16, 219
Wills Act 1963 ... 202

TABLE OF STATUTORY INSTRUMENTS

Administration of Insolvent Estates of Deceased Persons Order 1986 (SI 1986 1999) ... 304

Financial Services and Markets Act 2000 (Designated Professional Bodies) Order (SI 2001 1226) ... 47

Financial Services and Markets Act 2000 (Exemption) Order 2001 (SI 2001 1201) ... 44

Financial Services and Markets Act 2000 (Financial Promotion) Order 2005 (SI 2005 1529) ... 49, 52
  Art.55 ... 52
  Art.55A ... 53

Financial Services and Markets Act 2000 (Professions) (Non- Exempt Activities) Order 2001 (SI 2001 1227) ... 48

Financial Services and Markets Act 2000 (Regulated Activities) Order 2001 (SI 2001 544) ... 45, 53-5, 58, 298
  Art.22 ... 46
  Art.29 ... 46
  Art.60 ... 46
  Art.66 ... 46, 50, 298
  Art.67 ... 46, 50, 53, 57
  Art.72C ... 50
  Pt.III ... 46

Inheritance Tax (Delivery of Accounts) (Excepted Estates) (Amendment) Regulations 2011 (SI 2011 214) ... 277, 279

Inheritance Tax (Delivery of Accounts) (Excepted Estates) Regulations 2004 (SI 2004 2543) ... 277

Money Laundering Regulations 2007 (SI 2007 2157) ... 59-63
  reg.5 ... 61
  reg.5(a) ... 62
  reg.6 ... 62
  reg.7 ... 61-2
  reg.11 ... 62
  reg.16(4) ... 62
  reg.19 ... 61
  reg.20(1)(b) ... 61
  reg.20(2)(d)(i) ... 61
  reg.21 ... 61

Non-Contentious Probate (Amendment) Rules 1991 (SI 1991 1876) ... 242

Non-Contentious Probate Rules 1987 (SI 1987 2024) ... 242
  r.9 ... 261
  r.12 ... 273
  r.20 ... 245-7, 250-1, 257, 265, 268
  r.21 ... 246
  r.22 ... 246-7, 250-1, 257, 268, 271-2
  r.22(4) ... 246
  r.25 ... 249
  r.27 ... 246, 248, 264-5
  r.27(1A) ... 264
  r.35 ... 248
  r.37 ... 250
  r.37(2) ... 250

Proceeds of Crime Act 2002 (Business in the Regulated Sector and Supervisory Authorities) Order 2007 (SI 2007 3287) ... 61

Solicitors' (Non-Contentious Business) Remuneration Order 1994 (SI 1994 2616) ... 313

TABLE OF EU LEGISLATION

EU Treaties and Conventions

Charter of Fundamental Rights of the European Union 2000 ... 369

EC Treaty ... 368

Single European Act 1986 ... 328, 336

Treaty on European Union ... 369
Treaty of the European Union 2009
    Art.3 ... 342
    Art.4 ... 336
    Art.4(3) ... 336, 340
    Art.17 ... 328, 331
Treaty on the Functioning of the European Union ... 331
    Art.20 ... 347
    Art.21 ... 347
    Art.26 ... 342
    Art.28 ... 342
    Art.29 ... 342
    Art.30 ... 342
    Art.31 ... 342
    Art.32 ... 342
    Art.34 ... 342-6
    Art.35 ... 343
    Art.36 ... 342-4, 346-7
    Art.37 ... 343
    Art.45 ... 347–49, 351
    Art.45(2) ... 348
    Art.49 ... 351, 353
    Art.49-54 ... 352
    Art.49-62 ... 352
    Art.53 ... 353-4
    Art.54 ... 352
    Art.55 ... 350
    Art.56 ... 355
    Art.56-62 ... 352-3
    Art.57 ... 354-5
    Art.62 ... 352
    Art.101 ... 355-9, 361-8
    Art.101(1) ... 355-61
    Art.101(2) ... 359
    Art.101(3) ... 360-1, 363
    Art.102 ... 355, 362, 364-7
    Art.157(1) ... 334
    Art.216 ... 332
    Art.228 ... 334
    Art.258 ... 340, 342
    Art.259 ... 340, 342
    Art.263 ... 339, 342
    Art.265 ... 339, 342
    Art.267 ... 338, 341-2, 354
    Art.268 ... 340
    Art.277 ... 339, 342
    Art.288 ... 332
    Art.340 ... 340, 342
Treaty of Lisbon 2007 ... 328-9, 369
Treaty of Maastricht ... 369

TABLE OF EU SECONDARY LEGISLATION

Directives

Directive 67/227 on turnover taxes ... 159

Directive 77/388 on the harmonisation of the laws of the Member States relating to turnover taxes ... 159

Directive 98/5 to facilitate practice of the profession of lawyer on a permanent basis in a Member State other than that in which the qualification was obtained ... 354

Directive 2001/97 amending Council Directive 91/308 on prevention of the use of the financial system for the purpose of money laundering (Second Money Laundering Directive) ... 59

Directive 2004/38 on the right of citizens of the Union and their family members to move and reside freely within the territory of the Member States ... 347, 349

    Art.2(2) ... 349

    Art.6(1) ... 348

    Art.7 ... 347

    Art.16(1) ... 348

    Art.27(2) ... 350

    Art.28(1) ... 350

    Art.28(3) ... 351

Directive 2005/36 on the recognition of professional qualifications ... 353

Directive 2005/60 on the prevention of the use of the financial system for the purpose of money laundering and terrorist financing (Third Money Laundering Directive) ... 59

Directive 2006/123 on services in the internal market ... 352

    Art.4 ... 352

Regulations

Regulation 622/2008 amending Regulation 773/2004 on the conduct of settlement procedures in cartel cases ... 359

Regulation 1612/68 on freedom of movement for workers within the Community ... 347

    Art.7(2) ... 348

    Art.12 ... 349

TABLE OF INTERNATIONAL TREATIES AND CONVENTIONS

European Convention on Human Rights and Fundamental Freedoms 1950 ... 368-9, 373-4, 379
   Art.2 ... 375, 379
   Art.2(2) ... 375
   Art.3 ... 380
   Art.4 ... 380
   Art.5 ... 380-2
   Art.5(1)(c) ... 381
   Art.5(4) ... 381-2
   Art.6 ... 378, 382, 384-5, 387, 393, 395
   Art.6(1) ... 383, 385-7
   Art.6(2) ... 383
   Art.6(3)(b) ... 383
   Art.6(3)(c) ... 384
   Art.7 ... 390
   Art.8 ... 376, 387, 390-1, 393
   Art.8(1) ... 392
   Art.8(2) ... 376, 391, 393
   Art.9 ... 391
   Art.10 ... 377, 381, 392
   Art.10(2) ... 377
   Art.11 ... 381, 393
   Art.12 ... 393
   Art.14 ... 393
   Art.16 ... 393
   Art.17 ... 393
   Art.18 ... 394
   Art.56(1) ... 386
   Protocol I, Art.1 ... 394
   Protocol I, Art.2 ... 394
   Protocol I, Art.3 ... 394
   Protocol VI ... 394

General Agreement on Tariffs and Trade (GATT) ... 332

TABLE OF CODES OF CONDUCT

OFR code ... 3, 5-6, 8, 12, 14-22, 28-9
   Principle 5 ... 10
   Principle 6 ... 8
   Principle 7 ... 14
   Principle 8 ... 11, 15, 17
   Principle 9 ... 15
   Principle 10 ... 15
   s.1 ... 22-6
   s.4 ... 26-7

Recognised Bodies Regulations 2009 ... 12

Solicitors' Accounting Rules 1998 ... 12
Solicitors Code of Conduct 2007 ... 5, 9, 12, 14, 16, 28-9
   r.1 ... 12-13

r.1.01 ... 14
r.1.02 ... 14
r.1.03 ... 14
r.1.04 ... 14
r.1.05 ... 14
r.1.06 ... 14
r.2 ... 18-19, 21, 286
Solicitors Financial Services (Conduct of Business) Rules 2001 ... 51, 298
Solicitors Financial Services Scope Rules 2001 ... 48, 51, 54, 57, 298
   r.4(a) ... 52
   r.4(b) ... 52
   r.4(c) ... 52
Solicitors' Investment Business Rules ... 295

Professional conduct

INTRODUCTION

1.1 An era of change

The legal services market is undergoing an era of change and it was felt by many practitioners and regulators that the governance of legal service providers was also in need of modernisation. For solicitors in practice, this change comes almost on the back of what has already been a period of overhaul over the past few years.

The Solicitors Regulation Authority ('SRA') is the independent regulatory body of the Law Society in England and Wales. The SRA is preparing a new code of conduct: the SRA Code of Conduct. For the purposes of this chapter and to differentiate between the old and new codes, this new code will be referred to as the outcomes-focused regulation code ('the OFR Code'). The OFR Code will be contained in a handbook ('the Handbook'). This outcomes-focused approach to regulation is a change from the strict rules based on compliance regulations which are currently in force. You will see from this chapter that the OFR approach is intended to reduce the number of mandatory rules and provide a more flexible approach to the governance of legal service providers.

1.1.1 What will the OFR code mean for consumers?

The SRA envisages that the OFR Code will ensure consumers receive a professional service and encourage higher standards of service for consumers by making it clear what *outcomes* clients should expect from legal service providers. It is hoped that this will allow consumers to make informed decisions about the service provided and the options available to them.

The SRA has commented that it anticipates that this will free up law firms to do new and better things for clients, by providing more flexibility and reducing bureaucracy. Regulation will be risk-based, so the SRA intends to focus its resources on high-risk firms, and high-risk activities, to ensure consumers are protected.

However, at the time of writing this chapter, some concern has been expressed by practitioners and, in fact by the Law Society, that the timetable for bringing in the OFR Code was too tight. The Law Society has even gone so far as to suggest that the speed at which the new OFR Code is being introduced risks a breakdown in relations with the profession as a whole. The Law Society has been keen to express its support of the OFR approach in general; however, in a formal response to the SRA's final consultation on the draft OFR Code, the Law Society said that, despite progress in changing the SRA's structure, the culture change 'required to implement OFR successfully cannot be fully achieved in the time allowed'.

Whether or not this prediction will come to pass can only be seen in the coming year when the OFR Code is implemented on 6 October 2011, and once the profession has had time to respond to it.

1.1.2 What will the OFR code mean for you and the profession as a whole?

As students entering the profession in September 2011 you are in a unique position as you will study the new OFR Code before it is in fact implemented in practice (see timeline below).

You will also be seeing the emergence of the new alternative business structures ('ABSs') which are possible due to the Legal Service Act 2007 ('LSA'). These ABSs will allow for the ownership of legal service providers, currently restricted to lawyers, to be open to anyone deemed 'fit or proper'. This could be an insurance company or a supermarket—hence the much discussed term 'Tesco law' which has been widely commented on by the media and professionals alike.

Although there is some concern from existing legal firms that ABSs will have a detrimental effect on their business, the alternative and more positive view is that these new ABSs will mean that as new solicitors you will have broader options in progressing your careers and will no longer be limited to seeking partnership in a law firm in order to climb the career ladder, so the top end of the career ladder may look more diverse than it currently is.

It cannot at this stage be truly known what effect ABSs or the OFR Code will have on the profession. Only time will tell. But what is certain is that you are entering the profession at a very dynamic and challenging time.

The timeline for implementation of the outcomes-focused approach and introduction of ABSs is set out in the diagram below.

Figure 1.1 Timeline of SRA Handbook implementation

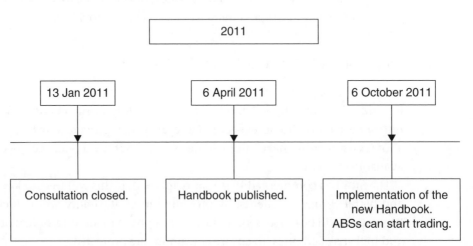

1.2 A brief history of legal ethics

One of the earliest examples of regulation of the legal profession can be found in Chapter 29 of the Statute of Westminster 1 (1275) in which 'deceit or collusion' by early lawyers was forbidden. *Re G Mayor Cooke* 5 TLR 407 is an example of common law identifying these ethical principles. In this case it was stated that an act of professional misconduct is committed by a lawyer who does something which is 'dishonourable to him as a man and dishonourable to his profession'.

These ethical principles which have been honoured by lawyers since medieval times were not committed to any real written form until the second half of the twentieth century. In 1960 the Law Society's *A Guide to the Professional Conduct and Etiquette of Solicitors* was first published; this contained the original set of rules. This was only superseded on 1 July 2007 by the implementation of the Law Society's Code of Conduct.

You will see from this chapter that you could argue the regulation of the legal profession has gone full circle. Originally a profession which required no absolute written code (as a lawyer acted within one rule—that being to act honourably) to a profession governed by the Code of Conduct 2007 (a set of mandatory rules of compliance often criticised as too detailed, complicated and rigid) to the OFR Code the intention of which is to revert back to lawyers upholding a number of basic principles. How they uphold those principles will not be strictly regulated. There is, of course, at this stage no practical evidence as to whether the new OFR approach will do what the SRA intended it to do, this being, the intention of better provision for the consumer, better support for the profession and flexible regulations for an ever-changing legal market.

1.2.1 Why the need for change—again?

The LSA was passed in 2007. It represented a key stage in the process of a number of Government reviews and recommendations which included the removal of restrictions on competition within the legal profession in relation to the structure, ownership and management of law firms and the development of ABSs for legal service firms. It was felt that the implementation of a new form of regulation, based on the firm rather than an individual solicitor, would be required in order to deliver the objectives of the LSA.

There were concerns that the existing regulations in the Code of Conduct 2007 (the '2007 Code') were too strict and inflexible for the changing legal market. The legal market was seeing a significant increase in the export of legal services, new technology, different and innovative ways of attracting new clients and developing the business and, as mentioned, the introduction of ABSs. These new developments are changing the legal market and, as such, it was felt by both practitioners and regulators that a new approach to regulation was needed to keep abreast of these changes.

There were also concerns, particularly from the City firms, that the existing regulation for the larger firms serving the corporate sector was not fit for purpose and the SRA's consumer focus did not protect adequately the needs of corporate clients. Many city firms mooted that they should be governed by an alternative set of rules. It is however hoped by the SRA that the OFR Code will be a 'one size fits all' regulation as it will allow for more flexibility—a regulation fit for all legal service providers from the large City firms to the sole practitioners and also the new ABSs.

The new regulation is intended to be flexible, wide-ranging and not static. The SRA felt a rules-based approach focused on strict compliance rather than on the primary aim, which is to achieve the best outcome for the client. The OFR Code is intended to provide a clear focus on the achievement of positive outcomes for consumers and give firms flexibility to decide how those outcomes are best achieved.

The OFR Code therefore focuses on the quality of what a solicitor is delivering to a client, rather than prescribing how legal service providers reach that stage. Suggested benefits by the SRA are an ability to adapt both to the operations of a firm and to the needs of the particular client base and the ability to eliminate some rules-driven bureaucracy which can create unproductive costs and sometimes interfere with clear and simple communication. However, this must all be read in the context of the concerns previously mentioned above by the Law Society and lawyers and the fact that there is no implementation in practice of these new regulations on which to base any theory as to whether the OFR Code has worked and achieved what it intended to achieve.

1.3 How this chapter is divided

In the first section of this chapter we will look at what being a member of the profession and a good solicitor means, the Handbook and the OFR Code in general.

In the second section of this chapter we will look at the practical application of the OFR Code and will look in detail at the principles (the 'Principles'), the outcomes (the 'Outcomes') and indicative behaviours ('Indicative Behaviours') in the OFR Code (reproduced with the kind permission of the Law Society) which are most relevant to you at this stage of your legal career as a student and trainee.

The OFR Code covers the following:

- 1st Section—You and your client;
- 2nd Section—You and your business;
- 3rd Section—You and your regulator;
- 4th Section—You and others; and
- 5th Section—Applications, waivers and interpretations.

We will be mainly concentrating on the 1st section of the OFR Code dealing with 'You and Your Client', as this is the area which you need to be very familiar with during the LPC and when you start your time in practice. We will also look in brief at areas in the 4th section—particularly in relation to undertakings. The other parts of the OFR Code are of course important and you must be aware of what they cover, but for your purposes at this level of your study we will not be concentrating on them.

The third section of this chapter highlights the areas in the core subjects which you will study on the LPC where professional conduct issues typically occur:

- property law and practice;
- litigation; and
- business law and practice.

Throughout the chapter, to assist you with your learning and knowledge of the OFR Code, there will be activities to do. There will also will be example scenarios from everyday practice where you will be asked to consider how you might achieve the Outcomes for your clients. **Suggested solutions** to these activities and scenarios will be provided at the end of this chapter at **(1.8)**. You should check your answers against these suggested solutions in **(1.8)** as you attempt each activity.

1.4 What being a member of the profession and a good solicitor means

> **Activity 1**
> What do you think clients want from their legal advisors? Try to think of as many diverse ideas as you can.

1.4.1 Act professionally

The public demands a high standard of professionalism from the legal profession, but the nature of what 'acting professionally' actually encompasses can be difficult to define. The standard is extremely high (as it should be!) not only in order to fulfil your professional duties and obligations, but also in order to satisfy ever-increasing client demands and expectations.

The following is a non-exhaustive list of what you should be aiming to achieve in order to maintain a high standard of professionalism.

- Have high ethical standards including honesty and integrity.
- Have respect for all people you deal with or work with.
- Be polite and have good manners.
- Have a positive attitude.
- Be confident but not arrogant.
- Be competent.
- Be flexible.
- Be commercially aware.
- Understand confidentiality.
- Have good communication skills.
- Have good time management.
- Be punctual.
- Understand financial management.

The maintenance of professionalism is constantly required both inside and outside the office. It is worth noting that many firms when recruiting for trainees often ask their staff members for reports or comments on the interviewees. This extends to comments from the receptionist, cleaner, canteen assistant and other trainees to partners who met the interviewees. Wherever you are and whoever you are speaking to, you should remember your ethical and professional standards.

1.4.2 Enrolling as a student member

All LPC students must enrol as students with the SRA. In order to enrol and be accepted by the SRA as a member of the profession you must confirm you are of good character and suitable for the profession. You will (if you are already studying the LPC) all have done this and seen the type of behaviour or past convictions which might preclude you from working as a lawyer. Even though you are not yet in contact with clients, the principles of professional conduct apply to all of you now as student members.

You must remember that as a law student a higher than normal standard of behaviour is expected from you. Look at Principle 6 set out in the OFR Code. You must 'behave in a way that maintains the trust the public place in you'. Professional rules are strictly enforced. It must be noted that you are already members of the profession and are subject to the same constraints and responsibilities which apply to qualified solicitors.

The SRA will take an interest in the behaviour of prospective solicitors. It is likely to take disciplinary action if issues such as criminal convictions, dishonesty, bankruptcy or LPC assessment offences arise. Examples of dishonesty and potential offences would include copying someone else's answer (including copying from a published work without proper attribution), making a false declaration that the assessment submission is your own work or dodging a fare on the tube or train!

The spirit of the OFR Code and its rules of professional conduct are summarised by the SRA in its introduction to the Handbook:

> This Handbook sets out the standards and requirements which we expect our regulated community to achieve and observe, for the benefit of the clients they serve and in the general public interest. Our approach to regulation (i.e. authorisation, supervision and enforcement) is outcomes-focused and risk-based so that clients receive services in a manner which best suits their own particular needs, and depending on how services are provided (e.g. whether in-house or through private practice).

1.4.3 Commercial and client awareness

In the increasingly competitive environment in which all solicitors now operate, it is more important than ever to provide outstanding service to clients. One of the key elements of continuing success for any lawyer, or his or her firm, is to recognise that they must put the needs of the client first. Reread the last sentence of the introduction to the Handbook set out above. You will note the emphasis on an individual client and his or her needs. Being a lawyer is not just about being technically good, it is also about being client-focused and ensuring your clients receive a service appropriate to their needs. What is suitable for one client may not be suitable for another.

The success or failure of a solicitor's practice depends largely on how it deals with its clients, in addition, of course, to the quality of the legal services delivered. Technical excellence is of course critical for a solicitor and clients will expect you to have this technical excellence but that is only the beginning. Clients in today's market expect you to provide so much more than technical ability.

Clients want their solicitors to:

- be attuned to their ever-changing needs;
- understand their individual situation and concerns;
- deliver on time at an appropriate cost;
- 'add value' to the relationship;
- (if they are corporate clients) be as commercially focused as they are; and
- (if they are corporate clients) understand their business.

By acting within the OFR Code you should be achieving these 'wants' but you should remember that the Outcomes in the OFR Code are a fluid concept: what may satisfy one type of client may not satisfy another. Each firm will need to review their client base and ascertain whether their existing systems and requirements will suit their specific clients under the OFR Code. A firm may have to have very different systems in place to meet different client type needs particularly if they are a firm practising a wide range of legal services. It will not be enough for firms to assume that, if they were meeting the rules of the 2007 Code, they will be achieving the Outcomes in the OFR Code.

Furthermore, client expectations of solicitors continue to increase as does the firm's drive to deliver continued excellence in client service. Even when you have satisfied a client it is vital to consider what else you can do to improve the relationship and add further value. This is because solicitors are working in an increasingly competitive market which looks certain to become even more challenging with the introduction of the ABSs.

1.4.4 Time and costs recording

A crucial part of your job will be recording your time. This is important both for the client and the firm in order to achieve the Outcomes of the OFR Code and act within the Principles of the Handbook. All firms have some form of time recording system. As a trainee this can be one of the hardest skills you need to learn. Time is recorded on a six minute basis. Each six minute period of time is one unit. If you write a letter and it is a short letter which only takes you two minutes to dictate you would charge one unit. So you round up to the nearest six minutes. If you spend half an hour writing or dictating a more complicated letter then you would record five units of time. Each activity you undertake as a solicitor will have a different code for time recording purposes; so there will be different codes for letter-writing, making or receiving a telephone call, attending court, attending on a client, preparation or perusing a file. All of these are examples of chargeable activities; that is, activities which you can charge to your client for work undertaken on their transaction or file.

You may also be surprised to hear that there will be codes which relate to non-chargeable activities. Examples of these might be training, internal meetings or marketing and networking. These are activities which you will have to attend to as part of your job but you cannot record these to a client's matter as they do not form part of the client retainer or rules of engagement.

Each client will have a number; it is to that client and number that time is recorded. This is necessary in order to provide the most accurate picture of how the firm spends time and to allow proper informed management and strategic decisions to be made. Most firms will have targets which they expect their fee-earners to achieve in relation to the amount of chargeable time which must be recorded in a day.

There are several different time recording and case management programmes used by firms and as part of your induction at any firm you work in you should be given separate training on how to operate the relevant system. The importance of accurate time recording is paramount. The purpose and value of time recording is not only so a client's costs can be recorded and billed accurately and correctly but also to provide financial information on the basis of which the partners can make sensible and informed decisions about their firm. If fee-earners do not record time accurately, the partners of the firm may, as a result, make decisions based on incorrect information. This could have a seriously detrimental effect on the profit and/or the overall financial stability of the firm.

Remember the firm is a business and it is for the partners to make decisions based on financial sense. The time recording system allows them to have at their finger tips information on the chargeable and non-chargeable time for all individual lawyers and departments. This will allow partners in a firm or managing directors of an ABS to identify departmental difficulties and allow better decisions to be taken on matters such as work allocation.

In the current competitive and difficult financial market, it will also give crucial information in relation to variations in fee-earner workloads, which will assist with recruitment and staffing decisions.

'Imaginative' and 'creative' time recording is fraudulent. From a business perspective, it also reduces the value of the relevant information and, as above, can lead to misconceived decisions being made. It will therefore be impossible to assess true productivity and profitability of fee earners and/or departments, types of work and clients. This will have a direct impact on the firm's ability to comply with the Principles of the OFR Code, particularly the last four Principles of the OFR Code relating to good business management (see (**1.5.3**) below).

1.4.5 Be organised

Under Principle 5 of the Handbook, you must provide a proper standard of service to your client. In order to achieve this you need to be organised and have excellent time management skills. Ensuring you have such skills will help you manage the stress and pressures of the job. You will find, in order to achieve the best of yourself on the LPC, you will similarly have to be self-disciplined and to manage your time. You should start trying to organise yourself so you give yourself enough time to complete your work but also to give yourself some 'downtime'. You will not be doing the best job you can, both on the LPC and in practice, if you are not able to relax. If you are very stressed it is likely you will be trying to do too much at the same time. You may feel like you are 'fire fighting, tackling issues as they arise rather than dealing with your tasks in a considered and organised fashion. Learning how to prioritise is crucial.

> **Activity 2**
>
> Spend a few minutes thinking of processes you could implement to ensure you have good time management skills.

> **Activity 3**
>
> Test your 'natural clock'. Use a clock or watch with a second hand. Shut your eyes for what you think is one minute. When you think a minute has passed open your eyes and check your watch or clock. Do you have a good natural clock? If not, you know this is a skill you will need to improve.
>   Most people naturally think sixty seconds lasts longer than it actually does.

1.4.6 Always be on time!

This is good manners, as well as professional conduct, but always make sure you are on time. This comes down to good time management. Do not arrive late with an excuse you are busy. So are your clients! Consider how you feel if any service provider fails to deliver their service to you on time.

More than just bad manners, you will not be complying with Principle 5 or Principle 6 of the OFR Code if you are late. A lack of punctuality could damage rapport with your client or could damage your professional reputation and that of the firm. You could also be opening yourself up to potential negligence claims arising from missed deadlines. What if a claim was time-barred because you missed the limitation period or you were charged a penalty or fine for paying stamp duty land tax late on behalf of a client? It is vital to implement an effective diary system to assist your file or work management and in turn to reduce stress levels and foster good organisational skills. Again, your firm may have already instigated systems to assist you with this as part of its own requirements. You will most certainly have access to an electronic diary in which, as a matter of habit, you should add all of your deadlines and dates which are relevant to your client files.

1.4.7 Dictation and note taking

Another vital skill that you will have to learn is dictation. Although some firms will expect you to do some of your own typing and administration jobs, most firms appreciate that it is more cost effective to employ support staff to help you with this aspect of your job. It is usually quicker for you to dictate a letter and/or document and have a secretary with excellent touch-typing skills then transfer this to paper. This is a much better use of your time and better for the client who is paying for your skills on a timed basis. This will ensure you are achieving the Principles not only in relation to providing your client with a proper standard of service (Principle 5) but also in relation to managers of the legal service provider ensuring that the business is run effectively (Principle 8).

It is also important you record by way of a note on your file each and every conversation with clients, other professionals or solicitors on each transaction. If it is not a communication in a written form (a copy of which can go on the file) there is no way to record what has been discussed other than a written record of the conversation. Again this would normally be dictated by the fee-earner and typed up and added to the file. But think commercially: if it is a very quick conversation then write the note by hand (neatly so it is legible!) so you are not needlessly taking up secretarial time and wasting paper! You must always bear in mind your firm is a business—do not waste resources. This business sense is at the heart of the new OFR Code.

1.4.8 Professional conduct and the LPC

Professional conduct cannot be considered in isolation. It pervades all aspects of a solicitor's life and work; for that reason it is also studied on the LPC as a pervasive topic. It will be covered in all of your core subjects and where applicable in your elective subject choices.

When considering whether you are complying with the OFR Code you need to ensure you are aware of the following:

Figure 1.2 Professional conduct diagram

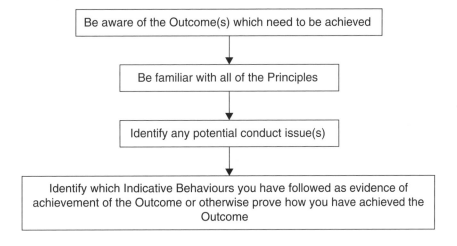

1.5 The Handbook

1.5.1 Structure of the Handbook

Until the implementation of the Handbook, the regulatory regime consisted of the Solicitors' Code of Conduct 2007, the Solicitors' Accounts Rules 1998, the SRA Recognised Bodies Regulations 2009 and the client financial protection (that is, indemnity insurance and compensation fund requirements). The Handbook replaces all of these regulations in a single structure and brings together the key regulatory elements in seven sections. The Handbook does not just regulate solicitors in traditional firms but will also regulate new entrants to the legal profession, for example the new ABSs. Clients of all types of legal practice will receive the same level of protection from the SRA.

There is no printed version of a 'rule book'. The Handbook is an online only resource. The benefit of this is that it will allow for flexibility without the need to reprint the Code with any updating changes. However, there has also been concern expressed that this flexibility will lead to problems. It will be easy for the SRA to update and change the OFR

Code and Handbook but more difficult for legal service providers to keep on top of the OFR Code and its current requirements.

You can access the OFR Code and other elements of the Handbook on the SRA website http://www.sra.org.uk. You will also be able to use the SRA website to check for any amendments. Please note that due to the flexible nature of the OFR Code there may have been minor amendments since this text book was published. In order to keep you up to date with amendments another resource available to you is http://www.oxfordtextbooks.co.uk/orc/foundations11_12/.

Figure 1.3 shows a snapshot of how the Handbook is structured. This was provided to practitioners by the SRA on 6 April 2011 when the final version of the Handbook was launched.

Figure 1.3 Code of conduct structure diagram

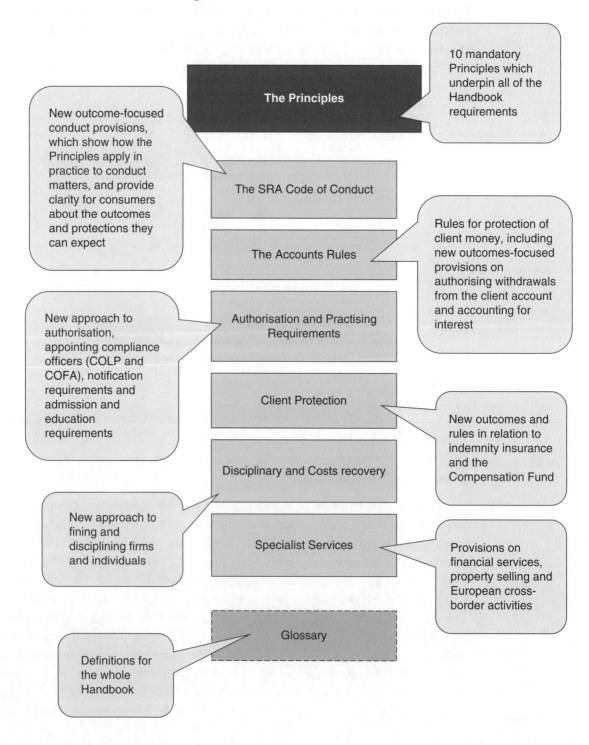

For the purposes of the rest of this chapter we will be focusing on the Principles and the SRA Code of Conduct (defined in this chapter as the OFR Code) as it is these, as a student and trainee, you need to be most familiar with as you carry out your studies and enter practice.

1.5.2 Background to the Handbook

In October 2008 Lord Hunt of Wirral was commissioned by the Law Society to write a report into the regulation of legal services and to consider what was needed to establish best modern practice. His findings confirmed the view that there needed to be a radical overhaul. He further concluded that the SRA needed greater expertise and understanding and a more sophisticated approach that recognised the varied needs of different sectors of the profession.

Lord Hunt advised a return to reinvigorated professional values—a return to principle-based regulation. He further went on to state that Rule 1 of the 2007 Code should become the overarching philosophy, a statement of core ethics that embrace the importance of justice and the rule of law, integrity, independence, the paramountcy of client's interests and standards of service. The writer was fortunate enough to attend one of Lord Hunt's presentations during the gathering of information and input from the profession for his report. The clear message from the presentation was the need to return to the early implied regulation governing the profession, that being, to act within the instinctive guiding principle of professionalism, decency, trusted adviser and duty to the client.

Set out below is Rule 1 from the 2007 Code. In addition to this Rule 1 there were then 24 rules to supplement this with extensive guidance for each rule. All rules and guidance were **mandatory**.

	Rule
1.01 **Justice and the rule of law**	You must uphold the rule of law and the proper administration of justice.
1.02 **Integrity**	You must act with integrity.
1.03 **Independence**	You must not allow your independence to be compromised.
1.04 **Best interests of clients**	You must act in the best interests of each client.
1.05 **Standard of service**	You must provide a good standard of service to your clients.
1.06 **Public confidence**	You must not behave in a way that is likely to diminish the trust the public places in you or the legal profession.

It is interesting to set out Rule 1 from the 2007 Code as you will see that the view of Lord Hunt of Wirral, and many other commentators and practitioners, was in fact widely adopted by the SRA when drafting the Principles for the Handbook.

1.5.3 The Principles

The new Handbook will be underpinned by ten overarching Principles, some of which are new and others which have been based on existing core duties. The Principles are amplified by Outcomes which firms are expected to achieve. The only **mandatory** parts of the Handbook are the Principles and Outcomes. These are intended to cover those areas which are genuinely needed to protect clients and the public and to deliver high standards of service. The rest of the Handbook including the Indicative Behaviours and guidance are **advisory** only (with the exception of specific areas such as accounts).

The ten Principles underpin the new regime and everything in the Handbook, not just the OFR Code. The OFR Code then sets the Principles in context. The Principles define the fundamental ethical and professional standards expected of all firms and individuals when providing legal services. The introduction to the Principles in the Handbook advises that the Principles should be your starting point when faced with an ethical dilemma.

The ten Principles of the OFR Code are set out in Figure 1.4.

Figure 1.4 Ten Principles of the OFR Code

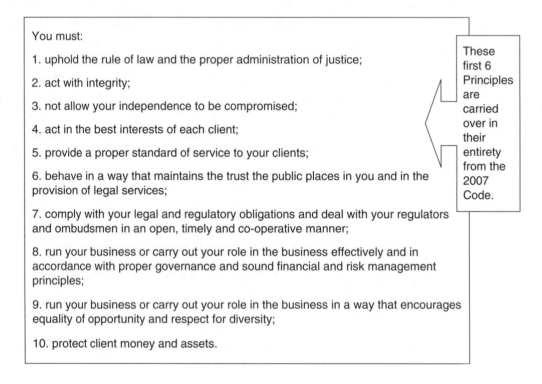

Consider these Principles next to the old Rule 1. You can see that the old Rule 1 has in its entirety been adopted, with the addition of four new Principles.

The first six Principles (being the same as from the old Rule 1) have long been established as the professional standards required from the legal profession. Indeed, the guidance to Rule 1 as set out in the 2007 Code confirms this approach:

A modern just society needs a legal profession which adopts high standards of integrity and professionalism The core duties contained in rule 1 set the standards which will meet the needs of both clients and society…

The aim of the Principles is to ensure a solicitor's responsibility to his or her clients and to society is upheld. As a rough guide, Principles 1 and 6 address the responsibility a solicitor has to society and Principles 2, 3, 4 and 5 address the responsibilities a solicitor has to his or her client.

The four new Principles have been included to assist with the new OFR approach.

Principle 7 adds as a mandatory obligation the need to comply with the regulator. There was under the old regime a high level of non-compliance in certain areas, including failure to disclose referral fees and non-payment of compensation awarded by the Legal Complaints Service. This Principle also assists the SRA with its gathering of information, which is a large part of the OFR approach, allowing the SRA to monitor risk as an ongoing relationship with firms rather than having to deal with an incident after it has happened or with a complaint once it has been made, or even in very serious cases having to shut down a firm once an incident has occurred.

Principle 8 has been included to try and tackle the large number of firm insolvencies in the last few years and the large number of firms in the Assigned Risk Pool. The Assigned Risks Pool provides indemnity insurance cover for firms which cannot get cover from qualifying insurers or cannot reasonably afford the terms available to them. This might be because the firm has a poor claims record, a major claim outstanding but not yet decided or other risk factors. This Principle therefore makes it mandatory that the firm is run based on sound commercial awareness.

Principle 9 is an important addition as it tries to differentiate between the different client types, whether they are sophisticated body corporates or vulnerable individuals. This Principle also covers the treatment of employees.

Principle 10 is also a valuable addition, particularly in the current climate with the increase in mortgage fraud. This goes to the heart of the duty in Principle 4, which is to act in the best interests of your client by protecting their assets which have been entrusted to your firm.

The last four new Principles are drafted very widely and look like catch-all provisions but they effectively duplicate duties already imposed on the legal profession through various legislative and regulatory frameworks.

You should review the Principles in the Handbook. In addition to the Principles there are notes which should be read in conjunction with the Principles providing additional guidance on what these mean.

If the Principles are breached then the enforcement approach by the SRA will depend on all of the circumstances of each individual case. The primary aim of the SRA is to achieve the right outcome for the consumer.

1.5.4 The Code of Conduct (referred to in this chapter as the OFR Code)

In addition to the ten Principles, the OFR Code will contain the Outcomes. The Outcomes are mandatory and when achieved will help ensure compliance with the Principles. It is hoped these will be an explanation of what the successful application of the Principles should look like to a client instructing a legal professional. It is anticipated that the mandatory Outcomes will be achieved in a variety of ways depending on the particular transaction and circumstances. Whereas previously the legal profession and firms had the detailed rules to guide them in their actions, the legal service providers are being allowed to decide for themselves and make considered decisions how to best translate the Principles into a successful client outcome. This will mean greater judgement on the part of the legal service provider. Some may say this is a positive step allowing solicitors to go it alone and make informed decisions as to how to best translate the Principles and Outcomes into a successful client outcome. This differs from the 'hand-held approach' of the 2007 Code. However, doubters of the OFR regime would say this widens the opportunity for some practitioners to avoid their professional duties without the strict rule-based requirements of old, thus keeping them in line.

The Outcomes have then been supplemented with the non-mandatory Indicative Behaviours to aid compliance and understanding by practioners. The Indicative Behaviours are not exhaustive. These are provided to give some assurance that if you follow the Indicative Behaviours your firm '*may*' be achieving the Outcomes. The word *may* is important. There is no certainty that even if you or your firm is following the Indicative Behaviours you will then be compliant with the OFR Code. Firms are encouraged to consider how they can best achieve the Outcomes, taking into account the nature and size of the firm, their particular circumstances and, crucially, the needs of their particular clients. It will be up to the legal service provider to prove how it has achieved the Outcome.

This new flexible, individualistic approach is intended to achieve the move away from the old detailed rule book which received so much 'bad press' amongst practitioners, especially City firms, and the new approach links to the new slogan of the OFR Code—'freedom in practice'. However, hand in hand with this approach it must be understood that you have no certainty your firm is compliant. The SRA has also stated that it will not act as a 'safe harbour' to firms seeking approval for an activity.

1.5.5 Compliance officers

One of the more substantial regulatory changes in the OFR Code is the new requirement for firms to appoint a Compliance Officer for Legal Practice (CoLP) and a Compliance Officer for Finance and Administration (CoFA). In order to hold these posts you would need to be of sufficient seniority and hold a position of sufficient responsibility to fulfil these roles. The person appointed must therefore, within the firm, have sufficient authority and credence to put in place systems, controls and governance of these systems and controls to ensure good compliance with the Handbook. It is for the firm to ensure that these nominated officers have sufficient authority to ensure the systems will work effectively. These officers will provide a point of contact for the SRA on matters concerning compliance. Even though these rules seem to impose ultimate responsibility on the CoLP and CoFA, the guidance notes state the existence of these compliance officers in a firm is not a substitute for the firm's and manager's responsibilities.

However, again, concern has been expressed in relation to these roles and how their responsibilities have been drafted in the Handbook. The Law Society is so concerned by the prospect of these officers becoming personally exposed under the Handbook that it is considering a scheme to shore up the position of these officers as it felt it was wrong that the officers should be held personally liable for the behaviour of others.

1.6 Practical application of the OFR Code

1.6.1 You and your client

Before you read this section of this chapter you should review the first Section of the OFR Code which covers 'You and Your Client'. The Outcomes in this section show how the Principles apply in the context of client care.

Section 1 of the OFR Code covers:

- client care;
- equality and diversity;
- conflicts of interest;
- confidentiality and disclosure;
- your clients and the court; and
- your client and introductions to third parties.

1.6.1.1 Client care (Chapter 1 of section 1 of the OFR Code)

There are sixteen Outcomes relating to client care. These cover: providing a proper standard of service, giving clients the appropriate level of information about the services they will receive and supplying information as to how much this will cost. For the purpose of this chapter we are going to concentrate on those areas of professional conduct which you will encounter during your LPC and training.

1.6.1.2 Client care and costs

You must remember that your firm is running a business and in order to comply with Principle 8, and the Handbook in general, the amount you can bill a client and the fees you are able to generate are crucial. As mentioned previously, it is no longer good enough to be an excellent technical lawyer: you need to be able to go out there and win clients and fees and then retain those clients. It is also worth noting that it is not negligence or errors which garner the most complaints from clients in relation to their lawyers, it is the costs associated with these services.

You may, when you enter practice, be shocked or embarrassed by your charge out rate. You may feel that you do not yet have the expertise to be charged out by your firm at such an expensive rate. An average trainee charge out rate is likely to be in the region of £100–£150. For City firms this figure could be much higher. However, your limited experience has been taken into account by your firm when they set your charge out rate. Partners and more senior lawyers will be charged out at substantially more. You should remember that you have studied for a long time to get to the position you are in. Do not get into the habit of undercharging. Record your time correctly. This reiterates the requirement to always act professionally as discussed in **(1.4.1)**. If you are surprised by your charge out rate, imagine how surprised a client might be, particularly if they have never had the need of a solicitor before. It is imperative that your client has its eyes wide open in relation to the likely cost of a matter. Better this is all laid out in the open and the client is kept up to date with this as the transaction continues rather than surprising the client with a large bill at the end. This is when the complaints start. You must get over any discomfort you may feel in discussing the potential cost of something.

1.6.1.3 Costs in general

Rule 2 in the 2007 Code governed all aspects of costs information and was very detailed setting out clear guidance on the information which clients had to be given at the outset and during a transaction. Information in relation to costs also had to be in writing. You will see from **O(1.13)** that this has been replaced by an obligation to provide the best possible information.

O(1.13)   *clients* receive the best possible information, both at the outset and when appropriate as their matter progresses, about the likely overall cost of their matter;

There is no obligation to provide this information in writing any more, but Indicative Behaviour **IB(1.19)** suggests this information should be in a clear and accessible form appropriate to the needs and circumstances of the client. The Indicative Behaviours also cover explaining to your client not only how your costs might be charged but also warning the client that they may have to pay another person's costs, perhaps in a litigation matter, and whether the client may be entitled to public funding or a conditional fee agreement. Remember that the Indicative Behaviours are not mandatory but if you do not follow them you may be asked to prove how you have otherwise met the Outcomes.

Activity 4

What different ways can you think of to ensure the following different client types have the best possible information in relation to costs and their transaction and thereby achieve O(1.13)?

(a) An illiterate client.

(b) A client who does not speak English.

(c) A medium sized corporate client.

(d) A large corporate experienced legal service user.

1.6.1.4 Publicly funded clients

It is important to think about your clients individually. Cost information for different types of clients will vary depending on the type of work you are doing for them, the nature of your firm and the type of client. Clearly you will be achieving **O(1.13)** if you do not discuss the possibility of public funding when acting on behalf of a corporate client (to do so would in fact be wrong). However, if you are acting for an individual whose financial situation would indicate they may be entitled to public funding and you do not discuss this option with them (which is covered in **IB(1.16)**) then it would be for you to prove to the SRA how you achieved **O(1.13)** without giving this information.

> **Activity 5**
>
> You are acting for a client whose father has just died. Your firm was instructed to deal with the probate. On the basis of your initial instructions you gave your client a quote confirming your costs would be £1,000 plus VAT. However, you have now received correspondence from another firm of solicitors advising they have been instructed to contest the will of your client's father. The matter is now clearly more complicated than originally anticipated. What should you do now to ensure you are achieving the Outcomes?

1.6.1.5 Conditional fee agreements

Conditional fee agreements only arise in litigation. **IB(1.17)** provides guidance suggesting that if you agree a fee agreement with your client then the client should be given all relevant information in relation to that agreement. Again, remember the Indicative Behaviours are not mandatory. They merely offer assistance to a solicitor to advise how they can achieve the Outcomes. However, if you have a conditional fee agreement with your client and your client does not have all the relevant information given to them in relation to the agreement then, because you did not follow the IBs (but may have achieved the Outcome in a different way), it will be for you to prove to the SRA how you have achieved the Outcome.

1.6.1.6 Client care and complaints

Outcomes **O(1.9)**, **O(1.10)**, **O(1.11)** and **O(1.14)** all cover how a client's complaints should be handled and the information which a client should be given at the outset of their matter. You will note in **O(1.9)** that the obligation to provide information to clients in relation to their right to complain confirms that this must be in writing and must be given at the outset of the matter.

O(1.9) *clients* are informed in writing at the outset of their matter of their right to complain and how *complaints* can be made;

Again, Rule 2 in the 2007 Code set out the rules in relation to providing complaints information to clients. This had the same requirement as **O(1.9)**. At the start of the matter the client had to be given in writing information that they could complain if they were unhappy with the service they received and who they could complain to. It was, however, also mandatory to have a written complaints procedure which had to be highlighted to the client and provided to them on their request. You will note this obligation to have a written complaints procedure is not in the Outcomes. However, look at **IB(1.22)**, which supports the new **O(1.9)**. This suggests that, by having a written complaints procedure, which should be brought to the client's attention, this may achieve the Outcome.

It would appear therefore on the surface that little has changed. Although it is no longer compulsory to have a written complaints procedure, most, if not all, firms will already have these in place, so will continue to do so under the new OFR regime in the knowledge that if this satisfied the old 2007 Code then it should for the most part continue to satisfy the Outcomes. By having the written procedure firms are following the Indicative Behaviours which albeit not mandatory are guidance as to how you can achieve the Outcomes. The difference will be in making sure the written complaints procedure is satisfying the needs of all client types.

> **Activity 6**
>
> On the information provided which of the following scenarios would not achieve the required Outcomes?
>
> (a) A client who has been referred to you e-mails you and gives you some background details on a transaction he wants to instruct you on. You send him a brief e-mail back just introducing yourself and commenting on his e-mail. The client responds and confirms he wants to instruct you. You e-mail him a letter and include within this letter information on the client's right to complain if there is an issue and the estimated cost of the matter.
>
> (b) An angry client contacts the firm's receptionist and says, 'I want to make a complaint and don't tell me I can't because I know I am entitled to because the solicitor told me I could in the first letter he ever wrote to me!' The receptionist gives very clear oral instructions about the procedure available to the client.
>
> (c) A client who has been referred to you comes into the office to see you. He decides on the spot he is so keen to instruct you that you discuss with him at this first interview the likely costs and the fact that if he so wishes in the future he can make a complaint, and how to go about that. You go back to your desk and open a file. Part of the firm's opening file procedure is a checklist. You tick the boxes in relation to the OFR Code's costs and complaints requirements as having been met.

> **Activity 7**
>
> You work for a firm that has in place a written complaints procedure. This runs to 20 pages and is very detailed. You act for a client who has had a very limited education and whom you know struggles with reading and writing. He rings up the receptionist to complain. She refers him to the letter sent out at the start of the transaction, which in fact contained a copy of the complaints procedure and advises him he needs to read this and follow the suggested procedure.
>
> Has your firm achieved O(1.9)? If not, how could you suggest amending this procedure for this client?

1.6.1.7 Client care and instructions and resources

Look at **O(1.3)**.

O(1.3) when deciding whether to act, or terminate your instructions, you comply with the law and the Code;

As a solicitor, you can decide whether you wish to act for a client or not, but when making that decision you need to comply with the law and the OFR Code. However, look at **IB(1.26)**. You may not have complied with the OFR Code if you terminate instructions with a client without good reason and without providing reasonable notice. You should not therefore refuse to act or terminate instructions based on any difference in political or social views with a client. You need to base your decision on good reason. It would be for you to prove to the SRA that your decision for refusing or terminating instructions was based on good reason.

Compliance with the Outcomes should ensure that both solicitors and clients are clear as to their responsibilities and expectations. Clients whose expectations have been properly managed are less likely to complain about the service they receive, but more likely to be impressed with the service and to re-instruct the solicitor or law firm in question.

> **Activity 8**
>
> Which of the following do you think would be reasonable reasons for refusing or terminating instructions and would therefore be achieving O(1.3)?
>
> (a) You have been acting on behalf of a client who has not paid her bills despite your accounts department having written to her twice and spoken to her four times in the last three months asking for payment.
>
> (b) You are contacted by a potential client who has been accused of criminal damage. He set fire to an abortion clinic as he is vehemently opposed to abortion. You in fact believe in a woman's right to choose and decide not to accept his instructions.
>
> (c) A potential client tells you that they have heard you are the best divorce lawyer in the country and that if you manage to agree a divorce settlement of over £15 million pounds for them they will give you a £5000 bonus at the end of the matter.
>
> (d) You acted previously for a client, Tom Smith. A new client wants to instruct you in bringing an action against Tom.
>
> (e) You have been acting on behalf of a client whom you don't like. This month when you sent her an interim bill she paid it late. You decide to terminate her retainer.

When deciding whether to accept instructions you should never allow your pride or incorrectly held embarrassment to take over when considering whether or not your firm has the resources to act on behalf of a client. Look at Principle 5. You must provide your client with a proper standard of service.

> **Activity 9**
>
> Read the following scenario. Then look at the Outcomes in the OFR Code. Is your firm able to act for him? Explain your answer.
>
> You are a trainee at a firm which only offers property advice services. A client for whom you have acted for many years in relation to his successful property investment business contacts you for advice on an employment matter. An employee is claiming constructive dismissal. He wants you to act because he trusts you.

1.6.1.8 Client care in general

Most firms will already have in place a client care letter. City firms tend to use the phrase 'terms and conditions of business' or 'engagement letters', which will contain the information required in relation to costs and complaints. These are sent out to clients at the start of each transaction or, if a firm acts for a client on a retainer basis, may simply be reviewed with the client each year rather than sent out for each and every transaction they are instructed on.

These satisfied the requirements in Rule 2 of the 2007 Code. It is anticipated that these will continue to be the procedure most firms will use in order to satisfy the Outcomes in section 1 of the Code 'You and your client'. However, there is a subtle shift in emphasis which you need to watch out for. Previously, a firm may have had a perfect client care letter which ticked all the rule boxes of the detailed Rule 2 in the 2007 Code. However, this may not be satisfactory for your particular client if they do not understand the information provided to them because it is too detailed or complex. In this scenario, under the OFR Code you will not have satisfied the Outcomes. Firms who already have effective and extensive systems in place to ensure that client care is the focus of their engagement will still under the new OFR Code have to carry out a thorough check of these systems and procedures to check they will be compliant with achieving the Outcomes.

Many larger firms will have in place rules of practice which they require their fee earners to comply with to ensure complete client satisfaction. These will be going a long way towards satisfying the subtle shift to ensuring each individual client is cared for rather than just a tick box system which was required under the 2007 Code.

Typical rules include:

- All incoming correspondence must receive a reply within 24 hours of receipt.
- Each incoming call must be dealt with as promptly and efficiently as possible.
- If a fee earner is unavailable or for some justifiable reason unable to take that call immediately, then the call must be returned on the same day.
- A fee-earner must sit down with a client and understand its business and needs and react and carry out its transaction accordingly.
- When a client file is removed from the office it must not be read whilst travelling on public transport.
- A client file or any matter relating to a client or the business of the firm must not be discussed in public where there is any likelihood of being overheard.
- Particular care should be taken in any communication to ensure that what is written or communicated is intended and in a suitable form for your particular client.

1.6.2 Equality and diversity (Chapter 2 of section 1 of the OFR Code)

As mentioned previously in this chapter you have a duty as a solicitor at all times to be seen to be polite, professional and to have integrity. Review the Outcomes in Chapter 2 of section 1 of the OFR Code in relation to this. None of the requirements to act within the Equality Act 2010 or to act in any way which would discriminate against any particular person or group of people should be a surprise to you. However, it is worth noting that these Outcomes are intended to cover both your relationship with clients and your relationship with your colleagues within your firm.

1.6.3 Conflicts of interest (Chapter 3 of section 1 of the OFR Code)

Conflicts of interests can be one of the most difficult areas to assess and do catch practitioners out. The problem is that there are circumstances, albeit limited, when you can act if there is a 'conflict of interest' and the decision as to whether a conflict exists can be fluid as the transaction progresses, so it must be an ongoing monitoring process. You should have Chapter 3 of section 1 on 'Conflicts of Interest' to hand as you read this so you can review the different Outcomes and Indicative Behaviours as they are mentioned.

Due to the practical difficulties of assessing and dealing with conflicts this was, in the drafting of the new OFR Code, one of the most contentious areas particularly in relation to property transactions. This will be covered in more detail later in **paragraph 1.7.1** when we look at conduct issues relating to property law and practice.

At the start of a transaction most firms will run what is called a conflict check. This checks a firm's database to assess whether the firm has had any dealing with either the instructing client or the other party to the transaction. This information is the starting point to ascertain if there is, or likely to be, a conflict of interest. Under the 2007 Code this conflict check was a requirement—a mandatory rule. In the draft versions of the OFR Code it had been intended that the requirement to have these systems in place was only to be an Indicative Behaviour and therefore not mandatory. However, during the consultation process carried out with practitioners it was clear that this was felt by many to be almost one step too far and cause for concern. In the final version of the OFR Code released on 6 April 2011 the original draft Indicative Behaviours were upgraded to Outcomes. Look at O(3.1)–O(3.3). Clearly, whether the firm is a sole practitioner with a small client base or an international City firm, the systems and procedures in place are likely to vary. The way in which such a conflict check will be undertaken will depend on the size and nature of the firm. It might be enough in a very small sole-practitioner firm to manually check a filing cabinet but clearly this is not going to be sufficient in a larger firm.

There is the basic rule that you cannot act if there is a conflict of interest between you and your client. See O(3.4). This is called an 'own interest conflict' in the OFR Code. So if you were buying property from a client this would be an 'own interest conflict' and you **could not** act.

Prohibition on acting in conflict situations

O(3.4) you do not act if there is an *own interest conflict* or a significant risk of an *own interest conflict*;

O(3.5) you do not act if there is a *client conflict*, or a significant risk of a *client conflict*, unless the circumstances set out in Outcomes 3.6 and 3.7 apply;

However, look at **O(3.5)**. You can act in limited circumstances if there is a conflict between two or more clients. This Outcome essentially reflects the rules and guidance of the 2007 Code. You can act in **O(3.6)** if there is a client conflict and the clients have a 'substantially common interest' or in **O(3.7)** if there is a client conflict and the clients are competing for the same objective.

It is necessary first to look at 'substantially common interest' and see what this means. It is defined in Chapter 14 of the OFR Code. There needs to be a strong consensus between the conflicting clients on how any common purpose is to be achieved and any area of conflict has to be peripheral to the common purpose. In addition you need to achieve **O(3.6) (a)–(d)**.

Exceptions where you may act with appropriate safeguards, where there is a client conflict

O(3.6) where there is a *client conflict* and the *clients* have a *substantially common interest* in relation to a matter or a particular aspect of it, you only act if:

(a) you have explained the relevant issues and risks to the *clients* and you have a reasonable belief that they understand those issues and risks;

(b) all the *clients* have given informed consent in writing to you acting;

(c) you are satisfied that it is reasonable for you to act for all the *clients* and that it is in their best interests; and

(d) you are satisfied that the benefits to the *clients* of you doing so outweigh the risks.

In other words, you can only act if the parties have had the relevant issues and risks explained to them, if all the clients have given their consent to your acting on behalf of both of them in writing, if you are satisfied that it is reasonable for you to act for all of the clients and if you believe that the benefits to the clients of your doing so outweigh the risks. You can see then that it is only going to be in limited circumstances that you will be able to satisfy all of these requirements.

You can also act for both parties competing for the same objective which is defined in Chapter 14 as *asset, contract or business opportunity* if you satisfy **O(3.7)(a)–(e)**. The Indicative Behaviours will help you to ascertain if there is a conflict or a potential conflict and whether you can act or whether you should refuse instructions.

Outcomes O(3.6) and O(3.7) are intended to apply to specialised areas of legal services where the clients are sophisticated users of those services and they conclude they would rather use their retained solicitors rather than seek out new advisors. Often the large City firms or small specialist firms will act for several of the large PLC companies and will find their existing clients both want to instruct them in relation to the same transaction because of their expertise in their business or the market place. The SRA anticipates it should be rare for a firm to rely on O(3.7). Indeed, this Outcome should be relied upon with extreme caution. It is likely to be only the City firms who will try and use this.

If you cannot satisfy either of the exceptions in O(3.6) or O(3.7), O(3.5) will apply and you will have to refuse to act for a client (if you have not already started acting). If you have already started acting for a client as no conflict existed at the start of the matter and a conflict arises during the transaction, you will have to stop acting for one of the clients. In deciding who you have to stop acting for, you would also at this stage need to think about your duty of confidentiality (duty of confidentiality is discussed in more detail below).

One area that City firms pushed for was to change the definition of 'conflict of interest' and 'client conflict' to relate only to current clients. This has not been incorporated and remains the same as the 2007 Code to include any client whether former or current. The definition of client in Chapter 14 of the OFR Code makes this clear.

It is also worth noting that there may be times where you should still refuse to act for two clients even if there is no conflict of interest because you would be breaching the Principles. This was discussed briefly in **Activity 8**. So, for example, if you were instructed to act on behalf of one client on the acquisition of a business where your firm had previously acted for that business and held confidential information in relation to it, there is no conflict per se. Remember conflict is defined as between clients in the ***same or related matter***. Here you acted for the business on a previous matter. Therefore it is not a conflict but you would hold information which was material to the new client. Therefore you would not be able to act because to do so would be breaching the overriding Principles 2, 4, 5 and 6.

> **Activity 10**
>
> Consider this scenario. Jot down whether or not you could act in this scenario.
>
> You are a trainee at a firm which is well known for expertise in the telecoms industry. You have two long-standing clients, Phone PLC and Broadband Unlimited PLC, both large telecoms companies. Both companies contact your firm asking you to act on their behalf in relation to a tender to purchase a recently liquidated telecoms business.

1.6.4 Confidentiality and disclosure (Chapter 4 of section 1 of the OFR Code)

Keeping the affairs of your client confidential is central to the relationship you have with a client and is fundamental to your ability to comply with the Principles. You should read Chapter 4 of section 1 of the OFR Code before you read this section of this chapter.

You should note that your duty to keep your client's affairs confidential continues even though the retainer between you and your client is terminated and even on the death of your client. It is also not just the individual solicitor who has a duty to keep the affairs of his client confidential but **all** members of the firm.

Your duty of confidentiality exists at all times. Do not discuss your day at work and inadvertently discuss your client's affairs while travelling home with your partner or friend on the tube or on the bus or train. Anyone could hear your conversation. If you work in an office building do not discuss with a colleague a transaction in the lift or while making a cup of coffee in the kitchen. Again, anyone else in the lift or kitchen could overhear your conversation.

Your duty of confidentiality is set out in O(4.1).

O(4.1) you keep the affairs of *clients* confidential unless disclosure is required or permitted by law or the *client* consents;

O(4.2) any individual who is advising a *client* makes that *client* aware of all information material to that retainer of which the individual has personal knowledge;

O(4.3) you ensure that where your duty of confidentiality to one *client* comes into conflict with your duty of disclosure to another *client*, your duty of confidentiality takes precedence;

As is, this is not difficult to comply with or complicated. However, this must be read in conjunction with O(4.2). You have a duty of confidentiality but you also have a duty to advise a client of any information which is material to them. The problem arises if you are acting for more than one client. A conflict may occur between the clients if your duty of confidentiality with one client conflicts with your duty to disclose information which is relevant and material to another client's matter. The Outcomes confirm how you need to deal with this situation. Look at O(4.3). The duty of confidentiality takes precedence. This is the same as was set out in the 2007 Code. The duty of confidentiality always overrides the duty of disclosure.

To achieve the Outcomes you must disclose material information to a client but you must also keep information confidential. If you are unable to do this because to achieve your duty of confidentiality in O(4.1) you are unable to tell the other affected client of the information which is material to them because of O(4.3), then you will need to cease acting for the client to whom you owe the duty of disclosure, and not tell that client why because of your duty of confidentiality to the other client.

Activity 11

Match up the following potential confidentiality situations with the suggested solutions or methods of achieving the Outcomes.

> You work in a criminal practice. You hear your client on his mobile negotiating to buy firearms for a planned burglary.

> You may be able to act but you would need to put in place safeguards, would need consent to act and should deem it reasonable to act with those safeguards in place.

> You outsource photocopying to an external printers. The next day an article in the press appears revealing information obtained from the material you outsourced.

> You should not reveal this information.

> You work for a large City firm. Your firm has acted for Client X who you know has financial issues. You are instructed by a private investor who intends to lend money to Client X.

> You may still be able to show you have achieved the Outcomes if you can prove to the SRA you made sufficient checks to ensure client confidentiality.

> An old client rings to say his mother has died and your firm prepared her will. He says his mother told him that she left her house to his son. He asks you to check this before he tells his son.

> You should contact the police.

Conflicts, confidentiality and disclosure is a lot about instinct and the more experienced you become in practice the more your instinct will become honed and your professional conduct warning chime will start to ring when situations do not feel right. You need to try and listen to this and assess every situation and scenario to make sure you are acting within the Handbook.

> **Activity 12**
>
> Read the scenario below and circle or underline areas when your conduct warning chime starts to ring. Have a look at the solution to see how your instinct is doing so far.
>
> Tony and Dougie McGovern come to see you and instruct you to act on behalf of them. They run a building firm together. Tony set the firm up when he left school at 16 and Dougie joined him three years later when he also left school at 16. Tony had built up a considerable amount of goodwill when he was on his own.
>
> Tony and Dougie tell you that up until now they have done building work to other people's houses but now want to take advantage of their skills and buy up properties, do them up and sell them on. They are hoping this will be more profitable. They tell you that they want all of the properties put into their joint names even though Tony will be the one funding the purchases initially. They also tell you that they want to hold the properties as tenants in common but to be held in equal parts.
>
> Tony says he is really busy and any correspondence whether by phone, letter or e-mail should be via Dougie. Dougie will discuss anything he needs to with Tony and will then get back to you.
>
> Several weeks later you receive the official copies from the seller's solicitor in relation to a property they want to buy and begin to do the work. Dougie rings you unexpectedly and says he wants to instruct you to act for him also in relation to a personal matter. He tells you his wife is threatening to divorce him as she has found out he has been having an affair. He says he is really worried as she has said she is going to take him for everything he has! He doesn't want Tony to know as he thinks Tony will be really angry with him and worried about the financial effect on their business. He tells you to press on buying the property and not to do anything at the moment as he is going to try and talk his wife round but he wanted to give you a heads up as he may need to instruct you if his wife refuses to listen.
>
> What should you do now? What conduct issues does this scenario raise?

1.6.5 Your client and the court (Chapter 5 of section 1 of the OFR Code)

It is essential when you are acting as a litigator or trainee in a litigation department that you understand the additional Outcomes you must achieve. These will be looked at later in this chapter when discussed in context with what you will cover on the LPC in your civil and criminal litigation core subject.

1.6.6 You and others: relations with third parties (Chapter 11 of section 4 of the OFR Code)

It is worth noting that in the preface to the Outcomes it is specifically set out that the conduct requirement dealing with your relations to third parties extends beyond professional and business matters. It also ensures you do not use your professional title of a lawyer to advance your personal interest. This is inherent in any event under the Principles but the importance of how you act in your personal capacity, not just professional capacity, is again reiterated here.

In the 2007 Code there were specific rules dealing with how you needed to deal with other solicitors or members of the profession but these detailed rules have not been reproduced in the OFR Code. You need to go back to your overarching Principles, note the requirement to act with integrity and behave in a manner which maintains the trust the public have placed in you. You may find dealing with one particular solicitor very frustrating, or find that another lawyer is underhand or very rude in his or her dealings but you should never sink to their level. Always be polite, if necessary polite but firm. Never be too informal. It is easy to forget if you have a very friendly relationship with another solicitor that your responsibility is to your client. Don't allow yourself, because of this social connection, to be too easy-going in a negotiation just because you don't want to upset your relationship with the other solicitor. It is very easy to fall into this trap.

You will also come to realise that, wherever you choose to practise whether it is the City of London, Leeds, Birmingham or a smaller town or city, the legal world is a very small community. Everyone knows somebody you went to college with, or worked with previously either in the same firm or on the other side of a transaction. You should also remember that any written communication you make may one day be read out in court. You do not want other legal professionals talking about you in a less than enthusiastic way or want something embarrassing you have written read out in court. This goes back to the overarching Principle; always act with integrity. Deal with other professionals in the same manner you would like to be treated.

The element of Chapter 11 on which we are going to concentrate for the purpose of this chapter is the undertaking point.

Look at the definition of undertaking as set out in Chapter 14 of the OFR Code. You will note how wide this extends. Anyone in a firm who gives a statement which someone else reasonably relies upon, whether given orally or in writing, will have given an undertaking. Relate this then to the Outcomes in Chapter 11.

O(11.2) you perform all *undertakings* given by you within an agreed timescale or within a reasonable amount of time;

Note the requirement to perform an undertaking within the agreed timescale or within a reasonable period of time. It is important therefore to ensure you never say you will do something when you have no control over whether or not that act can be achieved. Most firms will have very detailed guidelines as to when and how undertakings can be given. Note **IB(11.5)** which confirms your firm may be meeting the Outcomes if you have a record of each undertaking given. This can be administratively quite time consuming but it is very important so that a firm can keep track of what has been promised and ensure these are met.

Activity 13

Review this scenario.

It is eight o'clock and you are still in the office working – it has been a long day! You have just finished speaking with the solicitor on the other side of your transaction. You have finally managed to agree a contentious clause in a contract on behalf of a client. You tell the other solicitor while on the telephone that you will engross (prepare final versions of) the agreement and put them in the post, before you go home tonight, for signature by all parties. You also say that you will send with the documents some money for a survey which the other solicitor's clients had paid for and which your clients had said they would meet the cost of. Your clients had promised earlier in the day they would drop a cheque off for you in the morning for this amount. You follow your conversation up with an e-mail confirming the points discussed and confirming you would send the agreement and money.

At which point has an undertaking been given? What are the issues with this undertaking?

1.7 Professional conduct and the LPC core subject areas

1.7.1 Property law and practice

1.7.1.1 Introduction

In practice the specific areas of professional conduct which arise in relation to property arise in relation to acting for both the seller and buyer in property transactions, acting for both the lender and borrower in property transactions and dealing with more than one prospective buyer in a conveyancing transaction. The other more sinister aspect of professional conduct and property can be seen in the huge rise in the use of property transactions for mortgage fraud and money laundering. This will be considered in more detail in Chapter 3 of this textbook.

The conveyancing market has changed considerably over the last few years. Conveyancing was for many firms the 'bread and butter' of their income. However, this is no longer the case. The number of sole practitioners and smaller high street firms has dropped significantly over the last ten years and with this so has the traditional conveyancing model. This has been replaced to a large extent by bulk conveyancing. New 'all singing all dancing' case management software has replaced much of the personal contact between a client and lawyer. Clients now can access directly their file within the case management system to see how progress is and what stage of the transaction their file is at. The rise and then fall of the property market has also had a drastic effect on not only the residential property market but also the commercial property market and those law firms which rely on this type of work.

1.7.1.2 Conflicts of interest in property transactions

Professional conduct issues that arise in property transactions, whether residential or commercial conveyancing, centre on the issues of conflicts of interests or the potential for conflict. If you are a litigator then it is clear you cannot act for both the defendant and claimant as their requirements clearly conflict. However, this is not always so easy to spot in a non-contentious matter and you may feel able to act for both parties in such a scenario.

In the 2007 Code there were distinct rules dealing with acting for a buyer and seller and acting for a borrower and lender. Originally the SRA's intention had been to remove specific reference to property transactions from the conflict provisions, thereby ensuring that that situation was considered the same as any other potential conflict situation—that is, you cannot act if a conflict exists or arises except in limited circumstances. However, this was met with considerable concern from practitioners and the Law Society as to the confusion this would cause.

The final version of the OFR Code at the time of publication of this textbook does follow the SRA's initial intention to some extent, as it does not contain any specific Outcomes which deal with acting for buyer and seller but it does in fact contain some Indicative Behaviours. Look at **IB(3.3)** and **IB(3.4)** which would suggest you may have met the Outcomes if you decline to act for a buyer and seller when you would need to negotiate on price of a property or where a builder is selling to a non-commercial client. Note also **IB(3.14)** which confirms acting for a buyer and a seller may tend to show you have **not** met the Outcomes.

The position contained with the OFR Code actually reverses the 2007 Code where solicitors could act for a buyer and seller in specific limited circumstances. Under the new OFR Code the Indicative Behaviours would suggest you should not act—but always remember the Indicative Behaviours are not mandatory. Therefore, as with all new Outcomes, it will be for the firm to show how they have achieved the Outcomes when acting for a buyer and seller in any given circumstance. The lack of specific Outcomes therefore does mean you need to go back to basics and assess whether there is a conflict or a significant risk of a conflict occurring if you do act. If you are satisfied that no conflict exists then remember you would also then need to satisfy yourself that you can also achieve all of the Principles too. The SRA has noted it is important to ensure the benefit of your acting for both a buyer and seller should be a benefit to the clients and not in your firm's own commercial interests.

The SRA has confirmed that acting for a buyer and seller is an area which would carry a high risk and it would not expect firms to routinely act in those circumstances. The reasons why it is so high risk is because there would normally be some form of negotiating to be done over the price or some inequality in bargaining power which would make it very difficult for you to achieve Principle 4 on behalf of both clients. Remember also Principles 2, 3 and 5.

1.7.1.3 Acting for a borrower and lender

The position in relation to acting for a borrower and lender would seem to be not that far removed from the regulation in the 2007 Code, although far less detailed. If you look at **IB(3.7)** you may be showing evidence of complying with the Outcomes if when acting for a borrower and lender it is a standard mortgage and the certificate of title the lender asks you to use is in a form approved by the council of mortgage lenders. The basics would therefore appear to be the same—that you can act in a residential situation for the buyer of a house who is taking out a mortgage and act for the mortgage provider as well provided a conflict of interest does not arise of course during the transaction. You should not always assume you can act in these circumstances. You need to consider conflict in every scenario. Remember this is just an Indicative Behaviour and it only **may** show you have achieved the Outcomes.

> **Activity 14**
>
> Why should the following situations make you look more closely at acting for the borrower and lender?
>
> (a) You are acting for Simon buying a house. You are also acting for his mortgage provider. He tells you he is really relieved because the surveyor sent by the mortgage company to value the house missed the evidence of subsidence movement in his report to the mortgage provider so they have approved his loan. He doesn't think he would have got it otherwise!
>
> (b) You are still acting for Simon but this time there are no subsidence issues. However, this time he is not borrowing the money from a mortgage provider but from his father and his father has asked you to act for him too as it will make it easier.
>
> (c) You are doing your niece's conveyancing and you are lending her the money to buy her house. You are charging a commercial rate of interest.

1.7.1.4 Property law and practice and undertakings

We have already considered undertakings in **paragraph 1.6.6** above but it is worth noting that in conveyancing situations there are some undertakings automatically implied. Undertakings form part and parcel of the conveyancing transaction. For example, there are undertakings which assist with the procedure at exchange. You should be aware these exist even though they may not be explicitly referred to. You will deal with these in more detail in the property law and practice core module on the LPC.

1.7.2 Litigation

1.7.2.1 Introduction

When considering litigation, the areas of professional conduct which most commonly arise are advice about funding and costs, refusing instructions to act as an advocate, your duty of disclosure and duty to the court and appearing as an advocate. The most common question you will probably be asked by a layperson is: how can you defend a client if you know he or she is guilty? Your reading of the OFR Code will help you to answer this question.

The Outcomes you need to achieve in relation to your duties to the court and acting as an advocate are set out in section 1, Chapter 5 of OFR Code. You should have this to hand as you read the scenario below.

Activity 15

You work for a firm which specialises in criminal litigation. You are called to the police station late at night to represent a young man, Jack, in detention, who allegedly beat someone up last night. You take instructions from Jack and write down his story. He tells you that he didn't do it and the police have the wrong man and are trying to set him up because they don't like him and are always picking on him. He tells you that he doesn't work and is on benefits.

You agree to act on behalf of Jack. You tell him you will prepare his proof of evidence and have it ready for him to check at the first court hearing.

Jack enters a not guilty plea at the court hearing and afterwards you give him the proof of evidence which is several pages long, for him to read. He gives it back to you after one minute and says it is fine. You give him a pen and he signs it. The proof of evidence contains information from Jack which indicated he was at his girlfriend's when the incident took place and she will vouch for this. You draft Jack's defence statement on this basis and serve it on the prosecution.

Some weeks later when the matter is listed for a pre-trial hearing, you meet Jack outside court as arranged. Jack tells you his girlfriend is running late maybe, he says, because she is reluctant to back up his story. He says, 'Between you and me I bopped that lad but he deserved it. She is worried about lying in court—silly mare!'

You know that the 'other lad' who was allegedly beaten up by your client is a well-known drug dealer and actually you quite like Jack. He is just a scallywag rather than a criminal in your opinion! Anyway he told you all this as a friend and you want to keep on good terms with him. You decide not to do or say anything further based on the information he has just given you.

What conduct issues does the above scenario throw up?

The issues contained in the scenario above relate to criminal litigation but the issues will be similar for commercial litigation. Instead of public funding you may need to advise them in relation to conditional fee agreements and would need to advise them in full in relation to the possibility of having to meet the other parties' costs as well as your own. The other issues are the same as would face any litigator in court. Look at **O(5.1–5.8)** and remember too your overriding Principles 1, 2 and 6.

1.7.3 Business law and practice

1.7.3.1 Identifying your client

The main areas where you are going to come across conduct issues in a more corporate setting is in deciding who your client is and avoiding conflicts of interest. Deciding who your client is may sound quite straightforward but in a corporate or commercial sense this can actually be quite difficult.

> **Activity 16**
>
> You are instructed by Mr Red, Mr Green and Mr Orange to incorporate a new business called Colour Me Happy Limited. They all intend to be directors and shareholders in the business. Mr Orange currently owns a property which he is going sell to Colour Me Happy Limited to be used as its new head office.
>   Who is your client?

1.7.3.2 Conflicts of interest

In **paragraph 1.6.3** we already looked at the issues which you may encounter in relation to conflicts of interest in commercial transactions and the exceptions contained in O(3.6) and O(3.7) which are only likely to be utilised by sophisticated legal services users and therefore, more likely, the large corporate firms. This is a particularly tricky area and you should always remember that conflict warning chime which you should pay attention to.

> **Activity 17**
>
> You have been acting for Montgomery Limited for the past five years and have dealt with a number of legal issues for it, including incorporating the company initially and drafting the shareholders' agreement. You now receive instructions from one of the directors regarding a property he owns which is leased to the company. It appears the company is in financial difficulty and is in 6 months, arrears with its rent.
>   What professional conduct issues do you need to consider here?

Professional conduct: checkpoints

You should now be able to:

- Identify how you should behave as a member of the profession;
- Understand the overarching Principles which govern the legal profession;
- Find your way around the OFR Code and understand how it works; and
- Identify the areas of professional conduct which are most relevant to you at this stage of your studies.

1.8 Suggested solutions to Chapter 1 activities

> **Activity 1**
>
> - To do a good job!
> - To provide clear advice and explanations.
> - To be able to keep things confidential.
> - To be pro-active. A client does not want to feel it always has to ring you to find out what is happening or if anything is happening.

Activity 1—Continued

- To provide clear information as to how much the matter will cost.
- To communicate effectively.
- To understand how to treat a client—a client thinks he is like a consumer and therefore 'the customer is always right'.
- Note there are certain circumstances where this might not be true and following your client's instructions you may in fact be breaching Principle 4 to act in a client's best interest. Imagine if your client were getting divorced and told you to delay matters as much as possible because he wanted to make things difficult for his wife. This would be following a client's instructions but would not be in his best interests and you would have to explain your duty to him.
- To help and inform the client in its decision-making process.
- To have good problem solving skills.
- To be able to think outside the box and come up with innovative solutions or commercial recommendations.
- To always put the client's needs first.
- To be realistic and honest. It is better to tell a client at the outset they cannot win a case rather than let them litigate only to lose! This again goes directly to your ability to comply with the Principles. Don't waste your client's money or public funding!
- To follow instructions from the client. *Subject to the comments above.*
- To manage the client's expectations. Don't tell a client you will be completing next week, or will send a letter out tonight if you won't be able to meet that deadline.
- To appreciate the importance of timing. Remember to a client their transaction is the only transaction! They don't know you have a mountain of paperwork on your desk to deal with nor should they need to know. You need to have excellent time management skills.
- To ascertain and understand the client's objectives. This goes directly to the goal of the OFR Code which is to achieve Outcomes for individual clients. It is not just a tick box system the rules of which are applicable to all clients.
- To become familiar with the client's business in order to be able to always act in a client's best interests.

Activity 2

- Use a diary to keep track of all due dates, meetings and scheduled activities.
- Make and use 'to do lists' every day.
- Anticipate deadlines and high stress periods and work these into your day/week.
- Set priorities and deadlines. Categorise 'to do list' tasks into high, medium and low priorities and focus on high priorities first.
- Divide large tasks into several smaller parts. Focus on a small task to complete one part at a time. This will make a big project feel more manageable.
- Regularly ask yourself, 'What is the best use of my time right now?' Do that task.
- Schedule time for 10/15 min breaks and 'interruptions'. That will leave you some time for the inevitable 'unplanned' jobs you will have to undertake.
- Don't forget to sleep, exercise and eat! This will allow you to stay physically fit and mentally alert.

Activity 2—Continued

- Within limits learn to say no. Commit yourself only to those activities you have time for.
- Do one task at a time and finish it; avoid procrastination—get on and do the job.
- Many firms have clear desk policies so you will need to clear your desk at the end of the day. This is an excellent way of ensuring you are working in an organised and systematic fashion.

Activity 4

Remember under the OFR Code what will satisfy the Outcomes for one client will not necessarily satisfy the Outcomes for another.

(a) If your client is illiterate you will have to give them extra support and think of ways around this problem. You may initially advise them of the likely cost in a meeting with them and agree to phone weekly with an update. You may be able to set up an automated text service if your client can read numbers, updating him in relation to the costs during a transaction. A detailed letter discussing potential legal costs and disbursements is not going to meet this client's requirements and you would therefore not be achieving O(1.13).

(b) You will need an interpreter to either translate a letter setting out the costs into the client's language or to interpret in a face to face meeting and discuss the costs. Again remember the ongoing requirement to keep your client informed of the potential costs. This will all need to be done in their language.

(c) It will probably be appropriate for a firm to send out what has been called a client care letter in the 2007 Code to this type of client at the start of a transaction and send updates in a written format as necessary. This will be a fairly detailed letter explaining charge out rates, disbursements and estimates. Agree with your client how they would like this information—letter, e-mail, fax.

(d) A large corporate experienced legal service user may not want or need detailed information in relation to costs at the start of the transaction. You could provide access to its case management file on your computer systems so it can have an ongoing view of the costs. The company may ask to pay you a set fee per month for continuous legal advice and just ask you to provide a breakdown of costs as and when needed.

Activity 5

New information has been received which means the likelihood is that the costs will be greater than originally envisaged. To achieve the Outcomes clients must receive, when appropriate and as the matter progresses, the best possible information in relation to costs. **O(1.13)** sets out this requirement.

Since you have received this new information you need to give the client an update on the likely increase in costs and potential costs of the other side if this matter becomes litigious. Look at **IB(1.11)**. This suggests that you need to clearly explain your fees and if and when they are likely to change. **IB (1.12)** says you should give warnings about any other payments which the client may be responsible for.

Although the IBs are not mandatory, remember the preamble to them confirms that if you follow them, you may tend to show you have achieved the Outcomes. If you do not achieve the Outcome and have not followed the IBs, it will be for you to prove to the SRA how, by any alternative means, you have met the Outcome.

Activity 6

a) A client who has been referred to you e-mails you and gives you some background details on a transaction he wants to instruct you on. You send him a brief e-mail back just introducing yourself and commenting on his e-mail. The client responds and confirms he wants to instruct you. You e-mail him a letter and include within this letter information on the client's right to complain if there is an issue and the estimated cost of the matter.

b) An angry client contacts the firm's receptionist and says, "I want to make a complaint and don't tell me I can't because I know I am entitled to because the solicitor told me I could in the first letter he ever wrote to me!" The receptionist gives very clear oral instructions about the procedure available to the client.

c) A client who has been referred to you comes into the office to see you. He decides on the spot he is so keen to instruct you that you discuss with him at this first interview the likely costs and the fact that if he so wishes in the future he can make a complaint, and how to go about that. You go back to your desk and open a file. Part of the firm's opening file procedure is a checklist. You tick the boxes in relation to the OFR Code's costs and complaints requirements as having been met.

> This **achieves** the Outcomes as the fact a client can complain must under **O(1.9)** be given in writing at the start of the matter.

> This too may **achieve** the Outcomes. Note there is no requirement to have a **written** complaints procedure. You only have to tell a client that they can complain in writing. **IB(1.22)** suggests having one would achieve the Outcomes but remember the IBs are **not** mandatory.

> This **does not achieve** the Outcomes. Under **O(1.9)** the client must be informed in writing that he has the right to complain.

Activity 7

The Outcomes in Chapter 1 in relation to client care do not provide specific information as to how you should give the client the information he needs to understand his engagement of you as his solicitor. This is because you need to focus on the Principles and ensure you are achieving the right Outcomes for your particular client. What is right for one client is not necessarily right for another. You need to take into account in every case a client's particular needs and circumstances.

In this case it is likely you will not have met the Outcomes because the receptionist has suggested the client read a detailed letter and work out what he needs to do next. You know his reading and writing skills are limited so this needs to be taken into account when considering the Outcomes for this particular client. There is probably too much complex information contained in this lengthy letter and this would affect the client's ability to read and understand the information contained within it. In these circumstances it would have been better for the receptionist to have talked the client through what he needed to do in very clear steps. Another option would have been to invite the client in to talk through his complaint with a dedicated complaints handler at the firm who could discuss his options with him.

Activity 8

(a) It would be reasonable to stop acting for this client. She has consistently not been paying her bills despite your chasing her for them. A solicitor is entitled to be paid for his/her services!

(b) Your reasons for refusal must be reasonable. You cannot refuse instructions based on a personal dislike of something or someone or their beliefs. You would however have to think carefully whether you could act in a client's best interests if you felt very strongly about this issue.

Activity 8—Continued

(c) You are not allowed to accept gifts from clients unless they take independent legal advice. Look at **IB(1.9)**; you may be showing achievement of the Outcomes if you refuse to act in these circumstances. But in this instance this is more than a gift; this is almost a bribe which may affect your judgement when acting and would most certainly be in breach of Principles 3 and very likely 2 and 5.

(d) You may think this is a conflict but it is not because this is not the 'same matter' which is required for a conflict to exist. Look at the definition of 'client conflict' in Chapter 14. However, there is some professional embarrassment here and you would not be able to comply with the Principles. You might feel unable to act for the new instructing client because you may feel inhibited to act in your client's best interests because of your previous relationship with Tom. You may be able to show reasonable reasons for refusing instructions in such a scenario.

Activity 9

You are a trainee at a firm which only offers property advice services. You are being asked by a client to advise on an employment matter. Remember you must provide your client a good standard of service under Principle 5. Your firm does not appear to have the appropriate resources. **O(1.4)** states you must have the resources skill and procedure to carry out your client's instructions. You cannot achieve **O(1.4)**. **IB(1.7)** confirms you must decline to act if you can't act in the client's best interests. In this scenario you would not have the expertise to achieve the Outcomes or the Principles. You will need to tell your client they will need to appoint another solicitor. You could suggest solicitors who have the appropriate expertise.

Activity 10

This should have made your conflict warning bell chime. Here you have two clients who want to instruct you in relation to the purchase of a telecoms business.

You need to look at the conflict Outcomes to see if you can achieve them and the Principles.

To satisfy **O(3.1)** and **O(3.3)** you should ensure your systems and controls are sufficient and suitable for your client base. Here you are a trainee at a large City firm. The large numbers of clients and transactions which your firm is likely to be involved with, along with the number of fee-earners involved, would suggest you would need a very rigorous and tested technical software programme to cross check your large client base and assess if there is a conflict. This should reveal the fact that you are being asked to act for two clients who wish to purchase the same business. On this basis there would appear to be a potential conflict.

This would potentially be a 'client conflict'. Remember under **O(3.5)** that you cannot act if there is a conflict of interest or risk of conflict of two or more clients in relation to the same or related matter unless the situation falls within one of the limited exceptions set out in **O(3.6)** and **O(3.7)**.

> **O(3.6)** allows you to act subject to appropriate safeguards if the clients have a *substantially common interest*. If you look at the definition of substantially common interest in Chapter 14, you will see this means where there is a clear common purpose. This is not the case here. They are each wanting to buy the business, not buy the business together.
>
> **O(3.7)** allows you to act where the clients are *competing for the same objective*. You will note this is defined as 'asset, contract or business opportunity', which is the case here. You can only act if:

Activity 10—Continued

   (a) the clients are both aware you are acting for two clients and both clients have confirmed in writing their consent for you to act in this situation;
   (b) there is no other client conflict;
   (c) different solicitors act for each client unless the clients specifically agree otherwise; and
   (d) you are satisfied that it is reasonable for you to act and that your acting benefits the client more than any risk that might arise to them of your firm acting for both parties.

You also need to be aware of **IB(3.5)** and **IB(3.7)** which would suggest you may be achieving the Outcomes only if you act in the above circumstances, if there is no unequal bargaining power and if the clients are sophisticated users of legal services. Also look at **IB(3.12)** which goes further and would suggest you may not be achieving the Outcomes if you act under the exception in O(3.7) if there is an unequal bargaining power.

Before deciding whether to act, you would need to check all of this in addition to ensuring you would also be meeting the Principles.

Activity 11

Match up the following potential confidentiality situations with possible solutions or methods of achieving the Outcomes.

Situation	Solution
You work in a criminal practice. You hear your client on his mobile negotiating to buy firearms for a planned burglary.	You should contact the police. ***Such disclosure is permitted by law. Note IB(4.2).***
You outsource photocopying to an external printers. The next day an article in the press appears revealing information obtained from the material you outsourced.	You may still be able to show you have achieved the Outcomes if you can prove to the SRA you made sufficient checks to ensure client confidentiality. *See IB(4.3)*
An old client rings to say his mother has died and your firm prepared her will. He says his mother told him that she left her house to his son. He asks you to check this before he tells his son.	You should not reveal this information. ***See IB(4.6). If you disclose the content of a will, this may suggest you have not achieved the outcomes.***
You act for Client X who you know has financial issues. You are instructed by a private investor who intends to lend money to Client X.	You may be able to act but you would need to put in place safeguards, would need consent to act and should deem it reasonable to act with those safeguards in place. *See O(4.4)*

Activity 12

Read the scenario below and circle or underline areas when your conduct warning chime starts to ring. Have a look at the solution to see how your instinct is doing so far.

Tony and Dougie McGovern come to see you and instruct you to act on behalf of them. Together they run a building firm.	There is nothing wrong with acting for two clients so long as you keep in mind that you can't act if a conflict exists or arises.
	Don't forget to achieve all of the basic client care Outcomes in relation to costs and complaints procedures and go through this with them. You also need to make sure you do a conflict check (your firm should ensure they have the appropriate systems in place to achieve this). Remember **O(3.1 – 3.3)**.
Tony had built up a considerable amount of goodwill when he was on his own.	Your instinct (which should be quite honed by now!) should start to kick in. It would appear there is an imbalance in their interests in the business. Not an issue yet but you need to keep it in mind.
They tell you that they want all of the properties put into their joint names even though Tony will be the one funding the purchases initially. They also tell you that they want to hold the property as tenants in common but to be held in equal parts.	Your instinct should be in full mode now! Your instructions are to put the properties into joint names, albeit to be held as tenants in common but you are told this is to be on the basis of equal shares. So any equity in the property will be split equally even though it is Tony funding the purchases. Are you acting in each client's best interest? Will you be able to uphold the Principles?
Tony says he is really busy and any correspondence whether by phone, letter or e-mail should be via Dougie and Dougie will discuss anything he needs to with Tony and will then get back to you.	You should be concerned by this. How can you ensure that Dougie is checking anything with Tony. Look at **IB(1.25)**. You need to make sure that you are satisfied that the person providing the instructions has the authority to do so. Get Tony to confirm this in writing.
Several weeks later you receive the official copies from the seller's solicitor in relation to a property they want to buy and begin to do the work.	So long as you have satisfied yourself that there is no conflict and you have achieved the client care Outcomes it should be okay to go ahead and start

Activity 12—Continued

Dougie rings you unexpectedly and says he wants to instruct you to act for him also in relation to a personal matter. He tells you his wife is threatening to divorce him as she has found out he has been having an affair. He says he is really worried as she has said she is going to take him for everything he has! He doesn't want Tony to know as he thinks Tony will be really angry with him and worried about the financial effect on their business. He tells you to press on buying the property, not to tell Tony, and not to do anything at the moment as he is going to try and talk his wife round but he wanted to give you a heads up as he may need to instruct you if his wife refuses to listen.

What should you do now?

On the face of it this is okay. You can act for one client on another matter so long as you always keep in mind the Outcomes you need to achieve and Principles you need to abide by. Outcomes in relation to conflict and confidentiality should be issues you should be thinking about at this stage. At this point you should be very concerned. You know that Tony is funding the purchase of the property but that the equity will be held 50/50. The ownership of these assets would likely be taken into account in any financial settlement in a divorce.

Oh oh! You now hold information which is material to one client but which you are not able to tell him because of your need to keep affairs of a client confidential. **See O(4.1).** *Dougie has also specifically instructed you not to tell Tony.*

You should explain to Dougie what duties you need to comply with.

You need to explain your duty in **O(4.2)** *to tell Tony. However, remember you also have a duty to Dougie in* **O(4.1)** *to keep his information confidential. Note* **O(4.3).** *Your duty of confidentiality takes precedence over your duty of disclosure.*

You should tell Dougie that, unless he consents to your telling Tony of the threats from his wife, you will have to stop acting for Tony but you will not be able to tell Tony why you have to stop acting. Tony would obviously then be very suspicious! Dougie would probably have to end up telling his brother anyway! If Dougie gives you consent then you would be able to continue acting PROVIDED no conflict arose.

If Tony, on hearing of the problem, instructed you that he wanted the properties in his name only and Dougie did not agree with this, you should not continue to act for both of them! You could not act in both of their best interests!

Activity 13

At which point has an undertaking been given. What are the issues with this undertaking?

- As soon as you tell the solicitor on the telephone that you will put the documents in the post and send the money you have given an undertaking. Look at the definition in Chapter 14. An undertaking can be given orally and does not have to contain the word 'undertake'. You have at this point promised to do something which the other solicitor is relying on.

- It is 8 o'clock at night and therefore you cannot put the documents in the post. Last post in the UK is usually at 6pm. Therefore you will have breached this element of the undertaking. A breach but probably not too bad an error as you could make sure the documents were hand delivered the next day if the other solicitor's firm was close. Or you could ring the solicitor in the morning and confirm that you of course could not put them in the post last night but will do so today.

- More of an issue is the undertaking to send the money. You have given an undertaking to send some money based on a promise from your client to drop a cheque off in the morning. There are two issues with this. Firstly the client may not drop the cheque off at all whereby your firm will have to meet the costs of this undertaking! Your firm will not be very happy with you! Secondly even if the client does drop off the cheque in the morning, cheques take at least five working days to clear so you still won't have funds in the morning—and the cheque might bounce!

- You should never give an undertaking to send money unless you have cleared funds from your client in your client account.

Activity 14

Why should the following situations make you look more closely at acting for the borrower and lender?

(a) This goes back to your conflict issues. You are acting for two clients here: the lender and the borrower. Until Simon told you about the subsidence movement you could act for both of them as long as there was not a conflict. Now a conflict has arisen. You hold material information which you have a duty to disclose under **O(4.2)** and a duty to Simon under **O(4.1)**. Remember your duty of confidentiality overrides your duty of disclosure. You would therefore have to stop acting for the bank and not tell them why unless Simon let you disclose the information to the lender.

(b) You cannot act for two or more clients where there is a conflict of interest. From the facts there does not appear to be any conflict between the parties. But note **IB(3.7)(a)**. The IBs would suggest that you would only be satisfying the Outcomes if the lender is a normal institutional lender. Here Simon's father is not a normal institutional lender. This would therefore fall under the general conflict Outcomes and Principles—that you can act if you can act in the best interests of **each** client and their interests do not conflict. If Simon's father instructed you to add an unusually high interest rate to the mortgage document then this would not be in Simon's best interest and a conflict would arise at this point. You should then not act for both.

> **Activity 14—Continued**
>
> (c) This is an 'own interest conflict'. You would be lending the money. Remember you can never act where there is a conflict or significant risk of conflict between you and your client. It would be difficult for you to prove in this scenario that you have met your niece's needs as you had such an inherent interest in the matter. You should not act.

> **Activity 15**
>
> What if any conduct issues does the above scenario throw up
>
> He tells you he didn't do it.
>
> | | |
> |---|---|
> | You agree to act on behalf of Jack | *Don't forget to do your conflict check first!* |
> | You take instructions from Jack and write down his story. | *You should take care when taking instructions to ensure the information is true. You do not have an additional duty to investigate whether it is true. You can take the information given to you at face value but if there are obvious holes in your client's story you need to be careful. Look at **O(5.1)**. You must not knowingly or recklessly mislead the court.* |
> | You tell him you will prepare his proof of evidence. | *Make sure you draft this in language appropriate for your particular client. Use clear, plain English so your client can understand it.* |
> | He tells you that he doesn't work and is on benefits. | *You should be thinking about funding. Your client will probably be eligible for public funding. You need to satisfy **O(1.13)**.* |
> | He gives it back to you after one minute and says it is fine. You give him a pen and he signs it. | *Can your client really have read this in full in that time? Can he read? Is he too embarrassed to tell you? Remember you will be drafting his defence statement based on this and the defence statement is going to be relied upon in court!* |
> | Jack tells you his girlfriend is running late maybe, he says, because she is reluctant to back up his story. He says, 'Between you and me I bopped that lad but he deserved it, she is worried about lying in court—silly mare!' | *At this point you should be very concerned! You have knowledge that the client is misleading the court. You will be in breach of O(5.1). He had told you he was at his girlfriend's and you put this information in his defence statement. You now know this is not true.* |
> | You decide not to do or say anything further based on the information he has just given you. | *You **must** tell Jack of your duties to the court. Look at **O(5.2)** and **O(5.4)**. You can advise Jack that he can maintain a not guilty plea and make the prosecution prove the case against him, but you cannot advance the defence statement which suggests he can't have done it as he was at his girlfriend's, as you now know this is not true. The defence statement will need to be withdrawn or amended. Look at **IB(5.4), IB (5.5)** and **IB(5.9)**. You should advise Jack to allow you to withdraw or amend the defence statement. If he refuses to give you consent you should stop acting.* |

Activity 16

Who is your client?

It is important to work out who you are instructed by and acting for. If you do not, there is a risk you will be acting when there is a conflict of interests, or a significant risk of one which, as you know, will mean you are not achieving the Outcomes.

You could be acting for the directors of the company, you could be acting for the shareholders of the company or you could be acting for Mr Orange in his personal capacity as seller, or you could be acting for Colour Me Happy Limited, the company as the buyer.

You can see how in a business scenario it is not as easy as it may seem to answer the question of who is your client!

Activity 17

What professional conduct issues do you need to consider here?

Again it is important to consider who your client is. Is it the company Montgomery Limited as the tenant or is it the director who has contacted you as landlord? You would not be able to act for both here. Your conflict antenna should have suggested that there is going to be a conflict of interest here.

This is a contentious issue between a landlord and a tenant. Remember you cannot act for two clients where there is a conflict of interest or risk of a conflict. The tenant may argue there are good reasons for it withholding rent or dispute the fact entirely that it is in arrears!

The exceptions in **O(3.6)** and **O(3.7)** do not apply here as there is no common purpose nor are the clients competing for the same asset or business.

You should not act. It is very unlikely you would be achieving the Outcomes in the OFR Code or the Principles.

Visit the Online Resource Centre for more information and useful weblinks.
www.oxfordtextbooks.co.uk/orc/foundations11_12/

2

Financial services

GENERAL INTRODUCTION TO THE REGULATION OF FINANCIAL SERVICES

2.1 Introduction

The first part of this chapter is a general introduction to the regulation of financial services. The Financial Services and Markets Act 2000 (FSMA 2000) is put into context and the need for authorisation under the Act is explained. What is covered by the general prohibition is considered, as are the meanings of 'regulated activity' and 'specified investment'.

The second part discusses the position of solicitors, specifically those who are regulated by the Law Society, a 'designated professional body'.

To help you to assess your learning, a series of short-answer questions is included with space for your answers. Five scenarios are also set out to help you in the application of the financial services regulation to solicitors in their every day work.

In the final part of this chapter, what constitutes money laundering and the relevance of the legislation to solicitors is considered.

2.1.1 Investments

To appreciate the legislation and its effect fully it is helpful to understand what the legislation affects. The FSMA 2000 uses the term 'investment'. It helps, initially, to consider the word in its wider meaning, rather than in the narrower meaning which is given to it under the legislation.

A dictionary definition of 'investment' is 'monies *invested* for income or profit'. The definition of the verb 'to invest' is 'to commit monies to a particular use in order to earn a financial return'.

The meaning which is given to the word 'investment' in the FSMA 2000 does not include all investments in the wider meaning (the meaning of the word for the purposes of the FSMA 2000 is considered at **2.1.3.2**).

2.1.1.1 Financial return

The financial return—the income or profit—can be a return of income or capital, income being a recurring return and capital being a one-off benefit.

So an investment is something which will, it is hoped, bring in a return. Monies can be invested in a number of different ways. There are investments which will bring in solely income; investments which will bring in solely capital; and investments which will bring in a combination of both. The return received on an investment generally reflects the risk involved in making the investment.

2.1.1.2 The risk

The risk attached to an investment is the chance of the original money invested being lost to the investor. Some investments carry little (if any) risk and the return on these is usually predictable and on the low side, for example, a building society deposit account. A deposit account pays a lower rate of interest than that paid on the more usual building society account people invest in—a building society share account—but the deposit account has the advantage that should the society find itself in difficulties the account holder is guaranteed first repayment from the funds available and so the chances of the investor losing his capital are negligible.

Other investments carry a much higher risk, for example, shares on the stock market. The chance of a high return, by way of income (dividends) or capital growth, is there, but there is always a chance of the original investment being lost if, for example, the company goes into liquidation. An investor should always be aware of the risk attached to a particular investment, and investors should invest in those investments which carry a degree of risk only if they can afford to lose their original investment.

The diagram below shows various investments building up the layers in a pyramid. The higher in the pyramid, the more risky the investment. A lottery, with no real chance of the stake being returned, floats above the pyramid.

2.1.1.3 Other considerations

There are a great number of investments on the market—bank or building society accounts, gilts, equities, unit trusts—and which investment a person makes depends

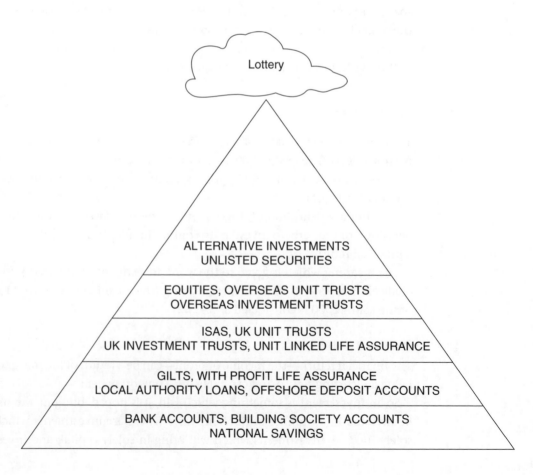

very much on the investor's individual circumstances and requirements. Risk is not the only factor to be taken into account on making an investment; other considerations are:

(a) Will the capital be needed with only a short period of notice?

(b) Are there tax advantages which should be considered?

(c) One consideration which should not be overlooked, what will give the investor peace of mind?

Appendix 2 to this book gives details of a number of investments. It also contains an explanation of some of the 'jargon' used in the financial services sector, with which it is useful to be familiar.

2.1.2 The background to the Financial Services and Markets Act 2000

With so many products on the market, investors often look for advice on which investment to make. Who can investors turn to?

Historically, and until 29 April 1988, investors could look to anyone for advice. The financial services industry was left to self-regulation with no one agency in overall control of the field. There was no requirement on financial advisers to have any qualifications, or for them to be registered or authorised. Anyone could advise a person about investments. This was found to be inadequate and gave rise, in the late 1970s and early 1980s, to a number of scandals in the investment sector, in which a number of investors lost considerable sums of money through poor advice. In addition the investment markets were rapidly changing. In 1981, the then Secretary of State appointed Professor LCB Gower to carry out a review of the law on investor protection.

This review resulted in the Financial Services Act 1986, an Act which introduced measures to regulate 'investment business' and those who gave investment advice (or, in the words of the Act, those who carried on investment business). It achieved this by prohibiting a person from carrying on investment business in the UK unless that person was authorised under the Act, or was an exempt person (s 3, 1986 Act). The Financial Services Act 1986 came into force on 29 April 1988 and, until 1 December 2001, any investment business carried on after that date was caught by that Act.

At midnight on 30 November 2001, the FSMA 2000 came into force, repealing the Financial Services Act 1986. It is this Act which provides the framework for the current statutory regime.

2.1.2.1 The effect of the Act

Under this regime there is a single regulator for the financial services industry. This single regulator is known as the Financial Services Authority (FSA). It has sole responsibility and powers for authorising, regulating, investigating, and disciplining authorised persons.

2.1.2.2 FSA's general duties

Set out in the FSMA 2000 are the four regulatory objectives that guide the FSA: market confidence; financial stability; the protection of consumers; and the reduction of financial crime (FSMA 2000, s 2). One of the aims of the FSA in meeting the 'protection of consumers' objective is to secure the appropriate degree of protection for consumers having regard to the differing degrees of risk involved with different kinds of investment. In addition, the differing degrees of experience and expertise that different consumers may have in relation to different kinds of regulated activity are to be taken into account. One concept to which the FSA will also have regard is the general principle that consumers should take responsibility for their own decisions (FSMA 2000, s 5).

2.1.2.3 The general prohibition

The FSMA 2000, s 19 prohibits a person from carrying on a regulated activity unless that person is authorised under the Act, or is an exempt person. Section 19 (2) refers to this prohibition as 'the general prohibition'.

2.1.2.4 Sanctions

The FSMA 2000 sets out the sanctions for breaching the general prohibition. It is a criminal offence (FSMA 2000, s 23). In addition, any agreement made by a person in contravention of the general prohibition is unenforceable, and action can be taken to recover money or property paid or transferred and for compensation for any loss (FSMA 2000, s 26). The amount of compensation to be paid is set out in s 28 of the Act. Further, it is a criminal offence to make a false claim to be, or falsely to hold oneself out as, an authorised or exempt person.

2.1.2.5 Authorisation and exemption

To be able to carry on a regulated activity without contravening the general prohibition a person must be either an authorised person or an exempt person.

Section 31 sets out the categories of authorised persons for the purposes of the FSMA 2000. There are four categories, but this chapter is concerned only with the first—that of being a 'person' who has been authorised by the FSA to carry on one or more regulated activities. The 'person' may be an individual, a body corporate, a partnership, or an unincorporated association (FSMA 2000, s 40). To become authorised an application is made to the FSA. If granted authorisation the authorised person is regulated by the FSA and is subject to the rules and regulations made by the FSA. These rules and regulations are set out in the FSA Rule Book.

The FSMA 2000, s 38 provides for the Treasury to permit specified persons or those falling within a specified class to be exempt from the general prohibition. An order has been made by the Treasury (the Financial Services and Markets Act 2000 (Exemption) Order 2001 (SI 2001 No 1201)) which provides for various persons to be exempt from the general prohibition. The exemptions are not comprehensive. However, the detail of the order is beyond the scope of this chapter.

The provision of relevance to most solicitors is that contained in FSMA 2000, Part XX. This grants an exemption from the general prohibition to members of the professions. This is explained in detail at 2.2 below.

2.1.3 The need for authorisation

When is a person carrying on a regulated activity with the consequence that authorisation under the Act is required?

The FSMA 2000, s 22 provides:

22.—(1) An activity is a regulated activity for the purpose of this Act if it is an activity of a specified kind which is carried on by way of business and—

    (a) relates to an investment of a specified kind or

    (b) in the case of an activity of a kind which is also specified for the purposes of this paragraph, is carried on in relation to property of any kind.

[...]
>   (4) 'Investment' includes any asset, right or interest.
>
>   (5) 'Specified' means specified in an order made by the Treasury.

For the activity to be a regulated activity and caught by the general prohibition it must generally:

(a) be an activity of a specified kind;

(b) be carried on by way of business; and

(c) relate to an investment of a specified kind.

There are some activities which do not have to relate to a specified investment (FSMA 2000, s 22(1)(b)).

Regulated activities and investments of a specified kind warrant further explanation (see **2.1.3.1** and **2.1.3.2** below).

2.1.3.1 Regulated activities

The FSMA 2000 does not itself define what activities are regulated activities. This is left to secondary legislation, in that the Act provides for the Treasury to make an order specifying activities that are to be included in the definition of 'regulated activities' (FSMA 2000, s 22(5)). To date, the Treasury has made one order specifying the kind of activities which are regulated activities—the Financial Services and Markets Act 2000 (Regulated Activities) Order 2001 (SI 2001 No 544) (the RAO).

The specified activities listed at present include:

(a) dealing in investments as agent;

(b) arranging deals in investments;

(c) managing investments;

(d) advising on investments;

(e) entering as provider into a funeral plan contract; and

(f) entering into or administering regulated mortgage contracts.

2.1.3.1.1 *Dealing in investments as agent*

This involves the buying, selling, subscribing for or underwriting of securities or contractually based investments as agent.

2.1.3.1.2 *Arranging deals in investments*

This could also be described as making arrangements for another person to *deal*. Simply recommending an investor to a broker would not be arranging. There must be some active participation.

2.1.3.1.3 *Managing investments*

This requires involvement in addition to just holding the investments, eg, receiving dividends on shares which form part of a trust fund which a solicitor is administering; or on a trust fund which a solicitor is administering, deciding whether or not a rights issue for shares, offered by a company in whom the trust has shares, should be taken up.

2.1.3.1.4 *Advising on investments*

This involves giving advice to an investor on the merits of making a particular investment. It may be distinguished from the giving of generic advice on investments. For example, giving advice on the benefits of a repayment mortgage compared with an endowment mortgage is generic advice and is not caught by the Act.

2.1.3.1.5 Entering as provider into a funeral plan contract

A funeral plan contract is a contract under which, in return for the customer making a payment, the provider undertakes to provide a funeral in the United Kingdom for the customer (or another person). Where it is expected, or intended, that the funeral will take place within one month of the contract then the funeral plan contract is not caught by the legislation.

2.1.3.1.6 Excluded activities

In addition to listing the specified activities, the RAO also sets out exclusions that are applicable. Where an exclusion applies (and this can be defined by the investment subject to the activity, or by the activity itself), the activity does not fall under the FSMA 2000 and so no authorisation is required. The person can engage in the activity without fear of prosecution. Examples include: dealing with or through authorised persons (RAO, Article 22), unless a commission is received for which he does not account to the client; arranging deals with or through authorised persons (RAO, Article 29), unless a commission is received for which he does not account to the client; funeral contract plans where the plan is covered by insurance or trust arrangements (RAO, Article 60).

In addition to the exclusions set out as applicable to individual activities the RAO also sets out a number of exclusions that apply to several specified kinds of activity. Three exclusions which will be of relevance to solicitors are 'trustees, nominees and personal representatives' (RAO, Article 66), 'Activities carried on in the course of a profession or non-investment business' (RAO, Article 67), and 'Provision of information on an incidental basis' (see **2.5.1**).

2.1.3.2 Specified investments

As with regulated activities, the Act does not itself define what investments are specified investments. This is also dealt with in the RAO (RAO, Part III). The investments listed in the RAO as specified investments include:

(a) deposits;

(b) contracts of insurance (This includes, for example, life policies, defective title indemnity, household, and buildings insurance, after the event legal expenses insurance. So far as exclusions are concerned contracts of insurance are dealt with differently to other types of investments and are excluded from some exclusions, notably RAO, Articles 66 and 67 (see **2.5.1**));

(c) shares;

(d) instruments creating or acknowledging indebtedness;

(e) government and public securities, but excluding National Savings products;

(f) instruments giving entitlement to investments;

(g) certificates representing certain securities;

(h) units in a collective investment scheme;

(i) options;

(j) futures;

(k) funeral plan contracts; and

(l) regulated mortgage contracts.

Some investments which are not included, and consequently are not regulated by the Act, are:

(i) land;

(ii) currency; and

(iii) tangible assets, eg art, classic cars, etc.

2.2 Relevance to solicitors

So far as solicitors are concerned, the FSMA 2000 impacts on them. They are carrying on a business; their work involves investments specified under the FSMA 2000 (shares in an estate which the solicitor is administering; an endowment policy being cancelled on the sale of a property and the redemption of the mortgage); and solicitors frequently engage in a specified activity—dealing, arranging, managing or advising. Furthermore, it is unlikely that the activity will be excluded under the Act. They are carrying on regulated activities. Consequently solicitors, on the face of it, need to be authorised to engage in their work which may fall to be regulated under the FSMA 2000.

2.2.1 The Law Society as a designated professional body

The regulated activities that most solicitors engage in are those which arise out of their main work as solicitors; they are incidental to their main work. For example, this would include selling shares in an estate that the solicitor is administering. Under the new regime these activities will be referred to as 'non-mainstream regulated activities'. Some solicitors do engage in regulated activities that are not incidental to their main work: for example, advising a client on what investments to make with an inheritance received. Such activities will be termed 'mainstream regulated activities'.

The majority of solicitors do not engage in mainstream regulated activities but in non-mainstream regulated activities. While it was accepted by the Law Society that consumers needed protection, the Society's view was that all solicitors are regulated by the Law Society, their professional body. For solicitors carrying on only non-mainstream regulated activities the requirement also to be regulated by the FSA would not be in a consumer's best interests. The dual regulation would be onerous and expensive. The Treasury accepted this argument and FSMA 2000, Part XX was added to the FSMA 2000 while it was still a Bill.

This Part of the FSMA 2000 contains provision for members of a professional body who are engaging only in non-mainstream regulated activities to be exempt from the requirement to be authorised persons in order to carry out certain regulated activities. It grants an exemption from the general prohibition.

There are a number of conditions before the exemption is available:

(a) the professional body must be a designated professional body (DPB); and

(b) the professional body must also supervise and regulate the way in which its members carry on non-mainstream investment business.

2.2.2 Designated professional bodies

The Treasury has the power to designate such bodies, and by SI 2001 No 1226, eight professional bodies, including the Law Society, were designated for the purposes of FSMA 2000, Part XX. Other professional bodies designated include the Law Society of

Scotland, the Law Society of Northern Ireland, the Institute of Chartered Accountants in England and Wales, and the Institute of Actuaries.

2.2.3 The Scope Rules

Although the Law Society is the designated professional body for solicitors in England and Wales, the Solicitors Regulation Authority, the independent regulatory body of the Law Society, supervises and regulates the way in which the non-mainstream regulated activities are carried on by practice rules, known as the Scope Rules. These fill in the detail of the DPB regime and are subject to approval by the FSA. The Scope Rules are considered in **2.5.2** below.

2.2.4 Additional conditions to be satisfied

In order for the carrying on of the non-mainstream regulated activities to be exempt certain conditions need to be met (FSMA 2000, s 327). These conditions include the following:

(a) The person carrying on the regulated activities must be a member of a profession.

(b) That person must not receive a commission from a third party in respect of the regulated activities, unless he accounts to his client for the commission.

(c) The regulated activity must be provided in a way that is incidental to the provision of professional services.

(d) The investment to which the regulated activity relates must not be an investment specified in an order by the Treasury for the purposes of FSMA 2000, s 327(6).

This last condition means that there will be some regulated activities that do not come under the exemption to the general prohibition. Members of DPBs will not be able to undertake these activities, even though they appear to fit within the DPB regime. The Treasury has made an order under FSMA 2000, s 327(6), the Financial Services and Markets Act 2000 (Professions) (Non-Exempt Activities) Order 2001 (SI 2001 No 1227) (NEAO). The detail of the NEAO is beyond the scope of this chapter.

2.2.5 Solicitors carrying on mainstream regulated activities

Such solicitors will be subject to dual regulation. The regulated activities they undertake will not be covered by the DPB exemption and so they will need to apply to the FSA for permission to carry on regulated activities. Once granted authorisation they will then be subject to the FSA Rule Book.

The authorisation can be for different types of regulated activities. Which activity will determine what 'permission' is required from the FSA. If the application is made in the name of a firm, approved person(s) will be named. The authorisation will also dictate what controlled functions the approved persons can undertake.

The detail of the application for authorisation by the FSA and the appropriate regulations to which authorised persons are subject to are beyond the scope of this chapter.

2.3 The regulatory regime

A diagrammatic representation of the regulatory regime and the role of the regulatory bodies is set out below.

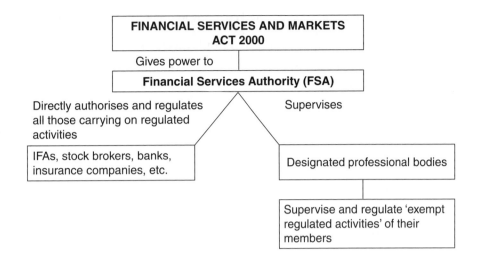

2.4 Financial promotions

In addition to the regulated activities regime and the general prohibition, the FSMA 2000 also sets out a second regime governing financial promotions. Section 21 (1) states: 'A person ('A') must not in the course of business, communicate an invitation or inducement to engage in investment activity.' As with the regulated activities regime, the detail of the financial promotions regime is set out in secondary legislation—the Financial Services and Markets Act 2000 (Financial Promotion) Order 2005 (SI 2005 No 1529) (FPO).

The terminology used in the financial promotions regime differs from that used in the regulated activities regime. For example, it uses the term 'controlled' rather than 'specified'. The activities and investments which fall within the legislation relating to financial promotions are similar to those falling within the regulated activities regime, but they are not identical.

The FPO defines 'communication' and distinguishes between 'real-time communications'—those made in a face-to-face situation or in a telephone conversation—and 'non-real-time communication'—which would include communications in writing (a letter, a publication or a website) or by e-mail.

The Part XX DPB regime does not cover financial promotions, and so solicitors undertaking non-mainstream regulated activities could still be caught by the financial promotions regime as they are not authorised by the FSA. There are several exemptions. Those relevant to solicitors engaging in exempt regulated activities under the DPB regime are discussed in more detail at **2.5.2.3** below.

SOLICITORS AND THE FINANCIAL SERVICES LEGISLATION

2.5 Solicitors regulated by the Solicitors Regulation Authority

The purpose of this part of the chapter is to explain in more detail the ways in which solicitors can comply with the financial services legislation.

There are three methods of complying with the legislation:

(a) seeking authorisation from the FSA directly (see **2.2.5**);

(b) ensuring that the only activities undertaken are those which are classified as excluded under the legislation; and

(c) taking advantage of the Part XX exemption, and ensuring that the only regulated activities undertaken are those deemed exempt regulated activities under the regulation of the Solicitors Regulation Authority as the independent regulatory body of the Law Society in its role as a DPB.

The majority of solicitors will undertake only non-mainstream regulated activities and so the first method will be inappropriate. The second and third of these methods are discussed in **2.5.1** and **2.5.2** below.

2.5.1 Excluded activities

The effect of carrying on only excluded regulated activities is that the activities do not come within the legislation and so no authorisation is needed. There are two types of excluded activities: those which apply depending on the investment which is subject to the activity; and those of a general application, which apply notwithstanding the investment. Examples of the first type are set out at **2.1.3.1.6**. Examples of the second type include trustees and personal representatives (RAO, Article 66), provision of non-investment services (RAO, Article 67), and provision of information on an incidental basis (RAO, Article 72C). These three exclusions are important to solicitors as many of the activities solicitors are engaging in on a day-to-day basis will come within their scope.

2.5.1.1 Trustees and personal representatives

Article 66 of the RAO provides for certain activities carried out by trustees and personal representatives to be excluded from the general prohibition. This means that solicitors acting in these capacities do not have to worry about authorisation. The activities excluded include arranging, managing, safeguarding and administering, and advising. There are two provisos to the exclusion. First, the investment to which the activity relates must not be a contract of insurance; and, second, the solicitor must receive only his costs for acting as trustee or personal representative; no additional remuneration must be received by him. In addition, the arranging or advising must be for, or to, a fellow trustee or personal representative, or for, or to, a beneficiary under the trust or will, or on intestacy.

2.5.1.2 Provision of non-investment services

The activities of dealing as agent, arranging, safeguarding and administering, and advising, when carried on in the course of a profession and when such that they might reasonably be regarded as a necessary part of other services provided in the course of that profession, are excluded from the general prohibition (RAO, Article 67). As with the exclusion for trustees and personal representatives, the investment to which the activity relates must not be a contract of insurance; and the solicitor must not receive additional remuneration for the activity. This exclusion will apply, for example, when arranging the sale of all the assets in an estate when administering it. However, where a decision has to be made as to which assets should be sold and which retained, it would be advisable to seek the advice of an authorised person.

2.5.1.3 Contracts of insurance

When the investment in question is a contract of insurance, the activities of arranging, managing, and safeguarding and administering are excluded from the general prohibition provided they are: (i) carried on in the course of a profession which does not otherwise consist of the carrying on of regulated activities; (ii) consist of providing information to a (potential) policyholder; and (iii) when the activity may reasonably be regarded as being incidental to that profession. The exclusion will apply, for example, when giving information to a conveyancing client with a view to arranging a defective title indemnity policy. The solicitor will be able to give the client the name and contact details of an authorised person who can advise the client. If more is involved, for example the filling in of forms, then the exclusion is not available.

2.5.2 Solicitors regulated by the Solicitors Regulation Authority as the independent regulatory body of the Law Society, a designated professional body

The Law Society is a designated professional body (DPB). The independent regulatory body of the Law Society, the Solicitors Regulation Authority (SRA), takes on the responsibility for regulating and supervising the way in which its members carry on non-mainstream regulated activities.

The Solicitors' Financial Services (Scope) Rules 2001 (the Scope Rules) and the Solicitors' Financial Services (Conduct of Business) Rules 2001 (the Conduct of Business Rules) set out the framework for the regulation. The Scope Rules set out the scope of the regulated activities which may be undertaken by solicitors. The Conduct of Business Rules regulate the way in which the exempt regulated activities are carried on.

The Scope Rules and Conduct of Business Rules are contained in the SRA Handbook in the Specialist Services section. The rules must be read in conjunction with the SRA Principles as the Principles apply to all aspects of practice, including the provision of financial services. The desired outcomes that apply to these specialist services are that financial services are provided to the same standard as required by the Financial Services Authority and in a manner that maintains confidence in the legal profession.

At the time of going to press the rules are subject to approval by the Legal Services Board. The key implementation date is 6 October 2011. Please refer to the online resource centre for updated information.

2.5.2.1 Scope Rules

The Scope Rules have been clearly drafted and are, with the Conduct of Business Rules, perhaps the most easily understood part of the financial services legislation affecting solicitors undertaking non-mainstream regulated activities.

The Scope Rules set out the conditions and restrictions with which solicitors' firms seeking to rely on the DPB regime must comply when carrying on regulated activities. They also prohibit solicitors from carrying on certain regulated activities and set out the effect of a breach of the Rules.

As, at the time of going to press, the Scope Rules are subject to approval by the Legal Services Board they are not reproduced here. They can be found on the Solicitors Regulation Authority website by using the following link: **http://www.sra.org.uk/solicitors/handbook/services/financial-scope-rules/content.page**

The Scope Rules should be read in full. However, three of the conditions warrant specific mention. A firm which carries on any regulated activities must ensure that:

   (a) the activities arise out of, or are complementary to, the provision of a particular professional service to a particular client;

(b) the manner of the provision by the firm of any service in the course of carrying on the activities is incidental to the provision by the firm of professional services; and

(c) the firm accounts to the client for any pecuniary reward or other advantage which the firm receives from a third party (Scope Rules 4(a), (b), (c)).

The effect of the condition contained in Rule 4(a) is that the solicitor must first be acting for the client with regard to another matter, and the activity in question must arise out of, or as a result of, that first instruction, or be complementary to it. It is not possible for the solicitor to undertake a regulated activity in isolation.

For the condition in Rule 4 (b) one factor that is taken into account is the proportion of the firm's work relating to regulated activities compared with the proportion of other professional services provided. If the proportion of regulated activity exceeds the other work, it is not incidental to it.

Under Rule 4 (c) accounting to the client means that the commission or reward must be held to the order of the client.

At **2.2.4** it was pointed out that FSMA 2000, s 327 sets out additional conditions which need to be met in order for the carrying on of the non-mainstream regulated activities to be exempt. Compliance with the Scope Rules will ensure that these additional conditions are also met.

2.5.2.2 Conduct of Business Rules

As with the Scope Rules, the Conduct of Business Rules should be read in full. They set out what information clients must receive, how transactions should be effected, what records must be kept (including records of the transactions and any commissions received), and details of the safekeeping of clients' investments.

As, at the time of going to press, the Conduct of Business Rules are subject to approval by the Legal Services Board they are not reproduced here. They can be found on the Solicitors Regulation Authority website by using the following link: **http://www.sra.org.uk/solicitors/handbook/services/financial-conduct-business-rules/content.page**.

The Conduct of Business Rules apply only to solicitors relying on the DBP regime. However, it is recommended that firms relying on an exclusion to ensure that they are not breaching the FSMA 2000 also comply with the Rules as the distinction between the two methods of compliance is very fine.

2.5.2.3 Financial promotions

Solicitors carrying on exempt regulated activities under the DBP regime must be aware of the implications of the financial promotions regime as regulated by the Financial Promotions Order (SI 2005 No 1529 as amended) (FPO: see **2.4**). As they are not authorised by the FSA they will be subject to the restriction on financial promotions. They will have to ensure either that the content of the communication is approved by an authorised person (if it is not a real-time communication, as authorised persons are prohibited from approving real-time communications for unauthorised persons), or that the communication comes within an exemption. There are two relevant exemptions, one dealing with real-time communications and the second dealing with non-real-time communications. Together these two exemptions should cover most communications to clients.

2.5.2.3.1 *Real-time communications*

The exemption covering these communications is contained in Article 55 of the FPO. Briefly, the communication will be exempt provided the solicitor is relying on the DPB exemption; the person to whom the communication is made is an existing client; and the activity to which the communication relates is incidental to the provision of professional services and either is excluded under Article 67 of the RAO (provision of non-investment services: see **2.5.1.2**) or is an exempt regulated activity by virtue of the DPB exemption.

2.5.2.3.2 Non-real-time communications

The exemption covering these communications is contained in Article 55A of the FPO as amended. Where non-real-time communications are concerned, the communication will be exempt provided the solicitor is relying on the DPB exemption and the communication includes a specified statement. The statement is as follows:

The firm is not authorised under the Financial Services and Markets Act 2000 but we are able in certain circumstances to offer a limited range of investment services to clients because we are members of the Law Society. We can provide these investment services if they are an incidental part of the professional services we have been engaged to provide.

2.5.3 Self-test questions

2.5.3.1 The purpose and scope of financial regulation

You should now have an understanding of the purpose and scope of financial services regulation. To test your knowledge and understanding answer the following short-answer questions. The answers are set out in Appendix one.

Q.1 What act provides the framework for the current financial services statutory regime?

Q.2 What is the name of the regulator for the financial services industry?

Q.3 What does the regulator have responsibility and power for?

Q.4 What are the four regulatory objectives that guide the regulator?

Q.5 What is the effect of the general prohibition set out in FSMA 2000, s 19?

Q.6 What are the sanctions if the general prohibition is breached?

Q.7 To carry on a regulated activity without contravening the general prohibition a person must be either an:

Q.8 What exemption to the general prohibition is contained in FSMA 2000, Part XX?

Q.9 What section of the FSMA 2000 sets out the definition of 'Regulated Activity'?

Q.10 For an activity to be a regulated activity and caught by the general prohibition it must generally:

Q.11 Name a statutory instrument which defines what activities are regulated activities. Give the full reference and the usual abbreviation.

Q.12 Name a statutory instrument which defines what investments are specified investments. Give the full reference, the part and the usual abbreviation.

Q.13 The majority of solicitors engage in non-mainstream regulated activities. What are non-mainstream regulated activities?

Q.14 The Law Society of England and Wales is a DPB. What is a DPB?

Q.15 FSMA 2000, Part XX states that a DPB must supervise and regulate the way in which its members carry on non-mainstream investments business. By what rules does the SRA, as the independent regulatory body of the Law Society, the

DPB, supervise and regulate its members? Give the full titles of the rules and the short titles.

Q.16 There are two types of excluded activities. Those which apply depending on the type of investment involved and those which apply irrespective of the investment involved. For the exclusions to be applicable what must the solicitor do with any related commission received by him?

Q.17 Give three examples of activities which are excluded under the RAO.

Q.18 Which article in the RAO sets out the exclusion for trustees and personal representatives?

Q.19 What do the rules referred to in question 15 set out.

Q.20 (a) What is a real-time communication?

(b) What is non-real-time communication?

2.5.3.2 Solicitors and the financial services legislation

The following scenarios help you to put the legislation into context. They should assist you in understanding how the legislation impacts upon solicitors in their work.

For each of the scenarios you should ask five questions (see the flow chart at **2.6**):

(a) Does the activity involve a specified investment?

(b) Is the activity capable of being a regulated activity under the RAO?

(c) If so, does it fall within any of the exclusions in the RAO?

(d) If not, is the activity capable of being an exempt regulated activity under Part XX?

(e) Does the activity fall within the Scope Rules?

Consider the scenarios. Assume that you are a trainee with Crookesmoor & Co, and that the firm has not sought authorisation by the Financial Services Authority. Identify any financial services issues that arise. Decide whether you can act as requested. If you can act, state whether you are relying on an exclusion to the FSMA 2000 or whether the activity is an exempt regulated activity.

1. You are acting for a client in her divorce. As part of the financial provision agreement an endowment policy in your client's name is to be transferred to her husband. Are we able to deal with this?

    (a) Does the activity involve a specified investment?

    (b) Is the activity capable of being a regulated activity under the RAO?

    (c) If so, does it fall within any of the exclusions in the RAO?

    (d) If not, is the activity capable of being an exempt regulated activity under Part XX?

    (e) Does the activity fall within the Scope Rules?

2. A client has received £20,000 in damages from a personal injury claim in which one of the assistant solicitors in the litigation department acted. The client has asked for some advice on where he should invest the money. Can we advise him?

    (a) Does the activity involve a specified investment?

    (b) Is the activity capable of being a regulated activity under the RAO?

    (c) If so, does it fall within any of the exclusions in the RAO?

    (d) If not, is the activity capable of being an exempt regulated activity under Part XX?

    (e) Does the activity fall within the Scope Rules?

3. Two of the partners in the firm are the trustees of the TG Wilford Deceased Will Trust. They are the only trustees. The trust assets comprise some land and a holding of unit trusts. They have always undertaken a review of the assets each half year, selling and buying assets as they think best for the trust. Under the FSMA regime, can they continue with this practice?
   (a) Does the activity involve a specified investment?
   (b) Is the activity capable of being a regulated activity under the RAO?
   (c) If so, does it fall within any of the exclusions in the RAO?
   (d) If not, is the activity capable of being an exempt regulated activity under Part XX?
   (e) Does the activity fall within the Scope Rules?

4. An existing client asks for advice on whether he should buy a particular plot of land, which he will then develop. Can/should we advise him?
   (a) Does the activity involve a specified investment?
   (b) Is the activity capable of being a regulated activity under the RAO?
   (c) If so, does it fall within any of the exclusions in the RAO?
   (d) If not, is the activity capable of being an exempt regulated activity under Part XX?
   (e) Does the activity fall within the Scope Rules?

5. You are acting on behalf of James and Philip, the executors of their grandmother's estate. The estate is relatively small. It includes a house, some accounts with the Nationwide Building Society and some shares in BG plc, Centrica and Abbey plc. Under the will the residue will be divided among four grandchildren, who are all adults. All the assets are to be sold or closed to enable the funeral account etc to be paid. Are we able to deal with these sales/closures?
   (a) Does the activity involve a specified investment?
   (b) Is the activity capable of being a regulated activity under the RAO?
   (c) If so, does it fall within any of the exclusions in the RAO?
   (d) If not, is the activity capable of being an exempt regulated activity under Part XX?
   (e) Does the activity fall within the Scope Rules?

2.6 Conclusion: solicitors and the financial services legislation

Where a solicitor is carrying on regulated activities the flow chart that follows sets out the questions to be asked to determine whether the activities come within the financial services regime, whether they are excluded and so no authorisation is required, or whether they will be exempt regulated activities under the DPB regime.

2.6.1 Checkpoints

You should now be able to demonstrate an:

- awareness of the purpose and scope of financial services regulation (**2.1; 2.2; 2.3**);
- understanding of the financial services regulatory framework in general (**2.3**);
- understanding of how the financial services regulatory framework applies and in particular in relation to solicitors' firms (**2.5**); and
- ability to identify when financial services issues are raised in the type of transactions that you are likely to encounter as a trainee in a solicitors' firm that has exempt professional firm status (**2.5; 2.6; 2.7**).

IS AUTHORISATION REQUIRED?

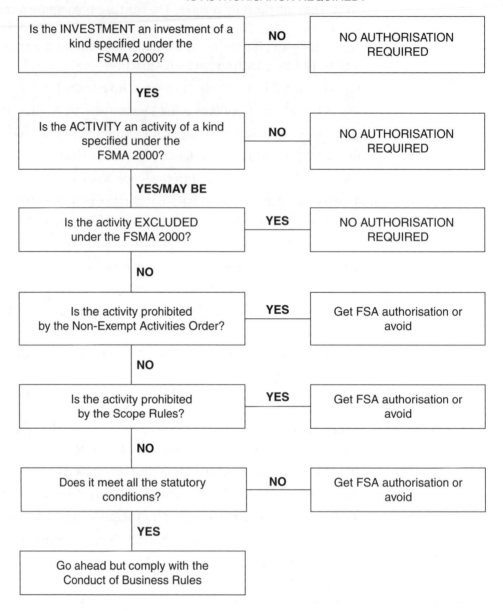

2.7 Commentary to scenarios

(*Scenarios set out at 2.5.3.2*)

1.
(a)	Does the activity involve a specified investment?	*Yes, a contract of insurance.*
(b)	Is the activity capable of being a regulated activity under the RAO?	*Yes, dealing.*
(c)	If so, does it fall within any of the exclusions in the RAO?	*No, there are no exclusions relating to dealing.*
(d)	If not, is the activity capable of being an exempt regulated activity under Part XX?	*In any event it does come within Part XX.*

(e)	Does the activity fall within the Scope Rules?	*Yes. You can actually advise on and/or arrange the acquisition or disposal by way of assignment.*

Conclusion: You can deal with the transfer.

2.

(a)	Does the activity involve a specified investment?	*Yes and to advise properly you need to be able to cover all types of investment as some will be specified investments.*
(b)	Is the activity capable of being a regulated activity under the RAO?	*Yes, advising (see conclusion regarding generic advice).*
(c)	If so, does it fall within any of the exclusions in the RAO?	*No, it does not fall within any of the exclusions. Article 67 (Provision of non-investment services) is not available as the activity could not be reasonably regarded as a necessary part of the other services provided to the client, ie acting in the personal injury claim.*
(d)	If not, is the activity capable of being an exempt regulated activity under Part XX?	*No, it cannot be said to be incidental to the personal injury claim.* *There is room for considering that the activity does 'arise out of, or is complementary to, the provision of a particular professional service to a client'. However, to give this advice would not be meeting the spirit of the legislation. If in doubt you should ask yourself whether you, or the firm, have the expertise to give best advice.*
(e)	Does the activity fall within the Scope Rules?	*Not applicable.*

Conclusion: You cannot advise him on specific investments. To do so will be a breach of the financial services legislation.

However, you can give generic advice on the different types of investment open to him and their different characteristics.

You will need to put him in touch with an independent financial adviser—someone who will be authorised by the FSA and so able to carry on a regulated activity.

In doing so you will be ensuring that your client receives best advice.

3.

(a)	Does the activity involve a specified investment?	*Yes, the unit trusts are. Land is not a specified investment however.*
(b)	Is the activity capable of being a regulated activity under the RAO?	*Yes, arranging, managing, administering and advising.*
(c)	If so, does it fall within any of the exclusions in the RAO?	*Yes, Article 66—trustees and PRs. Unlikely that additional remuneration, ie commission, would be received.*

(d) If not, is the activity capable of being an exempt regulated activity under Part XX?
(e) Does the activity fall within the Scope Rules?

Conclusion: Yes, they can continue with their twice-yearly reviews.

4.
(a)	Does the activity involve a specified investment?	No. Land is not caught by the FSMA. There is no need to ask any further questions.
(b)	Is the activity capable of being a regulated activity under the RAO?	
(c)	If so, does it fall within any of the exclusions in the RAO?	
(d)	If not, is the activity capable of being an exempt regulated activity under Part XX?	
(e)	Does the activity fall within the Scope Rules?	

Conclusion: You can give him the advice he is seeking. No authorisation is needed. You need to consider whether you have the specialist knowledge to do so. It depends on exactly what he is seeking advice on. As we are looking at this at trainee level, it may be that the partner does have the necessary knowledge—it is more a question of identifying the thought process.

5.
(a)	Does the activity involve a specified investment?	*Yes, shares*
(b)	Is the activity capable of being a regulated activity under the RAO?	*Yes, dealing or arranging.*
(c)	If so, does it fall within any of the exclusions in the RAO?	*Yes, Article 67—necessary.*
(d)	If not, is the activity capable of being an exempt regulated activity under Part XX?	*In any event it does come within Part XX.*
(e)	Does the activity fall within the Scope Rules?	

Conclusion: You can arrange the sale of the shares.

You do need to bear in mind the possible CGT implications of the PRs selling rather than transferring relevant assets to beneficiaries and letting them sell.

Also bear in mind that in an estate where not all the assets need to be sold to pay debt, legacies, etc, you should be advising the PRs to take independent financial advice, to ensure that the clients receive the best advice. It may be that being in a position where some assets need realising, but not all, you come outside the 'necessary' exclusion. Independent advice should be sought.

Visit the Online Resource Centre for more information and useful weblinks.
www.oxfordtextbooks.co.uk/orc/foundations11_12/

3

Money laundering

3.1 Introduction

This chapter considers money laundering. We look at:

- the process of money laundering
- the primary legislation and offences, and
- the relevance of the legislation to solicitors.

A concerted effort is being made within the EU to tighten up on money laundering. This was reflected by both the Second and the Third European Money Laundering Directives, which have led to changes in the UK legislation, in particular the Money Laundering Regulations (MLR) (see **3.8.3**). Without a concerted worldwide effort to eradicate money laundering, any European legislation will have limited effect. There are still jurisdictions where no questions are asked about the provenance of funds.

The breadth of the regulation encompasses large-scale laundering of drugs money, to relatively small-scale fraud, such as benefit fraud by an individual. Solicitors are usually unwittingly involved in a money laundering scheme. They will avoid this by being conversant with the requirements of the money laundering legislation and fully complying with it. Solicitors in all areas of practice must be aware of the impact of the legislation. It is equally important to a family practitioner as to a corporate lawyer.

In the UK, the Serious Organised Crime Agency (SOCA), which came into being in April 2006, is the body responsible within the United Kingdom for receiving and analysing all suspicious activity reports (SARs) about money laundering. More information about SOCA can be found at www.soca.gov.uk.

3.2 Money laundering

Before looking at details of the MLR it is helpful to understand what is meant by money laundering. Essentially it is the process by which 'dirty' monies, ie the proceeds of crime, are 'washed' to give them the appearance of 'clean' money.

There are three stages in a money laundering transaction: placement, layering, and integration.

3.2.1 Stage one: Placement

This is the stage at which the cash proceeds of the crime are put into a non-cash asset, for example, buying investments with cash or buying a property with cash. Alternatively the money may be initially paid into a series of bank accounts. This stage will be the most difficult for the criminal because he will be disposing of cash. The initial cash may also be taken and invested 'off shore', ie taken out of the country and reintroduced to the country at the layering stage. This asset is then sold, or the money withdrawn from the bank, to enable layering to take place.

3.2.2 Stage two: Layering

To avoid the money being readily traceable, the money will be passed through many transactions to create a trail which is not easily followed by the authorities. Money launderers may seek to pass money through a solicitor's client account as part of 'layering'. Law Society guidance makes it clear that money should be passed through the client account only where there is 'a genuine underlying legal transaction or some other valid reason to hold clients' money'.

3.2.3 Stage three: Integration

The final stage is for the money to pass into a legitimate business or investment. By this stage, from the criminal's point of view, the proceeds will, it is hoped, not be readily traceable back to the proceeds of the original crime.

The impact of the legislation is that the scope of money laundering has been widened. Not only does it encompass the above, but also covers matters such as tax evasion (even of a minor nature) and benefit fraud.

3.3 The legislation

The primary legislation is contained within the Proceeds of Crime Act 2002 (POCA 2002) as amended, the Terrorism Act 2000 and the Anti-Terrorism, Crime and Security Act 2001. The relevant legislation needs to be read in conjunction with the Money Laundering Regulations 2007 (SI 2007 No. 2157).

3.4 The offences

Each Act sets out various offences.

3.4.1 The Proceeds of Crime Act 2002

POCA 2002 defines money laundering (s 340(11)) and creates a number of money laundering offences.

Those offences fall broadly into three areas:

- The first involves the **laundering** of proceeds of crime (POCA 2002, ss 327–9).
- The second centres around the **failure to report** a knowledge or suspicion of money laundering (POCA 2002, ss 330–2).
- The final area relates to **tipping off** the person whom you know or suspect is laundering money about a money laundering disclosure or a money laundering investigation (POCA 2002, s 333A).

Everyone is subject to POCA 2002, but the offences of 'failing to report' and 'tipping off' apply only to those who are engaged in business in the 'regulated sector'. Certain activities carried on by solicitors fall within the definition of activities in the regulated sector (The Proceeds of Crime Act 2002 (Business in the Regulated Sector and Supervisory Authorities) Order 2007 paragraph 1(1)(n) (2007 SI No. 3287)).

3.4.2 The Terrorism Act 2000 and the Anti-Terrorism, Crime and Security Act 2001

The offences established under these acts are beyond the scope of this book.

3.4.3 The Money Laundering Regulations 2007 (SI 2007 No. 2157)

These regulations require the regulated sector to operate various systems with a view to minimising money laundering. A failure to comply with the requirements is a criminal offence.

The MLR 2007 apply to various persons, including independent legal professionals acting in the course of business in the UK.

3.5 Relevance to solicitors

As practising solicitors fall within the regulated sector and are independent legal professionals for the purposes of the MLR 2007 it is important that the requirements are understood and complied with.

To ensure that he does not commit an offence of money laundering under the POCA 2002 if a solicitor knows or suspects that the proceeds of crime are involved in a particular matter then he must disclose his concerns. This disclosure will initially be to the Money Laundering Reporting Officer (see **3.9.1**) who must then make a decision whether or not to report the concerns to SOCA. The disclosure is termed an 'authorised disclosure' for the purposes of both the legislation, and when considering matters of professional conduct (see **3.9.2**).

To avoid an offence of tipping off, a solicitor must not mention his concerns or the fact that the matter has been referred to SOCA to his client.

3.5.1 MLR 2007 key requirements

The key requirements imposed on solicitors by the MLR are:

- to appoint a nominated officer, usually known as a Money Laundering Reporting Officer (reg 20(2)(d)(i));
- to apply customer due diligence measures (reg 7);
- to establish reporting procedures (reg 20(1)(b));
- to train staff (reg 21); and
- to keep records (reg 19).

3.5.1.1 Customer Due Diligence Measures

Perhaps of most relevance to trainee solicitors are the customer due diligence (CDD) measures. Under MLR 2007 reg 5, 'Customer due diligence measures' means:

(a) identifying the customer and verifying the customer's identity on the basis of documents, data or information obtained from a reliable and independent source;

(b) identifying, where there is a beneficial owner who is not the customer, the beneficial owner and taking adequate measures, on a risk-sensitive basis, to verify his identity so that the relevant person is satisfied that he knows who the beneficial owner is, including, in the case of a legal person, trust or similar legal arrangement, measures to understand the ownership and control structure of the person, trust or arrangement; and

(c) obtaining information on the purpose and intended nature of the business relationship.

Regulation 6 expands on the interpretation of 'beneficial owner'. MLR 2007 reg 7 provides:

(1) ... a relevant person must apply customer due diligence measures when he—

(a) establishes a business relationship;

(b) carries out an occasional transaction;

(c) suspects money laundering or terrorist financing;

(d) doubts the veracity or adequacy of documents, data or information previously obtained for the purposes of identification or verification.

(2) Subject to regulation 16(4), a relevant person must also apply customer due diligence measures at other appropriate times to existing customers on a risk-sensitive basis. ...

The purpose of the CDD measures is to ensure that firms know their clients and the purpose of the clients' business relationship with the firm. The better a firm knows its clients the smaller the chance of the firm unwittingly being involved in money laundering. A client's identity is his name and address. Verifying that identify means seeing evidence of the name and address. It is important that this evidence is from a 'reliable and independent source' (MLR 2007 reg 5(a).) Where you are using original documents to verify the identity, it is usual to ask for evidence containing a photograph of the client, such as a photo-driving licence or passport. An original utilities bill, or bank statement, can be used to verify the client's address. Verification can also be completed electronically or by obtaining the information from others who are also regulated.

If the firm does not deal on a face to face basis with the client (and the client has not been physically present for identification purposes) then enhanced measures are called for. These will usually be met by seeking additional evidence for verification of name and address.

Under the MLR 2007 it is important that the firm retains records of the documents used for the CDD measures for five years.

MLR Reg 11 provides that CDD measures must be undertaken before conducting the work for the client. It also specifies what can or cannot be done if the firm is unable to apply the CDD measures.

3.5.2 Professional conduct issues

The money laundering legislation gives rise to a number of professional conduct issues.

3.5.2.1 Confidentiality

A solicitor is under a duty to keep confidential to his or her firm the affairs of clients and to ensure that the staff do the same.

When making an authorised disclosure (**3.8.4**) the duty of confidentiality is overridden and a solicitor will not be breaching the duty of confidentiality.

3.5.2.2 Privilege

When acting for a client, some documents and information are protected by way of a privilege against disclosure and this is called legal professional privilege. Again, when making an authorised disclosure (**3.8.4**) this is overridden and a solicitor will not be breaching the legal or professional restrictions upon him of legal professional privilege.

The Law Society issues detailed anti-money laundering guidance for solicitors. The guidance takes account of all new developments, including relevant cases, and can be found on the Law Society's website: http://www.lawsociety.org.uk under anti-money laundering. The latest practice note on anti-money laundering can be found in the practice notes section of the practice support area of the Law Society's website: www.lawsociety.org.uk/productsandservices/practicenotes/aml.page.

The Law Society has previously issued a warning to all solicitors alerting them to circumstances in which they might be assisting money laundering. The causes for concern include:

(a) unusual settlement requests, for example, settlements by cash, surprise payments by way of a third party cheque, or settlements which are reached too easily

(b) unusual instructions, for example, long-distance clients who have no apparent reason for instructing your firm, or if instructions change without a reasonable explanation

(c) use of solicitors' client accounts. Be cautious if you are instructed to do legal work, receive funds into your client account, but then the instructions are cancelled, and you are asked to return the money whether to your client or a third party

(d) suspect territory, for example, where a client is introduced by an overseas bank or third party based in a country where drug trafficking or terrorism may be prevalent

(e) loss-making transactions. Be alert to instructions which could lead to some financial loss to your client or a third party without a logical explanation, particularly where your client seems unconcerned.

3.6 Money laundering: checkpoints

You should now be able to:

- describe the process of money laundering (**3.8.2**)
- identify the primary offences (**3.8.4**)
- identify the relevance of the money laundering regime to solicitors (**3.9.1, 3.9.2**).

Further guidance and details of the relevant legislation can be found on the Law Society web site: http://www.lawsociety.org.uk.

Visit the Online Resource Centre for more information and useful weblinks.
www.oxfordtextbooks.co.uk/orc/foundations11_12/

Revenue law

4

An introduction to revenue law

4.1 The history of taxation

For centuries monarchs and, later, governments have had and used the power to raise money by way of taxes. This 'revenue' was originally required to fund the cost of maintaining an army and a navy and a relatively small amount of other public expenditure. Over the last century we have seen a vast increase in the amount of government expenditure on the provision of a wide range of services including healthcare, housing, education and roads and the provision of financial benefits like social security payments and pensions.

In order to pay for these services and benefits, governments raise money by imposing a number of different taxes and other payments. We would commonly associate taxes with, for example, income tax, but in the past there have been other, more unusual, taxes. Window tax, for example, was imposed at one time on the basis of the number of windows in a building. A less obvious tax which still exists and which you will consider in the LPC is stamp duty.

4.2 Changing taxes

Taxes have changed over the years. Income tax was imposed as a temporary measure in 1842 and has been with us ever since. However, each year it is customary for the Chancellor of the Exchequer to announce the government's financial requirements and proposed taxation measures for the forthcoming year in his annual Budget speech in November. These proposals then form the basis of the Finance Bill for that year which later becomes the Finance Act.

4.3 Taxes in the LPC context

The study of 'revenue law', as it is often called as an alternative to 'taxation', forms an integral part of the LPC. It is termed a 'core subject' because it should not be studied in isolation. It pervades many of the compulsory subject and elective subject areas.

4.4 The main taxes

The main taxes and their common abbreviations are:

(a) income tax (IT);

(b) capital gains tax (CGT);

(c) corporation tax (CT);

(d) inheritance tax (IHT); and

(e) value added tax (VAT).

4.5 The EC dimension

Membership of the European Community has meant the acceptance of measures which affect the extent to which a Member State can impose taxation and customs duties. It has also meant the harmonisation of indirect taxation and, in particular, the introduction of VAT in all Member States.

4.6 Sources of tax law

4.6.1 Statute and statutory instrument

The rules governing the taxes that you will be concerned with on this course are mainly contained in various Acts of Parliament but are also to be found in statutory instruments.

In the case of each tax there is a principal charging Act but, on occasions, provisions will also be contained in other Acts or statutory instruments which either contain administrative provisions or which amend the earlier legislation.

The principal charging Acts and their common abbreviations are as follows:

Tax	Act	Abbreviation
Income tax	Income Tax (Earnings and Pensions) Act 2003	ITEPA
	Income and Corporation Taxes Act 1988	ICTA
	Income Tax (Trading and other Income) Act 2005	ITTOIA
	Income Tax Act 2007	ITA
Capital gains tax	Taxation of Chargeable Gains Act 1992	TCGA
Corporation tax	Corporation Tax Act 2009	CTA
	Corporation Tax Act 2010	CTA 10
	Income and Corporation Taxes Act 1988	ICTA
Inheritance tax	Inheritance Tax Act 1984	IHTA
Value added tax	Value Added Tax Act 1994	VATA

Many of the administrative provisions relating to income tax, corporation tax and capital gains tax are contained in the Taxes Management Act 1970 (TMA). Similar provisions relating to VAT are contained in the Customs and Excise Management Act 1979.

4.6.2 Case law

Regard must also be had to case law which may assist in determining the meaning and extent of the statutory provisions.

4.6.3 HM Revenue & Customs statements

4.6.3.1 Statements of practice

Statements of practice indicate what view the Inland Revenue will take of the practical application of particular tax provisions.

4.6.3.2 Extra-statutory concessions

If a taxpayer satisfies the terms of an extra-statutory concession, then the Revenue will waive its right to collect tax which would otherwise be due.

4.7 Administration of income tax, capital gains tax, and corporation tax

4.7.1 Treasury

Broadly, all taxation is under the control of the Chancellor of the Exchequer. He is a politician and is not necessarily an expert in either taxation or economic matters. He relies heavily on his permanent civil servants who are members of the Treasury.

4.7.2 Board of HM Revenue & Customs

The members of the Board are known as the Commissioners of HMRC. They must not be confused with Special Commissioners and General Commissioners who are involved in the appeals system which is considered later at **5.12**. The Commissioners of HMRC are permanent civil servants appointed by the Treasury. The Board regulates the administration of direct taxation in the UK. It is the Board who issue statements of practice and extra-statutory concessions.

4.7.3 Tax districts and HM inspectors of taxes

The country is divided into tax districts, each headed by a district inspector. The inspector is responsible for examining the returns of individuals, unincorporated businesses and companies and computing the tax that is due. A notice of assessment is then raised and sent to the taxpayer showing the amount of tax that is due.

4.7.4 Collectors of taxes

Just as the country is divided into tax districts, so it is divided into areas served by a smaller number of accounts and collection offices. Each office operates under the authority of a collector of taxes. As the name suggests, the collector is responsible for the collection of tax, if necessary, through the courts.

Figure 4.1 Administration of direct taxation in the UK.

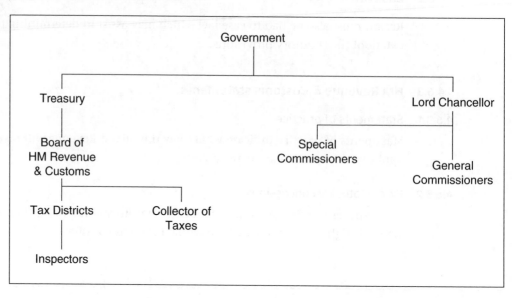

4.7.5 General and Special Commissioners

See **5.12** for the role of the Commissioners in the appeal process.

4.8 Administration of inheritance tax

4.8.1 Treasury

See **4.7.1**.

4.8.2 Board of HM Revenue & Customs

See **4.7.2**.

4.8.3 Capital taxes office

Unlike the taxes we have considered in **4.7** above, the Capital Taxes Office administers inheritance tax for the Board of HM Revenue & Customs. It also deals with the actual collection of the tax.

4.8.4 Special Commissioners

The appeal process is similar to that in respect of the other taxes mentioned at **4.7**.

4.9 Administration of value added tax

4.9.1 Treasury

See **4.7.1**.

4.9.2 Board of HM Revenue & Customs

The Commissioners of HM Revenue & Customs have overall responsibility for VAT. In addition, there are a number of VAT offices around the country which deal with registration and investigation work.

4.9.3 VAT tribunals

Appeal against a decision of the Commissioners is made to the VAT tribunal.

4.10 Who pays tax?

The following are potentially taxable in respect of the following taxes.

4.10.1 Individuals

- income tax on income;
- capital gains tax on chargeable gains;
- inheritance tax on lifetime chargeable transfers; and
- value added tax if the individuals carry on a business and register for VAT or become liable to pay VAT.

4.10.2 Partnerships

- income tax on income;
- capital gains tax on chargeable gains; and
- value added tax if the partnership registers for VAT or becomes liable to pay VAT.

4.10.3 Personal representatives

- the deceased's outstanding income tax and income tax chargeable during the administration of the deceased's estate;
- capital gains tax on any chargeable gain arising during the administration of the estate;
- VAT if they carried on the deceased's business and this was registered for VAT purposes; and
- inheritance tax on the value of the deceased's estate.

4.10.4 Trustees

- income tax on the income produced by the trust fund;
- capital gains tax on any chargeable gain arising;
- inheritance tax; and
- VAT if the trustees carry on a business and this is registered for VAT purposes or they become liable to pay VAT.

4.10.5 Companies

- corporation tax on income profits;
- corporation tax on capital gains;
- value added tax if the company is registered for VAT or becomes liable to pay VAT; and
- inheritance tax in certain very limited circumstances.

4.11 Tax planning

Solicitors and accountants are frequently asked to advise clients on ways in which to reduce their tax liability. Even if the client does not actually ask them to do so, potentially they will be negligent if they fail to take account of the tax implications of a certain course of action when giving other advice. In giving this advice, it is important to understand the difference between tax avoidance and tax evasion.

4.11.1 Tax avoidance

Tax avoidance is a legitimate exercise by which the potential taxpayer seeks to organise his/her affairs in such a way as to ensure either that no tax will be payable in respect of something which might otherwise have given rise to a tax liability, or that the amount of the liability is reduced to the lowest possible level by the use of the available tax concessions and reliefs.

4.11.2 Tax evasion

Tax evasion involves the taxpayer ignoring a tax liability or concealing it; for example, by failing to disclose the liability to the relevant authority by making a false return. Tax avoidance is legitimate; tax evasion is not.

Visit the Online Resource Centre for more information and useful weblinks.
www.oxfordtextbooks.co.uk/orc/foundations11_12/

Income tax

5.1 Introduction: basic structure of income tax

This chapter deals with the charge to income tax. In the chapter we explain in particular:

- the basic steps to calculate the liability to income tax (**5.2** to **5.10**);
- exempt income (**5.4**);
- classification of sources of income (**5.4**);
- how to gross up income received net of tax (**5.5**); and
- the rates of tax applicable to non-savings income, savings income and dividend income (**5.5** and **5.8**).

5.1.1 Sources of income tax law

Sources of income tax law are:

(a) Statute: the principal charging acts are the Income and Corporation Taxes Act 1988 (ICTA), the Income Tax (Earnings and Pensions) Act 2003 (ITEPA), the Income Tax (Trading and Other Income) Act 2005 (ITTOIA) and the Income Tax Act 2007 (ITA). The annual Finance Acts have made changes to ICTA, ITEPA and ITTOIA. Income tax is renewed annually by Parliament.

(b) Case law and Inland Revenue statements of practice and extra-statutory concessions.

5.1.2 Income

There is no statutory definition of income. But as income tax is charged on income and not capital profits, income needs to be distinguished from capital profits. Income profits are subject to income tax. Capital profits are not subject to income tax, but may give rise to a capital gains tax liability (see **6.1.2**). Generally, income is of a recurrent nature, eg salary received each month, interest regularly paid on a bank or building society account every quarter, or the annual profits of an unincorporated business.

5.1.3 Who pays income tax?

The following pay income tax:

(a) individuals (including minors);
(b) partnerships;

(c) personal representatives; and

(d) trustees.

5.1.4 Income tax year

The income tax year runs from 6 April to 5 April and is called the 'tax year' or 'year of assessment'. It is referred to by the calendar years which it straddles—eg the tax year beginning on 6 April 2011 is referred to as the tax year 2011/12.

5.1.5 Collection of tax

There are two methods of collection of income tax. These are:

(a) deduction at source (see **5.1.5.1**); and

(b) self-assessment (**5.1.5.2**).

5.1.5.1 Deduction at source

Certain types of income are said to be paid 'net of tax', ie, subject to deduction of income tax at source. Examples of types of this income are:

(a) dividends;

(b) salaries (Pay As You Earn—PAYE);

(c) trust income;

(d) interest paid by banks and building societies (except by the National Savings Bank); and

(e) debenture interest (loan interest payments paid by companies).

The payer of the income effectively acts as a tax collector by deducting the tax from the payment and handing the tax to HM Revenue & Customs—HMRC. (The recipient is given credit for the tax paid.) The payer then hands over the net amount to the recipient.

To prevent a multiplicity of claims for repayment of income tax by non-taxpayers there is a procedure whereby, if an investor meets certain criteria, he can register with the payer (eg the bank or building society) for the interest to be paid without deduction of any tax. This is done by filling in form R85 (see **Example 1**).

5.1.5.2 Self-assessment

The second method of collection of tax is self-assessment which will affect anyone whose income is not subject to deduction of tax at source. Examples of persons who will have to file income tax returns to HMRC are:

(a) self-employed;

(b) partners;

(c) company directors;

(d) individuals having more than one source of income; and

(e) individuals in receipt of investment income the receipt of which may make them liable to tax at the higher rate.

5.2 Calculation of income tax

Income tax is charged on an individual's taxable income.

There are a number of steps that must be followed to determine an individual's liability to income tax. These are as follows:

Step 1 You need to identify all sources of income to calculate total income (see **5.4** and **5.5**).

Step 2 Next you must ascertain net income by deducting any reliefs (see **5.6**).

Step 3 Once you have deducted reliefs you must deduct personal allowances treated as tax deductions to ascertain taxable income (see **5.7**).

Step 4 Having ascertained taxable income you can now apply the appropriate rates of tax (see **5.8**). You must remember that there are rules as to the order in which different sources of income are taxed (see **5.5 and 5.8**).

Step 5 Having applied the rates of tax you should identify and apply any allowances treated as tax reductions (see **5.9**).

Step 6 Lastly, you must deduct any tax deducted at source (see **5.10**).

To summarise the above:

Total income

less

Reliefs

=

Net income

less

Personal reliefs (personal allowance and blind person's allowance only)

=

Taxable income

We will be looking at each of the elements for calculating taxable income. It is *important* that you learn this formula.

5.3 Rates of tax

5.3.1 The rates and tax bands

Income tax is charged at basic and higher rates. For the tax year 2011/12 the rates of tax are as follows:

Slice of taxable income	Rate	Referred to as:
£0–£35,000	20%	basic rate
£35,001–150,000	40%	higher rate
Over £150,000	50%	additional rate

Therefore the basic rate of 20 per cent is charged on the first £35,000 of taxable income, the higher rate of 40 per cent is charged on all taxable income between £35,001 and £150,000, and 50 per cent is payable on anything over £150,000.

EXAMPLE 1

An individual has *taxable* income of £38,500. His tax liability is computed as follows:

Slice of taxable income	Rate	£
£35,000	at 20%	7,000.00
£3,500	at 40%	1,400.00
Tax liability		8,400.00

5.3.2 Exceptions

When calculating the tax liability of a taxpayer whose income includes savings and dividend income, the savings income and the dividend income must be treated as the top slices of income. This is looked at in more detail in **5.5**.

There are special rules for savings income, where there is a 10 per cent starting rate of tax. The starting rate applies to the first £2,560 of savings income but is not applicable if taxable non-savings income exceeds this threshold. Further consideration of the 10 per cent starting rate for savings income is outside of the scope of this book.

Dividend income attracts a basic rate of 10 per cent. If the taxpayer is a higher rate taxpayer the dividend income will attract tax at 32.5 per cent. If the taxpayer is liable to tax at the additional rate the dividend income will attract tax at 42.5 per cent. For this reason dividend income is treated as the top slice of income after savings income.

5.3.3 Personal representatives

Personal representatives are liable to the basic rate of tax only, 20 per cent for the tax year 2011/12.

5.3.4 Trustees

Trustees are liable to either the basic rate of tax or the trust rate (see **6.2.1.3** and **11.4.2**).

5.4 Total income

5.4.1 Calculating total income

Looking back at the calculation of taxable income (**5.2**), it can be seen that the first step is to calculate the individual's total income.

'Total income' is the total of an individual's income computed according to either ITEPA or ITTOIA. Until recently 'statutory income' was computed according to the rules contained in the various schedules set out in ICTA 1988. Details of the schedules and equivalent provisions of ITTOIA and ITEPA are set out below. Each part of ITTOIA and ITEPA sets out the rules for calculating income from that source. An individual may have, and often does have, more than one source of income which will fall into either ITEPA or into the different parts of ITTOIA.

However, certain types of income are exempt from income tax (exempt income), ie they are not included in calculating total income. These items include:

(a) child benefit and certain other social security benefits;

(b) the first £70 of National Savings Bank interest each year;

(c) interest on National Savings Certificates;

(d) scholarships;

(e) interest on damages for personal injuries or death;

(f) certain maintenance received;

(g) interest on a Tax Exempt Savings Account (TESSAs); [AQ2]

(h) dividends paid on a Personal Equity Plan (PEPs);

(i) all interest and dividends paid on an Individual Savings Account (ISA); and

(j) gross income up to £4,250 pa from renting a room (subject to certain conditions being satisfied).

5.4.2 Chargeable sources of income

Schedule of ICTA	Relevant provision of ITEPA or ITTOIA	Source of Income
A	Part 3 ITTOIA	Rent and other receipts from land in the UK. Furnished lettings.
D Case I	Part 2 ITTOIA	Profits of trade in the UK.
D Case II	Part 2 ITTOIA	Profits of a profession or vocation in the UK.
D Case III	Part 4 ITTOIA	Interest, annuities, and other annual payments.
E	ITEPA	Employment, pensions income, and social security income.
F	Part 4 ITTOIA	Dividends and certain other distributions by companies.

5.5 Grossing up

Certain types of income will be received by the taxpayer net of tax. (Remember collection of tax by deduction at source at **5.1.5.1**.) In order to calculate the taxpayer's liability to tax, it is necessary to include the gross amount of that particular source of income in the taxable income calculation.

The reason for this is that except in the case of salary, tax will only have been deducted at 20 per cent; however, it may well be that the particular circumstances of this taxpayer are such that his taxable income attracts tax at the higher rate or additional rate as well as the basic rate. It is therefore necessary to add the gross amount of this source of income to the taxpayer's other income in order to calculate the exact amount for which the taxpayer is liable. However, credit is then given for the tax deducted at source. The balance is the amount which the taxpayer must pay to HMRC.

Dividend income is treated differently from savings income in that the taxpayer will receive a tax credit of 10 per cent of the gross dividend as if tax had been deducted at that rate at source.

In order to calculate the gross income where tax has been deducted at source, the formula is as follows:

$$\text{Gross amount} = \text{Net amount} \times \frac{100}{(100 \text{ less the rate at which tax has been deducted})}$$

Grossing up should be applied to trust income, interest paid by banks and building societies (except the National Savings Bank), debenture interest (all of which are known as savings income), and dividend income.

Earned income taxed under the provisions of ITEPA should not be grossed up because, under the PAYE system, income tax at all rates will have been deducted by the employer using tables and information supplied by HMRC and taking into account the taxpayer's personal reliefs. A certificate of tax paid (Form P60) is given by the employer to the employee on a yearly basis showing the gross figure. If the taxpayer has other sources of income apart from salary, then he will put the gross figure in his tax return for the purposes of assessing what further tax liability (if any) he has.

Therefore, in order to calculate the gross amount which goes into the computation of statutory income, the formula is as follows for savings income:

$$\text{Gross amount} = \text{Net amount} \times \frac{100}{(100-20)} = \text{Net amount} \times \frac{100}{80}$$

The formula for grossing up dividend income is as follows:

$$\text{Gross amount} = \text{Net amount} \times \frac{100}{(100-10)} = \text{Net amount} \times \frac{100}{90}$$

EXAMPLE 2

Maria receives dividend income of £900.
The calculation to gross up the dividend income is:

$$\text{Gross dividend} = 900 \times \frac{100}{90} = £1{,}000$$

Once Maria's income tax liability is calculated she will be entitled to a credit of the income tax deducted at source. This is referred to as a tax credit. In this case she will be entitled to a tax credit of £100 against her final liability (ie the tax paid on the gross dividend of £1,000 at the rate of 10 per cent).

As stated earlier, at **5.3.1**, the basic rate of tax is normally 20 per cent. Therefore, if the taxpayer is a basic rate taxpayer, the tax paid by the body paying the interest will satisfy the taxpayer's liability to tax. If the taxpayer receiving savings income is a non-taxpayer or a starting rate taxpayer he will be able to make a repayment claim to the HMRC for the tax paid by the relevant body. However, if he is a higher rate taxpayer, then he will be liable to pay tax on the gross amount of the savings income at 40 per cent less the tax credit for the tax paid on his behalf by the relevant body.

The full amount of the savings income is treated as a top slice of income (but before dividend income). When the rates of tax are applied to the taxable income (which, do not forget, will include the gross amount of savings income) it is necessary to treat the full amount of the savings income included in the taxable income as a top slice of income and calculate the tax on it before calculating the tax on dividend income.

Dividend income attracts a basic rate of tax of 10 per cent, not 20 per cent. Therefore, if the taxpayer is a basic rate taxpayer the tax deemed to be paid by the company paying the dividend will satisfy the taxpayer's liability to tax. If the shareholder is a non-taxpayer or is unable to utilise the tax credit in full there is no right to make a repayment claim. Higher rate taxpayers and additional rate taxpayers will be liable to tax on the gross amount of the dividend income of 32.5 per cent and 42.5 per cent respectively, less the tax credit.

Trustees are taxed on dividend income at the rate of 42.5 per cent.

EXAMPLE 3

Daniel's taxable income has been calculated at £39,000. This includes gross dividend income of £6,000. This means that his non-savings income is £33,000 (£39,000 – £6,000).

Ignoring reliefs/charges on income for the purposes of this exercise, applying the rates of tax and using the non-savings income first:

Slice of taxable income	Rate	Tax £
£33,000 of non-savings income	at 20%	6,600.00

(ie £33,000 of non-savings income, leaving £2,000 of the basic rate band still available) then continuing to apply the rates of tax to the dividend income, remembering that dividend income attracts a basic rate of tax of 10%, not 20%:

£2,000 of dividend income	at 10%	200.00
£4,000 of dividend income	at 32.5%	1,300.00
		8,100.00
less tax credit (£6,000 ´ 10%)		(600.00)
Tax to be paid to the collector		7,500.00

Throughout this chapter we will be using an example to illustrate how income tax is calculated. The following example illustrates the principles that we have looked at in 5.4 and 5.5.

EXAMPLE 4

Anna is 34 years old. She is a partner in a firm of surveyors. In the tax year 2011/12 her share of the partnership profits are £29,000. She has shares in AZG Ltd on which she receives a net dividend of £600. She earns net interest on her account with the Rivelin Building Society of £400.

First, we must identify the three sources of income, which are:

Non-savings income
Partnership profits

Savings income
Building Society interest

Dividend income
Dividends

Second, we must identify whether the income received by Anna is net income or gross income. The partnership income will be received gross but the savings and dividend income will be received net of tax. We must therefore gross up the savings and dividend income when calculating total income.

Total income

	Net £	Gross £
Partnership profits		29,000.00
Building Society interest	400.00	500.00
$400 \times \frac{100}{(100-20)}$		
Dividends	600.00	666.67
$600 \times \frac{100}{(100-10)}$		
Total income		30,166.67

5.6 Reliefs

Once statutory income has been calculated, the next step is to calculate net income. Net income is derived by deducting reliefs from statutory income (previously known as 'charges on income'). These reliefs remove sums of money from the income tax calculation.

Reliefs are deducted from the taxpayer's income for the tax year in which they are paid. The type of reliefs within the scope of this book are payments of interest on qualifying payments.

Most interest payments do not attract tax relief and must be paid out of taxed income (eg credit card and overdraft interest). However, in certain cases, tax relief is available for interest paid on money borrowed. The qualifying payments for income tax purposes within the scope of this book are:

(a) a loan to invest in a partnership;

(b) a loan to invest in a close trading company; and

(c) a loan to personal representatives to pay IHT (inheritance tax).

You should, of course, bear in mind that there are other types of relief. We will look at those with which we are concerned in this chapter in more detail below.

5.6.1 Loan to invest in a partnership

The loan must be for a qualifying purpose. These are:

(a) to buy a share in a partnership; or

(b) to make a loan to a partnership provided the money is used for the purposes of its trade, profession or vocation; or

(c) to add to a partner's capital.

There is also a condition which must be satisfied. This is that the partner must be a partner (or become a partner) when the loan is made and must still be a partner when the interest is paid.

EXAMPLE 5

Sally is a partner in a firm of solicitors. Her statutory income is £30,000. She borrows £10,000 to make a loan to the partnership. This loan is to be used to buy new office equipment. Interest is charged on the loan at the rate of 10 per cent per annum. This means that she will pay interest of £1,000 each year on that loan.

As the interest on the loan is for a qualifying purpose (ie it is a loan to her partnership and the money is to be used for the purposes of its profession) and as she is a partner when the interest is paid, the interest paid will be treated as a charge on income.

Therefore, Sally will calculate her total income as follows:

	£
Total income	30,000
less	
Reliefs	1,000
equals	
Net income	29,000

5.6.2 Loan to invest in a close trading company

The loan must be for a qualifying purpose. These are:

(a) to purchase shares in a close trading company; or

(b) to lend money to a close trading company.

A close company is a company which is controlled by:

(a) five or fewer participators (ie shareholders); or

(b) participators (however many) who are also directors.

'Control' lies in the hands of those holding more than one-half of the votes at a general meeting of shareholders (ie a majority shareholding). Therefore, if a company has nine or fewer shareholders, then it will always be a close company. Whatever the distribution of shareholdings, there must always be five who, between them, own a majority of the shares. In assessing 'control', rights of shareholder's 'associates' (eg spouse, children) are also taken into account.

There are also some conditions which must be complied with. These are:

(a) the company must carry on a trade; and

(b) the borrower must either:

(i) own or acquire at least 5 per cent of the shares in the company; or

(ii) be a shareholder and work for the greater part of his time in the management or conduct of the company.

EXAMPLE 6

Colworth Engineering Ltd has nine shareholders, one of whom is Stephanie. She is also a full-time working director of the company.

Stephanie takes out a loan of £5,000 to lend to Colworth Engineering Ltd. Interest on the loan is charged at 10 per cent per annum. Therefore the annual interest paid by Stephanie is £500.

Colworth Engineering Ltd is a close trading company. It is a close trading company because it has only nine shareholders.

We do not know Stephanie's shareholding but as she is a full-time working director she meets the condition that 'the borrower is a shareholder and works for the greater part of her time in the conduct of the company'.

This means that the loan is for a qualifying purpose and the interest paid will be entitled to relief.

Stephanie will be able to deduct the £500 interest as a relief.

5.6.3 A loan to personal representative to pay inheritance tax

Personal representatives (PRs) are liable to income tax on the income received by the estate during the administration period at the basic rate of 20 per cent (or 10 per cent in the case of dividend income from companies). They are not liable to pay income tax at any higher rates but neither do they qualify for any allowances.

You will see in **Chapter 13** on entitlement that PRs often have to pay inheritance tax (IHT) in respect of part of the deceased's estate before they obtain a grant. The PRs, however, need to obtain the grant before they can dispose of assets in the estate which will then enable them to pay the IHT. The PRs will often need to take out a loan to pay this part of the IHT. If a loan is taken out then income tax relief is available to them to the extent that the loan was to pay IHT on personal property in the UK.

EXAMPLE 7

Using our earlier example of Anna, she now borrows £20,000 from the White Rose Bank on which she pays interest at 5 per cent per annum. Anna uses the loan to increase her capital in the partnership. The annual interest of £1,000 will be allowable as a relief. We are therefore able to build on the example to ascertain Anna's net income.

Total income

	Net £	Gross £
Partnership profits		29,000.00
Building Society interest	400.00	500.00
$400 \times \frac{100}{(100-20)}$		
Dividends	600.00	666.67
$600 \times \frac{100}{(100-20)}$		
Total income		30,166.67
Deduct reliefs		
Interest on loan from White Rose Bank		(1,000.00)
Net Income		29,166.67

5.7 Personal reliefs treated as income tax deductions

Once net income has been calculated, the next step is to deduct personal reliefs in order to compute the taxpayer's taxable income. It is important to differentiate between a tax deduction and a tax reduction (see **5.9**) because the treatment will make a difference to the amount of tax ultimately payable. Only tax deductions are taken into account at this stage.

5.7.1 Personal representatives and trustees

Personal representatives and trustees are not entitled to any personal reliefs.

5.7.2 Tax deductions

There are only two reliefs which are dealt with as tax deductions:

(a) the personal allowance (including the personal age allowance); and

(b) the blind person's allowance.

The remaining reliefs are dealt with as income tax reductions. These are dealt with in more detail in **5.9**.

Personal reliefs treated as deductions from total income are looked at in more detail below.

5.7.2.1 Personal allowance (PA)

Each individual is entitled to a personal allowance. For 2011/12 this is £7,475. This allowance is reduced by £1 for every £2 by which income exceeds £100,000. This is irrespective of age.

The personal age allowance is also treated as a tax deduction (see **5.9.1.1**).

Husband and wife and civil partners are taxed separately and are each entitled to a personal allowance. If one spouse/civil partner has a surplus personal allowance, the surplus cannot be transferred to the other spouse/civil partner, nor can it be carried forward and used in a later year. However, if one spouse/civil partner has an unused personal allowance, a tax saving could be made by transferring any assets producing income to that spouse/civil partner.

5.7.2.2 Blind person's allowance

A registered blind person can claim a relief in addition to his other allowances. The full relief may be claimed even if the blind person was so registered for only part of the tax year for which the claim is made.

For 2011/12, the relief is £1,980.

EXAMPLE 8

Using our earlier example of Anna we must now calculate her taxable income by deducting her personal allowances. She will be entitled to the basic personal allowance.

Total income

	Net £	Gross £
Partnership profits		29,000.00
Building Society interest	400.00	500.00
$400 \times \frac{100}{(100-20)}$		
Dividends	600.00	666.67
$600 \times \frac{100}{(100-10)}$		
Total income		30,166.67
Deduct reliefs		
Interest on loan from White Rose Bank		(1,000.00)
Net Income		29,166.67
Deduct personal allowance		
Personal allowance		(7,475.00)
Taxable income		**21,691,67**

5.8 Applying the rates of tax to statutory income

Having ascertained taxable income, the next step is to apply the rates of tax. Before this, the taxable income must be split down into non-savings income, savings income, and dividend income. This is because the rates of tax must be applied in the following order:

(a) non-savings income;

(b) savings income; and

(c) dividend income.

Savings income and dividend income are treated as the top two slices of income. (See **Example 3, Example 7,** and **5.5.**)

EXAMPLE 9

Using our earlier example of Anna we must now apply the rates of tax. Because of the top slicing rule it is important to apply the rates in the correct order. In order to do this we must ascertain

Anna's taxable non-savings income. This is ascertained by taking the taxable income of £21,691.67 and deducting from this the aggregate of her savings income and dividend income £1,166.67 (£500.00 + £ 666.67). This gives us taxable non-savings income of £20,525.00.

Total income

	Net £	Gross £
Partnership profits		29,000.00
Building Society interest	400.00	500.00
$400 \times \frac{100}{(100-20)}$		
Dividends	600.00	666.67
$600 \times \frac{100}{(100-10)}$		
Total income		30,166.67
Deduct reliefs		
Interest on loan from White Rose Bank		(1,000.00)
Net Income		29,166.67
Deduct personal allowance		
Personal allowance		(7,475.00)
Taxable income		21,691.67
Apply the rates of tax		
Non savings income		
£20,525 @ 20%		4,105.00
Savings income		
£500 @ 20%		100.00
Dividend income		
£666.67 @ 10%		66.67
Total tax		4,271.67

5.9 Personal reliefs treated as income tax reductions

Certain personal reliefs only attract tax relief at a particular rate. For the tax year 2011/12, the rate is 10 per cent. These reliefs are treated as income tax reductions.

The reliefs dealt with in this way relevant to this course are:

(a) married couples' and civil partners' age allowance; and

(b) qualifying maintenance payments.

If the reliefs were dealt with as a deduction, in the same way as the personal allowance and the blind person's allowance, then relief would be obtained at the taxpayer's highest rate, ie 50 per cent, 40 per cent or 20 per cent according to the taxpayer's individual circumstances, and not at the prescribed rate of 10 per cent of the relevant relief. Therefore, the reliefs are instead treated as income tax reductions. That is, the amount of the taxpayer's liability to tax for the relevant tax year is reduced by an amount equal to 10 per cent of the relevant relief.

The reduction can only reduce the taxpayer's tax bill to nil—there cannot be any repayment of tax.

The reliefs are covered in more detail at **5.9.1.** and **5.9.2.**

5.9.1 Age allowances

Individuals are entitled to higher personal (see **5.7**) and married couples'/civil partners' allowances (MCA) if they are of a certain age at the end of the tax year:

Personal allowance
Aged 65 to 74	For tax year 2011/12	£9,940
Aged 75 and over	" "	£10,090

Married couples'/civil partners' allowance
Aged 75 and over	For tax year 2011/12	£7,295

A man who is married and living with his wife for any part of a tax year is entitled to the married couples' allowance for that year in addition to his personal allowance. This principle also applies to civil partners. However, to qualify for the allowance at least one of the couple must have reached the age of 65 before 6 April 2000.

The MCA is automatically allocated to the husband but:

(a) the married couple may jointly elect that the MCA be allocated wholly to the wife (the election must be made before the beginning of the appropriate tax year); *or*

(b) the wife may elect independently that half of the MCA be allocated to her (again, the election must be made before the beginning of the appropriate tax year); *or*

(c) if any part of the MCA cannot be used fully by either the husband or wife then that spouse may give notice to the Inland Revenue to transfer the unused part to the other spouse (this election must be made within five years of 31 January next following the appropriate tax year).

There are special rules relating to the MCA for the year of marriage, separation and death which are outside the scope of this book. The rules relating to the allocation of the MCA for civil partners are also outside of the scope of this book.

5.9.1.1 Income limit for age-related allowances

The full age allowances are only available if the taxpayer's total income does not exceed £24,000 (2011/12). Above this limit:

(a) The PA is reduced by £1 for every £2 of the taxpayer's total income over £24,000 until it equals the normal PA.

(b) The MCA is similarly reduced by £1 for every £2 of the husband's total income above £24,000 less any reduction in his PA under (a) above until it equals £2,800, which will be the minimum MCA. The tax reduction is limited to 10 per cent of this sum (£280.00).

EXAMPLE 10

Henry is a married man aged 78 with a total income of £32,000. As Henry is over 75 he is entitled to the higher personal allowance of £10,090. As he is also married, he is also entitled to the higher MCA of £7,295. However, as his total income exceeds £24,000, a reduction in the PA and MCA must be made for the excess income.

To calculate the PA and MCA available to Henry we first calculate the reduction for the excess income. The excess income is calculated by deducting from his total income the limit of £24,000, giving a figure of £8,000. This is then halved as the reduction is £1 for every £2 of excess income, giving a reduction of £4,000.

We then look at the amount of PA available:

Personal allowance

	£
Age allowance	10,090
Less	
reduction for excess	(4,000)
	6,090

As this is below the normal PA of £7,475 the reduction is limited to £2,615, the difference between the age allowance and the normal PA. Henry gets relief equal to the normal PA of £7,475.

The amount of MCA available to him is then calculated:

	£
Married couple's allowance	
Age allowance	7,295
Less	
reduction for excess (the unused reduction £4,000 – £2,615)	(1,385)
	5,910

MCA age allowance available: £5,910.

As this is higher than the minimum MCA of £2,800 the higher figure of £5,910 is taken. Relief is limited to 10 per cent of this figure ie £591.00.

5.9.2 Maintenance payments

Tax relief for maintenance payments was withdrawn from the tax year 2000/1 unless one or both of the parties was born before 6 April 1935. Further consideration of maintenance payments is outside the scope of this book.

5.10 Deduction of tax deducted at source

The last step is to deduct any tax deducted at source (see **5.1.5.1** and **5.5**). This is to ensure that the taxpayer does not account again for the tax already deducted by, for example, the bank or building society. It is also important to remember that most employees will have had tax deducted under the PAYE system.

EXAMPLE 11

Using our earlier example of Anna our last step is to deduct any tax deducted at source. Anna has two sources of income on which tax will have been deducted at source. These are the building society interest and the dividend.

Total income

	Net £	Gross £
Partnership profits		29,000.00
Building Society interest		
$400 \times \frac{100}{(100-20)}$	400.00	500.00
Dividends	600.00	666.67

$600 \times \frac{100}{(100-10)}$		
Statutory income		30,166.67
Deduct reliefs		
Interest on loan from White Rose Bank		(1,000.00)
Net Income		29,166.67
Deduct personal allowance		
Personal allowance		(7,475.00)
Taxable income		21,691.67
Apply the rates of tax		
Non-savings income		
£20,525 @ 20%		4,105.00
Savings income		
£500 @ 20%		100
Dividend income		
£666.67 @ 10%		66.67
Total tax		4,271.67
Deduct tax deducted at source		
Building society interest	100.00	
Dividend	66.67	
	166.67	166.67
Tax payable		4,105.00

5.11 Date for payment

5.11.1 Taxpayers not subject to deduction of tax at source

For anyone not subject to deduction of tax at source, eg sole traders or partners, tax is payable in three tranches:

(a) an interim payment on 31 January during the relevant tax year;

(b) a further interim payment on 31 July following the end of the relevant tax year; and

(c) a balancing payment/repayment on 31 January following the end of the relevant tax year.

For the tax year 2011/12 tax will be payable as follows:

(a) first interim payment 31 January 2012;

(b) second interim payment 31 July 2012; and

(c) a balancing payment/repayment on 31 January 2013.

The amounts of each of the 'interim payments' will normally be based on half of the income tax liability (less any tax deducted at source) for the preceding tax year. However, the taxpayer will have the right to reduce payments on account where he believes that the amounts due for the current year will be less. Payments on account will not be required when substantially all of a taxpayer's income is subject to deduction of tax at source, for example PAYE, or where the amount is below a threshold to be determined by the Treasury from time to time.

Interest will run on tax from the date it is due to the date it is paid. HMRC will pay interest on amounts overpaid from the date of payment (or the due date, if later), to the date of repayment.

In addition, if a tax liability for a tax year is not paid by 28 February following the tax year, a surcharge of 5 per cent of the outstanding tax will be charged. There is a right of appeal against the surcharge on the grounds of reasonable excuse.

The taxpayer has a choice of when the tax return is submitted. If the taxpayer includes all information on the tax return and forwards this to HMRC no later than 31 October in the following tax year HMRC will calculate the assessment on his behalf (this deadline is extended if submitted electronically). Otherwise the filing deadline is 31 January following the tax year (or two months after HMRC have required him to make a return, if later) and the taxpayer must calculate the amount of the assessment. In either case the Inland Revenue may later amend the assessment if it was incorrect.

5.11.2 Deduction at source

Where income is received after deduction of income tax at source (eg dividends, interest) and the taxpayer is a higher rate taxpayer, the extra tax is due on 31 January following the tax year.

So far as earned income taxed under ITEPA is concerned (ie salary), tax is deducted and paid to the Inland Revenue under the PAYE system at lower, basic, and higher rates at the time the salary is paid. It is computed by use of personal tax codes, issued by the Inland Revenue to employers and employees, and deduction tables supplied to employers. If the taxpayer has no other sources of income, then the correct amount of tax should have been paid. However, if the taxpayer has other sources of income, then the taxpayer will need to complete a tax return.

Overdue tax will attract interest.

5.12 Appeals

If a taxpayer disagrees with an assessment an appeal may be possible: application should be made in writing, normally within 30 days of the issue of the notice of assessment.

The taxpayer can apply to postpone payment of the amount of tax considered to be excessive: if this is agreed by the Inspector, the tax not disputed becomes payable within 30 days after the Inspector's agreement to the postponement (unless this is before the normal due date for payment of the tax).

In practice, many appeals will be settled by reaching agreement with HMRC. If agreement is not possible, HMRC will normally then offer a review (by an officer not involved in the orginal decision). The taxpayer can reject this offer within 30 days.

However, it is open to a taxpayer who has appealed to ask for either of the following:

- a review by HMRC; or
- the appeal to be heard by an independent tribunal—the First-tier Tribunal (Tax)

These are alternative, not successive, steps. However, if the taxpayer initally opts for a review it is still possible to ask the tribunal to consider the matter once the review is finished.

Appeals from the decision of the First-tier Tribunal (Tax) lies to the Upper Tribunal (Tax and chancery) provided permission is First obtained from the First-tier Tribunal.

5.13 Back-duty cases

A back-duty case arises when HMRC discovers that a taxpayer has evaded tax, usually by not disclosing his true income, by supplying inaccurate information or by claiming reliefs and allowances to which he is not entitled.

On discovery of a back-duty case, HMRC can commence criminal proceedings and/or make assessments for the lost tax plus interest and/or claim penalties. However, criminal proceedings are rarely taken and HMRC prefer to reach some settlement with the taxpayer.

5.14 Conclusion: checkpoints

You should now be able to:

- calculate an individual's liability to income tax (**5.2** to **5.10** and **5.15**); and
- identify different types of income (**4.4**, **5.5** and **5.8**).

5.15 Income tax calculations

To test your understanding of Income Tax you should now complete the following exercise.

Thomas, aged 42, is a partner in a firm of architects. He borrowed £15,000 to invest in the partnership on which he pays annual interest of 9 per cent.

His partnership income for the tax year 2011/12 is £40,000. He also receives during the tax year 2011/12 dividend income of £3,250, net interest from the Rutland Building Society of £1,200 and net interest of £300 from Hallam Bank plc.

Thomas's wife, Elizabeth, aged 40, is employed as a solicitor. She receives a salary of £37,500. During the tax year 2011/12 she receives net interest of £5,000 from White Rose Bank plc; she also receives dividend income of £400 and net interest from the Rivelin Building Society of £350.

Calculate Thomas's and Elizabeth's respective tax bills for 2011/12.

Answer overleaf.

Thomas

Calculate total income.

Take in 'Thomas calculate total income' from previous page.

		£ Net	£	£ Gross
Salary				40,000.00
Building society interest (gross)	$(1200 \times \frac{100}{80})$	1,200.00		1,500.00
Bank interest (gross)	$(300 \times \frac{100}{80})$	300.00		375.00
Dividend (gross)	$(3,250 \times \frac{100}{90})$	3,250.00		3,611.11
Total income				**45,486.11**
Deduct reliefs				
Interest on loan from				
Hallam Bank plc £15,000 × 9%				(1,350.00)
Net income				**44,136.11**
less personal reliefs:				
personal allowance				(7,475.00)
Taxable income				**36,661.11**

Before the rates of tax can be applied Thomas's income must be divided into non-savings income, savings income and dividend income. This is because savings income and dividend income are treated as the top slice of income with dividend income being taxed last.

His savings income is £1,875, ie gross bank interest of £375 and gross building society interest of £1,500. His gross dividend income is £3,611.11. Therefore his taxable non-savings income is ascertained by deducting from his taxable income his aggregated gross savings income and gross dividend income, ie £31,175 (£36,661.11 – £5,486.11).

Taxable non-savings income £31,175 (£36,661.11 – £5,486.11).

			Income		Tax
Apply the rates of tax					
Tax liability					
Non-savings income					
Basic rate			31,175.00	@ 20%	6,235.00
Savings income*	Basic rate		1,875.00	@ 20%	375.00
Dividend income**	Basic rate		1,950.00	@ 10%	195.00
	Higher rate		1,661.11	@ 32.5%	539.86
			36,661.11		
Tax liability					**7,344.86**
Less:					
Tax deducted at source:					
Building society	(1,500 × 20%)			300.00	
Bank	(375 × 20%)			75.00	
Dividend	(3,611.11 × 10%)			361.11	
				736.11	(736.11)
Tax payable					**6,608.75**

*All of his savings income will be taxed at 20% because he has not exhausted his basic rate tax band.

**The first £1,950 of his dividend income will be taxed at 10 per cent because he has not exhausted his basic rate tax band. The remaining £1,166.11 will be taxed at the higher rate, which for the purposes of dividend income is 32.5 per cent as opposed to the higher rate of 40 per cent for all other types of income.

Elizabeth

Calculate total income.

		£ Net	£	£ Gross
Salary				37,500.00
Building society interest (gross)	$\frac{(350 \times 100)}{80}$	350.00		437.50
Bank interest (gross)	$\frac{(5000 \times 100)}{80}$	5,000.00		6,250.00
Dividend (gross)	$\frac{(400 \times 100)}{80}$	400.00		444.44
Total income				44,631.94
Deduct reliefs				
Net income				44,631.94
less personal reliefs:				
personal allowance				(7,475.00)
Taxable income				37,156.94

Taxable non-savings income £30,025 (£37,156.94 – £7,131.94)

			Income		Tax
Apply the rates of tax					
Tax liability					
	Basic rate		30,025.00	@ 20%	6,005.00
Savings income	Basic rate		4,975.00	@ 20%	995.00
	Higher rate		1,712.50	@ 40%	685.00
Dividend income	Higher rate		444.44	@ 32.5%	144.44
Tax liability			37,156.94		**7,829.44**
Less:					
Tax deducted at source:					
Building society	(437.50 × 20%)			87.50	
Bank	(6,250.00 × 20%)			1,250.00	
Dividend	(444.44 × 10%)			44.44	
				1,381.94	(1,381.94)
Tax payable					**6,447.50**

Visit the Online Resource Centre for more information and useful weblinks.
www.oxfordtextbooks.co.uk/orc/foundations11_12/

Capital gains tax

6.1 Introduction: basic structure of capital gains tax (CGT)

This chapter deals with the charge to CGT. In the chapter we explain in particular:

- who pays CGT (**6.2**);
- which assets are chargeable to CGT (**6.4**);
- when a disposal occurs for the purpose of CGT (**6.5**);
- how to calculate the gain (**6.6**);
- exemptions and reliefs from the charge to CGT (**6.8**);
- the treatment of assets held at 5 April 1998 (**6.11**); and
- disposals of part (**6.13**).

6.1.1 Sources of capital gains tax law

The sources of capital gains tax law are:

(a) Statute: the principal charging Act is the Taxation of Chargeable Gains Act 1992 (TCGA).
(b) Case law and HM Revenue & Customs statements of practice and extra-statutory concessions.

6.1.2 Capital profits

There is no statutory definition of capital profits. Capital profits need to be distinguished from income profits because capital profits may give rise to a charge to capital gains tax (CGT) as opposed to a charge to income tax. Generally, capital profits are of a non-recurring nature. The consequence of this is, usually, there will be no charge to CGT where there has been a charge to income tax.

6.1.3 Collection of taxes

CGT is subject to self-assessment in the same manner as income tax. This system has been discussed in more detail at **5.1.5.2**.

6.1.4 Payment of CGT

The normal due date for payment of CGT is 31 January following the end of the year of assessment in which the gain arose. Therefore, if a capital asset is disposed of in the tax year ending 5 April 2012, ie 2011/12, the tax falls due to be paid by 31 January 2013. Overdue tax attracts interest.

6.1.5 Appeals and back-duty cases

See 5.12 and 5.13.

6.2 Who pays CGT?

6.2.1 Chargeable persons

The following are liable to CGT:

(a) individuals;

(b) partners;

(c) personal representatives; and

(d) trustees.

6.2.1.1 Individuals

Individuals are liable to CGT.

6.2.1.2 Partners

Where there is a disposal of a partnership asset which results in a CGT liability, each partner is separately assessed for CGT upon his share of the partnership gains, ie a partner is liable for his share of the tax only—there is no joint and several liability.

For the tax year 2011/12 individuals and partners pay CGT at a rate of 18 per cent in the case of basic rate tax payers and 28 per cent in the case of higher rate and additional rate tax payers.

6.2.1.3 Personal representatives and trustees

Personal representatives may incur a liability to CGT during the administration period when they dispose of chargeable assets. Trustees may also incur a CGT liability if they dispose of chargeable assets from the trust fund. However, unlike individuals and partners, personal representatives and trustees pay tax on any chargeable gains arising at the trust rate. The trust rate for the tax year 2011/12 is 28 per cent.

6.2.2 Non-chargeable persons

The following are not liable to CGT:

(a) companies; and

(b) charities.

6.2.2.1 Companies

Companies do not pay CGT. They pay corporation tax on both their income and capital profits. The principles for calculating the company's capital profits which are liable to corporation tax are virtually the same as for calculating what gains are liable to CGT in the case of an individual.

Note that shareholders who are not companies are liable to CGT when they dispose of their shares in a company.

6.2.2.2 Charities

Charities are exempt from paying CGT.

6.3 The charge to CGT

CGT is charged on the amount of chargeable gains accruing to the taxpayer on the disposal of chargeable assets in a year of assessment. The year of assessment equates to the income tax year, ie 6 April to the following 5 April (see **5.1.4**). Where a taxpayer disposes of an asset a number of steps need to be followed to determine a taxpayer's liability to CGT. These steps are:

Step 1 You need to identify whether the relevant asset is a chargeable asset. If the asset does not come within the definition of chargeable asset, there is no liability to CGT and the subsequent steps may be ignored.

Step 2 Next you should identify whether there has been a disposal for CGT purposes of the relevant asset. If there has been no disposal for CGT purposes, there is no liability to CGT, and the subsequent steps may be ignored.

Step 3 Once you have identified that there has been a disposal of a chargeable asset, the gain realised by the taxpayer on that disposal needs to be calculated.

Step 4 Consider what, if any, exemptions or reliefs are available, other than the annual exempt amount.

Step 5 When calculating the gain, on some occasions it may transpire that the taxpayer has not made a gain but has suffered a capital loss. You should remember that there are rules as to how these losses are taken into account.

Step 6 Having taken into account any capital losses, if the taxpayer has made an overall gain you should utilise the annual exempt amount.

Step 7 Having followed these steps you will have determined the taxpayer's net chargeable gain for the relevant year of assessment. The liability to CGT on this net chargeable gain is calculated by applying the appropriate rates of tax.

To summarise, the steps are:

Step 1 Is the asset a chargeable asset?
Step 2 Has there been a disposal?
Step 3 Calculate the gain.
Step 4 Utilise any exemptions and reliefs other than that mentioned at Step 6.
Step 5 Utilise any losses.
Step 6 Utilise the annual exempt amount.
Step 7 Apply the appropriate rates of tax.

The remainder of this part of the book looks at these steps in more detail.

6.4 Chargeable assets

The basic rule is that all assets are chargeable assets unless they fall within an exemption. Exempt assets include:

(a) private motor cars (including certain vintage and veteran cars);

(b) UK sterling (ie cash);

(c) wasting assets (ie assets with a predictable life of less than 50 years). Examples are TVs, washing machines, and other consumer goods; and

(d) tangible moveable property (eg antiques) if the disposal consideration is £6,000 or less.

Chargeable assets are divided into two categories: business assets and non-business assets. It is important to determine into which category an asset falls as different levels of taper relief will apply (see **6.8.4.1** and **6.8.4.2**).

6.5 Disposal

A disposal occurs:

(a) on the sale of the whole or part of an asset which is not an exempt asset;

(b) on the gift of the whole or part of an asset which is not an exempt asset; and

(c) on the receipt of a capital sum resulting from the ownership of an asset which is not an exempt asset (even if the person paying the capital sum does not acquire the asset). An example of this would be if a valuable painting (ie worth more than £6,000) was destroyed by fire and the owner received a payment of its value under an insurance policy.

6.5.1 Death

On death, there is no disposal by the deceased and therefore no CGT liability. However, there is a deemed acquisition by the personal representatives for CGT purposes. They are deemed to acquire the deceased's assets at their market value at the date of death. A future disposal by the personal representatives may give rise to a CGT liability on any gains arising between the date of death and the date of the disposal. The effect of this rule is to wipe out any gains which accrued during the deceased's lifetime.

6.5.2 Spouses and civil partners

Where spouses and civil partners are living together, a disposal between them is treated as producing neither a gain nor a loss. There will therefore be no CGT payable on the transfer. However, the gains arising before the date of transfer are not wiped out. The payment of CGT on those gains is merely deferred. When the donee spouse or civil partner later disposes of the asset, then he will be charged to tax not only on his gain, but on the gains accrued during the period of ownership by the other spouse or civil partner as well (see **6.9.2**).

6.5.3 Relevant date of disposal

Where the disposal is by way of sale, the disposal occurs on exchange of contracts and not on completion of the contract. This is important for determining into which year of assessment the disposal falls.

For example, where Colin is selling a building plot and exchanges contracts on 30 March 2012 with completion on 21 April 2012, any gain made would fall to be taxed within the tax year 6 April 2011 to 5 April 2012.

6.6 Calculation of the gain

Once you have identified that there has been a disposal of a chargeable asset during the year of assessment, the next step is to calculate the gain arising from the disposal.

6.6.1 The gain

The gain arising on the disposal is the consideration for the disposal less allowable expenditure.

6.6.2 Consideration for the disposal

6.6.2.1 Sales at arm's length

Normally, where there is a sale and the sale is at arm's length (ie not between connected persons), then the sale price is taken to be the consideration for CGT purposes. If an asset is sold for payments by way of instalments, then the consideration is the aggregate of the payments.

6.6.2.2 Sales at an undervalue

If the sale is at an undervalue, then the sale for CGT purposes is deemed to be at the market value of the asset on the date of disposal (see **6.5.3**). The actual consideration paid is ignored. However, if it can be shown that the low sale price was only as a result of a bad bargain, then the actual sale price will be taken.

As will be seen when dealing with inheritance tax, a gift or sale at an undervalue may also lead to a charge to inheritance tax if the donor dies within seven years of the disposal. If the charge to inheritance tax does occur, then the inheritance tax attributable to the value of the asset can be treated as an expense which is deductible in calculating the gain on the donee's disposal.

However, the deduction of the inheritance tax can only reduce the donee's gain to nil; it cannot create a loss which the donee is then able to use to reduce other gains in the same tax year or carry forward to future tax years.

6.6.2.3 Sales between connected persons

If the sale is not at arm's length (ie it is between connected persons), then the gain, if any, will be calculated by reference to the market value of the asset on the date of the disposal. The actual consideration agreed between the parties is ignored. The purpose of the rules is to prevent taxpayers avoiding CGT by fixing an artificially low sale price which will correspondingly produce an artificially low gain.

Connected persons include:

(a) spouse and civil partner (note that transfers between spouses and civil partners are a special category and the transfer is treated as being on a no gain/no loss basis—see **6.5.2** and **6.9.2**);

(b) relatives (brothers, sisters, parents, grandparents, children, grandchildren, ie lineal descendants);

(c) spouses of any connected person; and

(d) business partners (except where partnership assets are disposed of under a bona fide commercial arrangement).

6.6.2.4 Gifts

If there has been a gift, then for CGT purposes, the consideration is the market value of the asset on the date of disposal.

6.6.2.5 Market value

Market value is the price the asset might reasonably be expected to fetch on the open market.

6.6.3 Allowable expenditure

Allowable expenditure is the total of the:

(a) initial expenditure;

(b) subsequent expenditure; and

(c) incidental costs of disposal.

6.6.3.1 Initial expenditure

'Initial expenditure' is:

(a) the acquisition cost of the asset, or where there is a disposal between connected persons, the market value of the asset at the date of acquisition; and

(b) the incidental costs of acquisition (eg legal and valuation fees, stamp duty, etc.); or

(c) (if the asset was created rather than acquired) expenditure wholly and exclusively incurred in creating the asset (eg the cost of building a weekend cottage).

6.6.3.2 Subsequent expenditure

Subsequent expenditure is:

(a) expenditure wholly and exclusively incurred for the purposes of enhancing the value of the asset, otherwise known as enhancement expenditure, ie expenditure which is reflected in the state or nature of the asset at the date of disposal (eg the cost of building an extension but not the cost of routine maintenance or insurance); and

(b) expenditure wholly and exclusively incurred for the purposes of defending title to the asset (eg legal fees in resolving a boundary dispute).

6.6.3.3 Incidental cost of disposal

Incidental cost of disposal is the cost incurred in disposing of the asset (eg legal and estate agent's fees, advertising costs).

EXAMPLE 1

David bought his holiday cottage in 2000, from his father, for £50,000. The market value of the cottage as at that date was £70,000. During the purchase, David incurred legal fees of £800 and stamp duty of £500. Since he purchased the cottage, David has spent £1,500 having double glazing put in the cottage and £600** on decorative repairs.

David now sells the cottage for £100,000, incurring legal fees of £700 and estate agent's fees of £1,400.

What is David's gain on the sale of the cottage?

	£	£
Consideration		100,000
Less: Allowable expenditure:		
Initial expenditure:		
Acquisition cost (market value)*	70,000	
Incidental costs of acquisition:		
Legal fees	800	
Stamp duty	500	
Subsequent expenditure:		
Improvements	1,500	
Incidental costs of disposal:		
Legal fees	700	
Estate agent's fees	1,400	(74,900)
Gain		25,100

*The acquisition cost is deemed to be market value because David bought the cottage from a connected person, his father.

**The decorative repairs do not form part of the allowable expenditure because they are a cost of routine maintenance.

6.7 Capital losses

It may be that the consideration received on the disposal is less than the cost of the asset. If so, there will be a capital loss arising from the disposal.

A capital loss is created when the cost of the asset is greater than the consideration received.

6.7.1 Setting losses against gains

If a loss arises on a transaction chargeable to CGT, it is first offset against other chargeable gains arising in the same tax year ('carry across' relief). Therefore, it is necessary to calculate the gain or loss on each disposal made during the tax year, using the principles which have been covered above. Once this has been done, the gains are added together to calculate the total gains for the tax year. Similarly, the losses are added together to calculate the total losses for the tax year. The total losses are then deducted from the total gains to calculate the gains (losses) for the tax year.

Since 6 April 1998 losses are deducted before applying the annual exempt amount (but after deducting other reliefs) and are allocated in the manner most beneficial to the taxpayer.

6.7.2 Carry-forward of losses

If, having offset the losses against other gains in the same tax year, there is still an unrelieved balance of loss, this can be carried forward. The losses can be set off to reduce gains to the level of the annual exempt amount. The loss can be carried forward in this way indefinitely until all the loss has been relieved in subsequent tax years ('carry forward' relief).

6.8 Exemptions and reliefs

There are a number of exemptions and reliefs that should be considered before the amount to be taxed can be determined. The main exemptions and reliefs are contained in paragraphs **6.8.1** to **6.8.9**.

It is important to realise that the exemptions and reliefs can interact with each other in different ways. The various interactions are highlighted and explained in the paragraphs dealing with the exemptions and reliefs. It is advisable to identify all appropriate exemptions and reliefs for any given scenario. Once the appropriate exemptions and reliefs have been identified, and the interaction between them determined, the exemptions and reliefs can be properly applied.

6.8.1 Annual exempt amount

6.8.1.1 Individuals

There is an exempt band available for each tax year, ie gains up to that limit are not liable to CGT. For the tax year 2011/12, the annual exempt amount is £10,600. The exemption or any unused part of it cannot be carried forward.

6.8.1.2 Personal representatives and trustees

Personal representatives and trustees have an annual exempt amount. For personal representatives the annual exempt amount for gains accruing in the year of death and the two following years of assessment are the same as for an individual (ie for the tax year 2011/12, £10,600). Beyond the third year they have no annual exempt amount. All chargeable gains are chargeable to CGT. For trustees the annual exempt amount is an amount equal to one-half of the individual's annual exempt amount (ie for the tax year 2011/12, £5,300).

6.8.2 Tangible moveable property

It has already been stated (see **6.4(d)**) that tangible moveable property (eg antiques) is exempt from CGT where the consideration on the disposal is £6,000 or less.

Where the consideration on the disposal exceeds £6,000, the chargeable gain is either the actual gain after taper relief or five-thirds of the difference between £6,000 and the value of the consideration, whichever is the lesser amount (obviously, it would be unfair if a disposal were wholly liable to CGT whereas if the consideration had been slightly less, the disposal would have been completely exempt).

Where a loss is made on the disposal of a tangible asset sold for less than £6,000 the sale price is deemed to be £6,000 to ensure that no capital loss is created.

6.8.3 Private dwelling house

A gain on the disposal by an individual of a dwelling house, including grounds of up to half a hectare, will be completely exempt provided it has been occupied as the taxpayer's only or main residence throughout his period of ownership (TCGA, ss 222–6). For the purposes of calculating an individual's period of ownership, the following may be ignored:

(a) the first year of ownership;

(b) the last three years of ownership; and

(c) certain periods of absence for job-related activities.

A married couple may only have one main residence. If more than one residence is owned then an election must be made as to which is the main residence. The election may be backdated up to two years from the date of acquisition of the second residence. If no election is made HMRC will decide which is the main residence. Similar rules apply for any individual who owns more than two properties.

6.8.4 Entrepreneurs' relief

The effect of this relief is that the first £10,000,000 of lifetime gains will be taxed at 10 per cent. Any gains in excess of this limit will be taxed at 28 per cent. The following assets will qualify for relief:

(a) the disposal of the whole or part of a business;

(b) the disposal of any assets which were used for the purpose of a business that has ceased within the three years immediately before the disposal and which were used for business purposes at the time of cessation; and

(c) the disposal of shares in a trading company or the holding company of a trading group of companies in which the taxpayer owns at least 5 per cent of the ordinary share capital carrying at least 5 per cent of the voting rights and who is an officer or employee of the company.

To qualify for the relief these conditions must have been met for at least a year ending on the date of disposal.

The relief does not have to be taken all at once and, except in limited circumstances outside the scope of this book, no account is taken of disposals prior to 6 April 2008.

Example 2

Danielle is a sole trader. She sells her business in September 2011. When she sells her business she makes a gain of £360,000. She has not previously claimed entrepreneurs' relief.

		£
Gain		360,000
Less		
Less		
Annual Exempt Amount		(10,600)
Chargeable Gain		349,400
Tax payable	£349,400 @ 10%	34,940

6.8.5 Hold-over relief (gifts and sales at an undervalue)

Hold-over relief is available where there has been a gift or a sale at an undervalue (TCGA, s 165). Where the disposal is a sale at an undervalue, the relief is available but only in respect of that part of the gain which is attributable to the 'gift' element. It is available in respect of business assets only.

Business assets include:

(a) goodwill;

(b) assets used in the business (including assets owned personally but used in the business);

(c) shares of a trading company not quoted on the Stock Exchange or the Alternative Investment Market; and

(d) shares in a trading company which is a personal company. A personal company is one where the taxpayer owns at least 5 per cent of the voting shares in that company.

Both donor and donee must elect for the relief as the effect is to postpone payment of tax and shift liability to the donee. The donor's gain arising from the disposal will not be charged to CGT but will be 'held over' until the donee's eventual disposal of the asset. The gains are not wiped out. Liability for the donor's gains during his period of ownership of the asset shifts to the donee in that when the donee eventually disposes of the asset, he will be charged to CGT on both gains, subject to any exemptions or reliefs available to the donee at that time.

If the donee does not dispose of the asset until his death, then the donor's gain will escape CGT altogether (as will the donee's gain). This is because there is no disposal (and therefore no charge to CGT) on death (see **6.5.1**). The donor's chargeable gain which is to be held over is calculated in the usual way.

The donee is deemed to acquire the asset at market value less the donor's chargeable gain. The effect of this is that when the donee eventually disposes of the asset, his gain will include the donor's gain.

The donor is not able to reduce the gain to be held over by applying his annual exempt amount. The effect of this rule is that unless the donor has other gains in the tax year against which he can use his annual exempt amount, that amount will be unused. Therefore, if the donor is not expected to make any other disposals in the tax year and the gain arising from the disposal is the same as or only marginally exceeds his annual exempt amount, then the donor and donee may decide not to elect for this relief so as to obtain a greater tax saving.

EXAMPLE 3 (hold-over relief)

Martin transfers his business to his son when the market value of the business is £50,000. Martin purchased the business on 1 April 1982 for £10,000. Ignoring indexation and any other exemptions and reliefs:

The net gain to be held over will be calculated as follows:

	£
Market value	50,000
Less: Acquisition cost	(10,000)
Net gain held over	40,000

If Martin's son later sells the business for £60,000 net of expenses of the sale, the net gain on disposal will be calculated as follows:

	£
Sale price (net)	60,000
Less: Acquisition cost*	(10,000)
Chargeable gain	50,000

* Acquisition cost is the market value at date of his acquisition less the held-over gain:
£50,000–£40,000 = £10,000

6.8.6 Roll-over relief on replacement of qualifying business assets

This relief encourages expansion and investment in business assets by enabling the sale of those assets to take place without an immediate charge to CGT provided the sale proceeds are invested in other business assets within a certain period (TCGA, s 152). The charge to CGT is postponed until the disposal of the new asset. There is a similar relief for companies (see **8.6.1.2**).

The relief is available to an individual who disposes of a qualifying asset used in or by a trade, profession, or vocation. For these purposes the definition of 'trade' includes a trade carried on by a personal company (ie a company in which the individual has not less than 5 per cent of the voting rights).

There are other circumstances which may qualify for relief but these are beyond the scope of this book.

Qualifying assets include:

(a) fixed plant and machinery not forming part of a building;
(b) land and buildings occupied for the purposes of a trade (NB the trade must not be the development of land);
(c) goodwill;
(d) milk quotas and potato quotas;
(e) ewe and suckler cow quotas; and
(f) ships, aircraft and hovercraft.

There are other qualifying assets for the purpose of roll-over relief (TCGA, s 155).

It is important to remember that both the 'old' and 'new' asset must be qualifying assets although not necessarily of the same kind. For example, a farmer could sell land occupied for the purpose of his business and roll over his gain into milk quota.

The replacement asset must be acquired within a period commencing one year before and ending three years after the disposal of the 'old' asset.

The 'old' asset must also have been used in the taxpayer's business throughout its ownership otherwise the roll-over relief will be apportioned pro rata to the period of such use.

The effect of roll-over relief is that the gain will be effectively postponed until either the disposal of the 'new' asset or any gain is no longer rolled over into the purchase of a further qualifying asset.

As with hold-over relief, the whole of the gain arising on the disposal of the business asset must be rolled over. Again, this means that unless the taxpayer has other disposals in the same tax year, his annual exempt amount will be wasted if he elects for the relief. This relief may be used in conjunction with taper relief. However, there are special rules as to the application of taper relief in these circumstances which are beyond the scope of this book.

6.8.7 Roll-over relief on incorporation of a business

The relief is available when an individual transfers an unincorporated business as a going concern to a limited company either wholly or partly in consideration for the issue of shares in that company (TCGA, s 162). The relief will be restricted if the consideration is only partly provided by the issue of shares. This relief may be used in conjunction with taper relief. However, there are special rules as to the application of taper relief in these circumstances which are beyond the scope of this book.

6.8.8 Life policies

Gains accruing on disposal of a life policy (which occurs on assignment, surrender or maturity) are exempt unless the disponor is not the original beneficial owner and acquired their rights or interest for consideration in money or money's worth.

6.9 Taxation of the chargeable gain (the applicable rates of tax)

6.9.1 Individuals

As has been stated previously, individuals are charged to CGT on their chargeable gains at rates the rate of 18 per cent or 28 per cent depending on their income tax status. For this reason it is necessary to consider the taxpayer's income tax position when deciding what rate of CGT to apply.

EXAMPLE 4

Laura has a taxable income of £34,000. After taking into account her annual exempt amount, she has chargeable gains of £10,000. Applying the rates of tax to calculate the CGT payable:

£	£
1,000 @ 18%	180.00
9,000 @ 28%	2,520.00
CGT payable	2,700.00

NB. The first £30,400 of the basic rate tax band has already been absorbed by Laura's taxable income for income tax purposes. Therefore the first £1,000 of her chargeable gain is taxed at 18 per cent and the remainder at 28 per cent.

6.9.2 Husband and wife and civil partners

A husband and wife and civil partners are taxed separately for CGT purposes. They each have an annual exempt amount of £10,600. A disposal between spouses or civil partners does not give rise to CGT.

The disposal is treated as neither producing a gain nor a loss. However, the gain is not wiped out altogether. When the donee spouse/civil partner disposes of the asset, then that spouse/civil partner will be charged to CGT not only on the spouse's/civil partner's own gain but also on the donor spouse's/civil partner's gain. The donee spouse/civil partner is deemed to acquire the asset at donor spouse's/civil partner's acquisition cost.

EXAMPLE 5

Andrew acquires a plot of land in June 1993 for £6,000. On 25 December 1995 he transfers the plot to his wife Ellen. Ignoring any other exemptions or reliefs:

On 10 June 2011 Ellen sells the plot for £20,000.

On the transfer from Andrew there will be no CGT payable because of the spouse exemption.

When Ellen disposes of the property CGT will be calculated as follows:

Her cost of acquisition is the price at which Andrew bought the land, ie £6,000.

Ellen's net gain will be calculated as follows:

	£
Consideration	20,000
Less: Allowable expenditure:	
Acquisition cost	(6,000)
Net gain	14,000

6.9.3 Personal representatives and trustees

Personal representatives and trustees pay CGT at the trust rate. For the tax year 2011/12 this is 28 per cent (see **6.2.1.3**).

6.10 Instalment option

There is an option to pay CGT by instalments in two cases:

(a) undue hardship (6.10.1); and

(b) gifts of land and certain shareholdings (6.10.2).

6.10.1 Undue hardship

If the consideration is payable by instalments over a period exceeding 18 months from the date of disposal and the Revenue is satisfied that the taxpayer would otherwise suffer undue hardship, the CGT may also be paid by instalments.

The Inland Revenue directs the period (not exceeding eight years) over which the CGT can be paid and what constitutes undue hardship.

6.10.2 Land and certain shareholdings

Where the disposal is a gift of:

(a) land,

(b) a controlling shareholding in any company or

(c) a minority holding in an unquoted company,

then the CGT may be paid by ten equal annual instalments *but* the option is only available provided hold-over relief is not available on the disposal. This applies even if hold-over relief is available but not claimed.

Interest on these instalments runs from the normal date for payment unless the gift is of agricultural property.

6.11 Assets held at 31 March 1982

There are also special rules for assets owned on the 31 March 1982 and for certain assets which may still attract an indexation allowance. These rules are beyond the scope of this book.

6.12 Disposals of part

When the disposal is of only part of the asset, the initial and subsequent expenditure must be apportioned when calculating the gain on the disposal of part.

To find out what proportion of the initial and subsequent expenditure is deductible in calculating the gain on the disposal of part, the formula is as follows:

$$\frac{A}{A+B}$$

where A = consideration received for the part disposed of, and B = market value (at the date of disposal) of the part retained.

EXAMPLE 6

Jill bought a large plot of land in 1985 for £400,000 including her costs of acquisition. She now sells part of it for £100,000. The market value of the retained part is £400,000. Her costs of disposal are £2,000. What is her gain on the disposal, ignoring indexation and any other reliefs? Proportion of initial expenditure deductible (there is no subsequent expenditure):

$$\frac{£100,000}{£100,000 + £400,000} = 1/5$$

In calculating the gain on the disposal of part, Jill is able to deduct 1/5 of the total initial expenditure.

	£	£
Consideration		100,000
Less: Allowable expenditure:		
Add:		
Initial expenditure (1/5 ´ £400,000)	80,000	
Incidental costs of disposal	2,000	(82,000)
Gain		18,000

6.13 Tax planning

6.13.1 Using the annual exempt amounts of both spouses or civil partners

Remember that both spouses or civil partners will be entitled to an annual exempt amount. Therefore, it may be worthwhile transferring assets to the other spouse or into the joint names of both, so as to make use of both exemptions. There will be no charge to CGT on the transfer.

6.13.2 Using the annual exempt amount of both spouses or civil partners

If one spouse has utilised his or her annual exempt amount, then it may be beneficial to transfer assets into the name of the other spouse.

When you are considering whether to transfer assets, however, remember that the cost of legally transferring the asset to the spouse may be more than the potential tax saving. This must be taken into account. You must remember also that you cannot utilise any unused income tax allowances when calculating the CGT liability on the chargeable gain.

6.14 Example

Example 7

Bharti buys a holiday cottage in June 2008 for £200,000. She incurs legal fees of £2,400 when she buys the cottage and surveyor's fees of £600. In September 2008 she builds a conservatory onto that cottage. The cost of building the conservatory is £12,000. Bharti sells the cottage in March 2014 for £400,000. She incurs estate agent's fees of £4,000 and legal fees of £900. Bharti is a higher rate tax payer. Assuming 2011/12 rates and allowances apply, calculate the gain.

	£	£
Consideration		400,000.00
Less		
Allowable expenditure		
Acquisition cost	200,000.00	
Incidental costs of acquisition:		
Legal fees	2,400.00	
Surveyor's fees	600.00	
Subsequent expenditure	12,000.00	
Incidental costs of disposal:		
Legal fees	900.00	
Estate Agent's fees	4,000.00	
	219,900.00	(219,900.00)
Net Gain		180,100.00
Less annual exempt amount		(10,600.00)
Chargeable gain		169,500.00
CGT payable	169,500 @ 28%	47,460.00

6.15 Conclusion: checkpoints

You should now be able to:

- ascertain who pays CGT (**6.2**);
- identify which assets are chargeable to CGT (**6.4**);
- identify when a disposal occurs for the purposes of CGT (**6.5**);
- calculate the liability to CGT (**6.6**);
- identify and apply relevant exemptions and reliefs from the charge to CGT (**6.8**); and
- calculate the liability to CGT on the disposals of part (**6.13**).

Visit the Online Resource Centre for more information and useful weblinks.
www.oxfordtextbooks.co.uk/orc/foundations11_12/

7

Inheritance tax

7.1 Introduction: basic structure of inheritance tax (IHT)

This chapter deals with the charge to inheritance tax (IHT). In the chapter we explain in particular:

- the charge to inheritance tax (**7.2**);
- potentially exempt transfers (PETs) (**7.3**); and
- the occasions to tax (**7.5**) and the basic steps to follow to calculate the liability to inheritance tax (**7.5.1** to **7.5.4**).

As the charge to IHT depends on what happened in the preceding seven years there are examples to show how the inheritance tax is calculated in the following circumstances:

- the charge to tax and a lifetime chargeable transfer (LCT) (**7.6**);
- the charge to tax and an LCT where the transferor dies within seven years of the LCT (**7.7**);
- the charge to tax and a PET (**7.8**); and
- the charge to tax and death (**7.9**).

IHT is commonly thought of as a tax paid only on death. Certainly, liability to the tax is triggered by death, but it is also triggered when a person (the 'transferor') transfers money or property into certain types of trust during their lifetime. A lifetime transfer which triggers a liability to IHT is known as a lifetime chargeable transfer (LCT).

There are currently (tax year 2011/12) two rates and bands of tax; £1–£325,000, where IHT is payable at 0 per cent—this is referred to as the nil-rate band (NRB)—and £325,001 and over, where IHT is payable at 40 per cent. Any liability to IHT on an LCT at the time of making the transfer (ie during the lifetime of the transferor) is charged at one-half of the rates applicable on death, so 0 per cent and 20 per cent.

Where there is a liability to IHT, the amount of IHT payable is linked to the value of any gifts of money or property ('transfers of value') made by the transferor in the seven years preceding the transferor's death or the date of the LCT. This seven-year period is known as the cumulation period and is an important consideration in calculating the charge to IHT. The fact that the amount of tax is calculated by reference to the cumulative total of the person dying or making the LCT, as opposed to the person inheriting the estate or gift, means that, to an extent, the name 'inheritance tax' could be considered to be a misnomer.

After reading this chapter you should be able to identify the occasions on which IHT is charged, and also calculate the liability to tax. There are five basic steps to follow to calculate the liability and at **7.5** the points common to all occasions are set out. The charge to IHT on each of the specific occasions identified at **7.5** are dealt with at **7.6** to **7.9**, and any additional points that need to be taken into consideration are identified. The worked examples illustrate the calculation on each of the occasions. If you use the examples to help you to calculate an IHT liability on a different scenario, you should ensure that you are using the relevant worked example to fit the circumstances of your scenario.

7.1.1 Sources of inheritance tax law

Sources of inheritance tax (IHT) law are:

(a) Statute: the principal charging Act is the Inheritance Tax Act 1984 (IHTA 1984). The true name of the statute is the Capital Transfer Tax Act 1984 but s 100, Finance Act 1986 provides that it may be known as the Inheritance Tax Act 1984 and it is by this title that it is generally referred to. However, as for income and capital gains tax, annual Finance Acts have made changes to the Act.

(b) Case law and HMRC statements. Again, as for income and capital gains tax, these may be relevant as sources of IHT law.

7.1.2 Administration

IHT is a direct tax and is administered in the same way as income and capital gains tax.

7.1.3 Collection of tax

7.1.3.1 Lifetime transfers

Tax due in respect of lifetime transfers liable to IHT is collected by direct assessment.

7.1.3.2 Death

Tax due on the death of a person is also collected by direct assessment. A form of self assessment is used.

7.1.4 Appeals and back duty cases

The same regime applies as for income tax and you should refer to **5.12** and **5.13**.

7.2 The charge to inheritance tax

Section 1 of the Inheritance Tax Act 1984 (IHTA 1984) states that 'Inheritance tax shall be charged on the value transferred by a chargeable transfer.' This raises two questions: what is a *chargeable transfer* and how is the *value transferred* calculated?

7.2.1 Chargeable transfers

7.2.1.1 The legislation

Section 2 of IHTA 1984 expands on s 1 and explains that, 'A chargeable transfer is a *transfer of value* which is made by an individual but is not . . . an *exempt transfer*.' The Act then goes on to expand this further stating what is meant by a transfer of value (IHTA 1984, s 3) and what is meant by an exempt transfer (see **7.5.2** and **7.6.3**).

A transfer of value:

is a disposition made by a person (the transferor) as a result of which the value of the transferor's estate immediately after the disposition is less than it would be but for the disposition; and the amount by which it is less is the value transferred by the transfer. (IHTA 1984, s 1(3))

The Act excludes some assets from the charge to tax and also details dispositions which are not transfers of value.

7.2.1.2 Excluded assets

Categories of excluded property are set out in ss 6, 47, and 48 of IHTA 1984. Section 6 includes property situated outside the UK where the person beneficially entitled to it is domiciled outside the UK. Sections 47 and 48 deal with reversionary interests in settled property. The term reversionary interest is used to describe the situation where X leaves some property in a settlement so that Y enjoys the income from that settlement during his lifetime, but, on Y's death, the property goes to Z absolutely. Prior to Y's death, Z's interest in the settled fund is referred to as a 'reversionary interest'. This interest is excluded property so far as Z is concerned. In some cases the reversionary interest will not be excluded property. One example would be if it was purchased for money or money's worth.

7.2.1.3 Dispositions which are not transfers of value

7.2.1.3.1 *Gratuitous benefit*

A disposition is not a transfer of value if the transferor had no intention to confer a gratuitous benefit. This principle is relevant where there has been a sale at an undervalue. If the transferor can prove that he made a bad bargain (for example, through not recognising how much the asset was really worth) and had no intention of conferring a gratuitous benefit on the transferee, then the loss resulting to the transferor's estate arising from the bad bargain will not have any IHT implications.

7.2.1.3.2 *Dispositions for family maintenance (IHTA 1984, s 11)*

Payments by a transferor to spouses, civil partners, children, and dependent relations which result in a loss to the transferor's estate are not chargeable in the following circumstances:

(a) if the payment is by one spouse or civil partner for the maintenance of the other (this provision includes any disposition for maintenance made on the occasion of a divorce); or

(b) if the payment is for the maintenance, education or training of a child of the marriage or civil partnership (or of any other child not in the care of its parents); or

(c) if the payment represents reasonable provision for the care and maintenance of a dependent relative.

7.3 Potentially exempt transfers

In addition to excluded assets and dispositions which are not transfers of value, some transfers of value made during a person's lifetime are classified by the Act as 'Potentially Exempt Transfers' (PETs) (IHTA 1984, s 3A). If a transfer of value is a PET, then if it is made seven years or more before the transferor dies it is an exempt transfer, otherwise, ie if the transferor dies within seven years of making the transfer, it is a chargeable transfer. While the transferor is alive, it is thus potentially exempt.

Currently, a PET is a *lifetime* transfer of value made on or after 22 March 2006 to one of the following:

(a) another individual; or

(b) the trustees of a trust for the benefit of the disabled.

Whereas before the Finance Act 2006 the majority of lifetime transfers were PETs, this is no longer the case. An outright gift by an individual to another individual is the PET you are most likely to come across.

With the exception of a gift into a disabled trust, gifts made during a person's lifetime into trust will be lifetime chargeable transfers. Such examples of transfers are:

(a) a lifetime transfer to a discretionary trust; and

(b) a lifetime transfer giving a beneficiary an interest in possession.

Lifetime chargeable transfers are subject to a different charging regime during the lifetime of the trust. The regime comprises a periodic charge and an 'exit charge'. The regime is referred to in **Chapter 11**, but the detail of the regime is not needed for this part of the course.

7.4 The transfer of value on death

There is a deemed transfer of value on death. This means that when a person dies they are treated as if immediately before their death they made a transfer of value.

7.5 The occasions to tax

There are, then, three occasions on which IHT is charged:

(a) on a chargeable transfer made during a person's lifetime (a lifetime chargeable transfer, LCT);

(b) on a PET or LCT when the transferor does not survive seven years from the date of the transfer; and

(c) on death.

Having identified that there has been a chargeable transfer, to calculate the IHT payable on a chargeable transfer there are five basic steps to follow:

(1) Calculate the value transferred.

(2) Identify any available exemptions and deduct them from the value transferred.

(3) Identify any available reliefs and deduct them from the value transferred.

(4) Calculate the transferor's cumulative total as at the date of the transfer and the amount of the nil-rate band remaining.

(5) Calculate the IHT payable by applying the appropriate rate (or rates) of tax to the value of the transfer for IHT purposes. The rate (or rates) will depend on whether the tax is being paid on the date of the transfer or on the death of the transferor.

The five basic steps remain the same regardless of the occasion on which the tax is being charged. Depending on which occasion is the relevant one, there are additional steps to go through. These are set out later when examples of calculating the tax are worked through for each of the three occasions on which IHT is charged.

Points which are common to all three occasions are discussed at each step below.

7.5.1 Step 1: Calculate the value transferred

The value transferred is usually the market value of the asset at the date of the transfer. Two provisos to this are set out below. There are other provisos to this which are set out when each occasion is looked at individually.

7.5.1.1 Related property

Some assets are worth more when valued together, as a set for example, than they would be if they were owned by more than one person. Six dining chairs could be worth £3,600 as a set, giving an individual value of £600. However, if they are not kept as a set the value of each chair would be only £200, giving a total value of only £1,200. A transferor could use this to his advantage. For example, Mr Evans owns a pair of antique side tables. The market value of the pair is £50,000 but if they were separated they would each be worth only £15,000. Mr Evans wants to give the side tables to his daughter. If he made a gift to her of the pair then he would have made a PET of £50,000 (ignoring any exemptions or reliefs). However, if Mr Evans were to give away one of the side tables to his wife the loss to his estate would be £35,000 (£50,000 less £15,000 being the value of the side table he retained). As the gift was to his wife it would be exempt for IHT purposes (see **7.5.2.1**). Mr Evans could then gift the remaining side table to his daughter; this would be a PET of £15,000 as the side table is no longer one of a pair and so has a lower value. His wife could gift the side table she received to their daughter, also making a PET of £15,000. The potential liability to IHT is therefore smaller than it would have been had Mr Evans made the gift to his daughter of both of the side tables.

Section 161 of IHTA 1984 prevents transferors from avoiding IHT in this way. Property in one spouse's estate is related to property in the other spouse's estate. Where any property in one spouse's estate would be worth more if valued together with related property in the other spouse's estate, the property is valued as a proportion of the related property valued together.

This means that, on the facts of Mr Evans above, when he makes the gift of one side table to his daughter the side table is valued with the side table in his wife's estate, as the related property rules apply, and so the loss to his estate is $1/2 \times £50,000 = £25,000$, rather than £15,000.

Shareholdings are a good example of assets affected by the related property rules. The related property rules apply mainly to property in the estates of spouses but the rules do cover other situations where the transferor makes gifts to other exempt transferees, for example charities, and stands to benefit from a similar tax advantage.

7.5.1.2 Joint property

When an individual has only a share in an asset it is more difficult to sell the share than it would be to sell the whole. To take account of this difficulty the value of the individual's share in the asset is reduced by between 10 per cent and 15 per cent. For example, Joan and Ruth own a house as tenants in common, in equal shares. The house has a market value of £64,000. The value of Joan's share in the property for IHT purposes is in the region of £28,800 (one-half of the property is worth £32,000; 10 per cent of this is £3,200, and so the discount leaves a value of £28,800). This can be an advantage to the transferor if the transferor's share in a property is gifted to another, or the transferor dies; the loss to the transferor's estate is smaller because of the discount. However, if a transferor owns an asset outright and chooses to gift a share in the asset, the loss to the transferor's estate is higher as the value of the share of the asset retained must be discounted before ascertaining the loss to the estate. For example, if Joan owned the house outright and chose to gift a half share to Ruth the loss to Joan's estate would not be £32,000, one-half of the value of the house. It would be £35,200, as the value of the share she has retained is worth only £28,800, after taking into account the discount.

When the joint owner is the transferor's spouse or civil partner the related property rules apply and no discount is given.

7.5.2 Step 2: Identify any available exemptions and deduct them from the value transferred

A transfer of value made by an individual will not be a chargeable transfer if it is an exempt transfer. There are a number of exemptions available; some cause the whole transfer to be exempt, others cause part of the transfer to be exempt with the remainder of the transfer being a chargeable transfer or a PET.

The transfer of value may qualify for exemption by virtue of the fact that it is a disposition to an exempt transferee (these are applicable on lifetime dispositions *and* on death) or because it comes within one of a number of limited *lifetime* transfers which qualify for exemption.

7.5.2.1 Exemptions available on lifetime transfers and on death

Given below is a list of the main exemptions available both on lifetime dispositions and on death. The statutory reference is given for the exemptions and the relevant section should be consulted for the full conditions applicable.

Exemptions available on lifetime dispositions only are set out at **7.6.3**.

(a) *Transfers between spouses or civil partners* (IHTA 1984, s 18): transfers between spouses or civil partners are exempt provided that the gift is immediate, ie the gift takes effect immediately. However, it is common for a spouse or civil partner to state in his will that his estate will pass to the other spouse or civil partner only if the other spouse or civil partner survives for a specified period. As long as the specified period does not exceed 12 months the spouse or civil partner exemption will still apply.

Provided both the transferor and the spouse or civil partner are domiciled in the UK there is no limit on the amount of the exemption. However, the exemption is limited if the transferor was domiciled in the UK but the spouse or civil partner was not. The current limit to the exemption in these circumstances is £55,000.

(b) *Gifts to charities* (IHTA 1984, s 23).

(c) *Gifts to political parties* (IHTA 1984, s 24).

(d) *Gifts for national purposes* (eg to British Museum or National Trust) (IHTA 1984, s 25).

7.5.3 Step 3: Identify any available reliefs and deduct them from the value transferred

Applicable reliefs available both on lifetime transfers and deemed transfers of value on death are business property relief (BPR) and agricultural property relief (APR). Generally, any exemption is deducted before any available relief. However, if the disposition is a lifetime disposition and BPR or APR is available at 50 per cent, the relief is given before deducting the annual and other exemptions. This ensures that the exemptions are maximised.

7.5.3.1 Business property relief

BPR relief operates to reduce the value transferred by a transfer of relevant business property by either 100 per cent (ie no charge to IHT) or 50 per cent. To qualify for the relief the transferor must have owned the relevant business property for two years prior to the transfer. However, if the relevant business property is a replacement for other relevant business property, then the relief will be available if the combined period of ownership is two years or more.

7.5.3.2 Relevant business property

The following categories of property qualify for BPR:

(a) a business or interest in a business, eg the business of a sole proprietor or a partner's interest in a business;

(b) shares in an unquoted company;

(c) shares in a quoted company which give the transferor control of the company, or

(d) land or building, machinery, or plant used for the purposes of a business carried on either:

(i) by a company (unquoted or quoted) of which the transferor has control; or

(ii) by a partnership of which the transferor was a partner.

The reduction in the value transferred is 100 per cent for business property coming within categories (a) and (b) and 50 per cent for business property coming within categories (c) and (d).

7.5.3.3 Related property

Under the related property rules (see **7.5.1.1**), holdings of spouses or civil partners are treated as one holding and if their total holding gives control then either will have control for the purposes of the relief. See **Example 3** below.

7.5.3.4 Additional rule for lifetime transfers

Where a lifetime transfer is made (either a lifetime chargeable transfer or a PET where the transfer does not survive by seven years) and IHT (or additional IHT) becomes payable because the transferor dies within seven years, then the relief is not available unless the property originally transferred (or replacement property which qualifies as relevant business property) is still owned by the transferee at the date of the transferor's death (or transferee's death, if earlier).

EXAMPLE 1

William has shares in a quoted company giving him control of the voting. The other shares are held by unrelated parties. He gives his holding away. It is valued at £240,000. William dies one year after the gift.

The gift is a PET when it is made. As William dies within seven years of making the gift it becomes a chargeable transfer. Provided the share holding originally transferred (or replacement property which qualifies as relevant business property) is still owned by the transferee at the date of the transferor's death the shares are relevant property for the purposes of BPR (category (c) at **7.5.3.2)** and so BPR is available. The value transferred is reduced by 50 per cent. Ignoring other exemptions which may be available, the value transferred is 50 per cent of the value of the shares at the date of the transfer: 50% × £240,000 = £120,000.

> **EXAMPLE 2**
>
> At the time of his death Mr Slater was the owner of a building used by an unquoted company in which he had a controlling shareholding. The value of the land at the date of his death is £350,000. The shareholding in the company has a value of £450,000.
>
> On his death there is a deemed transfer of value. The shares are relevant property for the purposes of BPR (category (b) at **7.5.3.2**) and so BPR is available. Their value transferred is reduced by 100 per cent. The value transferred is nil.
>
> As Mr Slater has a controlling interest in the company, the building is also relevant property for the purposes of BPR (category (d) at **7.5.3.2**) and so BPR is available. The value transferred is reduced by 50 per cent. The value transferred is 50 per cent × the value of the buildings at the date of death: 50% × £350,000 = £175,000.

> **EXAMPLE 3**
>
> Mr Exton holds 40 per cent of the shares in a quoted trading company. His wife holds 20 per cent of the shares in the same company. Mr Exton gives his holding to his son.
>
> This gift is a PET. Should Mr Exton die within seven years of making the gift then the PET will become a chargeable transfer. Due to the related property rules Mr and Mrs Exton's shareholdings are treated as one. Mr Exton is deemed to have a holding of 60 per cent and so has control of the company. The shares are relevant property for the purposes of BPR (category (c) at **7.5.3.2**) and so BPR is available. Their value transferred is reduced by 50 per cent.

7.5.3.5 Agricultural property relief

This relief operates in a similar way to BPR. It reduces the value transferred by a transfer of agricultural property by either 100 per cent (ie no charge to IHT) or 50 per cent. Agricultural property is defined in the IHTA 1984 and, basically, is agricultural land or pasture and farm buildings situated in the UK, the Channel Islands, or the Isle of Man. The agricultural value of the property is taken as the value at which the property would be valued if it was subject to a perpetual covenant prohibiting its use otherwise than as agricultural property.

To qualify as agricultural property, the property must have been:

(a) occupied by the transferor for agriculture throughout the two years immediately before the transfer (there is no condition on the time of ownership: the transferor may have rented the property initially and only purchased the property shortly before selling it—the transferor will still qualify for APR provided the total period of occupation was at least two years); or

(b) owned by the transferor for seven years before the transfer and occupied by someone for agriculture throughout that seven-year period.

Relief at 100 per cent is available for transfers on or after 10 March 1992 if:

(i) the transferor was the owner or tenant in possession; or

(ii) the transferor had the right to obtain possession within 12 months (by concession, if the transferor has the right to obtain vacant possession within 24 months, relief at 100 per cent is also given); or

(iii) where the transfer is after 1 September 1995, the transferor's interest fails to come within either of classes (i) or (ii) because of a new tenancy granted on or after 1 September 1995.

There are also rules governing the position where a tenancy is inherited.

Relief at 50 per cent is available on any other qualifying agricultural property.

7.5.3.6 Additional rule for lifetime transfers

Where a lifetime transfer is made (either a lifetime chargeable transfer or a PET where the transfer does not survive by seven years) and IHT (or additional IHT) becomes payable because the transferor dies within seven years, then the relief is not available unless the property originally transferred (or replacement property which qualifies as relevant agricultural property) is still owned by the transferee at the date of the transferor's death (or transferee's death, if earlier) and the property qualifies for the relief at the date of the transferor's death.

EXAMPLE 4

Joe owns his farm, which he works, and has done so for many years. The agricultural value of his farm is £160,000. If Joe were to gift the farm, or on his death, agricultural property relief at 100 per cent is available. The agricultural value of the farm in Joe's estate is reduced to nil.

EXAMPLE 5

Alistair owns a farm which has been let to a tenant farmer for the past twelve years. The agricultural value of the farm subject to the tenancy is £200,000. If there were to be a disposal by Alistair, agricultural relief would be available at 50 per cent and the value of the property would be reduced to £100,000 for IHT purposes.

7.5.4 Steps 4 and 5

Step 4: Calculate the cumulative total of the transfers at the date of the transfer and the amount of the nil-rate band remaining.

Step 5: Calculate the IHT payable by applying the rate (or rates) of tax to the value of the transfer for IHT purposes.

These two steps require some further explanation.

7.5.4.1 The rates of IHT

IHT is currently charged at two rates. For the tax year 2011/12 the first £325,000 is taxed at 0 per cent, the nil-rate band (NRB); the amount above £325,000 is taxed at 40 per cent (see the example on a lifetime chargeable transfer for the rate which applies to LCTs at the time they are made).

All calculations shown here have assumed that the current rates have always applied. This is not the case. The rates usually alter with each tax year, following an announcement in the budget by the Chancellor. Tax tables should be consulted to determine the rates of tax which were applicable at any given date.

7.5.4.2 The principle of cumulation

IHT operates on a cumulative basis, the cumulation period being seven years. The rate (or rates) of tax applicable to a chargeable transfer depends on the cumulative total of all chargeable transfers made by the transferor in the seven years preceding the transfer currently being charged. As a consequence of the cumulation principle, the transfer is taxed as the top slice of the aggregate of the cumulative total and the transfer. The cumulative total eats into the NRB. To calculate the rate (or rates) of tax at which the chargeable transfer is to be taxed, the cumulative total is deducted from the NRB. If, after deducting the cumulative total from the NRB, there is some NRB remaining then the amount of the transfer equal to the NRB remaining is taxed at 0 per cent and the remainder of the transfer is taxed at the rate applicable to the occasion of the charge.

It is important to emphasise that the cumulative total is relevant only in determining the rate (or rates) of tax. Once this has been determined, the rate(s) is then applied only to the value transferred by the current chargeable transfer. It is not applied to the cumulative total.

To calculate the transferor's cumulative total at the date of the current transfer it is necessary to look back over the seven years preceding the date of the transfer and identify the chargeable transfers, if any, which the transferor made during that period. Having identified the chargeable transfers the next step is to calculate the net value of those transfers for IHT purposes. This is achieved by following Steps 1 to 3 inclusive.

Both examples below assume that current rates apply.

EXAMPLE 6 (Calculating IHT on estate where the deceased made a transfer within seven years of death)

Isabelle dies; her estate is valued at £360,000 for IHT purposes. Three to four years before she died she gifted cash of £120,000 to her daughter, Jasmine. She made no other gifts.

When made, the gift to Jasmine was a PET. As Isabelle has died within seven years of making the gift it is a chargeable transfer. There are no other chargeable transfers within the seven years preceding Isabelle's death.

Ignoring any exemptions and reliefs which may be available on the gift to Jasmine the value transferred was £120,000. Isabelle's cumulative total at the date of her death is £120,000.

Deducting the cumulative total from the NRB, ie subtracting £120,000 from £325,000, leaves an amount of £205,000 of the NRB remaining. When the rate(s) of tax are applied to the value of the estate on Isabelle's death, there is £205,000 of the NRB available.

The rates of tax applied to the estate will be £205,000 taxed at 0% and the remaining £155,000 of the estate (total £360,000) taxed at 40 per cent giving a total of £62,000 of IHT to pay.

EXAMPLE 7 (Calculating IHT on an LCT where: (a) the transfer had made no other lifetime gifts; and (b) the transferor made an LCT within seven years of the later LCT)

Ignoring exemptions and reliefs:

(a) Philip makes a gift to a discretionary trust of £375,000. This is a lifetime chargeable transfer and is chargeable to IHT.

If this is the only gift Philip has made in the last seven years, Philip's cumulative total at the time of making the gift is nil, meaning that all of the NRB is available. The rates of tax applied will be £325,000 taxed at 0 per cent and the remaining £50,000 taxed at 20 per cent, giving a total of £10,000 of IHT to pay when the gift is made (see **7.6.1**).

(b) However, if, in the previous seven years, Philip has made chargeable transfers of £160,000, then the IHT payable is different. Philip's cumulative total is £160,000. Deducting this from the NRB leaves an amount of £165,000 of the NRB remaining. The rates of tax applied to the £375,000 will be £165,000 taxed at 0% and the remaining £210,000 taxed at 20 per cent, giving a total of £42,000 IHT to pay.

7.5.4.3 Summary

Steps 4 and 5 can be summarised as the following sub-steps:

(a) Identify any chargeable transfers in the seven years preceding the current transfer.

(b) Calculate the value of each of those chargeable transfers for IHT purposes, ie find their net value for IHT. This is done by following Steps 1, 2, and 3 for each chargeable transfer.

(c) Calculate the transferor's cumulative total at the date of the current transfer, by adding together the net value of all chargeable transfers made in the preceding seven years.

(d) Calculate the balance of the NRB remaining, if any, by deducting the cumulative total from the NRB.

(e) Apply the rates of tax to the current transfer.

7.6 The charge to tax and a lifetime chargeable transfer

In addition to the points mentioned above, when following the five steps to calculate the IHT payable on a chargeable transfer, some additional points should also be taken into account when the occasion is a lifetime chargeable transfer. These are identified as each step is considered.

7.6.1 The rates of tax

One matter which is best dealt with at this point is a mention of the rates of IHT charged on an LCT. Provided the transferor survives seven years from the date of the transfer then the rates of tax applicable to the transfer are one-half of the usual rates, that is 0 per cent on the NRB and 20 per cent on values exceeding the NRB. However, should the transferor fail to survive the seven-year period, then the usual rates of tax apply to the transfer, that is the NRB at 0 per cent and 40 per cent on values exceeding the NRB. The way this works in practice is that at the time of the LCT, IHT is paid at the reduced rates. If the transferor then dies within the seven-year period, the additional tax is paid. The five basic steps are applied to an LCT at the time of the transfer.

7.6.2 Step 1: Calculate the value transferred

For lifetime dispositions the value transferred is the amount by which the value of the transferor's estate is reduced by the disposition. That is the loss to the transferor's estate. The value transferred is normally determined by reference to market value. In the case of a gift, the loss will usually be the market value of the asset transferred. In the case of a sale at an undervalue, the loss will usually be the market value of the asset less the consideration received on the sale.

It is important to note that the loss to the transferor's estate will not always equal the gain to the transferee's estate.

EXAMPLE 8

Peter owns 51 per cent of the issued share capital of Crookesmoor Ltd. The total issued share capital amounts to 10,000 shares. Peter is able to pass an ordinary resolution at a shareholders' meeting on his own (an ordinary resolution is arranged by 51 per cent of the vote) and, because of this, his holding is deemed to carry control of the company and is valued accordingly. Peter's 51 per cent holding in the company is valued at £11 per share.

Peter wishes to give 200 of his shares (ie 2 per cent of the company), to his son, David. A stake of that size, being a very small minority holding in the company (ie one which does not carry control), is worth only £3 per share.

Assume that a 49 per cent holding in Crookesmoor Ltd, because it no longer carries control, is only worth £7 per share.

The diminution in Peter's estate is:

	£
Value of estate before gift (5,100 @ £11)	56,100
Less value of estate after gift (4,900 @ £7)	34,300
	21,800

This is a very different result from the £600, which is the value to David of the shares actually gifted (200 @ £3).

7.6.2.1 Related property

Do not overlook the effect of the related property rules (see **7.5.1.1**).

7.6.2.2 Grossing up

As mentioned earlier, the value transferred is the amount by which the transferor's estate is reduced by the disposition. The transferor is primarily liable for any IHT due on a lifetime chargeable transfer, but the transferee can pay. Usually it is the transferee who pays the IHT. This means that the loss to the transferor's estate is limited to the value of the gift itself. However, if the transferor pays the IHT due on a lifetime chargeable transfer then the loss to the transferor's estate will be the total of the gift and the IHT due on the transfer. The value of the gift must be grossed up to find the value transferred. If the transferor is paying the IHT, then the property gifted is generally described as the *net chargeable transfer* and the loss to the transferor's estate is described as the *gross chargeable transfer*, being the net chargeable transfer plus the attributable tax. The steps to follow when grossing up a transfer are:

(a) Calculate the net chargeable transfer (NCT); ie from the chargeable transfer deduct any exemptions or reliefs which may be available, eg the annual exemption, spouse exemption, BPR, or APR.

(b) Calculate the amount of the net chargeable transfer exceeding the transferor's NRB at the date of the transfer. To do this calculate how much of the transferor's NRB is available by calculating the transferor's cumulative total at the date of the transfer and deducting it from the full NRB. This will give the amount of the NRB available. Subtracting this amount from the NCT will leave the amount of the NCT exceeding the NRB.

(c) Calculate the IHT payable. The formula to use is:

$$IHT = 1/4 = amount\ of\ NCT\ exceeding\ NRB$$

This formula applies when the lifetime rate of IHT is 20 per cent. For periods when the rate of tax differed consult tax tables.

(d) Calculate the gross chargeable transfer (GCT). This is done by adding the net chargeable transfer to the IHT payable. $GCT = NCT = IHT$. This is the loss to the transferor's estate.

EXAMPLE 9 (Grossing up—assumes that the current rates apply)

Mr Teal transfers £160,000 into a discretionary settlement. He is to pay the IHT. He has made chargeable transfers in the last seven years amounting to £340,000 for IHT purposes.
Working through the steps:

(a) Calculate the net chargeable transfer (NCT). On the facts given here the only exemption or relief available is the annual exemption for the tax year in which the gift is made (see **7.6.3.1**). *Assume that the previous year's annual exemption was used elsewhere*. The NCT is £157,000 (ie £160,000–£3,000 annual exemption).

(b) Calculate amount of the net chargeable transfer exceeding Mr Teal's NRB. Mr Teal has a cumulative total of £340,000. His nil-rate band is used up and this means that all of the current chargeable transfer exceeds the NRB.

(c) Calculate the IHT payable. Applying the formula: *IHT* = 1/4 ´ £157,000 = £39,250.

(d) Calculate the gross chargeable transfer. The gross chargeable transfer is the total of the NCT and IHT, which is £196,250 ie (£157,000 + £39,250).

The loss to Mr Teal's estate is the amount of the gross chargeable transfer, £196,250.

EXAMPLE 10 (Grossing up—assumes that the current rates of tax apply)

Mrs Francis transfers £350,000 into a discretionary settlement. She is also to pay the IHT. She has made no chargeable transfers in the last seven years.

(a) Calculate the net chargeable transfer (NCT). On the facts given here the only exemption or relief available is the annual exemption for tax year in which gift is made. *Assume that the previous year's annual exemption was used elsewhere*. The NCT is £347,000 (ie £350,000 – £3,000 annual exemption).

(b) Calculate the amount of the net chargeable transfer exceeding Mrs Francis's NRB. Subtracting the full NRB of £325,000 from the NCT leaves an amount of £22,000 exceeding the NRB.

(c) Calculate the IHT payable. Applying the formula: *IHT* 1/4 ´ £22,000 = £5,500.

(d) Calculate the gross chargeable transfer. The gross chargeable transfer is the total of the NCT and IHT, which is £352,500 ie (£347,000 + £5,500).

The loss to Mrs Francis's estate is the amount of the gross chargeable transfer, £352,500.

EXAMPLE 11 (Grossing up—assumes that the current rates of tax apply)

Mr Frost transfers £270,000 into a discretionary settlement. He is to pay the IHT. He has made chargeable transfers in the last seven years amounting to £124,000 for IHT purposes.

(a) Calculate the net chargeable transfer (NCT). On the facts given here the only exemption or relief available is the annual exemption for tax year in which gift is made. *Assume that the previous year's annual exemption was used elsewhere*. The NCT is £267,000 (ie £270,000 – £3,000 annual exemption).

(b) Calculate amount of the net chargeable transfer exceeding Mr Frost's NRB. To do this, calculate how much of the transferor's NRB is available by calculating the transferor's cumulative total at the date of the transfer and deducting it from the full NRB. This will give the amount of the NRB available. Subtracting this amount from the NCT will leave the amount of the NCT exceeding the NRB.

Mr Frost has a cumulative total of £124,000. This leaves £201,000 of his nil-rate band available for this transfer. Subtracting the £201,000 from the NCT leaves an amount of £66,000 exceeding the NRB.

(c) Calculate the IHT payable. Applying the formula: *IHT* = 1/4 ´ £66,000 = £16,500.

(d) Calculate the gross chargeable transfer. The gross chargeable transfer is the total of the NCT and IHT, which is £283,500 ie (£267,000 + £16,500).

The loss to Mr Frost's estate is the amount of the gross chargeable transfer, £283,500.

Note: If transferor pays the tax, and should the transferor make other gifts or die within the next seven years, the *gross* figure must be brought forward as part of the cumulative total.

7.6.2.3 Incidental expenses of transfer and CGT

There may be expenses incurred in connection with the gift, or a sale at an undervalue (eg legal costs, stamp duty, etc). There may also be a liability to CGT as well as to IHT. The rules for deduction of expenses or CGT from the value transferred are as follows:

(a) If the expenses or CGT are paid by the transferor, they do not reduce the value transferred.

(b) If they are paid by the transferee, they reduce the value transferred.

7.6.3 Step 2: Identify any available exemptions and deduct them from the value transferred

In addition to the exemptions detailed at **7.5.2** there are additional exemptions to be taken into account. These are available for lifetime dispositions only.

7.6.3.1 The annual exemption

The first £3,000 of transfers made by a transferor in any one tax year are exempt. Where the transfers of value exceed £3,000, the first £3,000 is taken to be exempt. If the total transfers fall short of £3,000, the unused part of the exemption may be carried forward to the following tax year. However, in the following tax year the £3,000 exemption for that year must be used before the amount brought forward. There is no further carry forward if the amount brought forward cannot be used in the following tax year. The exemption is applied chronologically if there is more than one transfer of value in a tax year. If there are several gifts on one day, the exemption is apportioned among them in proportion to the values transferred.

EXAMPLE 12

In the tax year 2008/9 Maria makes transfers of value of £1,800. In the tax year 2009/10 she makes transfers of value of £3,500. In the tax year 2010/11 she makes transfers of value of £6,000. She has not made any other gifts. The transfers of value made in the tax year 2008/9 fall within the annual exemption for that year and so are exempt for IHT purposes. Maria has used £1,800 of the annual exemption for that tax year; she has £1,200 of the annual exemption unused.

In the tax year 2009/10 she will have to use the annual exemption for that year, 2009/10. If some of the transfers are unrelieved after applying the annual exemption, she can utilise the unused exemption from 2008/9:

Tax year 2009/10

	£
Transfers of value	3,500
Less exemption (2009/10)	(3,000)
Chargeable transfers	500
Less balance of unused AE 2008/9	500
Total chargeable transfers	Nil

In 2010/11 Maria can only use the annual exemption for that year. £3,000 of the transfers of value made in that year will be chargeable transfers and will form Maria's cumulative total.

Tax year 2010/11	£
Transfers of value	6,000
Less exemption (2010/11)	(3,000)
Chargeable transfers	3,000

The unused balance of the annual exemption from the tax year 2008/9 (£700) will be lost.

EXAMPLE 13

On 15 June 2011 Emily makes a gift of £325,000 to her daughter on trust for life (an LCT). On 7 September 2011 Emily makes a gift of £50,000 to a discretionary settlement (LCT). She had also made earlier gifts, using her annual exemptions for the years 2009/10 and 2010/2011.

The annual exemption for the tax year 2010/2011 is applied against the gift made on 15 June 2011, reducing the value transferred to £322,000.

There is no annual exemption to apply against the gift made on 7 September 2011, its value transferred remains at £50,000.

7.6.3.2 Small gifts exemption

A transferor is allowed to make any number of gifts of up to £250 provided they are to different people, without affecting the cumulative total (IHTA 1984, s 20). The gifts must be outright and not by way of settlement. The gift itself must be no more than £250—the exemption cannot be used to cover the first £250 of a larger gift, ie if the gift is greater than £250, it is not an exempt transfer.

7.6.3.3 Gifts in consideration of marriage or civil partnership

Gifts in consideration of marriage or civil partnership are exempt up to certain limits (IHTA 1984, s 22). The limits are dependent on the relationship of the donor to the parties to the marriage or civil partnership. If the value of the gift exceeds the limit, the excess is chargeable. The limits are:

(a) £5,000 if the gift is by a parent of one of the parties to the marriage or civil partnership;

(b) £2,500 if the gift is by a remoter ancestor of one of the parties to the marriage or civil partnership, eg a grandparent or great-grandparent;

(c) £2,500 if the gift is by one of the parties to the marriage or civil partnership; or

(d) £1,000 if the gift is by any other person (eg a guest).

The gift must be:

(a) before a specific marriage or civil partnership and conditional on it, ie the donor must have a right to recover the gift if the marriage or civil partnership does not take place; or

(b) on or contemporaneously with the marriage or civil partnership; or

(c) after the marriage or civil partnership provided it was given in satisfaction of a prior legal obligation.

The gift must also be an outright gift to either of the parties to the marriage or civil partnership or, if settled, it must comply with the conditions set out in s 22 of IHTA 1984.

Where the marriage or civil partnership exemption is available, it should be deducted before the annual exemption, so that the annual exemption can be used elsewhere, if required.

7.6.3.4 Normal expenditure out of income

Transfers of value are exempt if they can be proved to be part of the normal expenditure of the transferor, made out of income and of such a size that, after allowing for all such transfers, the transferor is left with sufficient income to maintain the standard of living which the transferor is used to (IHTA 1984, s 21).

7.6.3.4.1 Life policy written in trust

The most likely example of expenditure which falls into this exemption is where the transferor takes out a policy which assures the transferor's own life for the benefit of, say, the transferor's children. When the policy matures (on the death of the transferor), the proceeds of the life policy do not pass through the transferor's estate (and thus do not attract IHT), but instead they go directly to the children. The transferor is deemed to make a gift to the children every time a premium on the policy is paid. However, the transferor will frequently be able to establish that such a gift does not represent a transfer of value because it can be exempted under the 'normal expenditure out of income' provisions. The transferor is paying the premiums out of income and is left with sufficient income to maintain the transferor's usual standard of living. As the premiums are paid regularly the payments are part of the transferor's normal expenditure.

7.6.4 Step 3: Identify any available reliefs and deduct them from the value transferred

The only reliefs available are those set out at **7.5.3**. Do not forget the additional rules applicable to lifetime transfers for both BPR (**7.5.3.4**) and APR (**7.5.3.6**).

7.6.5 Steps 4 and 5

Calculate the transferor's cumulative total as at the date of the transfer and the amount of the nil-rate band remaining and calculate the IHT payable by applying the rate (or rates) of tax to the value of the transfer for IHT purposes.

As stated at **7.6.1**, lifetime chargeable transfers are initially charged at half the rates in force at the time of the transfer. The current 2011/2012 rates of tax are 0 per cent for the first £325,000 and 20 per cent for the balance over that amount. As before, the rate or rates of tax applicable will depend on the cumulative total of all previous chargeable transfers made in the last seven years. When a transferor makes an LCT the amount of IHT payable is calculated by following the five steps. The position if the transferor dies within seven years of making the transfer, with the result that the full rates of IHT are chargeable, is discussed at **7.7**.

EXAMPLE 14 (Assumes that the current rates of tax apply)

On 5 June 2011 Zac transfers a cash payment of £340,000 into a discretionary settlement. He has made no previous lifetime transfers. Any IHT is to be paid by the trustees of the settlement. Calculate the IHT payable on the transfer.

Zac has made a lifetime chargeable transfer. Following the five steps:

Step 1: the value transferred is the amount of the cash payment, £340,000.

Step 2: one exemption available is the annual exemption for the tax year in which the gift is made, 2011/2012. This means that the transfer is reduced by £3,000 to £337,000. As this is the first chargeable transfer Zac has made he also has available his annual exemption for the previous tax year, 2010/2011. This reduces the transfer to £334,000.

Step 3: there are no reliefs which are available to Zac.

Step 4: Zac's cumulative total is nil as he has made no chargeable transfers in the seven years preceding the transfer on 5 June 2011. The whole of his NRB remains (£325,000).

Step 5: as this is an LCT the rates of tax are one-half of the death rates, the NRB at 0 per cent and the balance of the transfer at 20 per cent. Applying the rates of tax, the first £325,000 is taxed at 0 per cent and the remaining £9,000 is taxed at 20 per cent. The trustees of the discretionary settlement have £1,800 of IHT to pay.

EXAMPLE 15 (Assumes that the current rates of tax apply)

Revisiting example 7(b) but without ignoring exemptions and reliefs:

Philip makes a gift to a discretionary trust of £375,000 on 29 April 2011. On 1 May 2009 Philip made lifetime chargeable transfers totalling £160,000. Any IHT is to be paid by the trustees of the settlement. Calculate the IHT payable on the gift made on 29 April 2011.

Philip has made a lifetime chargeable transfer.

As you are aware that Philip made LCTs before the LCT on 29 April 2011, you may find it useful to draw a time-line to establish what events occurred within the seven years before the LCT on 29 April 2011.

The time-line should help you to establish Philip's cumulative total immediately before he made the gift on 29 April 2011.

Following the five steps:

Step 1: the value transferred is the amount of the cash payment, £375,000.

Step 2: one exemption available is the annual exemption for the tax year in which the gift is made, 2011/12. This means that the transfer is reduced by £3,000 to £372,000. As Philip made no lifetime gifts in the preceding tax year, 2010/11, the annual exemption for that year is also available. This reduces the transfer to £369,000.

Step 3: there are no reliefs which are available to Philip.

Step 4: Looking at the time-line above Philip made an LCT of £160,000 within seven years of the gift on 29 April 2011. To calculate his cumulative total, we can apply steps one to three to the LCT on 1 May 2009.

Step 1: *the value transferred is the amount of the cash payment, £160,000.*

Step 2: *one exemption available is the annual exemption for the tax year in which the gift is made, 2009/10. This means that the transfer is reduced by £3,000 to £157,000. As Philip made no lifetime gifts in the preceding tax year, 2008/9, the annual exemption for that year is also available. This reduces the transfer to £154,000.*

Step 3: *There are no reliefs which are available to Philip.*

The value of the transfer made on 1 May 2009 for IHT purposes is £154,000.

Philip's cumulative total on 29 April 2011, immediately before he made the gift to the discretionary trust, was £154,000.

Step 5: Philip has £171,000 of his NRB available to him (£325,000–154,000). As this is an LCT, the rates of tax are one-half of the death rates, the NRB at 0 per cent, and the balance of the transfer at 20 per cent. Applying the rates of tax to the £369,000, the first £171,000 is taxed at 0 per cent and the remaining £198,000 is taxed at 20 per cent. The trustees of the discretionary settlement have £39,600 of IHT to pay.

Exercise 1

Exercise 1 illustrates the charge to IHT when a transferor makes a lifetime chargeable transfer where he has made other LCTs in the preceding seven years.

Work through this example to ensure that you understand the steps to be followed and that you can apply them correctly.

There is a commentary on the exercise at the end of the chapter.

cont.

On 28 May 2011 Mr Martin transfers a cash sum of £211,000 into a discretionary settlement and the trustees are to pay any IHT due as a result of the transfer.

Mr Martin had made a transfer into the settlement of £160,000 on 17 February 2004, just over seven years prior to the present gift.

He also made a cash payment into the settlement of £134,000 on 9 August 2004, between six and seven years prior to the present gift. The tax on each of those transfers was paid by the trustees of the settlement.

In addition to these LCTs Mr Martin also made a gift of £70,000 cash to his daughter on 1 June 2010. He made no other lifetime transfers. Any IHT is to be paid by the trustees of the settlement. Assuming that the current rates of tax apply, calculate the IHT payable on the transfer Mr Martin made on the 28 May 2011.

Follow the five steps.

You may find it useful to refer back to earlier examples to remind yourself of the steps. You may find **Example 14** useful for the basic calculation; **Examples 12** and **13** useful for the application of annual exemptions; and **Examples 6 and 15** useful for the situation where the transferor has a cumulative total at the date of the current transfer.

7.7 The charge to tax and a lifetime chargeable transfer where the transferor dies within seven years of the lifetime chargeable transfer

At **7.6.1** it was pointed out that, provided a transferor survived seven years from the date of making an LCT the rate of IHT charged on values exceeding the NRB was reduced to 20 per cent. If the transferor failed to survive the seven-year period, then IHT is charged at the full rate, 40 per cent. IHT at the reduced rate is paid at the time of the transfer and any additional liability is paid at the time of the transferor's death. In practice this means that if a transferor dies within the seven-year period there has to be a second calculation of IHT. The full calculation needs to be carried out as not only is the IHT payable at the full rates but also, due to the transferor's death, the transferor's cumulative total at the date of the LCT may have changed and so the amount of the NRB available may have altered. This would be the case if the transferor had made a PET within the seven years preceding the date of the LCT which was not included in the transferor's cumulative total at the time of the LCT because it was, at that time, a PET. If the PET was made within seven years of the transferor's death, then it will now be a chargeable transfer and so its value will be included in the transferor's cumulative total at the date of the LCT (see **Example 16**, below).

On occasions the value of the property gifted by the LCT may go down between the date of the gift and the date of the transferor's death. If this is the case, then, usually, the lower (date of death) value is used to calculate the additional tax payable (IHTA 1984, s 131). The lower value is not used if the property gifted was a lease with less than 50 years unexpired, or if the gift was of tangible moveable property which was a wasting asset (see **Example 18**, below).

The lower value is only used to calculate the additional charge to IHT as a result of the donor's death. The original date of gift value is used in all other calculations, for example the calculation of the donor's cumulative total.

In addition to the five basic steps there are two other steps which may be relevant.

7.7.1 Step 6: Taper relief

Although IHT is charged at the full rates if the transferor dies within the seven-year period, there is some relief so long as the transferor survived at least three years from the date of the gift. The relief is given by only a percentage of the IHT calculated being payable. The amount of the relief depends on how long the transferor survived after making the LCT.

If the transfer is made within three to four years of the transferor's death, only 80 per cent of the IHT calculated is payable. If the period between the transfer and the death is four to five years, 60 per cent of the IHT is payable; five to six years, 40 per cent; and six to seven years, only 20 per cent. This relief is known as taper relief, or tapering relief, as the amount of IHT payable tapers off the longer the transferor survives (see **Example 17**, below).

It is important to understand that taper relief reduces the IHT attributable to the transfer; it does not reduce the value transferred.

7.7.2 Step 7: Taking into account any IHT paid at the date of the LCT

After applying taper relief, account is taken of any IHT that was paid at the date of the transfer. Full credit is given for tax paid at the time of the transfer. However, if the amount of tax paid at the date of the transfer exceeds the amount of IHT payable due to the death of the transferor within the seven-year period then the balance of IHT payable is reduced to nil. There will be no refund of tax.

EXAMPLE 16 (Effect of death on an LCT made within seven years of the transferor's death assuming that the current rates of tax apply throughout)

Mr Martin dies on 10 October 2011.

On 28 May 2011 Mr Martin transferred a cash sum of £211,000 into a discretionary settlement and the trustees were to pay any IHT due as a result of the transfer.

Mr Martin had made a transfer into the settlement of £160,000 on 17 February 2004, just over seven years prior to the gift made on the 28 May 2011.

He also made a cash payment into the settlement of £134,000 on 9 August 2004, between six and seven years prior to the gift made on the 28 May 2011. The tax on each of those transfers was paid by the trustees of the settlement.

In addition to these LCTs Mr Martin also made a gift of £70,000 cash to his daughter on 1 June 2010. He made no other lifetime transfers. Any IHT was to be paid by the trustees of the settlement. Assuming that the current rates of tax apply, calculate the IHT payable on the transfer Mr Martin made on the 28 May 2011 as a result of Mr Martin's death.

The LCT made by Mr Martin on the 28 May 2011 was within the seven years preceding his death. IHT is now chargeable on the LCT at the full rates. The full calculation needs to be repeated.

Following the five steps:

Step 1: the value transferred is the amount of the cash payment, £211,000.

Step 2: one exemption available is the annual exemption for the tax year in which the gift is made, 2011/12. This means that the transfer is reduced by £3,000 to £208,000. The annual exemption for the previous tax year, 2010/11, is not available as it is applied against the PET made on the 1 June 2010. The PET is now chargeable due to Mr Martin's death within 7 years of the gift.

Step 3: There are no reliefs which are available to Mr Martin (as before).

Step 4: Going back for seven years from 28 May 2011 Mr Martin made one chargeable transfer, the transfer to the settlement on 9 August 2004. [The transfer on 17 February 2004 was made more than seven years before the transfer in 2011.] In addition, as Mr Martin has died within seven years of the gift to his daughter on 1 June 2010 the gift is no longer a PET; it becomes chargeable.

The value of the transfer made on 9 August 2004 was £134, 000. The only exemption available will be the annual exemption for the tax year in which the gift was made. This reduces the transfer to £131,000. The annual exemption for the previous tax year will not be available to Mr Martin as it will have been used on the gift made on 17 February 2004. There are no reliefs which are available to this transfer. The value of the transfer for IHT purposes is £131,000.

The value of the transfer made on 1 June 2010 was £70,000.

One exemption available is the annual exemption for the tax year in which the gift is made, 2010/11. This means that the transfer is reduced by £3,000 to £67,000. The annual exemption for the previous tax year, 2009/10, is also available. The transfer is reduced by £3,000 to £64,000.

Mr Martin's cumulative total on 28 May 2011 is £ 195,000. (ie £131,000 + £64,000).

Step 5: Mr Martin has £130,000 of the NRB available to him (£325,000 – £195,000). The first £130,000 of the transfer is taxed at 0%. The remainder £78,000 (£208,000 – £130,000) is taxed at 40 per cent. There is IHT of £31,200 for the trustees to pay.

Step 6: As Mr Martin died within three years of the LCT, taper relief is not available.

Step 7: IHT of £2,200 was paid at the time of the transfer. Credit is given for this payment. The amount of IHT payable by the trustee of the settlement due to Mr Martin's death within the seven-year period is £29,000 (£31,200 – £2,200).

EXAMPLE 17 (With taper relief)

On the same facts as **Example 16**, above, Mr Martin dies on 9 July 2015. The steps up to and including Step 5 remain as in **Example 16**, above. At Step 6, as the LCT was made within four to five years of his death taper relief is available. Only 60 per cent of the IHT is payable, 60 per cent of £31,200, giving an amount due of £18,720.

Step 7: IHT of £2,200 was paid at the time of the transfer. Credit is given for this payment. The amount of IHT payable by the trustees of the settlement due to Mr Martin's death within the seven-year period is £16,520 (£18,720 – £2,200).

Exercise 2

Exercise 2 illustrates the effect of death on the charge to IHT when a transferor makes a lifetime chargeable transfer where he has made other LCTs in the preceding seven years, and where the transferor subsequently dies within seven years.

Work through this example to ensure that you understand the steps to be followed and that you can apply them correctly.

There is a commentary on the exercise at the end of the chapter.

Mr Martin dies on 9 July 2016.

On 28 May 2011 Mr Martin transferred a cash sum of £211,000 into a discretionary settlement and the trustees were to pay any IHT due as a result of the transfer.

Mr Martin had made a transfer into the settlement of £160,000 on 17 February 2004, just over seven years prior to the gift made on the 28 May 2011.

He also made a cash payment into the settlement of £134,000 on 9 August 2004, between six and seven years prior to the gift made on the 28 May 2011. The tax on each of those transfers was paid by the trustees of the settlement.

In addition to these LCTs Mr Martin also made a gift of £70,000 cash to his daughter on 1 June 2010. He made no other lifetime transfers. Any IHT was to be paid by the trustees of the settlement. Assuming that the current rates of tax apply, calculate the IHT payable on the transfer Mr Martin made on the 28 May 2011 as a result of Mr Martin's death.

You may find it useful to refer back to earlier examples to remind yourself of the steps. You may find **Examples 14** and **16** useful for the basic calculation; **Example 12** useful for the application of annual exemptions; **Examples 6** and **15** useful for the situation where the transferor has a cumulative total at the date of the current transfer; and **Example 17** for the application of taper relief.

EXAMPLE 18 (Effect of death on an LCT made within seven years of the transferor's death where the value of the property gifted has fallen and assuming that the current rates of tax apply throughout)

On 15 November 2006 Jason makes a gift of a freehold property worth £472,000 to a discretionary settlement and the trustees are to pay any IHT due as a result of the transfer. He has made no previous lifetime transfers.

Jason dies on 10 February 2011. On that date the property has a value of only £412,000.

A: IHT on the occasion of the LCT

Following the five steps:

Step 1: The value transferred is the value of the property on the date of the transfer, £472,000.

Step 2: One exemption available is the annual exemption for the tax year in which the gift is made, 2006/7. This means that the transfer is reduced by £3,000 to £469,000. As this is the first chargeable transfer Jason has made he also has available his annual exemption for the previous tax year, 2005/6. This reduces the transfer to £466,000.

Step 3: There are no reliefs which are available to Jason.

Step 4: Jason's cumulative total is nil as he has made no chargeable transfers in the seven years preceding the transfer on the 15 November.

Step 5: As this is an LCT the rates of tax are one-half of the official rates, the NRB at 0 per cent and the balance of the transfer at 20 per cent. Applying the rates of tax, the first £325,000 is taxed at 0 per cent and the remaining £141,000 at 20 per cent. The trustees of the discretionary settlement have £28,2\00 of IHT to pay.

B: Supplementary charge

As the transfer was within the seven years preceding his death IHT is now chargeable on the LCT at the full rates. The full calculation needs to be repeated.

Following the five steps:

Step 1: The value transferred is the value of the property on the date of the transfer, £472,000. However, as the value of the property has fallen, the date of death value can be used to calculate the additional tax payable (IHTA 1984 s 131). The value of the property is £412,000.

Step 2: One exemption available is the annual exemption for the tax year in which the gift is made, 2006/7 This means that the transfer is reduced by £3,000 to £409,000. As this is the first chargeable transfer Jason has made he also has available his annual exemption for the previous tax year, 2005/6. This reduces the transfer to £406,000.

Step 3: There are no reliefs which are available to Jason.

Step 4: Jason's cumulative total is nil as he has made no chargeable transfers in the seven years preceding the transfer on the 15 November.

Step 5: Jason has available to him the full NRB; the balance of the transfer is taxed at 40 per cent. Applying the rates of tax, the first £325,000 is taxed at 0 per cent and the remaining £81,000 at 40 per cent. There is IHT of £32,400 for the trustees to pay.

Step 6: As Jason died within four to five years of the LCT taper relief is available. Only 60 per cent of the IHT is payable, 60 per cent of £32,400, giving an amount due of £19,440.

Step 7: IHT of £28,200 was paid at the time of the transfer. Credit is given for this payment. The amount of IHT payable by the trustees of the settlement due to Jason's death within the seven-year period is reduced to nil. There will be no repayment of the additional tax paid at the time of the transfer.

NB: The lower value of the property is used only to calculate the additional IHT payable by the trustee as a result of the donor's death. The original value is used when calculating the donor's cumulative total at the date of death (which in this case will be £466,000).

NB: Similar principles apply when calculating the IHT payable by the donee of a PET when the donor dies within seven years of the gift. Thus, if in **Example 18** Jason's original transfer had been a PET rather than an LCT, there would have been no charge to tax at the time of the gift. On his death within seven years, the PET would have become chargeable. The calculation described in Steps 1–6 of paragraph B above would be undertaken to establish the donee's liability to tax on the former PET. Jason's cumulative total of lifetime transfers, however, would remain at £466,000.

7.8 The charge to tax and a PET

IHT is charged on a PET when the transferor does not survive for a period of seven years from the date of the PET. If the transferor dies within that period, the transfer becomes a chargeable transfer and IHT is payable at the full rates at the date of death.

If a PET becomes a chargeable transfer, then the steps to follow to calculate the IHT payable are the five basic steps, taking note of the matters mentioned when the charge to IHT and an LCT was considered, and, in addition, Step 6, set out at **7.7.1** (Step 7 is not applicable as there will have been no IHT payable at the time of the PET). Looking at the steps as applicable to a PET which becomes chargeable, the following apply.

7.8.1 Step 1: Calculate the value transferred

The comments made when looking at Step 1 in the charge to tax and a lifetime chargeable transfer (**7.6.2**), the related property rules (**7.5.1.1**) and the comments on incidental expenses of transfer and CGT (**7.6.2.3**) are all relevant here. Also relevant are the comments at **7.7** on a fall in value of the gifted property between the date of the gift and the date of the transferor's death. The lower value, subject to the exceptions set out at **7.7**, is used in the calculation of IHT payable as a result of the donor's death within seven years of the date of the gift.

7.8.2 Step 2: Identify any available exemptions and deduct them from the value transferred

As with LCTs, in addition to the exemptions set out at **7.5.2.1**, the exemptions available for lifetime dispositions, set out at **7.6.3**, are all available to reduce the value transferred by a PET.

7.8.3 Step 3: Identify any available reliefs and deduct them from the value transferred

Only business property relief and agricultural relief are available. Again, do not overlook the additional rules applicable to lifetime transfers at **7.5.3.4** and **7.5.3.6** respectively.

7.8.4 Steps 4 and 5

Calculate the transferor's cumulative total as at the date of the transfer and the amount of the nil-rate band remaining and calculate the IHT payable by applying the rate (or rates) of tax at the date of death to the value of the transfer for IHT purposes.

If a PET becomes a chargeable transfer, then IHT is charged at the full rates of tax. The transferor's cumulative total at the date the PET was made must be calculated to determine the applicable rate or rates of tax.

> **EXAMPLE 19 (Assumes that the current rates of tax apply throughout)**
>
> Isabelle dies on 15 June 2011. Her estate is valued at £360,000 for IHT purposes. She gifted cash of £120,000 to her daughter, Jasmine, on 21 December 2007. This was in addition to a gift of cash of £218,000 she made on 5 November 2002 to the trustees of a discretionary settlement. The trustees paid any IHT. She made no other gifts.

When made, the gift to Jasmine was a PET. As Isabelle has died within seven years of making the gift it is a chargeable transfer. There are no other chargeable transfers within the seven years preceding Isabelle's death.

Step 1: Calculate the value transferred. As the gift was of cash the value transferred is £120,000.

Step 2: Identify any exemptions and deduct them from the value transferred. One exemption available is the annual exemption for the tax year in which the gift is made 2007/8 This reduces the transfer to £117,000. As Isabelle had made no lifetime gifts in the previous tax year, 2006/7, the annual exemption for that year is also available. This reduces the transfer to £114,000.

Step 3: Identify any reliefs and deduct them from the value transferred. There are no reliefs available as the gift is cash.

Step 4: Calculate the transferor's cumulative total at the date the gift is made and the amount of the NRB remaining. Going back seven years from 21 December 2007, the date of the PET which has become chargeable, Isabelle made one chargeable transfer, the gift to the settlement. This was an LCT. (Although the LCT has to be taken into account when calculating Isabelle's cumulative total in December 2007, no additional tax is payable on it as it was made more than seven years before her death.) To calculate Isabelle's cumulative total Steps 1 to 3 have to be applied to the LCT. The value transferred was £218,000. The exemptions available will be the annual exemption for the tax year in which the gift was made, 2002/3. This reduces the value transferred to £215,000. As she had made no transfers during the previous tax year, 2001/2, that year's annual exemption is also available reducing the value transferred to £212,000. No other exemptions are available and there are no reliefs available. The value of the LCT for IHT purposes is £212,000. Isabelle's cumulative total on 21 December 2007 is £212,000. She has £113,000 of the NRB available to her.

Step 5: Calculate the IHT payable by applying the rate (or rates) of tax to the value of the transfer for IHT purposes. £113,000 of the transfer falls within the NRB. The remainder of the transfer, £1,000, will be taxed at 40 per cent. There will be IHT of £400 to pay on the transfer. See **7.8.5.1** below for the final step in the calculation.

7.8.5 Step 6: Taper relief

The final step to be taken is to apply taper relief, if applicable. This applies to PETs which become chargeable in exactly the same way as the additional charge to IHT on LCT where the transferor dies within seven years of the transfer (see **7.7.1**).

7.8.5.1 Continuing Example 19

As the gift was made three to four years before Isabelle's death, only 80 per cent of the tax is payable. The amount of tax to pay is £320.

Exercise 3

> Exercise 3 illustrates the effect of death on the charge to IHT when a transferor makes a PET, and where the transferor subsequently dies within seven years.
>
> Work through this example to ensure that you understood the steps to be followed and that you can apply them correctly.
>
> There is a commentary on the exercise at the end of the chapter.
>
> You may find it useful to refer back to earlier examples to remind yourself of the steps. You may find **Examples 14** and **16** useful for the basic calculation. In addition, you may find **Exercise 2** and **Example 19** useful for cumulative total.
>
> On 1 March 2005 Vinny makes a cash gift of £175,000 to her daughter. On 23 April 2008 she makes a cash gift of £180,000 to her god-daughter. Vinny dies on 3 August 2010.
>
> Assuming that the current rates of tax apply, calculate the IHT due on the gift made on 23 April 2008 as a result of Vinny's death.

7.9 The charge to tax and death

As stated at **7.4**, there is a deemed transfer of value on death. Again the five basic steps need to be gone through to calculate the IHT payable on the occasion of a person's death. There are some additional points to be taken into account and these are mentioned as the five steps are considered.

7.9.1 Step 1: Calculate the value transferred

On death, the value transferred is the value of the deceased's *estate* immediately *before* the deceased's death (s 4 IHTA 1984).

7.9.1.1 The estate

The deceased's estate is the aggregate of all property to which, immediately prior to death, the deceased was beneficially entitled to, other than excluded property. This includes not only assets which the deceased owned as sole owner, but also the deceased's share of any property owned jointly, either as beneficial joint tenants or as tenants in common.

The deceased's estate also includes the value of any interest which the deceased had in settled property. Only property in which the deceased had an interest in possession is included. An example of a deceased having an interest in possession is where the deceased was the sole life tenant of a will trust. The value of the interest is included where either (i) the trust was set up before 22 March 2006, or (ii) the trust was set up on or after 22 March 2006 and was an immediate post death interest trust. The capital value of the trust fund will be aggregated with the deceased's estate for the purposes of calculating any liability to IHT.

Also included in the value of the deceased's estate will be the value of any property subject to a reservation of a benefit (see **7.10**).

7.9.1.2 Liabilities

The value of the estate is the total value of the assets which make up the estate, less any liabilities of the estate.

7.9.1.3 Excluded property

As mentioned at **7.2.1.2**, some assets are excluded for IHT purposes. Do not forget that a reversionary interest in settled property is excluded property.

7.9.1.4 The value of the estate

The general rule is that assets are to be valued at their market value immediately before death. The date-of-death value is usually referred to as the probate valuation. There are exceptions to the market value rule and these are set out below.

7.9.1.5 Related property

Do not overlook the effect of the related property rules (see **7.5.1.1**). A provision which should not be overlooked is the provision contained in s 176 of IHTA 1984. This gives some relief to the related property rules. If property in the deceased's estate is valued as related property and is sold within three years of the date of death, then, provided the sale meets the conditions set out in the section, s 176 of IHTA 1984 allows the property to be revalued without it being treated as related property. This means that the lower value can be substituted for IHT purposes.

7.9.1.6 Value immediately before death

Section 4 of IHTA 1984 states that 'the value transferred is the value of the deceased's estate immediately *before* death'. However, some assets are valued immediately *after* death in order that any changes in the value of the asset by reason of the death can be taken into account. One example would be a life policy. Where the deceased has taken out a life policy and the proceeds to be paid out on death form part of the estate, it is the policy proceeds which are taxable even though the proceeds are not due immediately before death; they are only due as a result of the death and the insurance company does not in fact pay out until after death! Another example is the loss of goodwill. Where the deceased was a proprietor of a business it will frequently be the case that the business will suffer as a result of the deceased's death through loss of goodwill and, consequently, the value of the business will fall. The legislation permits this factor to be taken into account when valuing the business at the date of death, even though the goodwill is not in fact lost until some time later.

7.9.1.7 Sale of land within four years of death

The usual market value rules apply to land held in a deceased's estate. However, if an interest in land is sold within four years of the date of death for less than the probate value the lower value can, in certain circumstances, be substituted for the probate value (IHTA 1984, ss 190–8).

7.9.1.8 Sale of qualifying shares within 12 months of death

Again, the usual market value rules apply to shares held in a deceased's estate. If the shares are shares in a company which is quoted on a recognised stock exchange or holdings in an authorised unit trust (qualifying shares) and are sold within 12 months of the date of death for less than the probate value, the lower value can, in certain circumstances, be substituted for the probate value (IHTA 1984, ss 178–89). When calculating the overall loss to the estate by virtue of the qualifying shares being sold for less than the probate value, it is the aggregate, or net, loss to the estate taking into account the proceeds of sale of all qualifying shares sold during the 12 months.

7.9.2 Step 2

Identify any available exemptions and deduct them from the value transferred.

The only exemptions available are the ones set out at **7.5.2.1**. Do not forget that the ones set out when looking at an LCT are *not* available on death.

7.9.3 Step 3

Identify any available reliefs and deduct them from the value transferred.

In addition to the reliefs set out at **7.5.3** there are two other reliefs available on death.

7.9.3.1 Woodlands relief

If the deceased's estate included land in the UK which was not eligible for agricultural property relief but on which trees and underwood are growing, woodlands relief may be available (IHTA 1984, s 125). The deceased must have been beneficially entitled to the land throughout the five years preceding the date of death or must have been beneficially entitled to the land otherwise than for consideration in money or money's worth (ie had been given or inherited the land on the death of another).

The relief operates in a different way to BPR and APR. Those reliefs operate by including the value of the asset in the value of the estate and applying a relief calculated as a percentage of the value of the asset. Woodlands relief operates by excluding the value of the woodlands from the estate. Any liability to IHT is deferred until there is a disposal of the woodlands.

For the relief to operate the beneficiary of the woodlands must elect to the Inland Revenue for the relief.

7.9.3.2 Quick succession relief

Quick succession relief offers some relief where a person dies within five years of receiving a chargeable transfer (IHTA 1984, s 141). For it to apply, the deceased's estate must have been increased by a chargeable transfer (either a lifetime gift or one which occurred on death) made to the deceased within five years of the deceased's death ('the first transfer'). In addition, IHT must have been paid on the first transfer. For the relief to be applicable there is *no* requirement that the property the deceased received as a result of the first transfer still forms part of the deceased's estate at the date of death.

The relief operates by giving a tax credit which then reduces the IHT payable on death ('the second transfer').

There are two stages to calculating the tax credit. First the calculation:

$$\frac{(G-T)}{G} \times T$$

where G is the gross amount of the first transfer and T is the amount of IHT paid on the first transfer.

A percentage of the figure arrived at is allowed as the tax credit, the percentage depending on the amount of time which has elapsed between the two transfers. The percentages are:

100 per cent if the first transfer was one year or less before death.
80 per cent if the first transfer was one to two years before death.
60 per cent if the first transfer was two to three years before death.
40 per cent if the first transfer was three to four years before death.
20 per cent if the first transfer was four to five years before death.

The amount of the tax credit cannot result in a refund of IHT.

EXAMPLE 20 (Assume that the current rates of tax apply throughout)

Ignoring exemptions and reliefs:

Gladys dies in August 2010. She leaves her estate, valued at £500,000, to her daughter, Barbara. Gladys made no lifetime gifts. The IHT payable on Gladys' estate is £70,000 (ie £325,000 @ 0% and £175,000 @ 40%). Barbara dies suddenly in October 2011. She has made no lifetime gifts. Her estate is valued at £750,000 and she leaves this to her sister. As Barbara dies within 5 years of inheriting her mother's estate QSR is available.

The amount of the QSR is:

Stage One:

$$\frac{(G-T)}{G} \times T \quad \frac{(500,000-70,000)}{500,000} \times 70,000 = 60,200$$

Stage Two:

As Gladys died one to two years before Barbara's death 80 per cent of this figure is available: 80% = 60,200 = £48,160.

The IHT payable on Barbara's estate is £170,000 (£325,000 @ 0% and £425,000 @ 40%) less the QSR of £48,160, leaving IHT to pay of £121,840.

7.9.4 Steps 4 and 5

Calculate the transferor's cumulative total as at the date of the transfer and the amount of the nil-rate band remaining and calculate the IHT payable by applying the rate (or rates) of tax to the value of the transfer for IHT purposes.

On death, the transferor's estate is liable to IHT. The rate or rates of tax will depend on the cumulative total of all chargeable transfers made by the transferor in the seven years before death. It must be remembered that the cumulative total will include all PETs which have now become chargeable transfers as a result of the transferor's death within seven years.

EXAMPLE 21 (Assumes that the current rates of tax apply throughout)

James dies on 31 May 2011. The value of his estate is £75,000; there are no exemptions or reliefs available to his estate. During his lifetime James made only one gift. He made a gift, on 1 April 2006, of £160,000 cash into a discretionary settlement with the trustees paying any IHT due as a result of the transfer.

Following the five steps to calculate the IHT payable on the estate:

Step 1: The value transferred is the value of the estate, £75,000.

Step 2: There are no exemptions available.

Step 3: There are no reliefs available.

Step 4: There is one transfer made in the seven years preceding his death which will make up his cumulative total. The value of the transfer made on 1 April 2006 was £160,000. One exemption available will be the annual exemption for the tax year in which the gift was made, 2005/6. This will reduce the value of the gift to £157,000. The annual exemption for the previous year, 2004/5, is also available and will reduce the value of the gift to £154,000. There are no reliefs which are available to this transfer.

James' cumulative total on the date of his death is £154,000.

Step 5: There is £171,000 of James' NRB remaining (£325,000 – £154,000). All the estate, £75,000, will be taxed at 0 per cent. There is no IHT to pay.

Exercise 4

> Exercise 4 illustrates the charge to IHT on a transferor's estate on the death of the transferor, when the transferor has made transfers of value during the preceding seven years.
>
> Work through this example to ensure that you understand the steps to be followed and that you can apply them correctly.
>
> There is a commentary on the exercise at the end of the chapter.
>
> You may find it useful to refer back to earlier examples to remind yourself of the steps. You may find **Examples 14** and **16** useful for the basic calculation. In addition, you may find **Exercise 3** and **Example 21** useful.
>
> James dies on 31 May 2011. The value of his estate is £60,000; there are no exemptions or reliefs available to his estate. During his lifetime James made several gifts. He made a gift, on 1 April 2006, of £157,000 cash into a discretionary settlement with the trustees paying any IHT due as a result of the transfer.
>
> On 25 June 2007 he made a gift of £100,000, cash, to his daughter.
>
> The only other gift he made was a gift of £45,000 cash on 4 July 2008 to his son. Assuming that the current rates of tax apply, calculate the IHT due on James's estate.

7.9.5 Transfer of unused nil-rate band

For deaths on or after 9 October 2007 a claim can be made for the part of the NRB unused on the death of a spouse or civil partner (s 8A IHTA 1984 as amended).

The effect of this is that where the first to die used none of the NRB available on the first death, the surviving spouse/civil partner has double the NRB available at the second death. If part of the NRB had been used on the first death, a proportion of the NRB at the date of the second death is available at the second death.

EXAMPLE 22 (Assumes that the current rates of tax apply throughout)

George died in May 2009. By his will he left all his estate to John, his civil partner. George had made no lifetime gifts. His cumulative total at the date of his death was nil.

John dies in October 2011. His estate has a net value after deduction of liabilities of £800,000. In his will he leaves his estate to his brother and sisters.

On George's death no IHT was payable as his estate passed to an exempt beneficiary, his civil partner, John. As George's cumulative total was nil, the full amount of his NRB at the date of his death was unused.

Following the five steps to calculate the IHT payable on John's estate:

Step 1:   The value transferred is the value of the estate, £800,000.

Step 2:   There are no exemptions available.

Step 3:   There are no reliefs available.

Step 4:   John's cumulative total at the date of death is nil as he has made no chargeable transfers in the seven years preceding his death.

Step 5:   The full NRB is available to John's estate, £325,000. As George did not use his NRB at the date of his death, there is a further 100 per cent of the NRB available to John's estate. Applying the rates of tax, the first £650,000 is taxed at 0 per cent and the remaining £150,000 at 40 per cent. There is IHT of £60,000 for the personal representatives to pay.

EXAMPLE 23 (Using the rates of tax for 2008/9 and 2010/11)

George died in May 2008. By his will he left £156,000 to his nephew. He left the remainder of his estate, with a net value of £500,000, to John, his civil partner. George had made no lifetime gifts. His cumulative total at the date of his death was nil.

John dies in October 2010. His estate has a net value after deduction of liabilities of £800,000. In his will he leaves his estate to his brother and sisters.

Following the five steps to calculate the IHT payable on the estate on George's death:

Step 1:   The value transferred is the value of the estate, £656,000.

Step 2:   There is one exemption available. The civil partner exemption is available on the £500,000 passing to John. The value is reduced to £156,000.

Step 3:   There are no reliefs available.

Step 4: George's cumulative total at the date of death is nil as he has made no chargeable transfers in the seven years preceding his death.

Step 5:   The full NRB, £312,000 in 2008/9, is available to George's estate. Applying the rates of tax, the £156,000 is all taxed at 0 per cent. There is no IHT to pay. George has used 50% of his NRB. On **John's** death his net estate is valued at £800,000.

Following the five steps to calculate the IHT payable on John's estate:

Step 1:   The value transferred is the value of the estate, £800,000.

Step 2:   There are no exemptions available.

Step 3:   There are no reliefs available.

Step 4:   John's cumulative total at the date of death is nil as he has made no chargeable transfers in the seven years preceding his death.

Step 5:   The full NRB is available to John's estate, £325,000. As George used 50 per cent of his NRB at the date of his death, there is a further 50 per cent of the NRB at the date of John's death

(50 per cent of £325,000) available to John's estate. Applying the rates of tax, the first £487,500 (£325,000 + £162,500) is taxed at 0 per cent and the remaining £312,500 at 40 per cent. There is IHT of £125,000, for the personal representatives to pay.

Where on the death of a surviving spouse or civil partner there are two, or more unused NRBs available for a transfer, the maximum that can be transferred is 100 per cent of the NRB at the date of death of the surviving spouse or civil partner. There are rules which set out how the amount available for transfer is calculated, but this is beyond the scope of this chapter.

7.9.6 LCTs and PETs made in the seven years preceding the date of death

Do not overlook the fact that when a person dies not only may there be a charge to IHT on the deceased's estate; there may also be additional IHT to pay on any LCT made in the seven years preceding the date of death. This is because, at the time of the LCT, IHT is paid at half the rates applicable on death, with the balance of any IHT being due if the transferor dies within seven years of the date of the transfer.

There may also be a liability to IHT on any PET made in the seven years preceding the date of death. This is due to the fact that a PET is treated as an exempt transfer at the time it is made and only becomes a chargeable transfer if the transferor dies within seven years of making the PET.

> **EXAMPLE 24 (Assumes that the current rates of tax apply throughout)**
>
> Jonathon dies on 17 February 2010. His estate comprises a house he owns jointly, in equal shares, with his sister. The market value of the house is £90,000. He also owned at the date of his death an interest in a partnership, his interest having a market value of £100,000. The other assets in his estate have a value of £100,000. By his will he has left a legacy of £10,000 to the Royal National Institute for the Blind (a registered charity) and the remainder of his estate passes to his sister.
>
> During his lifetime he made the following gifts. On 24 September 2001 a gift of £50,000 cash to one of his nieces, Jane. On 15 May 2003 a gift of £130,000 cash to his nephew, Mark, on the occasion of Mark's wedding. On 10 November 2004 a gift of £218,000 cash to the trustees of a discretionary settlement, on which he agreed to pay any IHT due. In addition to these gifts, on 2 June 2007 he gifted a building which was used by the partnership to his nephew, Andrew. The building was owned solely by Jonathon and had a market value of £100,000. Andrew still owned the building at the date of his uncle's death. What IHT was payable during Jonathon's lifetime and what IHT is payable on his death?
>
> During his lifetime only one of the gifts made was an LCT, the gift to the discretionary settlement. The other gifts were gifts to individuals and so were PETs.
>
> Following the five steps to calculate the IHT payable when the LCT was made on 10 November 2004:
>
> Step 1: The value transferred is the amount of the cash payment, £218,000.
>
> Step 2: One exemption is available, the annual exemption. Jonathon has available the annual exemption for the tax year in which the gift is made, 2004/5; this reduces the value of the gift to £215,000. The annual exemption for the previous tax year, 2003/4, is not available as it is applied against the PET made on the 15 May 2003.
>
> Step 3: There are no reliefs available.
>
> Step 4: Jonathon's cumulative total is nil as he has made no chargeable transfers in the seven years preceding this transfer. (The gifts on 24 September 2001 and 15 May 2003 are PETs.)
>
> Step 5: The whole of Jonathon's NRB is available. The value transferred, £215,000, falls within the NRB: there is no IHT payable when the gift is made.
>
> When Jonathon dies not only will there be a charge to IHT on his estate; there may also be additional IHT to pay on any LCT made in the seven years preceding his death and a charge to IHT on

any PETs made in the seven years preceding his death. The gift made on 15 May 2003 was made in the seven years preceding his death, as was the LCT on 10 November 2004 and the PET on 2 June 2007.

Following the five steps, beginning with the earliest gift:

Step 1: The value transferred was the value of the cash gift, £130,000.

Step 2: The gift was made in consideration of Andrew's marriage. The first £1,000 is exempt, reducing the value transferred to £129,000. One exemption available is the annual exemption for the tax year in which the gift is made, 2003/4. This means that the transfer is reduced by £3,000 to £126,000. As Jonathon had made no lifetime gifts in the previous tax year, 2002/3, the annual exemption that tax year is also available. This reduces the transfer by £3,000 to £123,000.

Step 3: There are no reliefs available.

Step 4: Jonathon's cumulative total on 15 May 2003 was nil. The gift made on 24 September 2001 was a PET. As it was made more than seven years before Jonathon died it is not chargeable.

Step 5: All the NRB is available and so there is no IHT to pay on the occasion of Jonathon's death on the gift made on 15 May 2003.

Looking next at the LCT made on 10 November 2004: Repeating the steps taken above when calculating the IHT payable at the time the gift was made:

Step 1: The value transferred is the amount of the cash payment, £218,000.

Step 2: One exemption is available, the annual exemption. Jonathon has available the annual exemption for the tax year in which the gift is made, 2004/5; this reduces the value of the gift to £215,000. The annual exemption for the previous tax year, 2003/4, is not available as it is applied against the PET made on the 15 May 2003.

Step 3: There are no reliefs available.

Step 4: Jonathon's cumulative total is £123,000, which is the value of the transfer made on 15 May 2003.

Step 5: £202,000 of Jonathon's NRB is available. £202,000 of the value transferred is taxed at 0 per cent; the remainder, £13,000, is taxed at 40 per cent, giving a total of £5,200 IHT.

As this is a calculation of the additional IHT due on an LCT due to the death of the transferor within seven years of the making of the gift:

Step 6: This provides for taper relief to be applied, if appropriate. The gift was made within five to six years of Jonathon's death and so only 40 per cent of the IHT is payable, £2,080.

Step 7: There was no IHT payable at the time the transfer was made and so the IHT due on the LCT as a result of Jonathon's death within seven years of the transfer is £2,080.

Following the steps for the transfer made on 2 June 2007: Step 1: the value transferred is the market value of the building, £100,000. Step 2: the annual exemption for the tax year in which the gift was made, 2007/8, is available, as is the annual exemption for the preceding tax year, 2006/7. However, Step 3: as the building was used for the purpose of the business carried out by the partnership of which Jonathon was a partner, the building qualifies for BPR at 50 per cent **(7.5.3.2)**. The BPR is given before deducting the annual exemptions **(7.5.3)**, leaving a value transferred of £44,000. Step 4: Jonathon's cumulative total on 2 June 2007 was £338,000 (£123,000 + £215,000). There is no NRB remaining and the whole £44,000 will be taxed at 40 per cent, making IHT of £17,600. Step 6: as the gift was made within two to three years of Jonathon's death there is no taper relief. Step 7 is not applicable as the transfer was a PET when originally made and so there will have been no IHT paid at the time of the gift.

The liability to IHT on the estate remains to be calculated.

Step 1: The value of the estate is the value of Jonathon's share in the house, which, as it was jointly owned, will have the joint owner's discount applied, giving a value of £45,000 − (10 per cent of £45,000) = £40,500. The remainder of the estate was valued at £200,000. The value of the estate is £240,500.

Step 2: There is one exemption, the gift to the charity of £10,000 is exempt, reducing the value transferred to £230,500.

Step 3: The interest in a partnership qualifies for BPR at 100 per cent, reducing the value of the estate to £130,500.

Step 4: The total value for IHT purposes of each of the chargeable transfers made in the seven years preceding the date of death will form Jonathon's cumulative total. At the date of his death this total is £382,000 (£123,000 + £215,000 + £44,000).

Step 5: All Jonathon's NRB has been used; all the estate, £130,500, will be taxed at 40 per cent, giving IHT of £52,200 to pay.

The IHT due on the gift made on 10 November 2004 to the discretionary settlement, £2,080, is payable by the trustees of the settlement, out of the trust monies.
The IHT due on the gift made on 2 June 2007 to Andrew, £17,600, is payable by Andrew.
　The IHT due on the estate, £52,200, is payable by Jonathon's personal representatives from the monies in his estate.

7.10 Gifts subject to a reservation

A gift of property is subject to a reservation if, after gifting the property, some benefit is still enjoyed or retained by the transferor. It would be tempting under the IHT legislation for the transferor to give away property to another individual but to continue to retain an interest in it. That way, the property would not form part of the transferor's estate liable to IHT on death. Also, provided the transferor survived seven years from the date of the gift the property would escape IHT altogether. (Even if the transferor died within seven years of making the gift then, provided the value of the gift fell within the transferor's NRB at the date the gift was made, and the rates of IHT remain the same, then no more IHT would be payable on the death than would have been paid had the gift not been made and the asset still formed part of the deceased's estate. If the transferor died within the seven-year period and the value of the property transferred exceeded the available NRB, then taper relief would operate to reduce the amount of IHT payable). A good example of a gift where a benefit is retained would be a parent who makes a gift of a holiday home to a child but continues to use the holiday home frequently throughout the year without paying any rent to the child.

There is legislation to prevent taxpayers trying to avoid IHT in this way (Finance Act 1986, s 102).

The original gift of the asset will be a lifetime transfer, an LCT or a PET depending on the recipient of the gift. In addition, if the property is still subject to a reservation at the transferor's death, then the property, at its value at the date of death, will be included in the transferor's estate and will be taxed as part of the transferor's estate on death. If the original gift was made in the seven years preceding the transferor's death, IHT or additional IHT may be payable on the original gift as a result of the death.

If, in the above example of the gift of a holiday home, the parent was still enjoying visits to the property at the time of death, which was six years after the original gift, the original PET would become chargeable as a result of the death. In addition, the value of the property would also be included in the value of the parent's estate at the date of death. There would be a double charge to IHT.

If the reservation ceases before death, then the transferor will be treated as making a PET on the date the reservation ceases. In the earlier example, if the parent ceased using the property five years after having made the original gift, there would be a PET at the date the parent stopped using it. The value of the PET would be the value of the property at that date. If the parent died one year after ceasing to use the property, both PETs would become chargeable as they would have been made in the seven years preceding the parent's death.

As the making of a gift with a reservation can result in a double charge to IHT there are provisions giving some relief for this.

Care should be taken to avoid giving advice to a client which could result in a gift with a reservation being made.

7.11 Liability, burden, and payment of tax

The question of *liability* is concerned with who will actually be required to send to the Revenue any IHT that is due: *burden* is concerned with who ultimately bears the tax (a matter of no concern to the Revenue but of considerable interest to, for example, the beneficiaries of a deceased's estate).

7.11.1 Lifetime chargeable transfers

7.11.1.1 Due date for payment

IHT due on the value transferred by a chargeable lifetime transfer normally falls due six months after the end of the month in which the transfer takes place. However, if the chargeable transfer occurs between 6 April and 30 September (inclusive) in the tax year, then the IHT is due on 30 April in the following year.

Overdue IHT attracts interest.

7.11.1.2 Liability and burden

The primary liability for (and burden of) IHT due in respect of a lifetime chargeable transfer lies with the transferor. The majority of LCTs will involve the transferor transferring property to trustees. If the tax is not paid by the transferor by the due date, then the trustees become liable. If the trustees are unable to pay the tax, then the Revenue has power to seek payment from persons who have an interest in the settlement.

It is possible for the transferee to agree to pay the tax instead of the transferor in this instance.

7.11.1.3 Additional tax due on death

Where a person dies within seven years of making a lifetime chargeable transfer, additional tax may become payable. If so, then this is due six months after the end of the month in which death occurred.

The primary liability for this additional tax lies with the transferee (ie the trustees). However, if the tax remains unpaid after the due date, the Revenue can seek payment from persons who have an interest in the settlement and, as a final recourse, from the personal representatives of the transferor's estate.

7.11.2 PETs which become chargeable

7.11.2.1 Due date for payment

IHT falls due six months after the end of the month in which the transferor's death occurs.

Overdue tax attracts interest.

7.11.2.2 Liability and burden

The transferee is primarily liable (and bears the burden of the tax). In the case of a trust, the transferee will be the trustees and the burden will fall on the trust property (effectively on the beneficiaries). If the tax remains unpaid 12 months after the date of death, then the personal representatives of the deceased's estate are liable, leaving them to try to recover the tax from those who have primary liability.

7.11.3 Death

7.11.3.1 Due date for payment

IHT due on death is due six months after the end of the month in which death occurs. Overdue tax attracts interest.

7.11.3.2 Liability and burden

This depends on the property bearing the IHT.

7.11.3.3 Deceased's free estate

The PRs are liable for the IHT on the deceased's free estate. If the will is silent as to burden, tax on the free estate in the UK is normally borne by the residue (in the case of foreign property, by that property itself). If the testator has specifically provided that particular gifts in the will are to bear their own tax, that direction will normally prevail.

7.11.3.4 Settled property in which the deceased had an interest

If IHT is due, as a result of the death, on assets in a trust fund in which the deceased had an interest, then the trustees of the settlement are liable for the IHT due. The burden falls on the trust property.

7.11.3.5 Property passing other than under the deceased's will or intestacy

If property passed outside the will, for example, the deceased's share of a house owned as beneficial joint tenants with the deceased's sister, then the beneficiary of the asset, the sister, bears the burden for the IHT attributable to it although the liability falls on the PRs.

7.11.4 Instalment option

In certain cases, IHT may be paid by ten equal annual instalments, the first instalment due on the normal due date for payment.

Only certain assets qualify for the instalment option. These are:

(a) land and buildings; or

(b) shares or securities giving control immediately before the transfer; or

(c) unquoted shares or securities of a company which did not give the transferor control provided the Inland Revenue is satisfied that the sum attributable to their value cannot be paid in one sum without undue hardship;

(d) unquoted shares (but not securities) of a company which did not give the transferor control where the value transferred attributable to the shares exceeds £20,000 *and* either the nominal value of the shares is not less than 10 per cent of the nominal value of all the shares of the company at the time of the transfer, *or* the shares are ordinary shares and their nominal value is not less than 10 per cent of the nominal value of all ordinary shares of the company at that time;

(e) (where the transfer is on death) unquoted shares or securities of a company which did not give the transferor control where the tax on the holding and on any other shares or securities qualifying for the instalment option comprises at least 20 per cent of the tax payable by a particular person; and

(f) a business or interest in a business.

7.11.5 Entitlement

The instalment facility is available in respect of:

(a) transfers on death; or

(b) lifetime chargeable transfers where the transferee pays the IHT (the transferor is primarily liable); or

(c) a PET which becomes chargeable, provided the transferee pays the IHT and still owns the property at the date of the transferor's death. If the property is sold, then the whole amount of IHT remaining becomes payable immediately.

EXAMPLE 25

Colin dies on 20 November 2010. Part of his estate comprises 20,000 shares in a quoted company which gave Colin control of the company. The shareholding is valued at £75,000 at the date of Colin's death. The IHT payable in respect of shares is, say, £27,400.

If the instalment option is not opted for, IHT falls due on 31 May 2011.

However, if the instalment option is opted for, £2,740 (1/10 × £27,400) is payable on each 31 May from 31 May 2011 until 31 May 2020.

7.11.6 Interest

Where land is concerned (other than land on which agricultural property relief is available), interest accrues on the balance of IHT outstanding from the date when the first instalment becomes due for payment.

However, in respect of the other categories of property qualifying for the instalment option, the general rule is that no interest is payable provided that each instalment is paid by the due date.

7.12 Tax planning

7.12.1 Lifetime gifts and taper relief

As a general principle, tax will be saved by making a transfer during one's lifetime rather than on death. This is due to the seven-year cumulation period.

If the transferor survives seven years after making the gift, then no tax will be payable on the gift if it was a PET and tax at only half the official rates will have been paid if it was a lifetime chargeable transfer.

Even if death occurs within seven years, the full charge to IHT may be mitigated by taper relief. However, it is important to understand that taper relief reduces the *IHT attributable* to the chargeable transfer *not* the value of the chargeable transfer itself. Therefore, taper relief is only applicable if IHT is payable on the chargeable transfer.

IHT will only be payable on the chargeable transfer if the value of the transfer, taking into account the transferor's cumulative total at the date the transfer was made, exceeds the transferor's NRB. If the chargeable transfer (taking into account the cumulative total at the date of the gift) does not exceed the NRB available at the date of chargeable transfer, no IHT is payable and so taper relief is inapplicable.

7.12.2 Appreciating assets

An asset which has potential for capital appreciation should be considered before other assets if the transferor is thinking of making lifetime gifts. This is because the value of the asset at the *date of transfer* is taken for IHT purposes. Should the asset remain in the estate its value at the date of death will have been higher (it is an appreciating asset) and a higher liability to IHT could result.

The instalment option may be available to reduce the burden of any IHT on lifetime gifts (and hold over relief may be available to hold over any CGT).

However, it may be not within the taxpayer's means to give away his assets several years before his death.

7.12.3 Utilising exemptions

7.12.3.1 Exemptions generally

Full use should be made of the available exemptions, of which the annual exemption is the most important. It allows property to be handed down tax-free over a period of time.

7.12.3.2 Spouse or civil partnership exemption

Each spouse or civil partner is liable for IHT. It may be worthwhile for the more wealthy spouse or civil partner to transfer property to the other spouse or civil partner to enable both spouses or civil partners to make full use of their annual exemptions and nil-rate band. For example, if the estates are of sufficient size, it may be beneficial for spouses or civil partners to arrange their estates such that each has an estate at least equal to the nil-rate band. This will mean that they will each be able to give away the maximum amount without paying tax.

7.13 Conclusion: checkpoints

You should now be able to:

- identify the occasions when a charge to IHT arises (**7.5**);
- calculate the IHT liability on a lifetime chargeable transfer (**7.6**);
- calculate the IHT liability on an LCT where the transferor dies within seven years of the LCT (**7.7**);
- calculate the IHT liability on a PET where the transferor dies within seven years of the PET (**7.8**); and
- calculate the IHT liability of death (**7.9**).

7.14 Commentary to exercises

Exercise 1

This exercise illustrates the charge to IHT when a transferor makes a lifetime chargeable transfer where he has made other LCTs in the preceding seven years.

Following the five steps:

Step 1: The value transferred is the amount of the cash payment, £211,000.

Step 2: One exemption available is the annual exemption for the tax year in which the gift is made, 2011/12. This means that the transfer is reduced by £3,000 to £208,000. As he had made no chargeable transfers during the previous tax year, 2010/2011, that year's annual exemption is also available, reducing the value transferred to £205,000. [The PET on the 1 June 2010 is ignored for the purposes of the annual exemption 9s19 (3A) IHTA 1984.]

Step 3: There are no reliefs which are available to Mr Martin.

Step 4: Going back for seven years from 28 May 2011 Mr Martin made one chargeable transfer, the transfer to the settlement on 9 August 2004. [The transfer on 17 February 2004 was made more than seven years before the transfer in 2011. The gift to his daughter on 1 June 2010 was a PET. As Mr Martin is still alive the PET is treated as (potentially) exempt and so can be ignored for the purposes of calculating his NRB.] The value of the transfer made on 9 August 2004 was £134,000. The only exemption available will be the annual exemption for the tax year in which the gift was made (2004/5). This reduces the transfer to £131,000. (The annual exemption for the previous tax year (2003/4) will not be available to Mr Martin as it will have been used on the gift made on 17 February 2004.) There are no reliefs which are available to this transfer. The value of the transfer for IHT purposes is £131,000. Mr Martin's cumulative total on 28 May 2011 is £131,000.

Step 5: Mr Martin has £194,000 of the NRB available to him (£325,000 – £131,000). The first £194,000 of the transfer is taxed at 0 per cent. The remainder, £11,000 (£205,000 – £194,000), is taxed at 20 per cent. There is IHT of £2,200 for the trustees to pay.

Exercise 2

Exercise 2 illustrates the effect of death on the charge to IHT when a transferor makes a lifetime chargeable transfer where he has made other LCTs in the preceding seven years, and where the transferor subsequently dies within seven years.

Following the steps:

Step 1: The value transferred is the amount of the cash payment, £211,000.

Step 2: One exemption available is the annual exemption for the tax year in which the gift is made, 2011/12. This means that the transfer is reduced by £3,000 to £208,000. The annual exemption for the previous tax year, 2010/11, is not available as it is applied against the PET made on the 1 June 2010. The PET is now chargeable due to Mr Martin's death within 7 years of the gift.

Step 3: There are no reliefs which are available to Mr Martin (as before).

Step 4: Going back for seven years from 28 May 2011 Mr Martin made one chargeable transfer, the transfer to the settlement on 9 August 2004. [The transfer on 17 February 2004 was made more than seven years before the transfer in 2010.] In addition, as Mr Martin has died within seven years of the gift to his daughter on 1 June 2010 the gift is no longer a PET; it becomes chargeable.

The value of the transfer made on 9 August 2004 was £134,000. The only exemption available will be the annual exemption for the tax year in which the gift was made. This reduces the transfer to £131,000. The annual exemption for the previous tax year will not be available to Mr Martin as it will have been used on the gift made on 17 February 2004. There are no reliefs which are available to this transfer. The value of the transfer for IHT purposes is £131,000.

The value of the transfer made on 1 June 2010 was £70,000. One exemption available is the annual exemption for the tax year in which the gift is made, 2010/11. This means that the transfer is reduced by £3,000 to £67,000. The annual exemption for the previous tax year, 2009/10, is also available. The transfer is reduced by £3,000 to £64,000.

cont.

Mr Martin's cumulative total on 28 May 2011 is £195,000 (ie £131,000 + £64,000).

Step 5: Mr Martin has £130,000 of the NRB available to him (£325,000 – £195,000). The first £130,000 of the transfer is taxed at 0 per cent. The remainder £78,000 (£208,000 – £130,000) is taxed at 40 per cent. There is IHT of £31,200 for the trustees to pay.

Step 6: As the LCT was made within five to six years of his death taper relief is available. Only 20 per cent of the IHT is payable, 20 per cent of £31,200, giving an amount due of £12,480.

Step 7: IHT of £2,200 was paid at the time of the transfer. Credit is given for this payment. The amount of IHT payable by the trustee of the settlement due to Mr Martin's death within the seven-year period is £10,280 (£12,480 – £2,200).

Had the amount of the IHT paid by the trustees at the time of the transfer exceeded the liability to IHT due to Mr Martin's death within the seven-year period then the amount payable as the result of his death would be reduced to nil. There would be no repayment of the additional tax paid at the time of the transfer.

Exercise 3

Exercise 3 illustrates the effect of death on the charge to IHT when a transferor makes a PET, and where the transferor subsequently dies within seven years.

Following the steps:

Step 1: Calculate the value transferred. As the gift was cash the value transferred was £180,000.

Step 2: Identify any exemptions and deduct them from the value transferred. One exemption available is the annual exemption for the tax year in which the gift is made, 2008/9. This reduces the transfer to £177,000. As Vinny had made no lifetime gifts in the previous tax year, 2007/8, the annual exemption for that year is also available. This reduces the transfer to £174,000.

Step 3: Identify any reliefs and deduct them from the value transferred. There are no reliefs available as the gift is cash.

Step 4: Calculate the transferor's cumulative total at the date the gift is made and the amount of the NRB remaining. Going back seven years from 23 April 2008, the date of the PET which has become chargeable, Vinny made one PET, the gift of £175,000, to her daughter on 1 March 2005. Although this was a PET, it was made within seven years of Vinny's death and so is now taken into account when calculating her cumulative total. To calculate Vinny's cumulative total **steps 1** to **3** have to be applied to the gift made on 1 March 2005. The value transferred was £175,000. The exemptions available will be the annual exemption for the tax year in which the gift was made, 2004/5. This reduces the value transferred to £172,000. As she had made no transfers during the previous tax year, 2003/4, that year's annual exemption is also available, reducing the value transferred to £169,000. No other exemptions are available and there are no reliefs available. The value of the gift made on 1 March 2005 is £169,000. Vinny has £156,000 of the NRB available to her (£325,000 – £169,000).

Step 5: Calculate the IHT payable by applying the rate (or rates) of tax to the value of the transfer for IHT purposes. £156,000 of the transfer falls within the NRB. The remainder of the transfer (£18,000) will be taxed at 40 per cent. There will be IHT of £7,200 to pay on the transfer.

Step 6: As the gift was made three to four years before Vinny's death taper relief is available. Only 80 per cent of the tax is payable. The amount of tax to pay is £5,760.

Exercise 4

Exercise 4 illustrates the charge to IHT on a transferor's estate on death of the transferor, when the transferor has made transfers of value during the preceding seven years.

Following the steps:

Step 1: The value transferred is the value of the estate, £60,000.

Step 2: There are no exemptions available.

Step 3: There are no reliefs available.

Step 4: There are three transfers made in the seven years preceding James's death. James's cumulative total will equal the total of the value for IHT purposes of each of the three transfers.

The value of the transfer made on 1 April 2006 was £157,000. One exemption available will be the annual exemption for the tax year in which the gift was made, 2005/6. This will reduce the value of the gift to £154,000. The annual exemption for the previous year, 2004/5, is also available and will reduce the value of the gift to £151,000. There are no reliefs which are available to this transfer.

The value of the gift made on 25 June 2007 was £100,000. Again, one exemption available will be the annual exemption for the tax year in which the gift was made, 2007/8. This will reduce the value of the gift to £97,000. The annual exemption for the previous year, 2006/7, is also available and will reduce the value of the gift to £94,000. There are no reliefs which are available to this transfer.

The value of the gift made on 4 July 2008 was £45,000. Again one exemption available will be the annual exemption for the tax year in which the gift was made, 2008/9. This will reduce the value of the gift to £42,000. The annual exemption for the previous year, 2007/8, has already been used. There are no reliefs which are available to this transfer.

James's cumulative total on the date of his death is £287,000 (£151,000 + £94,000 + £42,000). James has £38,000 of the NRB available to him (£325,000 − £287,000).

Step 5: Calculate the IHT payable by applying the rate (or rates) of tax to the value of the estate (£60,000). The first £38,000 of his estate is taxed at 0 per cent. The remainder £22,000 (£60,000–£38,000) is taxed at 40 per cent. There is IHT of £8,800 for the trustees to pay.

online resource centre Visit the Online Resource Centre for more information and useful weblinks.
www.oxfordtextbooks.co.uk/orc/foundations11_12/

Corporation tax

8.1 Introduction: basic structure of corporation tax (CT)

This chapter deals with the charge to CT. In the chapter we explain in particular:

- the basic steps to calculate the liability to CT (**8.3** to **8.13**);
- loss relief (**8.5**); and
- the rates of tax (**8.8**).

Corporation tax (CT) is charged on the profits of companies resident in the UK by reference to their taxable profits arising in each accounting period.

A company is not charged to income tax or capital gains tax; it is charged to CT on its profits. 'Profits' means both its income profits and capital gains.

This difference between companies and individuals is not as fundamental as first appears. The income profits of a company liable to CT are calculated in the same way as an individual's statutory income is calculated for income tax purposes (see **5.4**). The capital gains of a company liable to CT are calculated on the basis of similar principles to those which apply to CGT for individuals (see **Chapter 6**, above although there are a number of differences).

8.2 Taxable profits

The company's taxable profits are the figure upon which it pays CT.

Taxable profits are calculated by deducting what are known as 'charges on income' from the company's total profits.

The company's total profits are the aggregate of its income profits and its capital gains for the relevant accounting period.

8.3 Calculation of income profits

A company's income profits liable to CT are calculated in a similar way as an individual's statutory income (see **5.4**). However, the company's income continues to be assessed to tax under the rules of set out in the Corporation Taxes Act 2009 (CTA 2009) and Corporation Taxes Act 2010 (CTA 2010). The assessments under the various Schedules are then added together to calculate the net income profits liable to CT (see **5.4.2**).

The major source of the company's income is likely to be from a trade of one sort or another. It is important not to ignore the fact that a company may have other sources of income apart from trading income. For example, the company may well have investments from which it derives rental income.

Another source of income may be bank and building society interest. There is one important difference in the tax treatment of interest in relation to companies. Whereas individuals receive the interest net of income tax at the 20 per cent rate, companies receive interest gross. There is therefore no need to gross up the interest received in calculating the company's taxable profits.

8.3.1 Trading profits

The rules for assessment are the same for both companies and sole traders/trading partnerships. The trading profits liable to CT are those profits actually arising in the chargeable accounting period.

The profits liable to tax are the chargeable receipts less deductible expenditure.

8.3.1.1 Chargeable receipts

Chargeable receipts are those which:

(a) *derive from the trading activity,*

The receipt must derive from the trading activity rather than from circumstances not directly connected with the trade, eg sales or compensation received for cancellation of a trading contract, but not a gratuitous sum received on termination of a trading relationship as a gesture of goodwill.

(b) *and which are of an income nature.*

Income receipts must be distinguished from capital receipts. This distinction is very important in the case of sole traders and partnerships in view of the fact that capital receipts attract CGT, not income tax. It is less so in the case of companies because both capital receipts and income receipts are charged to CT.

If an item is purchased for the purpose of resale at a profit, the proceeds of sale will be of an income nature, eg stock. On the other hand, if the asset is purchased for the benefit or use of the business on a more permanent basis as opposed to resale, then the receipt will be of a capital nature, eg purchase of machinery for a factory or office equipment.

8.3.1.2 Deductible expenditure

Expenditure is deductible if it is:

(a) *of an income nature,*

If expenditure is incurred for the purpose of enabling the company/trader to resell the item at a profit, then the expenditure will be of an income nature, eg the expense to a company in buying its stock but not its expense in buying its permanent assets such as office equipment.

Another test is whether the expenditure is recurrent rather than once-and-for-all expenditure. If recurrent, it will generally be of an income nature, eg overheads (electricity, rent, telephone, interest paid on an overdraft). On the other hand, once-and-for-all expenditure such as the purchase of fixed assets (eg cars, office equipment), will generally be of a capital nature and not deductible.

(b) *and if it has been incurred wholly and exclusively for the purposes of the trade.*

Expenditure is not 'wholly' incurred for the purposes of the trade if it is excessively large such that it partly represents a gift, eg excessive remuneration to a director.

Expenditure is not 'exclusively' incurred for the purposes of the trade if the motive for incurring the expenditure includes an element of personal enjoyment, eg a trip to the USA partly for business purposes but also for a holiday, will not be a deductible business expense.

8.3.2 Calculation of income profits

The steps required are:

(a) take total chargeable receipts (income);

(b) deduct expenditure which is allowable; and

(c) deduct capital allowances.

8.4 Capital allowances

Companies like sole traders/partnerships may be able to reduce their trading profits by claiming capital allowances on expenditure on machinery and plant and on industrial buildings. The capital allowances system works in a similar way for both companies and sole traders/partnerships (see **Chapter 10**, below).

8.5 Trading loss relief

It may well be that after deduction of trading expenses and capital allowances, that a trading loss is produced. If so, then loss relief may be available in respect of that loss. It may also be that although a trading profit has been made in the current accounting period, that there have been trading losses in previous accounting periods for which loss relief is available in this accounting period.

For companies, there are two types of loss relief available. If available, they are taken before charges on income are deducted.

8.5.1 Carry-across and carry-back relief for trading losses

A company's trading loss for an accounting period can be carried across to be deducted from profits (income or capital) from any source for the same accounting period (CTA 2010, s 37).

If the income profits or capital gains of the same accounting period are insufficient to absorb the loss (either wholly or in part), then the unrelieved loss can be carried back to be deducted from income or capital profits from the 12 months immediately preceding the accounting period in which the loss was made, provided that the company was then carrying on the same trade. This provision applies to losses incurred in any accounting period ending on or after 2 July 1997 and which require time apportionment in respect of an accounting period which starts before and ends after that date. In respect of losses arising prior to 2 July 1997 the carry-back may be effected and deduction made against income or capital profits during the previous three years, providing the company was carrying on the same trade. The loss must be set against the profits of the later accounting periods first. Again, if the carry-back would involve setting the losses against profits of an accounting period commencing earlier than a date three years previously the profits must be time-apportioned.

If carry-back relief is taken, then it will mean that the company will recover CT previously paid.

There is a temporary extension of carry-back relief for accounting periods ending between 24 November 2008 and 23 November 2010. This allows trading losses to be carried back to the preceding three-year period. There are conditions about how the extended relief is applied and caps on how much can be carried back. Further consideration of the extended relief is outside the scope of this book.

EXAMPLE 1

A company makes its accounts up to 31 December in each year. In the year ended 31 December 2010 it makes a profit of £80,000 and chargeable gains of £10,000. In the year ended 31 December 2011 it makes a trading loss of £160,000 and chargeable gains of £60,000. It only carries on the same trade during each period.

Its profits chargeable to corporation tax will be:

	£
Year ended 31 December 2011	
Trading profit for year	Nil
Chargeable gains	60,000
Less: carry-across relief	(60,000)
Taxable profit for year	Nil

Unrelieved losses to carry back of £160,000 − £60,000 = £100,000

	£
Year ended 31 December 2010	
Trading profit for year	80,000
Chargeable gains	10,000
	90,000
Less: carry-back relief	(90,000)
Taxable profit for year	Nil

Unrelieved losses to carry forward of £100,000 − £90,000 = £10,000

8.5.2 Carry-forward relief for trading losses

Alternatively, or to the extent that a loss is not relevant under s 37 above, a company's trading loss for an accounting period can be carried forward to be deducted from the first subsequent profits which that trade produces (CTA 2010, s 45).

This relief is not available against non-trading income or against capital gains. Further, if the company has two or more trades, then the relief can only be taken against the profits of the trade which produced the loss.

8.6 Calculation of chargeable gains

8.6.1 Normal CGT principles apply

A charge to CT may arise when the company disposes of a chargeable asset in the accounting period which results in a chargeable gain.

The chargeable gain is calculated in the same way as for individuals, but as the company is not an individual, it is not entitled to an annual exemption. When calculating the gain, however, an allowance (indexation allowance) is made to some elements of the allowable expenditure. This allowance is made to remove from the charge to CT any increase in the value of the asset which is solely due to the effects of inflation since the asset was acquired or the expense incurred. The effect of inflation on the value of the asset, or expenditure incurred, is calculated by using the retail prices index (RPI) which is published monthly by the government.

The only capital gains reliefs to which the company may be entitled are:

(a) capital loss relief; and

(b) roll-over relief on replacement of qualifying business assets.

8.6.1.1 Capital loss relief

If a company makes a capital loss, then it may be set off against capital gains of the same accounting period. If the loss is unrelieved, either wholly or in part, then the loss may be carried forward and set off against capital gains of later accounting periods.

8.6.1.2 Roll-over relief on replacement of qualifying business assets

This relief is also available to sole traders and partnerships. See **Chapter 10**, below, for further details.

If a company disposes of a qualifying business asset used for the purposes of its trade and reinvests all of the proceeds in the purchase of another qualifying business asset, then the gain is not taxable at the time of the disposal but is deducted from the acquisition cost of the new asset (see **6.8.6**).

The main types of qualifying business asset are:

(a) land and buildings;

(b) fixed plant and machinery;

(c) goodwill; and

(d) ships, aircraft, and hovercraft.

Both the old and the new assets must be qualifying business assets. The new assets must have either been acquired within one year before or three years after the disposal of the old asset.

The relief operates by deferring the payment of tax on the gain arising from the disposal. However, the charge to tax is not escaped altogether. The gain arising on the disposal is deducted from the acquisition cost of the new asset. When the new asset is disposed of, unless roll-over relief is further available to defer the payment of tax, the company will be charged to tax on the gain arising from the disposals of both the old and new assets.

There are special rules for the tax treatment of intangible assets such as goodwill. This form of roll-over relief is beyond the scope of this book.

8.7 Charges on income

A company's income profits and capital gains for an accounting period will be added together to produce the company's total profits for the accounting period. Charges on income are then deducted to arrive at the taxable profits, which is the figure upon which CT is paid.

Note that charges on income can be deducted from income profits from all sources and from capital gains, whereas trading expenses can only be deducted from trading receipts.

Therefore, it is important not to confuse those expenses which qualify as charges on income and those which are merely trading expenses. See also **Chapter 10**.

The main charge on income is certain charitable donations.

Charges on income are payable by the company subject to deduction of income tax at the basic rate. This tax is paid to the Inland Revenue and the recipient of the payments will be assessed on the grossed up amount but will receive a tax credit for the income tax already paid. Further consideration of charges on income is outside of the scope of this book.

8.8 Rates of tax

CT rates are fixed by reference to financial years, being the period from 1 April in one year to the following 31 March. This is marginally different from the income tax year which runs from 6 April to 5 April in the following year.

It is important to appreciate that CT is calculated by reference to each accounting period of the company. An accounting period is normally 12 months ending with the company's accounting date, ie the date to which the company's accounts are made up.

In view of the fact that rates of tax are fixed for financial years, if the accounting period does not match the financial year and the rates of tax change, then in order to calculate the company's CT liability, the profits of the accounting period must be apportioned on a time basis between the two financial years.

EXAMPLE 2

A company makes up its accounts to 31 December in each year.

Its profits for the accounting period ending 31 December 1999 are £1,650,000.

The full rate of CT for the financial year 1998 (ie 1 April 1998 to 31 March 1999) is 31 per cent but the rate changes to 30 per cent for the financial year 1999. CT will be payable as follows:

	£
3/12 ´ £1,650,000 ´ 31%	127,875
9/12 ´ £1,650,000 ´ 30%	371,250
	499,125

Rates of tax for the financial year 2011 (ie 1 April 2011 to 31 March 2012) are:

	£	%
Small companies' rate	0–300,000	20
Effective marginal rate	300,001–1,500,000	27.5
Main rate	Over 1,500,000	26

8.8.1 Main rate

This applies where the company's profits are equal to or exceed the upper limit of £1,500,000. The standard rate applies to all of the taxable profits.

EXAMPLE 3

Company has taxable profits of £2,000,000.

Taxable profits exceed upper limit.

All £2,000,000 taxed at main rate (26%) = £520,000.

8.8.2 Small companies' rate

This will apply to all of the taxable profits if they do not exceed the lower limit of £300,000.

EXAMPLE 4

Company has taxable profits of £250,000.
  Taxable profits below £300,000.
    All profits taxed at small companies' rate (20 per cent) = £50,000

8.8.3 Marginal rate

The marginal rate applies if the company's profits fall between the relevant limits namely, £300,001 and £1,500,000.

For these companies, there is an effective marginal rate of 27.5 per cent, the profits up to the lower limit being taxed at the small companies' rate and the profits above that amount being taxed at the upper marginal rate. For the financial year 2011, the first £300,000 will be taxed at 20 per cent and the balance up to £1,500,000 at 27.5 per cent.

The reason why the marginal rate is higher than the standard rate is because the first band (£300,000) is taxed at only 20 per cent. Therefore, it is necessary to apply to the balance of the profits a rate higher than the standard rate so that the combined average of both rates will progressively approach the standard rate as the profits reach the upper limit.

EXAMPLE 5

Company has taxable profits of £1,000,000.
  Taxable profits between lower and upper limits.
  First £300,000 taxed at small companies' rate (20 per cent) and balance at the effective marginal rate (27.5 per cent).

	£
CT = £300,000 × 20%	60,000
£700,000 × 27.5%	192,500
	252,500

8.9 Distributions of profit

A distribution of profit will normally be by way of dividend but if a company buys back or redeems its shares for a price over and above the original allotment price, it may also be treated as making a distribution of profit of the excess over and above the allotment price, which will then be treated as if it was a dividend.

Individual shareholders are entitled to some reduction in the rate of tax payable on dividends received, to reflect the fact that those dividends are being paid by the company out of profits which have themselves already been subject to CT. The dividends will be taxed at a rate of 10 per cent, 32.5 per cent or 42.5 per cent depending on the individual's income tax status. (see **5.5**). Shareholders receiving dividends who are themselves companies no longer have the benefit of any reduction in the rate of CT payable on their own profits.

8.10 Calculating the liability

The steps to be followed are:

(a) Calculate income profits = trading receipts less trading expenses.

(b) Calculate chargeable capital gains.

(c) Calculate taxable profits = Total profits (income profits + chargeable gains) less charges on income.

(d) Apply the appropriate rate or rates of tax.

(See the example at **8.14**.)

8.11 Payment of CT

8.11.1 CT

CT is normally payable nine months after the end of the company's accounting period to which it relates. A 'pay and file' system applies. Under this system, companies make their own assessments of their liability to CT. Companies are required to complete a CT return in which the company calculates its own CT liability. The return must be delivered to the Revenue within 12 months of the end of the period to which it relates. There are graduated penalties for late filing of returns. A new self-assessment regime was put into effect for accounting periods ending on or after 1 July 1999. Companies with taxable profits exceeding £1.5 million now have to pay CT quarterly.

8.11.2 Interest

Unpaid or underpaid CT which is overdue attracts an interest charge payable in addition. This interest cannot be treated as a charge on income.

8.12 Close companies

A close company is a company which is controlled by five or fewer 'participators' (shareholders) or by 'participators' (however many) who are also directors.

'Control' effectively means a majority shareholding. Remember that in assessing control, the rights of 'associates' must be added to the rights of the participator. 'Associates' include, amongst others, spouse, parents, remoter forebears, children, remoter issue, brothers and sisters.

Nearly all private companies will be close companies. Indeed, if a company has nine or fewer shareholders, then it will always be a close company, whatever the respective shareholdings, since it must be under the control of some five of them, even if none of them are related to each other.

Close companies are subject to special tax rules which are designed to prevent their use as a vehicle for tax avoidance.

8.12.1 Loans to participators or their associates

When a close company makes a loan to a participator or his associate, a charge to CT is imposed. For the financial year 2011, the company must pay HMRC CT equivalent to 25 per cent of the amount of the loan.

The charge will only be refunded if and when the loan is repaid, written off or released.

In the recipient's hands, the loan is not taxable so long as it remains a loan. If and when the loan is written off, it is treated as if a dividend in the recipient's hands, ie the CT paid by the company is treated as satisfying the recipient's income tax liability save in so far as the recipient is a higher rate taxpayer. A shareholder who is not even liable for starting rate income tax is not able to make a repayment claim to HMRC to recover the tax paid by the company.

8.12.2 Exceptions

The charge to CT does not arise if:

(a) the loan is made in the ordinary course of a money lending business, eg a finance company making a loan on commercial terms to someone who just happens to hold shares in the company; or

(b) if the loan (together with any outstanding loan to the same person), does not exceed £15,000, the borrower works full time for the company and owns less than 5 per cent of the shares.

8.12.3 Gifts and other transfers of value by close companies

Inheritance tax is generally only charged on transfers of value made by individuals. However, if a close company makes a transfer of value, then this is deemed to be a gift by all the participators in the company in proportion to their shareholdings.

Each shareholder is then treated as having personally made a gift of the appropriate fraction of the company's gift. Unless covered by a relief and/or exemption available to that individual, the gifts will be taxed as though they were chargeable transfers. The rules relating to potentially exempt transfers (see **Chapter 7** above), meaning that there would be no liability to inheritance tax if the donor survives for a full seven years and with a sliding scale of liability for lesser periods, do not apply. Therefore, inheritance tax becomes payable immediately.

The company is primarily liable for the IHT due. This is one exception to the general rule that companies are not liable for inheritance tax.

This provision does not apply if the transfer is a dividend or a benefit in kind provided to a director or employee of the company. The aim of the legislation is to ensure that gifts or other transfers of value do not escape tax. However, dividends are already assessed to tax and benefits in kind to directors and employees under IT(EP)A.

8.12.4 Provision of benefits in kind to a participator or associate

If close companies provide benefits in kind (eg living accommodation) for a participator or his associate, then the company will be treated as making a distribution. The cost to the company of providing that benefit in kind will be treated for tax purposes as though it were a dividend. The recipient will be assessed to income tax under.

This provision will not apply, however, if the participator or his associate is a director or employee of the company.

Again, the aim of the legislation is to ensure that benefits in kind are assessed to tax. If the participator or associate is a director or employee of the company, then the benefit is already assessed to tax under IT(EP)A.

8.12.5 Close investment holding companies: rates of tax

A 'close investment holding company' is a company which exists purely for the purposes of holding investments. If a company is a 'close investment holding company', then the small companies' rate of CT will not be available and the company will pay CT on all of its taxable profits at the standard rate.

This only applies to close companies which exist purely for the purposes of holding investments. Trading companies or companies which deal in land, shares, or securities and companies carrying on investment on a commercial basis or group holding companies which hold investments by way of shares in their own subsidiary companies are not affected by these anti-avoidance provisions.

8.13 Steps to calculate CT, including chargeable gains

1. Calculate income profits for CT purposes as follows.
    1.1 Calculate income profits from main activity.
    1.2 Deduct capital allowances and/or apply any balancing charges or allowances.
    1.3 Deduct any available trading losses.
    1.4 Add any income from other sources.
2. Add together all the chargeable gains for the accounting period calculated as follows:
    2.1 Take the disposal consideration.
    2.2 Deduct allowable expenditure being:
    - acquisition cost;
    - costs of acquisition;
    - subsequent improvements;
    - indexation allowance on the above three items only; and
    - costs of disposal.
    2.3 Deduct any capital losses for the accounting period.
    2.4 Deduct any capital losses carried forward (if utilised).
    2.5 Deduct any available trading losses.
3. Deduct charges on income from the aggregate of 1 + 2.
4. Apply the appropriate rate or rates of tax.

8.14 Example of CT calculations

EXAMPLE 6

Moorvale Ltd has five shareholders. It has profits and losses as follows:

Accounting period ended	Trading profits £	Other income profits £	Capital gains £
31 March 2010	(100,000)	10,000	Nil
31 March 2011	50,000	10,000	(20,000)
31 March 2012	100,000	10,000	30,000

NB: figures in brackets denote income/capital losses.

Moorvale Ltd has no charges on income in any accounting period.

In 2011/12, Moorvale Ltd:

Declares a dividend of £5,000 (£1,000 paid to each of the five shareholders).

Makes a loan of £10,000 to a shareholder, Sally Barnett, who is a part-time employee.

Claims capital allowances of £20,000.

Calculate Moorvale Ltd's corporation tax liability for each of these years. Assume for this example that CT rates remain the same as in 2011/12 for all three years.

Year ended 31 March 2010:

Taxable profits:	£
Trading income	Nil
Other income	10,000
Capital gains	Nil
	10,000
Less trading losses carried across	(10,000)
	Nil

No corporation tax liability.

Unrelieved trading losses of £90,000 to carry forward.

Year ended 31 March 2011:

Taxable profits:		
Trading income	50,000	£
Less trading loss b/f*	(50,000)	Nil
Other income		10,000
Capital gains		Nil
		10,000

Corporation tax *due* = £2,000 (£10,000 × 20%)

(Capital losses cannot be set against income. Capital loss of £20,000 will be carried forward together with the unrelieved trading loss of £40,000.)

* Trading losses can only be brought forward against income profits of the same trade and not other income profits.

Year ended 31 March 2012:

Total profits:

	£	£
Trading income	100,000	
Less capital allowances	(20,000)	
	80,000	
Less trading losses b/f	(40,000)	40,000
Other income		10,000

			50,000
Capital gains		30,000	
Less capital losses b/f		(20,000)	10,000
			60,000

Taxable profits:
Taxable profits are less than £300,000 so all profits taxed at 20 per cent.
Corporation tax *due* = £12,000 (£60,000 × 20%)
CT paid on *loan** = £2,500 (25% × £10,000)

  * Moorvale Ltd is a close company and so must pay CT on the loan in addition to CT on the taxable profits.

8.15 Conclusion: checkpoints

You should now be able to:

- calculate a company's liability to CT (**8.3** to **8.13**); and
- identify how to apply loss relief (**8.5**).

Visit the Online Resource Centre for more information and useful weblinks.
www.oxfordtextbooks.co.uk/orc/foundations11_12/

9

Value added tax

9.1 Introduction to value added tax (VAT)

This chapter deals with the charge to VAT. In the chapter we explain in particular:

- the classification of different types of supply of VAT (**9.4**);
- input and output tax (**9.5**);
- requirements for registration for VAT purposes (**9.7**); and
- how VAT is calculated.

Value added tax (VAT) is a tax levied on supplies of goods and services made by a supplier who is or is required to be registered for VAT purposes. It was introduced into the UK in 1973. It is also applied by all other EC Member States under various names, although the rates of tax and the types of goods and services to which it applies do vary between member states.

It is payable on taxable supplies of goods or services made in the UK by a 'taxable person' in the course of business. It is also charged on imports of goods into the UK from outside the EC and on goods and some services obtained elsewhere in the EC.

9.2 Sources of VAT law

The principal charging statute is the Value Added Tax Act 1994 (VATA 1994). Detailed provisions relating to implementation of the Act are contained in a large number of statutory instruments. Many of these deal with the effect of VAT in very specific situations. Because of the complexity of the VAT legislation, the practitioner faced with a VAT issue will have to research all of this legislation to determine the application of VAT in particular circumstances. This book only deals with the basic principles of VAT which are of general application.

Additionally, HM Revenue & Customs (HMRC) issue VAT Notices. Whilst they lack legal force, they express the views of HMRC on the law as it applies to specific transactions. These can be a valuable source of information.

Like income tax and capital gains tax, VAT is subject to a number of extra-statutory concessions where HMRC allow relief from VAT on an extra-statutory basis.

EC Directives 67/227 and 77/338 are also relevant sources, VAT having been introduced in 1973 in order to bring UK law in line with European Community law.

9.3 Administration of VAT

VAT was until recently administered by HM Commissioners of Customs & Excise and not by the Inland Revenue. However, in April 2005 the Inland Revenue and HM Customs and Excise amalgamated into HM Revenue & Customs.

The Customs arm of HMRC operates from a headquarters in London with a central accounts and computer centre in Southend and a number of local VAT offices throughout the country.

Apart from the submission of periodic returns of VAT to the central office in Southend, most of a VAT-registered trader's dealings will be with the local offices who deal with matters concerning registration and compliance with VAT legislation. They also have teams of officers who carry out what are known as 'control visits', inspecting the records of businesses to ensure they are properly recording all transactions and implementing VAT correctly.

In addition, there are teams of specialists who carry out investigations work where there are believed to be more serious breaches of VAT legislation. These officers often carry out lengthy and detailed investigation and surveillance work before using their powers to seize relevant records.

Appeal from a decision of the HMRC is made to an independent VAT Tribunal. Appeals from decisions of the VAT Tribunals can be made to the High Court or direct to the Court of Appeal with the consent of the Tribunal.

9.4 Classifications of supply

In order to understand the operation of VAT it is important to recognise that goods and services fall into four distinct categories:

(a) Standard rated: these are subject to VAT at the standard rate of 20 per cent.

(b) Lower rated: these are subject to VAT at lower rate of 5 per cent.

(c) Zero rated: these are technically subject to VAT but at a rate of 0 per cent.

(d) Exempt: these are not subject to VAT at all.

9.4.1 Standard-rated supplies

Standard rated supplies comprise anything which does not fall within one of the other categories.

9.4.2 Lower-rated supplies

Supplies of domestic heat and power attract VAT at a lower rate, currently 5 per cent. However, the lower rate does not apply to supplies for non-domestic purposes. Since 1 July 2006 the lower rate also applies to contraceptive products bought over the counter.

9.4.3 Zero-rated supplies

Full details of supplies which will be zero rated for VAT purposes are contained in Sch 8 to VATA 1994. Zero-rated supplies include the following:

(a) food, other than non-essential food (eg chocolate) and food supplied in the course of catering (eg restaurant food or hot take-away food);

(b) water and sewerage services;

(c) construction of residential buildings, but generally not alterations or repairs to existing buildings;

(d) books and newspapers;

(e) exports made outside the EC;

(f) public transport; and

(g) children's clothing and footwear and supplies of protective safety helmets and boots.

9.4.4 Exempt supplies

Full details of supplies which will be exempt from VAT are contained in Sch 9 to VATA 1994. The principal categories of exempt supplies are as follows:

(a) supplies of land (including buildings) or of any interest in land or any rights over land (this does not apply to certain matters such as car parking rights or the letting of holiday cottages and it is also possible to waive the exemption in respect of supplies of land and so to elect to charge VAT);

(b) provision of insurance or reinsurance;

(c) postal services provided by the Post Office;

(d) betting, gaming, and lotteries (which are usually subject to betting licence duty);

(e) finance (which covers a wide range of transactions such as banking, money-lending and the sale and purchase of shares);

(f) education and vocational training provided by non-profit-making establishments;

(g) provision of health services;

(h) burial and cremation;

(i) trade unions and similar bodies providing they are non-profit making;

(j) sports competitions and physical education (basically, provided the organisation is non-profit making and returns all fees as prizes);

(k) certain works of art; and

(l) one-off fundraising events by charities and other similar bodies.

9.5 Inputs and outputs

The idea underlying VAT is that it is a tax on the value added to goods at each stage in the production process or on the whole value of services provided. In other words, a VAT-registered business will be able to reclaim the VAT paid on the goods or services which it purchases ('input tax') and will only pay VAT on the value of the goods it sells ('output tax').

The VAT which it actually pays to the Customs & Excise will be as follows:

Output tax minus input tax = tax payable.

There are certain restrictions on the reclaiming of input tax, which is not recoverable in respect of the following:

(a) motor vehicles unless they are used exclusively for business purposes. If there is any element of non-business use, no VAT is recoverable (however, if the vehicle is leased then 50 per cent of the VAT on the leasing payment can be recovered if there is non-business use);

(b) business entertainment or hospitality; and

(c) certain fittings acquired by a builder for a new dwelling.

EXAMPLE 1

A VAT-registered business purchases standard-rated goods and services of £174,000 plus VAT and zero-rated supplies of £2,000. It makes sales of £620,000, all of which are standard-rated items. The VAT which it pays over to Customs & Excise at the end of the relevant VAT period will be:

		£
Output tax	£620,000 × 20%	124,000
Less: Input tax	£174,000 × 20% = £34,800	
	£2,000 × 0% = £0	(34,800)
Net VAT payable		89,200

9.6 The charge to VAT

VAT is charged on the taxable supply of goods and services by a taxable person (see **9.7.1**) in the course of a business carried on by him. The amount on which the tax is charged is the value of the supply.

9.6.1 Taxable supply

All supplies of goods and services are taxable supplies except those supplies which are exempt supplies.

9.6.2 Supply of goods

A supply of goods takes place in any transaction where the whole property in the goods is transferred (eg sale or even a gift of goods exceeding £50 in value, such as a business giving a Christmas hamper to a customer) or where the agreement expressly contemplates that the property will be transferred, as in the case of a hire-purchase agreement. In addition to goods in the more obvious sense, the definition includes the supply of any form of power, heat, refrigeration, or ventilation or the grant, assignment, or surrender of a major interest in land (ie the freehold or a lease for a term exceeding 21 years).

9.6.3 Supply of services

Generally any supply which is not a supply of goods (as defined above) and which is done for consideration, is a supply of services (eg solicitors' services). However, gifts of services are not considered to be a supply.

9.6.4 Taxable person

A taxable person is any individual, partnership, or company making or intending to make taxable supplies and registered, or required to be registered, for VAT.

Note that taxable person includes any person who ought to be registered but has failed to take the necessary steps to register.

9.6.5 Business

'Business' is a wide term which covers any trade, profession, or vocation. It includes the disposal of a business or any of its assets. It would include, for example, a supply of services by a firm of solicitors who are registered for VAT. If that firm were then to sell their old office computers, they would also have to charge VAT on the sale price because there would be a sale of business assets, although not a common transaction for that particular business.

9.6.6 Value of supply

VAT is charged on the value of the supply of goods or services. This is what the goods or services would cost were VAT not charged. Often, the value of the supply is given as part of the price. For example, a service may be advertised as costing £100 plus VAT, £100 being the value of the supply.

On the other hand, the price of the supply quoted may be the VAT-inclusive amount. If so, then the value of the supply will be the total price less the VAT element. To find this amount multiply the gross amount by the appropriate VAT fraction, namely 1/6 for the standard rate of 20 per cent. For instance, if the total price is £1,000 then £1,000 × 1/6 = VAT element (£166.67).

A price is always deemed to include VAT, unless the contrary is stated.

If the supply is one of goods and is not for a consideration (ie a gift), then the value of the supply is the market value of the gift.

9.7 Registration

9.7.1 Taxable persons

VAT is only charged on persons who are registered or required to be registered for VAT. It is the person (ie individual, company, or partnership) and not the business who is required to register for VAT. That person's VAT registration will cover all his business activities and he is taxable on all his taxable supplies, however diverse his different business interests may be. Where, however, there are separate business entities, separate registrations will be allowed. For example, a person trading as a sole trader is separate from a limited company of which he is a director and majority shareholder, or from a partnership in which he is a partner with others.

In the case of groups of companies, a group VAT registration is normally effected so that one of the companies is designated as the 'representative member' to be responsible for all VAT returns and payments for the whole group, with the other companies remaining jointly and severally liable for payment. Individual companies which have several separate trading divisions are able to seek separate registration for each trading division.

9.7.2 Compulsory registration

Under Sch 1 to VATA 1994, a person is required to register for VAT at the end of any month if the value of his taxable supplies (including zero rated supplies) in the past 12 months has exceeded a certain threshold. Further, a person is required to register for VAT at any time if there are reasonable grounds for believing that the value of his taxable supplies in the next 30 days will exceed that threshold.

The registration threshold from 1 April 2011 is £73,000. If, however the annual limit has been exceeded but HMRC is satisfied that taxable turnover will not exceed £71,000 in the following 12 months, registration will not be needed.

Registration is effected by submitting Form VAT1 to HMRC. In the case of registration of a partnership Form VAT2 must also be submitted, giving details of all of the partners. On registration, the taxable person is issued with a VAT registration number.

9.7.3 Voluntary registration

It is possible for persons who make or intend to make taxable supplies of less than the current compulsory registration threshold to register for VAT voluntarily.

9.7.3.1 Advantages of voluntary registration

The main reason why a business may wish to register for VAT voluntarily is to enable it to reclaim VAT charged to it by its suppliers. If the business is not registered, then it is not able to do so.

9.7.3.2 Disadvantages of voluntary registration

When deciding whether to register voluntarily, the business must consider the disadvantage that VAT may affect its selling position in that it will have to charge its customers higher prices including the VAT element. This will not be a problem if the customers are themselves exclusively VAT–registered persons as all VAT charged can be reclaimed by them. It will also not be a problem if the business makes predominantly zero-rated supplies. However, it may affect the selling position of a small business which is not currently VAT registered and is able to undercut its larger rivals who are obliged to charge VAT, where the customers are not themselves VAT registered or are otherwise unable to reclaim the input VAT by virtue of making only exempt supplies (see **9.7.3.3**).

The business should also not ignore the additional administrative costs associated with accounting for VAT.

9.7.3.3 Exempt and zero-rated suppliers

It is not possible for a person who makes or intends to make only exempt supplies to register for VAT voluntarily. That person falls wholly outside the VAT net. He makes no charge to customers for VAT but at the same time, because he is unable to register for VAT, cannot reclaim the VAT charged by suppliers.

Therefore, although zero-rated and exempt suppliers are similar in that the customer does not actually pay any VAT, the distinction is important in the sense that a zero–rated supplier can register for VAT and reclaim VAT charged on his supplies. An exempt supplier is not able to do so.

9.8 Rates of tax and tax points

9.8.1 The tax point

The tax on a supply of goods and services becomes chargeable at a definite time which is known as the 'tax point'. The rate of tax charged is the rate applicable at the date of the tax point and the tax must be accounted for in the tax period into which the tax point falls (see **9.9.1**).

So far as goods are concerned, the basic rule is that the tax point is the date on which the goods are removed to give effect to the transaction (ie the date of despatch). If goods are not actually removed (eg machines built on site), the tax point is the date on which they are made available to the customer.

In the case of services, the basic rule is that the tax point is the date on which the services are performed. In practice, this means the date on which the services are completed.

However, the basic tax point can be altered by invoicing and payment arrangements:

(a) If the supplier issues a tax invoice or receives payment before the basic tax point, then the tax point can be brought forward to the date of the invoice or date of payment (whichever is earlier).

(b) If the supplier issues a tax invoice within 14 days after the basic tax point, then the tax point can be delayed to the date when the invoice is issued.

9.8.2 Rates of tax

For the financial year 2011/12 (ie 1 April 2011 to 31 March 2012), the rates of tax are as follows:

Standard rate:	20 per cent
Lower rate:	5 per cent
Zero rate:	0 per cent

9.9 Accounting for VAT

9.9.1 Tax invoices

When a registered person supplies goods or services taxable at a positive rate (ie any supply other than one which is zero rated) to another taxable person, he must, within 30 days of the time of the supply, issue a 'tax invoice' to that person obtaining certain specified details. The tax invoice is an important document, since it is the principal evidence available to the customer to support a claim for the reclaim of input tax. The customer must keep the original, and the supplier must retain a copy.

It is not necessary to issue a tax invoice for zero-rated supplies (except if the customer is in another EC member state), or for supplies to customers who are not taxable persons, although such persons may request one.

The tax invoice must clearly show the following:

(a) a number identifying the tax invoice;

(b) date of supply, ie the tax point;

(c) supplier's name, address, and VAT registration number;

(d) customer's name (or trading name) and address;

(e) type of supply;

(f) description sufficient to identify the goods or services supplied;

(g) for each description, the quantity of goods or the extent of the services, the rate of tax, and amount payable (excluding VAT);

(h) rate of any cash discount offered;

(i) the total tax chargeable at each rate, with the rate of tax to which it relates; and

(j) the total amount of tax chargeable.

If there is more than one date on a tax invoice, the tax point must be clearly identified.

9.9.2 VAT records

The taxable person must record in books of account all output tax charged by him and all input tax reclaimed by him in each three-month period (known as the 'tax period').

There are special rules which allow businesses to deal with their VAT accounting on a monthly basis if they so wish.

9.9.3 Due date for payment

Within one month of the end of the tax period, the taxable person must submit a VAT return in form VAT 100 for the tax period together with a cheque for the VAT due.

9.9.4 The amount of VAT payable

The amount of VAT payable is the VAT charged on all supplies of goods and services made in the course of the business (output tax) less any VAT paid in the course of the business (input tax).

Where input tax exceeds output tax, a repayment of the difference will be made by HMRC.

When a person makes both exempt and taxable supplies, special rules provide that only part of his input tax will be deductible from the output tax charged on the taxable supplies.

There are also special rules concerning self-supply of goods and services. For example, if an insurance company (exempt and therefore unable to recover input tax) also has its own printing business to supply it with printing upon which it would pay VAT if it purchased the supplies elsewhere, there will be a potential charge to VAT on the supply made.

EXAMPLE 2 (periodic VAT calculation)

Hallam Wholesale Ltd operate a cash-and-carry warehouse, selling both food and household goods. They are a VAT-registered supplier. Their sales in the last VAT quarter amounted to £2,500,000 net of VAT of which £1,500,000 was zero rated and £1,000,000 was standard rated. Their purchases in this period were zero-rated food of £1,100,000 and other standard-rated goods for resale of £700,000 plus VAT. In addition they have, in the same period, received invoices for the following sums plus VAT where appropriate, from VAT-registered suppliers:

	£
Accountants	15,000
Solicitors	1,500
Telephone	1,000
Electricity	2,000
Water charges	2,400
Buffet lunch for customers	1,400

The VAT payment which should accompany Hallam Wholesale's VAT return in respect of this period will be calculated as follows:

Output tax:

	£
£1,500.000 × 0%	0.00
£1,000.000 × 20%	200,000.00

		£	
Less Input tax:			
Goods £1,100,000 × 0%		0.00	
Goods £700,000 × 20%		140,000.00	
Accountants £15,000 × 20%		3,000.00	
Solicitors £1,500 × 20%		300.00	
Telephone £1,000 × 20%		200.00	
Electricity £2,000 × 20%		400.00	
Water £2,400 × 0%		0.00	(143,900.00)
Net VAT due			56,100.00

Electricity is for non-domestic use and is charged at standard rate.
Water charges are zero rated.
Buffet lunch is entertainment and so input tax is not allowable.
The return must be submitted and VAT paid within 30 days of the end of the period.

9.10 Penalties

A person who fails to comply with the VAT legislation is liable to a range of criminal and civil penalties in addition to being required to pay any unpaid tax with interest. The main penalties are as follows.

9.10.1 Late notification of liability to register

Where a person who is liable to register for VAT fails to do so, he will be liable to a civil penalty of the greater of £50 and a percentage of the net tax for which he was liable during the period when he should have been registered (in addition to the tax itself plus interest). This percentage rises according to the period of delay and is:

- 5 per cent for a period of up to 9 months;
- 10 per cent between 9 and 18 months; and
- 15 per cent where the failure lasts more than 18 months.

9.10.2 Default surcharge

If a registered person submits a return late or submits the return on time but fails to pay the VAT on time, HMRC can apply a default surcharge which can range from £30 to 15 per cent of the tax due. The detailed provisions are outside the scope of this book.

9.10.3 Serious misdeclaration penalty

Serious misdeclaration penalty applies when the VAT liability is understated on the return or where HMRC assess less than the total tax which should be due and the taxpayer fails to point this out to them within 30 days. In order to attract the penalty, the underdeclaration or overstatement of repayment must exceed the lesser of £1,000,000 or 30 per cent of the relevant amount for the period. The rate of penalty is 15 per cent of the tax underdeclared.

9.10.4 Persistent misdeclaration penalty

Persistent misdeclaration penalty is at the rate of 15 per cent of the tax due and relates to circumstances where there is a material inaccuracy, namely an underdeclaration which exceeds the greater of £500,000 and 10 per cent of the gross amount of VAT for the period. Again the detailed rules are outside the scope of this book.

9.10.5 Interest on VAT unpaid

Interest is also payable on VAT which is unpaid, the rate currently being 2.5 per cent in excess of the average of bank base lending rates. This is not treated as an allowable expense for the purposes of calculating liability of the business to income tax or to corporation tax.

9.11 Conclusion: checkpoints

You should now be able to:

- classify different types of supply (**9.4**);
- distinguish between input and output tax (**9.5**);
- recognise when registration is required for VAT purposes (**9.7**); and
- make a simple VAT calculation.

 Visit the Online Resource Centre for more information and useful weblinks.
www.oxfordtextbooks.co.uk/orc/foundations11_12/

10

Taxation of sole proprietors and partnerships

10.1 Introduction to the taxation of sole proprietors and partnerships

This chapter deals with the taxation of sole proprietors and partnerships. In the chapter we explain in particular:

- the opening-year rules (**10.5**);
- the closing-year rules (**10.6**);
- overlap relief (**10.7**);
- changes in membership of a partnership (**10.8**);
- capital allowances including balancing allowances and balancing charges (**10.9**); and
- loss relief (**10.11**).

Taxable income is calculated by deducting reliefs and personal allowances from the taxpayer's statutory income. The taxpayer's total income is the total of his income computed according to Part 9 of the Income Tax (Trading and Other Income) Act 2005 (IT-TOIA) (see **Chapter 5**).

It is assumed for the purposes of this chapter that the sole trader or partnership has no other income apart from their trade or vocation income. When calculating the income tax liability of a sole trader or partner, it is important to appreciate the fact that the sole trader/partner may well have other sources of income apart from income from the business/partnership. For example, the sole trader/partner may receive bank or building society interest which is assessed to tax under the rules of ITTOIA. That income must also be included in the statutory income calculation.

Details of the charges on income and personal reliefs to which the sole trader/partner may be entitled, and more detail on the calculation of income tax, are contained in **Chapter 5**.

10.2 Income tax liability of partnerships

10.2.1 Liability

Each individual partner is required to include his share of the partnership income in his own tax return and will be separately assessed for income tax on that partnership income on an individual basis. The partners are not jointly and severally liable for the tax due in respect of the partnership income. An individual partner is liable for the tax due on his share of the partnership income only.

10.2.2 Calculation of trading profits

The rules for assessing a sole trader/partnership's trading profits liable to income tax under ITTOIA are, briefly, that the trading profits are calculated by deducting deductible expenditure and capital allowances from the sole trader's/partnership's chargeable receipts.

10.2.2.1 Chargeable receipts

Chargeable receipts are those which:

(a) *derive from the trading activity*,

The receipt must derive from the trading activity rather than from circumstances not directly connected with the trade, eg sales, or compensation received from cancellation of an order, would be a trading receipt, but this would not apply to a gratuitous sum received on termination of a trading relationship as a gesture of goodwill.

(b) *are of an income nature.*

Income receipts must be distinguished from capital receipts. This distinction is very important in the case of sole traders and partnerships because capital receipts attract capital gains tax (CGT) and not income tax. If an item is purchased for resale at a profit, the proceeds of sale will be an income receipt, eg purchase and sale of stock by an antique dealer. If the asset is purchased for the benefit or use of the business on a more permanent basis, as opposed to resale, the receipt will be of a capital nature, eg purchase and sale of shelves and counters in a shop.

10.2.2.2 Deductible expenditure

Expenditure will be deductible if it:

(a) *is of an income nature*,

If the expenditure is incurred for the purposes of enabling the business to resell the item at a profit, the expenditure will be of an income nature, eg the purchase of stock but not the cost of buying permanent assets such as office equipment.

Another test is whether the expenditure is recurrent rather than once-and-for-all expenditure. If recurrent, it will generally be of an income nature. Examples would be rent, rates, telephone, and interest on an overdraft. Once-and-for-all expenditure like the purchase of cars or office equipment will not be deductible as it is of a capital nature.

(b) *has been wholly, exclusively and necessarily incurred for the purposes of the trade.*

Expenditure is not wholly incurred for the purposes of the trade if it is excessively large, so that it is, effectively, in part a gift. Expenditure is not exclusively and necessarily incurred if it has a dual purpose, eg a trip to America which is part business and part holiday will not be an allowable deduction.

10.2.2.3 Capital allowances

These are explained at **10.9**.

10.3 Basis of assessment: accounting basis

The business will have to produce accounts on a consistent basis each year. In respect of accounting periods ending on or before 5 April 1999 there were three ways in which the accounts of a sole trader or partnership could be prepared and the method used will have to be agreed with the Revenue. The bases which could be used to determine trading profit (loss) were as follows.

10.3.1 Earnings basis

Accounts include all income earned whether or not it is actually received and all expenses incurred whether or not actually paid. There is no requirement for invoices to have been issued or received. The value of stock and work in progress at the end of the accounting period is taken into account.

This method is used by a trader or trading partnership and the Revenue normally insisted on this method being used by professionals for the first three years. In respect of accounting periods beginning on or after 6 April 1999, all businesses will have to use this basis to comply with the requirement that the accounts show 'a true and fair view' of the profits for the accounting period.

10.3.2 Cash basis

Accounts include only the items actually received and paid. Income earned but not paid and expenses incurred but not paid are not included. The value of work in progress at the end of the accounting period is not taken into account. Some solicitors operated on this basis. With limited exceptions for barristers during early years of practice, the cash basis of assessment was abolished with effect from 6 April 1999. Special adjustment rules apply to the transition but these are outside the scope of this book. The resulting additional income tax charge may be spread over ten years.

10.3.3 Bills delivered basis

Accounts include all bills delivered to customers or clients and all invoices received whether or not actually paid. Other items such as the value of work in progress are often disregarded. This basis was commonly used by solicitors. Like the cash basis, this basis ceased to apply in respect of accounting periods commencing on or after 6 April 1999. Special adjustment rules and the ability to spread the additional tax charge over ten years apply as for the cash basis.

10.4 Basis of assessment: taxation basis

The basis of assessment determines the basis period for the relevant tax year, that is, the period in respect of which trading profits will be assessed to tax in that particular tax year. A sole trader/partnership is assessed to income tax on the current year basis (CYB), that is, on the profits of the accounting period ending in the current tax year (the 'basis period').

EXAMPLE 1

A partnership makes up its accounts to 31 May in each year. Its trading profits are as follows:

	£
2008	10,000
2009	15,000
2010	20,000
2011	30,000
2012	35,000

The income for income tax purposes is as follows:

Tax Year	Income
	£
2008/9	10,000
2009/10	15,000
2010/11	20,000
2011/12	30,000

Income tax becomes payable in three instalments as follows:

(a) first interim payment on 31 January during the tax year in which the accounting period ends;

(b) second interim payment on 31 July immediately following the end of the tax year; and

(c) final payment/repayment on 31 January following the end of that tax year or 30 days following assessment (if later).

The interim payments will be estimated by the Revenue and based on the income tax payable in respect of the previous tax year but it is possible for the taxpayer to have the figures amended if there has been a significant change in the income which has not had income tax deducted at source.

10.5 Starting a new business: the opening-year rules

There are special rules which apply to determine the basis of assessment in the early years of the business.

10.5.1 The rules

For the purposes of this book, it is assumed that the sole trader/partnership's first accounts are made up to a date which falls in either the first or second tax year of the trade and that the business does not change its accounting date. If not, then the opening-year rules are more complex and are outside the scope of this book.

The opening-year rules are as follows:

Tax year	Basis of assessment
Year of commencement	Profits from date of commencement to following 5 April.
Second year	Profits for 12 months ending with accounting reference date in second tax year *or* if the period from commencement to that date is less than 12 months, the actual profits of first 12 months' trading.
Third and subsequent years	Current year basis (ie normal basis).

Always find out what tax year you are concerned with and the accounting period applicable. Do not forget that it is rare for a business to have an accounting year which coincides with the tax year. If profits are taxed twice under these rules then this will be corrected later (see **10.7** overlap relief).

10.5.2 Apportionment of profits on a time basis between accounting periods

Where, under the opening-year rules, the profits to be assessed in a particular tax year are the actual profits arising in a given period, the profits are calculated by apportioning the profits of one or more accounting periods on a time basis. For the sake of simplicity in the examples, apportionment will be on a monthly basis although, in practice, the calculation will be done upon a daily basis.

EXAMPLE 2

Mark starts his business on 1 November 2011, making up accounts to 31 October in each year. The tax year in which he starts business is therefore the tax year 2011/12.

His trading profits are as follows:

Year ended	Profits £
31/10/12	18,000
31/10/13	39,000
31/10/14	44,000

His assessments are as follows:

Tax year	Basis of assessment	Basis period	Income
2011/12	Actual from commencement to 5/4/12	1/11/11–5/4/12 (approx. 5 months)	£7,500 (5/12 × £18,000)
2012/13	12 months to a/c ref date in tax year	1/11/11–31/10/12	£18,000
2013/14	CYB	1/11/12–31/10/13	£39,000
2014/15	CYB	1/11/13–31/10/14	£44,000

EXAMPLE 3

Anne starts in business on 1 July 2011. She makes up her first set of accounts for the six months ended 31 December 2011 and then for calendar years thereafter. The tax year in which she starts her business is the tax year 2011/12.

Her trading profits are as follows:

	£
6 months ended 31/12/11	3,000
Year ended 31/12/12	7,600
Year ended 31/12/13	8,200
Year ended 31/12/14	6,400

Her assessments are as follows:

Tax year	Basis of assessment	Basis period	Income
2011/12	Profits from commencement to 5/4/11	1/7/11–5/4/12	£4,900 (£3,000 + [3/12 × £7,600])
2012/13	12 months to a/c ref date in tax year	1/1/12–31/12/12	£7,600
2013/14	CYB	1/1/13–31/12/13	£8,200
2014/15	CYB	1/1/14–31/12/14	£6,400

10.6 Ceasing business: the closing-year rules

As for the opening years of business, there are special rules which apply in the final years of a business.

10.6.1 The rules

The closing-year rules are as follows:

Tax year	Basis of assessment
Final year	Actual profits from day after end of basis period in penultimate tax year to date of discontinuance.
Penultimate and previous years	CYB.

EXAMPLE 4

Peter is in partnership with Tim and Bob. Peter takes 4/10 of the profits (both income and capital) with the balance being shared equally between Tim and Bob. Partnership accounts are made up to 31 July in each year.

Peter retires with effect from the end of the current accounting period, 31 July 2011. The partnership's profits for the last two years are as follows:

Accounting period (Year ending)	Profits £
31/7/10	70,000
31/7/11	100,000

The partners' assessments for 2010/11 and 2011/12 will be as follows:

2010/11
Tax year before retirement:
For all partners:
Basis of assessment: CYB. Profits = £70,000

	£
Peter (4/10)	28,000
Tim (3/10)	21,000
Bob (3/10)	21,000

2011/12
Tax year of retirement:
Peter:
Basis of assessment: Actual profits from day after last basis period (ie 1/8/10) to retirement (31/7/11)

Profits = £100,000
Peter (4/10): £40,000

Tim and Bob
Basis of assessment: CYB. Profits = £100,000

Tim (3/10)	£30,000
Bob (3/10)	£30,000

10.6.2 Apportionment of profits on a time basis between accounting periods

As for the opening-year rules, if the profits to be assessed in a tax year under the closing-year rules are the actual profits arising in that period, then if necessary, the profits are calculated by apportioning the profits of one or more accounting periods on a time basis. Again, for the sake of simplicity in this book, apportionment will be done on a monthly rather than daily basis.

10.7 Overlap relief

The intention under the rules is that over the lifetime of the business, its profits should be taxed in full once and once only. However, the Revenue recognises that during the first two years of a business under the opening-year rules, the sole trader/partnership will have some of its profits taxed more than once if it makes up its accounts to a date other than 5 April in each year. To compensate a form of relief exists whereby the profits that have been taxed more than once in the opening years of the business can be deducted from profits in the final tax year. This form of relief is known as 'overlap relief'. If the overlap relief is greater than the profits from which it is deducted in the final tax year, then the Revenue will allow the excess overlap relief to be treated as a loss.

EXAMPLE 5

Jane starts business on 1 August 2005, making up her accounts to 31 July in each tax year. She ceases to trade on 31 July 2012. Jane's trading profits for the first accounting period to 31 July 2006 are £15,000.

In her first tax year of trade (2005/06), Jane will be assessed to tax under the opening-year rules on her actual profits from the date of commencement 1 August 2005 to 5 April 2006 (ie actual profits during that eight-month period).

Jane's income assessment for 2005/06 will therefore be £10,000 (8/12 × £15,000).

In her second tax year (2006/07), Jane will be assessed to tax under the opening-year rules on her actual profits of the first 12 months of trade (ie the 12-month period from 1 August 2005–31 July 2006). This corresponds with Jane's first accounting period.

Jane's assessment for 2006/07 will therefore be £15,000.

It can be seen that the profits of the period 1 August 2005–5 April 2006 have been assessed to tax in both the tax years 2005/06 and 2006/07. Therefore, when Jane ceases to trade, she will be entitled to deduct £10,000 (the profits for that period) from her assessment for her final tax year (2012/13).

If, for example, her assessed profits in the final tax year are £30,000, then overlap relief will operate to reduce her assessable income to £20,000.

10.8 Changes in the membership of a partnership

10.8.1 Introduction

Where there is a change in the composition of the partnership and there is at least one person who is common to both the old and the new firms, there will be a deemed automatic continuation of the partnership for income tax purposes. However, the new opening-/closing-year rules will apply, on an individual basis, to the partner who is joining/leaving the partnership.

10.8.2 New partner(s): opening-year rules apply

New partner(s) only will be treated for income tax purposes in the tax year in which they are admitted as though they have just started to trade as sole traders. The opening-year rules (see 10.5) will therefore apply to the new partner(s) only for the tax year in which they are admitted and for the following tax year, as follows:

Tax year	Basis of assessment
Year of admission	Profits from date of admission to following 5 April.

Taxation of sole proprietors and partnerships

Tax year after admission	Profits for 12 months ending with accounting year end in tax year after admission *or* if the period from commencement to that date is less than 12 months, the actual profits of first 12 months' trading.
Third and subsequent tax years	CYB.

The new partner will be assessed in the opening years on his share of profits for the relevant basis period (ie the period which is assessed to tax in the relevant tax year). This will be determined by the relevant profit-sharing ratio for that basis period.

EXAMPLE 6

Angela and Brian have been in partnership for many years sharing profits equally. They make up their accounts to 31 December in each year. On 1 January 2012, they admit Clare as a partner. Thereafter, Angela, Brian and Clare share profits equally. The partnership's profits are as follows:

Accounting period (Year ending)	Profits £
31/12/11	20,000
31/12/12	30,000
31/12/13	45,000
31/12/14	60,000

2011/12
Tax year of admission
Angela and Brian will be assessed to tax as follows:
Basis of assessment: CYB (ie 1/1/11–31/12/11)
Profits = £20,000
   Angela (1/2) £10,000
   Brian (1/2) £10,000
Clare will be assessed to tax as follows:
Basis of assessment: Profits from date of admission to following 5 April (ie 1/1/12–5/4/12)
Profits for the three months since admission = £7,500 (3/12 × £30,000)
   Clare is entitled to a one third share of those profits (1/3 × £7,500) = £2,500

2012/13
Tax year following admission
Angela and Brian will be assessed to tax as follows:
Basis of assessment: CYB (ie 1/1/12–31/12/13)
Profits = £30,000
Angela (1/3) £10,000
Brian (1/3) £10,000
Clare will be assessed to tax as follows:
Basis of assessment: Profits of 12 months ending with a/c ref date in 2012/13 (ie 1/1/12–31/12/12)
Profits = £30,000
Clare (1/3) = £10,000

2013/14
Third tax year
Angela, Brian and Clare will be assessed to tax as follows:
Basis of assessment: CYB (ie 1/1/13–31/12/13)
Profits = £45,000
Angela (1/3) £15,000
Brian (1/3) £15,000
Clare (1/3) £15,000

10.8.3 Retiring/expelled/deceased partners: closing-year rules apply

Similarly, retiring, expelled, or deceased partners only, will be treated for income tax purposes in the tax year in which they leave as though they have just ceased trading as sole traders. The closing-year rules will apply to the outgoing partner(s) only for the tax year in which they leave.

Tax year	*Basis of assessment*
Tax year of leaving	Actual profits from day after last basis period to date of leaving.
Penultimate and previous tax years	CYB.

As on admission of a new partner, the retiring/expelled/deceased partner will be assessed in the closing years on his share of the profits for the relevant basis period for that tax year. His share will be calculated by reference to the relevant profit-sharing ratio for that basis period.

EXAMPLE 7

Stephen, Mary, and Sarah have been in partnership for many years, sharing profits equally and making up their accounts to 31 December in each year. On 31 December 2011, Sarah retires as a partner. Thereafter, Stephen and Mary continue to share profits equally. Sarah retires therefore in the tax year 2011/12.

The partnership's profits are as follows:

Accounting period (Year ended)	Profits £
31/12/10	30,000
31/12/11	45,000

Sarah will be assessed to tax as follows:

2010/11
Tax year prior to retirement
Basis of assessment: CYB
Profits = £30,000
    Sarah (1/3) = £10,000

2011/12
Tax year of retirement:
Basis of assessment: Actual profits from day after last basis period (ie 1/1/11) to date of retirement (31/12/11)
Profits = £45,000
    Sarah (1/3) = £15,000

10.9 Capital allowances

Ordinarily, expenditure which is of a capital, as opposed to income, nature is not deductible in calculating the sole trader/partnership's trading profits liable to tax. However, certain types of assets, principally plant and machinery and industrial buildings, do attract relief in the form of capital allowances. The provisions relating to capital allowances are contained in the Capital Allowances Act 2001 (as amended). The effect is that, in each accounting period, a proportion of the value of the asset is deductible when calculating the taxable profits of the trade when statutory income is calculated.

10.9.1 How the allowances are given

Capital allowances for sole proprietors and partnerships and also for limited companies are given by reference to accounting periods. This means that the business will calculate its entitlement to capital allowances by reference to capital expenditure and capital disposals arising in each accounting period of the business and will deduct them when calculating the trading profits of each accounting period. Balancing charges, which are explained below, will also now be treated as a trading receipt of the relevant accounting period, ie added to trading profits for the relevant accounting period.

10.9.2 Plant and machinery (except cars which are not used solely for business purposes and long life assets)

10.9.2.1 The writing-down allowance

If expenditure is incurred on an item of plant and machinery within this category, it will qualify for a 'writing-down allowance' (WDA) 20 per cent of the written-down value on a reducing balance basis. However, most businesses will qualify for a new annual investment allowance (AIA) for the first £100,000 spent on plant and machinery. The AIA will allow businesses to claim a 100 per cent allowance up to this sum.

EXAMPLE 8

Mr Evans has been in business for many years as a baker, preparing accounts to 31 December in each year. On 1 October 2011, Mr Evans purchases some machinery for £10,000. It is assumed, for the purposes of this example, that Mr Evans has no other items of plant.

The accounting period ending 31 December 2011 will fall to be assessed in the tax year 2011/12 (CYB). For this accounting period, Mr Evans is entitled to the AIA of 100 per cent of the cost of the machinery.

His capital allowance for this accounting period will be:

100% × WDV(£10,000–nil) = £10,000

The above capital allowance is deducted in calculating Mr Evans' trading profits for the accounting period ending 31 December 2011.

If, as is likely, the sole trader/partnership owns more than one item of plant and machinery, then the position is more complicated. For the purposes of calculating the WDA, the assets are aggregated in a 'pool' of assets and treated as if they are all one asset. Therefore, the amount of the WDA (subject to the AIA) will be up to 20 per cent of the total of expenditure on machinery and plant less all allowances so far claimed (ie the written-down value of the 'pool' of capital assets).

10.9.2.2 Disposals: balancing allowances and balancing charges

When an asset is sold (or on cessation of trade) there will be a balancing adjustment to be made to ensure that the business does not get tax relief for more than has actually been lost by depreciation in the value of the asset.

If the business has just one item of plant and machinery, the position is relatively straightforward.

(a) If the asset is sold for less than the written-down value, there will be a balancing allowance (effectively an additional WDA) of an amount equal to the difference between the sale price and the written-down value. This will be deducted from trading profits in the same way as for other capital allowances.

(b) If, on the other hand, the asset is sold for more than the written-down value, there will be a balancing charge of the amount equal to the difference between the sale price and the written-down value. A balancing charge is added to trading profits and is therefore effectively a negative capital allowance clawing back part of the capital allowance already received. However, the balancing charge will be restricted to the amount of the allowances which have been given on the asset. Therefore, if the sale price exceeds the original cost of the asset, then the original cost of the asset is substituted for the sale price in computing the charge.

The excess of the sale price over the original cost will be liable to be taxed as a capital gain and so liable to CGT in the case of individuals and partnerships.

If, on the other hand, there is a general 'pool' of assets, then the position is as follows.

(a) The sale price of the item disposed of is deducted from the written-down value of the 'pool' brought forward from the previous accounting period. This will be done before the WDA is calculated on the remaining assets. The effect of the deduction of the sale price of the asset which is sold is that smaller allowances will be available on the 'pool' in that and subsequent accounting periods.

(b) As for a single item, the sale proceeds deducted from the 'pool' cannot exceed the original cost of the asset sold. Any excess of sale proceeds over original cost represents a capital gain that will be liable to be taxed as a capital gain.

(c) If the sale price is greater than the balance brought forward on the 'pool' (the WDV of the 'pool'), then a balancing charge is made, restoring the 'pool' value to zero.

(d) On cessation of trade, the difference between the total sale proceeds of the assets and the WDV of the 'pool' will give rise to a balancing charge or balancing allowance as appropriate.

10.9.3 Motor cars

These are subject to special rules for motor cars purchased after 6 April 2009 that relate to the CO_2 emissions of the car. Motor cars which are not used solely for business purposes may also qualify for capital allowances. Further consideration of these allowances is outside the scope of this book.

10.9.4 Industrial buildings

Historically, a writing-down allowance of 4 per cent of the original cost of construction or purchase of an industrial building (ie a factory, mill or similar, but not offices) could be claimed for every accounting period when the building is in use. As the WDA is a percentage of the original cost of the building (unlike the reducing balance basis applied to other assets), full relief is obtained after 25 accounting periods. This allowance was withdrawn from April 2011. Further consideration of industrial buildings is outside the scope of this book.

10.10 Partnerships: allocation of profits/losses between partners

In the case of partnerships, once the partnership's trading profits (loss) have been calculated, the next step is to allocate these profits (losses) between the partners in the firm in the relevant profit (or loss) sharing ratio.

The profit (loss) ratio to be applied in allocating the profit (loss) between the partners for a particular tax year will be determined by reference to the ratio for the accounting period which is assessed in that tax year.

EXAMPLE 12

An existing business makes up its accounts to 31 December in each year. For the tax year 2011/12, under the current year basis, the business will be assessed on the profits for the accounting period ending 31 December 2011. The profit (loss) sharing ratio for that accounting period will govern how the profits (losses) are allocated amongst the partners in the tax year 2011/12.

10.11 Trading loss relief

It may well be that the partnership or sole trader has suffered a trading loss under the rules of the Income Taxes Act 2007 (ITA). This may be because deductible expenditure is greater than chargeable receipts or because, even though trading profits have been made, the deduction of capital allowances creates a trading loss. Under the current year basis, it will generally result in a nil assessment for the current tax year.

However, in addition, relief for the trading loss made in that accounting period is given in a number of ways. If a partnership makes a loss, each partner can choose what type of loss relief to claim in respect of his share of the loss.

10.11.1 'Carry across' against other income

Under s 64 of ITA 2007, the loss made in that accounting period may be set off against any of the taxpayer's other income taxable in the year of the loss, if the taxpayer so elects—'carry across'.

The 'year of the loss' is the tax year in which the loss-making period of account ends. For example, if a taxpayer makes a loss in his accounting year ending 31 December 2010, that loss will be treated as arising in the tax year 2010/11, since that is the tax year in which the loss-making accounting period ends. Under s 64, the loss made can be set off against any income of the taxpayer which falls to be assessed in the tax year 2010/11.

If a trading loss is not fully relieved under s 64, either because the taxpayer did not elect to take the relief or because the taxpayer's other income in the year of the loss was insufficient, then the taxpayer may elect to set off the loss (or unrelieved loss) against any income taxable in the preceding tax year (ie 2009/10) under s 64.

Note that use of either relief means a deduction from total income (ie statutory income less charges on income) and so can result in a loss of allowances which are treated both as a deduction (eg personal allowance) and as a reduction (eg CA).

There is a temporary extension of carry-back relief for accounting periods ending between 24 November 2008 and 23 November 2010. This allows trading losses to be carried back to the preceding three-year period. There are conditions about how the extended relief is applied and caps on how much can be carried back. Further consideration of the extended relief is outside the scope of this book.

EXAMPLE 13

Alan has been in business since 1998, making up his accounts to 30 September each year. His trading profits for the two years ended 30 September 2011 were:

Year ended 30 September 2010: Profit £60,000
Year ended 30 September 2011: Loss (£48,000)

In addition, he has dividend income which amounts to £9,800 (gross) annually.

The year of the loss is the tax year in which the loss-making period of account ended ie 2011/12.

Therefore he can make a claim under s 64 of ITA 2007 to offset his loss of £48,000 against any of his income for that tax year, as follows:

2011/12

	£
Income	Nil
Dividend	9,800
	9,800
Less s 64 loss relief	(9,800)
	Nil

Unclaimed loss £38,200 (£48,000–£9,800)

He can then elect to set the balance of his loss against any of his income taxable in the previous tax year (ie 2010/11) as follows:

2010/11

	£
Income	60,000
Dividend	9,800
	69,800
Less s 64 loss relief	(38,200)
	31,600

The loss is now fully relieved.

10.11.2 'Carry-across' and 'carry-back' against capital gains

Under s 72 of the Finance Act 1991, any trading loss remaining after a s 64 claim has been made may be set off against the taxpayer's net capital gains (ie capital gains before the annual exemption is taken) for the tax year of the loss and/or the preceding tax year, provided that the trade which gave rise to the loss is still being carried on.

10.11.3 'Carry-forward' against future profits

If s 64 relief is not claimed (or is claimed but there is still an unrelieved balance of loss), then the loss (or unrelieved balance) may, if the taxpayer so elects, be carried forward and set off against the first available profits of the same trade (ITA 2007, s 83). There is nothing to prevent the taxpayer leaving a gap of several years before the year in respect of which the relief is first claimed.

Once the election has been made in respect of a tax year, there are two important points to note.

(a) Under s 83, losses can only be offset against profits from the same trade, not against non-trading income or trading income other than from the trade which produced the loss.

(b) The loss must be set against profits for the year in respect of which the election is made and then the next year in which there are those profits and so on until all the loss is relieved.

10.11.4 Terminal loss relief

A loss sustained in the final 12 months' trading can be carried back and set against profits of the same trade for the three tax years preceding the tax year of discontinuance, taking later years before earlier years (ITA 2007, s 89). Note that s 89 does not allow relief against non-trading income or capital gains, or trading income other than income from the trade which produced the loss. The loss must be set against the profits from later years before earlier years.

10.11.5 Start-up loss relief

Losses made in the first four tax years of a new business may be carried back and set against other income of the taxpayer (not capital gains) for the three tax years preceding the tax year of the loss (ITA 2007, s 72). Unlike s 64, income from earlier years must be relieved before later years.

10.11.6 Carry-forward relief on incorporation of business

When an unincorporated business is transferred to a company in consideration wholly or mainly in exchange for the allotment of shares in the company to the former proprietor(s), he/they can set off their unabsorbed trading losses against any income (eg dividends, salary) which they receive from the company for any year throughout which they own such shares (ITA 2007, s 86).

10.12 Statutory income

Once the sole trader/partner's partnership income has been assessed, it is then necessary to calculate the sole trader/partner's statutory income. If the sole trader/partner has other sources of income apart from partnership income, then his statutory income will be the total of his partnership income added to his other sources of income which will have been assessed under either I(TE)PA or ITTOIA.

If the sole trader/partner has made a trading loss, then he will be entitled to set off that loss against his other income under s 64 of ITA 2007 as mentioned above. This will have the effect of reducing his statutory income.

10.13 Taxable income

Once the sole trader/partner's statutory income has been calculated then, as normal, any charges on income attracting full relief to which the sole trader/partner is entitled are deducted to calculate total income. Personal reliefs attracting full relief are then deducted to calculate taxable income. Once the taxpayer's tax liability has been calculated, reductions are made for any personal reliefs attracting relief at 10 per cent only and for any tax which has been collected at source. For a more detailed consideration of these principles see **Chapter 5**, above.

10.14 Conclusion: checkpoints

You should now be able to:

- apply the opening-year rules (**10.5**);
- apply the closing-year rules (**10.6**);
- recognise when overlap relief is available (**10.7**);
- recognise the implications of a change in the membership of a partnership (**10.8**);
- calculate capital allowances, balancing allowances, and balancing charges (**10.9**); and
- apply the rules relating to loss relief (**10.11**).

Visit the Online Resource Centre for more information and useful weblinks.
www.oxfordtextbooks.co.uk/orc/foundations11_12/

Taxation of trusts and settlements

11.1 Introduction and background

11.1.1 Introduction

This chapter is an introduction to the taxation regimes of the main types of trusts and settlements.

Each of the three main taxes are considered separately:

- inheritance tax
- capital gains tax and
- income tax.

11.1.2 Background

Settlements may be created by settlors in their lifetime, or by will, or they may arise under the intestacy rules. It is our purpose here to consider the tax implications of such settlements from the viewpoint of both the trustees and the beneficiaries.

The three main taxes to be considered are inheritance tax, capital gains tax, and income tax. Each tax must initially be considered separately as, although the Finance Act 2006 gives a common definition of 'settled property', 'settlement', and 'settlor' for capital gains tax and income tax, there is no overall integrated approach to the taxation of trusts.

There is some consistency in the method of taxing the trust. However, as mentioned at **11.5**, you may find it a useful exercise, to aid your understanding, to draw up and complete a grid detailing the different types of trust and the taxation treatment they are subject to.

Examples of the main types of trust include:

Those which can be created both during the settlor's lifetime or on death:

- Discretionary trust. This is a trust where no beneficiary has the immediate right to receive any income (etc) from the property: for example, where the settlor settles the property on trust for a class of beneficiaries and gives the trustees the discretion as to which of the beneficiaries, if any, receives any of the income from the trust property, or any of the capital.

- Interest in possession trust. Here a beneficiary has the immediate right to the income from, or the use or enjoyment of, the property: for example, David, in his will, leaves his residuary estate to his wife, Susan, for life, and on her death to his children equally. On David's death Susan has an interest in possession in the residuary estate.

- Contingent interest trust. Under such a trust the beneficiary does not have the immediate right to receive any income (etc) from the property. The beneficiary has the right when the contingency is fulfilled: for example, during his lifetime, Gordon settles £250,000 on trust for such of his grandchildren, alive at the date of the settlement, who attain the age of 18 years and if more than one then in equal shares. If at the time the settlement is created Gordon's grandchildren are seven, nine, and 11 none of them will have the immediate right to receive the income from the property. Once the eldest reaches 18 then that grandchild will have the right to receive the income from a one-third share of the property.

Those created only on death, either in the settlor's will or on intestacy:

- trusts for bereaved minors
- trusts for bereaved young persons
- trusts with an immediate post-death interest.

These types of trust were created by the amendments made to the Inheritance Tax Act 1984 by the Finance Act 2006. The trusts are described in more detail at **11.2.3.2**. They enjoy a more favourable, or different, taxation for IHT purposes than other types of trust.

11.2 Inheritance tax

On 22 March 2006 the Chancellor announced major changes to the inheritance tax regime for trusts and settlements. These changes were embodied in the Finance Act 2006. As a result of the changes it is useful to distinguish between those trusts and settlements created during the settlor's lifetime and those created on death, either under a will or on an intestacy.

It is not the place of this chapter to reflect the inheritance taxation treatment before 22 March 2006, merely to record the position as it now stands.

Statutory references in this section are to Inheritance Tax Act 1984 (as amended) unless otherwise indicated.

11.2.1 Definition of 'settlement'

For the purposes of inheritance tax, the term 'settlement' is defined by s 43(2). It includes a disposition whereby property is for the time being:

(a) held in trust for persons in succession (eg 'to Lesley for life, remainder to Rosalind');

(b) held for a person subject to a contingency (eg 'to Charles provided he attains the age of 25');

(c) held on trust to accumulate the whole or part of the income, or to make payments from income at the discretion of the trustees or some other person;

(d) charged or burdened with the payment of an annuity.

There is no settlement for inheritance tax purposes where property is held behind a trust for sale as beneficial joint tenants or tenants in common, nor where it is held in a bare trust.

Where chargeable events occur, the primary liability for the payment of the tax lies with the trustees—the burden falling upon the trust property. In appropriate cases, the instalment option will be available if the charge arises on a death or, in other situations, if qualifying property remains settled.

11.2.2 Creation of a settlement

When a settlement is created it constitutes a transfer of value by the settlor and its chargeability will be determined in the normal way. As mentioned at **11.2**, it is useful to distinguish between those trusts and settlements created during the settlor's lifetime and those created on death, either under a will or on an intestacy. For the purposes of considering the taxation of the various types of trust and settlements for inheritance tax purposes this chapter considers the various types under those two headings.

11.2.2.1 Created during the settlor's lifetime

See **11.1.2** for examples of the types of trust and settlements that can be created during the settlor's lifetime.

A transfer into one of these constitutes a transfer of value by the settlor and, unless covered by an exemption, it is a lifetime chargeable transfer.

As we saw (in **7.3** and **7.6**) the *inter vivos* creation of a settlement is an LCT, chargeable at half the rate(s) which would have applied on a death at that time, with the possibility of a supplementary charge should the settlor then die within seven years. Grossing up will apply on creation, unless the settled fund pays the tax. There are special rules which apply where a settlor creates 'related settlements' (basically, several settlements on the same day) and where property is subsequently added to the settlement.

11.2.2.2 Created on death

See **11.1.2** for examples of the types of trust and settlements that can be created on death, either under the deceased's will, or on intestacy.

Whether the trust is created by the settlor's will or the operation of the intestacy rules the property involved is part of the transfer deemed to take place on death and so chargeable (unless, again, covered by an exemption).

11.2.3 Liability of the trustees during the continuance of the trust

11.2.3.1 Created during the settlor's lifetime

For the purposes of this chapter, all trusts and settlements created during a settlor's lifetime are subject to the same inheritance tax treatment. The exception, being gifts into a disabled trust, is beyond the scope of this chapter.

Property in the trust is defined in s 58 IHTA 1984 as 'Relevant Property', and so the phrase 'relevant property regime' has been coined to describe the regime applied.

Under the relevant property regime the property in the trust or settlement is subject to two categories of chargeable events:

(a) The periodic charge. This is imposed at ten-yearly intervals, the first occasion of the charge normally being the tenth anniversary of the creation of the trust. Basically, the charge is upon the value of 'relevant property' in the settlement at the time.

(b) The exit charge. This is imposed when capital 'leaves' the settlement during the first ten years or between periodic charges (eg because the trustees exercise a discretion to distribute capital; or a beneficiary fulfils a contingency and becomes absolutely entitled; or the trustees appoint out capital in the fund to a beneficiary). The value to be charged is the value leaving the settlement. However, no exit charge will apply where the capital leaves the settlement within three months of the creation of the trust or of a periodic charge (s 65), or if it does so within two years of the creation of the settlement where this happened on death (s 144).

11.2.3.1.1 *Rates of tax and cumulation*

The periodic charge is levied at 30 per cent of the lifetime rate of inheritance tax—ie, at a maximum rate of 6 per cent (30 per cent of 20 per cent). The exit charge is levied at a proportion of the charge which would have been levied on a periodic charge had it occurred at the time—the precise method of calculation depending upon whether the exit charge arises before the trust's first ten-year anniversary or subsequently.

In all cases, in calculating the tax payable the settlor's cumulative total of chargeable lifetime transfers in the seven years prior to the creation of the settlement is the starting point of the settlement's cumulative total. This is so however long the settlement has been in existence.

11.2.3.2 Created on death

Again, generally, trusts created on the death of the settlor are subject to taxation under the relevant property regime. See **11.2.3.1**.

However, the following trusts are not subject to the relevant property regime, but are taxed in a more favourable, or different, way. They are considered separately.

11.2.3.2.1 *Trusts for bereaved minors*

This type of trust is excluded from the relevantv property regime provided various conditions are met. These are set out in s 71A IHTA 1984, inserted by the Finance Act 2006. A bereaved minor is defined as a minor of whom at least one parent has died. The conditions are that:

1. the trust must be created by the will of a deceased parent of the bereaved minor, arise on intestacy, or be established under the Criminal Injuries Compensation scheme;
2. the beneficiary will, on attaining the age of 18 years, or before, become absolutely entitled to the settled property and the income arising from it; and
3. whilst the beneficiary is alive and under 18 any income from the trust is applied for the benefit of the bereaved minor.

Provided these conditions are met, then, when the settled property vests in the beneficiary on attaining the age of 18, or earlier, no exit charge applies. In addition, no matter how long the period between the commencement of the trust and the date the beneficiary attains a vested interest, no periodic charges shall apply (s 71A–C IHTA 1984, as amended).

11.2.3.2.2 *Trusts for bereaved young persons/Age 18-to-25 trusts*

This type of trust is covered by s 71D–F IHTA 1984, as amended. A trust to which s 71D IHTA 1984, as amended, applies falls under a 'light touch' relevant property regime. Provided the conditions of the section are met then no periodic charges apply and the basis for the exit charge when the beneficiary attains a vested interest is limited. The conditions are that:

1. the beneficiary has not attained the age of 25 years;
2. at least one parent of the beneficiary has died; and
3. the trust is established under the will of a deceased parent or the Criminal Injuries Compensation Scheme.

In fact, if the beneficiary attains an absolute interest on or before attaining 18 then there is no exit charge. If the beneficiary attains the absolute interest after 18 but no later than his/her 25th birthday then the period over which the exit charge is calculated is limited to the period commencing on the beneficiary's 18th birthday, ceasing on the date the beneficiary is entitled to an absolute interest, which will be on or before reaching 25 years.

There is also no exit charge should the beneficiary die before attaining an absolute interest or on any advancements made before attaining an absolute interest.

11.2.3.2.3 *Trusts with an immediate post-death interest*

Where, under a will or on intestacy, a beneficial entitlement in the trust property arises on the death of the settlor (and where s 71A does not apply and it is not a disabled person's trust) s 49A IHTA 1984, inserted by the Finance Act 2006, provides that the charging basis set out in s 49 applies. The trust will not be taxed under the relevant property regime. The charging basis is set out at **11.2.3.2.4**. This type of trust is an interest in possession trust, but when the beneficial entitlement arises on the death of the transferor it is taxed in a different way for IHT purposes.

11.2.3.2.4 *Charging basis (s 49)*

A beneficiary who has an immediate post-death interest is treated as if beneficially entitled to the property in which that interest subsists. In other words, if under a trust created by Toby's will, Laurence is the life tenant entitled to the income from a trust fund whose capital is valued at £500,000, that capital value is treated as part of Laurence's estate for tax purposes. If he were entitled to half of the income from the fund then £250,000 would be deemed to be part of his estate.

11.2.3.2.5 *Chargeable events for the s49 Charging basis of Trusts with an immediate post-death interest*

Chargeable events occur whenever, and to the extent that, the interest in possession terminates—since this will (effectively) be treated as a disposition of the property by the person with the interest in possession. The chargeable events will be:

(a) Death of the life tenant—a chargeable event

Thus, the deemed transfer on the death of the life tenant includes the trust property. The trustees are primarily liable for the tax attributable to this part of the estate, and the burden of that tax will fall upon the trust property. However, the tax payable on both the unsettled and settled estate will be affected by the need to cumulate both with any chargeable lifetime transfers made by the life tenant in the seven years prior to the death to fix the rate(s) of tax payable.

(b) Termination during the lifetime of the life tenant—chargeable events

The termination may occur during the lifetime of the life tenant—eg, on the sale, gift or surrender of the life interest, or the consent by the life tenant to the advancement of the remainderman. Normally, unless exempt, such lifetime terminations will be treated as PETs made by the life tenant and thus only actually chargeable to tax if the life tenant dies within the next seven years.

Notice that a tax charge may arise on a sale of the life tenant's interest. A transfer of value will occur even if the sale has been for the full market value of the life tenant's interest—because the life tenant has been treated as 'owning' the property, whereas the value of the life interest will be determined on an actuarial basis.

EXAMPLE 1

Lisa is the life tenant of a fund of £100,000 and she sells her life interest to Penelope for £25,000 (its full actuarial value). There will be a transfer of value (normally a PET) of the amount by which her estate goes down in value—£75,000. This demonstrates the fact that inheritance tax is not merely a tax on gifts or transactions at an undervalue.

(c) Termination during the lifetime of the life tenant—no chargeable event

If on the termination of the interest in possession the life tenant becomes absolutely entitled to the settled property, no charge will arise. This is because the value of the life tenant's estate does not change, and so there can be no transfer of value. Thus suppose that trustees advance £10,000 from capital to the life tenant under a power given to them by the trust instrument (this would not, of course, be possible under the general law). Prior to the advancement, this sum would have been deemed to be part of the life tenant's estate; it now is the life tenant's absolutely.

Again, no charge will arise on a partition of the settled property to the extent of the property taken by the life tenant under the arrangement.

EXAMPLE 2

Lucas is the life tenant and Roger the remainderman of a settled fund worth £500,000, and they agree to break the settlement on terms that Lucas will take £100,000 absolutely and Roger the remaining £400,000. The amount taken by Lucas does not affect the value of his estate; however, there is a transfer of value (normally a PET) by Lucas of the amount taken by Roger.

However, if the life tenant purchases a reversionary interest, special rules apply to prevent avoidance of tax.

EXAMPLE 3

Lois is the life tenant under a settlement of £500,000. Ronald is the remainderman, and Lois agrees to purchase his reversion for its full actuarial value of (say) £100,000. Her estate both before and after the transaction includes the value of the settled property, but the estate of Lois has now been depleted by the £100,000 paid to Ronald. She has, in effect, bought something which was already regarded as hers for tax purposes and reduced the value of her estate in the process. By s 55 she is prevented from gaining any tax advantage from such a deal: she will be deemed under this provision to have made a transfer of value (normally a PET) of the amount paid to Ronald.

11.2.3.3 Charitable and similar trusts

Trusts for charitable and similar purposes and those for the benefit of mentally disabled persons and those in receipt of an attendance allowance are not subject to the rules described above. Nor are pension fund trusts (s 151), employee trusts (s 86), or protective trusts even after forfeiture (ss 73 and 88).

11.2.3.4 Survivorship clauses

These are commonly included in wills for a variety of tax and succession reasons. A standard provision of this kind is: 'To Benedict provided he survives me for 28 days but if he fails to do so then to Clarissa'.

Because Benedict's interest is contingent, a settlement with no interest in possession arises on the death of the testator. At the end of the survivorship period (or on Benedict's earlier death) this will come to an end because Benedict (or Clarissa should Benedict fail to survive) becomes absolutely entitled to the property. In principle, therefore, an exit charge should then arise. However, provided the survivorship period does not exceed six months, this will not happen (s 92).

11.3 Capital gains tax

Statutory references in this section are to Taxation of Chargeable Gains Act 1992 (as amended) unless otherwise stated.

11.3.1 The basic position

As we shall see, the creation of a settlement is a disposal for the purposes of the tax. Thereafter, so long as the property remains within the definition of 'settled property'—with the possibility of an 'exit charge' when it ceases to do so—it is subject to a special charging regime. Disposals (actual or notional) by the trustees of the trust property may trigger a charge to tax; disposals by the beneficiaries of their beneficial interests generally do not.

11.3.2 Definition of 'settled property'

'Settled property', is defined (s 68) as 'any property held in trust' except in those situations excepted from the definition by s 60. This excludes from the definition property held by a person:

(a) as nominee for another person; or

(b) as trustee for another person who is absolutely entitled as against the trustee (ie, someone who has the exclusive right—subject only to the payment of trust expenses—to direct how the property should be dealt with). Such a situation (sometimes called a 'bare trust') might arise where a remainderman has become absolutely entitled on the death of the life tenant, or a beneficiary has fulfilled a contingency; or

(c) as trustee for any person who would be absolutely entitled as against the trustees but for infancy or other disability. This must be the only reason why the person concerned is not able to call immediately for the property to be 'handed over'—ie that person's interest must be vested. If a contingency (eg attaining 18) still has to be fulfilled, the property remains settled property.

Where one of the three exceptions applies, the trust property is for tax purposes dealt with as if it were vested in the beneficiary concerned, and acts of the nominee or trustee are treated as those of the beneficiary.

If two or more persons hold property as joint tenants or tenants in common, the property is not 'settled property' for the purposes of capital gains tax provided they are together absolutely entitled to the property.

11.3.3 Settlor's liability

This will depend upon whether the settlement is created in the lifetime or on death.

11.3.3.1 Lifetime settlement

Whenever property is transferred to trustees, there is a disposal for capital gains tax purposes by the settlor to the trustees. This is so whether the settlement is revocable or irrevocable, and even if the settlor (or the settlor's spouse or civil partner) is a trustee (even the sole trustee) or a beneficiary.

The disposal (and corresponding acquisition by the trustees) is at the then market value of the property concerned. Any gain or loss will essentially be computed in the ordinary way. However, as the settlor and the trustees are connected persons (s 18(3)) any loss can only be relieved by setting it against gains made on subsequent disposal(s) to the trustees. If hold-over relief is available (either because the assets are put into the trust by a transfer which is an LCT for inheritance tax purposes (s 260) or are business assets (s 165), it may be claimed by the election of the settlor alone.

11.3.3.2 Settlement created on death

Here, there will be no disposal (in line with the general scheme of the Act that death is not a chargeable event for capital gains tax purposes). The deceased's personal representatives will (as we have seen in **6.5.1**) be deemed to acquire the assets concerned at their market value at the date of death, and this will also be the value at which the trustees will be deemed to have acquired them.

11.3.4 Liability of trustees

As in the case of income tax, trustees are a single and continuing body for tax purposes; thus a change of trustees is not a chargeable event for capital gains tax purposes. For the tax year 2011/12 the rate of CGT that trustees pay is 28 per cent.

11.3.4.1 Actual disposals

Where the trustees sell trust assets, any chargeable gain or allowable loss is calculated in the normal way. The exemptions and reliefs to which they may be entitled include:

(a) *Annual exempt amount* (s 3 and Sch 1). This is available normally at half the rate to which an individual is entitled in the year in question (for the tax year 2011/12 it is £5,300). However, where the same settlor has created more than one settlement, the available exempt amount is divided equally between them—subject to the proviso that each trust is entitled to a minimum exemption of 10 per cent of the exemption available to individuals (for the tax year 2011/12, therefore, £1,060).

(b) *Main residence* (s 225). Trustees may claim this exemption on the disposal of a property which has been the only or main residence of a person entitled to occupy it under the terms of the settlement.

(c) *Roll-over relief* (s 152). This will be available only if the trustees are carrying on an unincorporated business.

Where trustees incur a loss on the disposal, it can be relieved against any gains which they have in the same tax year, with any surplus being carried forward to future years.

11.3.4.2 Notional disposals (s 71)

When someone becomes absolutely entitled to (any part of) the trust property as against the trustees (or would become so entitled but for infancy or other disability) such property (or part) ceases to be 'settled property'. This may occur, for example, where the trustees exercise a power of advancement—though not where cash is advanced, since sterling is an exempt asset for tax purposes; when a beneficiary obtains a vested interest on fulfilling a contingency; where the remainderman becomes absolutely entitled on the *inter vivos* termination of a life interest (eg on the surrender of the life tenant's interest).

On the happening of any such event, the trustees are deemed to dispose of the property concerned and immediately reacquire it (as nominee of the beneficiary) at its then market value. Any chargeable gain or allowable loss is calculated in (essentially) the ordinary way. Hold-over relief may be claimed in appropriate circumstances on a joint election by the trustees and the beneficiary.

If the trustees incur an allowable loss for which they are unable to obtain relief, the loss may effectively be transferred to the beneficiary who becomes absolutely entitled.

Where the event causing the property to cease to be 'settled property' is the death of the life tenant, there is no chargeable disposal; but (as is generally the case for capital gains tax purposes on death) there is nonetheless a deemed disposal and reacquisition by the trustees at the then market value of the property (s 73). The effect is that the remainderman acquires the property at this value. However, tax must now be paid on any gain held over when the property was put into the settlement.

If on the death of the life tenant the property remains settled property (eg because another life tenant becomes entitled, or because a remainderman is only contingently entitled), the position is governed by s 72. There is again no chargeable disposal, but there is a deemed disposal and reacquisition of the property by the trustees which will form the basis of any future charge. However, tax will again be payable on any gain held over when the property was put into the settlement.

11.3.5 The beneficiaries

The tax position of the beneficiaries will depend upon whether the trust property is within the definition of 'settled property' or not.

11.3.5.1 Settled property (s 76)

On the disposal by a beneficiary of the beneficial interest there is no chargeable event—unless that beneficial interest was acquired by the beneficiary or a predecessor in title for consideration in money or money's worth (other than consideration consisting of another interest under the settlement).

11.3.5.2 Bare trust

If the property has ceased to be 'settled property', the beneficiary is effectively treated as already the 'owner' of the property. The result is that any subsequent disposals by the trustees are treated and taxed as if made by the beneficiary.

11.4 Income tax

11.4.1 The basic position

As we will see, income arising under a trust will normally suffer tax in the hands of the trustees in a manner not dissimilar (in general terms) to that applicable to personal representatives. Beneficiaries under the trust may have to include trust income in their tax returns, thus perhaps (according to their circumstances) enabling them to make a repayment claim or causing them to be liable to higher rate tax.

However, in relation to certain *inter vivos* trusts there are anti-avoidance provisions which effectively require the income from the settlement still to be taxed as part of the settlor's income. These provisions affect (broadly) the following categories of settlement, a term which is for these purposes very widely defined:

(a) where the settlor has made a settlement under which the settlor's minor children benefit;

(b) where the settlor or the settlor's spouse or civil partner have retained an interest in the settlement, whether or not actual benefits are received by them;

(c) where the settlor, the settlor's spouse or civil partner, or minor child have received a capital payment or benefit from the settlement.

These provisions, which do not apply to trusts arising on death, are complex and are not further discussed in this book.

11.4.2 Liability of trustees

11.4.2.1 Generally

Trustees (who are for tax purposes a single and continuing body) are liable to income tax at the basic rate on all of the income arising to the trust (other than dividends where the rate is 10 per cent), without any deduction for any trust expenses. Their statutory income is calculated in essentially the same way as that of individual taxpayers; they cannot, however, claim personal reliefs—but are not liable to higher rate tax.

11.4.2.2 Dividend Trust Rate and Trust Rate

For the tax year 2011/12 this is 42.5 per cent for dividend income and 50 per cent on other income and is payable on all income which (under s 31, Trustee Act 1925 or the trust instrument) is to be accumulated, or is payable at the discretion of the trustees or some other person—and (in either case) is not to be treated (before distribution) as the income of either the settlor (see above) or a beneficiary.

In practice, the liability to pay tax at this special rate applies to most cases where there is a settlement without an interest in possession.

The special rate is in effect only levied on the amount of trust income actually available for accumulation or for the exercise of the discretion, since the trustees are able to deduct expenses 'properly' chargeable to income under the general law (whatever the trust instrument may actually provide). Such expenses must, however, be claimed against dividends in priority to other income.

The trust rate is not applied to all income. In April 2005, where income is taxed at the trust rate, a standard rate band was introduced.

From 6 April 2006 the first £1,000 of income received net of tax or with a tax credit will be liable at only the basic rate depending on the type of income (10 per cent for dividends, 20 per cent for other income).

Any income in excess of the £1,000 is taxed at the dividend trust rate and trust rate (42.5 per cent for dividend income and 50 per cent on other income).

Where any of the net income of the trust is paid to, or applied for the benefit of, a beneficiary, the trustees must provide a tax deduction certificate for the tax paid by them.

11.4.3 Beneficiaries with a right to trust income

In cases where beneficiaries have a vested interest in the income of the trust it will be taxed as part of their income when it arises, whether it is accumulated, applied for their benefit, or distributed to them.

A beneficiary who has a vested interest in the capital will (unless the trust instrument otherwise provides) normally also have a vested interest in the income—even if under 18. A beneficiary whose right to capital is contingent on attaining an age greater than 18 will (unless s 31, Trustee Act 1925 has been excluded or modified by the trust instrument) effectively receive a vested interest in the income at 18. From that age until either the capital vests or the interest fails (eg because the beneficiary dies before fulfilling the contingency), the trustees (under s 31) must pay the income to the beneficiary. It must be returned, therefore, as part of the beneficiary's statutory income.

Where beneficiaries have vested interests, it is their share of the income (after trustees' expenses have been met) grossed up at basic rate which must be included in their returns. They have tax credits for the tax paid by the trustees.

Capital payments by the trustees will, in principle, not be liable to income tax. However, where the beneficiary is entitled to have income augmented from capital such 'topping-up' payments will be taxed in the hands of the beneficiary—*Brodie's Will Trustees v IRC* (1933) 17 TC 432; *Cunard's Trustees v IRC* [1946] 1 All ER 159.

11.4.4 Beneficiaries with no right to trust income

This situation arises where the beneficiary's entitlement to the income depends upon the fulfilment of a contingency, or the exercise of a discretion in the beneficiary's favour.

In these cases, the trust income will be taxed at the trust rate, in the hands of the trustees as it arises (**11.4.2.2**). If such income is simply accumulated, it is not taxable as part of the beneficiary's income; and the accumulations, when finally paid over to the beneficiary, are effectively capital and therefore not then liable to income tax. However, if any of the income is advanced to, or applied for the benefit of, the beneficiary the amounts so paid or applied (grossed up at the rate paid by the trustees) are then treated as part of the beneficiary's income for tax purposes—with the benefit of a tax credit for the total tax effectively already paid by the trustees.

11.5 Conclusion: checkpoints

You should now be able to explain to a client:

- inheritance tax;
- capital gains tax; and
- income tax;

and treatment of the following types of trusts and settlements:

- discretionary;
- interest in possession;
- bereaved minors;
- bereaved young persons;
- immediate post-death interest; and
- bare.

You may find it useful to draw up and complete a grid, as shown below, with the taxation treatment of the various trusts as a useful exercise and revision tool.

	Discretionary	Interest in possession	Bereaved minors	Bereaved young persons	Immediate post-death interest	Bare
Inheritance tax—settlor	11.2.2.1/ 11.2.2.2	11.2.2.1/ 11.2.2.2	11.2.2.2	11.2.2.2	11.2.2.2	11.2.2
Inheritance tax—during life of trust	11.2.3.1/ 11.2.3.2	11.2.3.1/ 11.2.3.2	11.2.3.2	11.2.3.2	11.2.3.2	11.2.3
Capital gains tax—settlor	11.3.3	11.3.3	11.3.3	11.3.3	11.3.3	11.3.3
Capital gains tax—during life of trust	11.3.4	11.3.4	11.3.4	11.3.4	11.3.4	11.3.5.2
Income tax—during life of trust	11.4.4	11.4.3	11.4.4	11.4.4	11.4.3	11.4.3

Visit the Online Resource Centre for more information and useful weblinks.
www.oxfordtextbooks.co.uk/orc/foundations11_12/

Wills and administration of estates

12

Introduction to wills and administration of estates

12.1 Introduction

The aim of this part of the book is to provide you with a basis for understanding the practice and procedure of obtaining a grant of representation and the administration of an estate.

When someone dies, their relatives or friends will usually have dealt with the most pressing matters—registering the death and arranging the funeral—before consulting a solicitor. In simple cases, or where the deceased has left little property, it may well be that a solicitor is not consulted at all. Commonly, however, the advice of a solicitor will be sought as to who is entitled to the deceased's property, as to the liability of the estate to tax, and generally as to 'what has to be done' in order to pass the deceased's property to those now entitled to it.

12.2 Breakdown of the task

- *Chapter 13 Entitlement to the estate:* To a large extent, who is entitled to the deceased's property will depend upon whether or not there is a valid will (**13.2**). To the extent that there is not, the intestacy rules apply (**13.10**). Some property, however, passes independently of the will or the operation of the intestacy rules (**13.18**). Sometimes, relatives or dependants may be able to make a claim for provision to be made for them which if successful would have the effect of 'varying' the dispositions made in the deceased's will or taking effect under the intestacy rules (**13.23**).

- *Chapter 14 Application for a grant of representation:* We begin this chapter with a consideration of the nature and effect of grants of representation (**14.2**) and a summary of the practice involved in obtaining a grant (**14.12**). This chapter ends with a more detailed consideration of the court's requirements (**14.19**) followed by those of HMRC (**14.26**).

- *Chapter 15 Post-grant practice:* The duties and powers of personal representatives are considered first (**15.2**). The administration of the estate begins in earnest with the collection/realisation of the assets, following which the debts and other liabilities must be discharged (**15.6**). The final steps involve the distribution of the estate to those entitled (**15.14**).

 Visit the Online Resource Centre for more information and useful weblinks.
www.oxfordtextbooks.co.uk/orc/foundations11_12/

13

Entitlement to the estate

13.1 Basic structure of entitlement to the estate

In this chapter, we will be discussing the law underlying the entitlement to a person's property on his or her death. To do this, we shall need to consider aspects of:

- the law of 'testate succession' where the deceased has left a will (**13.2** to **13.9**);
- the law of 'intestate succession' if there is no will, or if any will left by the deceased is not wholly effective to dispose of their estate (**13.10** to **13.17**);
- the law governing devolution of property not passing under the terms of the deceased's will or the operation of the intestacy rules (**13.18** to **13.22**); and
- the law enabling members of the family or dependants of the deceased to make claims for provision against the estate (**13.23** to **13.31**).

13.2 Wills

In the following paragraphs we are assuming that a person has died leaving a will. You may have been instructed by a relative or friend of the deceased who has been appointed as executor by the will, or your firm may have been appointed. The role of executors is, in effect, to manage the deceased's estate until it can be distributed to those entitled. Normally, these entitlements will be determined by the deceased's will, but this is subject to a number of important provisos, ie that:

(a) the will is valid (**13.3**); that is, that the deceased (the testator) was both capable of and had the intention to make this will, and that it was properly executed. If the will is invalid it will be wholly ineffective, and the deceased's property will pass to those entitled under the intestacy rules (see **13.10** to **13.15**);

(b) the will has not been revoked (**13.4**). If so, again the deceased's property will pass to those entitled on intestacy;

(c) where the will has been altered, whether such alterations are effective (**13.5**);

(d) if the will refers to any other documents, whether these documents have been 'incorporated' and thus become part of the will (**13.6**);

(e) the will effectively deals with the whole of the deceased's estate capable of passing by will. Any such property that does not pass under the will, because, for example, the clause dealing with the residue of the deceased's estate fails (**13.7**), again passes under the intestacy rules;

(f) certain of the deceased's property may not have been capable of being disposed of by will, but will pass as of right to those entitled (**13.18** to **13.22**); and

(g) the will has not been varied after the testator's death. This may seem a surprising concept, but it is possible for the court to vary entitlements under a will if a successful claim is made under the Inheritance (Provision for Family and Dependants) Act 1975 (**13.23** to **13.30**). It is also possible for beneficiaries under a will (and those entitled under the intestacy rules) to vary their entitlements by consent, and indeed to reject outright gifts which would otherwise pass to them (**15.12**).

13.3 Validity of wills

13.3.1 Generally

English law will generally recognise a will as valid (Wills Act 1963) if it accords with the internal law of either:

(a) the country in which it was executed; or

(b) the country in which the deceased was domiciled or of which he was a national—either at the time of its execution or of the deceased's death.

So far as English domestic law is concerned, a valid will requires that the testator should have the *capacity* and *intention* to make the will, and compliance with the prescribed *formalities*.

13.3.2 Capacity

At the date of making the will, the testator must not (normally) have been under the age of 18 (being of age is, however, not a requirement if the testator was in a position to make a 'privileged' will as a soldier on actual military service or a seaman at sea). Additionally, the testator must have had the necessary mental capacity. The common law position has been somewhat altered by the Mental Capacity Act 2005.

13.3.2.1 The common law test

The traditional test for mental capacity to make a will was laid down in *Banks v Goodfellow* (1870) LR 5; QB 549. Testators must have understood three things:

(a) the nature of the act (ie the making of a will) and its effects;

(b) the extent of their property; and

(c) the claims to which they ought to give effect.

Generally, it had to be shown that the requisite understanding existed at the date of execution of the will. However, the rule in *Parker v Felgate* (1883) 8 PD 171 laid down an acceptable alternative where that could not be done. Under this rule, it was sufficient to show that:

(a) the requisite capacity existed at the date of giving instructions for the preparation of the will;

(b) the will was prepared in accordance with those instructions; and

(c) at the time of execution the testator understood that he was signing a will for which instructions had previously been given (though it is not necessary for the testator at that time to be able either to remember what those instructions were, or to understand the will if read over to him).

13.3.2.2 Position under the Mental Capacity Act 2005

The Mental Capacity Act 2005 was fully implemented in October 2007. The Act provides a new single test of capacity and reforms the law and procedures relating to decision-making on behalf of people who are unable to make decisions for themselves. A Code of Practice was issued in April 2007 giving further guidance on the Act.

Section 1 of the Act provides, among other things, for a statutory presumption of capacity, i.e. it is assumed that a person has capacity until the contrary is proved.

Section 2 sets out a single test of capacity, i.e. that a person lacks capacity in relation to a matter if at the material time he is unable to make a decision for himself in relation to the matter because of an impairment of, or a disturbance in the functioning of, the mind or brain.

Section 3 defines when a person is unable to make decision for the purposes of Section 2—for example, that a person is unable to understand the information relevant to the decision.

How will this new statutory test of capacity relate to the common law test of capacity to make a will as set out in *Banks v Goodfellow*? According to the Code of Practice, the Act's new definition of capacity is in line with the common law tests and the Act does not replace them. Such post-2007 case law as we have also indicates that s 3 is largely a restatement of the *Banks v Goodfellow* test.

It also seems likely that the rule in *Parker v Felgate* has survived the Mental Capacity Act 2005.

13.3.2.3 Proof of capacity

At common law the onus of proving the existence of the necessary mental capacity lay with the person seeking to prove the will, i.e. to have it accepted by the court as valid. Two rebuttable presumptions were of assistance here, namely that capacity was assumed where the will appeared to be rational and that mental states continued.

As noted above, under the Mental Capacity Act 2005, it is to be assumed that a person has capacity until the contrary is proved (s 1). The burden of proof is thus now on the person who challenges the will.

EXAMPLE 1

Ann, aged 80, made a will shortly before her death. She was known to be suffering from Alzheimer's disease. Ann's solicitor obtained her consent to consult her doctor who confirmed that Ann was only suffering from a mild form of the disease, and that there were times when Ann would have the necessary mental capacity to make a will. The doctor agreed to be present when the will was executed, and supplied the solicitor with a short note confirming that (at that time) Ann was capable of understanding the nature and effect of the will. The solicitor also kept an attendance note of the circumstances at the time of execution. If a person wished to challenge the will on the basis of Ann's lack of testamentary capacity, then the burden of proof would rest with them. In the light of the evidence gathered by Ann's solicitors, it looks unlikely that they would succeed.

13.3.2.4 Lack of capacity

Where capacity is not presumed or proven, the will cannot be admitted to probate.

For completeness, you should note that where a person lacks the necessary mental capacity to make a valid will for him or herself, the Court of Protection is able (under the provisions of s 16 of the Mental Capacity Act 2005) to make a 'statutory will' on behalf of that person.

13.3.3 Intention

13.3.3.1 The requirement

The testator must have had a general intention to make a will, and a specific intention to make the particular will. Put another way, the testator must know and approve the contents of the will. To the extent that such knowledge and approval are lacking, the will cannot be admitted to probate.

The necessary knowledge and approval must normally have existed at the date of the execution of the will: however, the rule in *Parker v Felgate* (**13.3.2.1**) also applies in this context.

13.3.3.2 Proof

The onus of proof lies on the propounder of the will. There is generally a rebuttable presumption that a testator with the necessary mental capacity executed the will with the requisite knowledge and approval of its contents. Those who seek to challenge the will would have to prove that the testator made the will (or perhaps a particular provision in it) as a result of force, fear, fraud, or undue influence; or that the necessary knowledge and approval were lacking because of a mistake.

There is no such presumption of knowledge and approval in two situations:

(a) The testator is blind or illiterate, or someone has signed the will on the testator's behalf. As we will see (**13.3.4.2**) a suitably drafted attestation clause will assist in supplying the necessary evidence of knowledge and approval.

(b) There are suspicious circumstances—in particular where the will substantially benefits the person who prepared it (or a close relative of that person). In such cases, evidence will be required of the testator's knowledge and approval of the contents of the will, otherwise the gift will fail.

13.3.4 Formalities

13.3.4.1 Section 9 of the Wills Act 1837 (as substituted by s 17 of the Administration of Justice Act 1982)

This section provides that:

No will shall be valid unless—

(a) it is in writing, and signed by the testator, or by some other person in his presence and by his direction; and

(b) it appears that the testator intended by his signature to give effect to the will; and

(c) the signature is made or acknowledged by the testator in the presence of two or more witnesses present at the same time; and

(d) each witness either—

(i) attests and signs the will; or

(ii) acknowledges his signature, in the presence of the testator (but not necessarily in the presence of any other witness), but no form of attestation shall be necessary.

The section does not apply to privileged wills, which can be made informally—even orally. Nor does it apply to statutory wills under the Mental Health Act 1983, for which that Act lays down special rules.

13.3.4.2 Attestation clause

Most wills will contain an attestation clause (it is to be hoped that all those professionally drawn will do so), although it is not a requirement for validity. If so, your task in proving the formal validity of the will is straightforward, as it will be presumed that the will has been executed in accordance with s 9 of the Wills Act 1837, ie there is a presumption of due execution.

There are a number of different forms of attestation clauses in common use, but all should show (as a minimum) compliance with the statutory requirements.

EXAMPLE 2

Hugh Jones has died. At the end of his typewritten will there is an attestation clause; the signatures are in ink.

> SIGNED by Hugh Jones as his
> last will in our joint presence   *Hugh Jones*
> and then by us in his
>
> *Jean Fredericks*
> 18, Westway, Barchester
> *Alan Price*
> 2, The Grove, Barchester

Unless there is evidence to the contrary, the will is presumed to be formally valid.

Where the testator was blind or illiterate, or someone else signed on behalf of the testator, we saw (in **13.3.3.2**) that there is no presumption of knowledge and approval and that this will have to be established if the will is to be admitted to probate. The simplest way of doing this is by the inclusion of a special attestation clause showing that:

(a) the will was read over to the testator in the presence of the witnesses;

(b) that the testator understood and approved the will;

(c) that the testator then signed the will or that it was signed by another in the testator's presence and at his direction; and

(d) that the witnesses attested the will as before.

If the will does not include an attestation clause (or only an inadequate one) compliance with the requirements of s 9 will have to be proved. This will also be necessary if there is something on the face of the will, for example, the testator's signature is not complete, to show that there were unusual circumstances at the time of execution. The 'mechanics' of how this is done are discussed at **14.24**, but it is convenient to consider below the requirements of s 9 in greater detail.

13.3.4.3 In writing

A will may be typed or handwritten (in ink or pencil—though the use of both will raise a rebuttable presumption that the parts written in pencil are 'deliberative only' and they will only be admitted to probate if there is evidence that the testator intended them to be final). There is no restriction as to the material upon which a will may be written, nor as to the language used: it may even be written in code, provided there is evidence available enabling it to be deciphered.

13.3.4.4 Signature

The testator's usual signature is ideal, but any mark (eg a thumbprint or rubber stamp) made by the testator and intended to be a signature will suffice. One of the leading cases on this point is *In the Goods of Chalcraft* [1948] P 222; 1 All ER 700, where a dying testatrix managed to sign 'E. Chal' but was unable to complete her full signature. It was held that this was sufficient; the testatrix intended what she had written (as much as she could manage in the circumstances) to be her signature. In another case, *In the Estate of Cook* [1960] 1 WLR 353; 1 All ER 689, the will began with the name of the testatrix and ended with the words 'Your loving mother'. The court accepted that the testatrix intended this to be her signature.

However, testators do not need to sign their own wills; the Act allows signature by another—at the testator's direction and in the testator's presence. The person so signing (who may be one of the witnesses) may sign their own name or that of the testator, and ideally, as noted above, the attestation clause should recite this.

13.3.4.5 With intent to give effect to the will

It is usual (and logical) for the signature to appear at the end of the will, but this need not necessarily occur. In *Wood v Smith* [1993] Ch 90, the testator had made his signature at the beginning of the will, intending this to give effect to his will, but written before he had made any provisions disposing of his estate. The Court of Appeal held that this could constitute a valid execution of the will provided the signing and the subsequently written dispositions all formed part of one transaction.

13.3.4.6 Signature made/acknowledged in the presence of two or more witnesses present at the same time

Where the testator is (as is usually the case) signing the will, the signature must be completed in the presence of at least two witnesses, present at the same time. The witnesses do not need to be able to see the contents of the will, or even to know that the testator is signing a will. They must, however, be able to see the testator writing the signature (for this reason a blind person cannot act as a witness), though it is not necessary for them to see the signature itself. Alternatively, the testator may sign the will and then acknowledge that signature (by words or conduct) in the presence of the (two or more) witnesses, who must be present at the same time and be able to see the signature. Again, ideally, this will be recited in the attestation clause. There are no special rules as to the capacity of the witnesses, but they must be bodily and mentally present (not, eg drunk or asleep). Although, by s 15 of the Wills Act 1837, a beneficiary will normally lose a gift under a will where that beneficiary or their spouse has witnessed the will (**13.7.5**), this does not affect the formal validity of the will.

13.3.4.7 Witnesses attest and sign (or acknowledge their signatures) in the presence of the testator

Attestation is, in effect, the validation of the testator's signature. The witnesses need not sign (or acknowledge) in each other's presence, though in practice this is what usually happens. However, the presence of the testator (bodily and mentally) is required when the signature/acknowledgement is made.

13.3.5 Codicils

A codicil is used to add to, amend, or partially revoke the terms of an existing will. The requirements for a valid codicil are the same as those required for a valid will.

13.4 Revocation of a will

13.4.1 The general position

Provided a testator retains testamentary capacity, a will is revocable at any time during the testator's lifetime. This is so even if the testator has entered into a contract not to revoke the will (though if the will is revoked the estate may be liable for the breach of contract).

13.4.1.1 Circumstances in which revocation may occur

Revocation may occur:

(a) automatically by operation of law:
   (i) marriage (see **13.4.1.3**) or civil partnership (see **13.4.1.4**);
   (ii) divorce, dissolution, or nullity (see **13.4.1.5** and **13.4.1.6**)

(b) by deliberate act of the testator:
   (i) later will or codicil (see **13.4.1.7**);
   (ii) destruction (see **13.4.1.8**).

Sometimes, revocation is regarded as conditional only. This is considered in **13.4.2**.
The law relating to alterations is discussed in **13.5**.

13.4.1.2 Mutual wills

A qualification to the principle of revocability is the equitable doctrine of mutual wills. The law in this area was recently confirmed in *Charles v Fraser* [2010] EWHC 2154, including the following

> Mutual wills are wills made by two or more persons, usually in substantially the same terms and conferring reciprocal benefits, following an agreement between them to make such wills and not to revoke them without the consent of the other.
>
> (a) For the doctrine to apply there has to be what amounts to a contract between the two testators that both wills shall be irrevocable and remain unaltered. The agreement may be incorporated in the will or proved by extraneous evidence which may be oral or in writing.
>
> (b) The agreement is enforced in equity by the imposition of a constructive trust on the property which is the subject matter of the agreement. The beneficiaries under the will that was not to be revoked may apply to the court for an order that the estate is held on trust to give effect to the provisions of that will.

It should be noted that such wills can be problematic and are not 'popular' with practitioners.

13.4.1.3 Marriage

If the testator has married after executing a will, that marriage will generally revoke that will (Wills Act 1837, s 18 (both in its original form and as substituted by Administration of Justice Act 1982)).

The scope of the exceptions to this general rule depends upon whether the will was made before 1983 or after 1982. Normally wills are dated at the time of execution, and we shall only deal here with wills made after 1982. The principal exceptions are found in s 18(3) and (4) of the Wills Act 1837 (as substituted):

(a) Section 18(3) provides that where 'it appears from the will that at the time it was made the testator was expecting to be married to a particular person and that he intended that the will should not be revoked by the marriage, the will shall not be revoked by his marriage to that person'.

(b) Section 18(4) provides that where 'it appears from a will that at the time it was made the testator was expecting to be married to a particular person and that he intended that a disposition in the will should not be revoked by his marriage to that person . . .' then that particular disposition will not be revoked by the marriage, and the rest of the dispositions will also be 'saved' unless the contrary appears from the will.

Only intrinsic evidence is admissible to establish the testator's expectation and intention, and an express declaration included in the will covering the points will prevent revocation.

EXAMPLE 3

John Kent married Avril Brown in September 2009, and died in April this year. His will, dated 8 August 2009, contained the following declaration:

'I DECLARE that I make this will in the expectation of my marriage to Avril Brown and that I intend that this will shall not be revoked by that marriage.'

John's will is effective despite his marriage.

It is possible for a testator to make a will conditional upon marriage, ie the will does not take effect unless and until the marriage takes place. Clearly, in such cases the question of revocation by subsequent marriage does not arise.

13.4.1.4 Civil partnerships

The Civil Partnership Act 2004 came into force on 5 December 2005, enabling same-sex couples to form an official 'civil partnership'. In broad terms, registered civil partners enjoy the same benefits as spouses. Civil partners, for example, have the same inheritance rights as married couples and enjoy the same benefits for taxation purposes. Changes of particular relevance to us are indicated below, but civil partners also have similar rights to married couples for employment, welfare benefit, maintenance, and child support purposes, etc.

So far as the topic of revocation is concerned, the Act inserts a new s 18B into the Wills Act 1837. A civil partnership between a testator and another person will generally revoke the testator's existing will, just as we have seen a marriage does. There are similar exceptions to those set out in **13.4.1.3** above, ie revocation will not occur if it appears from the will that the testator was expecting to form a civil partnership with a particular person and intended that the will, or a disposition in the will, should not be revoked by the formation of that civil partnership.

13.4.1.5 Divorce/nullity of marriage

Here, s 18A(1) of the Wills Act 1837 provides (subject to contrary intention in the will) for a sort of 'limited revocation' on a decree absolute of divorce or nullity. Any provisions in the will as to the appointment of the former spouse as executor or trustee take effect as if the former spouse had died on the date upon which the marriage is dissolved or annulled, and will thus be ineffective. Further, any property which is given by the will to the former spouse passes as if that spouse had died on that day, and will thus not pass to the former spouse.

Under s 6 Children Act 1989 (again, subject to expressed contrary intention) any appointment of the spouse as guardian of the testator's children is similarly 'revoked' on decree absolute of divorce.

Note that these provisions do not apply on separation, nor do they affect any provisions of the will other than those indicated.

13.4.1.6 Dissolution/nullity of civil partnerships

So far as civil partnerships are concerned, there is a court-based procedure for dissolving the civil partnership which is similar to the current divorce process for married couples. A new s 18C inserted into the Wills Act 1837 makes provision similar to that outlined in **13.4.1.5**. If the civil partnership is dissolved or nullified by the court, then the former civil partner will be treated as if they had died on the day upon which the dissolution or nullity takes effect, and, subject to a contrary intention in the will, any gift or appointment of them as an executor will be ineffective.

Any appointment of the former civil partner as guardian of the testator's children is also 'revoked'—see s 6 Children Act 1989.

13.4.1.7 Later will/codicil

By s 20 of the Wills Act 1837 a will is revoked (wholly or partially) by a later will or codicil; or 'by some writing declaring an intention to revoke the same and executed in the manner' of a will—as in *Re Spracklan's Estate* [1938] 2 All ER 345, where the Court of Appeal held that a letter (signed by the testatrix and duly attested) to her bank manager asking him to destroy the will which the bank was keeping for her satisfied this requirement.

A later will or codicil impliedly revokes an earlier testamentary disposition only to the extent that it is inconsistent with or merely repeats the terms of the earlier document. However, it is common—and helpful for the avoidance of doubt—for a will to contain an express revocation clause, such as, 'I hereby revoke all previous wills and codicils made by me'.

Clearly, a codicil to a will should not contain such a revocation clause!

The doctrine of conditional revocation may apply (see **13.4.2**).

13.4.1.8 Destruction

By s 20 of the Wills Act 1837 a will is also revoked by 'burning tearing or otherwise destroying the same by the testator or by some person in his presence and by his direction with the intention of revoking the same'.

There are thus two essential elements for an effective revocation:

(a) *An act of destruction*. An act of destruction is necessary; merely writing 'cancelled' or 'revoked' across the will is not enough. Nor is putting a line through parts of the will, or even the signature of the testator (though it will be otherwise if there has been an effective obliteration). In *Re Adams (Dec'd)* [1990] Ch 601, the testator's signature had been heavily scored through with a ball-point pen so as to render it illegible. The court held that a material part of the will had been destroyed with the intention to effect a revocation of the whole. Where part only of the will is destroyed, this may amount to a revocation of that part of the will only, or of the whole will if of a sufficiently substantial or vital part (eg the testator's or witnesses' signatures, *Hobbs v Knight* (1838) 1 Curt 769).

The court will admit extrinsic evidence of the testator's intention in determining the extent of any revocation, and may infer this from the state of the will at the date of death.

A destruction by someone other than the testator must, to be effective, be done in the testator's presence and at the testator's direction; if not, it is not possible for the testator subsequently to 'ratify' the act.

(b) *An intention to revoke.* The testator must have the intention to revoke at the time of the will's destruction. The necessary mental capacity is the same as that required for the making of a will (see **13.3.2**). Accidental revocation is, therefore, an impossibility; so is one based upon a mistaken belief that the will is invalid or has already been revoked. If a will is found mutilated at the date of death, this will be rebuttably presumed to have been done by the testator with the intention of revoking it (wholly or partially, depending upon the extent of the mutilation). There is a further rebuttable presumption that a will last known to have been in the testator's possession, but which cannot be found at the date of death, has been destroyed by the testator with the intention of revoking it.

The doctrine of conditional revocation may again apply (see **13.4.2** below).

13.4.2 Conditional revocation

This topic is generally beyond the scope of this book. Suffice it to say that we were considering above the situation where a testator has an absolute intention to revoke an existing will, in which case the revocation is immediately effective (assuming the other essential elements are present). There may be evidence, however, that the intention to revoke is conditional only, when the revocation will not be effective unless and until the condition is met. The condition might be, for example, the validity of a new will. Difficult questions may arise in such cases, both as to admissibility of evidence and as to construction (especially where revocation clauses appear to have been mistakenly included in wills or codicils) and specialist practitioner's books should be consulted.

The doctrine of conditional revocation may also apply in the context of alterations (see **13.5.1.3**).

13.5 Alterations in wills

13.5.1 Section 21 of the Wills Act 1837

This lays down the basic rule, which is that:

no obliteration, interlineation, or other alteration made in any will after the execution thereof shall be valid or have any effect, except so far as the words or effect of the will before such alteration shall not be apparent, unless such alteration shall be executed in like manner as hereinbefore is required for the execution of a will . . .

13.5.1.1 Effective alterations

An alteration will be effective if:

(a) it is made (or is presumed to have been made without evidence to the contrary) before execution. An unattested alteration is rebuttably presumed to have been made after execution (except where the 'alteration' is the filling in of a blank space, when the rebuttable presumption is that this was done prior to execution). Either presumption is rebutted by intrinsic or extrinsic evidence to the contrary;

(b) it is made after the will but duly executed. In practice, it is sufficient if the testator and the witnesses initial the alteration; or

(c) the original wording or effect of the will is, as a result of the 'alteration', not apparent (ie is not decipherable by natural means, see **13.5.1.3**(b)).

13.5.1.2 Ineffective alterations

An alteration will be ineffective if:

(a) it is unattested and made by the testator after (or it cannot be established to have been made before) execution and does not amount to an obliteration;

(b) it is made by someone other than the testator and without his knowledge and approval; or

(c) it is made by the testator without an intention to revoke.

13.5.1.3 Consequences of invalid alteration

This will depend upon whether the original wording is 'apparent' or not. The wording is apparent if it can be deciphered by 'natural means' (such as holding up to the light or using a magnifying glass) without resort to 'forbidden' methods (such as the use of chemicals, infra red photography or extrinsic evidence):

(a) If the original wording is so apparent, it will be admitted to probate.

(b) If it is not so apparent, the will is prima facie admitted to probate with a blank space where the obliteration has occurred. However, where there has been an attempted substitution in place of what has been obliterated the doctrine of conditional revocation may apply; this will allow the courts to employ any of the forbidden methods mentioned above in an attempt to ascertain and give effect to the original wording.

13.5.2 Precautions

It is clearly sensible to have all alterations (even those made before execution of the will) initialled by the testator and the witnesses. Further, testators should be discouraged from attempting to make their own 'adjustments' to their wills.

13.6 Incorporation by reference

As we have seen (**13.3.4**), for a document to be admitted to probate it must be executed in accordance with the requirements of s 9 of the Wills Act 1837. However, a document not so executed may, in effect, become part of the will under the doctrine of incorporation by reference.

For this to happen, three conditions must be met:

(a) The document must be clearly identified in the will.

(b) The document must already exist at the date of the will. The onus of proving this fact lies with the person seeking incorporation of the document.

(c) The document must be referred to in the will as already in existence at the time of execution. If this is not the case (eg because the statement is equivocal or the reference is to a document to be prepared in the future) the document in question cannot be incorporated.

EXAMPLE 4

Clause 3 of a recently deceased testator's will (made in 2009) states 'I leave £10,000 to be held on the trusts set out in clause 5 of the Trust Deed dated 8 March 2005 and made between myself of the one part and Daniel Thomas and Ruth Brown of the other part'. The deceased's executor, Daniel Thomas, tells you that he has the trust deed mentioned in the will at home in his safe. It would seem that all the requirements for incorporation are satisfied; the gift under the will is prima facie valid. The trust deed would thus be submitted to probate with the will (see **14.24**).

13.7 Failure of gifts by will

There are a number of reasons why gifts contained in wills may fail. We shall only deal (at **13.7.3** to **13.7.5**) with three of those reasons, and with the consequences of failure at **13.7.6**. You should additionally note, however, that a gift will fail if the wording is uncertain, as do gifts contrary to public policy. In the last category, for example, a person convicted of murdering the testator is not permitted to take a benefit under the victim's will (or intestacy). Again, a beneficiary of a gift under a will is entitled to refuse that gift (ie to disclaim it), and a gift offending the rules against perpetuity and accumulation will also fail. None of these issues is considered further here.

First, a mention of terminology that you may encounter in wills. Technically, a 'legacy' is a gift of personalty (eg money, shares, chattels) and a devise is a gift of realty (eg freehold land). The term 'legacy' is commonly used to encompass both types of gift, as we will in the remainder of this chapter.

Legacies can further be classified as specific, general, demonstrative or residuary (**13.7.2**), relevant when considering whether a legacy fails and the consequences of failure. Before considering the 'hallmarks' of these legacies, we should briefly note two rules of construction as to the date from which the will speaks.

13.7.1 Date from which the will speaks

Unless there is a contrary intention in the will, then:
(a) as to property, the will speaks and takes effect 'as if it had been executed immediately before the death of the testator' (Wills Act 1837, s 24). Thus a gift of the contents of the testator's house will prima facie be construed as a gift of the contents as at the date of death (rather than at the date of the will).

The use of words such as 'my', 'now', or 'at present' in describing the gift may be sufficient to indicate a contrary intention. For example, a gift of 'my 500 shares in ABC plc' would probably be construed as a gift of the shares owned at the date of the will. On the other hand, a gift of 'all my shares in ABC plc' would prima facie pass the shares owned at the date of death; the subject matter of the gift here is generic and so described as to be capable of increase or decrease between the date of the will and the date of death.

(b) As to the objects of the gift (ie the beneficiaries), the will speaks from the date of execution. In other words, s 24 does not apply (unless a contrary intention appears from the will). As a result, a gift to 'the vicar of St Luke's Church Barchester' is prima facie a gift to the person fulfilling that description at the date of the will. This rule does not apply to 'class gifts' or to identified gifts to each member of a class (see further at **13.8.2**).

13.7.2 Legacies: Specific, general, demonstrative, pecuniary, or residuary

13.7.2.1 Specific legacy

This is a gift of particular property owned by the deceased distinguished from any other property of the same kind which may be owned by the deceased, eg 'my 500 shares in XYZ plc', 'my freehold property Greenacre'. Such gifts are subject to the doctrine of ademption if the testator does not own the property concerned at the date of death (see **13.7.3**).

13.7.2.2 General legacy

This is a gift of property not distinguished by the testator from other similar property, eg '500 shares in XYZ plc'. This constitutes a gift of *any* 500 shares in the company (even if in fact that was the number which the testator owned at the date of the will). Such gifts are not subject to the doctrine of ademption, so that if in the example the testator did not own any XYZ plc shares at the date of death, the beneficiary is entitled to require estate funds (provided these are sufficient) to be used to buy 500 such shares.

13.7.2.3 Demonstrative legacy

Such legacies (not commonly encountered today) are essentially general in character, but a specific source is identified from which it is to be paid, eg '£1,000 to Ambrose to be paid from my Newtown Building Society Account'. Such legacies are not ademeed if the account has been closed during the testator's lifetime, or there is insufficient in the account at the date of death to pay the legacy in full. In such circumstances, the beneficiary is entitled to any balance at that time, and to have the deficiency paid as a general legacy.

13.7.2.4 Pecuniary legacy

This is a gift of money, and usually is general in character, eg a gift of '£5,000'. However, it may be specific (eg a gift of 'the £5,000 which I keep in my safe' or 'the £5,000 which Xavier owes me'); or demonstrative (eg '£5,000 payable from my current account at Newtown Bank').

13.7.2.5 Residuary legacy/devise

Residuary gifts embrace all the rest of the deceased's property (ie not disposed of by any specific, general, or demonstrative gifts).

13.7.3 Failure of legacies: ademption

To the extent that a testator no longer owns the property which is the subject of a specific legacy at the date of death, the gift is ademeed, ie it fails, and the disappointed beneficiary is not entitled to any compensation. Ademption may occur because the testator has sold the property, or given it away before death.

> **EXAMPLE 5**
>
> Clause 3 of Paul's will states, 'I give my 800 shares in PQR plc to my brother Robert'. It is likely that this will be construed as a specific gift of the 800 shares that Paul owned at the date of the will in PQR plc. If Paul sold 300 of those shares before he died, Robert would only take the remaining 500 shares.

Ademption can also occur where there has been a change in substance (ie in the very nature of the property) as opposed to a mere change in name or form. This distinction is not always easy to see.

> **EXAMPLE 6**
>
> Clause 4 of Paul's will provides, 'I give my 100 shares in BCD plc to my sister Susan'. Again this is likely to be construed as a specific gift. Suppose before Paul died BCD plc subdivided its shares so that one original share was represented by five new shares. It is likely that this would be construed as a mere change in the form of the shares, and Susan would take the 500 (new) shares in BCD plc. If, however, BCD plc were taken over by another company (say FGH plc), and FGH plc issued shares in FGH plc to replace those held in the original company, it is likely that this would be seen as a change in substance (ie shares in an entirely different company) and the gift of the BCD plc shares to Susan would fail.

Note that ademption only applies to specific legacies; it has no application to general legacies (eg '500 shares in XYZ plc', see **13.7.2.2**) or where the subject matter of the gift is ascertained at the date of death (eg 'the contents of my house', see **13.7.1**).

13.7.4 Failure of legacies: lapse

13.7.4.1 Beneficiary dying before testator

As a general rule, a beneficiary must survive the testator in order to take a gift under that testator's will, otherwise the gift lapses—in which event (unless there is an effective substitutional provision, see **13.7.4.3**) the subject matter of the intended gift will fall into residue, or (if itself a share of residue) pass under the intestacy rules (see **13.7.6**).

We saw at **13.4.1** that if the testator's marriage/civil partnership has been dissolved, then, unless the will provides otherwise, gifts in the will to the former spouse/civil partner will in effect lapse.

A class gift (see **13.8.2**) only lapses if all members of the class predecease the testator: the rule is similar in the case of gifts to beneficial joint tenants.

13.7.4.2 Commorientes

Usually there is no problem in determining who died first—the testator or the beneficiary—and thus whether the gift has lapsed. What, however, if they die in a common accident (eg a plane crash), and the order of death is uncertain? Unless the will provides that the beneficiary must survive the testator for a certain period (28 days is common) the *commorientes* rule (Law of Property Act 1925, s 184) applies. Under this rule, where there is no evidence as to the order in which deaths have occurred then, for succession purposes, the younger is deemed to have survived the elder. Thus a gift in the younger's will to the elder would lapse, but not *vice versa*. The *commorientes* rule generally applies both where there is a will, and where there is no will so that the estate will be distributed under the intestacy rules (see **13.12**).

13.7.4.3 Substitutional gifts

Although it is not possible to prevent the operation of the doctrine of lapse, the will may specifically provide as to what is to happen to the gifted property if the original beneficiary dies before the testator. This is particularly common so far as residuary gifts are concerned.

EXAMPLE 7

Della's will leaves, '£2,000 to my niece Jane and the rest of my estate to my husband Neil but if he fails to survive me then to my son Mark'. Only Della's son Mark survives her; the gifts to Jane and Neil therefore lapse. Jane's gift will thus fall into residue, and Mark will take Della's entire estate.

13.7.4.4 Substitution by statute

Section 33 of the Wills Act 1837 in effect provides a sort of statutory substitutional clause—but only where the original gift is to the testator's issue (ie child or remoter lineal descendant). This section applies where:

(a) a will contains a gift to the child or issue (ie grandchild, great-grandchild, etc) of the testator; and

(b) the intended beneficiary dies before the testator, leaving issue; and

(c) issue of the intended beneficiary are living (including *en ventre sa mère*) at the testator's death.

If these conditions are met then, in the absence of a contrary intention shown by the will, the gift takes effect as a gift to such issue, who take (in equal shares if more than one) the gift which their parent would have taken. It is not clear whether if the original gift is contingent the gift 'substituted' by s 33 is subject to the same contingency.

The section also applies (in the absence of a contrary intention in the will) to a class gift to the testator's children or remoter issue. It is important to appreciate that s 33 cannot prevent the failure of gifts in favour of beneficiaries who predecease but who are not issue of the testator. Thus in the example of Della's will at **13.7.4.3**, s 33 would not operate to save the gift of £2,000 for any of Jane's children who survived Della. However, if Mark had also predeceased but his two children survived Della, then under s 33, Della's entire estate would pass to those two children in equal shares.

13.7.5 Failure of gifts to witnesses

A gift in a will fails if the beneficiary or the beneficiary's spouse or civil partner witnesses the will, though the validity of the will as such is not affected (Wills Act 1837, s 15). However, the gift will not fail if, ignoring the attestation by the beneficiary or spouse or civil partner, the will is duly executed, ie because there are at least two other witnesses who are not beneficiaries or their spouses or civil partners. Further, a gift within the terms of s 15 may be 'saved' if the will is subsequently confirmed by a codicil which is independently witnessed.

If the will appoints solicitors (or other professionals) to act as executors, it will invariably also contain a charging clause, enabling them to be paid for their work in administering the estate. On a death prior to 1 February 2001, s 15 would cause the charging clause to fail if a member of the firm appointed was one of the (two) witnesses to the will. However, where the deceased died after 31 January 2001, by virtue of s 28(4)(a) of the Trustee Act 2000, such a provision is treated as remuneration for services (and not as a gift) so that the charging clause would not fail in such circumstances.

Where the beneficiary's spouse or civil partner has witnessed the will, s 15 applies only if the beneficiary and the witness were married or civil partners at the date of the execution of the will; there will be no problem where they married or entered into a civil partnership after that date.

13.7.6 Consequences of failure of legacies

If the gift fails then clearly the original intended beneficiary will not take. Who will take instead?

13.7.6.1 Alternative provision in will or by statute

First, it is necessary to consider whether the will itself has made alternative provision in the event of failure of the original gift. Thus, in the case of ademption, has the testator provided that the beneficiary is to receive alternative property if the original gifted property is no longer in the estate at death? In the case of lapse, does the will contain an effective substitutional clause (**13.7.4.3**)? Alternatively, is the gift saved by statute (see Wills Act 1837, s 33, **13.7.4.4**) or the saving provisions of s 15 of the Wills Act 1837 or s 28(4) of the Trustee Act 2000?

13.7.6.2 No alternative provision

Save where the gift has adeemed, the property which was the subject matter of the failed gift will form part of the deceased's estate. Who is now entitled to this property? The answer will depend on the type of gift which has failed. Unless the failed gift was a gift of residue, then (assuming there is an effective residuary gift) the gifted property will 'fall into residue', ie swell the property that would otherwise pass under the residuary legacy.

If a gift of residue wholly fails, the entire residuary estate will pass to those entitled under the intestacy rules (see **13.10** to **13.17**). If, however, the gift of residue only fails in part, there is a 'partial intestacy' as to the property comprised in the failed gift: this part will again pass to those entitled on the deceased's intestacy. A partial intestacy will also arise where the will contains effective non-residuary gifts, but either there is no gift of residue or it fails wholly or in part.

EXAMPLE 8

Jack's will contains the following gifts, '£1,000 to my godson Stephen Smith and the residue of my estate to be divided equally between my daughter Harriet and my late wife's son Keith Jones'. Both Stephen and Keith have predeceased Jack, but Harriet and Keith's daughter Rachel survive.

The pecuniary legacy lapses, and this sum will now form part of the residuary estate. Harriet will take one-half of the residue in accordance with the will, but what will happen to Keith's lapsed one half share? It will not pass to Harriet as the gift was to Harriet and Keith as tenants in common in equal shares and the will does not provide what is to happen if one of them predeceases the testator. Section 33 of the Wills Act 1837 will not save the remaining one-half share for Rachel (because Keith is not Jack's issue). Jack is thus partially intestate, and the failed gift will pass to those entitled on Jack's intestacy.

In this example, a partial intestacy would have been avoided if:

(a) the will had included an express substitutional gift in favour of Keith's issue in the event of the gift to Keith failing; or

(b) the will had provided that the residue was to be divided 'equally between such of my daughter Harriet and my late wife's son Keith Jones as survive me'. In this case, the effect would have been to pass the whole of the residuary estate to Harriet; or

(c) the will had left the residuary estate to Harriet and Keith 'jointly' (ie as joint tenants) rather than 'equally'. Here again the effect would have been that Harriet would take the whole of the residuary estate.

> If Jack's daughter had also died before him leaving no children alive at the date of his death, then Jack's entire estate would pass under the intestacy rules.

13.8 Gifts to children in wills

We do not intend to cover the law on construction of wills—a major topic in itself. Gifts to children are so common in wills, however, that it is worth noting a few points of construction in relation to such gifts.

13.8.1 Meaning of 'children'

In the absence of contrary intention in the will, gifts to a person's 'children' (whether that person is the testator or anyone else) will include all children of that person (whether legitimate, illegitimate or adopted by them). It will not include a natural child of that person who has been adopted by someone else. Relevant legislation includes the Legitimacy Act 1976, the Adoption Act 1976 and (for wills made after 3 April 1988), Family Law Reform Act 1987.

13.8.2 Class gifts

Class gifts are particularly used in wills to leave property to children where it is not desired to name the children individually. Class gifts do raise a number of construction issues. You will be relieved to know that we do not intend to explore the complex cases, but merely to explain briefly the basic rules and highlight points that may need further research.

13.8.2.1 How to recognise a class gift

A class gift is a gift of property to be divided among beneficiaries who fulfil a general description, for example, '£50,000 to the children of Zoe', '£50,000 to the children of Zoe who attain the age of 18'. In such cases, the total value of the gift is clear: the problem is to know how to share it among those entitled. This will obviously depend upon how many people fit the description. In the examples given, it would not be possible to answer this question with certainty at least until the death of Zoe; in the meantime, no distribution would be possible.

A similar problem arises where the gift in the will takes the form of an individual gift to the members of a class, eg '£5,000 to each of the children of Zebedee'. Here, what the prospective beneficiaries are to take is identified but until the death of Zebedee it cannot be known how many children will qualify.

13.8.2.2 Class-closing rules

The courts have invented class-closing rules to overcome these problems and allow distribution at an earlier date. The various rules (which one applies to a given case depends upon the type of gift involved) determine when the class will close. In principle, this will generally happen when there is one person fitting the description who has a vested interest. At whatever point the class closes, it does so to the exclusion of any potential beneficiary not then 'living'—a term which includes a child conceived and subsequently born alive. This is obviously 'unfair' to those thus excluded from benefit, but this disadvantage is considered to be outweighed by the advantage of earlier distribution.

The class-closing rules may be excluded by a clear provision in the testator's will, such as 'to the children of Zoe living at my death', or 'to the children of Zebedee whenever born'.

As indicated above, the rules (if not so excluded) differ in detail according to the type of gift involved. We shall only mention here the types of class gift most commonly encountered.

(a) Immediate vested gift, eg '£5,000 to the children of Arthur'. The class closes at the date of the testator's death if there is any child of Arthur then living. If there are none, the class remains open until the death of Arthur.

(b) Immediate contingent gift, eg '£5,000 to the children of Arthur who attain the age of 18'. Here the class closes at the testator's death if any such child has already reached the age of 18. The class will include any of Arthur's children who are 18 plus any others then living who subsequently attain that age. If a 'class member' dies before 18, then they will not share in the gift. If at the date of the testator's death no child of Arthur has fulfilled the contingency (ie attained 18), the class remains open until one does; the class will then close around that child and any others then living who subsequently attain the age of 18.

(c) Individual gift to members of a class, eg '£5,000 to each of the children of Arthur', or '£5,000 to each of the children of Arthur who attain the age of 18'. In these cases, unless there is a contrary intention in the will, the class will close at the date of the testator's death. If there are no children of Arthur then living, the gift fails.

13.9 Wills: checkpoints

1. Formal validity:
    (a) Is the will signed by the testator and two witnesses (**13.3.4.1**)?
    (b) Does the will contain an appropriate attestation clause (**13.3.4.2**)?
    (c) If no/inadequate attestation clause, has s 9 of the Wills Act 1837 been complied with (**13.3.4.3** to **13.3.4.7**)?
    (d) Is there any suggestion that the testator lacked capacity (**13.3.2**)? Note that the burden of proving that the testator lacked capacity rests with the person(s) who challenged the will (**13.3.2.3**).
    (e) Is there any suggestion that the testator did not know and approve of the contents of the will (**13.3.3**)? Note presumptions (**13.3.3.2**).
2. Revocation:
    (a) Is the will the most recent one (**13.4.1.7**)?
    (b) Does it contain a revocation clause (**13.4.1.7**)?
    (c) Has the testator married (**13.4.1.3**) or entered into a civil partnership (**13.4.1.4**) since the date of the will?
    (d) Has the marriage/civil partnership of the testator been dissolved/annulled (**13.4.1.5** and **13.4.1.6**)?
3. Alterations:
    (a) Are any alterations effective (**13.5.1.1**)?
    (b) Are any alterations ineffective (**13.5.1.2**)?
4. Incorporation:
    (a) If the will refers to another document, has that document been incorporated and is it available (**13.6**)?

5. Failure of gifts:
    (a) Does the testator's estate include property specifically gifted by the will (**13.7.3**)?
    (b) Have any named beneficiaries predeceased the testator (13.7.4.1)?
    (c) If so, is there an effective substitutional gift (13.7.4.3) or is the gift saved by s 33 of the Wills Act 1837 (13.7.4.4)?
    (d) Has a beneficiary or their spouse/civil partner acted as witness (**13.7.5**)?
6. Class gifts
    (a) Does the will contain class gifts (13.8.2.1)?

(b) If so, have the class-closing rules (13.8.2.2) been excluded by the terms of the will?
    (c) If not:
        (i) Does the will contain an immediate vested class gift and, if so, is any person within the class alive at the date of the testator's death?
        (ii) Does the will contain an immediate contingent class gift and, if so, has any person fulfilled the contingency at the date of the testator's death?
        (iii) Does the will contain an individual gift to members of a class and, if so, is any person within the class alive at the testator's death?

13.10 Intestacy

We have already made reference to the 'intestacy rules'. Distribution of a deceased's estate is governed by these rules when the deceased has died either:

(a) wholly (or totally) intestate, ie without having effectively disposed of any of their property by will. This may be because the deceased never made a will or the will is invalid; or

(b) partially intestate, ie having made a valid will but this does not dispose of the whole of the estate. This situation may arise where the will contains no residuary gift, or where there is a gift of residue but this has wholly or partly failed (eg because a residuary beneficiary has predeceased the testator, and there is no effective substitutional gift, either in the will or by the operation of s 33 of the Wills Act 1837—see **13.7**).

In the first case, the distribution of the whole of the deceased's succession estate will be in accordance with the intestacy rules: in the second, these rules will only apply to such of the deceased's property as does not pass under the will. In both cases, however, certain types of property will pass on death quite independently of the intestacy rules; for example, property held by the deceased as a beneficial joint tenant (see **13.19**).

The Law Commission's Consultation Paper No 191—*Intestacy and Family Provision Claims on Death*—published in October 2009 proposes a number of changes which, if enacted, would significantly alter the position set out below. For example, a surviving spouse or civil partner would take the entire estate where the intestate died without issue; and in some circumstances a surviving cohabitant would be treated as if a spouse or civil partner for the purposes of the intestacy rules. Consultation on the proposals closed at the end of February 2010 but it will be some time before it is known what changes, if any, are likely to be made.

13.11 Intestacy: the basic position

Where the deceased left a will, its effective provisions will be implemented. To the extent that the estate is not disposed of by will, its distribution is governed by the rules in Part IV of the Administration of Estates Act 1925 (as amended).

13.11.1 Section 33(1) of the Administration of Estates Act 1925 (as amended)

Section 33(1) provides that the personal representatives hold the intestate's estate not disposed of by will on trust with a power to sell. The personal representatives must pay the funeral, testamentary and administration expenses, debts, and other liabilities of the deceased out of the intestate's ready money and from the net proceeds of any part of the estate which is sold.

The residuary estate (what is left after all the liabilities and expenses have been discharged) is then to be shared among those entitled according to the statutory rules.

13.11.2 Entitlement

As we will see, the position of a spouse (provided that spouse survives the intestate by 28 days) is considered first under the intestacy rules. The surviving spouse may take the whole of the intestate's estate. If not, or the spouse does not so survive, the rules then set out in order of entitlement categories of the deceased's blood relatives who are entitled to (or to a share in) the intestate's estate. Earlier classes take to the exclusion of later classes of relatives, and generally children of a predeceasing relative take their parent's share. If the deceased was partially intestate, the surviving spouse or some of these relatives may also benefit under the will, but this will not affect any entitlement that they may have under the intestacy rules. **Figures 13.1** and **13.2** at pages 278 and 279 set out the various entitlements.

By virtue of the Civil Partnership Act 2004 a civil partner has similar rights to the intestate's estate as those enjoyed by a spouse.

13.11.3 The statutory trusts

In the case of certain classes of relatives—namely, issue, brothers and sisters, uncles, and aunts—it will be seen that the class takes on 'the statutory trusts'. Section 47 of the Administration of Estates Act 1925 defines this expression as meaning:

(a) equally for all members of the class of relatives concerned living or *en ventre sa mère* (ie conceived) at the date of the intestate's death who attain the age of 18 or marry or enter into a civil partnership under that age;

(b) the issue of any class members who predecease take *per stirpes* their parent's share provided they (ie the issue) attain 18 or marry or enter into a civil partnership earlier.

Where the potential beneficiary dies before the intestate (regardless of whether that person had attained the age of 18 or was married or had entered into a civil partnership), but leaves issue, then the substitution referred to in (b) above applies. Where, however, the potential beneficiary is living at the date of the intestate's death (a) but subsequently dies before attaining a vested interest (ie before attaining the age of 18 or earlier marriage or entry into a civil partnership), the estate will be dealt with as if that person had never existed (even if survived by their issue).

This latter, slightly anomalous, position would be altered if the Estates of Deceased Persons (Forfeiture Rule and Law of Succession) Bill 2011 is enacted. The Bill (a Private Members' Bill currently before Parliament and supported by the Government) proposes that if a minor child survived the intestate but died before attaining 18 or earlier marriage/entry into a civil partnership, but was survived by issue, then such issue should take their parent's share.

Until any such change is enacted it is, therefore, important to note whether the potential beneficiary dies before or after the intestate, as **Example 9** illustrates.

13.12 Entitlement where there is a surviving spouse (or a surviving civil partner) of the intestate

To be entitled the spouse (ie a person to whom the intestate was lawfully married at the date of death) must survive the intestate by 28 days. There is no entitlement under the intestacy rules for a divorced spouse (ie after decree absolute) or one who is judicially separated.

Similar provisions apply where the deceased left a surviving civil partner—to be entitled the civil partner must survive by 28 days and there is no entitlement once the civil partnership is dissolved.

We noted in **13.7.4.2** that the *commorientes* rule (where the order of death is uncertain) relates also to cases where there is a total or partial intestacy. So far as intestate succession between spouses/civil partners is concerned, the spouse/civil partners must survive the deceased by 28 days, so that the point cannot arise. In the case of intestate succession between other relatives, the *commorientes* rule will apply in the usual way, as there is no requirement that they survive the deceased by 28 days in order to become entitled.

Assuming that the deceased's spouse or civil partner so survives, that spouse's or civil partner's entitlement will depend on whether the deceased's issue also survive, and if not, whether certain of the deceased's other close relatives survive (see **Figure 13.1** at page 278).

EXAMPLE 9

Ian has recently died intestate, leaving the following issue:

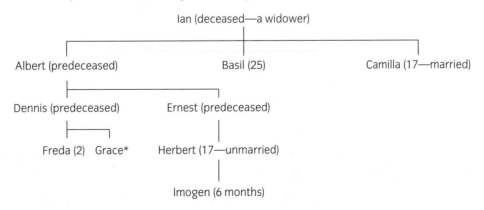

* Grace was *en ventre sa mère* at the date of Ian's death.

Ian's estate will pass to his issue on the statutory trusts. As he had three children it will prima facie be divided into three shares.

Both Basil and Camilla will take a vested one-third share each—they have satisfied the contingency. Note that Camilla, although she has fulfilled the contingency, is under 18 and so will not be able to give an effective discharge to the personal representatives. The capital of her share will have to be held for her until she attains her majority. She will, however, be entitled to receive the income in the meantime, as a married infant can give a good receipt for income. Were she to die before attaining 18, her one-third share would pass as part of her estate to those entitled on her intestacy.

Albert's share will pass under the statutory trusts to his issue, ie his one-third share will be subdivided into two equal shares. The (one-sixth) share which Dennis would have inherited had he survived Ian, will be held on the statutory trusts for Freda and Grace; Ernest's one-sixth share will similarly be held for Herbert (he does not obtain a vested interest because he is not married).

If both Freda and Grace were to die before attaining vested interests (eg they both die aged 15) their one-sixth share would accrue to Herbert, provided he in turn survives to attain a vested interest. If he also fails to do so, the estate will be distributed as if Freda, Grace and Herbert had never existed. The whole of Albert's share will therefore accrue to Basil and Camilla, since these will be the only interests under the statutory trusts which vest. Imogen will not be entitled as her father (Herbert) was alive at the date of Ian's death.

13.12.1 Spouse (or civil partner) alone

Where there are no issue, parents, or brothers or sisters of the whole blood (or their issue), the personal representatives hold the whole of the residuary estate for the surviving spouse (or civil partner) absolutely.

13.12.2 Spouse (or civil partner) and issue

13.12.2.1 The spouse (or civil partner)

The spouse or civil partner is entitled to:

(a) the personal chattels absolutely;

(b) statutory legacy of £250,000, free of costs, with interest (currently at 6 per cent) from the date of death until payment; and

(c) life interest in one-half of the residuary estate. Thus, if anything remains after the personal chattels and the statutory legacy have been paid, the spouse or civil partner is entitled to the income for life from one-half of the balance of the estate.

All property passing to the surviving spouse or civil partner under these rules (including the half of the residuary estate invested to fund the life interest) passes tax free as it enjoys the benefit of the inheritance tax spouse/civil partner exemption.

13.12.2.2 The issue

The issue are entitled (on the statutory trusts, see **13.11.3**) to the other one-half of the residuary estate and to the remainder interest in that half in which the spouse or civil partner has a life interest.

13.12.2.3 Personal chattels

The term 'personal chattels' is defined by s 55(1)(x) of the Administration of Estates Act 1925 as including:

carriages, horses, stable furniture and effects (not used for business purposes), motor cars and accessories (not used for business purposes), garden effects, domestic animals, plate, plated articles, linen, china, glass, books, pictures, prints, furniture, jewellery, articles of household or personal use or ornament, musical and scientific instruments and apparatus, wines, liquors and consumable stores, but do not include any chattels used at the death of the intestate for business purposes nor money or securities for money.

In spite of this definition showing signs of its age, it is clear that it is intended to cover items of personal and domestic use and ornament. In most cases there is unlikely to be much difficulty in determining whether a particular item, by its nature, falls within the definition. However, use is sometimes relevant: assets used for business purposes are excluded, so that it would appear that a car used for both business and private purposes falls outside the definition.

The phrase 'articles of household or personal use' has been held to include, for example:

(a) a 60-foot yacht used by the deceased for pleasure (*Re Chaplin* [1950] Ch 507; 2 All ER 155);

(b) a stamp collection made by the deceased as a hobby (*Re Reynold's Will Trusts* [1966] 1 WLR 19; 3 All ER 686); and

(c) a collection of watches worth some £50,000 out of an estate of approximately £80,000 (*Re Crispin's Will Trusts* [1975] Ch 245; [1974] 3 WLR 657; [1974] 3 All ER 772).

13.12.3 Spouse, (or civil partner), no issue but parent(s) or brothers/sisters of the whole blood (or their issue)

In this case, the spouse or civil partner takes (free of tax as a result of the inheritance tax spouse/civil partner exemption):

(a) the personal chattels absolutely;

(b) statutory legacy of £450,000, free of costs and with interest (as before); and

(c) one-half of the residuary estate (ie the capital) absolutely.

The other one-half of the residuary estate passes to the intestate's parent(s) or, if neither survives, to the brothers and sisters of the whole blood or their issue on the statutory trusts.

13.12.4 Special rules applying to spouses (or civil partners)

There are two possible elections which may be open to the surviving spouse or civil partner and, if exercised, will affect the distribution described above. These relate to the surviving spouse/civil partner's life interest and to the 'matrimonial home'.

13.12.4.1 Redemption of life interest

Where the surviving spouse/civil partner has a life interest in the residuary estate, an election may be made, in writing, to the personal representatives to capitalise that life interest (Administration of Estates Act 1925, s 47A). If the spouse/civil partner is the sole personal representative, the election is made to the Senior District Judge of the Family Division. The time limit for making the election is 12 months from the date of the grant, but the court can, in its discretion, extend the time limit.

The effect of making the election is that, instead of receiving the income only from one-half of the residuary estate for life, the spouse/civil partner takes a capital sum (inevitably less than half of the residuary estate) absolutely. The balance of the residuary estate (after the deduction of the costs of the capitalisation) will then be held for the issue on the statutory trusts.

There is a complex statutory formula for arriving at the capitalised value. However, if the issues are all *sui juris* the figure may be arrived at instead by agreement between the spouse/civil partner and the issue.

13.12.4.2 Appropriation of the matrimonial home

Schedule 2 to the Intestates' Estates Act 1952 enables the surviving spouse/civil partner, in effect, to purchase the matrimonial home (or the deceased's interest in it where they were beneficial tenants in common). The election is not necessary where the deceased and the surviving spouse/civil partner were beneficial joint tenants because the deceased's interest accrues automatically to the survivor, independently of the intestacy rules.

The 'matrimonial home' is defined as that in which the surviving spouse/civil partner was resident at the date of death of the intestate; it does not matter whether the deceased was also so resident.

The Act gives the spouse/civil partner the right to require the personal representatives to appropriate the matrimonial home (at its value at the date of appropriation, see *Re Collins* [1975] 1 WLR 309; [1975] 1 All ER 321) in partial or total satisfaction of the spouse/civil partner's statutory legacy and/or absolute or capitalised life interest in the residuary estate. If these are not adequate to 'purchase' the deceased's interest, the deficiency may be made up out of their own resources by the spouse/civil partner.

This election too must be made in writing to the personal representatives within 12 months of the grant (the court having again a discretion to extend the time limit). Normally, during this period the personal representatives cannot sell the matrimonial home without the consent of the spouse/civil partner. If the spouse/civil partner is one of two or more personal representatives, the notice should be given to the others. The Schedule does not say what is to happen if the spouse/civil partner is the sole personal representative.

In four cases, the consent of the court is required before the election can be made. Broadly, this would be when the home was only part of a building owned by the deceased, or if the home was part of a farm or other business premises, and specialist texts should be consulted in these circumstances.

The general power of appropriation (**15.4.2.1**) is also available to the surviving spouse/civil partner if also the personal representative of the intestate—but note the 'self-dealing' rule mentioned in **15.4.2.3**.

13.13 Issue of the intestate

Subject to the entitlement of any surviving spouse/civil partner, the residuary estate is held for the issue of the intestate on the statutory trusts.

Effectively, children take to the exclusion of remoter issue, except where a child predeceases the intestate leaving issue, when, as we have seen, the issue take their parent's share on the statutory trusts.

An adopted child is treated as a legitimate child of its adoptive parent(s) and not as the child of its natural parents (Adoption Act 1976, s 39). A legitimated child is treated as if born legitimate (Legitimacy Act 1976, ss 5 and 10). Note, however, that step-children have no entitlement to the estate of their step-parent under the intestacy rules.

Section 18 of the Family Law Reform Act 1987 provides that (on a death on/after 4 April 1988) the distribution of assets on intestacy is to be determined without regard to whether the parents of a particular person were (or were not) married to each other. In other words, illegitimacy is ignored—and this applies not only to the intestate's issue but to all other relatives who may be entitled under the intestacy rules (on a death before 4 April 1988 different rules applied).

The Family Law Reform Act 1987 provides no special protection for personal representatives who distribute in ignorance of illegitimate claimants. However, under s 18(2) there is a presumption that an illegitimate child is not survived by its father, or any person related to that child only through its father, unless the contrary is shown.

13.14 Other relatives of the intestate

If there are no surviving spouse/civil partner or issue, the order of entitlement to share in the estate is as follows:

(a) parents (equally if both alive); but if none then

(b) brothers and sisters of the whole blood (ie who share the same parents as the deceased) on the statutory trusts; but if none then

(c) brothers and sisters of the half blood (ie who share only one parent with the deceased) on the statutory trusts; but if none then

(d) grandparents (equally if more than one); but if none then

(e) uncles and aunts of the whole blood (ie brothers and sisters of the whole blood of one of the intestate's parents) on the statutory trusts; but if none then

(f) uncles and aunts of the half blood (ie brothers and sisters of the half blood of one of the intestate's parents) on the statutory trusts. It is blood relatives of the intestate who are entitled, not those related only by marriage.

Apart from parents or grandparents, members of each class take on the statutory trusts. For example, Harry (a bachelor) dies intestate. His only surviving relative is a niece, Isla, the daughter of his late sister Gwen. Isla will be entitled to all of Harry's estate provided she attains 18 (or marries under that age). Of course, if Gwen had survived Harry, Isla would have no entitlement.

13.15 The Crown

If the intestate is not survived by any relatives qualifying to share in the estate in any of the above categories then the Crown takes the residuary estate as *bona vacantia*. If the intestate died resident within the Duchy of Lancaster or in Cornwall, the Duchy or Duke of Cornwall respectively take as *bona vacantia*.

Section 46 of the Administration of Estates Act 1925 gives the Crown, etc a discretion in such cases to make provision for the intestate's dependants (who need not be related to the deceased) and for 'any other person for whom the intestate might reasonably have been expected to make provision'.

13.16 Inheritance tax and intestacy

It is not our purpose here to go into this topic in any detail, but merely to stress again that any property passing to the deceased's spouse/civil partner under the intestacy rules (even if only for life) will be wholly exempt from inheritance tax (as it will be covered by the spouse/civil partner exemption).

13.17 Intestacy: checkpoints

1. Does any of the deceased's estate pass by will (**13.11**)?
2. As to property undisposed of by any will and passing under the intestacy rules:
   (a) Has the deceased's spouse/civil partner survived by 28 days?
   (b) If so, see **Figure 13.1** below and **13.12**.
   (c) If the surviving spouse/civil partner does not take the entire residuary estate, is:
      (i) redemption of life interest
      (ii) appropriation of matrimonial home
   relevant or necessary (**13.12.4**)?
3. If spouse/civil partner does not survive for 28 days:
   (a) are there issue (**13.12** and **13.13**)? (NB the statutory trusts (**13.11.3**));
   (b) if not, are there other relatives qualifying to share in the estate (**13.14**)? (NB the statutory trusts (**13.11.3**).)

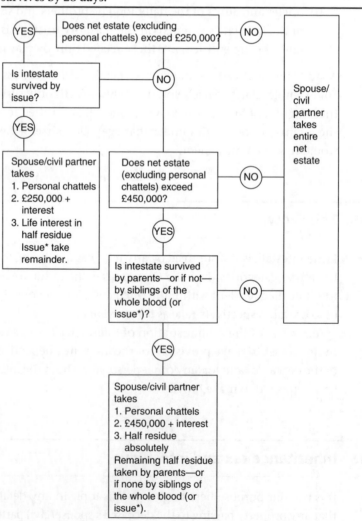

Figure 13.1 Destination table where intestate's spouse/civil partner survives by 28 days.

* On the statutory trusts (13.11.3).

Figure 13.2 Destination table where intestate's spouse/civil partner does not survive by 28 days.

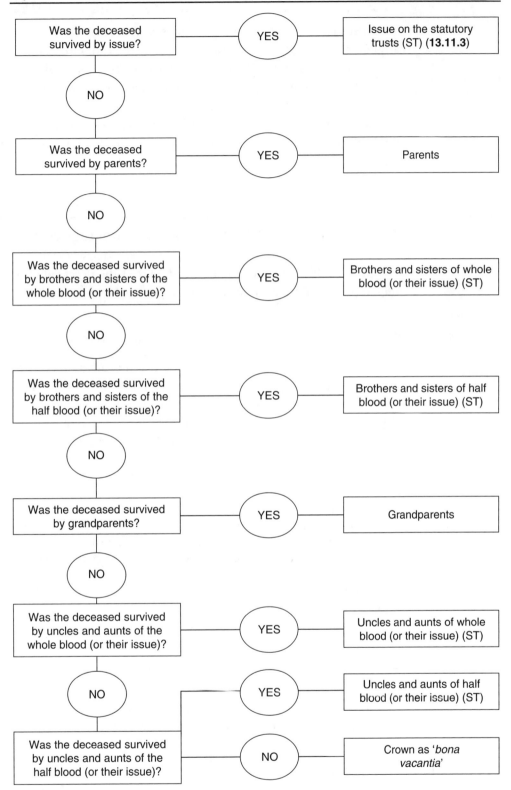

13.18 Property not passing under the will or the intestacy rules

We noted above that certain property passes on death quite independently of the will (if any) or intestacy rules. This is the case even if the will purports to gift such property, as it is simply not capable of being passed by will. The value of such property may well be significant, and knowledge of how such property passes will be relevant when advising on entitlements to property owned by the deceased. Depending on the type of property, it may or may not be part of the deceased's taxable estate chargeable to inheritance tax on death (see **7.9**). Although not of immediate concern, for ease of reference, such property is listed at **13.20** and **13.21**, and see also **Table 13.1** at page 283.

13.19 Property passing outside the will or intestacy rules

The property listed below does not form part of the deceased's 'succession estate' and therefore is not payable to the deceased's personal representatives.

13.19.1 Property owned by the deceased as beneficial joint tenant

Where the deceased was a beneficial joint tenant of any property, the deceased's interest accrues automatically on death to the surviving joint tenant(s). This is the case whether the property is personalty (eg a bank account) or land (eg the matrimonial home).

Where the jointly owned property is held as beneficial tenants in common, however, the share of each joint owner will pass under their will (or the intestacy rules).

> **EXAMPLE 10**
>
> Joyce and John, who are not married, live together with their daughter Kelly (aged 18) who is Joyce's only child. Joyce has a joint bank account (beneficial joint tenancy) with John, and they jointly own their home as tenants in common. Joyce dies intestate, survived by John and Kelly. Joyce's share of the money in the bank account will pass by survivorship to John, and can be claimed by producing a copy of her death certificate to the bank. Her share in the home, however, will form part of her succession estate, which here passes under the intestacy rules to Kelly.

We will see at **13.20** that although a deceased's interest as beneficial joint tenant *does not* form part of the deceased's succession estate, it *does* form part of the deceased's estate for inheritance tax purposes. The deceased's interest as tenant in common, however, forms part of the succession estate and also the taxable estate.

13.19.2 Trust policies

If the deceased had taken out life assurance on his own life, then the sum assured may, under the terms of the policy, be payable to the deceased's estate. If so, the proceeds payable on death will be paid to the deceased's personal representatives as part of the estate passing under the will or intestacy rules.

Alternatively, the life policy may be held for the benefit of other person(s) either as a result of an express assignment or trust of the policy, or as a result of being written under s 11, Married Womens' Property Act 1882. The latter case is only applicable if the intended beneficiaries are the life assured's spouse or, since the Civil Partnership Act 2004 came into force, civil partner and/or children; in other cases, an express assignment or trust of the policy will be required. In either case, the policy 'belongs' to the beneficiaries and the policy monies are payable directly to them (or trustees for them) on proof of death, by sending a death certificate and completed claim form to the insurance company.

EXAMPLE 11

Peter has taken out two policies of life assurance. The Eversure Assurance Co policy is written in trust for his wife, Pam. The other policy, which is with the Longlife Assurance Co, is payable to his estate. Peter's will leaves his estate to his wife and children in equal shares. Pam survives Peter and is able to obtain the proceeds of the Eversure policy shortly after Peter's death. She finds this sum a useful means of support, pending the distribution of her late husband's estate (which includes the proceeds of the Longlife policy) in accordance with the will.

13.19.3 Pension scheme benefits

Many occupational pension schemes are drafted in such a way that a lump sum payable on death 'in service' does not form part of the estate of the deceased member of the scheme. This is achieved by making any such sum payable to family members entirely at the discretion of the trustees of the scheme—though usually the member is allowed to make a (non-binding) 'nomination' of his preferred recipient—not to be confused with the sort of nomination discussed at **13.19.4**. The deceased has no interest in such lump sum (and thus it cannot form part of his succession estate). The trustees of the scheme only require proof of death to enable payment to be made.

Again, it must be stressed that not all pension schemes operate in this way; frequently, any 'death in service' benefit is part of the estate of the deceased passing under the terms of the will or the intestacy rules.

13.19.4 Statutory nominations

In the case of certain investments, a person who is aged 16 or over may pass the property concerned on death under a statutory nomination made in writing and attested by one witness. Such a nomination is revoked by subsequent marriage, a later nomination, or if the nominee predeceases the nominator; however, it is unaffected by any subsequent will.

It is now only possible to make such a nomination of monies deposited in friendly societies and industrial and provident societies up to a limit in each case of £5,000. It used to be possible to nominate funds in trustee savings banks (withdrawn 1 May 1979) and National Savings Certificates and the National Savings Bank (withdrawn 1 May 1981). However, nominations made before these dates remain effective (unless revoked).

If property capable of nomination in this way is not so nominated, it forms part of the property passing on death under the terms of the deceased's will or the intestacy rules.

13.19.5 Donationes mortis causa

You will no doubt have encountered this type of gift in earlier studies of trust law and you will recall that they are gifts made in contemplation of death. We do not intend to go into further detail here, but only to mention that property passing under a valid *donatio mortis causa* passes directly to the donee on death.

13.19.6 Life interests in trust property

Where the deceased was possessed of such an interest at the date of death, the trust property will pass in accordance with the terms of the trust instrument.

13.19.7 Gifts with the reservation of benefit

This is an inheritance tax concept—it basically means that the deceased has given away property in their lifetime, but has retained some benefit in the gifted property (see 7.10). Regardless of the tax position, if the property has been effectively gifted in their lifetime, it will no longer belong to the deceased for succession purposes.

13.20 Property not forming part of the succession estate but forming part of the deceased's estate for inheritance tax purposes

Although the following property is not payable to the deceased's personal representatives, it nevertheless must be included in calculating the value of property passing on death for inheritance tax purposes, ie it forms part of the deceased's taxable estate:

(a) Property held by the deceased as beneficial joint tenant—the value of the deceased's share only, not the whole value of the property. Thus in the example at **13.19.1**, the value of Joyce's share of money in the bank account (not the total amount in the account) would be included in her estate for tax purposes. The value of her interest in the house (part of her succession estate) would, of course, also form part of her taxable estate on death. If Joyce and John had been married, any property passing to John would, of course, enjoy the benefit of the spouse exemption for inheritance tax purposes. See also **Table 13.1**.

(b) Nominated property (**13.19.4**).

(c) *Donationes mortis causa* (**13.19.5**).

(d) Life interests in trust property (**13.19.6**).

(e) Gifts with a reservation of benefit (**13.19.7**).

13.21 Property not forming part of the deceased's estate for succession or inheritance tax purposes

These are:

(a) Trust policies (**13.19.2**). Policies payable to the deceased's estate would, however, form part of the taxable estate.

Table 13.1 **Summary chart of commonly encountered property referred to in 13.20 and 13.21.**

Asset	Does the asset form part of succession estate?	Does the asset form part of taxable estate?
Deceased's interests as beneficial joint tenant	No	Yes (but exempt if passing to spouse/civil partner)
Deceased's interests as tenant in common	Yes	Yes (but exempt if passing to spouse/civil partner)
Life policy not written in trust	Yes	Yes
Life policy written in trust	No	No
Pension benefits passing to estate	Yes	Yes
Discretionary pension benefits	No	No

(b) Pension scheme benefits payable at the discretion of the pension trustees (**13.19.3**). If the lump sum benefit is payable to the deceased's estate, again it will be included in the estate for inheritance tax.

13.22 Property not passing under the will or the intestacy rules: checkpoints

1. Is there property which does not pass as part of the deceased's succession estate (**13.19**)?
2. If so, does such property:
   (a) form part of the deceased's taxable estate (**13.20**)?
   (b) not form part of the deceased's taxable estate (**13.21**)?

13.23 Provision for family and dependants

In this section we will consider, in outline, how a successful claim under the Inheritance (Provision for Family and Dependants) Act 1975 may alter the distribution of property that would otherwise be in accordance with the deceased's will, the operation of the intestacy rules, or a combination of both in the case of partial intestacy. In some cases, orders can be made which affect certain types of property which pass outside the deceased's succession estate, or even property disposed of by the deceased in the lifetime.

The Act enables certain classes of persons to apply for provision from the deceased's estate on the basis that the deceased's will or intestacy fails to make adequate financial provision for them, and only applies if the deceased dies domiciled in England and Wales.

You may be asked to advise a potential applicant under the Act, or to advise the personal representatives about the merits of a claim made against the deceased's estate. In the latter case, any statements by the deceased (or, indeed, any other evidence) as to why no provision was made for the claimant should be carefully preserved; such statements will be relevant if the claim goes to court, and may be useful in negotiations with the claimant.

As mentioned at **13.10** above, consultation on the Law Commission's Consultation Paper No 191 closed at the end of February 2010. This also contained proposals for changes to the family provision legislation—for instance, equating the position of cohabitants to that of spouses' civil partners in some cases. Again, we shall have to wait to see what changes (if any) may be made.

All statutory references in the remainder of this part of the chapter are to the Inheritance (Provision for Family and Dependants) Act 1975 unless otherwise stated.

13.24 The basis of the claim for provision

In order to succeed an applicant must:

(a) apply within the time limit (**13.25**);

(b) fall within one of the categories of applicant set out in s 1(1) (as amended) (**13.26**); and

(c) satisfy the court that the will or intestacy fails to make reasonable financial provision for the applicant (**13.27**).

The court may then order financial provision to be made out of the deceased's net estate (**13.30**). The deceased may have anticipated that a claim might be made under the Act and may have disposed of property prior to death in an attempt to defeat such a claim. The Act contains anti-avoidance provisions (ss 10 and 11) enabling an order to be made relating to such property in limited circumstances, although this is not further discussed here.

The Act also sets out certain guidelines which the court must take into account both when deciding whether or not reasonable financial provision has been made for the applicant and, if not, whether any order should be made (**13.28**).

13.25 The application

13.25.1 The time limit for making applications

Applications should normally be made within six months from the grant of representation (the document which confirms or grants authority to act as personal representatives) to the deceased's estate. A late application is only permitted if the court gives leave.

13.25.2 Protection of personal representatives from personal liability

Linked to the six-month time limit is the protection against personal liability granted by the Act to the personal representatives. If no claim has been made within the time limit, then the personal representatives may distribute the deceased's estate, and will not be liable personally even if the court allows a late application. Until the time limit has expired, the personal representatives run the risk of personal liability if the claim is successful and property distributed to beneficiaries has been dissipated by them. As claims can only be made against the net estate, the deceased's debts can, however, safely be paid.

13.25.3 Ascertaining whether a grant of representation has been issued

A claimant under the Act will need to know whether a grant of representation has been issued to enable the application to be made within the time limit. There is a procedure, known as a standing search, which will enable an applicant to find this out, and to obtain a copy of the grant. Specialist texts should be consulted for details of the procedure.

13.26 The applicant

13.26.1 Categories of applicant

The onus is on applicants to show that they come within one of the categories set out in s 1(1) in order that they can apply for an order to be made in their favour.

Applications under the Act are personal actions. If the applicant dies before the matter is determined by the court, then the application cannot proceed.

13.26.1.1 The deceased's spouse (or civil partner) (s 1(1)(a))

The marriage or civil partnership must have subsisted at the time of the deceased's death. A judicially separated spouse can apply, unless an order has been made under s 15 by the matrimonial court, preventing an application under the Act.

13.26.1.2 The former spouse (or former civil partner) of the deceased who has not 'remarried' (s 1(1)(b))

The marriage may have ended by decree of divorce or nullity. Again, no claim can be made if the matrimonial court has barred an application under the Act (ss 15 and 15A) by the former spouse—commonly part of a 'clean break' order. Since 5 December 2005 former civil partners are included in this category, but similarly are not able to apply if the court has barred an application under the family provision legislation.

13.26.1.3 A cohabitant (s 1(1)(ba))

This provision enables a claim to be made by a person who has lived in the same household as the deceased, as their husband or wife, throughout the two-year period immediately prior to the deceased's death. Since 5 December 2005 this category is extended to include a person who had lived with the deceased in the same household throughout the two years prior to the death as part of a same-sex couple without a formal civil partnership being registered.

In *Gully v Dix* [2004] 1 FCR 453 the Court of Appeal considered whether a claimant could still be 'living in the same household as the deceased' at the time of his death— even though they were in fact living separately at that time. The couple had been living together for 27 years, but the deceased (who was an alcoholic) had become increasingly erratic in his behaviour and the claimant had been advised to move out temporarily for the sake of her health some three months before his death. It was held that they could still be living 'in the same household' if they were still 'tied by their relationship' and *neither* of them had 'demonstrated a settled acceptance or recognition that the relationship (was) . . . at an end'. This was the case in this instance and the claimant was eligible to make an application under s 1(1)(ba).

13.26.1.4 A child of the deceased (s 1(1)(c))

Note that adult children can apply, but are unlikely to be successful if the applicant is able-bodied and in employment.

13.26.1.5   A person who has been treated as a child of the family in relation to any marriage (or civil partnership) of the deceased (s 1(1)(d))

In effect, the Act is here usually referring to stepchildren of the deceased, although the relevant 'treatment' may occur when that child is an adult. Again, claims by adult stepchildren are possible, but unlikely to be successful unless something more is shown.

13.26.1.6   A dependant (s 1(1)(e))

A dependant is any person (not included in the foregoing paragraphs) who immediately before the death of the deceased was being maintained, either wholly or partly, by the deceased.

In *Gully v Dix* (see **13.26.1.3** above) the Court of Appeal held that Mrs Gully also had a claim under s 1(1)(e). Although the deceased was not actually maintaining her at the moment of his death, the 'settled basis' of maintenance by the deceased had not been terminated by the abnormal situation existing in the three months prior to his death.

Broadly, this category allows claims by those financially dependent on the deceased. The Act lays out a two-stage test (s 1(3)) which must be satisfied by an applicant to come within this category. Suffice it to say here that the applicant must demonstrate that the financial support received was in excess of the value of any consideration provided by the applicant in return for such support.

EXAMPLE 12

Joy's aunt provides her with rent-free board and lodging while she is completing her LPC course. In return, Joy helps her with some housework. The aunt dies. It is likely that Joy would be able to establish that she comes within s 1(1)(e), although this of itself does not mean that her claim will succeed.

EXAMPLE 13

Two widowed brothers decide to pool their resources and live in the same house. Ted pays the rent, but Tom pays for their food. If the value of their contributions to running the house are roughly equal, then neither would be able to bring a claim under s 1(1)(e) against the estate of the other.

13.27   Reasonable financial provision

The Act (in s 1(2)) sets out a two-stage process:

(a) Has the will or the intestacy rules, or in appropriate cases a combination of the two, failed to make reasonable financial provision for the applicant?

(b) If so, the court considers what would amount to such reasonable financial provision.

What amounts to reasonable financial provision will depend on who is making the application, as the Act sets out two standards. One is applicable to an application by the surviving spouse, and the maintenance standard applies to other categories of applicant.

13.27.1   The surviving spouse/civil partner standard (s 1(2)(a))

13.27.1.1   The surviving spouse/civil partner

If the applicant is the surviving spouse/civil partner, the standard is such financial provision as would be reasonable in all the circumstances, whether or not that provision is required for maintenance.

This standard is thus more generous than the maintenance standard (below). The intention is that the surviving spouse/civil partner will have a claim on the family assets at least equivalent to that of a divorced spouse, and the court is directed to have regard to the provision which would have been awarded in divorce proceedings (s 3(2), see **13.28.2.1**).

13.27.1.2 Discretion to apply surviving spouse standard to judicially separated spouses and former spouses or civil partners

By s 14 the court has a discretion to apply the surviving spouse standard to judicially separated and former spouses if the death occurs within 12 months of the final decree in the judicial separation or divorce proceedings—and no final order has been made (or refused) in those proceedings. A similar discretion will apply to applications by former civil partners.

13.27.2 The maintenance standard

The standard is such provision as would be reasonable in all the circumstances for the applicant to receive for maintenance (s 1(2)(b)). Case law establishes that reasonable provision for maintenance is such that enables the applicant to live decently and comfortably according to his situation.

13.27.3 The test

The question for the court, judged objectively on the basis of facts known at the time of the hearing (s 3(5)), is whether the will or intestacy makes reasonable financial provision for the applicant. The court is not bound by testators' views as to whether they felt they were acting reasonably in making no, or only limited, provision for the applicant.

13.27.3.1 Evidence of a testator's reasons

If there is evidence (including hearsay evidence) of the reasons why a testator has not made provision in the will for an applicant, however, this is admissible (s 1, Civil Evidence Act 1995 and see **13.28.1.5**). For instance, the testator may have placed a written statement with the will, giving reasons as to why no provision has been made for an adult child. The court will judge what weight should be given to this evidence. It will clearly be given more weight if it is considered judgement (eg 'my son has a well-paid job; my daughter's accident has prevented her earning her own living'), but the court will also take into account those children's circumstances at the time of the hearing.

The will, once admitted to probate, is a public document, and thus open to inspection. A written statement of reasons, placed with the will and not referred to in it, will not be admitted to probate, and thus remains confidential.

13.28 The guidelines

The court must take into account the guidelines in s 3(1), both when determining whether the applicant has established that no reasonable financial provision has been made (13.27.3), and in determining what order, if any, should be made under s 2 (13.29). It is entirely in the court's discretion as to whether any order should be made at all.

Some of the guidelines are relevant to all applicants; some only relate to a particular category of applicant.

13.28.1 Guidelines relevant to all applicants

13.28.1.1 Financial resources and needs of the applicant, any other applicant, and any beneficiary whether now or in the foreseeable future

The court will assess the relative financial position of persons with any claim on the estate. Thus a needy applicant will have greater prospects of success if the beneficiaries are well off. In *Re Collins* [1990] Fam 56, it was held that the fact that the applicant was in receipt of social security benefits did not preclude the court from making an order out of her mother's estate.

13.28.1.2 Any moral obligation of the deceased to any applicant or beneficiary

In *Re Callaghan* [1984] Fam 1, for example, a claim was made by an adult child of the family against his stepfather's estate. The stepfather died intestate and his estate passed to his three sisters whom he had not seen for ten years. The court held that the deceased's greatest obligation was owed to the applicant who had kept in close touch with him and looked after him in his last illness. The court also took into account that many of the assets of the estate came from the applicant's mother who had died some years previously, and ordered a lump-sum payment of £15,000 to the applicant to enable him to buy his council house outright.

13.28.1.3 The size and nature of the net estate of the deceased

The larger the estate the easier will it be for the court to order reasonable provision for an applicant. Conversely, as costs will usually be awarded out of the estate, the court will discourage claims where the estate is small (*Re Coventry* [1980] Ch 461).

The source of the deceased's estate may be relevant, as in *Re Callaghan* (**13.28.1.2**).

13.28.1.4 Physical or mental disability

Any physical or mental disability of any applicant or beneficiary will be taken into account.

13.28.1.5 Any other relevant matter including the conduct of the applicant or any other person

Clearly the court has a wide discretion as to the matters it can take into account under this heading. As already mentioned, any statement (whether oral or written) by the deceased as to the reasons for the disposition of the estate can be considered (**13.27.3.1**). In *Re Callaghan* (**13.28.1.2**) the caring conduct of the applicant assisted his claim.

13.28.2 Guidelines relevant to particular categories of applicant

In addition to the factors set out above, the court must also take into account the points covered in the following paragraphs.

13.28.2.1 Where the applicant is the surviving spouse (or civil partner) (s 3(2))

The following factors are relevant:

(a) the age of the applicant and the duration of the marriage;

(b) the applicant's contribution to the welfare of the deceased's family; and

(c) the provision which the applicant might reasonably have expected to receive if, at the date of death, the marriage had instead been terminated by divorce.

Note that the likely provision on divorce is only a starting point; a different award may be appropriate on a financial provision application. For instance, the divorce court will have to consider the future needs of both parties—clearly this will no longer be relevant.

Where the estate is significant, the recent decisions in the family law cases of *White v White* [2003] 3 WLR 1571 (HL), *Miller v Miller; McFarlane v McFarlane* [2006] UKHL 24 and *Charman v Charman* (No 4) [2007] 1 FLR 1246 (CA) may have the effect of increasing the size of the award to the surviving spouse. Principles emerging from those cases indicate that in allocating assets between the couple on divorce, the court needs to achieve a fair outcome, bearing in mind the concepts of need, sharing, and, on occasion, compensation. Any proposed financial order should be tested against the 'yardstick of equality': any departure from that yardstick should only be made for good reason.

Similar factors will apply where the application is made by the deceased's civil partner.

13.28.2.2 Where the applicant is a former spouse (or civil partner) (s 3(2))

The guidelines (a) and (b) set out at **13.28.2.1** apply. Guideline (c) (what the divorce court would order) only applies if the court exercises its discretion to apply the surviving spouse standard (see **13.27.1.2**). Even if an application by a former spouse has not been barred by the matrimonial court (**13.26.1.2**), the Court of Appeal has indicated that only rarely would post-decree applications be successful. This is because the matrimonial court will have already considered the issues of maintenance and the allocation of assets between the parties.

Again, similar factors and principles will apply in the case of civil partnerships.

13.28.2.3 Where the applicant is a cohabitant (s 3(2A))

The following factors are relevant:

(a) the age of the applicant and how long they have lived in the same household as husband or wife of the deceased; and

(b) the applicant's contribution to the welfare of the family of the deceased, including by looking after the home or caring for the family.

13.28.2.4 Where the applicant is a child (s 3(3))

Here the court must consider the manner in which the applicant was being or might be expected to be educated or trained.

13.28.2.5 Where the applicant is a child of the family (s 3(3))

As well as considering the education guideline (in **13.28.2.4**), the court must also consider:

(a) whether the deceased had assumed any responsibility for the applicant's maintenance and, if so, the extent and the basis upon which the deceased assumed responsibility and for how long;

(b) whether in assuming and discharging that responsibility the deceased did so knowing that the applicant was not his own child; and

(c) the liability of any other person to maintain the applicant.

13.28.2.6 Where the applicant was maintained by the deceased (s 3(4))

Here the court must, in addition to the general guidelines, consider the extent to which and the basis upon which the deceased assumed responsibility for the applicant.

13.29 Family provision orders

13.29.1 Types of financial provision orders

The court must take into account the guidelines set out in **13.28** in deciding whether to make an order under s 2 and, if so, the type of order. The most common order is for a lump-sum payment, either in cash or by way of a transfer of a particular asset, but periodical payment orders (eg £200 per month) can also be made. Interim periodical payment orders are possible pending the determination of the final order.

13.29.2 Inheritance tax

How is the inheritance tax position affected if the court makes an order varying the disposition of the deceased's estate? The Act provides (s 19(1)) that for all purposes, including inheritance tax, the variation is deemed to be effective as from the deceased's death. In effect, the order is 'read back', as if the deceased had made the provision ordered by the court. If, for example, the court orders that provision be made for a surviving spouse, the estate's liability for inheritance tax will be reduced. This is because the property passing to the surviving spouse will be exempt from inheritance tax.

If an award is made the court can direct whether any inheritance tax is to be borne by the applicant or the estate.

13.30 Property available for financial provision orders

The deceased's 'net estate' from which any order for financial provision orders is made is widely defined in s 25(1). It comprises the following:

(a) all property of the deceased owned at the date of death and which could have been disposed of by will, less:

   (i) funeral testamentary and administration expenses;
   (ii) debts and liabilities; and
   (iii) inheritance tax.

(b) the deceased's severable share of a joint tenancy (which normally passes by survivorship, see **13.19.1**) but only if the application is made within the six-month time limit (**13.25.1**) and the court so orders (s 9);

(c) any property which the court has ordered under the anti-avoidance provisions to be available (under ss 10 or 11, which are not further discussed here); and

(d) any property in respect of which the deceased made a statutory nomination (**13.19.4**), a *donatio mortis causa* (**13.19.5**), or which the deceased could have appointed in lifetime under a general power of appointment which has not been exercised.

13.31 Family provision: checkpoints

1. Advising the personal representatives:
   (a) Has notice of any claim under the Act been received within the prescribed time limit (**13.25**)?
   (b) Does the claimant prima facie fall within any of the categories within s 1(1) of the Act (**13.26**)?
       (i) If so, do the dispositions taking effect on death make any provision for the claimant and could this be regarded as reasonable financial provision (13.27) to the relevant standard (13.27.1 and 13.27.2)?
       (ii) Is there any evidence as to why the deceased failed to make more generous provision for the claimant (13.27.3.1)?
       (iii) Do any of the general or special guidelines have any particular relevance to the claim (**13.28**)?

2. Advising the claimant:
   (a) Has a grant been issued and, if so, how long ago (see 13.25)?
   (b) Does the claimant prima facie fall within any of the categories within s 1(1) of the Act (13.26)?
   (c) If so, do the dispositions taking effect on death make any provision for the claimant and could this be regarded as reasonable financial provision (13.27) to the relevant standard (13.27.1 and 13.27.2)?
   (d) Is there any evidence as to why the deceased failed to make more generous provision for the claimant (13.27.3.1)?
   (e) Do any of the general or special guidelines have any particular relevance to the claim (13.28)?

online resource centre

Visit the Online Resource Centre for more information and useful weblinks.
www.oxfordtextbooks.co.uk/orc/foundations11_12/

14

Application for a grant of representation

14.1 Introduction

In this chapter we will be discussing the law and procedure relating to the issue of a grant of representation to the personal representatives of someone who has died. We will be considering:

- the nature, effect and the principal types of grant; the position of the personal representatives; and the responsibilities of solicitors instructed to act in the administration of an estate (**14.2** to **14.11**);
- obtaining the grant—practice (**14.12** to **14.18**);
- the court's requirements; oaths for executors, for administrators with will annexed and for administrators; and further affidavit evidence that may be required (**14.19** to **14.25**); and
- HMRC's requirements; excepted estates; Form IHT 400 and its Schedules; and the calculation of inheritance tax (**14.26** to **14.31**).

Figure **14.2** at page 309 sets out pre-grant procedures.

14.2 Grants of representation

In **14.2** to **14.18** we begin our consideration of the practice and procedure relating to the issue of a grant of representation. Such grants are court orders and are evidence of the personal representative's title to deal with the deceased's estate.

We will begin by examining briefly the court's jurisdiction in probate matters (**14.2.1**) and the responsibilities of solicitors instructed to act in the administration of an estate (**14.3**). We will then consider the effect of grants (**14.4**) and those cases where a grant is not necessary (**14.5**). The principal types of grant will then be examined (**14.6**). The following paragraphs (**14.7** to **14.11**) will look at various aspects of the position of personal representative. Finally, in **14.12** to **14.18** we will deal with a number of practical issues involved in obtaining the grant.

14.2.1 Background

14.2.1.1 Probate jurisdiction

The probate jurisdiction of the court is concerned with three issues:

(a) whether a document may be admissible to probate;

(b) who is entitled to a grant of representation; and

(c) should a grant already made be revoked.

Most probate business is non-contentious (in the probate lawyer's jargon, 'common form') and is exclusively the province of the Family Division of the High Court. Where there is a dispute concerning any of the above issues, the matter becomes contentious. Contentious (or 'solemn form') business is conducted in the Chancery Division, the County Court having a concurrent jurisdiction where the value of the estate is below the County Court limit at the date of death (currently this is £30,000). However, even in these cases, once the dispute is resolved the grant issues from the Family Division.

A grant is normally made by the English courts where the deceased left property situated in England and Wales (Administration of Justice Act 1932, s 2).

14.2.1.2 Non-contentious business

Common form business is mostly conducted in either the Principal Registry of the Family Division in London (headed by a senior district judge and a number of district judges) or in one of the District Probate Registries (or sub-Registries attached to most of them), each headed by a registrar. The jurisdiction of the Registries is not restricted to any geographical area. On the death of someone living (say) in Bristol there is no reason why the grant should not be applied for in Newcastle-upon-Tyne (or indeed anywhere else). However, it will normally in practice be more convenient to use the local Registry.

Application for a grant may be made by a personal representative in person or through a practising solicitor.

Non-contentious business is regulated by the Non-Contentious Probate Rules 1987, as amended by the Non-Contentious Probate (Amendment) Rules 1991. For convenience, these are hereafter referred to as 'the Rules' or 'NCPR'.

14.3 Responsibilities of solicitors instructed by personal representatives

It is not essential for personal representatives to instruct solicitors to act for them in obtaining a grant or in the administration of the estate. However, where a solicitor is instructed it is important to appreciate that the personal representatives are the solicitor's clients. Clearly, there is a potential for a conflict of interest if the solicitor also advises members of the family or the beneficiaries—especially if any hint of a dispute emerges.

It is also important to remember that the personal representatives will often be close relatives of the deceased and therefore (particularly initially) experiencing a degree of distress. The solicitor acting must be sensitive to this in dealings with the client, tempering efficiency with sympathy and understanding of the client's feelings.

14.3.1 Initial duties

On receiving instructions, the solicitor's first responsibilities will relate to the obtaining of the grant. There are basically three types of grant, which are discussed in more detail in **14.6**:

(a) *Probate*. This grant normally only issues to an executor duly appointed by the will or a codicil.

(b) *Letters of Administration with will annexed.* This grant is appropriate where there is a will but for some reason it is not possible to make a grant of probate to an executor.

(c) *Letters of Administration.* This grant, often called 'simple administration', is issued where the deceased died intestate.

Whichever is the appropriate grant, details will be required of the various assets and liabilities of the estate so that their value can be established. If there is a will, this will need to be obtained and its validity and admissibility to probate considered. Any application for a grant has to be supported by certain papers which will have to be prepared: these include the appropriate Oath (**14.19** to **14.23**) and in some cases other affidavit evidence (**14.24**); and either a Return of Estate Information (**14.27**) or an Inheritance Tax Account (**14.28** to **14.30**).

Once all the documentation is complete and any tax has been paid, application for the grant is made by lodging the various papers (including any will and codicils) at the selected Registry, either in person or by post, together with a cheque for the appropriate court fees. On receipt by the Registry, the papers are examined to check that they are in order and any testamentary documents are photocopied. The court records are searched to check, inter alia, that no grant has already been made and that no application has been made to another Registry. If all is in order, the grant is prepared, signed by a duly authorised signatory and sealed with the seal of the Family Division or of the District Registry. The grant is then sent, together with any office copies requested on making the application, to the 'extracting solicitor'—usually some 10 to 14 days after the application is lodged.

14.3.2 Later duties

Once the grant has been obtained, it will be necessary to advise the personal representatives as to their powers and duties. The various assets will need to be realised and the liabilities discharged. There may be a need to advise on a variety of matters, including beneficial entitlement, interim distribution, and possible changes in the disposition of the estate, before the estate can be finally wound up. These matters are considered in **Chapter 15**.

14.4 The effect of the issue of a grant

A grant of representation issued by the court is conclusive evidence as to the terms and due execution of any will (and codicil), or that the deceased died intestate.

From the viewpoint of the personal representatives, the effect of the grant depends upon whether they are executors or administrators.

14.4.1 Executors

An executor's title to act derives from the will (or codicil). The deceased's property vests in the executor on death, and the executor has full authority to deal with it without a grant. An executor may even commence court proceedings prior to the issue of a grant, though it may be necessary to obtain a grant before judgment.

The grant of probate, then, merely confirms the executor's title to act. However, a grant (or an office copy) is the only acceptable proof of the executor's title, and except in cases considered in **14.5** below will in practice always be required to enable the executor to deal with the deceased's property.

14.4.2 Administrators

Whether the grant is with will annexed or of simple administration, the issue of the grant actually confers authority to act upon the administrator; prior to this not even the person with the best right to a grant has any authority to act. It is only on the issue of the grant that the deceased's property vests in the administrator; in the interim it has been vested in the Public Trustee. What is more, the grant once made does not relate back to the date of death so as to confirm any action taken in the interim—except for the limited purpose of protecting the deceased's estate from wrongful injury in that period.

14.5 Grant not necessary

As we saw in **13.18** to **13.22** there are a number of situations where property passes on death directly to those entitled and not through the hands of the personal representatives; in these cases, since the personal representatives do not need to make title to the assets, a grant is not necessary.

It may also sometimes be possible for property which does pass to the personal representatives to be obtained or dealt with by them without the need for a grant.

14.5.1 Small sums due to the estate

Under the Administration of Estates (Small Payments) Act 1965, it may be possible for the personal representatives to obtain payment of sums due to the estate on production of a copy of the death certificate. However, where orders have been made under this Act, there is an upper limit (currently £5,000) in respect of each item—and if this is exceeded a grant will be necessary to establish title to the whole sum, not just the excess. The Act allows such payment to be made to the person appearing to be entitled to the grant or to be beneficially entitled to the asset concerned. The Act merely permits payment without a grant, however; it is not obligatory. Monies which are covered by orders under this Act include:

(a) money held in the National Savings Bank, National Savings Certificates, or Premium Savings Bonds (NB small balances in accounts with the high street clearing banks are not covered by orders under the Act);

(b) monies payable on the death of a member of a trade union, industrial or provident society, or a friendly society;

(c) civil servants' salaries, wages, or superannuation benefits; and

(d) service, police, and firemen's pensions.

Similar provisions apply under the Building Societies Act 1986 to funds invested in a building society.

The Law Commission's Consultation Paper No 191 (see **13.10**) has recommended that the £5,000 limit should be increased, but it will be some time before it is known whether this change will be made.

14.6 Types of grant

We have already identified the three types of grants. Entitlement to these will now be more fully considered, and is set out diagrammatic form in Figure **14.1** at page 303.

14.6.1 Probate

This grant can only be made to an executor, who is usually expressly appointed by the will or a codicil. If a firm of solicitors is appointed, unless the will clearly provides to the contrary (as it should), it will be the partners at the date of the will (or codicil containing the appointment) who are entitled to act. The appointment of an executor may be implied (in which case the appointee is described as 'executor according to the tenor of the will') where the will shows an intention that a particular person should perform the functions of an executor.

Appointments of executors are usually 'unlimited' as to property and time. However, it is possible for the appointment to be limited in either of these respects, eg 'I appoint X to be executor as to my business of . . .'; 'I appoint Y to be executor until my son Z attains his majority'. A grant issued to any such executor will be similarly limited.

14.6.2 Letters of administration with will annexed

This grant is appropriate where there is a valid will but it is not possible to make a grant of probate in favour of an executor. It may be that the will fails to appoint an executor, or that those appointed are dead or are unwilling or unable to act. Other situations where this grant will issue include cases where the appointed executors are minors or otherwise incapable of taking a grant (see **14.7** below).

14.6.2.1 Rule 20 of the NCPR

This governs the order of entitlement to a grant where the deceased left a valid will. At the head of the list is an executor (who as we have seen is entitled to a grant of probate). Where such a grant is not possible, the rule lays down the order of entitlement to a grant of letters of administration with will annexed. For a person in a later category to establish title to the grant it will be necessary to account satisfactorily for all those (including executors) who would have a better right (see **14.22.3**).

Under r 20 the full order is:

(a) an executor;

(b) a trustee of the residuary estate;

(c) any other residuary beneficiary (including one for life), or (where there is a partial intestacy because the residue is not wholly disposed of by the will) anyone entitled to share in the undisposed of residue. Normally, a residuary beneficiary whose interest is vested will be preferred to one whose interest is contingent only;

(d) the personal representative of anyone in (c) other than a life tenant of residue;

(e) any other beneficiary (including a life tenant or one holding as a trustee) or a creditor. Again, a person with a vested interest is normally preferred to one whose interest is contingent only; and

(f) the personal representative of anyone in (e) other than a life tenant or person holding as a trustee.

As can be seen, the order mainly depends upon entitlement to the deceased's property under the terms of the will, with the residuary interest being treated as the principal interest, whatever its value in relation to the other gifts under the will.

14.6.2.2 Rule 21 of the NCPR

Where a gift in a will fails by virtue of s 15 of the Wills Act 1837 (because the beneficiary or the beneficiary's spouse/civil partner has witnessed the will, see **13.7.5**), that beneficiary loses the right to a grant under r 20 as a beneficiary named in the will—though may still claim in any other capacity (eg as a person entitled on intestacy or as a creditor).

14.6.3 Letters of administration

A grant of 'simple administration' is appropriate where there is no valid will.

The order of entitlement to the grant is governed by r 22 of the NCPR, which as will be seen broadly follows the order of entitlement to share in the estate of the intestate (discussed at **13.10** to **13.17**). Again, for anyone in a lower category to be able to establish title to the grant it will be necessary to satisfactorily account for all those with a better right (see **14.23.2**).

14.6.3.1 Rule 22 of the NCPR

The order under r 22 is:

(a) the surviving spouse (or civil partner);

(b) the children of the deceased and the issue of any child who has predeceased;

(c) the deceased's parents;

(d) the deceased's brothers and sisters of the whole blood and the issue of any who have predeceased;

(e) the deceased's brothers and sisters of the half blood and the issue of any who have predeceased;

(f) grandparents;

(g) uncles and aunts of the whole blood and the issue of any who have predeceased;

(h) uncles and aunts of the half blood and the issue of any who have predeceased;

(i) the Treasury Solicitor where the Crown claims *bona vacantia*; and

(j) a creditor of the deceased.

14.6.3.2 Personal representatives

Basically, the personal representatives of a person have the same right to a grant as the deceased whom they represent. This is subject to r 27 of the NCPR (**14.8**) and to r 22(4) which gives preference to persons within categories (b) to (h) in **14.6.3.1** over the personal representative of a surviving spouse who has died before obtaining a grant—unless the spouse was beneficially entitled to the whole estate.

14.6.4 Limited grants

There are a number of situations in which a limited grant may be appropriate. These include grants where the only person entitled to a grant is a minor or suffering from mental incapacity (**14.7**).

14.6.5 Special grants

The most commonly encountered special grant is administration *de bonis non*. Such a grant is made to allow the completion of the administration of the deceased's estate following the death of the sole, or last surviving, personal representative to whom a grant has been issued who has died leaving part of the estate unadministered. It is also the appropriate grant following the revocation of a previous grant.

A *de bonis non* grant is not necessary where one of several proving personal representatives has died; the remaining grantees have full authority to complete the administration of the estate. Nor is it appropriate on a death before a grant has been issued; a *de bonis non* grant is always a 'second grant'.

Further, it will not be necessary to obtain such a grant where the so-called 'chain of representation' exists. This occurs where a sole, or last surviving, proving executor (ie one to whom a grant of probate has been issued) dies and that executor's executor duly takes a grant of probate.

EXAMPLE 1

Suppose that Toby dies appointing Tabitha to be his executor. Tabitha proves the will but dies before completing the administration of Toby's estate, appointing Trevor to be her executor. By proving Tabitha's will, Trevor automatically becomes also the executor by representation of Toby and able to complete the administration of Toby's estate. The 'chain' only operates through proving executors. If, in the example, Tabitha had failed to appoint an executor, or if Trevor had renounced or died before taking a grant to Tabitha's estate, or either Toby or Tabitha had died intestate, there would have been no chain and a grant *de bonis non* would have been needed to complete the administration of Toby's estate.

The order of entitlement to a *de bonis non* grant is governed by r 20 (**14.6.2.1**) if the original grant was of probate or administration with will annexed; or r 22 (**14.6.3.1**) where it was a grant of simple administration.

14.7 Personal representatives: capacity

In principle, a testator is free to appoint anyone as executor. Equally, any person who under rr 20 or 22 of the NCPR has the right to a grant is entitled to apply for a grant of letters of administration. There is no rule automatically debarring (say) someone who is insolvent or who has a criminal record. However, there are a number of qualifications to this general principle, which are considered in the following paragraphs.

14.7.1 Minors

A minor cannot take a grant. If the minor is one of several executors or potential administrators, the practice is to make a grant immediately to the adult executors or administrators, with, in the case of a grant of probate, power being reserved to the minor to apply for a grant of 'double probate' on attaining 18. Where the minor is the only or last surviving executor or potential administrator, a grant of letters of administration (with will annexed if there is a will) is made (normally to the minor's parent or guardian) for the use and benefit of the minor until age 18, when it automatically terminates and a grant can then be made to the executor/administrator now entitled.

14.7.2 Mental incapacity

Where executors or potential administrators are suffering from mental incapacity such as to render them incapable of managing their own affairs, the position is broadly similar to that applying in the case of minors, and where it is the only executor/potential administrator who is so incapacitated a grant for the use and benefit of that person will be made to the persons specified in r 35 of the NCPR.

14.7.3 Section 116 of the Senior Courts Act 1981

Section 116 gives the court a discretion, where it considers that 'by reason of any special circumstances' it is necessary or expedient, to issue a grant to someone other than the person who is prima facie entitled under the Rules. A grant in these circumstances may be issued to anyone (not necessarily the person with the 'next best right'), and may be general or limited in any way in which the court sees fit.

This power has been used, for example, to pass over a potential grantee shown to be unfit to administer the estate (eg because bankrupt) or otherwise unsuitable or unable to act (eg because in prison, or missing and whereabouts unknown).

14.7.4 Section 50 of the Administration of Justice Act 1985

This allows the court to remove any existing personal representative and appoint a substitute. Such substitute will be an executor if replacing an executor; otherwise the grantee will be an administrator.

14.8 Personal representatives: several claimants

14.8.1 Probate

On an application for a grant of probate, all the executors appointed by the will or any codicil (and whose appointments have not been revoked by a later codicil) must in some way be accounted for. How this is achieved will be discussed at **14.21**. Subject to this, the grant may issue to any one or more of them, up to the limit imposed by s 114 of the Senior Courts Act 1981 (**14.9**). Rule 27 of the NCPR requires that notice of the application shall normally be given to any executors to whom power is being reserved (see **14.10.2**).

14.8.2 Administration

When a grant of letters of administration with will annexed or simple administration is applied for, all those having a better right to a grant than the applicant(s) must be 'cleared off' (ie accounted for). We will consider how this should be done at **14.22** and **14.23**. Where there are several potential grantees in the same degree of priority, r 27 allows the grant to be made (again, subject to the limits imposed by s 114 of the Senior Courts Act 1981) to any one or more of them, but this time without any requirement for notice to the others entitled in the same degree.

However, r 27 further provides that preference should normally be given to:

    (a) an adult rather than someone on behalf of a minor entitled in the same degree; and

    (b) a living person rather than the personal representative of a deceased person who, if living, would have been entitled in the same degree.

14.9 Personal representatives: number

14.9.1 Executors

A sole executor always has full authority to act, even in cases where minority or life interests arise (contrast the position of administrators at **14.9.2**).

A testator can appoint any number of executors, but a grant of probate cannot issue to more than four (Senior Courts Act 1981, s 114). Those who have not predeceased the testator or renounced have 'power reserved' to them (see further **14.10.2**).

However, s 114 does not prevent the possibility of a grant to a maximum of four executors in respect of part of the deceased's estate and another grant to four different executors in respect of another part. Thus, if the deceased had appointed four executors to deal with his business and four further executors to deal with the rest of the estate, two grants in respect of the different parts of the estate can be made to them all.

14.9.2 Administrators

Here, whether the grant is with will annexed or simple administration, s 114 again provides for a maximum of four grantees. However, in certain cases, it also requires that there should normally be a minimum of two (or a trust corporation, such as the Public Trustee or a bank). This minimum requirement arises whenever, under any will or on the intestacy, a beneficiary is an infant, or there is a life interest. However, if a grant is made to two grantees as a result of this requirement and one of them then dies, there is no requirement for a replacement to be appointed: the survivor has full authority to act henceforth alone (though the court may on application appoint a 'replacement').

14.9.3 Additional personal representatives

14.9.3.1 Rule 25 of the NCPR

A person entitled to a grant of administration may, without leave, apply for a grant together with a person entitled in a lower degree, provided there is no other person entitled in priority to the person to be joined—or, if there are any such persons, they have all renounced. If the person sought to be joined does not have any (or any immediate) right to a grant, an *ex parte* application to a district judge or registrar will normally be required.

14.10 Personal representatives: renunciation/power reserved

No one can be forced to accept office as an executor or administrator, though a person entitled to a grant can be forced to make up their mind whether to take a grant or not. Executors or administrators are free to renounce their rights to a grant provided they have not accepted office. As an alternative to renunciation, an executor who does not wish to act in the administration may have 'power reserved' (see **14.10.2**).

14.10.1 Executors: renunciation

An executor accepts office, thus losing the right to renounce, by taking a grant, or even before this by 'intermeddling' in the estate, ie by doing something which shows an intention to accept office. Acts of charity, humanity, or necessity are not sufficient to constitute such acceptance. Thus, for example, arranging the funeral will not be enough; but writing to request payment of monies due to the estate will.

A renunciation must be in writing, signed by the renouncing executor, and containing a statement that the executor has not intermeddled. It becomes effective on being filed at the Registry (usually with the papers to lead the grant to some other person).

An executor cannot generally renounce part of the office. The office must be accepted in full, or renounced in full.

Under r 37 of the NCPR, a renunciation by an executor of the right to a grant of probate does not operate as the renunciation of any rights that person may have to a grant of letters of administration (whether as beneficiary or creditor), unless there is also an express renunciation of those rights.

14.10.2 Executors: power reserved

Rather than renounce, one of several executors appointed by the will/codicil who does not wish to act in the administration can instead have 'power reserved' (see further **14.21.7.3**). This, in effect, means that the executor concerned will not be involved in the application for the grant and thus will not be entitled/required to take part in the process of dealing with the testator's affairs. However, if circumstances change (eg a proving executor falls ill or dies, or the non-proving executor changes his mind) the executor to whom power has been reserved can apply for a grant at a later stage—and thereafter be involved with the administration.

14.10.3 Administrators: renunciation

An administrator accepts office only by taking a grant: no amount of 'intermeddling' prior to this will constitute acceptance. Renunciation is again effected in writing, signed by the renouncing 'administrator' (no declaration that there has been no intermeddling being required in this case), and this is filed (usually) with the other papers to lead the grant to someone else. Rule 37(2) provides that an administrator who has renounced in one capacity (eg as a residuary beneficiary) can claim a grant in another (eg as a creditor).

14.11 Grants of representation: checkpoints

1. Effect of the issue of a grant (**14.4**).
2. Is a grant necessary (**13.19** and **14.5**)?
3. If yes, which one is appropriate:
    (a) Is there a will?
        (i) If so, probate (**14.6.1**) or letters of administration with will annexed (**14.6.2**).
        (ii) Entitlement to grant governed by r 20 of the NCPR (**14.6.2.1**).
    (b) If no will:
        (i) Letters of administration (**14.6.3**).
        (ii) Entitlement to grant governed by r 22 of the NCPR (**14.6.3.1**).
4. Are any potential grantees?
    (a) Minors (**14.7.1**)?
    (b) Mentally incapable (**14.7.2**)?

5. Is more than one person entitled to the grant (**14.8**)?
6. How many may/must apply (**14.9** and **14.10**)?
7. May a potential applicant renounce (**14.10**)?

Figure 14.1 Application for a grant of representation.

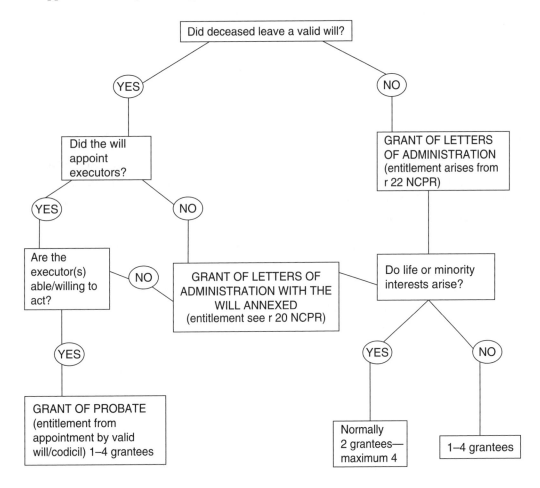

14.12 Obtaining the grant: practice overview

14.12.1 The early stages

We have already outlined some of the issues to be considered in the early stages of the administration of an estate. At **14.12.2** to **14.12.4** we will endeavour to put those matters in context and consider other practical issues which may arise in the pre-grant period of the matter.

14.12.2 Early stages: instructions

The personal representatives may (and frequently do) instruct a solicitor to act for them in the conduct of the administration. You may yourself be appointed an executor, or be a partner in a firm which has been appointed to act. In all of these cases you will have to ascertain the information you need to begin the task from the personal representatives or family members who may (especially initially) be in a distressed state. Whilst it is, of course, important that you perform your role efficiently, it is equally important that you conduct matters with sensitivity and with a proper concern for those who may not only be very upset but perhaps in temporary difficult financial circumstances resulting from the death.

14.12.2.1 What do you need to know?

Much of the information required to enable you to complete the first stage of the administration of the estate (obtaining the grant) will be apparent from the discussions in the previous sections of this chapter. In addition, you will also need to establish how and to whom the estate is to be distributed (**Chapter 13**), and whether any problems are likely to be encountered in this connection. There may, for example, be missing beneficiaries (see **15.7.2**) or the possibility of a claim under Inheritance (Provision for Family and Dependants) Act 1975 (see **13.23** to **13.30**).

14.12.2.2 Checklists

The best way to ensure the efficient collection of the information you need from the personal representatives or family members is to use a suitable checklist. Most firms will have their own version of such a checklist, which should prompt you to discover the details appropriate to any given case relating to the following matters:

(a) full personal details relating to the deceased, the immediate family, and any dependants;

(b) full personal details relating to the proposed personal representative(s), and to beneficiaries entitled to share in the estate. In both cases, as we have seen, who these people are will very much depend upon whether or not there is a will;

(c) details of the various assets:

   (i) in the deceased's succession estate (ie passing under the will or the intestacy rules);

   (ii) not in the succession estate but in the taxable estate (ie any property of which the deceased was a beneficial joint tenant, or in respect of which he/she had made a statutory nomination or a *donatio mortis causa*; any settled property of which the deceased had been a tenant for life);

   (iii) not forming part of the estate for either succession or taxation purposes (such as s 11 of the Married Women's Property Act 1882 and other trust policies, or certain lump sum pension scheme benefits);

(d) details of the various liabilities due from the estate or charged upon any of the assets listed above

(e) details of any lifetime gifts within the seven years prior to the death (or at any time if a benefit was reserved).

14.12.3 Early stages: what else will you need?

In addition to the information identified above, you will need (as appropriate) the following:

(a) The death certificate—you will need this to register the death (see **14.13** below).

(b) The original will and any codicil(s). Your firm may already be holding these, or perhaps they have been lodged for safe keeping with the deceased's bank. Once obtained, it will be necessary to consider any issues of validity etc which may arise (see **13.3** to **13.8**) and whether affidavit evidence may be required to support the application (see **14.24**).

(c) Any 'paperwork' associated with the various assets and liabilities. Thus, for example, you will need the title deeds relating to any land (or at least to discover their whereabouts). Similarly, such things as share certificates, insurance policies, bank and building society account details, outstanding bills, etc should be obtained.

(d) Details of any insurances (eg house and contents cover) effected by the deceased. Arrangements should be made, as soon as possible, either to have the interest of the personal representatives noted on any such policies, or for fresh cover in their name to be taken out. In the case of motor insurance, ensure (if needed) that appropriate cover is (or has been) arranged to enable family members to continue to use the vehicle.

14.12.4 Early stages: financial difficulties?

Always check at the first interview whether members of the deceased's family have any immediate financial needs as a result of the death. It will be some weeks (perhaps months) before significant funds will become available from the estate; do any surviving spouse/civil partner and children have access to adequate funds in the meantime?

What sources of funds might there be to assist here? Where the deceased had a joint bank or building society account with the surviving spouse/civil partner, or the survivor has adequate funds of their own the problem may not be acute. Where there are funds which could be released without a grant (in particular, any s 11 of the Married Women's Property Act 1882 or other trust policies, or certain pension fund lump-sum benefits payable at the discretion of the trustees of the scheme) try to take the necessary steps to enable payment to be made as quickly as possible. Similarly, where a state- or employment-related 'pension' may be payable, deal with this as a matter of priority.

14.13 Registering the death

The first task upon receipt of instructions is to register the death with the various banks, building societies, insurance companies, etc in which the deceased had investments and to establish the amounts due to the estate as at the date of death.

This is done by sending a copy of the death certificate (solicitors may alternatively send a letter certifying the death) to the various institutions, with a request for information as to the amount due to the estate. The Law Society has agreed a protocol with the British Bankers Association, the Building Societies Association and the Association of British Insurers which allows solicitors to send instead a 'death certificate verification' form certifying that they have in their possession and inspected an original certificate. However, not all institutions accept this alternative procedure.

In the case of shareholdings, you should register the death with the various companies and ask them to confirm the extent of the deceased's holding; it may be that the personal representatives have not in fact located all the share certificates. You may then wish to instruct a stockbroker to prepare a valuation for you. Where the deceased owned land, the assistance of a surveyor may be required; it will be helpful in such a case if the surveyor can also give a valuation of the household and personal effects. Expert assistance in valuing the deceased's assets will also be necessary where, for example, the deceased was 'in business', whether as a sole trader or partner, or the business was conducted through the medium of a company.

The deceased's Inspector of Taxes should also be notified of the death. You will then usually receive a tax return to be completed in due course in respect of the pre-death period of the tax year in question and another relating to the post-death period; if the administration period stretches beyond the end of that tax year, further returns for the later years will be required.

At an early stage, you should also notify the various creditors of the death and that the estate is now responsible for the debts due to them. This should stop the family being further distressed by demands for payment.

If there is a will and there are beneficiaries other than those instructing you, you should inform them of their 'interest' under the will and that—subject to the will being admitted to probate and the needs of the administration—you will be contacting them again as soon as you are able to deal with their legacies. It will be helpful if you give them an estimate of the timescale involved, being as realistic as possible in this. It is important to be cautious in what you say because the will might prove not to be admissible and/or there might not be sufficient funds to enable payment in full of all the legacies after the various liabilities have been discharged.

14.14 Preparing the papers to lead the grant

As confirmation of the amounts due to the estate is received, the appropriate Oath (see further **14.21** to **14.23**) and Inheritance Tax forms (see further **14.27** to **14.30**) can be drafted, along with any other supporting evidence (such as affidavits and copy testamentary documents) which may be required in the particular case (see further **14.24**). Fair copies will have to be prepared for swearing or signature (as appropriate) before being lodged at the selected Registry.

14.15 Funds for payment of inheritance tax

In order to obtain the grant the personal representatives will have to pay any inheritance tax due on the delivery of the Inheritance Tax Account. However, they normally need the grant as evidence of their title—without which those holding the deceased's funds will be unwilling to part with them! How can the deceased's personal representatives solve this 'circular' problem?

HMRC has agreed a process with the British Banker's Association and the Building Societies' Association which allows personal representatives to draw on money held in bank/building society accounts in the deceased's sole name to pay the inheritance tax that is due on delivery of Form IHT 400. The scheme is voluntary on the part of the financial institutions, and where the deceased had a number of accounts with a bank/building society—including loan and credit card accounts—only the net balance is likely to be available.

If taking advantage of this scheme, a separate Schedule—IHT 423 (see **14.28.3.3**) must be completed and submitted to the bank or building society concerned in respect of each account from which it is sought to transfer funds in payment of the tax due.

We saw in **14.5** that it is possible to obtain amounts due to the estate without production of a grant under Administration of Estates (Small Payments) Act 1965 and any such funds could be used to help pay the tax bill.

However, it is likely in many cases that much more will be needed than can be raised in this way. In the following paragraphs we consider other sources of funding which may be available to the personal representatives.

14.15.1 Bank loan

Either the deceased's or the personal representatives' bank will normally be happy to lend whatever is needed to pay the inheritance tax. The bank will usually insist upon an undertaking from the personal representatives to account to it from the first proceeds of the realisation of the estate assets once the grant has been obtained. An undertaking may also be required from the solicitor acting for the personal representatives, in which event the solicitors should first obtain an irrevocable authority from the personal representatives.

The bank will of course charge interest, so that, irrespective of the terms of any undertaking, the loan should be discharged as soon as possible. Provided the arrangement with the bank takes the form of a loan (rather than an overdraft facility) the personal representatives may be entitled to income tax relief for the interest payable.

14.15.2 Loan from beneficiary

A beneficiary may well be prepared (in order to mitigate or avoid the cost of bank borrowing) to lend money to help pay the inheritance tax (either interest-free or at a rate less than the commercial rate charged by the bank). If interest is paid, it will also qualify for income tax relief in the manner described in **5.6.3**.

This approach will only work, of course, if the beneficiaries have money readily available—either from existing resources, or from monies passing to them on the death but outside of the will or the intestacy rules (such as the proceeds of a s 11 of the Married Women's Property Act 1882 or other trust policy, jointly held property accruing by survivorship, nominated property, or lump-sum benefits under a superannuation scheme payable at the discretion of the trustees of the scheme).

14.15.3 Sale of assets

We saw in **14.4.1** that an executor's authority derives from the will, the grant merely confirming this; administrators, on the other hand, actually have their authority conferred by the grant. In principle, therefore, it is possible for an executor (but not an administrator) to sell estate assets prior to the issue of the grant: in practice, however, purchasers may well wish to see confirmation of the vendor's title before parting with their money! In particular, although it is possible to enter into a contract to sell land 'subject to probate', the grant will be needed to make the executor's title before the sale can be completed.

However, it may be possible for an executor to sell some assets before grant. A grant is not needed to pass title to chattels; this is achieved by delivery coupled with the necessary intention. Further, under Stock Exchange rules an executor can sell quoted shares before the grant is issued, subject to an undertaking for its production being given.

14.15.4 Direct payment to the HMRC

Where the deceased's assets include policies of life assurance whose proceeds are payable to the personal representatives, the insurance company may be prepared to release some/all the monies due to the estate direct to HMRC in payment of inheritance tax.

14.16 Swearing or affirming the oath

This must be done before an independent solicitor (or Justice of the Peace), and it will be a necessary formality also for any other affidavit evidence required. The fees payable are currently £5.00 per deponent for each Oath or other affidavit, plus £2.00 per deponent for marking each will, codicil, or exhibit to any other affidavit.

14.17 Lodging the papers

When all is ready, it is necessary to lodge (by post or in person) at the selected Registry:

(a) the appropriate Oath;

(b) the will and codicil(s) (if any) plus <u>two</u> A4 copies of each such documents;

(c) if an excepted estate, Form IHT 205 (see **14.27.2**); otherwise the receipted Probate Summary (Schedule IHT 421—see **14.28.3.2**);

(d) any further supporting documents, such as further affidavits, copy testamentary documents (eg because the originals contain unattested alterations) and renunciations; and

(e) a cheque for the probate fees. Where the <u>net estate</u>–ie the amount remaining in the deceased's sole name after funeral expenses and debts have been deducted (joint assets passing automatically to the surviving joint owner are ignored for the purposes of the fee calculation) – does not exceed £5,000, no fee is payable. For larger estates, the fee is currently £45. Normally, the issue of one or more Office Copies of the grant should be requested on lodging the application. This will (inter alia) help to speed up the process of registering the grant: the fee payable is £6.00 for the first copy and £1.00 for each additional copy ordered at the same time.

14.18 Obtaining the grant: practice overview: checkpoints

1. When taking instructions, what information/documentation, etc, do you need (**14.12.2** and **14.12.3**)?
2. With whom do you need to register the death (**14.13**)?
3. How is any IHT payable on delivery of the account to be funded (**14.15**)?
4. What do you need to lodge at the selected Registry to lead the grant (**14.17**)?

See further Figure **14.2**.

Figure 14.2 Estate administration—pre-grant procedure

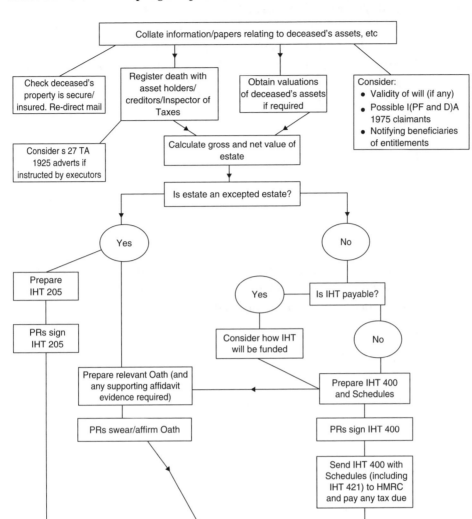

14.19 The court's requirements: oaths

Every application for a grant of representation must be supported by an Oath—in effect, evidence in the form of an affidavit—sworn or affirmed by the personal representatives, usually before a solicitor holding a current practising certificate and who is not a partner or employee of the firm preparing the Oath.

The essential purposes of the Oath are:

(a) to identify the applicants and the deceased;

(b) (in the case of a grant of letters of administration) to account for those who have a better right to a grant under rr 20 or 22 of the NCPR; and

(c) to establish the applicant's title to the grant sought.

14.20 The requirements generally

Increasingly, firms are now using commercial software packages to produce 'customised' Oaths for the particular case in which they may be acting. Alternatively, pre-printed forms are completed and adapted to meet the circumstances of the particular case. In this event, it is important to make sure that the 'finished document' reads as a piece, ie it should make proper sense in the same way as if it had been specifically drafted for the case concerned.

There are a number of different versions of pre-printed forms available from Law Stationers, which may vary slightly, eg in the order in which information is presented, or in what is actually pre-printed, but whose basic structure is essentially similar. They all contain marginal notes to assist in their completion. In cases of doubt or difficulty the guidance of the court should be sought.

We will here consider the completion of Oaths for executors (**14.21**); for administrators with will annexed (**14.22**); and for administrators (**14.23**). In **14.24** we will consider some of the situations in which it may be necessary to provide the court with further affidavit evidence. In all cases, the heading will be the same:

IN THE HIGH COURT OF JUSTICE
FAMILY DIVISION
THE PRINCIPAL REGISTRY (or)
THE DISTRICT PROBATE REGISTRY AT
In the estate of deceased (See **14.21.1**)

The details of the extracting solicitor should also be given; the Registry will then address any correspondence or queries to the solicitor rather than the personal representatives. It will be convenient (especially in the case of larger firms) for the solicitor's reference also to be given. This will then appear on the grant when issued and thus make it easier to identify who is dealing with the matter when this is received in the extracting solicitor's office.

14.21 Oath for executors

This is the appropriate Oath where a grant of probate is sought by an executor appointed by the will or a codicil.

14.21.1 'In the estate of . . . deceased'

This is, in effect, the final part of the heading. The true full name of the deceased should be entered here. In most cases, this will present no difficulty.

However, sometimes it may be necessary to include an alternative 'alias' name, for example, because the will was not executed in the deceased's full name, because the deceased's name has changed since making the will, or because the deceased held property in different names.

The inclusion of an 'alternative' name will not, however, be necessary unless one of the indicated circumstances applies. Thus the fact that the deceased was named 'John' but was habitually called 'Jack' does not require any reference or explanation in the oath, unless, for example, he made his will in the name of Jack, or held property in that name.

Application for a grant of representation

Oath for Executors

IN THE HIGH COURT OF JUSTICE

Extracting Solicitor
Address

Family Division

DX

*"Principal" or "District Probate". If "District Probate" add "at.........................".

The*   Registry

† If necessary to include alias of deceased in grant add "otherwise (alias name)" and state below which is true name and reason for requiring alias.

IN the Estate of †

(1) "I" or "We". Insert the full name, place of residence and occupation or, if none, description of the deponent(s). State the postcode of the deponent(s) and deceased's place of residence, if known.

(1)

deceased.

(2) Or "do solemnly and sincerely affirm".

(3) Each testamentary paper must be marked by each deponent, and by the person administering the oath.

make Oath and say,(2)   that
(1)   believe the paper writing   now produced to and marked by (3)

to contain the true and original last Will and Testament (4)
of †

(4) "with one, two (or more) Codicils", as the case may be.

of

deceased,

(5) This should be the date of birth as shown in the Register of Deaths.

(6) If exact age is unknown, give best estimate.

(7) Where there are separate legal divisions in one country, the State, province, etc., should be specified.

(8) Delete "no", if there was land vested in deceased which remained settled land notwithstanding his or her death.

(9) Include the names of the executors who have renounced. Or delete if no executors are to renounce.

who was born on the (5)   day of
and who died on the   day of
aged   years (6) domiciled in (7)
and that to the best of   knowledge, information and belief there was (8) [no] land vested in the said deceased which was settled previously to h   death (and not by h   Will
(4)   )
and which remained settled land notwithstanding h   death

And (1)   further make Oath and say (2)
that (9)

executor(s) named in the said Will (4)
have renounced probate thereof
Notice of this application has been given to

the executor(s) to whom power is to be reserved, [save

(10) Delete or amend as appropriate. Notice of this application must be served on all executors to whom power is to be reserved unless dispensed with by a Registrar under Rule 27 (3), or unless Rule 27(1A) applies. All executors to whom power is to be reserved should be named.

(11) "I am" or "we are". Insert relationship of the executors to the deceased only if necessary to establish title or identification.

(12) "The sole", or "the surviving", or "one of the", or "are the", or "two of the", etc.

](10)

And (1)   further make Oath and say (2)
that (11) (12)
                                                            Execut
named in the said

[P.T.O.
PRO4/1

260 Application for a grant of representation

(13) If there was settled land the grant should exclude it. Insert "save and except settled land".

and that (1)   will (i) collect, get in and administer according to law the real and personal estate (13) of the said deceased; (ii) when required to do so by the Court, exhibit in the Court a full inventory of the said estate (13) and when so required render an account thereof to the Court; and (iii) when required to do so by the High Court, deliver up the grant of probate to that Court; and that to the best of   knowledge, information and belief

(14) Complete this paragraph only if the deceased died on or after 1 April 1981 and an Inland Revenue Account is not required; the next paragraphs should be deleted.

(15) The amount to be inserted here should be in accordance with the relevant figure shown in paragraph 1 of the PEP List.

(16) The amount to be inserted here should be the net value of the estate, rounded up to the next whole thousand.

(17) Complete this paragraph only if an Inland Revenue Account is required and delete the previous and following paragraph.

(18) Complete this paragraph only if the estate qualifies under paragraph 2 of the PEP List and delete the previous two paragraphs.

(19) The amount to be inserted here is the exact amount of the gross estate.

(20) The amount to be inserted here is the exact amount of the net estate.

(14) [the gross estate passing under the grant does not exceed (15) £   , and the net estate does not exceed (16) £   and that this is not a case in which an Inland Revenue Account is required to be delivered]

(17) [the gross estate passing under the grant amounts to £ and the net estate amounts to £   ].
†

(18) [the gross estate passing under the grant amounts to (19) £   and the net estate amounts to (20) £   and that this is not a case in which an Inland Revenue Account is required to be delivered]

SWORN by

the above-named Deponent at

this   day of

Before me,

                  A Commissioner for Oaths/Solicitor.

SWORN by

the above-named Deponent at

this   day of

Before me,

                  A Commissioner for Oaths/Solicitor.

SWORN by

the above-named Deponent at

this   day of

Before me,

                  A Commissioner for Oaths/Solicitor.

Oyez 7 Spa Road, London SE16 3QQ
© Crown copyright.

Probate 4

11.2009

5073580
PRO4/2

Whenever an alias is necessary, the deceased (wherever his name is to be mentioned in the Oath) should be described by the true full name, followed by the alternative(s), eg 'John Edward Smith otherwise John Smith'. To comply with the requirements of r 9 of the NCPR it will also be necessary to furnish an explanation for the 'alias'.

14.21.1.1 The true full name

Normally, this will be the name on the birth certificate or, in the case of a married woman, the name of her husband (assuming she had adopted his surname). Similar principles will prima facie apply in the case of a divorced woman.

14.21.1.2 Common problems

14.21.1.2.1 Will in 'incorrect' name

This might arise, for example, because the deceased whose full name is Jane Elizabeth Smith has made her will in the name of Jane Smith. In such a case, she should be described as 'Jane Elizabeth Smith (otherwise Jane Smith)'. It will also be necessary to swear, in the Oath (at the end of the printed form) or in a separate affidavit, that 'the true name of the deceased is Jane Elizabeth Smith but that she made and executed her will in the name of Jane Smith'. In such a case, the grant will normally issue in the true name only.

14.21.1.2.2 Property in different names

Where the deceased held property in different names, again the full true name should be given first, followed by the 'alias'. It will also be necessary, at the end of the Oath form or in a separate affidavit, to indicate which is the true name and to include a statement that the deceased held property in the alternative name(s)—identifying (at least one item of) property held in the alternative name(s). For example, at the end of the pre-printed form might be added 'And that the true name of the deceased was Jonathan Smith and that he held Blackacre in the name of John Smith.' The grant will then be issued showing both names.

14.21.2 The applicants

The first paragraph of the Oath identifies those who are applying for the grant. The order should be the same as that in the will, but, in practice, if it is desired to change the order (eg to place a solicitor who has been appointed first) this can be done.

14.21.2.1 Names

The true full name of each applicant should be given. If this differs from the name in the will/codicil containing the appointment, an explanation will be required.

If the discrepancy is slight, the matter is usually easily dealt with, eg 'Susan Jones (in the will called Sue Jones)'. If the name has been misspelled, again the solution is simple, eg 'Jonathan James (in the will written Jonathon James)'. If the name has changed on marriage the explanation (eg) 'Ann Evans, married woman (formerly and in the will called Ann Brown, spinster)' will suffice.

Sometimes, the Registry may require further proof of the identity of an applicant. This might arise, for example, where the will appoints 'my wife' without naming her. In such a case, the (short) further evidence needed can usually be incorporated into the Oath (eg by including a statement that the applicant 'was the lawful wife of the deceased at the date of the will').

14.21.2.2 Addresses

The full postal address (including postcode) of the true place of residence of each applicant should be given. Solicitors (and others acting in a professional capacity) may give their business addresses. Former addresses need not be given unless relevant in establishing the executor's identity (where this is an issue).

14.21.2.3 Occupations or descriptions

The occupation of each applicant, male or female, should be given (eg 'schoolteacher' or, if retired, 'retired schoolteacher'). If the applicant has no occupation, this should be stated.

14.21.3 ' ... make Oath and say ... '

It is not necessary for the Oath to be sworn. Applicants may, instead, affirm—in which event, the words 'make Oath and say' whenever they appear should be deleted and replaced with 'do solemnly and sincerely affirm'. It will also be necessary to alter the jurat at the end of the form (in some prints this appears on the back of the form) by deleting the word 'SWORN' and substituting 'AFFIRMED'.

14.21.4 ' ... That [I/We] believe the paper writing now produced to and marked by [Me/Us] to contain the true and original last will and testament ... '

The purpose of this statement is to identify the document(s) which are being put forward as admissible to probate. This is achieved by 'marking' the document(s) concerned. The deponents (the applicants for the grant swearing the oath or making the affirmation) and the solicitor administering the oath or taking the affirmation sign the documents, thus exhibiting them to the affidavit evidence which the Oath comprises. If there is a codicil, after the word 'testament' there should be added 'with (one) (two, or as the case may be) codicil(s)'.

14.21.5 Details of the deceased

This part of the form requires basic information regarding the deceased testator. This must now include their date of birth and gender.

14.21.5.1 Name

As already discussed (in **14.21.1**) the deceased's full true name should be given here, with any alias.

14.21.5.2 Address

The last residential (postal) address (including post code, where known) of the testator should be given. If this is different from the address in the will or codicil, the previous address should be added after the words 'formerly of ...' (any intervening changes of address are ignored). If the addresses are the same, the words 'formerly of' should be deleted.

14.21.5.3 Date of birth and death

Usually, the birth and death certificates will give the relevant dates; however, it is not normally necessary to submit copies of the certificates.

14.21.5.4 Age

The testator's age should be stated (the best estimate being sufficient where this is uncertain).

14.21.5.5 Domicile

Normally, the deceased's domicile at the date of death must be included in the Oath. Where the deceased died domiciled in England or Wales domicile should be sworn as 'England and Wales'. The sworn domicile will appear in the grant; this may have important consequences in relation to the recognition of grants within the different jurisdictions in the UK.

14.21.6 Settled land

You will not often in practice encounter an estate where the deceased had an interest in settled land governed by the Settled Land Act 1925; this is even more unlikely now that no new strict settlements can be created (Trusts of Land and Appointment of Trustees Act 1996). However, in all cases the personal representatives must state whether there is/is not any settled land. It is quite wrong simply to delete the whole paragraph where there is no such land in the estate. In fact, the only permissible deletion is of the word '(no)' where there is, in fact, such land—for which a separate grant will be needed. In this event, it is enough to disclose in the Oath its existence: it is not necessary to give details of the settlement.

14.21.7 Executor's title

The purpose of this part of the form is to establish the 'capacity' in which the proving executors claim to be entitled to the grant. The discussion which follows indicates some of the more commonly met situations.

14.21.7.1 Relationship to the deceased

As we have seen (**14.4.1**), an executor's 'title' essentially depends upon appointment as executor by the will or codicil, the grant strictly only being required as evidence of that title. The fact that an executor is related to the deceased is therefore normally immaterial and need not be stated. However, it will be necessary to state the applicant's relationship to the deceased where identity is an issue, for example, if the will appoints 'my daughter' without naming her. If the will appoints 'my wife' or 'my husband' without naming the spouse concerned, the Oath should include a statement to the effect that the applicant is the lawful widow(er) and was lawfully married to the deceased at the time of the making of the will.

14.21.7.2 Where all appointed are applying

The wording to be used to describe the title of the proving applicant(s) will obviously depend upon the circumstances of the particular case. For example:

Only one appointee	*the sole executor/executrix*
All male, or male and female	*the executors*
All female	*the executrixes*
Implied appointment	*the executor according to the tenor*

14.21.7.3 Not all applying

Again the wording to be used to describe the entitlement of those applying will depend upon the circumstances. For example:

Some have died	*the surviving executor(s)/executrixes*
Some have renounced	*one (or two, etc) of the executors/executrixes*

In this case it is not necessary to recite the fact of renunciation by the other executor(s), but it helps the Registry if this is done. However, the renunciation itself must be filed with the papers to lead the grant.

Power is to be reserved   *one (or two, etc) of the executors/executrixes*

In this situation, the name(s) of the executor(s) to whom power is to be reserved must be indicated: further, the Oath must normally also state (NCPR, r 27) that notice of the application for the grant has been given to such executor(s).

14.21.7.4 Partners in a firm

Where partners in a firm (eg of solicitors) are appointed by name and some have predeceased or renounced, or power is to be reserved to one or more of the named partners, the procedures described in **14.21.7.3** above should be followed.

Where, however, the appointment is of partners in a firm without naming them (eg 'the partners at the date of my death in Solicitor & Co.') and not all of them wish to apply, it is sufficient for the Oath to contain a statement that the applicant is/was a partner (or the applicants are/were partners) at the appropriate date. Power can be reserved to 'the other partners' without naming them, and notice need not be given to those not wishing to act (NCPR, r 27(1A)).

14.21.8 Duties of the personal representatives

In practice little needs to be done with this paragraph of the Oath, except where there is settled land (see **14.21.6**), when it will be necessary to insert the words 'save and except settled land'.

14.21.9 Value of the estate passing under the grant

This is the deceased's free estate (ie unsettled property) in the UK in respect of which a grant is needed as evidence of the personal representatives' title. Property which does not pass to the personal representatives (ie in that capacity) is not relevant here (see **13.18** to **13.22**).

In this part of the Oath the appropriate inheritance tax certificate must be completed. There are now three possibilities, depending upon whether or not the estate is an 'excepted estate' for tax purposes. As we will see, if an estate is excepted it is necessary to file a Return of Estate Information in Form IHT 205 (see **14.27**), but a formal Inheritance Tax Account in Form IHT 400 (see **14.28**) is not required. Where the printed form offers alternatives for completion, those not relevant to the particular case should be deleted.

14.21.9.1 Excepted estate—gross value not exceeding inheritance tax threshold
(first paragraph on the OYEZ printed form)

If the estate is excepted (ie a formal account is not required) because its gross value does not exceed the inheritance tax threshold at the date of the application (in 2011/12 this is £325,000), the gross and net figures are not stated in the Oath precisely, but rather as not exceeding:

- (in the case of the gross estate) the appropriate tax threshold; or
- (in the case of the net estate) the value of that estate, rounded up to the next whole thousand pounds.

> **EXAMPLE 2**
>
> If in the case of a death in 2011/12 the value of the estate passing under the will is £150,000 (gross) and £144,500 (net), the figures to be inserted would be £325,000 (gross) and £145,000 (net). The certificate must also include the words 'and this is not a case in which an Inland Revenue Account is required to be delivered'.

14.21.9.2 Estate not an excepted estate (second paragraph on the OYEZ printed form)

Here, the exact gross and net values should be shown, but in this situation the words 'and this is not a case in which an Inland Revenue Account is required to be delivered' are, of course, inappropriate.

14.21.9.3 Excepted estate—gross value exceeds tax threshold but does not exceed £1 million and the chargeable estate after deducting spouse/charity exemption(s) does not exceed the tax threshold (third paragraph on the OYEZ printed form)

Here, again, the exact gross and net values should be given but the certificate must also include the words 'and this is not a case in which an Inland Revenue Account is required to be delivered'.

14.21.9.4 Other matters

The blank space at the end of the printed form can be used to provide any further information which might be required, eg as to an alias (see **14.21.1**); as to the identity of the applicant (see **14.21.2**); or as to the notice required under r 27 of the NCPR (see **14.21.7.3**) if not dealt with earlier. If the matter cannot be dealt with concisely, it will be necessary to file a separate affidavit.

14.21.10 Jurat

Each deponent must swear, or affirm, the Oath before an independent solicitor (or Justice of the Peace). It is not necessary for the names of all the deponents to be inserted if they are all swearing or affirming at the same time. Otherwise, a separate jurat should be drawn and completed for each deponent.

14.22 Oath for administrators with will annexed

As we saw in **14.6.2**, a grant of letters of administration with will annexed is appropriate whenever there is a will and a grant is for some reason not going to be made to an executor (because, perhaps none were appointed, or those appointed are all dead, or have renounced).

Many of the points discussed at **14.21** above regarding the completion of an Oath for executors apply equally to the Oath for administrators with the will. In this section we will concentrate upon the points of difference.

14.22.1 The applicants

Entitlement to apply for a grant of administration with will annexed is determined by r 20 of the NCPR (see **14.6.2.1**). The order in which the applicants' names appear in the Oath should follow that order.

Application for a grant of representation

Oath for Administrators with the Will

IN THE HIGH COURT OF JUSTICE
Family Division

Extracting Solicitor
Address

DX

The*   Registry

*"Principal" or "District Probate".
If "District Probate" add
"at _____"

† If necessary to include alias of deceased in grant, add "otherwise (alias name)" and state below which is true name and reason for requiring alias.

(1) "I" or "We". Insert the full name, place of residence and occupation or, if none, description of the deponent(s). State the post code of the deponent(s) and deceased's place of residence, if known.

(2) Or "do solemnly and sincerely affirm".

(3) Each testamentary paper must be marked by each deponent, and by the person administering the oath.

(4) "With one, two (or more) Codicils", as the case may be.

(5) This should be the date of birth as shown in the Register of Deaths.

(6) If exact age is unknown, give best estimate.

(7) Where there are separate legal divisions in one country, the State, province, etc., should be stated.

(8) Complete both blanks. When either such interest arises, two grantees may be required unless a trust corporation is applying.

(9) Delete "no", if there was settled land vested in deceased which remained settled land notwithstanding his death.

(10) If there was settled land such land may no longer be included in the scope of the grant.

(11) Here state manner in which all prior rights are satisfied, e.g., residuary legatees/devisees must show that no executors were appointed, or that those appointed either died before deceased or survived him and have since died without taking probate, or that they have renounced probate, or have failed to take a grant after being cited so to do (the order authorising a grant to citor being quoted).

(12) "I am" or "we are" and state title of applicants to the grant, including their relationship to the deceased only if necessary to establish title or identification.

(13) If there was settled land, insert "save and except settled land".

(14) Complete this paragraph only if the deceased died on or after 1 April 1981 and an Inland Revenue Account is not required; the next paragraphs should be deleted.

(15) The amount to be inserted here should be in accordance with the relevant figure shown in paragraph 1 of the PEP List.

(16) The amount to be inserted here should be the net value of the estate, rounded up to the next whole thousand.

(17) Complete this paragraph only if an Inland Revenue Account is required and delete the previous and following paragraphs.

(18) Complete this paragraph only if the estate qualifies under paragraph 2 of the PEP List and delete the previous two paragraphs.

(19) The amount to be inserted here is the exact amount of the gross estate.

(20) The amount to be inserted here is the exact amount of the net estate.

IN the Estate of †

(1)

deceased,

make Oath and say (2)
that (1)   believe the paper writing   now produced to and marked by (3)

to contain the true and original last Will and Testament (4)
of †

of

deceased,

who was born on the (5)   day of
and who died on the   day of   ,
aged   years (6) domiciled in (7)

and that (8)   minority and (8)   life interest arises in the estate of the
said deceased; and that to the best of   knowledge, information and belief there
was (9) [no] land vested in the deceased which was settled previously to h   death
(and not by h   Will (4)   ) and
which remained settled land notwithstanding h   death (10)

and (1)   further make Oath and say (2)
that (11)

that (12)   ; and that
(1)   will (i) collect, get in and administer according to law the real and personal estate
(13)   of the said deceased;
(ii) when required to do so by the Court, exhibit in the Court a full inventory of the said
estate, (13)   and when so required
render an account thereof to the Court; and (iii) when required to do so by the High Court,
deliver up the grant of letters of administration with Will annexed to that Court; and that
to the best of   knowledge, information and belief
(14) [the gross estate passing under the grant does not exceed (15) £
and the net estate does not exceed (16) £   , and that this is not a
case in which an Inland Revenue Account is required to be delivered]

(17) [the gross estate passing under the grant amounts to £
and the net estate amounts to £   ].
†

(18) [the gross estate passing under the grant amounts to (19) £
and the net estate amounts to (20) £   and that this
is not a case in which an Inland Revenue Account is required to be delivered]

[P.T.O.
PRO11/1

Application for a grant of representation   267

SWORN by

the above-named Deponent
at

this   day of
Before me,

              A Commissioner for Oaths/Solicitor.

SWORN by

the above-named Deponent
at

this   day of

Before me,

              A Commissioner for Oaths/Solicitor.

SWORN by

the above-named Deponent
at

this   day of

Before me,

              A Commissioner for Oaths/Solicitor.

SWORN by

the above-named Deponent
at

this   day of

Before me,

              A Commissioner for Oaths/Solicitor.

14.22.2 Minority and life interests

We have already seen (in **14.9.2**) that if a minority or life interest arises, a grant of letters of administration (whether or not with will annexed) will normally only issue to two grantees (or a trust corporation). An oath for administrators with will annexed must contain a statement as to whether or not there are minority or life interests arising—either under the terms of the will, or under the intestacy rules where the deceased died partially intestate. This part of the Oath form must, therefore, always be appropriately completed.

14.22.3 Clearing

The Oath must always 'clear off'—in effect, account for—all those who under r 20 of the NCPR have a 'better right' to the grant than the applicant(s). There is no need to account for anyone else in the same category as the applicant(s), nor to give notice of the application to any such person(s). All oaths for administration with will annexed will, therefore, have to account for the fact that no executor is applying by showing (as the case may be) that no executors were appointed, or that they are all dead or have renounced.

What further clearing is required will then depend upon how far down the list the applicant comes. Where there is a partial intestacy and an applicant is seeking a grant as a person entitled to share in the undisposed of property under the intestacy rules, anyone under r 22 of the NCPR having a 'better' claim than the applicant will also have to be cleared. Thus, in the second example in **14.22.4** below, it would be necessary to account for the fact that the deceased's spouse/civil partner (who would have a better right under r 22 than his children) was not applying.

14.22.4 Capacity

The Oath must then state the precise capacity in which the applicant claims to be entitled to the grant. This, remember, depends essentially upon entitlement to share in the estate rather than relationship to the deceased. Thus, for example:

(a) 'the residuary legatee and devisee under the said will';

(b) 'the daughters of the deceased and two of the persons entitled to share in the undisposed of estate of the said deceased';

(c) 'one of the specific legatees and devisees named in the said will'.

14.23 Oath for administrators

The grant of simple administration is appropriate where the deceased died wholly intestate. The entitlement to the grant essentially depends (as we saw in **14.6.3.1**) upon the applicant's relationship to the deceased. Many of the comments made in explanation of the practice in completing the Oath for executors (**14.21**) and the Oath for administrators with will annexed (**14.22** above) are equally relevant in this case also. Again, we will here concentrate upon the differences.

Application for a grant of representation

Oath for Administrators

Extracting Solicitor

Address

IN THE HIGH COURT OF JUSTICE

Family Division

DX

*"Principal" or "District Probate". If "District Probate" add "at-----".

The*   Registry

†If necessary to include alias of deceased in grant, add "otherwise (alias name)" and state below which is true name and reason for requiring alias.

IN the Estate of †

deceased,

(1) "I" or "We". Insert the full name, place of residence and occupation or, if none, description of the deponent(s). State the post code of the deponent(s) and deceased's place of residence, if known.

(1)

(2) or "do so solemnly and sincerely affirm".

make Oath and say (2) that †

(3) This should be the date of birth as shown in the Register of Deaths.

of

deceased,

(4) If exact age is unknown, give best estimate.

(5) Where there are separate legal divisions in one country, the State, province, etc., should be stated.

who was born on the (3)   day of
and died on the   day of   ,
aged (4)   years domiciled in (5)
intestate (6)

(6) Here give the status of deceased- "a spinster", "a widower", etc., and where necessary clear off the classes entitled in order of priority to applicant, e.g., "without issue or parent".

(7) The words which follow clear illegitimate, legitimated and adopted children and should be deleted if application made by surviving spouse or the civil partner (unless in the special circumstances it is necessary to clear issue) or a child. If appropriate substitute "without" for "or".

                                                                  (7) [or]   any other
person   entitled in priority to share in h   estate by virtue of any enactment and that
(8)   minority (8)   life interest arises under the intestacy; and
that to the best of   knowledge, information and belief there was (9) [no] land
vested in the said deceased which was settled previously to h   death and which
remained settled land notwithstanding h   death (10)

(8) Complete both blanks. When either such interest arises two grantees may be required unless a trust corporation is applying.

And (1)   further make Oath and say (2)
that (11)   the (12)

(9) Delete "no", if there was land vested in deceased which remained settled land notwithstanding his death.

(10) If there was settled land such land may no longer be included in the scope of the grant.

(11) "I am" or "we are".

(12) Show applicant's title, e.g., "brother of the whole blood and one of the persons entitled to share in the estate".

(13) If there was settled land, insert "save and except settled land".

                                                              of the said Intestate,
and that (1)   will (i) collect, get in and administer according to law the real and
personal estate (13)
of the said deceased; (ii) when required to do so by the Court, exhibit in the Court a full
inventory of the said estate (13)
and when so required render an account thereof to the Court; and (iii) when required to
do so by the High Court, deliver up the grant of letters of administration to that Court;
and that to the best of   knowledge, information and belief

(14) Complete this paragraph only if the deceased died on or after 1 April 1981 and an Inland Revenue Account is not required; the next paragraphs should be deleted.

(15) The amount to be inserted here should be in accordance with the relevant figure shown in paragraph 1 of the PEP List.

(16) The amount to be inserted here should be the net value of the estate, rounded up to the next whole thousand.

(14) [the gross estate passing under the grant does not exceed (15) £   , and
the net estate does not exceed (16) £   , and that this is not a case
in which an Inland Revenue Account is required to be delivered]

(17) Complete this paragraph only if an Inland Revenue Account is required and delete the previous and following paragraphs.

(17) [the gross estate passing under the grant amounts to £
and the net estate amounts to £   ].
†

(18) Complete this paragraph only if the estate qualifies under paragraph 2 of the PEP List and delete the previous two paragraphs.

(18) [the gross estate passing under the grant amounts to (19) £   and the
net estate amounts to (20) £   and that this is not a case in which an
Inland Revenue Account is required to be delivered]

(19) The amount to be inserted here is the exact amount of the gross estate.

(20) The amount to be inserted here is the exact amount of the net estate.

[P.T.O.
PRO8/1

Application for a grant of representation

SWORN by

the above-named Deponent
at

this   day of

Before me,

                    A Commissioner for Oaths/Solicitor.

SWORN by

the above-named Deponent
at

this   day of

Before me,

                    A Commissioner for Oaths/Solicitor.

SWORN by

the above-named Deponent
at

this   day of

Before me,

                    A Commissioner for Oaths/Solicitor.

SWORN by

the above-named Deponent
at

this   day of

Before me,

                    A Commissioner for Oaths/Solicitor.

14.23.1 The applicants

The order in which the names of the applicants are set out in the Oath should follow the order of priority in r 22 of the NCPR (see **14.6.3.1**). In the case of simple administration, no question of a discrepancy with the will can, of course, arise.

14.23.2 Clearing off

Following the words ' ... *domiciled in ... Intestate*' it is necessary to account for those with a better right to the grant than the applicant. Specifically, three matters must here be addressed:

14.23.2.1 Status of the deceased

The deceased's marital status must first be indicated, for example:

(a) 'a bachelor/spinster';

(b) 'a married man/woman/lawful civil partner';

(c) 'a widow/widower'; or

(d) 'a single man/woman' (where the deceased's marriage had been ended by a decree absolute of divorce). The details of the divorce (including the name of the court and the date of the decree) must be recited and it must also be sworn or affirmed that the deceased had not remarried/entered into a further civil partnership.

14.23.2.2 Clearing off those entitled under r 22 of the NCPR

It is not necessary to clear anyone entitled under this Rule in the same category as the applicant (nor is it necessary to give notice of the application to any such person). Thus, for example, if the deceased had four children, an application may be made by one of them (two if a minority or life interest arises) without reference to the others. However, it is essential to account for all those who might have a better right to the grant. This is, in effect, normally done by showing that the deceased was not survived by any relative(s) in the categories higher than that of the applicant(s), or that any survivors have since died or renounced.

In the simplest case, ie where there are no surviving relatives with a better right to the grant, the wording used is as follows:

To clear	*Swear that deceased died*
Spouse/civil partner	a bachelor, spinster, lawful widow(er), lawful civil partner, single man/woman
Children/issue	without issue
Parents	(or) parent
Brothers/sisters/their issue	(or) brother or sister of the whole [or half] blood or issue thereof
Grandparents	(or) grandparent
Uncles/aunts/their issue	or uncle or aunt of the whole [or half] blood or issue thereof

Where a relative in a higher category has survived but has since died/is not seeking a grant (eg having renounced) the wording of the Oath must deal with this, for example: ' ... Intestate leaving ... his lawful widow and the only person entitled to his estate him surviving who has since died/duly renounced letters of administration'. (In the latter case, the renunciation must be lodged with the papers to lead the grant.)

14.23.2.3 Clearing off 'any other person entitled in priority . . . by virtue of any enactment'

These words are designed to clear any illegitimate, legitimated, and adopted children and remoter issue of the deceased; they cannot be used as a 'short cut' formula for clearing those entitled under r 22.

If the application is being made by the surviving spouse or children/issue of the deceased, these words should normally be deleted.

If the applicant is from any category in r 22 below children or other issue, the words 'or any other person entitled . . . by virtue of any enactment' must always be left in.

14.23.3 Minority and life interests

The Oath for administrators must (as with the application for a grant with will annexed) contain a statement as to whether or not any such interests arise. A minority interest may of course arise whenever a beneficiary entitled to a share under the intestacy rules is under 18. A life interest will arise under the intestacy rules where the deceased is survived by a spouse/civil partner and issue and the value of the estate is greater than the relevant statutory legacy (see **13.12**).

14.23.4 Capacity in which grant sought

Essentially, as we have seen, the applicant's title depends upon relationship to the deceased and entitlement to the estate. The Oath must contain a precise statement as to both these matters.

14.23.4.1 Relationship

Some of the more commonly met descriptions to be used here are:

Spouse	*Lawful husband/lawful widow*
Civil Partner	*Lawful civil partner*
Child	*Son/daughter*—note that this is the appropriate description whether the child's parents were (or were not) married at the time of its birth.
Adopted child	*Lawful adopted son/daughter*—note that the Oath should contain a statement giving details of the adoption order and that it is still subsisting.
Grandchild	*Grandson/granddaughter*—note that the Oath will have to show that the grandchild's parent had predeceased so as to give the grandchild a beneficial interest under the statutory trusts.
Brother or sister	*Brother/sister of the whole [or half] blood.*
Nephew or niece	*Nephew/niece of the whole [or half] blood*—again, it will be necessary for the Oath to show that the applicant's parent has predeceased so as to give the applicant a share of the estate.
Parent	*Father/mother*
Grandparent	*Grandfather/grandmother*

Uncle or aunt	*Uncle/aunt of the whole [or half] blood*
Cousin	*Cousin german of the whole [or half] blood*—again, the Oath must show that the applicant's parent has predeceased so as to give the cousin a share of the estate.

14.23.4.2 Entitlement to the estate

The Oath must show the applicant'(s) entitlement to the estate. For example: 'the only person(s) entitled to the estate'; 'one [two, etc] of the persons entitled to share in the estate'.

Where a surviving spouse/civil partner is solely entitled, it should be stated in the Oath that the net estate does not exceed (as the case may be) £250,000 or £450,000 (see **13.12.2.1** and **13.12.3**).

14.24 Further affidavit evidence

In the vast majority of cases, a properly completed Oath is the only affidavit evidence that the court will require. Sometimes, however, the district judge or registrar will require further affidavit evidence to be submitted before issuing a grant. Some of the situations where such additional evidence may be required are considered briefly below: in such circumstances you will need to consult relevant practitioner works and perhaps the court itself as to the nature of the evidence required.

14.24.1 Due execution (r 12 of the NCPR)

We saw in **13.3.4.2** that the inclusion in a will of an attestation clause prima facie showing compliance with the requirements of s 9 of the Wills Act 1837 raises a presumption of due execution. If no attestation clause is included, or that included is insufficient, due execution will have to be proved—as it will if there is any reason for possible doubt as to the will's due execution (eg where the signature is imperfect or appears in an unusual position). Evidence of due execution may also be required where the deceased was blind, or executed the will with a mark, or where the will was signed by someone on behalf of the testator, though in all these cases the matter is in practice most effectively dealt with by an adjustment to the attestation clause in the will. If this has not been done, an affidavit as to knowledge and approval will also be required (see **14.24.2** below).

Ideally, the evidence of due execution should be given by one of the attesting witnesses or (failing this) anyone else present at the time of execution.

14.24.2 Knowledge and approval (r 13 of the NCPR)

Where a will has been signed by a blind or illiterate person, or by someone else on the testator's behalf, or for any reason (eg signs of extreme feebleness in the signature) there is a possible doubt as to whether the testator had the necessary knowledge and approval of the contents of the will (see **13.3.3.2**), the court must be satisfied on these points before the will can be admitted to probate. These matters are (as we have already seen at **13.3.4.2**) best dealt with by appropriate adjustments to the attestation clause; if this has not been done, affidavit evidence will be required to support the application for the grant.

14.24.3 Terms, condition, and date of will (r 14 of the NCPR)

The more commonly met possibilities here are set out below.

14.24.3.1 Alterations

We discussed the problems connected with alterations in **13.5**, where we saw that (except in the case of the filling in of a blank space) any unexecuted obliteration, interlineation, or other alteration is presumed to have been made after execution of the will and thus to be inadmissible. Where a will contains any such unexecuted alterations, etc it will normally be necessary (unless the district judge or registrar decides that the alteration is of no practical importance) for affidavit evidence to be provided as to whether or not each and every such alteration existed at the date of the execution of the will. Ideally this should be given by one of the witnesses or (failing this) by anyone else present at the time of execution. A copy of the will, omitting any inadmissible alterations (and showing a blank space where an obliteration has rendered the original wording not apparent), will have to be prepared and lodged with the other papers to lead the grant.

14.24.3.2 Incorporation

Where a will refers to another document in such terms as to suggest that it should be incorporated in the will (see **13.6**) the document will have to be produced and identified by (usually) affidavit evidence.

14.24.3.3 Date

Where there is doubt as to the date upon which a will was executed affidavit evidence will normally be required (ideally from one of the witnesses or anyone else present at the time) to establish the date of its execution. If possible, this should establish the exact date of execution; however, if this is not possible it should seek to establish execution between two definite dates.

14.24.4 Attempted revocation (r 15 of the NCPR)

Where there are circumstances which suggest the possibility of attempted revocation (whether by burning, tearing, or otherwise destroying, or by possible later will or codicil, eg suggested by the presence of pin or staple marks) the court must (in effect) be satisfied that the will has not been revoked. To this end, an affidavit of 'plight and condition' will often be required.

14.25 The court's requirements: checkpoints

1. Oath for executors:
    (a) Are there any 'alias' problems (**14.21.1**)?
    (b) Are there any problems in identifying the applicant(s) (**14.21.2**)?
    (c) Do any of the applicants wish to affirm rather than swear (**14.21.3**)?
    (d) What was the deceased's domicile (**14.21.5.5**)?
    (e) What is the position regarding settled land (**14.21.6**)?
    (f) How should the title of the applicant(s) be stated (**14.21.7**)?
    (g) Have all non-proving executors been accounted for in some way and any required notices given (**14.21.7.3** and **14.21.7.4**)?

(h) Which of the statements relating to the estate passing under the grant should be included (**14.21.9**)?

2. Oath for administrators with will annexed:
   (a) Are there any 'alias' problems (**14.21.1**)?
   (b) Are there any problems in identifying the applicant(s) (**14.21.2**)?
   (c) Do any of the applicants wish to affirm rather than swear (**14.21.3**)?
   (d) What was the deceased's domicile (**14.21.5.5**)?
   (e) Are there any minority or life interests—if so, minimum of two applicants normally needed (**14.22.2**)?
   (f) What is the position regarding settled land (**14.21.6**)?
   (g) Have those with a better right under r 20 been cleared off (**14.22.3**)?
   (h) How should the title of the applicant(s) be described (**14.22.4**)?
   (i) Which of the statements relating to the estate passing under the grant should be included (**14.21.9**)?

3. Oath for administrators:
   (a) Are there any 'alias' problems (**14.21.1**)?
   (b) Do any of the applicants wish to affirm rather than swear (**14.21.3**)?
   (c) Have those with a better right under r 22 been cleared off (**14.23.2**)?
   (d) What was the deceased's domicile (**14.21.5.5**)?
   (e) Are there any minority or life interests—if so, minimum of two applicants normally needed (**14.22.2** and **14.23.3**)?
   (f) What is the position regarding settled land (**14.23.6**)?
   (g) How should the title of the applicant(s) be described (**14.23.4**)?
   (h) Which of the statements relating to the estate passing under the grant should be included (**14.21.9**)?

4. Further affidavit evidence; are there any circumstances which may call for further evidence to be submitted, for example:
   (a) query as to due execution of will (**14.24.1**);
   (b) query as to knowledge and approval of contents of will (**14.24.2**);
   (c) alterations in will (**14.24.3.1**);
   (d) incorporation (**14.24.3.2**);
   (e) query as to date of will (**14.24.3.3**);
   (f) query as to attempted revocation of will (**14.24.4**).

14.26 HMRC's requirements

*Before studying the material in this section (**14.26** to **14.30**), you will find it helpful to have considered **Chapter 7** on inheritance tax, and especially **7.9**, which relates to the charge to tax on death.*

Unless the estate is an 'excepted estate' (see **14.27** below), it will not normally be possible for the personal representatives to obtain a grant of representation until they have submitted a formal Inheritance Tax Account (see **14.28** below), giving details of all the property in the deceased's taxable estate and its value, and (subject to the instalment option) paid any inheritance tax for which they are liable (Senior Courts Act 1981, s 109).

The personal representatives are under a duty to deliver an account (normally) within 12 months after the end of the month of death. However, they will in practice want to be in a position to do so much earlier than this, because:

(a) until they have paid the tax due on the delivery of the account they will be unable to obtain the grant and thus will be unable effectively to deal with the estate; and

(b) interest will begin to run six months after the end of the month of death.

The account form currently in use is known as **IHT 400**, which comprises a core account (considered in **14.28**) supported by Schedules as required in the circumstances of each particular case (considered in **14.29**). The steps involved in the actual calculation of the tax are identified in **14.28.6** and **14.29**.

In order to satisfy HMRC's requirements, it will be necessary for the solicitor acting for the personal representatives to obtain details of the various assets and liabilities of the estate, including property which passes on the death otherwise than through them (see **13.18** to **13.22**). The value of all such assets and liabilities as at the date of death must be established. This is a straightforward enough process in many cases, simply involving correspondence (eg with the bank, building society, insurance company, etc.) to ascertain the amount due to/from the estate. In other cases, expert assistance may be required (eg from an accountant, surveyor, or stockbroker) in order to establish the open market value of the property concerned at the date of death.

In ascertaining the extent and value of the estate, the personal representatives (and the solicitor acting for them) are required to make the fullest enquiries that are reasonably practicable in the circumstances—failure to do so may lead to penalties being imposed. Where an account is required, this must be completed to the best of the personal representatives' knowledge and belief. Again, there may be penalties (and even the liability to prosecution) for failure to disclose property on which tax may be payable.

The system is essentially one of 'self-assessment' of the taxable estate and calculation of any tax payable. The values shown in the account will ultimately have to be 'agreed' with HMRC (in the case of land with the local District Valuer), but this is usually done after the grant has been issued. Where tax is payable, this must be calculated by the solicitor acting for the personal representatives, who should then send the completed account to HMRC, together with all necessary Schedules—including the Probate Summary (IHT 421: see **14.28.3.2**)—and a cheque for the amount of the tax (plus any interest) due from the personal representatives. If tax etc is to be paid from the deceased's bank or building society account(s) it will also be necessary to submit a (separate) Schedule IHT 423 in respect of each such account to be used to the bank or building society concerned (see **14.15** above). When IHT 421 is returned, it is lodged at the selected Registry with the other papers to lead the grant (see **14.17**). If the estate does not qualify as an excepted estate, but nonetheless in the circumstances of the case no inheritance tax is in fact payable, IHT 421 is lodged with the other papers to lead the grant, and at the same time Form IHT 400 and relevant Schedules are sent to HMRC.

14.27 Excepted estates

If the estate is an 'excepted estate' there is no requirement to file a formal account in order to obtain a grant of representation, unless:

(a) HMRC so requires by notice in writing within 35 days of the issue of the grant; or

(b) it is subsequently discovered that the estate is not, after all, an excepted estate, in which event an account must be filed within six months of that discovery.

However, it will be necessary to file a 'Return of estate information'—Form IHT 205—see **14.27.2**.

In very broad terms, an excepted estate is one where no IHT is payable, either because the 'gross estate' (as defined) does not exceed the tax threshold, or does not exceed £1 million and no IHT is payable because of the operation of the spouse/civil partner and/or charity exemptions (for the detailed definition, see **14.27.1** below).

The present version of the rules is to be found in Inheritance Tax (Delivery of Accounts) (Excepted Estates) Regulations 2004 [SI 2004 No 2543] as amended particularly by Inheritance Tax (Delivery of Accounts) (Excepted Estates) (Amendment) Regulations 2011 (SI 2011/214).

14.27.1 Definition

An excepted estate includes one where all the following conditions are met:

(a) the deceased died domiciled in the UK; and

(b) the estate comprises only property which passes under the deceased's will or under the intestacy rules, or by statutory nomination, or beneficially by survivorship, or is settled property (not exceeding £150,000 in value) in which the deceased was entitled (immediately prior to death) under a single trust to an interest in possession, and

(c) not more that £100,000 of the gross value of such property is attributable to property situate outside the UK; and

(d) the deceased had not made any chargeable transfers (ie excluding exempt transfers but including former PETs) during the seven years prior to death, other than 'specified transfers' not exceeding in aggregate £150,000; and

(e) the total gross value (ie ignoring exemptions and liabilities) of the deceased's estate, plus 'specified transfers' and 'specified exempt transfers', does not exceed

either

the inheritance tax threshold at the time of the application for the grant (if the application is made on/after 6 April but before 6 August in any year, the relevant figure will be the tax threshold for the previous tax year);

or

£1 million and the net chargeable estate (after deduction of any exempt transfer on death to a spouse/civil partner and/or charity (but not any other 'specified exempt transfer') and the liabilities of the estate) does not exceed the relevant tax threshold. In relation to deaths prior to 6 April 2010 it was possible for an estate to be an "excepted estate" even though in the event the exemptions did not in fact apply because, after taking into account liabilities etc., no property actually passed to an exempt beneficiary. This unintended anomaly has been removed for deaths on/after 6 April 2010.

'Specified transfers' are chargeable transfers (including former PETs) consisting only of cash and/or quoted shares or securities and/or an interest in land (plus furnishings and chattels intended to be enjoyed with the land) unless the property concerned is subject to a reservation of benefit or becomes settled property. Thus, for example, if the estate of the deceased includes trust property exceeding £100,000 in value, or the deceased had an existing cumulative total at the date of death exceeding £100,000 the estate cannot be an excepted estate.

'Specified exempt transfers' include transfers between spouses/civil partners and gifts to charities (and also, eg, transfers to qualifying political parties or to provide maintenance funds for historic buildings etc).

In deciding whether conditions (d) and (e) are met, neither business property relief nor agricultural property relief are taken into account in determining the value of a chargeable transfer. In respect of deaths on/after 1 March 2010, transfers within the normal expenditure out of income exemption (**7.6.3.4**) made within seven years prior to death and which exceed £3,000 in a given tax year are to be treated as chargeable transfers in determining whether the estate qualifies as "excepted". In determining whether condition (e) is met, where the deceased was a beneficial joint tenant, only the value of the deceased's interest is taken into account.

For deaths on/after 6 April 2010, an estate which can benefit from the transferable nil rate band (**7.9.5**) may be able to qualify as an excepted estate—see **14.27.3** below. There is also a category of excepted estates for persons who have never been domiciled in the UK. In such cases, there will be no need to deliver a formal account if the deceased's UK estate is attributable solely to cash and/or quoted shares or securities the gross value of which does not exceed £100,000.

14.27.2 Form IHT 205

Although a formal account is not required, all applications for a grant in respect of an excepted estate must be accompanied by a 'Return of estate information'—IHT 205 (or IHT 207 where the deceased died domiciled abroad). The current version of this return is a 4-page document—IHT 205 (2006)—which (along with explanatory notes IHT 206 (2006)) can be downloaded from http://www.hmrc.gov.uk/cto/forms/iht205-2006-2.pdf and http://www.hmrc.gov.uk/cto/forms/iht206-2006-1.pdf respectively.

14.27.2.1 Page 1

Once it is established that completion of IHT 205 is indeed appropriate, the relevant box at the top of this page should be ticked.

Question 1 requests information about the deceased.

Questions 2–6 are concerned with various issues relating to the estate designed to ascertain (in effect) whether it is indeed an excepted estate. They require a 'No' or 'Yes' answer and identify various indicators that will mean completion of a formal account—IHT 400 (see **14.28**).

14.27.2.2 Page 2

Questions 7 and 8 continue this process.

Question 9 relates to assets to be added to the estate for inheritance tax purposes but for which a grant is not required—lifetime transfers made within seven years of death; deceased's share of joint assets passing automatically to the surviving joint tenant; any assets held in trust for the benefit of the deceased during their lifetime; nominated assets; and assets outside the UK. Pence should be ignored. Leave blank any box where the deceased did not have assets of the type specified. The total of figures in Boxes 9.1–9.6 is entered in Box A—Gross value of assets for which a grant is not required.

Question 10 relates to debts payable from the assets declared in Question 9. Again, pence should be ignored and the debts may be rounded up to the nearest pound. The total of the figures in Boxes 10.1–10.4 should be entered in Box B. This figure is then deducted from that in Box A and the result entered in Box C—Net value of assets for which a grant is not required.

14.27.2.3 Page 3

Question 11 requests similar information about the deceased's own assets for which a grant is required, the total value of which is identified in Box D—Gross value of assets for which a grant is required.

Question 12 is concerned with debts of the deceased. The total is entered in Box E. The Net estate in the UK for the purposes of the grant (D–E) is shown at Box F. The net estate for inheritance tax purposes (Box C + Box F) is shown at Box G and the Gross estate for inheritance tax purposes (Box A + Box D) is shown at Box H.

14.27.2.4 Page 4

Question 13 gives an opportunity for the applicants to provide any further information asked for by HMRC or which they wish to be taken into account.

Question 14 is concerned with the deduction of exemptions for property passing to the deceased's spouse and/or charities. If the figure at Box H (see **14.27.2.3** above) is less than the inheritance tax threshold, there can be no tax to pay and so it is not necessary to deduct any exemption that may be due—in which case enter "0" in Box J and copy the figure from Box G to Box K. Otherwise, the exemptions should be itemised and then totalled at Box J and at BoxK show the 'Net qualifying value for excepted estates'—Box G less Box J.

The figure at Box K must not exceed the inheritance tax threshold if the estate is to be an excepted estate. If it does, Form IHT 205 is not appropriate and a formal account will be required (IHT 400—see **14.28**).

. . . The Declaration at the bottom of the page is completed, and the Form signed by the applicant(s).

14.27.3 Claim to transfer unused nil rate band for excepted estates

The Inheritance Tax (Delivery of Accounts) (Excepted Estates) (Amendment) Regulations 2011 also provide for the possibility of an estate which is an excepted estate benefitting from the transfer of unused nil rate band of a pre-deceased spouse/civil partner. The effect of the claim will be to increase the available nil rate band on the occasion of the second death by 100 per cent–ie on a (second) death in 2011/12 to £650,000 – and the second estate remains an excepted estate so that completion of Form IHT 205 is appropriate. A claim can be made in respect of one earlier death only.

14.27.3.1 Conditions

(a) The second deceased must have survived the earlier death of their spouse/civil partner and have been married to, or in a civil partnership with, the first deceased at the time of the earlier death;

(b) The first deceased died

- on or after 13 November 1974 if the spouse of the second deceased, or
- on/after 5 December 2005 if the civil partner of the second deceased, or
- domiciled in UK at the date of their death.

(c) **None** of the nil rate band was used on the earlier death—so that 100 per cent is available for transfer.

(d) The first deceased's estate:

- consisted only of property passing under their will/ intestacy and jointly owned assets passing to an exempt beneficiary;
- did not include foreign assets whose gross value exceeded £100,000, settled property, or gift(s) with reservation of benefit to anyone other than the second deceased;
- did not qualify for agricultural property or business property reliefs either

on death or during their lifetime;

- (for deaths after 1 March 2011) did not include "normal expenditure out of income gifts" exceeding in total £3,000 in any of the seven years prior to their death.

If any of the conditions are not met then it will be necessary to complete Form IHT 400 (see **14.28** below).

14.27.3.2 The claim

If all the conditions are met, the claim to transfer the unused nil rate band is made by completing Form IHT 217 and sending it with the completed IHT 205, along with the other papers to lead the grant, to the Probate Registry. Form IHT 217 can be downloaded from http://www.hmrc.gov.uk/cto/forms/iht217.pdf.

14.28 Form IHT 400

14.28.1 Introduction

Where the estate is not an excepted estate, this account must be completed in all cases, together with any appropriate Schedules, which will always include the Probate Summary—IHT 421 (see **14.28.3.2**).

The current version of the account is a 16-page document, which (along with the Schedules and explanatory Notes to aid completion) can be downloaded from http://search2.hmrc.gov.uk/kb5/hmrc/forms/view.page?formid=3309&record=ID-K_xN6ens and http://www.hmrc.gov.uk/inheritancetax/iht400-notes.pdf.

The form contains a series of questions that must be answered; where there is nothing to be recorded in a particular box insert a dash or write in the figure '0'.

In showing the value of assets and liabilities and in identifying the taxable estate on the form, pence are ignored. Assets should be rounded down and liabilities rounded up to the nearest pound. However, when it comes to the actual calculation of tax (and any interest) due, pence are not ignored!

There are certain types of grant where it may not be necessary to fully complete IHT 400: for example, where the grant is to be limited to certain assets or is required only in respect of settled land. Such cases are beyond the scope of this book and are not considered further.

14.28.2 Pages 1 to 4 (Boxes 1–28)

Pages 1 and 2 are concerned with the deceased's details (Boxes 1–16) and Page 3 requires information regarding the person(s) dealing with the estate and details relating to any will and codicil(s) (Boxes 17–26). Boxes 27 and 28 on Page 4 need only be answered if there is a will.

14.28.3 Pages 4 and 5 (Boxes 29–48)

The rest of Page 4 and Page 5 contain a series of questions designed to identify which of the listed Schedules will be needed in the particular case. These should be completed before proceeding to the completion of the rest of IHT 400.

The information required to be included in the various Schedules is indicated in the forms and further assistance can be found in the explanatory Notes. It is proposed here only to refer to three cases.

14.28.3.1 IHT 402—Claim to transfer unused nil rate band

This Schedule should be submitted by the personal representatives (not later than 24 months after the end of the month in which the deceased died) if:

- the deceased died on/after 9 October 2007; and
- their spouse/civil partner died before them; and
- when the spouse/civil partner died their estate did not use up all of the nil rate band available to it; and
- it is desired to transfer the unused amount to the deceased's estate.

For the IHT nil rate band in force at the date the spouse or civil partner died reference can be made to IHT 400 Rates and Tables (which can be downloaded from http://www.hmrc.gov.uk/inheritancetax/).

The effect of the claim is that, on the deceased's death, the nil rate band available is increased by the percentage of the nil rate band (not the amount) unused on the earlier death of their spouse/civil partner (see **7.9.5**). Thus, if on the first death which occurred when the nil rate band was £300,000 the deceased left £150,000 to their only child and the residue to their surviving spouse, who dies in May 2011 when the nil rate band is £325,000, the available nil rate band is increased to £475,000. If all of the estate had been left to the surviving spouse the available nil rate band on the second death would be £650,000.

14.28.3.2 IHT 421—Probate summary

This Schedule must be completed in every case (other than an excepted estate) where application is being made for a grant in England and Wales (or Northern Ireland).

On page 2, the figures are taken from IHT 400 and Schedules. They are used to identify the gross and net estate for probate purposes (at Boxes 3 and 5 respectively). These figures are needed to complete the appropriate Oath (see **14.21.9** above); they will also appear in the grant itself when issued by the relevant probate registry, along with the figure for the total tax and interest paid on the account shown at Box 6.

14.28.3.3 IHT 422—Application for inheritance tax reference

This Schedule is required if there is any inheritance tax to pay on the estate: a reference number is required before a payment can be made and if it is intended to do so by cheque a payslip will also be needed. Alternatively, application can be made online.

If it is intended to pay by transferring money from the deceased's bank or building society account(s) it will also be necessary to submit a Schedule IHT 423 in respect of each such account to be used (see **14.15** above).

14.28.4 Pages 6 and 7 (Boxes 49–79)

This section of the account is concerned with the assets owned by the deceased in the UK—ie all those owned outright by the deceased and the deceased's share of jointly owned assets. Figures from the various Schedules are copied as appropriate to the various Boxes. The figures in Column A (relating to property not enjoying the benefit of the instalment option for the payment of tax) are totalled at Box 77 and those in column B (relating to property in respect that option is available—whether or not it is to be exercised) at Box 78. This gives, at Box 79, the gross estate in the UK.

14.28.5 Pages 8–10 (Boxes 80–108)

On page 8, deductions from the estate in the UK incurred up to the date of death are identified. In Box 80, details should be given of mortgages, secured loans and other debts payable out of property or assets owned outright by the deceased and included in Column B on pages 6 and 7. Details of funeral expenses should be shown in Box 81 and other liabilities in Box 82.

A Deductions summary (Boxes 83–91) occupies the first part of page 9, identifying at Box 91 the total estate in the UK.

Exemptions and reliefs are dealt with in Boxes 92–96. In Box 92 at the bottom of page 9 exemptions and reliefs claimed against assets in the deceased's sole name shown in Column A on pages 6 and 7 are identified. In Box 93 at the top of page 10 a similar exercise is conducted in relation to claims against assets in the deceased's sole name shown in Column B on pages 6 and 7. (In both cases, exemptions and reliefs relating to jointly owned assets should not be included here but deducted on IHT 404.) The section ends with the total net estate in the UK after exemptions and reliefs at Box 96.

The remainder of page 10 is devoted to identifying other assets taken into account to calculate the tax (Boxes 97–106). These are totalled at Box 107 and added to the total net estate (Box 96) to identify the total chargeable estate at Box 108.

14.28.6 Page 11 (Boxes 109–117)

This page is concerned with the calculation of the tax: if no tax is payable it can be ignored. At Box 110 indication must be given as to whether the instalment option (where available) is to be exercised. If so, the tax will have to be calculated using Form IHT 400 Calculation (see **14.29** below).

The 'Simple Inheritance Tax Calculation' (Boxes 111–117) can be used if *all* the specified preconditions are met. Otherwise, the Form IHT 400 Calculation must be used (again, see **14.29** below).

14.28.7 Pages 12 and 13 (Boxes 118 and 119)

On page 12, Box 118 is concerned with whether the direct payment scheme for the tax is to be used.

Box 119 is the declaration that all those delivering the account must complete and sign (on page 13).

14.28.8 Page 14 Checklist

A useful reminder of action to be taken and the additional information to be included when sending the forms to HMRC.

14.28.9 Pages 15 and 16

These pages identify return addresses and contact details and provide space for providing additional information.

14.29 Form IHT 400 Calculation

This form should be used where IHT 400 has been completed up to and including Box 109 and the simple tax calculation is not available to work out the inheritance tax payable.

A detailed consideration of the calculations that may be involved in completing this Form is beyond the scope of this book. However, the Form does contain useful brief summaries of:

- successive charges relief;
- double taxation relief;
- the calculation of interest on late payment of inheritance tax; and
- 'interest-free' instalments.

14.30 Summary

In completing, where required to do so, Form IHT 400 and any necessary Schedules, you are, in effect, presenting the details of the taxable estate and (where tax is payable) the calculation of the tax in the manner which HMRC prefers and, indeed, requires. However, in essence, the process is that described in **7.9** to **7.11**. In summary, this involves:

(a) Identifying the chargeable value (ie after any available exemptions and reliefs have been claimed) of any lifetime chargeable transfers (including former PETs) within the seven years prior to the death.

(b) Identifying the value of the chargeable estate on death, which involves:
   (i) establishing the gross value of all assets within the succession estate
   (ii) establishing the gross value of all property (of the kinds identified in **13.20**) which is not part of the succession estate but is part of the taxable estate
   (iii) deducting the value of any allowable debts, etc
   (iv) deducting the value of property covered by an available exemption or relief from tax.

(c) Cumulating the chargeable estate on death with the total of lifetime chargeable transfers.

(d) Applying the current inheritance tax rate scale to that (combined) cumulative total.

(e) Identifying the tax for which the personal representatives/others are accountable:
   (i) lifetime chargeable transfers (supplementary charge)—normally the trustees
   (ii) former PETs—normally the donees
   (iii) gifts with reservation of benefit—normally the donees
   (iv) trust property—normally the trustees
   (v) deceased's free estate—normally the personal representatives.

(f) Identifying the amount of tax to be paid by the personal representatives on delivery of the account:
  (i) tax on the non-instalment option property in full
  (ii) tax on instalment option property
    (1) if option not being exercised, in full
    (2) if option being exercised, any instalment(s) already due
  (iii) any interest where payment late.

14.31 HMRC's requirements: checkpoints

1. Is the estate an 'excepted estate' requiring completion of Form IHT 205–and if transfer of unused nil rate band is claimed, IHT 217 (**14.27**)?
2. If not, use Form IHT 400 and Schedules as required (**14.28**).
3. Calculate any tax due—Simple tax calculation—if available (**14.28.6**); otherwise, Form IHT 400 Calculation (**14.29**).

online resource centre Visit the Online Resource Centre for more information and useful weblinks.
www.oxfordtextbooks.co.uk/orc/foundations11_12/

15

Post-grant practice

15.1 Introduction

In this chapter we consider the law and practice relating to the administration and winding up of an estate once the grant has been issued by the court. We will be considering:

- the duties and powers of personal representatives (PRs) (**15.2** to **15.5**);
- administering the estate (**15.6** to **15.13**); and
- distributing the estate (**15.14** to **15.21**).

15.2 Duties and powers of personal representatives

As we have seen, it is generally necessary for personal representatives to obtain a grant of representation to establish title to the deceased's estate. Once the grant has been obtained, the personal representatives will need to know what duties and powers they have in the administration of the estate.

The Trustee Act 2000, which came into effect on 1 February 2001 but *in general applies to all trusts whenever created*, has significantly affected a number of the duties and powers discussed in **15.3** and **15.4** below. The 2000 Act, which by virtue of s 35 *also applies to personal representatives*, does not override any express provisions of the will or trust instrument. These may extend, modify, or exclude the statutory provisions.

15.3 Duties of personal representatives

15.3.1 The fundamental duty of personal representatives

The fundamental duty of a personal representative is to 'collect and get in' the deceased's estate, and then 'to administer it according to law' (Administration of Estates Act 1925, s 25, as amended). This duty must be performed 'with due diligence'.

15.3.1.1 Duty to collect the deceased's assets

Within a reasonable time, taking such steps as may be reasonably necessary, the personal representatives must collect the monies due and other assets belonging to the deceased which vest in them. There is no absolute rule as to what is a 'reasonable' in this context. Personal representatives will only be liable for loss resulting from their unreasonable conduct.

In practice, it will generally be necessary for the personal representatives to produce the original (or office copy) grant of representation to the persons who hold the deceased's assets, in order to establish entitlement to deal with such assets (see **14.4**).

15.3.1.2 Property of the deceased which does not vest in the personal representatives

The above duty only relates to the deceased's interests in property which devolve on the personal representatives. As we saw at **13.19**, certain types of property pass direct to those entitled on death and therefore do not vest in the personal representatives.

15.3.1.3 The duty to administer

Reasonable steps must be taken to preserve the deceased's estate, and within a reasonable time (prima facie within the 'executor's year'—the period of 12 months from the date of death) the personal representatives must realise any investments which it is not proper for them to retain.

Once the assets have been realised, administration of the estate thereafter involves the payment of debts, etc and any legacies, and the distribution of the residue according to the terms of the will and/or the intestacy rules (see further **15.6** to the end of this chapter).

15.3.1.4 Other duties

Duties imposed by s 25 of the Administration of Estates Act 1925 relate to the preparation (when required to do so by the court) of an inventory and account, and the delivery up to the court of the grant issued (eg so that it can be revoked and a new grant issued) if called upon to do so. We have seen that the various forms of Oath which constitute (in effect) the application for the grant (discussed in **14.19** onwards) contain statements acknowledging these duties.

15.3.2 The duty of care—Trustee Act 2000

Section 1 of the Trustee Act 2000 creates a new defined statutory duty of care applicable to trustees and personal representatives when carrying out their functions under the Act or equivalent functions under powers conferred by the will or trust instrument. They must act with such care and skill as is reasonable, bearing in mind any special knowledge or experience they have and, for professional trustees or personal representatives, any special knowledge or experience it is reasonable to expect them to have. This duty is in addition to the existing fundamental duties of trustees—eg to act in the best interests of the beneficiaries and to comply with the terms of the trust.

It is probable that the statutory duty does no more in effect than codify the common law duty of care so that the 2000 Act may make little difference in practical terms.

The statutory duty is a 'default' provision that may be excluded or modified by the trust instrument. Many professionally drafted wills and trust documents contain a clause excluding liability for breach of the standard of care, and it is anticipated that this practice will continue, with the effect that the beneficiaries of professionally drafted wills and trusts may be 'entitled' to a lower standard of care than that applicable to home-made efforts or on intestacy. The Solicitors' Code of Conduct 2007, Rule 2 (guidance note 67) indicates that where a solicitor/firm is considering acting as a paid executor/trustee a clause having the effect of excluding or limiting liability for negligence should not be included in the will/trust instrument without having first taken reasonable steps to ensure that the testator/settlor is aware of the meaning and effect of the clause.

The Trust Law Committee has recommended that paid trustees should not be able to rely on a clause excluding liability for negligence.

15.3.3 Statutory and equitable apportionments

Personal representatives may be under a duty to apportion income by virtue of s 2 of the Apportionment Act 1870, or under various equitable rules (such as the rules in *Howe v Earl of Dartmouth* (1802) 7 Ves 137, *Re Earl of Chesterfield's Trust* (1883) 24 ChD 643, and *Allhusen v Whittell* (1867) LR 4 Eq 295). The former are designed to solve questions of ownership of, for example, dividends received after the date of death but which relate to a period partly before and partly after the death. The equitable rules only apply where property is left to persons in succession (for example, to Albert for life, remainder to Victoria) and are designed to achieve fairness between the interests of life tenants and remaindermen. You will doubtless have encountered the apportionment rules in your study of Equity and the Law of Trusts, and will perhaps be relieved to know that both the statutory and equitable rules of apportionment are commonly excluded by contrary provision in the will—it being generally considered that the inconvenience and cost of implementing them outweighs any benefit to the beneficiaries.

15.3.4 Liability of personal representatives

Having accepted office, a personal representative is liable to beneficiaries or creditors for loss resulting from his own breach of duty (whether that arises from a misappropriation of estate assets, maladministration or negligence). A personal representative is not liable for loss resulting from a breach of duty by fellow personal representatives, unless negligent in allowing such breaches to take place.

15.4 Administrative powers of personal representatives

The Administration of Estates Act 1925 confers upon personal representatives a number of powers in connection with the administration of an estate. In addition, the Trustee Act 1925, the Trusts of Land and Appointment of Trustees Act 1996 and the Trustee Act 2000 give certain powers to trustees—and since the definition of 'trustee' for the purpose of these Acts effectively includes a personal representative, personal representatives also have these powers. These statutory powers are implied in all cases, ie whether the deceased died testate or intestate. In some cases they are subject to awkward limitations and professionally drawn wills usually give the personal representatives wider powers. The principal statutory powers are outlined below, together with an indication, where appropriate, of the type of modification or express clause that will commonly be contained in a will.

15.4.1 Power of personal representative to sell, mortgage, or lease

Section 39 of the Administration of Estates Act 1925 (as amended by the Trusts of Land and Appointment of Trustees Act 1996 and the Trustee Act 2000) confers upon personal representatives wide powers enabling them to sell or exchange any property, raise money by mortgage or charge, and grant or accept surrender of leases. These wide powers are necessary to enable the personal representatives to raise monies to pay a range of administration expenses (for instance, the payment of debts, funeral and testamentary expenses, inheritance tax, and pecuniary legacies). The personal representatives must decide which assets should be sold (see further **15.9**).

15.4.2 Power to appropriate

15.4.2.1 The power

Section 41 of the Administration of Estates Act 1925 provides that personal representatives may appropriate any part of the estate in or towards satisfaction of any legacy or interest or share in the estate, provided no specific beneficiary is thereby prejudiced. The 'appropriate consents' are necessary: thus, if the beneficiary is absolutely and beneficially entitled, the consent of that beneficiary is required (or of the beneficiary's parent or guardian if a minor). The asset to be appropriated must be valued for this purpose at the date of appropriation rather than at death (*Re Collins* [1975] 1 WLR 309).

EXAMPLE 1

Tom leaves a pecuniary legacy of £5,000 to Beth. The residue includes shares now worth £3,000. Provided Beth consents, the shares can be appropriated to her in partial satisfaction of her legacy, the balance being paid in cash. However, this would not be possible if (for example) the shares concerned had been specifically bequeathed to Beatrice.

15.4.2.2 Provision in will

Wills commonly dispense with the need for the consents required by s 41 on the grounds of convenience.

15.4.2.3 Application of the 'self-dealing' rule

We hope that you will recall this rule (ie that a trustee may not purchase trust property) from your earlier study of the law of trusts. The justification for the rule lies in the potential conflict of interest that may arise.

In *Kane v Radley-Kane* [1998] 3 WLR 617 it was held that this rule applies equally to personal representatives. In this case, a widow took out letters of administration to her husband's estate. The assets included some shares in a private company which she appropriated to herself in partial satisfaction of her statutory legacy. She subsequently sold the holding for almost ten times its value at the date of appropriation. It was held that the appropriation without the consent of the court or the other beneficiaries was invalid.

Thus, it will not be possible (unless authorised in the particular case by the will) for a personal representative to make an appropriation in his/her own favour in satisfaction of a pecuniary legacy—unless the assets appropriated are cash or the equivalent of cash (eg government stocks, plc shares).

15.4.3 Power to accept receipts for a minor's property

Unless the will provides otherwise, a minor is unable to give a valid receipt for monies or assets transferred to him or her in satisfaction of a legacy. A commonly held view is that parents (or guardians) are only able to give a valid receipt on behalf of their minor child if so authorised by the will. In the absence of such provision, the personal representatives have to retain the legacy until the minor has reached adulthood, thus preventing the estate from being wound up—for what might be a comparatively small amount of money. To overcome this difficulty, s 42 of the Administration of Estates Act 1925 enables personal representatives to appoint trustees of the property for the minor, provided the minor had a vested interest.

An alternative view, mentioned in the *Law Society's Probate Practitioner's Handbook* (5th edition, p 263), is that there is no longer a problem with receipts for minors as a result of s 3 of the Children Act 1989. This section provides that persons with 'parental responsibility' under the Act have the rights and duties which a parent has in relation to a child and his property. These rights include 'the right . . . to receive and recover in his own name, for the benefit of the child, property . . . which the child is entitled to receive or recover' (s 3(3)). The parent (or guardian) would recover such monies in a fiduciary capacity for the child. It is probable that not all practitioners are aware of this provision, however; it was not mentioned, for instance, as a possible alternative in response to a question about who could give a good receipt on behalf of a minor in *the Law Society Gazette* of 6 April 2006 (p 34).

If the gift is contingent (eg on the minor attaining 18) then it cannot, of course, be paid until the contingency is satisfied.

15.4.3.1 Express provision in the will

It is not uncommon, despite the statutory provisions mentioned above, for wills expressly to provide that a parent or guardian may give a valid receipt for a gift to which the minor is entitled, especially when the legacy is relatively small. Alternatively, the will may provide that the minor can personally give a valid receipt having reached a specified age (usually 16).

A further possibility is that the will directs that the legacy be held on trust for the minor. This might be particularly appropriate if significant sums are involved, and/or there are concerns about the parent etc being able to receive the legacy on behalf of the minor.

15.4.4 Section 15 of the Trustee Act 1925

This section gives personal representatives (and trustees) wide powers to settle claims made by or against the estate. This very useful power enables personal representatives to make a reasonable compromise instead of having to litigate in order to protect themselves against claims for breach of duty—subject to them having exercised the standard of care in Trustee Act 2000, s 1.

15.4.5 Power to insure

By s 19 of the Trustee Act 1925 (as amended by the Trusts of Land and Appointment of Trustees Act 1996 and the Trustee Act 2000, s 34) personal representatives may insure land and other property comprehensively and for its full value.

Insurance monies received under a policy of insurance are held as capital. They may be used to reinstate the property lost or damaged providing that the consent of any person whose consent is required to investment is obtained (Trustee Act 1925, s 20).

15.4.5.1 Express provision in the will

It is common for a will to provide for insurance of land and other property to full value, or reinstatement value, and against all risks. It may also provide that the property may be reinstated at the discretion of the personal representatives.

15.4.6 Power to delegate

15.4.6.1 Power to appoint agents

By s 11 of the Trustee Act 2000, personal representatives may collectively delegate all or any of their 'delegable functions' to an agent (such as a solicitor). 'Delegable functions' are any functions other than those relating to whether or in what way the estate assets should be distributed; decisions as to whether fees or other payments due should be made from capital or income; any power to appoint new trustees; and any power to delegate. By s 12, anyone (other than a beneficiary) can be appointed as agent, and if two or more people are appointed agents they must act jointly. Agents may be remunerated and employed on such terms as the personal representatives may determine (s 14) and s 15 directs that where an agent is engaged in 'asset management functions' (ie investment, acquisition or management of trust property) there must be an agreement evidenced in writing, to include a 'policy statement'—in effect, guidance as to how the agent should act in the best interests of the trust.

15.4.6.2 Review of and liability for agents

By virtue of s 21 of the Trustee Act 2000, the will may restrict the liability of personal representatives for the acts or omissions of their agent(s)—whether appointed under the authority of the statute or of a power in the will.

Subject to any inconsistent provision in the will, by virtue of Trustee Act 2000, s 22, personal representatives must keep under review the arrangements under which their agents act and how those arrangements are being put into effect. If asset management functions have been delegated, they have a duty to consider whether there is a need to revise or replace the policy statement (and if they consider there is such a need then to do so) and must assess whether the policy statement is being complied with by the agent(s). Further, if the circumstances make it appropriate to do so, the personal representatives must consider whether there is a need to exercise their power of intervention (in effect, to give directions to the agent(s) or to revoke the appointment), and if necessary to exercise such power.

Under s 23 of the Trustee Act 2000, personal representatives will not be liable for any act or default of the agent(s) unless they have failed to comply with the statutory duty of care applicable to them when appointing the agent or in carrying out their duties under s 22.

15.4.6.3 Section 25 of the Trustee Act 1925 (as substituted by s 5 of the Trustee Delegation Act 1999).

This allows personal representatives individually to delegate by power of attorney (on/after 1 March 2000) for a period not exceeding 12 months any of the duties, powers, and discretion vested in them. In this case, however, the personal representative remains fully liable for the acts of the delegate.

15.4.7 Indemnity for expenses

By s 31 of the Trustee Act 2000, trustees and personal representatives may reimburse themselves for all expenses properly incurred when acting on behalf of the trust or estate on or after 1 February 2001.

15.4.8 Power to run the deceased's business

The position here will depend upon whether the deceased was a sole trader or ran the business through the medium of a partnership or limited company.

15.4.8.1 Where the deceased was a sole trader

The general rule is that personal representatives have no authority to carry on the deceased's business. As an exception to this rule, however, they may do so with a view to the proper realisation of the deceased's estate, for example, to enable it to be sold as a going concern. This would not enable them, normally, to carry on the business for more than the executor's year.

A power to carry on the business may be implied from the terms of the will, but it seems in such cases that personal representatives will only have authority to utilise assets used in the business at the date of death and will not be entitled to have resort to any other part of the estate for additional funds.

Personal representatives are personally liable for debts incurred in running the deceased's business after his death, though they are entitled to an indemnity from the estate.

15.4.8.2 Express provision in the will

The will may confer wider powers on the personal representatives—for instance, to run (indefinitely) the business as a going concern and to use a wider range of estate assets in running the business.

15.4.8.3 Where the deceased traded as a partner

The personal representatives will usually have no power to intervene in the business. The partnership agreement must be consulted as it will normally contain provisions relating to the succession to a deceased partner's share, which will therefore pass outside the terms of the will.

15.4.8.4 Where the deceased was a shareholder in a limited company

In such a case the company will, of course, continue despite the death of its shareholder. The Articles of Association should be consulted, as these may give other shareholders rights to purchase the deceased shareholder's shares.

15.4.9 Power to invest

15.4.9.1 The general power of investment

Like the other provisions of the Trustee Act 2000, the statutory power of investment is a default power: it is expressed to be additional to powers conferred by, but subject to any restrictions in, the trust instrument.

The 'general power of investment' contained in s 3 of the Act authorises trustees and personal representatives to make any kind of investment that they could make if they were absolutely entitled to the assets of the trust. However, it explicitly excludes investments in land other than by way of loan (though see further **15.4.9.3** below).

Most professionally drawn wills (and trust instruments) are likely to contain express powers of investment in terms similar to the default power, so that this will in practice be most beneficial to older trusts lacking appropriately wide express powers, home-made wills, and cases of intestacy. It is likely that draftsmen will in future continue to use express investment clauses for a number of reasons. 'Investment' is not defined by the 2000 Act and the term will, as a result, cover whatever the common law from time to time determines. There could still, therefore, be doubt as to whether non-income producing assets constitute 'investment'. Alternatively, the testator may wish to restrict the trustees by ethical investment clauses preventing investment in, for example, the tobacco or arms industries.

15.4.9.2 The standard investment criteria

By virtue of s 4 of the Trustee Act 2000, trustees and personal representatives (whether exercising the statutory power or one conferred by the trust instrument) must have regard to 'the standard investment criteria'. They must also from time to time review the investments and consider whether, having regard to the standard investment criteria, they should be varied.

The standard investment criteria are:

(a) the suitability to the trust of the investment; and

(b) the need (to the extent that is appropriate in the circumstances) for diversification of the trust's investments.

Unless they reasonably conclude that in all the circumstances it is unnecessary or inappropriate to do so, personal representatives, before exercising the new statutory power or one conferred by the trust instrument, must (under Trustee Act 2000, s 5) obtain and consider proper advice about the way in which, having regard to the standard investment criteria, the power should be exercised. A similar requirement is imposed when reviewing the trust's investments. Proper advice is that of a person who is reasonably believed by the trustee to be qualified to give it.

15.4.9.3 Purchase of land

The purchase of land may be authorised by an express power. The default powers are given by s 6(3) of the Trusts of Land and Appointment of Trustees Act 1996 (as amended) and s 8 of the Trustee Act 2000. By these provisions, personal representatives are empowered to acquire freehold or leasehold land in the UK as an investment, for occupation by a beneficiary or for any other reason. These powers are additional to any conferred by, but subject to any restriction contained in, the will.

Personal representatives are not given an express duty to take 'proper advice' when buying land, unless they are acquiring it as an investment when s 5 (**15.4.9.2** above) will apply.

Again, it seems likely that professional draftsmen will continue to use express clauses relating to the purchase of land containing powers to repair, improve and maintain property, matters which are not covered in the Act.

15.4.10 Power to maintain a minor

Section 31 of the Trustee Act 1925 provides that where property is held for a minor beneficiary and the gift carries the right to the intermediate income, the trustees or personal representatives may apply the income for the maintenance education or benefit of the minor, and must accumulate the income not so applied. The following points should be noted:

(a) It does not matter whether the minor's interest is vested or contingent.

(b) The trustees or personal representatives are empowered to apply such income as is reasonable and in exercising their discretion must consider the age and requirements of the minor and the circumstances of the case generally, including what other income is applicable for the same purpose.

(c) Once the beneficiary attains the age of 18, accumulated income is normally added to capital and devolves with it (s 31(2)).

(d) If, although the minor has attained 18, the interest remains contingent, the discretion to use income for maintenance, etc ceases, and henceforth the income *must* be paid to the beneficiary until such time as the contingency is fulfilled or the interest fails (s 31(1)).

(e) The statutory power is only available to permit maintenance where the gift carries the intermediate income; most testamentary gifts will (in the absence of contrary provision in the will) carry such income. However, contingent pecuniary legacies generally do not, in which event s 31 will not apply; the intermediate income belongs in this case to the residuary beneficiaries.

EXAMPLE 2

In her will Tessa leaves £100,000 to her niece, Penny, contingently upon her attaining the age of 18, and the residue of her estate upon trust for her son, Rex, contingently upon his attaining the age of 25.

Both Penny and Rex are minors when Tessa dies.

The gift to Penny is a contingent pecuniary legacy, and unless it is one of the exceptional cases, or there is specific provision in the will, the statutory power to maintain is not available. The income will form part of the residue.

So far as Rex is concerned the statutory power is available, and the trustees may choose to pay the income yielded by the residue for Rex's maintenance. Any income not so paid over must be accumulated. When Rex reaches the age of 18 the power to maintain ceases, and the trustee must pay the current income to Rex until he reaches 25, or dies without having satisfied the contingency. If Rex attains the age of 25, he is then entitled to capital and accumulations.

15.4.10.1 Express provision in the will varying s 31

The statutory power may be considered to be adequate. The will may, however, commonly make the following modifications:

(a) conferring an absolute discretion on the trustees as to the amount of income available;

(b) removing the restriction as to the amount of income applicable where other funds are available; and

(c) where the gift is contingent on the beneficiary attaining an age greater than 18, removing the right to receive income at 18.

15.4.11 Power to advance capital

Section 32 of the Trustee Act 1925 gives trustees and personal representatives a discretion to apply capital for the advancement or benefit of a beneficiary (whether or not a minor) who has a vested or contingent interest in capital. The following points should be noted:

(a) up to one-half of the beneficiary's vested or presumptive share may be advanced;

(b) any person with a prior interest (eg a life tenant) must consent in writing to the advance;

(c) any advance made must be brought into account when the beneficiary becomes absolutely entitled;

(d) if a beneficiary contingently entitled receives an advance but fails to fulfil the contingency (eg the beneficiary dies before attaining the age specified for vesting) the amount advanced is not recoverable from the beneficiary's estate; and

(e) an advancement is a substantial payment made with a view to setting the recipient up in life: the term 'benefit' has been construed extremely widely. It may include (for example) a saving of tax: *Pilkington v IRC* [1964] AC 612.

15.4.11.1 Express provision in the will

The will may amend the statutory power by removing the first three limitations referred to in **15.4.11** above. The statutory power does not of course enable advancements to be made to a life tenant, but this power may be granted by the will.

15.4.12 Exercise of personal representatives' powers

A sole personal representative (whether originally so appointed or by survivorship) has the same powers as two or more personal representatives. A sole personal representative may thus give a valid receipt for the proceeds of sale of land (Law of Property Act 1925, s 27). Joint personal representatives generally have joint and several authority, so that the act of one binds the others and the estate. However, there are statutory exceptions in relation to the conveyance of land and the transfer of shares: in these cases, the conveyance or transfer will normally require all living personal representatives (ie to whom a grant has been issued) to join in.

Personal representatives' powers are in nature fiduciary and, therefore, must be exercised in good faith in the interest of the estate as a whole.

15.5 Duties and powers of personal representatives: checkpoints

1. Duties of personal representatives:
   (a) to collect the deceased's assets (**15.3.1.1**);
   (b) to administer the estate according to law (**15.3.1.3**); and
   (c) statutory and equitable apportionments (**15.3.3**).
2. Powers of personal representatives:
   (a) Does the will contain modifications/additions to the statutory powers?
   (b) If not, statutory authority for power:
      (i) to sell, etc. (**15.4.1**);
      (ii) to appropriate (**15.4.2**);
      (iii) to appoint trustees of a minor's property (**15.4.3**);
      (iv) to settle claims (**15.4.4**);
      (v) to insure (**15.4.5**);
      (vi) to delegate (**15.4.6**);
      (vii) for indemnity (**15.4.7**);
      (viii) to run the deceased's business (**15.4.8**);
      (ix) to invest (**15.4.9**);
      (x) to maintain a minor (**15.4.10**); and
      (xi) to advance capital (**15.4.11**).

15.6 Administering the estate

In **15.6** to **15.12**, we will begin our consideration of what happens once the personal representatives have received the grant from the issuing Registry. In **15.7** we will consider how the personal representatives may protect themselves against claims from potential beneficiaries or other claimants against the estate. In **15.8** we will outline the implications for personal representatives and solicitors acting for them of the compliance requirements under the Financial Services Act 1986 and the Solicitors' Investment Business Rules. The steps necessary to collect and realise the estate's assets are then identified (**15.9**). In **15.10** we look at the rules governing the payment of debts where the estate is solvent; the position where the estate is insolvent is outlined in **15.11**. The section concludes with a brief look at ways in which post-death changes may be effected to the deceased's dispositions (**15.12**). **Figure 15.1** on page 309 sets out the steps from obtaining the grant to ascertainment of the residue.

15.7 Protection of personal representatives

15.7.1 Against claims of unknown beneficiaries/creditors (Trustee Act 1925, s 27)

Even though they were not aware of the claims of a beneficiary or creditor at the time of distribution, the personal representatives remain personally liable to any unpaid beneficiary or creditor (*Knatchbull v Fearnhead* (1837) 3 M & C 122; 1 Jur 687). By complying with the requirements of s 27 the personal representatives can protect themselves against such liability. It is important, however, to appreciate that s 27 only affords protection to the personal representatives as such. Any disappointed beneficiary or creditor may recover from the person(s) to whom the personal representatives have distributed, including themselves if they are also beneficiaries.

In the case of an executor, whose authority derives from the will, advertisements under this section can (and to save time should) be made even before the grant is issued. Where the personal representatives are administrators they cannot properly do this, since they are authorised to act only by the grant itself. Once this has been issued, however, the placing of the required advertisements should be a matter of priority.

15.7.1.1 The advertisements

These are usually made by the solicitor acting for the personal representatives and on their behalf, requiring any person interested (as beneficiary or creditor) to send particulars to the personal representatives' solicitor within a stated time, which must not be less than two months from the date upon which the advertisement appears, after which time the estate will be distributed on the basis of claims of which the personal representatives then have notice (whether from a response to the advertisements or otherwise).

Such advertisements must be placed in:

(a) the *London Gazette*; and

(b) a newspaper circulating in the district in which any land forming part of the estate is situated (in practice, this will often be a local newspaper); and

(c) (in effect) any other newspaper, etc (whether in this country or abroad) as might be appropriate to the particular case. Thus, for example, where the deceased had been in business it might be appropriate to advertise in a relevant trade journal. If the personal representatives are in doubt they should apply to the court for directions.

15.7.1.2 Searches

The personal representatives should also make such searches as a purchaser of land would make (s 27(2)). Searches should therefore be made in the Land Registry or Land

Charges Registry; in the Local Land Charges Register; and a bankruptcy search against the deceased and the beneficiaries.

15.7.2 Against claims of missing beneficiaries/creditors

No protection, however, is afforded to personal representatives by s 27 where they are aware of the existence of claimants who simply cannot be found. In practice, the personal representatives should still make s 27 advertisements, but some further steps will be necessary to safeguard their position.

15.7.2.1 Payment into court

The personal representatives could pay the amount due to the missing beneficiary or creditor into court and distribute the rest of the estate in the normal way. The personal representatives will thereby achieve total protection, but from the viewpoint of the beneficiaries this is far from an ideal solution!

15.7.2.2 Indemnity

The personal representatives could distribute the whole of the available estate against an agreement by the beneficiaries to indemnify them in the event of the missing beneficiary or creditor subsequently appearing to claim their entitlement. This will certainly be more attractive to the beneficiaries, but is obviously risky from the standpoint of the personal representatives.

15.7.2.3 Benjamin Order

This is an order of the court giving the personal representatives leave to distribute the estate on the basis of an assumption set out in the order. In the case from which the order takes its name (*Re Benjamin* [1902] 1 Ch 723) the assumption was that a missing beneficiary had predeceased.

Before an application for such an order can be made, it will be necessary to make full enquiries for the missing claimant. In addition to the s 27 advertisements, the personal representatives should advertise for information in a newspaper circulating in the locality where the missing beneficiary was last heard of. The court may direct further enquiries and advertisements if it considers them to be necessary.

If the assumption in the order subsequently turns out to be wrong, the personal representatives are fully protected. The (no longer) missing beneficiary will have to seek his remedies against those to whom the estate has been distributed.

15.7.2.4 Insurance

As an alternative to a *Benjamin* Order, the personal representatives could seek cover against the risk of the missing beneficiary or creditor subsequently appearing. The insurance company will almost certainly require the same sorts of enquiries, etc as the court might require before making a *Benjamin* Order. However, where the risk is not great (eg because the sum involved is not large or the chances of a claim being made are remote) this may be a cheaper and quicker solution than an application to the court. Indeed, the use of 'missing beneficiary insurance' in the case of small estates was specifically approved in *Evans v Westcombe* (*Law Society's Gazette*, 10 March 1999) with the cost of the premium being a proper expense of the administration.

15.7.3 Other protection for the personal representatives

In relation to claims under the Inheritance (Provision for Family and Dependants) Act 1975, we have already seen at **13.25.2** that personal representatives are protected (should the court allow an 'out of time' application) if they have refrained from distributing the estate for six months after the issue of the grant. This does not, however, protect the beneficiaries to whom the assets may have been distributed.

There are a number of situations where the personal representatives need protection against other possible claims from potential beneficiaries, creditors or other claimants. These include the following.

15.7.3.1 Future and contingent liabilities

Where personal representatives distribute with knowledge of such liabilities, they receive no protection under s 27 of the Trustee Act 1925. Where there is a known future liability, therefore, a fund should be set aside by the personal representatives to meet it.

A contingent liability might arise, for example, where the deceased had acted as a guarantor for the repayment of a loan, or there is a threat of legal proceedings against the estate. There are several possible courses open to the personal representatives to deal with such a problem:

(a) They could estimate the amount of the possible liability and set aside an appropriate amount—distributing the rest of the estate. This is really unsatisfactory on two counts:

  (i) an accurate estimate may be difficult (even impossible) to make;
  (ii) the beneficiaries will have to wait for payment of the full amount due to them until the danger of the liability arising has passed.

(b) They could distribute the whole estate subject to an agreement from the beneficiaries to indemnify them should the liability actually materialise. This (again) is not a course which should appeal to the personal representatives for (we hope) fairly obvious reasons!

(c) If they wish to be able to distribute the whole estate (which is certainly what the beneficiaries would want) they could safely do so if they can arrange suitable (ie not too expensive) insurance cover.

(d) Failing this, the only other approach is an application to the court for directions.

15.7.3.2 Inheritance tax

The personal representatives can become liable for the inheritance tax on former potentially exempt transfers (PETs—and for the supplementary charge in respect of lifetime chargeable transfers) where the transferor dies within seven years, and the transferee has not paid the tax concerned within 12 months after the end of the month in which the transferor dies (**7.11**). A similar liability can also arise in respect of gifts with a reservation.

This potential liability is obviously something of which the personal representatives must take account. The trouble is, however, that (for example) the existence of a PET might not come to light until after they have distributed the estate (there is no obligation to report PETs in the transferor's lifetime). Further, the tax position on death may have been calculated on the assumption that there were no lifetime transfers; the discovery of the former PET may mean that the tax liability of the personal representatives in respect of the estate deemed to be transferred on death will also be increased.

The position of the personal representatives in such circumstances has been clarified by HMRC (see statement in *the Law Society's Gazette*, 13 March 1991). Broadly, it seems that the Capital Taxes Office will not normally pursue the personal representatives for any further inheritance tax where they have made 'the fullest enquiries that are reasonably practicable in the circumstances' to discover lifetime transfers, and have obtained a certificate of discharge (see further **15.16.2.4**) and distributed the estate before the former PET comes to light.

Where the personal representative is a practising solicitor, some protection may be afforded by the Solicitors' Indemnity Fund (see *the Law Society's Gazette*, 7 March 1990).

15.7.3.3 Other cases

There are a number of other situations in which the personal representatives may be afforded protection; these are described in various practitioner works which you will need to consult in appropriate circumstances. These include:

(a) s 45 of the Adoption Act 1976 (distribution of estate in ignorance of an adoption order of which they do not have notice);

(b) liability for rent and breaches of covenant where the estate includes leasehold interests; and

(c) where the court grants an application for rectification of a will under s 20 of the Administration of Justice Act 1982.

15.8 Financial services

We do not propose here to examine in any detail the framework of the Financial Services and Markets Act (FSMA) 2000 and the Financial Services and Markets Act 2000 Regulated Activities Order 2001 (RAO) discussed in **Chapter 2**. Remember that, in the case of solicitors who are exempt (under Pt XX of the FSMA 2000) as members of a profession regulated by a Designated Professional Body (DPB), the Act must be read in conjunction with the Solicitors' Financial Services (Scope) Rules 2001 (the Scope Rules) and the Solicitors' Financial Services (Conduct of Business) Rules 2001 (see **Appendix 3** and **Appendix 4**).

Our purpose here is to consider briefly the impact of the regime upon personal representatives and the solicitors acting for and advising them.

15.8.1 Personal representatives

Under s 19, FSMA 2000, there is a general prohibition against undertaking a 'regulated activity' (dealing, arranging, managing, or advising) in relation to investments unless the person carrying out the activity is authorised by the Financial Services Authority (FSA) or is exempt. Under the RAO, Article 66 exempts personal representatives (and trustees), provided that they receive no separate remuneration for such investment business and provided (in some cases involving professional personal representatives/trustees) that they do not advertise investment services. Note, however, that Article 66 does not apply where solicitors are not themselves personal representatives/trustees but are merely acting for them.

15.8.2 Solicitors

In practice, it is highly unlikely that any firm of solicitors engaging in probate and administration work could avoid carrying out investment business as defined by the

FSMA 2000. Thus, whether partners or employees of a firm are themselves the personal representatives, or are simply acting for the personal representatives, it is virtually impossible for them not to be managing investments—unless the particular estate comprised only assets that are not 'investments' for the purposes of the FSMA 2000 (eg, land, works of art). Similarly, in whatever capacity partners or employees of the firm are involved, it is more likely than not that at some stage they may be called upon to give investment advice (eg, as to whether to sell certain investments), or to arrange deals in investments (eg by arranging for the sale of certain shares by a stockbroker). It should be stressed that there is no bar on solicitors giving purely generic advice on investments (as opposed to advising in relation to a specific investment).

The question then arises as to whether the investment business is 'mainstream investment business'—such as advising a beneficiary on what investments to make with an inheritance received—or is 'non-mainstream investment business', namely business that is incidental to the solicitor's main work, such as selling shares in an estate that the solicitor is administering. Mainstream investment business requires regulation by the FSA. Subject to certain conditions, solicitors carrying out only non-mainstream investment business can avoid this requirement provided they fall within the exemption in Pt XX of the 2000 Act for members of a profession regulated by a Designated Professional Body (DPB)—in the case of solicitors, The Law Society. For this exemption to apply:

(a) the investment business must be incidental to other services being provided by the solicitors which do not themselves constitute mainstream investment business;

(b) the solicitor accounts to the client for *all* commission received; and

(c) the solicitor does not hold himself/herself out as offering investment services to clients.

Further, to avoid the need for regulation by the FSA, if the solicitor does in fact arrange or advise investments, this must be on the advice of an authorised person (such as a stockbroker or an independent financial adviser).

Rule 5 of the Scope Rules sets out further restrictions. For example, solicitors relying on the DPB exemption cannot recommend clients to buy packaged products (unit trusts, life policies, and stakeholder pensions), though it is possible to arrange such a transaction where the client is relying on independent advice from an authorised person. In addition, a solicitor managing the administration of an estate/trust must be careful to delegate the day-to-day decision-making in relation to investments to an authorised person (such as a stockbroker).

15.9 Collecting/realising the assets

15.9.1 Registering the grant

On the issue of the grant, the personal representatives now have their evidence of title and should proceed apace to register the grant with the various institutions (banks, building societies, insurance companies, etc) holding the deceased's assets and obtain from them the sums due to the estate.

Office copies of the grant, bearing the seal of the Registry, should be used rather than the original: photocopies are not acceptable evidence! The original is an important document of title and therefore should so far as possible be protected from the risk of loss and kept in the file. However, HMRC certainly like to see the original.

It is hoped that you will have obtained enough office copies of the grant to enable this process to be completed swiftly. The absolute priority should be the release of sufficient funds to discharge any loan to pay the inheritance tax (**14.15**). After this has been done, normally you should aim to discharge interest-bearing liabilities first so as to minimise the 'cost' to the estate.

As we have seen, the personal representatives' duty is to 'collect and get in' all the deceased's real and personal estate (and then administer it according to law). This must be done with 'reasonable diligence'. Unsecured debts due to the deceased should be collected as soon as practicable—the personal representatives taking proceedings for their recovery if necessary. There is no need to call in or realise loans secured on mortgages of land which are authorised investments, unless the money is needed to discharge the funeral, testamentary and administration expenses, debts, and pecuniary legacies.

Where the estate's assets include a reversionary (ie future) interest under a trust, this should not be sold unless there is some special reason for doing so (eg that there are no other funds available for the payment of the various expenses and debts of the estate).

Generally, causes of action vested in the deceased at the date of death survive for the benefit of the estate (as do those subsisting against the deceased against the estate) (Law Reform (Miscellaneous Provisions) Act 1934, s 1(1)). The main exceptions relate to contracts for the provision of personal services and the tort of defamation.

The personal representatives may also have an action to recover damages on behalf of certain dependants where the deceased's death has been caused by a wrongful act in respect of which the deceased could have sued if still alive (Fatal Accidents Act 1976). Any damages recovered under this Act do not form part of the deceased's estate for any purpose, but 'belong' to the dependants concerned.

The personal representatives (as we saw at **15.4.4**) have wide powers of settling claims made by or against the estate, so that they are not obliged to litigate every possible point or risk being held liable for not doing so.

15.9.2 Sales of assets

In order to be able to pay taxes and other liabilities, the personal representatives may have to sell assets in the estate. In principle, they are at liberty to use any assets coming into their hands for this purpose (see further **15.10** below). However, in practice there are a number of 'constraints' which they should bear in mind.

15.9.2.1 The will

The terms of any will should very much influence their decision. Thus, if the will makes specific gifts the property so given should not be sold unless other assets have been exhausted. Further, beneficiaries may have indicated a wish to receive particular assets in partial or total satisfaction of (as the case may be) a pecuniary legacy or share of residue. The personal representatives should endeavour to respect those wishes and avoid selling the assets concerned, if possible to do so.

15.9.2.2 Tax implications

You will have already encountered (in **7.9.1.7** and **7.9.1.8**) what are sometimes called 'loss on sale' reliefs for land and quoted securities sold within the prescribed statutory periods for less than their probate values. Where there are assets which might qualify for such relief, the personal representatives should consider whether to sell them and thus be able to reclaim any inheritance tax paid on the 'difference'. If this relief is claimed, remember that no loss relief is available for capital gains tax purposes.

Where personal representatives sell any assets during the course of the administration, there will prima facie be a charge to capital gains tax on gains accruing since the date of death. Such gains may be relieved from charge by the annual exempt slice: personal representatives have the same exemption as an individual (currently £10,100) for gains made on disposals in the tax year in which the death occurs and in the following two tax years. Thus, for example, if in March they are contemplating selling shares which show a gain of £11,000 since the date of death, they would be well advised to consider selling immediately sufficient to utilise the current year's exemption and the rest after 6 April.

Where personal representatives realise an allowable loss on a sale of estate assets, it may be set against their gains of that year and any amount not thereby absorbed is carried forward to be set against their gains in future tax years. Their loss cannot be passed on to the beneficiaries, so if it is possible that the personal representatives will not have sufficient gains to absorb any loss an alternative strategy should be considered. Where the asset concerned, instead of being sold, is vested in a beneficiary this is not a chargeable event and the beneficiary acquires at the value at the date of death. The beneficiary can then sell realising a loss to be set against any chargeable gains of the beneficiary.

15.10 Payment of debts (solvent estate)

A solvent estate is one where the assets are sufficient to cover in full the funeral, testamentary and administration expenses, debts, and other liabilities. It is immaterial whether or not legacies can also be paid in full.

So far as the creditors (including secured creditors) are concerned, they are entitled to be paid what is due to them from any part of the estate available for the payment of debts. As long as they are paid, it does not matter to them upon what part of the estate the burden of the payment falls. However, this is a matter of considerable importance from the viewpoint of the beneficiaries. Thus, to take a simple example, if the will leaves Blackacre to Beatrice and the residue of the estate to Rosalind, it will matter very much to them who has to bear the burden of the debts—particularly if Blackacre is subject to a mortgage at the date of the testator's death. It is with the resolution of such problems that this section is concerned. As we shall see, the answer will depend upon whether (and what) provision is made in any will.

15.10.1 Secured creditors

We are here concerned with the situation where a debt has been charged on the deceased's property during the deceased's lifetime (eg, a mortgage on Blackacre).

Subject to the testator showing contrary intention (see **15.10.4**), by s 35 of the Administration of Estates Act 1925 the property so charged is liable for the payment of that debt. So, in the example above, Beatrice will prima facie take Blackacre subject to the mortgage debt. If the value of Blackacre is insufficient to cover the mortgage debt, the 'deficit' would have to be met by the residuary estate, so that Rosalind's entitlement would be correspondingly reduced.

15.10.2 Other debts: the statutory order etc

So far as unsecured creditors are concerned (again, subject to any express provision in the will (see **15.10.4**) the order in which the estate's assets should be used is laid down by s 34(3) and Part II of the First Schedule to the Administration of Estates Act 1925. These provisions draw no distinction between realty and personalty.

The order is as follows (if there is nothing in a given 'category', or what there is proves insufficient, you move on down the list):

(a) Property undisposed of by the will (subject to the setting aside of a fund from which to pay any pecuniary legacies). Thus, where a partial intestacy arises (because the deceased's will contains no residuary gift, or where such residuary gift has totally or partially failed) the property not disposed of by the effective provisions of the will is primarily liable for the payment of the unsecured debts of the deceased. However, it is only so much of such undisposed of property as is not set aside to pay any pecuniary legacies (see **15.15.2**) that is so liable.

(b) Residue (again, subject to the setting aside of a fund from which to pay any pecuniary legacies, ie to the extent that these are not fully covered by the retention made under (a) above).

In most cases, this is as far down the order as you will need to go. However, if the assets comprised in (a) and (b) are insufficient, the list continues:

(c) Property specifically given for the payment of debts. Property is within this category if the will contains a direction that the identified property (eg Greenacre) is to be used to fund the payment of debts, but nothing is said as to what is to happen to any surplus.

(d) Property specifically charged with the payment of debts. Property falls within this category where the will contains a direction as in (c) above, but goes on to provide what is to happen to any surplus.

You may be pardoned for thinking that where the deceased has taken the trouble to identify specific property in the estate to fund the payment of debts, this would place such property firmly at the head of the list! Faced with the problem of reconciling logic with the statutory order, the courts have concluded that such a provision can only make the specifically given or charged property primarily liable where the will shows an intention to exonerate any property falling within categories (a) and (b) above (see further **15.10.4**).

(e) The pecuniary legacy fund (retained under (a) and/or (b) above). At this point, any such fund will be used to help pay the debts. Unless the testator has indicated that any such legacies are to be paid in priority, they will abate proportionately, so that each legatee bears a share of the burden of the payment.

(f) Property specifically devised or bequeathed, rateably according to the property's value (ie to the deceased) at the date of death. Thus, if Whiteacre (the subject of a specific gift in the will) is worth £100,000 and is subject to an outstanding mortgage of £25,000, its value for the purposes of this exercise will be £75,000.

(g) Property expressly appointed under a general power of appointment (again, rateably according to value). This category is rarely encountered in practice.

If needed, certain other categories of property may also be available for the payment of debts, but only after all the above categories have been exhausted. The categories include:

(a) *donationes mortis causa;*

(b) nominated property; and

(c) property in respect of which an option to purchase has been given by the will (*Re Eve* [1956] Ch 479; 3 WLR 69; 3 All ER 321).

15.10.3 Marshalling

Where (as they are entitled to do) the personal representatives discharge a debt out of property within a category which is not—as between the beneficiaries—liable to bear the burden of that debt, the equitable doctrine of marshalling can be invoked by the disappointed beneficiary so as to ensure that the debt is (at the end of the day) borne by the appropriate property. Thus, if the will makes a specific gift of some shares (within (f) in the list in **15.10.2**) to Peter and these are in fact sold to pay the debts (although the residuary estate—which is listed at (b) in **15.10.2**—is sufficient to cover them), Peter will be entitled to 'compensation' from the residue.

15.10.4 Contrary provision

The above rules only apply in the absence of contrary provision in the will. What constitutes such provision?

15.10.4.1 Secured creditors

The effect of s 35 of the Administration of Estates Act 1925 can be avoided in several ways. Thus, the gift of Blackacre in our earlier example (in **15.10**) might have been expressed to be 'free of mortgage', in which event the mortgage would be repayable out of the residue. Alternatively, the will might have contained a direction to pay debts 'including any mortgage charged on Blackacre' out of residue. It is important to appreciate, however, that a simple direction to pay 'debts' from residue without specifically mentioning the charge on Blackacre would not oust s 35. On the other hand, where the testator has identified a particular fund other than residue for the payment of 'debts', this is prima facie sufficient to cover all debts including the mortgage on Blackacre. However, Blackacre would remain charged with the payment of any deficit if the particular fund proved insufficient to discharge the debt completely.

15.10.4.2 Unsecured creditors

There are three formulae likely to be met in practice for varying the statutory order, the first two being most commonly encountered. They are:

(a) gift of residue on trust or trust for sale with a direction for payment of debts out of the proceeds (before division amongst the beneficiaries); and

(b) gift of residue 'subject to' or 'after' payment of debts.

In both of these cases, the effect will be to make the residue as a whole, including the property undisposed of by the will in the case of a partial intestacy, primarily liable for the payment of the debts.

(c) property 'given for' or 'charged with' payment of debts with intention to exonerate residue.

As we saw in **15.10.2** above, without some evidence of intention to exonerate residue such property remains in the third and fourth categories in the statutory order. However, provided this intention is clear, the property given or charged will become primarily liable.

15.11 Payment of debts (insolvent estate)

An estate is insolvent if the assets are insufficient to pay in full all the funeral, testamentary and administration expenses, debts and liabilities. Clearly, in such a case, the beneficiaries can receive nothing, and the creditors will not be paid in full. In what order are the creditors entitled to be paid?

This is a question of crucial importance for the personal representatives because if they pay 'out of order' they will prima facie incur personal liability for debts in a higher category that have not been paid (see further **15.11.3**). As a result, if there is any risk that the estate may prove to be insolvent it is necessary to be extremely careful strictly to observe the prescribed order for payment.

15.11.1 Secured creditors

Such creditors will in practice have a choice:

(a) They may simply rely on their security. Thus, for example, the mortgagee will rely on the (eventual) proceeds of sale of the mortgaged property to obtain repayment of the loan.

(b) They may realise their security (ie sell the property) and to the extent that this proves inadequate to join the 'queue' of unsecured creditors (see further **15.11.2**).

(c) They may (without selling) place a value on their security and seek payment of any deficit as unsecured creditors.

There is, in principle, a fourth choice—unlikely in practice often to be adopted: they could surrender their security and simply be treated as unsecured creditors!

To the extent that secured creditors rely upon their security to obtain repayment, they enjoy priority over the unsecured creditors.

15.11.2 Unsecured creditors

The order of priority—which cannot be varied by the testator—is governed by Administration of Insolvent Estates of Deceased Persons Order 1986.

The order of priority is as set out in the following paragraphs.

15.11.2.1 Reasonable funeral, testamentary, and administration expenses

By tradition, reasonable funeral expenses take precedence.

15.11.2.2 The bankruptcy order

Within each of the categories identified below debts rank equally. Personal representatives have no right to 'prefer' one creditor above the others in the same category, so that if there is insufficient to pay all the creditors in the given category in full, those debts abate proportionately, so that everyone receives (for example) 50p in the £ (see further **15.10.3**).

Under the bankruptcy order, debts rank as follows:

(a) Preferred debts. These include wages and salaries of the deceased's employees in the period of four months prior to the death, up to a maximum in the case of each employee of (currently) £800.

(b) Ordinary debts. These are all other debts (except deferred debts) including amounts owed to HMRC and the balance of any claim that does not rank as a preferred debt. Thus, for example, an employee who was owed wages of £1,000 could (subject to meeting the conditions above) claim £800 as a preferred creditor and the balance as an ordinary creditor.

(c) Interest on preferred and ordinary debts. The rate of interest will be the greater of the rate specified in s 17 of the Judgments Act 1838 at the date of death (currently 8 per cent) or the contractual rate applicable to the particular debt. Interest is payable from the date of death until payment, and the two categories rank equally for this purpose.

(d) Deferred debts. These are loans from the deceased's spouse, ie spouse at the date of death (the position at the date of the loan is irrelevant).

15.11.3 Protection of the personal representatives

If personal representatives pay (say) an ordinary debt having knowledge that there are preferred debts, the payment is an implied 'warranty' that there are sufficient assets to meet all the preferred debts of which they have notice (whether as a result of s 27 of the Trustee Act 1925 advertisements (**15.7.1**) or otherwise). If there are not sufficient funds to do this, the personal representatives are personally liable.

However, it has long been settled that they will not be personally liable where, without undue haste, they have paid an inferior debt without notice of a debt in a higher category (*Harman v Harman* (1686) 2 Show 492; 3 Mod Rep 115; Comb 35).

We have seen that personal representatives must not 'prefer' one creditor in a given category above any other in the same category. By s 10(2) of the Administration of Estates Act 1925, personal representatives are protected from liability to creditors of the same class where payment to others in that class has been made in full should the estate subsequently prove to be insolvent, provided that at the time of the payment the personal representatives were acting in good faith and had no reason to believe that the estate was insolvent. This protection is available even where a personal representative has paid a debt due to himself, unless the grant was taken as a creditor.

15.12 Post-death changes

At the beginning of the chapter we saw that the devolution of a person's estate will largely depend on whether that person has left a valid will or not. It may be, however, that when that person dies the dispositions effected by the will or intestacy, or otherwise, are unsuitable in some way. For example, they may fail to make adequate provision for the surviving spouse or another relative or dependant of the deceased; or it may be that the person entitled does not want the property which is left to them. Another possibility is that tax-saving opportunities will be wasted if the estate is distributed in accordance with the will or intestacy rules.

We have already noted (at **13.23** to **13.30**) the provisions of Inheritance (Provision for Family and Dependants) Act 1975. There are two further methods whereby alterations can be made to the dispositions of a deceased person's property after that person's death, and generally such alterations can be achieved without adverse inheritance and/or capital gains tax consequences.

15.12.1 Disclaimers

In the much quoted words of Abbot CJ 'the law is not so absurd as to force a man to take an estate against his will' (*Townson v Tickell* [1819] B & Ald 31). A beneficiary under a will or intestacy can disclaim an interest that is not wanted provided no benefit has been taken from the gift. The right to disclaim is lost once any benefit has been accepted by the beneficiary, who cannot generally disclaim part only of a single gift (but may disclaim one of several gifts). All that is necessary for a disclaimer to be effective is for disclaiming beneficiaries to indicate their intention to refuse the gift either orally or in writing to the deceased's personal representatives. However, if the disclaimer is to be effective for inheritance tax or capital gains tax purposes, it must be in writing. The effect of a disclaimer is that the property will pass as if the disclaiming beneficiary had predeceased the testator or the intestate. In the case of a specific or pecuniary gift in a will, on disclaimer this will normally fall into residue. In the case of a residuary gift, the subject matter will pass under the intestacy rules (except in the case of a class gift or gift to joint tenants, when it will accrue to the other class members/joint tenants as appropriate). In both cases this is subject to contrary intention in the will.

A disclaimer of a gift under a will does not operate so as to prevent the person disclaiming receiving the property under the intestacy rules.

EXAMPLE 3

If residue is left by Tom, a widower, to his two children Ann and Ben in equal shares and Ann disclaims her share under the will, one-half of the residue will pass on Tom's intestacy. Ann's disclaimer of her entitlement under the will does not operate to prevent her taking under the intestacy, however, and if this is desired she will also have expressly to disclaim her entitlement on intestacy.

The disadvantage of a disclaimer is, then, that the original beneficiary has no control over the ultimate destination of the gift. If the intention is to benefit someone other than the person next entitled under the will or intestacy rules, a 'variation' (see **15.12.2**) will be more appropriate.

15.12.2 Variations

A variation is a direction by the original beneficiary to the personal representatives to transfer property that would otherwise be taken by the beneficiary to someone else. Normally a variation will be in writing, and commonly by deed.

Unlike a disclaimer:

(a) a variation is possible even though the original beneficiary has accepted a benefit;

(b) a partial variation of a gift is possible; and

(c) the original beneficiary can control the destination of the property following the variation. Those taking under the variation do not have to be other beneficiaries or members of the deceased's family.

15.12.3 Inheritance tax and capital gains tax consequences

Prima facie, a disclaimer or a variation will constitute a transfer of value (usually a PET) for inheritance tax purposes and a disposal for capital gains tax. However, under s 42 of the Inheritance Tax Act 1984 and s 62 of the Taxation of Chargeable Gains Act 1992, it is possible to effect a disclaimer or variation without either of these consequences.

The conditions to be met are:

(a) the disclaimer/variation must be:

   (i) in writing;
   (ii) made within two years of death;
   (iii) not made for any consideration (other than another disclaimer/variation) in money or money's worth;

(b) in the case of a variation only:

   (i) in the case of variations made on/after 1 August 2002, the instrument of variation should contain a statement of intent that s 142 and/or s 62 relief(s) are to apply. If the variation results in more inheritance tax being payable, a copy of the instrument must be sent to HMRC within 6 months, together with a statement of how much extra tax is payable;
   (ii) if the variation results in more inheritance tax being payable, the personal representatives must join in the election.

If all the relevant conditions are met, then:

(a) the disclaimer/variation is not itself a transfer of value and/or disposal; and
(b) the inheritance tax and/or capital gains tax position will be determined as if the deceased had made the disposition now effected.

15.13 Administering the estate: checkpoints

1. Protection of personal representatives:
   (a) against claims of unknown beneficiaries/creditors (**15.7.1**);
   (b) against claims of missing beneficiaries/creditors (**15.7.2**);
   (c) against future or contingent liabilities (**15.7.3.1**);
   (d) against liability for inheritance tax (**15.7.3.2**);
   (e) against claims of unknown, adopted/illegitimate beneficiaries (**15.7.1, 15.7.3.3**);
   (f) against liability for rent and other breaches of leasehold covenants (**15.7.3.3**); and
   (g) against claims under the Inheritance (Provision for Family and Dependants) Act 1975 (**13.25.2**).

2. Financial services issues:
   (a) for personal representatives (**15.8.1**);
   (b) for solicitors acting as, or advising, personal representatives (**15.8.2**).

3. Collecting/realising the assets:
   (a) registering the grant (**15.9.1**);
   (b) which assets to sell (**15.9.2**).

4. Payment of debts—solvent estate:
   (a) secured creditors (**15.10.1**);
   (b) unsecured debts—the statutory order and other property (**15.10.2**);

(c) marshalling (**15.10.3**); and

(d) contrary provision in will (**15.10.4**).

5. Payment of debts—insolvent estate:

(a) secured creditors (**15.11.1**);

(b) unsecured creditors (**15.11.2**); and

(c) protection of personal representatives (**15.11.3**).

6. Post-death changes:

(a) Inheritance (Provision for Family and Dependants) Act claims (**13.22** to **13.29**);

(b) disclaimers (**15.12.1**);

(c) variations (**15.12.2**); and

(d) inheritance tax and capital gains tax consequences (**15.12.3**). (*See also* **Figure 15.1** at page 309.)

15.14 Distributing the estate

In **15.6** onwards, we examined various practical issues surrounding the early and 'middle' stages of the administration of an estate once the grant has been issued—to the point where the various debts and liabilities were discharged. We also considered how personal representatives might protect themselves against claims for breach of their duty, and how changes might be effected to the deceased's dispositions otherwise taking effect on death.

In the remainder of this section, we will now consider the 'endgame'—the distribution of the estate to those entitled under the terms of the will or the operation of the intestacy rules and the procedures are set out at **Figure 15.2** on page 323.

Although we have arbitrarily divided up our consideration in this way, it is of course an artificial division; the process of winding up an estate is a continuum with no 'natural breaks' or (necessarily) clearly definable stages (except, perhaps, 'pre-grant' and 'post-grant').

We will first look at some practical issues concerning the payment of the various legacies in any will (**15.15**). We will then consider how the residue (to which the residuary beneficiaries are entitled) is ascertained (**15.16**). Next, we will discuss estate accounts (**15.17**), assents (**15.18**), and financial services issues (**15.19**). Lastly, we will briefly discuss beneficiaries' rights and remedies (**15.20**).

15.15 Payment of legacies

Once the personal representatives are satisfied that assets are not needed for administration purposes (ie to pay the debts etc), they can give effect to the various specific, general, and pecuniary gifts made by the will. An indication by them that a particular asset is not needed for the purposes of the administration is technically 'an assent' (see further **15.18**).

15.15.1 Specific legacies and devises

The property which has been specifically given by the will is vested in the beneficiaries entitled by the method appropriate to the assets concerned. Thus, for example, chattels

Figure 15.1 Estate administration—from grant to ascertainment of estate available for distribution.

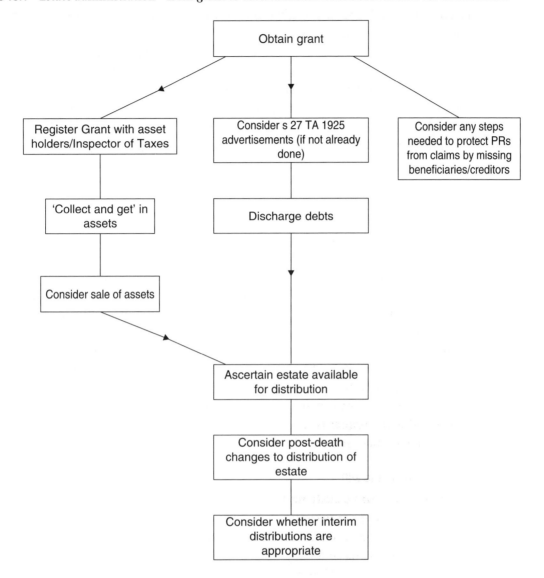

will be transferred by delivery, and company shares by the completion of the appropriate stock transfer form—which, with the share certificate(s), is lodged with the company's Registrar for registration of the change of ownership and the issue of a new share certificate. In the case of land, an assent in writing will be needed (see further **15.18.2**).

Unless the will otherwise provides, beneficiaries entitled to specific gifts will have to bear the costs of the transfer of the gifted property, and also the cost of its preservation and upkeep between the date of death and assent or actual transfer (*Re Rooke* [1933] Ch 970; *Re Pearce* [1909] 1 Ch 819).

However, specific beneficiaries are entitled to the income (if any) produced by the asset since the date of death. Thus, for example, on a specific gift of shares or land, the assent retrospectively passes to the beneficiary concerned any dividends or rent arising since the date of death.

15.15.2 Pecuniary legacies

In s 55(1)(ix) of the Administration of Estates Act 1925 the term 'pecuniary legacy' is defined so as to include general legacies, demonstrative legacies insofar as they cannot be paid from the designated fund, and any general direction for the payment of money (such as the inheritance tax on a specific gift which is to be free of tax). In this section we will use the term 'pecuniary legacy' as so defined.

The problem for the personal representatives in all these cases is essentially the same: from what part of the estate should they take the money to pay the beneficiary, or to purchase the subject matter of the general legacy, or to pay the inheritance tax? We have seen that there is a similar problem for the personal representatives in relation to the payment of the various debts and liabilities of the estate (see **15.10** and **15.11**).

Unfortunately, the general law regarding the incidence of pecuniary legacies is sometimes far from clear. The problems centre upon the extent to which the pre-1926 rules have been displaced by the provisions of s 33 of the Administration of Estates Act 1925—an issue still not entirely resolved more than 80 years on!

The rules can be briefly summarised as follows.

15.15.2.1 Provision in the will

The will may (and if you ever have to grapple with the complexities which can arise you will doubtless (rightly!) conclude *should*) contain express provision as to the property to be used to fund the payment of pecuniary legacies. In practice, the formulae usually adopted for dealing with the payment of debts (**15.10.4.2**) are simply adapted to include legacies as well. So, if residue is to be the chosen source, the trust or trust for sale of the residuary estate will direct the payment out of the proceeds of 'debts and legacies' before division. Alternatively, the residue may be given 'subject to' or 'after payment of' the 'debts and legacies'. Any of these provisions will make the residue as a whole (including any lapsed share) primarily liable. Where a specific fund is identified, it can similarly be made liable for the payment of the legacies in addition to the debts.

15.15.2.2 No provision in the will

In practice, you will usually find that the rules effectively identify the residuary estate as the fund from which pecuniary legacies should be paid. However, the situation is not quite as simple as this statement implies, and there can be especially difficult problems where there is a partial intestacy. In any case where the will does not provide for which part of the estate should bear the burden of pecuniary legacies you will need to consult appropriate practitioner works to make sure you get it right!

15.15.3 Abatement

If the property identified under the rules discussed in **15.15.2** is insufficient to meet the pecuniary legacies in full, they will abate proportionately.

15.15.4 Appropriation

If a beneficiary wishes to have a particular asset from the estate in total or partial satisfaction of a pecuniary legacy given by the will, the personal representatives will normally be able to accede to the request by exercising the power of appropriation in s 41 of the Administration of Estates Act 1925, or that conferred by the will (see **15.4.2**).

15.15.5 Receipts

The personal representatives are entitled to a discharge from the beneficiaries, which normally is obtained by getting them to sign a receipt.

Beneficiaries who are under 18 cannot (unless the will otherwise provides) give a good receipt, nor (although, as we have seen at **15.4.3**, there is an alternative view) can their parent, guardian, or spouse do so for them. In such cases, it will be necessary for the personal representatives to adopt one of the following solutions:

(a) hold the gifted property until the infant attains the age of 18 (in the case of a pecuniary legacy in the meantime investing in an authorised investment);

(b) use the power of appropriation (in s 41 of the Administration of Estates Act 1925 or the will), with the infant's parent, guardian, or (if none) the court giving any necessary consent (see **15.4.2**);

(c) use the power in s 42 of the Administration of Estates Act 1925 to appoint trustees to receive and hold the property for the infant until 18 (see **15.4.3**); and

(d) obtain their discharge by payment of the legacy into court under s 63 of the Trustee Act 1925.

15.16 Ascertainment of residue

Once the various legacies have been paid, the personal representatives can direct their attention to establishing the amount available for distribution to the residuary beneficiaries. In order to do this, they will have to finalise the tax position and deal with the expenses of the administration.

15.16.1 Income tax and capital gains tax

The personal representatives will need to have dealt with two matters here.

15.16.1.1 The deceased's tax affairs

The deceased's income tax and capital gains tax liability must be finalised—with any further tax payable being paid, or any repayment due being recovered. In either event, an inheritance tax corrective account may be required (see **15.16.2.3** below).

15.16.1.2 The administration period

The personal representatives must make tax returns for each of the tax years which the administration spans and discharge any assessments.

15.16.2 Inheritance tax

Various issues concerning this tax will also need to be resolved.

15.16.2.1 The deceased's liability

Where the deceased at the date of death had an outstanding liability to inheritance tax, this will need to be discharged—and if met by the estate is an allowable deduction in arriving at the taxable estate on the death.

15.16.2.2 Recovery of tax

The personal representatives may be liable to pay tax on property where the burden of the tax is in fact to be borne by the beneficiary to whom the property passes on the death. This may happen, for example, because the will expressly makes the beneficiary responsible for the tax attributable to the value of the gifted property. It may also happen where the property passes outside of the will (for example, where the deceased's interest as a beneficial joint tenant accrues by right of survivorship to the surviving joint tenant(s)—though this is not a problem, of course, where it accrues to a surviving spouse). How can the personal representatives ensure that they recover for the benefit of the residuary estate the tax ultimately to be borne by others?

Where a pecuniary legacy is given 'subject to tax' the problem is easily resolved: the personal representatives simply withhold the appropriate amount and pay the net legacy to the beneficiary.

That solution is clearly not appropriate where there has been a specific legacy of, for example, Blackacre or a diamond necklace. In such cases, the personal representatives should not vest the asset in the beneficiary concerned until the tax has been paid or satisfactory arrangements have been made for their reimbursement.

If the property has passed by survivorship, the personal representatives may have a ready solution if other assets are due to the beneficiary concerned under the will or the intestacy rules: before they part with any such assets, they should ensure that they are paid, eg by deducting the amount due. Where there are no other amounts due to the beneficiary concerned, they may ultimately have to sue to recover the amount due.

15.16.2.3 Corrective accounts

Any variations in the value or content of the estate will need to be reported to HMRC on a corrective account (or by letter if the adjustments are minor). Any further inheritance tax then due will have to be paid, or any repayment due claimed.

15.16.2.4 Certificates of discharge

When the inheritance tax position has been finalised, the personal representatives should seek a discharge from any further liability to inheritance tax on Form IHT 30. This requests the issue of a Certificate of Discharge of the property in the estate and all persons liable from any further claims to inheritance tax. When given, the Certificate is an effective discharge except in the case of fraud, failure to disclose material facts, the subsequent discovery of further assets, or changes in the 'tax bill' arising as a result of any variations etc. discussed at **15.12**.

If the personal representatives have paid all the tax other than that attributable to instalment option property, a limited form of Certificate may be issued, expressed to be a complete discharge except for the outstanding tax on the instalment option property. In such cases, the personal representatives will need to ensure that there are appropriate arrangements to protect them against claims for future instalments. No Certificate of Discharge is necessary (nor should it be sought) where the estate is an 'excepted estate' (see **14.27**). In such cases, there is, as we saw, normally an automatic discharge 35 days after the issue of the grant, unless the HMRC calls for an account or it is subsequently discovered that the estate is not, after all, an excepted estate.

15.16.3 Administration expenses

The expenses of the administration, ie (in addition to reasonable funeral expenses) the properly incurred expenses of the personal representatives themselves in the carrying out of their duties, will have to be ascertained and met.

15.16.3.1 Reasonable funeral expenses

The estate is only liable for 'reasonable funeral expenses'; any excess will be the personal responsibility of the person incurring those expenses. What is reasonable is a question of fact; matters to be taken into account would include the deceased's position in life, religious beliefs and expressed wishes as to funeral arrangements.

15.16.3.2 Legal costs

The personal representatives are, as we have seen, at liberty to instruct solicitors to act for them in the administration of the estate. The costs (including disbursements) of such solicitors are part of the expenses of the administration.

Solicitors' charges in non-contentious probate matters are governed by the Solicitors' (Non-Contentious Business) Remuneration Order 1994. Under the Order, a solicitor is entitled to charge and be paid 'such sum as may be fair and reasonable' having regard to all the circumstances of the case, and in particular to:

(a) the complexity of the matter or the difficulty or novelty of questions raised;

(b) the skill, labour, specialised knowledge, and responsibility involved on the part of the solicitor;

(c) the number and importance of the documents prepared or perused, without regard to length;

(d) the place where and circumstances in which the business or any part of it is transacted;

(e) the time expended by the solicitor;

(f) the nature and value of the property involved; and

(g) the importance of the matter to the client.

In *Jemma Trust Company Ltd v Liptrott* [2004] 1 WLR 646 the Court of Appeal considered whether it was now anachronistic and wrong for solicitors to charge a 'value element', depending on the size of the estate, in addition to an hourly rate. It was held that it was still open to solicitors to make a separate charge based on value, or a value addition to the hourly rate, provided the charges overall were fair, reasonable, and transparent.

15.16.3.3 Fees of other professionals

Where, for example, stockbrokers or surveyors are employed to assist with valuations of the deceased's assets their fees are also part of the expenses of the administration. Where such professionals have been instructed by the solicitors acting for the personal representatives, the solicitors will—as a matter of professional conduct—incur liability to meet their proper fees, which will then feature as disbursements in the solicitors' bill of costs.

15.16.4 Remuneration

Personal representatives, like trustees, are not entitled to remuneration for their services unless in some way this is authorised.

15.16.4.1 Legacy to proving executors

There is a presumption that any specific or general legacy (but not a gift of residue) given to someone appointed as executor is intended to be conditional upon that person accepting the office (*Re Appleton* (1885) 29 ChD 893). The presumption is rebuttable (eg by the testator indicating some other motive for the legacy, such as 'in recognition of a lifetime's friendship', or making it clear that the legacy should be payable whether or not the beneficiary proves the will).

15.16.4.2 Charging clause in the will

In practice, this will be the usual means by which authority to charge for their services will be conferred upon the personal representatives. Such clauses are routinely included where professionals (such as solicitors and accountants) or institutions (such as banks) are appointed.

Section 28 of the Trustee Act 2000 introduces new rules for the interpretation of charging clauses in favour of trust corporations or personal representatives acting in a professional capacity:

(a) The services for which charge may be made include those that could be provided by a lay trustee and are not confined to strictly professional services (as in the past).

(b) In the case of deaths on or after 1 February 2001, an express charging clause is not treated as a gift for the purposes of the Wills Act 1837, s 15 (see **13.7.5**).

Further, s 29 creates an 'implied' professional charging clause in certain circumstances. Trust corporations are generally entitled to receive 'reasonable remuneration' for services provided on behalf of a trust even if they could have been provided by lay trustees. Other professional trustees (but not a sole trustee) may be entitled to such remuneration provided each of the other trustees has agreed in writing.

It seems likely that draftsmen will continue to include express charging clauses both to cover sole professional trustees and to remove the need for agreement to payment by the other trustees where the professional is one of several trustees.

15.16.4.3 Agreement with beneficiaries

Remuneration can be paid to the personal representatives as a result of an agreement with the beneficiaries (being *sui juris*) out of assets to which they are entitled. There must, of course, be no hint of undue influence.

15.16.4.4 The court

The court, as part of its inherent jurisdiction, has power to authorise remuneration for the personal representatives, whether for past, present, or future services. There are also various statutory provisions which enable the court to authorise a personal representative to charge eg s 42 of the Trustee Act 1925 (trustees to hold minor's legacy) and s 50 of the Administration of Justice Act 1985 (substituted personal representative).

15.16.4.5 Rule in Cradock v Piper (1850) 1 Mac & G 664

This rule applies where a solicitor (being one of two or more personal representatives) acts in connection with litigation on behalf of all the personal representatives. Such a solicitor (or his/her firm) may charge for such work provided the bill is not 'inflated' by virtue of the solicitor being one of the parties.

15.16.4.6 Foreign remuneration

Where the law of a foreign jurisdiction entitles the personal representatives to remuneration, they will it seems be entitled to receive it (*Re Northcote's Will Trust* [1949] 1 All ER 442).

15.17 Estate accounts

If beneficiaries are left, for example, 'Blackacre' or '£1,000' by the will, they are clearly able to identify their entitlement. Unlike pecuniary or specific beneficiaries, the residuary beneficiaries have no ready means of knowing what they are entitled to receive. The estate accounts are, in effect, the means whereby the personal representatives identify the property available for distribution to the residuary beneficiaries, and they will also show how that entitlement is to be met.

15.17.1 Form

There are no particular rules, save that the accounts should be clear and easy to follow.

15.17.1.1 The accounts

Three accounts will, in practice, be needed: an income account (**15.17.2**), a capital account (**15.17.3**) and a distribution account (**15.17.4**). In the case of small estates, the income and capital accounts will often be combined; indeed, sometimes all three are combined in a single account. This is perfectly acceptable as long as the end result is clear and easy to follow.

15.17.1.2 Apportionments

Separate income and capital accounts will certainly be needed where there is (under the will or the intestacy rules) a life interest in the residue. Unless excluded by the terms of the will, the Apportionment Act 1870 (**15.3.3**) will require the apportionment of income received after death which relates partly to a period before and partly to a period after the death: the former will be shown in the capital account and the latter in the income account. The equitable apportionment rules (unless excluded) will also affect the entries to be made in the income and capital accounts.

15.17.1.3 Commentary

The accounts are in practice often accompanied by a commentary to explain the various entries, so as to assist the beneficiaries to understand how their entitlement has been arrived at. Thus, for example, the commentary will:

(a) identify the gross and net values of the estate;

(b) indicate its disposition (whether under the terms of the will or under the intestacy rules); and

(c) deal with any other relevant matters, such as interim distributions and distributions *in specie* (eg as a result of the personal representatives exercising a power of appropriation).

15.17.2 Income account

This should essentially do three things:

(a) give details of income receipts, itemising receipts from different sources (eg building society interest, bank interest, dividends, rent, etc);

(b) itemise details of expenditure from income (eg income tax, interest paid on legacies, and legal costs properly attributable to income such as the cost of preparing income tax returns); and

(c) show the net amount available for distribution.

15.17.3 Capital account

This will in practice need to do four things:

(a) itemise all the assets of the estate at their probate values. It may be more convenient to give the details required in a schedule or schedules to the account, simply bringing in the total(s);

(b) show realisations by the personal representatives during the course of the administration. The proceeds of sale may well differ from the probate valuation of the asset(s) concerned and any such variations have to be taken on board when accounting to the residuary beneficiaries;

(c) give details of all the liabilities discharged, pecuniary and specific legacies and expenses paid, including inheritance tax, capital gains tax, and income tax; and legal costs properly attributable to capital; and

(d) show the balance available for distribution.

15.17.4 Distribution account

This should show how the beneficiary's entitlement (whether this be to income or capital) is to be met. It should show details of any interim distribution(s) and indicate how the balance is to be paid (perhaps partly *in specie* and partly in cash).

15.17.5 Discharge

The estate accounts are the personal representatives' accounts and where you or your firm are not yourselves the personal representatives they should, therefore, first be presented to them for their approval. The personal representatives' acceptance of the accounts is usually signified by an endorsement to that effect signed by them.

The approved accounts are then presented (usually in duplicate) to the residuary beneficiaries, from whom the personal representatives are entitled to a discharge. Again, this is achieved by requesting the beneficiaries to return one of the copies of the accounts sent to them with an appropriate endorsement, such as 'I . . . agree to accept the amount due to me as shown by the within written accounts', duly signed. The endorsement will usually also contain a formal discharge of the personal representatives and an agreement to indemnify them against all claims and demands.

If a beneficiary refuses to approve the accounts, there are in practice ultimately only two possible solutions:

(a) an administration action for the examination of the accounts by the court may be commenced; and

(b) the personal representatives may pay the beneficiary's share into court under s 63 of the Trustee Act 1925.

It may not be possible for acceptance to be signified because the beneficiary is a minor or suffering from some other disability (eg mental incapacity).

In the case of a minor beneficiary, the solution may be the appointment of trustees under s 42 of the Trustee Act 1925 (**15.4.3**). If this section cannot be used (because the beneficiary's interest is contingent only) the personal representatives will in practice have to continue to hold the assets concerned until the beneficiary concerned attains the age of 18.

If the beneficiary is suffering from mental disability, the personal representatives should inform any receiver appointed by the Court of Protection to manage the beneficiary's affairs of the entitlement, and then proceed in accordance with the court's directions. If no receiver has been appointed, ideally application should be made for this to be done (usually by a close relative of the person concerned). If not, the personal representatives may be forced to consider payment into court to obtain their discharge.

If approval cannot be obtained because a beneficiary is missing, we saw (in **15.7.2**) that the personal representatives should (at an earlier stage of the administration) have taken steps to overcome this difficulty. In practice, this will have probably involved either obtaining a 'Benjamin Order' or some insurance cover, so that the full amount of the residue can be distributed to the other beneficiaries.

15.17.6 Transfer of assets

Once the personal representatives have obtained their discharge, they can arrange for the transfer of the assets to the residuary beneficiaries. As we saw in **15.15** above, the method of doing this will depend upon the nature of the assets concerned (see also **15.18**).

15.18 Assents

An assent occurs when the personal representatives acknowledge that they do not require an asset for the purposes of the administration (see **15.15**). Prior to this, the beneficiaries do not generally have any legal or equitable proprietary interest in the asset, but merely the right to have the deceased's estate duly administered (see further **15.20**).

15.18.1 Pure personalty

At common law, an assent may be in writing, made orally, or implied from conduct. Although the equitable title passes by virtue of such assent, if there are particular formalities needed to transfer the legal title, these must also be complied with—the personal representatives holding in the meantime as trustees for the beneficiary concerned.

15.18.2 Land

Here, the position is governed by s 36 of the Administration of Estates Act 1925. All assents relating to unregistered land are now subject to compulsory first registration under the terms of the Land Registration Act 2002 under which the duty to register (within two months of the disposition) lies with the transferee. However, if the application for registration is not made within this period, the disposition is void and the title will revert to the personal representatives who will (pending re-execution of the assent) hold it on trust for the transferee. In practice, therefore, the personal representatives should ensure that first registration takes place with the cost being a testamentary expense.

15.18.2.1 The power to assent

By s 36, Administration of Estates Act 1925 personal representatives are enabled to vest any interest in freehold or leasehold land in any person entitled to it—whether beneficially, as trustee, as personal representative of a beneficiary who has died before the assent can be made, or otherwise (such as a purchaser under a contract made by the deceased: *GHR Co Ltd v IRC* [1943] KB 303). An assent should not, in practice, be used where the personal representative is selling, or is asked to give effect to a contract for sale entered into by a beneficiary.

15.18.2.2 Form

By s 36(4), an assent must be in writing, signed by the personal representative(s) and naming the person(s) in whose favour it is given. Although technically a form of conveyance, an assent does not bear *ad valorem* stamp duty (except where being used to give effect to a contract).

Sometimes, a deed will in practice be needed, eg because indemnity covenants are required from the beneficiary.

It has been held that an assent complying with the requirements of s 36(4) is needed even where the personal representative is the person in whose favour the assent is being made, whether as beneficiary, trustee, or as personal representative of a deceased beneficiary: *Re King's Will Trusts* [1964] Ch 542.

15.18.2.3 Effect

By s 36(2), unless there is evidence of a contrary intention, an assent relates back to the date of the deceased's death. Thus, the beneficiary will now be entitled to rents or profits produced by the land since the date of the deceased's death.

15.18.2.4 Protection of beneficiaries

Anyone in whose favour an assent is made is entitled to require (at the expense of the estate) a memorandum of the assent to be endorsed upon the (original) grant of representation—and to call for the production of the grant to prove that this has been done (s 36(5)).

15.18.2.5 Protection of purchasers

There are two provisions affording protection to purchasers from personal representatives:

(a) Section 36(6): If a purchaser takes in good faith a conveyance from personal representatives containing a statement that the personal representatives have not previously made any assent or conveyance relating to the legal estate, the purchaser will take priority over any beneficiary in whose favour a prior assent or conveyance had been made unless notice of the earlier transaction had been endorsed upon the (original) grant. It is essential, therefore, that the purchaser ensures that the conveyance contains such a statement and that the grant is inspected to check for previous memoranda. Further, an endorsement on the grant relating to the conveyance to the purchaser should also be insisted upon.

(b) Section 36(7): The protection here is, again, afforded to the purchaser in the absence of any memorandum relating to a previous assent or conveyance endorsed on the grant. Subject to this, an assent or conveyance by a personal representative is sufficient evidence that the person in whose favour it is given or made is the person entitled to the legal estate. Thus the purchaser is not concerned, for example, to see the terms of the will to check that the recipient of the property was indeed entitled to it. However, the section does not provide that the assent or conveyance is 'conclusive' evidence, so that a purchaser in possession of information which indicates that the assent or conveyance was given or made to the wrong person will not be protected: *Re Duce and Boots Cash Chemists (Southern) Ltd's Contract* [1937] Ch 642.

15.18.2.6 Protection of personal representatives

By s 36(10), personal representatives may—as a condition of giving an assent or conveyance—require security for the discharge of any debts or liabilities to which the property is subject (such as a mortgage or liability to instalments of inheritance tax). However, personal representatives cannot refuse to give an assent once 'reasonable arrangements' have been made.

15.19 Financial services

We have seen (in **15.8**) that, in the context of probate and administration most investment business will in practice be non-mainstream investment business. However, where solicitors advise beneficiaries as to, for example, the investment of their inheritance, such advice will be prima facie mainstream business. Avoiding this consequence will normally involve taking the advice of, and making arrangements through, an authorised person.

15.20 Beneficiaries' rights and remedies

The beneficiaries will want to know that the estate is being efficiently administered by the personal representatives, and will be concerned to receive their entitlements under the will or intestacy as quickly as possible. In this section we will consider the nature of the beneficiaries' rights, and how they may be enforced.

15.20.1 The beneficiaries' right to compel due administration

The deceased's assets vest in the personal representatives 'in full ownership without distinction between legal and equitable interests' (*Commissioner of Stamp Duties (Queensland) v Livingston* [1965] AC 694).

Thus, until the administration is complete the beneficiary (whether under the will or intestacy rules) has neither a legal or equitable interest in the deceased's assets. It is only at this point that the personal representatives will know which of the deceased's assets have had to be sold to pay debts and administration expenses, and which are available for distribution to beneficiaries.

The beneficiary does, however, have a chose in action, the right to have the deceased's estate properly administered.

15.20.2 Date for payment of entitlement under will or intestacy

We have seen that personal representatives cannot be compelled to distribute the estate before the end of the executor's year (**15.3.1.3**). Beneficiaries will want to know whether they are entitled to income or interest between the date of death and the date of distribution. Whether the beneficiary is entitled to income from, or interest on, the value of the asset(s) during this period will depend on the provisions of any will, on the nature of the asset (ie whether or not it is income producing) and on the nature of the gift.

15.20.2.1 Specific gifts

Where the entitlement of the beneficiary is immediate, such gifts carry the right to any income accruing between the date of death and the vesting of the property in the beneficiary. The assent by the personal representatives vesting the property in the beneficiary (see **15.18**) operates retrospectively to give the beneficiary the right to such income. If the beneficiary has a contingent or future (deferred) entitlement, again such gifts carry the intermediate income which will be added to capital (and devolve with it) for so long as the rules against indefinite accumulation permit (thereafter, the income either falls into residue or passes under the intestacy rules).

15.20.2.2 Residuary gifts

Whether the beneficiary's entitlement is immediate or contingent, and whether of personalty or realty, such gifts carry the intermediate income. Where the beneficiary has a future (deferred) interest, devises (ie gifts of realty) probably carry the intermediate income: bequests (ie gifts of personalty) do not carry such right and the income passes under the intestacy rules.

15.20.2.3 Contingent pecuniary legacies

Where the will contains such a legacy, so that the sum involved has to be invested pending the fulfilment of the contingency, the gift does not normally carry the intermediate income; the income from the investment therefore belongs to the residuary beneficiaries. There are exceptions to this rule where the gift is to the child or person to whom the testator stands *in loco parentis*, and the contingency is attaining an age not greater than 18 (or earlier marriage); or where the gift is to any child made with the intention of providing for that child's maintenance.

All the rules stated above apply in the absence of provision to the contrary in the will.

15.20.2.4 Pecuniary legacies

As a general rule, a pecuniary legatee, general legatee, or demonstrative legatee (if the designated fund is exhausted) is entitled to interest at 6 per cent only from the date upon which such legacy is payable. In the absence of any direction to the contrary in the will, such a legacy is payable at the end of the executor's year. Any interest payable is regarded as an administration expense, payable therefore normally from residue.

Exceptionally, however, interest on such legacies is payable from the date of death (unless the will otherwise provides). For example:

(a) if the legacy is in satisfaction of a debt;

(b) if the legacy is charged on realty;

(c) if the legacy is to testator's infant child or to an infant to whom he stands *in loco parentis;* or

(d) if the legacy is to any infant with the intention to provide for that child's maintenance.

15.20.3 Remedies available to beneficiaries

Where difficulties arise during the administration of an estate, there are a number of formal remedies available to a beneficiary. Essentially, they fall into two categories:

(a) 'Administration proceedings', designed to ensure that the administration of the estate is properly conducted. Such actions may be general, or for specific relief, and need not necessarily be 'contentious', in that the personal representatives are equally entitled to seek the court's assistance in this way.

(b) Actions to 'recover loss' suffered.

The latter include the following.

15.20.3.1 Personal action against the personal representatives

Instead of commencing administration proceedings a personal action may be brought against the personal representatives. A failure by a personal representative to carry out the duties of the office is a *devastavit*, for which the personal representative is personally liable to the beneficiaries or creditors, unless they have acquiesced in or encouraged the breach. Personal representatives may, however, be relieved from liability:

(a) by provisions in the will relieving personal representatives from liability, eg where mistakes are made in good faith;

(b) by s 61 of the Trustee Act 1925 the court may wholly or partly relieve the personal representative from personal liability where it is satisfied that the personal representative acted 'honestly, reasonably and ought fairly to be excused'; or

(c) by agreement with the beneficiaries, being *sui juris* and fully aware of the breach, the personal representatives may be released from liability.

15.20.3 Tracing

A beneficiary (whether under a will or the intestacy rules) or a creditor may have the right to trace and recover property of the estate (or property representing such property) from the personal representatives or any other recipient of it, other than a bona fide purchaser for value or person deriving title from such purchaser. The right to trace is also lost if the property has been dissipated, or where to allow tracing would be inequitable. This remedy may be sought whether or not a personal action has been brought against the personal representative, though in so far as such action has been 'successful' the right to trace is clearly not also going to be available.

15.20.3.3 Personal action against recipients of estate assets

Where all other remedies of a beneficiary (whether under the will or intestacy rules) or creditor have been exhausted, a personal action may be brought against a person who has wrongly received the assets of the estate (*Ministry of Health v Simpson* [1951] AC 251).

15.21 Distributing the assets: checkpoints

1. Payment of legacies:
    (a) Specific legacies/devises (**15.15.1**).
    (b) Burden of pecuniary legacies (**15.15.2**):
        (i) provision in the will (**15.15.2.1**);
        (ii) no provision in the will (**15.15.2.2**).
    (c) Abatement (**15.15.3**).
    (d) Appropriation (**15.15.4**).
    (e) Receipts (**15.15.5**).
2. Ascertainment of residue:
    (a) Finalising the tax position:
        (i) income tax and capital gains tax (**15.16.1**);
        (ii) inheritance tax (**15.16.2**):
            (1) corrective accounts (**15.16.2.3**); and
            (2) certificates of discharge (**15.16.2.4**).

(b) Administration expenses:
   (i) funeral expenses (**15.16.3.1**);
   (ii) legal costs (**15.16.3.2**); and
   (iii) other professionals' fees (**15.16.3.3**).
(c) Remuneration of personal representatives:
   (i) legacy to proving executors (**15.16.4.1**);
   (ii) charging clause in will (**15.16.4.2**); and
   (iii) other possibilities (**15.16.4.3** to **15.16.4.6**).

3. Estate accounts:
   (a) Income account (**15.17.2**).
   (b) Capital account (**15.17.3**).
   (c) Distribution account (**15.17.4**).
   (d) Discharge of personal representatives (**15.17.5**).

4. Assents:
   (a) Pure personalty (**15.18.1**).
   (b) Land (**15.18.2**).

5. Beneficiaries' rights and remedies:
   (a) Right to compel due administration (**15.20.1**).
   (b) Date for payment of entitlement under will/intestacy (**15.20.2**).
   (c) Remedies:
      (i) personal action against the personal representatives (**15.20.3.1**);
      (ii) tracing (**15.20.3.2**); and
      (iii) personal action against recipients of estate assets (**15.20.3.3**).

See also **Figure 15.2** below.

Figure 15.2 Estate administration—the final stage.

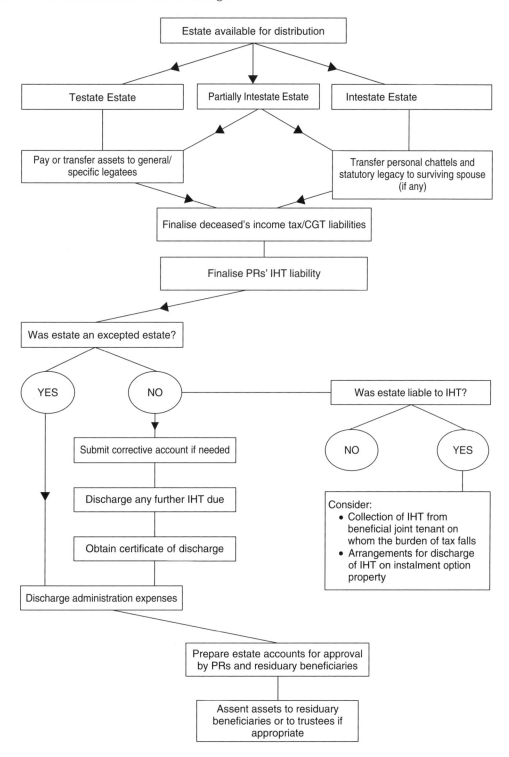

 Visit the Online Resource Centre for more information and useful weblinks.
www.oxfordtextbooks.co.uk/orc/foundations11_12/

EU law

16

EU law

THE EUROPEAN UNION, ITS INSTITUTIONS AND SOURCES OF LAW

16.1 Introduction

It is imperative that all lawyers today have an understanding of the law within the European Union (EU) as it impacts on many areas of current law, and failure to advise on EU law could open solicitors to negligence claims and disciplinary actions.

This section deals with the institutions of the EU and looks at the sources of EU law.

16.2 The institutions

The EU is made up of the following institutions:

(a) the European Commission (**16.2.1**);

(b) the Council of Ministers (**16.2.2**);

(c) the European Council (**16.2.3**);

(d) the European Parliament (**16.2.4**);

(e) the European Court of Justice, the General Court (formerly known as 'the Court of the First Instance') and specialised courts (**16.2.5**);

(f) the European Court of Auditors (**16.2.6**);

(g) the European Investment Bank (**16.2.7**);

(h) the Economic and Social Committee (**16.2.8**);

(i) the Committee of the Regions (**16.2.9**);

(j) the European Ombudsman (**16.2.10**); and

(k) the European System of Central Banks and the European Central Bank (**16.2.11**).

The Council of Ministers and the Commission provide the main day-to-day impetus in the EU's decision-making process. The Commission makes policy proposals after consulting a wide range of experts or interested parties; the Council of Ministers takes the final decision after consulting the European Parliament and the Economic and Social Committee and after discussions in the Committee of Permanent Representatives (COREPER).

16.2.1 The European Commission

The Commission is made up of one member from each Member State who is appointed jointly by the member governments for a five-year renewable term. One of the 27 Commissioners is also the High Representative of the EU for Foreign Affairs and Security Policy. The Commission is headed by a President proposed by the European Council and appointed by the European Parliament for a two-year renewable term. Once appointed, the Commissioners become independent of their national government and are required to act in the interests of the Union as a whole. Each Commissioner is responsible for a particular area of EU policy, eg the environment or competition law.

The Commission has four main functions as set out in Article 17 of the Treaty of the European Union ('TEU'):

(a) legislative and quasi-legislative powers;

(b) to activate EU policies (as proposed by third parties such as national governments, industry and non-governmental organisations);

(c) collecting revenue for the EU and committing EU expenditure; and

(d) supervisory powers—to ensure Member States and others adhere to EU law by referring matters to the European courts.

Decisions within the Commission are taken on a simple majority vote and the Commission is collectively answerable to the European Parliament.

16.2.2 The Council of Ministers

The Council of Ministers, or the 'Council of the European Union' as it is sometimes called, is the decision-making body of the EU and has a wide remit. One of its most important purposes is legislative—it decides whether or not to adopt legislation proposed by the Commission. It is organised into ten subject matters; each Council consists of one representative from each Member State appointed by its government who can commit the Member State on the matter in question. The various Councils of Ministers (determined by subject area) meet typically every one to two months. Each Council's composition depends on the matter under discussion—for example education ministers will consider education matters. The Presidency of the Council is held for a term of six months by each Member State in an order determined by case law. Voting can be by simple majority, qualified majority, or unanimity depending on the matter to be agreed: simple majority for a few non-contentious or procedural matters; unanimity (which allows any Member State to veto a decision) for certain politically sensitive decisions; and qualified majority voting for all other matters. The latter permits different Member States different weighted voting rights determined by their population. The TEU changed the way qualified majority voting rights are calculated. This has proved contentious and therefore transitional arrangements have been agreed to 1 November 2014.

16.2.3 The European Council

The European Council is made up of the Heads of States of the Member States, the President of the European Council and the President of the Commission. It meets at least four times a year and, although originally referred to in the Single European Act 1986, it was only formally recognised as a separate institution by the Treaty of Lisbon 2007. Its role includes:

(a) to make decisions about the EU constitution and propose reforms to the EC treaties;

(b) to appoint various important EU officers eg its President, the President of the Commission, the Commissioners and the High Representative;

(c) to set out informal agendas—proposing legislative matters it wants the Commission to consider;

(d) resolving issues which cannot be agreed by the Council of Ministers; and

(e) setting the EU's Common Foreign and Security Policy.

The office of the President of the European Council was introduced by the Treaty of Lisbon. The President sits as an additional member of the European Council and is appointed by qualified majority voting rights by the members of the European Council for a 30-month term renewable once.

16.2.4 The European Parliament (sometimes called the 'European Assembly')

This is the only EU institution that meets and debates in public. Its members are directly elected by the citizens of each Member State. Each Member of the European Parliament (MEP) serves for a five-year term. Members sit in political groups of which there are currently seven, not in national delegations. The number of MEPs that each Member State has depends on its size and changes have been made to the way this is calculated as a result of the Lisbon Treaty. Each MEP is required to vote on individual and personal bases. The European Parliament is now attempting to create pan-European political parties, and almost all members have joined at least a federation of national political parties.

The main task of the Parliament is to monitor the work of the Council of Ministers and the Commission. This is done by following one of two procedures depending on the matter in question: by consultation where the Parliament must be consulted on the Commission's proposals before the Council of Ministers gives its final approval; or where the Parliament can veto certain proposals. The Parliament has three other powers:

(a) appointment and dismissal of the Commission—it must approve the Commissioners proposed by the President of the Commission; it can dismiss all the Commission by a two-thirds majority (although it has never done so); and it can require the President of the Commission to sack a Commissioner if it has no confidence in that particular Commissioner;

(b) it is responsible for drawing up the preliminary draft budget which the European Council must then adopt. If the European Council subsequently adopts detailed budgets which the Parliament disapproves of the Parliament can veto those detailed budgets; and

(c) it has the right to bring actions against EU institutions before the European Court of Justice (ECJ).

The Parliament can also ask the Commission to act or can propose amendments to the Commission's proposals.

16.2.5 The European Court of Justice, the General Court (formally called 'the Court of First Instance') and Specialised Courts

The European Court of Justice was the first court established under the various EC treaties. There is one independent judge for each Member State assisted by eight Advocates-General and a President of the court. They are all appointed jointly by Member States for six-year renewable terms. The President is elected from among the judges for a three-year term. The function of an Advocate-General is to assist the judges in reaching their decision. He will present his submissions being a detailed analysis of the relevant issues of law and fact together with his recommendations. The court is not bound to follow these but they are useful for understanding the reasoning behind the court's decision. The court deals with disputes between Member States, Member States and EU institutions, EU institutions and firms, individuals or EU officials. It can hear appeals from Member States, the Commission, the Council, or from an individual, on all of whom its rulings are binding. At the request of national courts, it can give preliminary rulings on the interpretation of EU law. It has general jurisdiction with three exceptions/limitations covering the Common Foreign and Security Policy, criminal matters and in relation to the expulsion of a Member State.

The Single European Act provided for the setting up of a new court originally called the Court of First Instance (CFI) in 1989. This is now called the General Court. It consists of one judge from each Member State and one of them sits as Advocate General. Its jurisdiction was originally limited but it is now the main administrative court. There is a right of appeal on matters of law to the ECJ. Specialised courts can also be set up to hear disputes in specific areas. At the moment there is only one.

16.2.6 The European Court of Auditors

This was set up in 1977 to examine the revenue, expenditure and accounts of the EU and also to establish links with national audit bodies. Situated in Strasbourg, it comprises one member for each Member State, appointed by the Council, for six years. The court produces reports showing the management of the Union's finances which are a source of pressure on the institutions and others with administrative responsibility to manage them soundly.

16.2.7 The European Investment Bank

This is the Union's financing institution. It provides loans for capital investment promoting the Union's balanced economic development and integration.

16.2.8 The Economic and Social Committee

The Committee advises the Commission, the Council and the European Parliament. Its members are divided into the three groups of workers, employers, and various interests which represent the different categories of economic and social activity in the Union. It draws up opinions on draft EU legislation and the main issues affecting society.

16.2.9 The Committee of the Regions

This is the Union's youngest institution. There is now a legal obligation to consult this committee of representatives of local and regional authorities on a variety of matters that concern it directly. Historically its influence has been limited but it has now been given increased powers following the Treaty of Lisbon.

16.2.10 The European Ombudsman

As each citizen of each Member State is both a national and a European citizen, each has the right to apply to the European Ombudsman if he is a victim of an act of 'maladministration' by the EU institutions or bodies. The Ombudsman has wide-ranging powers of enquiries; for example, the EU institutions and bodies are required under certain conditions

Figure 16.1 Institutions of the European Union.

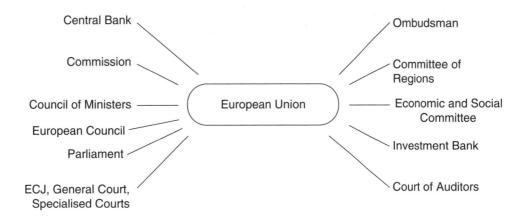

to provide all evidence he may request. The Ombudsman may also make recommendations to EU institutions and he can refer the case to the European Parliament for it to draw political conclusions from it if appropriate.

16.2.11 The European System of Central Banks and the European Central Bank

The European System of Central Banks ('ESCB') was set up to make monetary unification and creation of a single European currency possible. The ESCB is made up of the European Central Bank ('ECB') (originally called 'the European Monetary Institute') and the national central banks of each Member State. The ECB has certain powers reserved to it. For example it is responsible for the issue of euros and setting the interest rate for the euro. The UK has opted out of monetary unification and has so far chosen not to join the euro.

16.3 The sources of EU law

The sources of EU law are set out below.

16.3.1 The Treaties

Technically all the various treaties entered into since what was then called the European Economic Community came into being following the signing of the Treaty of Rome in 1957 are all sources of EU law. However, the main treaties which set out EU law are the two consolidated, revised and updated treaties introduced following the Treaty of Lisbon ie:

(a) the Treaty of the European Union; and

(b) the Treaty on the Functioning of the European Union ('TFEU').

16.3.2 EU secondary legislation

EU secondary legislation consists of:

(a) regulations;

(b) directives;

(c) decisions;

(d) recommendations; and

(e) opinions.

The legislative powers of the EU are laid down in Article 288 TFEU. This lists the five kinds of acts (secondary legislation) set out in the list above and also contains a short statement of the characteristics of each kind of act.

A regulation shall have general application. It is binding in its entirety and directly applicable in all Member States, ie a Member State does not need to pass any legislation implementing the contents of the regulation. In fact, national implementing measures are deemed improper unless the regulation requires Member States to take action to implement it.

A directive shall be binding as to the result to be achieved, upon each Member State to which it is addressed, but shall leave to the national authorities the choice of form and methods, ie a directive lays down an objective and allows each national government to achieve it by the means that they regard as most suitable. Directives require implementation by Member States before being fully effective in law.

A decision shall be binding in its entirety upon those to whom it is addressed, ie it does not require implementing legislation and is binding on Member States and individuals.

A recommendation and an opinion are not binding at all although they have been seen to have been of persuasive authority in certain cases.

Figure 16.2 Sources of EU Law.

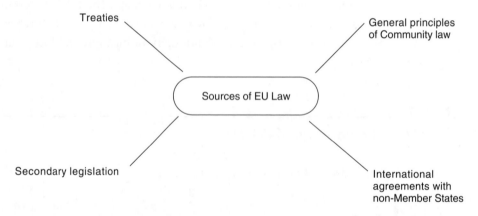

16.3.3 International agreements with non-Member States

International agreements with non-Member States are also a source of EU law to the extent they fall within the competences covered by the EU treaties (Article 216 TFEU). For example the EU is bound by the General Agreement on Trade and Tariffs (GATT) which was concluded before the establishment of the EU and all Member States are party to it.

16.3.4 General principles of EU law which encompass the entire jurisprudence of the European Courts

General principles of EU law are an important source of law. They are derived from a number of sources but the most important are the treaties and the legal systems of the Member States.

Other sources of law (such as resolutions and guidelines) from the Commission and other EU institutions are also very influential. Whilst not technically binding they are usually followed by the European Courts. These miscellaneous non-binding sources are often referred to as 'soft law'.

16.4 The European Union, its institutions and sources of law: checkpoints

In this section we have looked at:

- the institutions that comprise the European Union; and
- the sources of EU law.

You should now have an overview to the EU institutions, their functions and the sources of EU law.

THE RELATIONSHIP BETWEEN EU AND NATIONAL LAW

16.5 Introduction

All Member States have their own national law and are now subject to the law of Europe so it is necessary to understand how they work together. This section deals with the relationship between EU law and national law. It encompasses:

- the concept of direct effect; and
- supremacy.

16.6 The concept of direct effect

16.6.1 Meaning

The EU treaties were originally incorporated into UK law by the European Communities Act 1972 ('ECA') whereby EU law became directly applicable, ie part of our internal system. But the wording 'directly applicable' has created a problem because this phrase also covers provisions of EU law capable of application by national courts at the suit of individuals. The definition of a regulation provides that it is . . . 'directly applicable and can be relied on by an individual litigant . . . '. Therefore, we use the term 'directly effective' where a provision grants rights to individuals which must be upheld by the national courts.

Whether a particular provision will have direct effect is a matter of construction and each Member State will apply criteria such as clarity of language and the extent to which the provision has been incorporated into national law. Unfortunately, Member States are not always consistent. It is important to know whether a provision is directly effective because if it is, domestic courts must apply it, and in priority, over any conflicting provisions of national law.

Section 2(1) of the ECA provides that:

> All such rights, powers, liabilities, obligations and restrictions from time to time created or arising by or under the Treaties, and all such remedies and procedures from time to time provided for by or under the Treaties, as in accordance with the Treaties are without further enactment to be given legal effect or used in the United Kingdom shall be recognised and available in law, and be enforced, allowed and followed accordingly; and the expression 'enforceable EU right' and similar expressions shall be read as referring to one to which this subsection applies.

16.6.2 Treaty Articles

The doctrine of 'direct effect' was first developed in the case of *Van Gend en Loos v Nederlandse Administratie der Belastinge* (26/62) [1963] ECR 1 when a Dutch firm sought to invoke a provision of EU law against Dutch Customs Authorities. The firm had imported urea-formaldehyde from Germany into the Netherlands and had been charged a customs duty. This breached the EU rules on free movement of goods and the firm sought reimbursement from the Dutch government. A Dutch tribunal requested the ECJ to determine whether what is now Article 228 TFEU could be relied upon by an individual rather than a Member State. The ECJ held that the Article was directly effective, ie it gave rise to rights or obligations which individuals may enforce before their national courts. A provision will be directly effective provided it meets certain criteria:

(a) it must be sufficiently clear and precise; and

(b) it must be unconditional and leave no room for the exercise of discretion in implementation by Member States or EU institutions.

Van Gend dealt with an individual invoking an Article against an organ of the state and this is known as 'vertical' direct effect. But what about an individual invoking a Treaty Article against another private party or individual, known as 'horizontal' direct effect?

This was dealt with in *Defrenne v Sabena* (43/75)[1976] ECR 455. Ms Defrenne was an air hostess with Sabena Airlines. She brought an action based on what is now Article 157(1) TFEU which provides that men and women should receive equal pay for equal work. Sabena were in breach of this provision as male stewards were paid more for the same work. Sabena argued that Article 157(1) was not directly effective as it is concerned with the relationships between individuals and not between Member States and individuals. The ECJ disagreed and provided that Treaty provisions could have 'horizontal' direct effect provided they met the same criteria, ie clear and precise obligations with no discretion left to Member States as to implementation.

16.6.3 Directives

The problem with directives is that they require implementation by Member States, unlike regulations, and therefore it was thought that they could not have direct effect. The ECJ disagreed in *Grad v Finanzamt Traunstein* (9/70) [1970] ECR 825 where a haulage company sought to challenge a tax levied by the German authorities which the company claimed was in breach of an EU directive. The German government argued that only regulations were directly applicable and directives required implementation. The ECJ disagreed. The fact that only regulations were described as directly applicable did not mean that other binding acts were incapable of such effects.

This decision was confirmed in *Van Duyn v Home Office* (41/74) [1974] ECR 1337. Ms Van Duyn was a Dutch national and a member of the Church of Scientology. She wanted to enter the UK to work for the Church. The UK government had decided that the Church was undesirable and tried to exclude her on the ground of public policy. The Dutch government had implemented a directive dealing with the grounds for exclusion which were based on the personal conduct of the individual. Ms Van Duyn argued that it was not her personal conduct. The ECJ held that Ms Van Duyn was entitled to invoke the directive directly before her national court, thus confirming that directives can be directly effective. However, a directive will still have to satisfy the criteria set down in the Treaty cases. Remember that a directive has to be implemented by the Member State and, therefore, it cannot be directly effective until the time limit for implementation has expired. This was considered in the *Ratti* case (C148/78) [1979] ECR 1629) where S Ratti, a solvent manufacturer, labelled his solvents in line with an EU directive. This was contrary to the old Italian law and he was prosecuted for infringing national law. The ECJ ruled that once the time limit for the implementation of a directive has expired, a Member State may not apply internal law to someone who has complied with a directive. S Ratti was able to rely on one directive as that time limit had expired but not on the one for which the time limit was still running.

These cases illustrate 'vertical' direct effect, ie individual against the state, but what about 'horizontal' direct effect, ie can an individual invoke a directive against another individual?

16.6.3.1 Horizontal direct effect

There are many cases discussing the horizontal direct effect, the first of which was *Marshall v Southampton and South-West Hampshire Area Health Authority* (152/84) [1986] ECR 723. Mrs Marshall sought to challenge the AHA's compulsory retirement age of 65 for men and 60 for women as discriminatory. The ECJ held that the AHA was acting in its capacity as an 'emanation of the State' and so Mrs Marshall was able to recover damages, ie the AHA was not seen as an individual. In *Foster v British Gas plc* (C-188/89) [1990] ECR I-3313 a claim was made in respect of different retirement ages. The ECJ held that a directive might be relied on against organisations or bodies which were 'subject to the authority or control of the state or had special powers beyond those which result from the normal relations between individuals and which is carrying out a public service'. This therefore extended the concept of direct effect to a body or organisation with special powers carrying out a service or controlled by the state.

However, this spread of the concept of direct effect of a directive was halted in *Rolls Royce v Doughty* [1987] IRLR 447. Here, although the plaintiff was in the same situation as Mrs Foster, the ECJ held that Rolls Royce did not exercise any special powers, unlike British Gas, and Mrs Doughty was unsuccessful. The public services which it provided, eg defence, were provided to the state and not to the public. In 1995, in *Griffin v South West Water Services* [1995] IRLR 15, a privatised water company was held to be within the *Foster* definition. The case of *Faccini Dori v Recreb Srl* (C-91/92) [1994] ECR I-325 concerned doorstep selling and here, the ECJ halted the concept of 'horizontal' direct effect. 'A directive cannot itself impose obligations on an individual and cannot therefore be relied on by an individual.'

16.6.3.2 Indirect effect

Meanwhile, the court has tried various solutions to the problem of 'horizontal' direct effect. The first one of these was suggested in *Von Colson and Kamann v Land Nordrhein-Westfalen* (14/83) [1984] ECR 1891 which was based on a directive concerning equal treatment. Ms von Colson was employed in the prison service as a social worker. The authorities at a totally male prison would not engage her because of her sex on the grounds that it would cause too many problems and be too risky. The matter was referred to the ECJ. Instead of dealing with the vertical–horizontal problem, the ECJ turned instead to Article 4(3) TEU (formerly Article 10 of the EC Treaty). This provides that Member States should take all appropriate measures to ensure fulfilment of their obligations arising under EU law or from the acts of any of the EU institutions and that therefore national courts should interpret national law in such a way as to give effect to a directive by ensuring its objectives are met. The result of this case is that although EU law is not directly effective, it may still be applied indirectly as domestic law by means of interpretation. This gave rise to the concept of 'indirect effect'. However, the success of this principle depends on the Member State's discretion to interpret national law. In *Marleasing SA v La Comercial Internacional de Alimentacion SA* (C-106/89) [1990] ECR I-4135, the Spanish court was confronted with a national law on the constitution of companies which conflicted with an EU directive not implemented in Spain. The ECJ ruled specifically and without qualification that national courts were 'required' to interpret domestic law in such a way as to ensure that the objectives of the directive were achieved.

16.6.4 Regulations

Regulations will have direct effect provided they are sufficiently precise.

16.6.5 Decisions

Decisions may be directly effective provided the criteria for direct effect are satisfied.

16.6.6 Recommendations and opinions

These are non-binding measures and it is thought that at best they can only be taken into account in order to resolve ambiguities in domestic law.

16.7 Supremacy

We have seen that the courts are supposed to interpret domestic law so as to ensure the objectives of a directive are met, but what if there is a conflict between EU law and national law? The EU treaties are silent on this therefore it has been developed through case law. The question needs to be considered from the perspective of the EU and from that of the UK.

16.7.1 EU

In 1964, the court made a very brave ruling in *Costa v ENEL* (6/64) [1964] ECR 585 which concerned the compatibility with EU law of the nationalisation of the Italian electricity industry. It was very brave because the foundations of EU law were barely established. The court held that EU law must be supreme over conflicting national law. This was cited in *Van Gend en Loos* and the court went further to state that a Member State, by joining the EU, had limited its sovereign rights and Article 4 of the TEU underlined the Member State's commitment to observe EU law. The conflict went further in *Internationale*

Handelsgesellschaft GmbH v Einfuhr- und Vorratsstelle für Getriede und Futtermittel (11/70) [1970] ECR 1125 where there was a conflict between a regulation concerning the requirement under the Common Agricultural Policy for an export licence which conflicted with an Article in the German Constitution on German fundamental rights. The ECJ ruled that the provisions of EU law will always prevail over the provisions of national law no matter what has passed earlier. The court went further in *Simmenthal SpA v Commission* (92/78) [1979] ECR 777 where a number of regulations provided for the common organisation of the market in veal and beef by controlling the price of frozen beef. Here it was suggested that EU law is to be given priority over national law as soon as it comes into force, otherwise there can be no uniformity throughout the EU. Where a conflict exists, a judge should shut his eyes to national law and must not wait for it to be changed.

16.7.2 UK

Problems arise with the concept of supremacy from a UK perspective because, first, the UK has a dualist attitude, ie international and national law are different, and second, it has a largely unwritten constitution. In 1979, the case of *Macarthys Ltd v Smith* (129/79) [1980] ECR 1275, which concerned equal pay reached the Court of Appeal where it took the European view, ie that 'the courts have a bounden duty to give priority to EU law'. This was followed in 1983 by *Garland v British Rail Engineering Ltd* (12/81) [1982] ECR 359 which concerned sex discrimination, where the House of Lords adopted the 'rule of construction' approach. It said that the words of a statute passed after the Treaty are to be construed, if reasonably capable of bearing such a meaning, as to be intended to carry out the obligation which is imposed by the Treaty, and not to be inconsistent with it. In *R v Secretary of State for Transport, ex parte Factortame* (C-213/89) [1991] 1 AC 603, the House of Lords was confronted with the Merchant Shipping Act 1988 which was enacted to stop Spanish fishermen's quota-hopping measures. The Spanish fishermen said that it discriminated on the grounds of nationality. The House of Lords went further to suggest that if a British Act is in breach of a claimant's directly effective EU rights, these would prevail over the contrary provisions of the Act. In a further case, *Webb* (279/80) [1981] ECR 3305, which concerned discrimination based on pregnancy, the House of Lords, after making an application for a ruling, held that it should construe domestic legislation so as to accord with a directive.

These cases dealt with directly effective provisions but in *Duke v GEC Reliance Ltd* [1988] AC 618, there was a clash between a statute and a non-directly effective provision. The court acknowledged that it ought to interpret the statute in line with the directive even though it was not directly effective but went on to set aside the directive and apply the UK statute even though it was contrary to EU law. Therefore, unless a provision is directly effective it will have no force in the UK courts unless it is given effect by UK Parliament.

16.8 The relationship between EU and national law: checkpoints

In this section we have looked at:

- how EU law has been incorporated into national law; and
- what happens when there is a conflict between the two.

You should now be able to identify the main characteristics of direct effect and the issues affecting supremacy.

REMEDIES

16.9 Introduction

As can be seen from the above, the relationship between national and EU law has not been an easy or straightforward one. It has necessitated clarification and, consequently, it is important for us to address the area of remedies, namely the rights of individuals and Member States to review the acts and judgments of European institutions. At the same time, this extends to the rights of the institutions to review the acts of Member States.

This section looks at remedies, and covers:

- relevant Articles;
- judicial review;
- enforcement of law against Member States; and
- seeking a remedy in national courts.

16.10 Article 267 reference procedure

Under Article 267 TFEU the ECJ can give preliminary rulings on the following:

(a) interpretation of the Treaty; and

(b) validity and interpretation of acts of EU institutions.

The purpose of the procedure was commented on in *Rheinmühlen-Dusseldorf v Einfuhr- und Vorratsstelle für Getriede und Futtermittel* (146/73) [1974] ECR 139. This case concerned an attempt by a German cereal importer to obtain an export rebate under EU law. A question was raised as to whether what is now Article 267 gave an unfettered right for national courts to refer to or whether it is subject to national provisions whereby lower courts are bound by the judgments of superior courts. The ECJ replied quite strongly that '[Article 267] is essential for the preservation of the EU character of the law established by the Treaty and has the object of ensuring that in all circumstances the law is the same in all Member States in the EU.'

There are two situations where the Article 267 procedure works:

(a) Where a case is being heard before a court from which there is no appeal, the national court *must* make a reference if it believes clarification of EU law is required to decide the case. It is not necessary to make a reference where the point is so obvious as to leave no scope for reasonable doubt. This latter point was made in *CILFIT Srl v Ministry of Health* (283/81) [1982] ECR 341 and is known as the doctrine of *acte claire*. This case concerned a dispute between wool importers and the Italian Ministry of Health over payment of an inspection levy in respect of wool imports from outside the EU.

(b) Where a case is being heard by a court or tribunal which is exercising a judicial function, that court or tribunal *has the discretion* to make a reference. The ECJ's opinion must be required to decide the case. In *R v Bouchereau* (30/77) [1977] ECR 1999 the magistrates' court made a reference. M Bouchereau, a French national, was convicted of possessing a small quantity of drugs. He was fined £35 but the magistrate was minded to recommend deportation. The ECJ ruled that the crime was not sufficient to justify deportation.

Once the court has given its judgment, it is too late to ask for a reference.

Article 267 relies on a willingness to refer. The ECJ usually accepts any references to it. It will only refuse references occasionally when it considers the system is being abused. For example the case of Foglia v Novello (No 1) (104/79) [1980] ECR 745 and Foglia v Novello (No 2) (244/80) [1981] ECR 3045 where the ECJ stated that it had no power to rule on national law and it should not be used as a method for testing the compatibility of EU and national law.

16.11 Judicial review

Article 267 is not the only way to challenge the legality of an EU act. Article 263 TFEU provides that the court has a duty to review the legality of:

(a) legislative acts;

(b) acts of the Council, Commission, and European Central Bank; and

(c) acts of the European Parliament, European Council and bodies and offices of the Union intended to produce legal effects vis-à-vis third parties.

There are four grounds of review:

(a) lack of competence or *ultra vires*;

(b) infringement of essential procedural requirement or procedural *ultra vires*, for example, failure to give reasons;

(c) infringement of the EU treaties or any rule of law relating to their interpretation (which includes non-discrimination and human rights); and

(d) misuse of power.

In order to bring an action for judicial review under Article 263 the applicant must show they have the relevant standing to do so and the Article distinguishes between so called 'privileged' and 'non-privileged' applicants. Privileged applicants are, broadly speaking, Member States and the EU institutions and provided they bring an action within the relevant time limit (see below) they will always have standing. Non-privileged applicants are other natural or legal persons and they will only have standing if:

(a) the act is addressed to them or is of direct or individual concern to them (such as regulations, decisions and directives); or

(b) a regulatory act is of direct concern to them and does not require an implementing measure.

The right to bring an action for the judicial review of regulatory acts is a new right introduced by the Treaty of Lisbon. It is not yet clear what acts will be caught as 'regulatory acts' and therefore what the effect of this right of review will be.

All applicants (privileged or non-privileged) must bring the action within two months of the date of publication of the measure or notification to the claimant or, in the absence thereof, the date on which it came to the knowledge of the latter.

Article 277 TFEU does allow persons who are affected by an act of general application to challenge it indirectly, ie where, for example, a person is subject to a later decision based upon a regulation. In addition, Article 265 TFEU provides that the ECJ may bring an action against the European Parliament, the Commission, the Council of Ministers, the European Council or the European Central Bank where they have failed to act. Articles 268 and 340 TFEU provide that an institution may be sued where one of its servants has acted wrongfully in the performance of its functions or the institution itself has so acted. Rather than bring an action directly against a defendant, an applicant may make a complaint to the Commission. This procedure is free, but it does take rather a long time.

16.12 Enforcement of law against Member States

The Commission has the power to commence proceedings against a Member State for failure to implement EU law under Article 258 TFEU. It has to deliver a *reasoned opinion* on the matter after giving the state concerned an opportunity to submit its observations. If the state does not comply within the time period set down by the Commission, the matter is taken before the ECJ.

Other Member States can bring an action against another defaulting Member State by reason of Article 259 TFEU. Before bringing such an action the complaining Member State must first refer it to the Commission. Again, the Commission gives a reasoned opinion to which the offending state can submit its observations. If the Commission has not delivered an opinion within three months of the complaint being referred to it by the Member State, the matter can still go before the ECJ. The absence of an opinion does not matter.

Although Member States have been reluctant to use Article 259, the Commission is increasingly using Article 258 as part of the process of achieving a single market.

16.13 Seeking a remedy in the national courts

Article 4(3) TEU requires Member States to cooperate by taking all appropriate measures to ensure fulfilment of the obligations arising under EU law. This includes ensuring national remedies are available for breach of EU law. In the UK claims can therefore be brought for damages against the UK government for non-implementation and also between private individuals for breach of the provisions of the Treaties. Injunctions can also be sought.

The EU treaties do not make any provision as to what national remedies should be made available and over time the ECJ has become concerned to ensure the effectiveness of the remedies granted by the national courts for breach of EU law. In doing so it has sought to balance respect for the autonomy of the national courts against the need to ensure the remedies are sufficiently effective to ensure the supremacy of EU law and to ensure that Member States do not prejudice EU nationals compared to home nationals. Originally the ECJ took a non-interventionist approach when trying to balance these competing interests. For example it held in *Comet BV v Produktschap voor Siergewassen* (45/76) [1976] ECR 2043 that national remedies should be 'no less effective' than those available to deal with a breach of national law but that national courts should not be required to impose new remedies. However, the court's view has changed over the years such that in the *Factortame* case, it held that a national court should create an appropriate legal remedy if none exists.

An interim order was considered in the *Factortame* case which concerned a group of Spanish fishermen who owned British registered trawlers. The Merchant Shipping

Act 1988 had the effect of preventing these fishermen from fishing in British waters. This conflicted with EU legislation and so the fishermen applied for judicial review of the Act. Such a reference to the ECJ would take two years. In the meantime, the fishermen would lose their livelihood. Therefore, they applied for interim relief pending a judgment disapplying the Merchant Shipping Act. The House of Lords refused the application stating that they could not obtain an injunction against the Crown. A reference under what is now Article 267 TFEU was made and the ECJ disagreed and stated that the House of Lords must set aside the national law that precluded the granting of interim relief. Therefore, the House of Lords had to suspend the Merchant Shipping Act.

At the same time the ECJ developed a new separate remedy of state liability under which individuals can seek reimbursement from Member States for failing to implement EU law. This remedy was first established in *Francovich v Republic of Italy* (C-6 and 9/90) [1991] ECR I-5357. In this case, an Italian company went into liquidation leaving its employees with unpaid salary arrears. A directive was in existence which required Member States to set up a compensation scheme to deal with this situation but Italy had not complied. S Francovich sought compensation from the Italian court and the Italian government was obliged to make good the damage suffered as a result of the non-implementation of a directive. This finding was upheld in *Factortame* with the result that a person who has suffered loss as a result of a breach of EU law by a public body is not obliged to go down the judicial review route with its two-month time limit provided that the result pursued by the directive involved the conferring of rights for the benefit of individuals, the content of those rights could be determined by reference to the directive and there was a causal link between the failure to implement the directive and the harm suffered by the individual. The case of *Factortame* added a further point that a national court must set aside national procedural laws that represent an obstacle to the implementation of EU law.

The more interventionist approach of the ECJ to the effectiveness of national remedies has meant that on occasion EU nationals have been placed in a better position than home nationals. Recognising this, the ECJ has recently taken a slightly less stringent approach in reviewing the effectiveness of national remedies.

From the case of *Garden Cottage Foods v Milk Marketing Board* [1984] AC 130 it is clear that where there is a directly effective provision and an individual has suffered loss, he can claim for damages against the individual who caused the loss. This case concerned an application for an interlocutory injunction to restrain the defendants from refusing to supply milk to the plaintiffs. The refusal was alleged to be an abuse of a dominant position by the Milk Marketing Board. The compensation must be proportionate and where national measures do not allow for adequate compensation, they should be ignored. This has particular relevance in sex discrimination cases.

16.14 Remedies: checkpoints

In this section we have looked at:

- how to challenge a EU act;
- how the Commission enforces law against defaulting Member States; and
- how an individual can seek a remedy in the national courts.

You should now be able to identify the relevant Articles for review and how they operate.

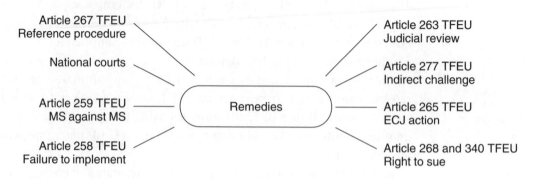

Figure 16.3 Remedies.

FREE MOVEMENT OF GOODS

16.15 Introduction

Fundamental to rights of a European citizen are the freedoms to move around, live, work, and trade more easily within the Union. This section deals with the free movement of goods. It looks at:

- the relevant Treaty provisions;
- customs duties;
- quantitative restrictions; and
- the rule of reason and Article 36 TFEU.

16.16 Treaty provisions

One of the main points of the internal market is free movement of goods and as such it is a 'cornerstone' of the EU. Its aim is to create a single market free of all restrictions on trade. This is achieved through a number of Articles:

(a) Article 3 TEU and Article 26 TFEU: the creation of an internal market. This aim is set out in Article 3 TEU and is supplemented by Article 26 TFEU which requires Member States to adopt measures ensuring the functioning of an internal market ie 'an area without internal frontiers'.

(b) Articles 28 and 29 TFEU: the creation of a Customs Union providing for the free circulation of goods throughout the EU whatever their place of origin once they are within the EU. A Common Customs Tariff applies to all products imported into the EU from outside the EU.

(c) Article 30 TFEU: the internal aspects of Common Customs Tariff: Member States should not introduce any new customs duties.

(d) Articles 31 and 32 TFEU: external aspects of Common Customs Tariff, ie how it works. Products are divided into lists which have applicable tariff rates (tariff rates are average of duties applied in four customs areas).

(e) Article 34 TFEU: prohibits quantitative restrictions on imports and measures having equivalent effect.

(f) Article 35 TFEU: prohibits quantitative restrictions on exports and measures having equivalent effect.

(g) Article 36 TFEU: exceptions to Articles 34 and 35 TFEU where restrictions are justified on the grounds of public morality, public policy, public health, public security, protection of national treasures, and protection of intellectual property rights.

(h) Article 37 TFEU: requires Member States to adjust any state monopolies to ensure that no discrimination as to the conditions under which goods are procured and marketed exists between nationals of Member States.

The meaning of 'equivalent effect' depends on whether it is in relation to customs duties or quantitative restrictions.

16.17 Customs duties

Customs duties come in many guises and are often called a tax. An example was given in the Gingerbread case of *Commission v Luxembourg and Belgium* (2, 3/62) [1962] ECHR 425. These Member States put a tax on imported gingerbread. They claimed the tax was to compensate for tax on rye (an ingredient of gingerbread). The ECJ held that the charge jeopardised the objectives of the EU and was a result of a unilateral decision. When applied to imports but not to similar national products it had the same effect as a customs duty and was unlawful.

16.18 Quantitative restrictions

This is the rule in *Dassonville*, ie 'all trading rules enacted by Member States that are capable of hindering, directly or indirectly, actually or potentially, intra-union trade' have the same effect as quotas (*Procureur du Roi v Dassonville* (8/74) [1974] ECR 837). In this case, a Belgian importer of Scotch whisky was prosecuted for selling it with false certificates of origin. He had imported the whisky from France and it was difficult to obtain certificates. He argued that Belgian law made it more difficult to import whisky if it came from a state other than the state of origin and this therefore breached Article 34.

Examples of measures which fall within this rule, ie are not allowed, include:

(a) a requirement that a certificate or licence be obtained prior to import or export, for example, a certificate of origin;

(b) measures encouraging purchase of national products on the basis of national origin. For example, in *Commission v Ireland* (248/81) [1982] ECR 4005, a 'buy Irish' campaign was not allowed, as it discouraged the purchase of other goods rather than merely drawing a consumer's attention to the specific qualities of the products; or

(c) measures which affect the domestic product as well (so called 'indistinctly applicable' measures). The leading case in this area is *Cassis de Dijon (Rewe-Zentral AG v Bundesmonopolverwaltung für Branntwein* (120/78) [1974] ECR 649) where a French company wanted to export blackcurrant liqueur to Germany. The liqueur had an alcohol content of 15–20 per cent. German law set down a minimum alcohol content of 25 per cent for fruit liqueurs and therefore the Germans sought to prevent the importation of the French product. The ECJ applied *Dassonville* and found the German law to be in breach of Article 34.

The effect of *Cassis de Dijon* was very wide and all kinds of indistinctly applicable measures such as labelling requirements, advertising rules etc were argued to be measures having equivalent effect to quantitative restrictions ('MEQRs'). The ECJ began to develop its rule of reason (see below) to try to limit such claims but in 1993 it decided to try to further limit the effect of Cassis in the important case of *Keck* (C-267 and 268/9) [1993] ECR 1-6097. In that case Keck was prosecuted for selling goods below their purchase price. The court held that selling arrangements would not constitute MEQR 'provided they effect in the same manner, in law and in fact, the marketing of domestic products and those from other Member States'. Note the ruling only applies to 'selling arrangements', that is measures that affect how a product is marketed and sold (such as rules setting opening hours or advertising restrictions). Rules which relate to the products themselves will still fall within *Cassis* and therefore within Article 34. Note also that selling arrangements may still fall within Article 34 and be construed as MEQR if, in law and in fact, they adversely affect imports over and above domestic products.

16.19 Exceptions to Article 34 TFEU

16.19.1 Article 36 TFEU

This Article applies to all MEQRs whether indistinctly applicable (applying to both imported and domestic goods) or distinctly applicable (only applying to imported goods). It allows restrictions on the free movement of goods to be imposed by Member States on certain grounds.

3.19.1.1 Public morality

This will be a matter for individual states but restrictions must not constitute a means of arbitrary discrimination against the import or a restriction on trade. Therefore, the exception can only be used where such a measure would affect a home-produced product in the same way. In *R v Henn & Darby* (34/79) [1979] ECR 3795 the defendants were convicted of being 'knowingly' concerned in the fraudulent evasion of the prohibition on the importation of indecent or obscene articles. These consisted of boxes of obscene films and magazines which were illegal. In *Conegate v Customs and Excise Commissioners* (121/85) [1986] ECR 1007 the goods consisted of sex dolls which could be sold lawfully throughout the UK.

16.19.1.2 Public policy

This can only be used where there is a serious threat to the fundamental interests of society. In *R v Thompson and others* (7/78) [1978] ECR 2247 the defendants traded in coins, some of which were no longer legal tender. They were convicted of being knowingly concerned in the fraudulent evasion of the prohibition on the importation of gold coins into the UK.

16.19.1.3 Protection of the health and life of humans, animals, and plants

Again this is a matter for individual states but the need must be real (backed up with relevant scientific evidence to demonstrate the dangers to health) and must not constitute arbitrary discrimination. Such discriminatory measures include import bans, import licences, health inspections, and prior-authorisation requirements. The actual measure must be considered carefully as it may not be for the protection of health but may actually constitute discrimination. In *Commission v UK* (40/82) [1982] ECR 2793, the UK government prohibited the import of poultry from France which adopted a policy of vaccination rather than slaughter. This was ostensibly to prevent the spread of Newcastle Disease. The ECJ ruled that the ban was unnecessarily restrictive and not part of a well-thought-out health policy but rather a measure to protect the UK poultry industry.

16.19.1.4 Public security

This cannot be readily called upon as a defence to a breach of Article 34. In *Campus Oil Ltd v Ministry for Industry and Energy* (72/83) [1983] ECR 2727 the Irish government required petrol importers to buy 35 per cent of their needs from an Irish refinery at government-fixed prices. This was so as to preserve the national refinery. The ECJ ruled that the measure was justified on the grounds of public security to maintain the national stocks in times of crisis.

16.19.1.5 Protection of national treasures

This ground has not yet been successfully revoked but it was suggested in *Commission v Italy* (7/68) [1968] ECR 423 that a wish by a Member State to prevent an art treasure from leaving that country may have been acceptable even though it may constitute a quantitative restriction.

16.19.1.6 Protection of industrial and commercial property

Intellectual property covers both industrial property and artistic property. 'Industrial property' means rights related to the production and distribution of goods such as trademarks and patents. 'Artistic property' means literary and artistic property such as copyrights. Intellectual property rights provide for the enjoyment of valuable property rights as against the world. It has usually been left to the national authorities to grant their own rights which relate to each national territory. Such individuality is really contrary to the spirit of the EU and, therefore, the ECJ has restricted the use of this as a defence to a breach of Article 34. It has distinguished between the ownership of these rights and their exercise. National rules must not constitute arbitrary discrimination or a restriction on the free movement of goods. The court will consider the 'specific subject matter' of the right. For example, the specific subject matter of a patent is 'to use an invention with a view to manufacturing industrial products and putting them into circulation for the first time' (*Centrafarm BV v Sterling Drug Inc* (15/74) [1974] ECR 1147). Sterling Drug Inc held the British and Dutch patents for a drug called NEGRAM. This drug was marketed either by Sterling Drug Inc or companies licensed to do so. Centrafarm, an independent Dutch company, bought supplies of the drug in Britain and Germany where it was much cheaper and resold it in the Netherlands. Sterling Drug Inc and its subsidiaries invoked their patent and trademark rights before the Dutch court to prevent NEGRAM being marketed in the Netherlands by Centrafarm. The ECJ held that once the patented goods are circulated in another Member State the right to exclude those goods is 'exhausted' and the patentee cannot prevent the import of the patented product. A similar approach has been adopted for trademarks and copyright.

16.19.2 The 'rule of reason'

The rule of reason permits Member States to claim certain additional grounds to justify a restriction of the free movement of goods but only in respect of indistinctly applicable measures. It is therefore important to identify whether a measure affects the equivalent domestic product as well as the imported one. Such restrictions can be justified provided they meet what are called the 'mandatory requirements'. Mandatory requirements are also sometimes referred to as the 'public interest objectives' and include the:

(a) protection of public health;
(b) fairness of commercial transactions;
(c) defence of consumer; and
(d) protection of environment.

However, in order for the measure to be necessary, it must be proportionate to the aim ie not go beyond the minimum that is necessary to meet the mandatory requirement concerned. In *Cassis*, the German government argued the defence of 'protection of the consumer' but the ECJ held that the measure was disproportionate to the aim as clear labelling was an acceptable alternative.

Therefore, when dealing with free movement of goods, the following should be borne in mind:

(a) Look to see whether the measure falls within Article 34. If it does not, then there's no issue.
(b) If yes, consider whether the measure is distinctly applicable or indistinctly applicable (*Cassis*).
(c) If the measure is distinctly applicable consider the defences under Article 36. If none applies the measure will be unlawful.
(d) If the measure is indistinctly applicable consider if it is a selling arrangement or a non-selling arrangement (*Keck*). If it is a selling arrangement it does not fall within Article 34 and there is no issue provided the measure does not, in law and in fact, adversely affect the imported product compared to domestic products.
(e) If the measure is a non-selling arrangement or a selling arrangement that adversely affects imported goods in law and in fact, consider the defences in Article 36 and the rule of reason. If none apply the measure is unlawful.

Figure 16.4 Exceptions to Article 34.

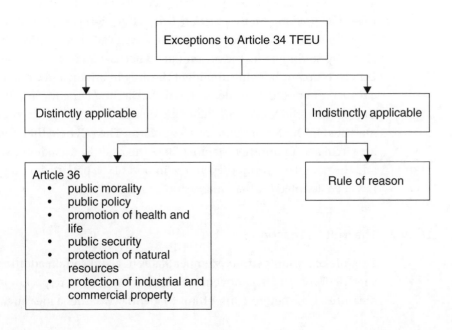

16.20 Free movement of goods: checkpoints

In this section we have looked at:

- the free movement of goods;
- which prohibitive measures are legal; and
- which prohibitive measures are illegal.

You should now be able to identify the relevant treaty articles, the factors which constitute a customs duty or quantitative restriction and the circumstances in which such a restriction will be permitted.

FREE MOVEMENT OF PERSONS

16.21 Introduction

Article 20 TFEU states that every EU national shall now be a citizen of EU. Each Union citizen has the right to move and reside freely within the Member State, subject to the limitations in the treaties and in other legislation (Article 21 TFEU).

Note that the right to EU citizenship is dependent on the individual being an EU national or a family member of an EU national (see further below). The case of *Micheletti v Delegacion del Gobierno en Cantabria* (C-396/90) [1992] ECR I-4239 established that 'it is for each Member State, having due regard to EU law, to lay down the conditions for acquisition and loss of nationality'.

The concept of EU citizenship has supplemented the rights of workers to free movement as originally envisaged in the Treaty of Rome and added other citizenship rights in addition to the right of free movement. Over time there have been a number of regulations and directives that have added to these rights including Regulation 1612/68 on workers and Directive 2004/38 on EU citizens.

This section sets out what constitutes a worker and deals with:

- a worker's rights;
- a worker's family; and
- the grounds for restricting the free movement of a person.

16.22 Workers

Article 45 TFEU provides for free movement of workers within the EU, but what is a 'worker'? The Treaty provides no definition but the ECJ has developed a definition through case law. In the case of *Sotgiu v Deutsche Bundespost* (152/73) [1974] ECR 153 the German Post Office's decision to pay increased separation allowances only to workers living away from home was held to be capable of breaching Article 7 (now repealed). The court referred to a worker as 'a person engaged in activities of an economic nature'. In *Lawrie-Blum v Land Baden-Württemberg* (66/85) [1986] ECR 2121 the applicant was a trainee teacher employed by the Minister of Education with the status of a civil servant. A worker was defined as someone who 'provides services of some economic value, for and under the direction of another person, for which he receives remuneration'. In *Levin v Staatssecretaris van Justitie* (53/81) [1982] ECR 1035 the Court held that part-time workers could be protected provided their activities were 'genuine and effective' and provided they were not 'marginal or ancillary'. In *Kempf* (139/85) [1986] ECR 1741 the court made it clear that even very low paid workers receiving wages that were far below subsistence level could still be undertaking genuine and effective work.

16.22.1 Workers' rights

Article 45 sets out the rights of workers.

16.22.1.1 Right to migrate

Under Article 45 a worker can go to another Member State to accept a job offer. Job seekers are also protected by Article 45 (*R v Immigration Appeal Tribunal ex parte Antonissa* (C-292/89) [1991] ECR 1-745). Accordingly a worker can go to another Member State for the purpose of seeking employment but only for a reasonable time. In the UK, immigration rules allow a person to stay for this purpose for six months.

16.22.1.2 Right to reside

Article 45 gives a worker the right to stay in another Member State for the purpose of employment. This has now been supplemented by various provisions in Directive 2004/38. An EU citizen and their family members (see below) have the right to reside within another Member State for a period of up to three months without any formalities other than the production of a valid passport or ID card (Article 6(1) Directive 2004/38). After the initial three-month period the workers and their family members can remain provided they meet certain conditions such as having sufficient financial resources not to be a burden on the host Member State and having comprehensive sickness cover (Article 7 Directive 2004/38). If the workers and their family members do stay beyond the initial three-month period the host Member State may require them to obtain a residency period. EU citizens who have resided legally for a continuous period of five years in the host Member State shall have the right of permanent residence there (Article 16(1) Directive 2004/38). This right also applies to family members who are not nationals of the host Member State and who have legally resided with the EU citizen for a continuous period of five years.

16.22.1.3 Right to remain

A retired worker has the right to remain, ie to stay in the host Member State, if they have permanent residency rights having stayed in the host Member State for more than five years (see above). If not then generally the retired worker can only remain if they have sufficient financial resources and comprehensive sickness insurance.

The right to remain is extended to workers who are temporarily unable to work due to illness or accident, workers who are involuntarily unemployed (but not voluntarily unemployed) and workers who are voluntarily unemployed who have entered into vocational training. Conditions apply.

16.22.1.4 Right to equal treatment

Workers have a right to equal treatment (Article 45(2) TFEU) and therefore the right not to be discriminated against. A migrant worker is also entitled to the same tax and social advantages as a national worker, whether or not these are attached to the contract of employment (Article 7(2) Regulation 1612/68). The case law on social advantages is complex and beyond the scope of this book.

16.23 Families of workers

Directive 2004/38 defines a family member as including spouses, civil partners (if recognised by Member States), children and grandchildren under 21 or dependents of the EU citizen or their spouse/civil partner, and parents or other direct ascendents of the EU citizen, their spouse or civil partner (Article 2(2)).

Member States are to facilitate entry to and residence to (a) other dependants and family members of the EU citizen where serious health grounds strictly require the personal care of that family member by the Union citizen; or (b) to the partner of the EU citizen being a partner that is not a recognised civil partner and with whom the EU citizen has a durable relationship, duly attested.

16.23.1 What about divorce or termination of a registered partnership?

By Article 13(2) this does not entail loss of residence of:

(a) EU citizen's family members who are themselves nationals of a Member State provided the marriage/civil partnership lasted for at least three years including one year in the host Member State prior to the initiation of the proceedings for the divorce, annulment or the termination of the registered partnership; or

(b) by agreement the spouse or partner who is not a national of a Member State but who has custody of the EU citizen's children; or

(c) this is warranted by particularly difficult circumstances, such as having been the victim of domestic violence while the marriage or registered partnership was subsisting.

16.23.2 What about dependants?

Dependants have the same rights as a worker even after a divorce and this includes children of the family even though they may not be descendants. They have the right to work in the host state if they have the necessary qualifications. In *Gül v Regierungspräsident Düsseldorf* (131/85) [1986] ECR 1573, a Turkish Cypriot doctor was married to an Englishwoman who was employed as a hairdresser in Germany. He was refused permission to practise medicine. This decision was overturned by the ECJ. Dependants are also entitled to be admitted to educational, apprenticeship, and vocational training courses (Article 12 Regulation 1612/68). Grants to cover the costs and maintenance during such education, apprenticeship and vocational training courses are part of the social advantages referred to in **3.22.1.4** above and are subject to certain conditions.

16.24 Exceptions to Article 45

Article 45 is not applicable to employment in public service. This has been exploited by Member States and so has been limited to 'posts involving the exercise of official authority and functions related to safeguarding the general interests of the State'.

Article 45 is about granting rights of access and residence when a worker moves from one Member State to another—there has to be a cross-border element—and therefore does not apply to 'wholly internal situations'. Similarly it will not apply when an EU national enters another Member State direct from a non-EU country.

Article 55 permits Member States to deny residence on the grounds of:

(a) public policy;

(b) public security; or

(c) public health.

On all these grounds it must be the personal conduct of the individual that is relied on for the purposes of the exception and the restriction must be proportionate, that is it must not go beyond that necessary to meet the public policy, security or health concerns.

16.24.1 Public policy and public security

Member States may argue that the past conduct of the worker is such that they wish to deny them access to or continued residence in the host Member State. There are a number of cases which illustrate the working of these exceptions. The first is *Van Duyn* where it was said that there must be a 'genuine and sufficiently serious threat to public policy affecting one of the fundamental interests of society'. In *Adoui and Cornuaille v Belgium* (115, 116/87) [1982] ECR 1665 it was added that 'membership of an organisation may constitute conduct but must be such that the government has recently taken steps to curb such activities'. In this case, Adoui and Cornuaille worked in a Belgian café with a rather questionable reputation. They were refused residency on the grounds of public policy. In *Rutili v Minister for the Interior* (36/75) [1975] ECR 1219, the ECJ held that, to use the public policy restriction, there must be a total ban on the conduct in question and the fundamental interests of society must be affected.

The exceptions must be used proportionately and therefore it is only in exceptional cases that past conduct will in itself justify deportation. This is also to be borne in mind when using the grounds to refuse entry, as a former terrorist will be allowed entry provided he or she is no longer a threat. In *Rutili*, he had been involved in trade union and political activities. He was an Italian working in France and the French government tried to restrict his movements to certain areas of France without success.

It must be the personal conduct of the individual concerned. In *Bonsignore v Oberstadtdirektor of the City of Cologne* (67/74) [1975] ECR 297, the applicant, who was an Italian working in Germany, was found guilty of causing the death of his brother by the negligent handling of a firearm. He was directed to be deported for its deterrent effect. The ECJ said that a Member State could not use a EU worker as a 'scapegoat'.

Previous criminal convictions do not in themselves constitute a ground for expulsion or exclusion. In *R v Bouchereau* (30/77) [1977] ECR 1999, the authorities sought to deport Bouchereau, a French national working in the UK, on the grounds of his conviction for the unlawful possession of drugs. The conviction must constitute a serious threat to the fundamental interests of society.

These decisions have now been incorporated into Article 27(2) of Directive 2004/38. When using the grounds of public policy or security, the host Member State must take account of various factors including how long the EU citizen has lived in the Member State, his age, health, family and extent of links with his country of origin (Article 28(1)).

16.24.2 Public health

The diseases to fall within the ground of public health must be highly infectious or contagious, eg TB.

16.24.3 Further restrictions on the right to exclude on the grounds of public policy or security

Although border controls are being reduced, Member States are still entitled to take such measures as are considered necessary for the purpose of combating terrorism, crime, the traffic of drugs and illicit trade in works of art. However, an expulsion decision may not be taken against an EU citizen if the citizen has resided in the host Member State for the previous ten years. In addition, no expulsion can be made of (a) a minor or (b) an EU citizen who has resided in the host Member State for the previous ten years unless there are imperative grounds of public security (Article 28(3) Directive 2004/38).

Persons excluded on the grounds of public security or public policy may apply for 'the lifting of an exclusion order after a reasonable period, depending on the circumstances, and in any event after 3 years from enforcement of the final exclusion order which has been validly adopted in accordance with EU law, by putting forward arguments to establish that there has been a material change in the circumstances which justified the decision ordering their exclusion' (Article 32(1)).

Figure 16.5 Article 45: worker.

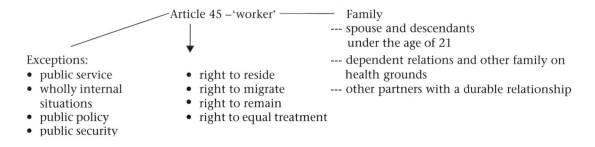

16.25 Free movement of persons: checkpoints

In this section we have looked at the free movement of persons. You should now be able to identify:

- the rights of workers and their families; and
- when a citizen's right of free movement might be restricted.

FREEDOM OF ESTABLISHMENT AND PROVISION OF SERVICES

16.26 Introduction

Articles 49 to 62 TFEU extend the freedom of movement of workers to include the free movement of a person who is self-employed to establish himself in another Member State or to provide services there. These rights do not just apply to a person but also extend to companies.

In this section we look at:

- freedom of establishment;

- freedom to provide services and its limitations; and
- freedom to receive services.

16.27 Freedom of establishment

Articles 49 to 54 TFEU cover the right of establishment. This means the right to 'set up shop' in another Member State either permanently or semi-permanently. Article 49 TFEU provides for the restrictions on establishment of a national in another Member State to be progressively abolished. It includes the right to take up and pursue self-employed activities and to set up and manage in other Member States undertakings, companies and firms and agencies, branches and subsidiaries under the conditions laid down by the law of the country where such establishment is effected. Equal treatment and principles of non-discrimination are therefore built into this freedom. Companies or firms are defined in Article 54 TFEU as 'companies or firms constituted under civil or commercial law, including cooperative societies, and other legal persons governed by public or private law, save for those which are non-profit-making'. Therefore, a UK company wishing to set itself up in Germany can do so provided it is properly constituted under UK law. If its main office is outside the EU it must have an effective link with a Member State.

16.28 Freedom to provide services

Articles 56 to 62 deal with the right to provide services such that restrictions on providing services are to be abolished. The 'right to provide services' means the provision of services by an individual in another Member State without residing there. For example, to provide mail order or internet services. It also includes the right of an individual to temporarily visit another Member State for the purpose of providing services in that Member State. Note there must be a cross-border element—wholly internal situations confined within one Member State are therefore not covered.

Services are defined as those 'normally provided for remuneration, in so far as they are not governed by the provisions relating to freedom of movement for goods, capital and persons'. This makes the freedom to provide services residual— it will only apply if the other free movement of goods or workers or if the freedom of establishment do not apply. Directive 2006/123 on Services in the Internal Market came into force in December 2009 and lays down general provisions relating to the provision of certain services (but note not the provision of all services). Under Article 4 of that Directive services must be provided for economic consideration.

16.29 Limitations

The freedom of establishment and the freedom to provide services are not absolute rights. Article 62 TFEU allows Member States to restrict those freedoms on the grounds of public policy, security, or health. However, following case law developed by the ECJ the Member States can only invoke such restrictions if they can justify them. The test for justification is whether the restriction on the freedom meets the so called 'imperative requirements' (sometimes called 'objective justification'). The restriction must:

(a) meet a legitimate public interest;

(b) be non-discriminatory and equally applicable to all EU nationals;

(c) proportionate; and

(d) not in breach of fundamental rights.

In addition, the freedoms do not apply to activities connected with the exercise of official authority in that Member State. 'Official authority' has a similar scope to 'public services' (see **16.24** above).

A further limitation is that the freedom of establishment and the freedom to provide services can only be exercised 'under the conditions laid down for its own nationals by the law of the country where such establishment is effected; or under the same conditions as are imposed by that state on its own nationals'. The problem for a non-national trying to establish himself or provide a service in another Member State is that he may not comply with the conditions laid down in that particular state for the practice of the particular trade or profession he wants to exercise. He may not be suitably qualified according to that Member State. The relevant conditions are those laid down by a trade or professional body relating to education, training and professional conduct. These vary from state to state and have proved to be a barrier.

16.29.1 Education and training

Article 53 TFEU envisaged a series of directives for the mutual recognition of qualifications from hairdressers to lawyers. Unfortunately, the issue of directives has proved to be a slow and difficult task. Since the rights of establishment and provision of services appeared to be conditional on the issuing of directives, it was thought those rights could not be invoked by individuals until the directives were issued. This point was tested in *Reyners v Belgium* (2/74) [1974] 2 CMLR 305. Mr Reyners was a Dutchman born, educated, and resident in Belgium. He was a doctor of Belgian law but was refused admission to the Belgian Bar because he was not a Belgian national. He claimed that this decision was in breach of what is now Article 49 TFEU. The Belgian government argued that Article 49 was not directly effective, it could not be relied on by an individual as against a Member State, because it depended on the issuing of directives under Article 53. The court held that the Article was in itself directly effective and that the provisions of Article 53 were complementary to Article 49 and not a necessary precondition. The same principle was applied in the context of services in *Van Binsbergen v Bestuur van de Bedrijfsvereniging voor de Metaalnijverheid* (33/74) [1974] ECR 1299. Here, Van Binsbergen, a Dutchman, qualified as an advocate in Holland. He had been living and working there but then moved to Belgium. He challenged a rule of the Dutch Bar that persons representing clients before certain tribunals must reside in the state in which that service is supplied. He argued that this rule was in breach of Articles 49 and 57. Again, no harmonising directives had been enacted. The court held he was entitled to rely on the Articles which were directly effective.

The harmonisation process has been extremely slow and, therefore, eventually the Commission approved Directive 2005/36 on the Recognition of Professional Qualifications which imposes a system for mutual recognition of qualifications. Three kinds of mutual recognition exist: qualified mutual recognition to professions (competence or aptitude tests may be required and the host Member States may require checks on the equivalence of the home qualifications); automatic mutual recognition for certain professions listed in an annexe to the directive based on a length of prior experience; and mutual recognition for certain sectors (mainly health) requiring evidence of the home qualification together with a minimum period of training.

16.29.2 Professional conduct

In addition to the rules governing training and education, there are also rules of professional conduct for certain professions. These can constitute barriers to the free movement of persons. In *Van Binsbergen*, it was acknowledged that professional rules of conduct relating to the legal profession do not infringe Articles 56 and 57 TFEU provided they do not discriminate against a non-national. In *Gullung v Conseils de l'ordre des advocats du barreau de Colmar et de Saverne* (292/86) [1988] ECR 111, a registration requirement with the German Bar for all barristers wishing to establish themselves in Germany was held to be permissible as such registration was required of its own nationals. However, there is still a problem for lawyers seeking to establish themselves in France. A law was passed in 1990 requiring foreign lawyers to become a member of a local Bar before being able to provide legal services even where French law does not require compulsory assistance of the lawyer. This would seem to contradict the directives for mutual recognition; however, it is still the intention in France that all lawyers must qualify under the French system. A foreign lawyer must present himself before an appropriate local Bar before he is free to practise. Directive 1998/5 (Practice of the profession of lawyers on a permanent basis) now gives EU lawyers a permanent right of establishment under their home title in another EU country.

16.30 Freedom to receive services

The freedom to provide services under Articles 56 and 57 has now been extended to receive services. In *Luisi & Carbone v Ministero del Tesoro* (286/82) [1984] ECR 377 which concerned a breach of Italian currency regulations, the court interpreted Article 56 to include the freedom for recipients of services to go to another state to receive that service there. Recipients were held to include tourists, persons receiving medical treatment and persons travelling for the purposes of education and business. This equality principle was developed in the case of *Cowan v French Treasury* (186/87) [1989] ECR 195. This concerned a British tourist who was the victim of a criminal assault while on holiday in Paris. His claim for compensation from the French Criminal Injuries Compensation Board was rejected as he was not a French national. On a reference under Article 267 TFEU the court held that he was entitled to receive compensation as a recipient of services. Compensation could not be denied on the ground of nationality. The principle of non-discrimination has been extended to access and funding for education and vocational training under the social advantages case law referred to above.

16.31 Freedom of establishment and provision of services: checkpoints

In this section we have looked at:

- the right to set up shop in another Member State;

- the right to provide services in or to another Member State even if you do not reside there and the limitations to this; and
- the right to receive services in another Member State.

You should now be able to identify the main criteria for freedom of establishment, freedom to receive and provide services and when such freedoms may be restricted.

COMPETITION LAW

16.32 Introduction

As has been seen, one of the main objectives of the EU is the creation of an internal market. Although competition may stimulate economic activity and provide freedom of choice, it can impede the freedom of businesses to trade between Member States. Where competition is not properly controlled, the markets may become divided. In this part of this section we will consider:

- anti-competitive practices (Article 101 TFEU);and
- abuse of a dominant position (Article 102 TFEU)).

To help you assess your learning, a number of checkpoint questions are asked at the end of the chapter.

16.33 Article 101 TFEU

Article 101(1) prohibits:

all agreements between undertakings, decisions by associations of undertakings, and concerted practices which may affect trade between Member States and which have as their object or effect the prevention, restriction or distortion of competition within the internal market.

Examples of agreements which fall within the prohibition in Article 101(1) are set out in the Article and include price fixing, limiting production or markets, and sharing sources of supply.

The wording of the Article needs to be considered more carefully. It is necessary to consider if there is:

(a) an agreement between undertakings

(b) which may affect trade between Member States, and

(c) which has as its object or effect the prevention, restriction, or distortion of competition.

16.33.1 Agreements between undertakings

16.33.1.1 Agreement

Although not defined in the TFEU, the word 'agreement' has been widely defined to include not only contracts but also formal and informal understandings and gentlemen's agreements whether written or oral. In *BMW Belgium v Commission* BMW's Belgian subsidiary attempted to prevent Belgian car dealers from selling cars to other

Member States. BMW Belgium issued a circular to the Belgian dealers asking them not to make such sales. The dealers were to signal their assent by returning a signed copy of the circular although it was made clear to them this would not constitute a contract. The ECJ decided this was an agreement under Article 101. The authorities will look at the intention of the parties when considering whether there is an agreement or not.

16.33.1.2 Undertakings

Again this is not defined in the TFEU but has been widely interpreted to include any entity engaged in economic or commercial activity regardless of its legal status or the way it is financed (*Höfner and Elser v Macrotron GmbH* (C-41/90) [1991] ECR I-1979). Examples of undertakings include companies, individuals, trade associations, state-owned corporations, public authorities engaged in commercial activities, transport organisations, and non-profit-making organisations.

Agreements between undertakings that form a single economic unit will not infringe Article 101(1) so an agreement between a parent company and a subsidiary will not amount to a decision between undertakings unless the subsidiary acts independently of the parent. Commission guidelines have made it clear that genuine agents will not be considered a separate undertaking from their principal and therefore agency agreements will generally fall outside Article 101(1). The Commission considers an agent to be a genuine agent unless the agent accepts a significant financial or commercial risk in carrying out its agency.

16.33.1.3 A decision by an association of undertakings

The most common association caught by Article 101(1) is a trade association but Article 101 can also extend to trade unions. Trade associations are often used for promotional campaigns or to set standards, etc. However, where an association coordinates its activities, for example, by standardising pricing or by imposing standards which are designed to exclude competitors, this may have an anti-competitive effect. For example, in 2010 the Commission fined the French Ordre National des Pharmaciens ("ONP") (the French professional body regulating pharmacists) for indirectly imposing minimum prices through its use of its disciplinary proceedings. The Commission found the ONP was an association caught by Article 101.

The decision of an association does not have to be binding. Recommendations from an association to its members may be sufficient to be in breach of Article 101(1).

16.33.1.4 Concerted practice

This occurs where there is coordinated action between businesses in the same sector which distorts competition in the market place, for example, raising prices at the same time or exchanging information on future price increases.

For example, in the *Banana Suppliers Cartel* it was found that four banana importers supplying leading brands of bananas into eight EU Member States regularly phoned each other over a three-year period sharing information about their proposed prices shortly before the weekly prices for bananas were announced by each of them. It was found that during those phone calls the importers would discuss with each other how they thought the price would develop and whether they proposed to increase, reduce, or maintain their prices. The Commission found the cartel had fixed prices (IP/08/1509). Parallel behaviour will amount to a concerted practice if it leads to competition which does not correspond to the normal conditions of the market.

16.33.2 Effect on trade between Member States

The agreement or concerted practice must affect intra-union trade or be capable of having such an effect. Therefore, an agreement which only affects the trade of countries outside the EU will not breach Article 101(1).

The test for intra-union effect was set out in *Société Technique Minière v Maschinenbau* (56/65) [1966] ECR 235:

> It must be possible to foresee with a sufficient degree of probability on the basis of a set of objective factors of law or fact that the agreement in question may have an influence, direct or indirect, actual or potential, on the pattern of trade between Member States.

Trade is a concept which covers not only the movement of goods and services and their prices but also the structure of the market and the parties competing within it. It is the pattern of that trade, ie where people can buy from or can sell or supply to and on what terms, which is considered.

vWhen the parties to an agreement are based in different Member States or the agreement relates to goods or services in several Member States a potential intra-union effect may be clear. However, an intra-union effect can occur even where the parties are based outside the EU provided the agreement or practice is implemented within the EU. The *Wood Pulp* cases [1985] 3 CMLR 474 concerned forestry practices in Finland, Sweden, and Canada which had an effect on the wood pulp prices in the EU. Similarly in the *LCP Panel* case 2010 (IP/10/1685) two Korean companies and four Taiwanese companies agreed prices and shared production information thereby preventing free competition in the market for flatscreens. The Commission found the majority of flatscreens used in the European computer, notebook and TV industry were supplied from Asia. The Commission fined the companies €648 million and the Competition Commissioner stated, "Foreign companies, like European ones, need to understand that if they want to do business in Europe they must play fair'.

Even agreements which relate to one Member State can contravene Article 101 if they have the effect of shutting off the national market from potential competitors from other Member States or if they reinforce the division of the internal market. An example of the latter was a scheme to fix the price of industrial and medical gases in the Netherlands. The scheme included price fixing and members agreeing not to deal with each other's customers for certain periods in the year. The potential effect on imports and exports of the gases to other Member States was evidence of an intra-union effect (*Industrial and Medical Gases* [2003] OJ L84/1).

Note that as long as the agreement *may* affect the pattern of interstate trade it is enough to satisfy the test of intra-union effect. It does not have to have an *actual* effect.

The Commission has issued guidelines on the effect of trade which set out the methodology to be used in deciding whether an agreement is capable of affecting trade between Member States.

16.33.3 The object or effect of preventing, restricting, or distorting competition

Having considered whether there is an agreement between undertakings which has an actual or potential intra-union effect, it is then necessary to decide if that agreement has the object or effect of preventing, restricting, or distorting competition.

European competition law takes a purposive approach and looks at the object of or effect any agreement has on competition rather than the form in which it is expressed. If an agreement distorts competition then, whether or not that was its intention, there will be a breach of the prohibition. If the object of the arrangement is not intended to restrict competition then a full market analysis of its actual effects will be required to establish whether or not it is anti-competitive.

Even if an agreement is likely to increase trade it may still be in breach of Article 101(1). This was considered in the important case of *Etablissements Consten SA v Commission* (56 and 58/64) [1966] ECR 299 where a German manufacturer (Grundig) appointed a sole distributor (Consten) for France who was granted exclusive use of the Grundig trademark in France. Consten brought a trademark action to prevent the resale in France of Grundig products bought by a French company in Germany. Consten and Grundig argued that the effect of Consten's appointment as distributor was to increase trade not to reduce it. The ECJ upheld the Commission's view that the agreement breached Article 101 as it had been used to divide the market and to prevent parallel trade.

16.33.4 Agreements likely to breach Article 101

When considering Article 101 it is necessary to assess what type of agreement is being dealt with. Both vertical agreements and horizontal agreements potentially fall foul of Article 101(1).

A vertical agreement is an agreement between undertakings which operate at different levels of the production or distribution chain, for example, an agreement between a manufacturer and a distributor or a distributor and a retailer. Examples include distribution, supply, franchise, and purchase agreements. Very often such agreements will include provisions which breach Article 101(1) in order to make the agreements commercially viable, for example, exclusive customer groups, geographic territories, or exclusive supply, or purchase obligations.

A horizontal agreement is an agreement between undertakings that are at the same level in the production or distribution chain, for example, an agreement between one manufacturer and another or between a number of retailers. Examples include research and development agreements, specialisation agreements, and information sharing agreements. Such agreements often include provisions in breach of Article 101(1) to make them commercially viable, for example, agreements to share markets, fix trading conditions, or joint buying and selling arrangements.

Generally, the Commission and the ECJ have looked more favourably on vertical agreements recognising that their pro-competitive effects outweigh the effects of the provisions in breach of Article 101(1).

16.33.5 De minimis Notice

Only agreements which affect competition to an appreciable extent will fall foul of the prohibition in Article 101(1) even if they intend to restrict competition. The Commission has issued a Notice on Agreements of Minor Importance which provides that certain agreements will not breach Article 101(1) provided:

(a) the undertakings' combined market share must not exceed 10 per cent for horizontal agreements or 15 per cent for vertical agreements. If in doubt as to the category of the agreement the 10 per cent threshold applies;

(b) the thresholds in (a) above are reduced to 5 per cent in the case of parallel networks of agreements affecting more than 30 per cent of the relevant market in the EU; and

(c) certain so called 'hard-core' restrictions such as price fixing are not contained in the agreements. These hard core restrictions mirror those imposed in the relevant block exemptions for vertical and horizontal agreements (see **3.34.2** below).

The Notice also makes it clear that agreements between small and medium-sized enterprises are rarely capable of appreciably affecting trade between Member States. SMEs are defined as undertakings with fewer than 250 employees and either an annual turnover of less than 50 million euro, or an annual balance sheet value of 43 million euro or less. Further helpful guidance on appreciability is included in the Commission's guidelines on the effect of trade.

16.33.6 Sanctions for breach of Article 101

Any agreement which is in breach of Article 101(1) is void by Article 101(2) and therefore unenforceable. The competition authorities can impose fines of up to 10 per cent of the annual turnover of the relevant undertakings. Lastly, aggrieved third parties who are adversely affected by the anti-competitive behaviour can bring proceedings against the undertakings to prevent the behaviour and/or to claim damages. A parent company can be liable to fines for the anti-competitive behaviour of its subsidiary even if it is not itself a party to those activities (see for example *Akzo Nobel* (C97/08)).

The Commission is taking an increasingly hard line with the fines that it issues. The most recent guidance on the level of fines (OJ 2006/C 298/11) increases the fines the Commission can impose for breaches of Article 101. In addition, the Commission is keen to encourage aggrieved third parties to bring actions for damages for breach of competition rules. It has adopted a white paper proposing changes to the civil laws of Member States which it hopes will permit such cases to be more easily brought before the national courts.

The power to fine heavily is used widely by the competition authorities. In 2008 the Commission imposed the highest cartel fines it has ever imposed when it fined four companies 1.3 billion euros for their part in a cartel sharing information and markets in the car glass market (IP/08/1685). The largest individual fine on a company of 896 million euros was also imposed in that case. In commenting on the fines issued in this case the then Competition Commissioner said, 'Management and shareholders of companies that damage consumers and European industry by running cartels must learn their lessons the hard way—if you cheat, you will get a heavy fine.'

To discourage cartels that fix prices, restrict supply and/or share markets illegally, the Commission has adopted a leniency policy encouraging 'whistle-blowing' and cooperation with the competition authorities. This abolishes or reduces liability to fines on a decreasing basis depending on whether a cartel member first notified the Commission of the cartel and the order in which cartel members began to cooperate with the Commission. Most national competition authorities have adopted similar leniency schemes. The Commission has also introduced a settlement procedure for cartels which will allow the early settlement of cartel cases when companies admit their involvement and liability in a cartel (Regulation 622/2008 and Commission Notice OJ C167, 02.07.08). In return for simplifying the conviction procedure and speeding up the decision process, cartel members will benefit from a further reduction in their fine.

16.34 Exemptions to Article 101(1)

As the scope of the prohibition in Article 101(1) is so wide it can catch many commercial agreements thereby making them unenforceable and the parties potentially liable to fines. However, the TFEU recognises that the pro-competitive effects of some agreements outweigh their anti-competitive effect. It provides, in Article 101(3), that exemptions to the prohibition can be granted if the four conditions in the Article are met:

(a) the agreement must contribute to improving the production or distribution of goods or to promoting technical or economic progress;

(b) the agreement must allow consumers a fair share of the resulting benefit;

(c) there must be no unnecessary restrictions; and

(d) there must be no elimination of competition.

To give certainty to parties to commercial agreements, it is necessary to ensure the agreements do not breach Article 101(1) or that an exemption under Article 101(3) is available.

16.34.1 The exemption scheme

Under a modernised exemption scheme introduced in 2004 the responsibility for ensuring an exception under Article 101(3) rests with the undertakings concerned. Under this system Article 101(3) is directly applicable and undertakings can assume they are exempt from Article 101(1) if the conditions in Article 101(3) are met. Businesses, and their advisers, must decide for themselves whether an agreement and its restrictions have an anti-competitive effect on the market having regard to any relevant block exemptions (see **3.34.2** below), notices, guidelines and competition case law. If businesses are concerned they are not within Article 101(3) they can either rely on a block exemption or seek an individual exemption from national competition authorities (see **16.34.3** below).

The Commission is not, generally, involved in applications for individual exemptions. Its primary role is to focus on investigating severe violations of competition law; to oversee a system of cooperation between the national competition authorities; and to provide guidance to businesses and competition authorities on the application of competition law. The notice on effect on trade and the notice on the application of Article 101(3) are examples of such guidance. The Commission has also indicated that it will provide guidance letters to companies on novel questions arising under Article 101.

16.34.2 Block exemptions

Block exemptions provide certainty to businesses and competition authorities that certain types of agreement are within Article 101(3) and are designed to reduce the number of applications which would otherwise need to be made for individual exemptions. They take the form of regulations issued for certain types of agreement considered to be generally beneficial rather than anti-competitive. Where an agreement falls within a block exemption, an undertaking need not apply for individual exemption.

Block exemptions are issued by the Commission. In the past, the Commission adopted a formulistic and regulatory approach to the drafting of block exemptions which prescribed the form agreements could take, the restrictions which could be included, and the restrictions which were prohibited. The Commission has moved away from the prescriptive approach to an economics-based approach, which uses market effect and, in particular, market share as the criteria for intervention.

The block exemptions on vertical agreements and horizontal agreements are examples of this approach. In these exemptions, certain agreements falling below specified market share thresholds are presumed to fall within Article 101(3) provided certain prohibited restrictions are not included. Above the relevant market share thresholds, such agreements are not covered by the relevant block exemption, but they are not necessarily presumed illegal under Article 101(1). Instead the parties have to assess the negative and positive effect of such agreements on competition within the relevant market.

Guidelines to accompany the market-based block exemptions have been issued by the Commission. They provide guidance as to whether or not to notify agreements falling outside the block exemptions to the national authorities for individual exemption. Some also consider the application and interpretation of the block exemptions themselves.

It should be noted that specific rules still apply to certain sectors; for example, the insurance and motor vehicle sectors. It should also be remembered that the benefit of a block exemption may be withdrawn from an agreement falling within it if the authorities consider that the agreement has, on balance, an anti-competitive effect.

As market share is becoming increasingly important to block exemptions, it is necessary to be able to correctly identify relevant markets. This is considered in more detail in **16.36.1.1** below.

The detailed terms of the Commission's block exemptions are beyond the scope of this book.

16.34.3 Individual exemptions

As has been stated above, if no block exemption applies and the parties are unsure as to whether or not they fall within the exemption in Article 101(3) they can apply to the relevant national competition authorities for an individual exemption. These may be granted for specific periods, conditions may be attached and the exemption may be renewed or revoked. Some of the national authorities will issue informal, non-binding, 'comfort letters' or written opinions as to whether or not the agreement does or does not infringe Article 101 or does or does not benefit from the exemption in Article 101(3).

16.35 Article 101: Flow chart

The flow chart opposite sets out the questions to ask to decide whether or not anticompetitive agreements have been entered into in breach of Article 101 and whether the benefit of notices or exemptions can be claimed to avoid sanctions.

16.36 Article 102 TFEU

Article 102 regulates the activities of undertakings in a dominant position. It provides that:

Any abuse by one or more undertakings of a dominant position within the internal market or in a substantial part of it shall be prohibited as incompatible with the internal market in so far as it may affect trade between Member States.

An example of such abuse would be directly or indirectly imposing unfair purchase or selling prices or other unfair trading conditions. As with Article 101, it is important to consider the wording carefully, as for a breach of Article 102 three elements must be established. These are as follows:

(a) a dominant position;

(b) an abuse of that position; and

(c) the abuse must affect trade between Member States.

The Commission has recently published guidance on how it uses an effects-based approach to decide whether to pursue breaches of Article 102.

16.36.1 Definition of dominant position

A dominant position was defined in *United Brands v Commission* (27/78) [1978] ECR 207 as 'a position of economic strength enjoyed by an undertaking which enables it to hinder the maintenance of effective competition on the relevant market by allowing it to behave to an appreciable extent independently of its competitors and customers and ultimately of consumers'.

The question of whether an undertaking holds a dominant position needs to be considered in the context of the relevant market for the goods or services in question. It is only when the relevant market has been correctly defined that it can be established whether or not an undertaking has a dominant position in that market. The Commission has issued a notice on the definition of the relevant market for the purposes of competition law which provides useful guidance on defining the relevant market.

16.36.1.1 Relevant market

The Commission's notice makes it clear that it is necessary to define the relevant product and geographic market. The relevant product market is determined by reference to the product in question and the goods or services which are interchangeable or substitutable for them by reason of their characteristics, price, and intended use. There are two kinds of product substitution: demand-side substitution and supply-side substitution. Demand-side substitution is the extent to which a consumer can obtain alternative goods. Supply-side substitution is the extent and ease with which other undertakings can supply alternative goods in competition with the undertaking in a dominant position.

In the *United Brands* case the Commission decided the relevant product market in question was bananas and not the fruit market and that United Brands had abused a dominant position within that market. At the time of the case, United Brands was a conglomerate which handled 40 per cent of the EU trade in bananas. United Brands had argued that it did not enjoy a dominant position in the fruit market and this was the proper context for examining its position. The Commission disagreed and contended that there is a demand for bananas which is separate from the demand for other fresh fruit. The consumer buys bananas specifically for their nutritional and other qualities and would not readily accept other fresh fruit as a substitute. In particular, bananas cannot be easily substituted for other fruit due to their suitability for the young and elderly. Therefore, the Commission found the market to be bananas and not fresh fruit generally. The ECJ upheld the Commission's position.

The relevant product market can sometimes be quite small. In *Hugin Kassaregister AB v Commission* (22/78) [1979] ECR 1869, Hugin was held to be in breach of Article 102 as it refused to supply spare parts for independent repair of cash registers. The Commission defined the relevant product market as consisting of spare parts for Hugin machines for which Hugin was the sole supplier. This was upheld by the ECJ despite arguments from Hugin that such a definition was too narrow.

It is also necessary to consider the relevant geographic market. The geographic market will be influenced by factors such as costs and feasibility of transport and consumer preferences. It extends to the area within which consumers are likely to search for alternatives.

Figure 16.6 Article 101 Flow chart.

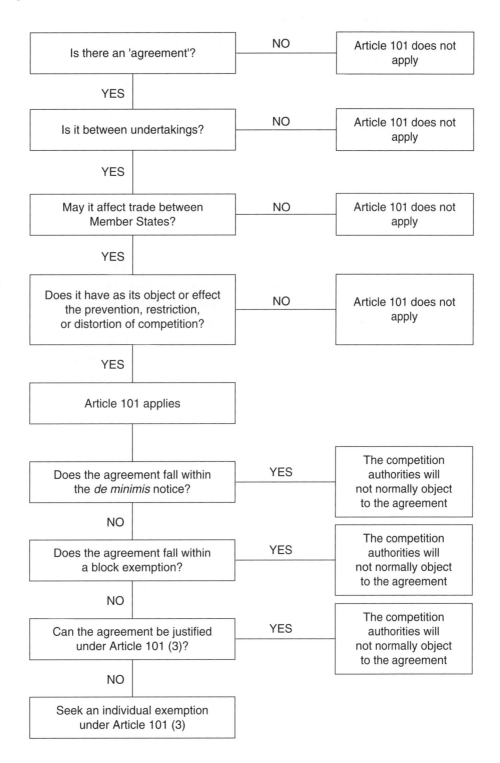

16.36.1.2 Dominant position

Once the relevant market has been determined it is necessary to establish whether the undertaking has a dominant position within that market. To help decide whether the undertaking holds a dominant position, a number of factors will be considered:

(a) market share of undertaking;

(b) market share of competitors;

(c) future actual or potential competition;

(d) financial and technical resource;

(e) control of production and distribution;

(f) conduct and performance; and

(g) strength of customers' bargaining position.

Market share is a useful indication (but only a first indication) as to whether or not an undertaking is likely to have a dominant position. In its guidance on Article 102 the Commission has indicated undertakings having a market share of less than 40 per cent of the relevant market are unlikely to have a dominant position.

16.36.2 Abuse of a dominant position

It is acceptable to hold a dominant position but not to abuse it. In doing so the Commission looks at the actual effect of the behaviour in the market rather than presuming certain types of behaviour are likely to be abusive. This is because in different markets with different trading conditions the same behaviour may have very different results. Once the Commission has established evidence of negative effects, the undertaking accused of abuse can defend itself if it can show either its conduct is objectively necessary or that the conduct creates efficiencies which, overall, benefit the consumer. In both cases the undertaking would have to show its behaviour is proportionate.

Examples of abuse of a dominant position have been held to include the following:

(a) unfair prices: where, on the facts, the price bears no relation to the economic value of the product or service, whether excessively high or low;

(b) discriminatory prices, where different customers are charged different prices without objective justification;

(c) refusal to supply: in *United Brands*, the undertaking had refused to supply a previous customer which had participated in an advertising campaign for a rival undertaking; or

(d) tying practices: obliging customers to take ancillary products for no objectively justifiable reason, to discourage customers from taking competitors' products.

In *Intel* (IP/09/745) the Commission found that Intel had abused its dominant position in computer chips in two ways. Firstly by hidden rebate payments requiring customers to buy all or a substantial part of their stock of chips from Intel and not its competitors. Secondly, by making payments to certain computer manufacturers to halt or delay the introduction of certain computers using chips supplied by an Intel competitor. The Commission fined Intel 1.06 billion euros.

16.36.3 Affecting trade between Member States

This phrase has the same meaning as for Article 101 such that the effect of the abuse would be to partition the markets in the EU.

16.36.4 Merger control

Abuse of dominant position under Article 102 will extend to mergers which eliminate competition. Some undertakings have attempted to reinforce their position by having, for example, tying agreements between an undertaking and its subsidiary. Although this may not constitute a breach of Article 101, it may constitute a breach of Article 102 if it has the effect of driving competition from the market. In addition, a merger between two or more undertakings which brings them under common control may amount to a breach of Article 102.

Regulations exist that empower the Commission to investigate mergers considered to have an EU dimension. The EU's merger regime is complicated. A more detailed consideration of it is beyond the scope of this book.

16.36.5 Exemptions and sanctions

Lastly, there are no exceptions to Article 102 equivalent to those under Article 101. The sanctions for breach of Article 102 are similar to those for breach of Article 101. The Commission can impose fines and aggrieved third parties can claim damages and/or seek injunctive relief.

Just as in Article 101 the Commission does use its powers to fine widely. In *Microsoft* (IP/04/382) the Commission found the computer company had abused its dominant position in the PC market in two ways: first by bundling its Windows Media Player with its Windows package thereby restricting competition from other media players and secondly, by restricting access to technical information to prevent the development of non-Microsoft equipment that worked with Windows PCs. The Commission fined the computer company 492.7 million euros and ordered Microsoft to disclose the relevant interface information and to offer a version of its Windows PC software without its Windows Media Player. In 2008 Microsoft was fined a further 899 million euros for failing to properly comply with the ruling.

16.36.6 Article 102: Flow chart

The flow chart overleaf sets out the questions to be asked to decide whether or not a business has a dominant position and whether it has abused that position in breach of Article 102 (remember, no exemptions can be claimed to avoid sanctions for breach of this Article).

16.37 Competition law: checkpoints

You should now be able to:

- describe the prohibition in Article 101 (16.33);
- identify the questions to be considered to decide if an agreement is in breach of Article 101 (16.33.1–16.33.3);
- give examples of anti-competitive agreements in breach of Article 101 (16.33);
- explain the various exemptions from Article 101 that are available and how they may be obtained (16.34);
- describe the prohibition in Article 102 (16.36);
- identify the questions to be considered to decide if a business is in breach of Article 102 (16.36.1 to 16.36.3);
- give examples of abuses of a dominant position (16.36.2); and
- list the sanctions and remedies available for breach of Article 101 and 102 (16.33.6 and 16.36.5).

Figure 16.7 Article 102 Flow chart.

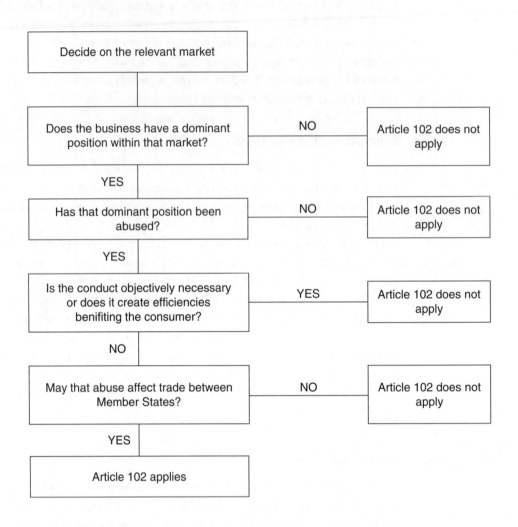

16.38 UK competition law

In private practice you are most likely to come across anti-competitive agreements and abuses of dominant position within the context of UK competition law rather than EU competition law. By way of background information only, there follows a short overview of UK competition law.

16.38.1 The prohibitions

Following the introduction of the Competition Act 1998, UK and European competition law is now largely similar. Section 2 of the Competition Act sets out what is known as the 'Chapter I prohibition' which is the English equivalent to Article 101—anti-competitive agreements. Section 18 of the Competition Act sets out what is known as the 'Chapter II prohibition' which is the English equivalent to Article 102. The wording of the sections is similar to the wording of Articles 101 and 102.

The Competition Act and the policies surrounding it are modelled on the EU system. The courts and the UK competition authorities are required to interpret the Act in a way that it is consistent with the policies adopted by the European courts and the Commission. Various notices and guidance have been issued by the Office of Fair Trading (OFT, which currently enforces the Act) which adopt similar principles to those enshrined in notices and guidance issued by the Commission. For example as with Article 101, exemptions are available from the Chapter 1 prohibition, the OFT has adopted appreciability tests that are similar to the *de minimis* principles and a leniency policy has been adopted when fining members of the cartel. In addition many of the notices issued by the OFT refer to EU competition cases and use them by way of precedent.

16.38.2 Which competition regime (UK or European) applies when?

The Competition Act is only concerned with behaviour which affects trade 'within the United Kingdom'. The Act applies when anti-competitive behaviour affects trade only in the UK, or a part of it. That part can be quite small. For example the OFT has investigated taxi firms for price fixing in certain towns in Lancashire, bus companies for creating supply monopolies for specific bus routes in Leeds and bus companies in Cardiff for eliminating a new 'no frills' bus service provider.

The European competition regime applies when there is or may be a cross-border effect on trade between Member States, so clearly, an agreement which only affects mainland Europe would be covered by the EU regime and not by the Act. Agreements which affect trade between the UK and another part of the Union would be caught by the EU regime. It follows that agreements/practices which have an effect or a potential effect internal to the UK *only* and which do not prevent others from entering the UK market are covered by the UK regime.

16.38.3 Differences

While the UK competition regime is very similar to the EU regime there are important differences in the detail of the various statutory provisions, notices and guidance. You will need to familiarise yourself with the provisions of the relevant Acts and the detail of the relevant notices and guidance etc if you come across UK competition law. Copies of the notices and guidance documents can be obtained from the OFT and are available to download from its website.

The remedies for entering into an anti-competitive agreement or abusing a dominant position are largely similar in UK law to the EU regime but there are two differences of particular importance.

16.38.3.1 Limited immunity

As with EU law, the OFT has a range of remedies available to it including fining companies up to 10 per cent of their worldwide turnover. However, to avoid the financial penalties being unduly burdensome on small companies, limited immunity from fines has been granted in certain circumstances. The immunity is in addition to the appreciability principle which applies in the UK competition regime. You may need to familiarise yourself with the detail of the immunity in private practice.

16.38.3.2 Criminal offences for cartel arrangements

The other main difference is that certain criminal offences have been introduced by the Enterprise Act 2002. Under these provisions any person who dishonestly agrees with other persons that two or more undertakings be involved in prohibited cartel arrangements is guilty of an offence. They may be liable to fines and/or imprisonment.

'Prohibited cartel arrangements' covers only horizontal agreements (see **16.33.4** above) and only certain anti-competitive practices—not all Chapter 1 prohibition behaviour. It covers price fixing, bid rigging, market sharing, and limitation of production or supply whether in domestic or international cartels. Powers of investigation are wide. The first ever convictions for cartel offences were obtained in September 2008 when three UK businessmen were imprisoned for between two and a half to three years for their involvement in an international cartel sharing markets and fixing prices for marine hose (used for transporting oil between oil tankers and storage facilities).

There are no equivalent criminal sanctions for breach of Article 101.

16.39 The EU and fundamental rights

16.39.1 Pre-Maastricht

Over time individuals began to use fundamental rights to challenge the acts of EU institutions and Member States: in particular, to use human rights to challenge Member States' efforts to restrict the freedoms you have considered in this chapter. In doing so they often referred to rights under the European Convention on Human Rights and Fundamental Freedoms (ECHR), which was drawn up under the direction of the Council of Europe in 1950. It came into force in 1953 before the Treaty of Rome. However, although the convention pre-dates the EU, the EU treaties as originally drawn did not refer to any such rights. Instead the ECJ began to allow people to assert such rights as general principles of law to follow when interpreting and applying EU law. Similarly it began to recognise rights conferred by the national constitutions of the Member States.

This new doctrine was announced in *Stauder v City of Ulm* (26/69) [1969] ECR 419, which concerned an EU scheme to provide cheap butter for recipients of war benefits. Herr Stauder received war victim benefits and therefore was entitled to cheap butter. He had to provide a coupon with his name and address on which he felt to be humiliating and a violation of fundamental human rights and that therefore the EU decision requiring this was invalid. The court held that this measure did not require the production of a person's name and address: 'Interpreted in this way the provision at issue contains nothing capable of prejudicing the fundamental human rights enshrined in the general principles of EU law and protected by the Court'. This judgment recognised that fundamental human rights are a general principle of EU law.

In *Internationale Handelsgesellschaft* (11/70) [1970] ECR 1125, the court went one step further, such that the concept of human rights applied by the court, while deriving its validity solely from EU law is, nevertheless, 'inspired' by national constitutional traditions. *Nold (J) KG v Commission* (4/73) [1974] ECR 491 concerned a decision under ECSC which provided that coal wholesalers could not buy German Ruhr coal direct from the selling agency unless they purchased a certain minimum quantity. Herr Nold could not do this and claimed the decision was a violation of human rights and deprived him of a property right and partly infringed his right to the free pursuit of an economic activity. The court recognised these rights but said they were subject to limitations:

(a) An EU measure in conflict with fundamental rights as expressed in the constitutions of Member States will be annulled.

(b) International treaties can supply guidelines which should be followed within the framework of EU law.

16.39.2 Maastricht

The position was regularised, to a certain extent, by the Treaty of Maastricht 1991. It inserted into the then TEU a principle that the EU 'should respect fundamental rights as guaranteed by the ECHR and as they result from the constitutional traditions common to the Member States as general principles of EU law'. This made the ECHR and national constitutional rights influential 'soft law' for the courts and Member States to take into account.

Not only has the Court found individuals can use their fundamental rights to challenge restriction on their freedoms but also Member States can use fundamental rights to justify restrictions they impose on the freedoms; for example, in *Omega Spielhallen* (C-36/02) [2004] ECR 1-9609 Germany used its constitutional tradition of 'human dignity' to prevent a laser company from establishing a laser game business in Germany that simulated murdering people.

16.39.3 The position post Lisbon

The amended TEU, as provided for by the Treaty of Lisbon, takes the recognition of fundamental rights further. It repeats that rights under the ECHR and national constitutions are general principles of law to be observed. In addition, it also states that the Union will accede to the ECHR although 'such accession shall not affect the Union's competences'. The effect of the accession on the Union, the EU institutions and the Member States is complex and not yet fully clear.

The amended TEU not only recognises the ECHR as a general principle but it also refers to the Charter of Fundamental Rights of the EU which was adopted by the Commission in 2000. This is distinct from the ECHR and not to be confused with it.

For a discussion of the European Convention and the Human Rights Act 1998, see **Chapter17**.

FURTHER INFORMATION

16.40 Bibliography and further reading

Chalmers, Damian, Davies, Gareth and Monti, Giorgi, *European Union Law* (2010) Cambridge University Press.

Craig, Paul and De Búrca, Gráinne, *EU Law Text Cases and Materials,* (2008) Oxford University Press.
Jones, Alison and Sufrin, Brenda, *EC Competition Law: Text, Cases and Materials* (2004) Oxford University Press.
Steiner, Jo, Woods, Lorna, and Twigg-Flesner, Christian, *EU Law* (2009) Oxford University Press.
Whish, Richard *Competition Law* (2009) Oxford University Press.

 Visit the Online Resource Centre for more information and useful weblinks.
www.oxfordtextbooks.co.uk/orc/foundations11_12/

Human rights

17

Human rights

17.1 Introduction

This chapter aims to provide an introduction to the following:

- the Convention and the Human Rights Act 1998, taking into account the origins of the Convention and the Human Rights Act 1998 and its incorporation into UK legislation;
- general principles of European jurisprudence;
- the Articles and the Protocols themselves; and
- areas where potential breaches may occur.

When the Human Rights Act came into force on 2 October 2000 there was much anticipation and speculation on its potential ramifications. All areas of law were affected by the incorporation—in particular the areas of criminal, family and employment law. All courts from the lowest to the high were required to have a thorough working knowledge of the contents of the Articles and Protocols and their application. The profession needed to do more than just have an understanding of the contents of the Convention, as European case law played, and still plays, a significant part in the application of the Convention. In order to interpret and apply case law effectively lawyers and courts alike needed to have a grasp of the European jurisprudence that was current when the European Court came to a decision.

Eight years on from its incorporation into UK legislation, the political climate is substantially changed and differing forces now come to bear upon the view that is taken of the human rights legislation. The growth of terrorism and the public outcry at the mismanagement over the release from prison of foreign criminals who should have been considered for deportation have shifted the balance towards issues of security and the protection of the public as opposed to the protection of individuals seeking to uphold their specific human rights.

Consequently there have been calls from all sides for the Human Rights Act to be reviewed or even dispensed with altogether. This would inevitably mean a review of the approach of the judiciary in interpreting convention rights in the light of UK legislation. There is now a wealth of case law in relation to many of the Articles which would now be reviewed. However, as a foundations manual, this chapter simply seeks to provide an overview of the Articles themselves with relevant case law highlighted where appropriate. Readers need to view this chapter in the light of the potential review of the Act and perhaps the possible ramifications that dispensing with the legislation altogether may bring.

For the present, however, the Act remains an integral part of the judicial make up of the UK and what is clear is that not only can legislative provisions be challenged, but also the way in which they have been applied. Practitioners should be clear about whether they are arguing that the law is incompatible, and therefore attempting to invoke ss 3 or 4 of the Act, or whether they are arguing that the relevant law itself is compatible but the way in which it has been applied violates the defendant's rights under the Convention.

17.2 General principles

17.2.1 The Human Rights Act 1998

The Human Rights Act 1998 has made the Convention central to the practice of law in the United Kingdom.

Section 2(1) of the Act requires all courts and tribunals to take into account the Convention and decisions by the institutions of the Convention, whether the European Court of Human Rights, the Commission of Human Rights, or the Council.

The Act creates a general statutory requirement that all legislation (past or present) be read and given effect in a way which is compatible with the Convention. It does this by providing, in s 3, that all legislation, primary and secondary, whenever enacted, must be read and given effect in a way which is compatible with Convention rights wherever possible.

Section 6(1) and (3) require public authorities to act in compliance with the Convention unless they are prevented from doing so by statute. This means that the courts have their own primary duty to give effect to the Convention unless a statute positively prevents this. It would therefore be unlawful for public authorities to act in a way which is incompatible with a Convention right. Courts themselves are included in the definition of public authorities.

It is generally perceived that it is only the actual decision of a court in a criminal or civil case that is subject to the right of appeal. This is true, but under the 1998 Act it is not just the decision of a court that is open to challenge but the way in which the courts actually function. For example, the administrative element of the Magistrates' Court Service or clerks who are exercising judicial functions conveyed upon them by national legislation are open to challenge. Clearly the management of the court itself by the Chief Executive and the Magistrates' Courts Committee has a direct effect upon the public and public funds and those decision-making processes are also open to scrutiny. As a result, any court, committee or individual must act compatibly with the Convention both in the decisions that it comes to and the process that it uses.

All courts and tribunals must have a working knowledge of the content of the Convention and the relevant case law to any given Article in order to be able to apply it correctly in accordance with UK legislation. To apply the decisions of cases brought down by Strasbourg, the courts and tribunals need to understand how decisions at Strasbourg are actually reached, so as to give the appropriate weight to any decision. In order to be able to effectively interpret Convention legislation and case law, the courts must understand the 'European jurisprudence' that exists when the judges come to a decision in Strasbourg.

17.3 European and international doctrines

A common misconception about the rights conveyed by the Convention is that if there is a breach by a public authority or Member State, the acts of that authority or Member State must be amended to bring them within the Convention. This is too draconian and would throw national law and procedures into a state of confusion. Although rights are conveyed to individuals, the rights contained within the Articles are rarely absolute and can be limited or qualified. The majority of rights are subject to limitations and qualifications; however, the right to freedom from torture is an absolute right and an act of torture could never be justified by acting in the interests of the state.

17.3.1 Limited rights

Some of the rights conveyed under the Articles of the Convention have limitations placed upon them so that in some circumstances an infringement of a guaranteed right does not amount to an infringement. For example, Article 2 contains the right to life. This right is limited by Article 2(2) which allows the use of force, but the amount used cannot be more than is absolutely necessary in the defence of a person from unlawful violence, to prevent escape from lawful detention, or to effect an arrest or quell a riot or insurrection. See the case of *McCann v United Kingdom* (1995) 21 EHRR 97, where suspected terrorists were shot dead in Gibraltar by British security agents. The Court held that there had been a breach of Article 2 as the state had failed to give adequate training or instructions to agents likely to use lethal force. This failure to plan and control was the central issue in deciding whether the force used had been absolutely necessary.

Article 2 is wider in its application than simply the right to life however. *Amin v Secretary of State for the Home Department* [2003] UKHL 51 which, in citing *Osman v UK* [1998] 29 EHRR 245 confirmed the primary purpose of Article 2 involved substantive obligations—the protection and safeguarding of life—and procedural aspects, namely, the 'minimum requirements of a mechanism, whereby the circumstances of a deprivation of life by the agents of a state may receive public and independent scrutiny'. Not only should there be an effective investigation where there had been a death where agents of the state were directly responsible for the death, but also where the system itself permits or fails to prevent a death ie in cases where there had been a life-threatening injury. This approach was confirmed in *R(D) v Secretary of State for the Home Department* [2006] 3 All ER 946 CA; [2005] UKHRR 917 where it was held that there was a duty to carry out an Article 2 investigation where there had been an attempted suicide by a prisoner. More recently the case of *Van Colle v Chief Constable of Hertfordshire* [2008] UKHL 50 confirmed that the test laid down in Osman was invariable and was not intended to impose a fluctuating standard to be applied on a case by case basis.

17.3.2 Qualified rights

Some Articles contain qualified rights, and as such the Convention permits them to be infringed in certain circumstances.

Once a victim has been shown to have established a primary right, the Convention seeks to balance the rights of the individual against other public rights. However, rights such as the right to respect for private life and the right to freedom of expression may sometimes compete with one another. Equally, some rights may be in direct conflict with public interest considerations. These sorts of rights, which impinge on the rights and freedoms of others, are necessarily qualified, and the Convention permits them to be limited by the state.

17.3.3 How far can a state limit the rights contained within the Convention?

The Convention permits these limitations only where they are:

(a) prescribed by law;

(b) intended to achieve a legitimate objective; and

(c) necessary in a democratic society (that is, proportionate to the ends to be achieved).

For example, Article 8 states that, 'Everyone has the right to respect for his private and family life, his home and his correspondence'. This is a presumed right, but a number of limitations and exceptions to it are set out in Article 8(2):

There shall be no interference by a public authority with the exercise of this right except such as is in accordance with the law and is necessary in a democratic society in the interests of national security, public safety or the economic well-being of the country, for the prevention of disorder or crime, for the protection of health or morals, or for the protection of the rights and freedoms of others.

The precise terms of the limitations in respect of the Articles vary but the judicial method for considering them is the same:

(a) Is the interference prescribed by law?

(b) Does it serve a legitimate objective?

(c) Is it necessary in a democratic society?

17.3.3.1 Is the interference prescribed by law?—The rule of law

No interference with a right protected under the Convention is permissible unless the citizen knows the basis for the interference because it is set out in ascertainable law. In the absence of any such detailed authorisation by the law, any interference, however justified, will violate the Convention—see *Malone v United Kingdom* (1984) 7 EHRR 14 where the applicant's telephone was tapped by the police. When this took place the only authorisation was an internal code of guidance produced by the police which was not available to the public. The European Court took the view that Mr Malone was unable to assess whether or not his telephone would be listened to, or what the basis in law for the surveillance might be. The common law position was inadequate, as could be seen from his failure in the High Court. The interference violated the Convention because it was not prescribed by law.

17.3.3.2 Does it serve a legitimate objective?

Legitimate objectives are:

(a) the interests of public safety;

(b) national security;

(c) the protection of health and morals; and

(d) the economic well-being of the country, or the protection of the rights and freedoms of others.

17.3.3.3 Is it necessary in a democratic society?—Proportionality

The Convention's approach is to decide whether a particular limitation from a right is justified in the sense of being 'proportionate to the legitimate aim pursued'.

This means that even if a policy which interferes with a Convention right might be aimed at securing a legitimate social policy, for example, the prevention of crime, this will not in itself justify the violation if the means adopted to secure the aim are excessive in the circumstances. *Soering v United Kingdom* (1989) 11 EHRR 439 stated:

> inherent in the whole of the Convention is a search for the fair balance between the demands of the general interest of the Community and the requirements of the protection of the individual's human rights. (para 89)

17.3.4 The margin of appreciation

A state is allowed a certain freedom to evaluate its public policy decisions, but this is subject to review by the Strasbourg institutions. The court has to ensure that the Member State's own political and cultural traditions are respected. When determining whether a social policy aim is legitimate therefore, or whether the means adopted to achieve it are 'necessary in a democratic society', the Commission and the Court have recognised limits as to their own competence to judge the issue. They have done this by giving the state a so called 'margin of appreciation' when assessing the extent to which a signatory has violated the Convention.

The most notable case in this area is *Handyside v United Kingdom* (1976) 1 EHRR 737. This case arose because of the intention to publish *The Little Red Schoolbook*, intended for children, but which included a chapter on sex. The books were seized by the police under the Obscene Publications Act 1959 and a forfeiture order obtained against the publishers. The publishers claimed a breach of their right to freedom of expression under Article 10.

Was the seizing of the books proportionate to the legitimate aim that the state sought to protect? The Court recognised that there was a margin of appreciation in this case which justified the interference with Article 10. It stated:

> By reason of their direct and continuous contact with the vital forces of their countries, state authorities are in principle in a better position than the international judge to give an opinion on the exact nature of these requirements as well as on the necessity of a restriction or penalty intended to meet them . . . Nevertheless Article 10(2) does not give the contracting state an unlimited power of appreciation. The Court which is responsible for ensuring the observance of those states' engagements is empowered to give the final ruling on whether a restriction or penalty is reconcilable with the freedom of expression as protected by Article 10. The domestic margin of appreciation thus goes hand in hand with a European supervision.

17.3.5 Derogations and reservations

In times of war or other public emergency it is open to a Member State to enter into derogation in respect of certain obligations. These cannot be general derogations. A derogation simply allows a state not to comply with the Article in question to the legitimate extent of the derogation. However, derogations in respect of the right to life (except arising from the lawful prosecution of war) or from the prohibitions against torture are not permitted.

Reservations differ from derogations in that they are merely conditions upon acceptance of a particular Article.

17.3.6 Equality of arms

This principle, laid down in the case of *Neuminster v Austria* (1968) 1 EHRR 91, was created in order to ensure that both parties to a case, whether in civil or criminal proceedings, were not placed at a procedural disadvantage. The principle can be more easily explained with reference to a practical example.

In the case of a summary-only offence which must be tried in the magistrates' court, the defence has no right to advance information from the prosecution. This differs from an either-way offence where such information is readily available. The defence must conduct its case ignorant of evidence in the prosecution's possession and it is therefore deprived of the opportunity of investigating and testing the strength of the prosecution's case. This may well have given rise to an application in the magistrates' court that there has been a breach of Article 6 of the Convention because the principle of equality of arms has been infringed (given that the majority of summary-only offences do carry the threat of a custodial sentence). However, this potential breach is effectively dealt with by para 43 of the Attorney-General's Guidelines: Disclosure of Information in Criminal Proceedings, where such advance information is now provided.

17.3.7 Horizontality

As mentioned earlier, s 6 of the Human Rights Act 1998 incorporates courts and tribunals into the definition of public bodies. When two individuals come to court for a decision to be made about their dispute, the court needs to act compatibly with the Convention. This will therefore have an indirect effect upon the two individuals who are not themselves covered by the Convention. The court's adherence to the Convention will have a *horizontal* effect on their relationship. In *Hokkanen v Finland* (1994) 19 EHRR 139, the European Court held that where grandparents failed to abide by court orders for contact and custody in favour of the father, Article 8 imposed upon the state a positive obligation to assist, so far as possible, the father's relationship with his child.

Douglas and Others v Hello! Ltd CA: Brooke, Sedley and Keene LJJ; reported: 21 December 2000 [2001] QB 467 involving Michael Douglas and Catherine Zeta Jones again illustrated that the court had a duty under s 6 to protect their private life. The case involved proceedings against *Hello!* magazine which threatened to publish unauthorised photographs from the couple's wedding when they had in fact sold the exclusive rights to *OK* magazine. While all three judges agreed that an injunction should be refused because the couple had in fact traded their right to private life like a commodity, the judgment is notable in confirming the effect that the Human Rights Act 1998 has had upon legal relations between individuals as opposed to legal relations between individuals and the state.

17.3.8 Living instrument

The Convention was drafted more than 40 years ago and, unlike usual pieces of legislation, it has not been amended, repealed, or replaced by more up-to-date legislation. To use the UK model of precedent would bind the court to adhere to decisions which are outmoded and probably unfair. It is primarily for this reason that the doctrine of precedent is not a main feature of Convention case law. The Convention is a 'living instrument' and cases are decided in line with the up-to-date economic and moral conditions of the

Member States. Although this creates some uncertainty when relying on previous decisions handed down, it at least ensures that the decisions are modern in their approach.

17.3.9 Protocols

Protocols can be thought of as extensions to the Convention where Member States can agree to add to the rights contained within it. The procedural method for doing this is to draw up a Protocol setting out the additional rights. The First Protocol provides for rights to the peaceful enjoyment of property, to education, and to free elections. The Human Rights Act 1998 allows the government to incorporate future Protocols into national law using rules of Parliament. The rights contained within the Protocols carry as much weight as the provisions contained in the Articles themselves.

17.3.10 Where to find Convention case law

The Council of Europe publishes individual judgments and decisions under the title *Publications of the European Court of Human Rights*. Court judgments are published in Series A and the pleadings, oral arguments, and documents are published in Series B.

Decisions of the Commission and judgments of the Court can be found at http://www.echr.coe.int.

Another source is the European Human Rights Reports (EHRR), which publishes all judgments and important decisions. The European Human Rights Law Review (EHRLR) appears six times a year, and has a case law section which highlights interesting cases and recent decisions.

17.4 The Convention rights

This section contains commentary on the main Articles of the Convention which affect legal practice. It should be viewed only as an introduction to some of the possible effects of the Convention and is no substitute for empirical research.

Schedule 1 to the Human Rights Act 1998 lists the Convention rights by reference to the relevant Articles of, and Protocols to, the European Convention on Human Rights, as follows.

17.4.1 Article 2—Right to life

1. Everyone's right to life shall be protected by law. No one shall be deprived of his life intentionally save in the execution of a sentence of a court following his conviction of a crime for which this penalty is provided by law.

2. Deprivation of life shall not be regarded as inflicted in contravention of this Article when it results from the use of force which is no more than absolutely necessary:

    (a) in defence of any person from unlawful violence;

    (b) in order to effect a lawful arrest or to prevent the escape of a person lawfully detained;

    (c) in action lawfully taken for the purpose of quelling a riot or insurrection.

This is a limited right: see *McCann v United Kingdom* (1995) 21 EHRR 97.

17.4.2 Article 3—Prohibition of torture

No one shall be subjected to torture or inhuman or degrading treatment or punishment.

This is an absolute right although there is a minimum level of severity required before Article 3 will be contravened. The case of *Ireland v United Kingdom* (1978) 2 EHRR 25 gave guidelines as to what constituted prohibited treatment. Torture was defined as deliberate inhuman treatment causing very serious and cruel suffering; inhumane treatment or punishment as treatment or punishment which causes intense physical and mental suffering; degrading treatment or punishment as treatment or punishment that arouses in a victim a feeling of fear, anguish, and inferiority capable of humiliating and debasing the victim and possibly breaking his or her physical or moral resistance.

17.4.3 Article 4—Prohibition of slavery and forced labour

1. No one shall be held in slavery or servitude. [This is an absolute right.]
2. No one shall be required to perform forced or compulsory labour. [This is a limited right.]
3. For the purpose of this Article the term 'forced or compulsory labour' shall not include:
   (a) any work required to be done in the ordinary course of detention imposed according to the provisions of Article 5 of this Convention or during conditional release from such detention;
   (b) any service of a military character or, in case of conscientious objectors in countries where they are recognised, service exacted instead of compulsory military service;
   (c) any service exacted in case of an emergency or calamity threatening the life or well-being of the community;
   (d) any work or service which forms part of normal civic obligations.

17.4.4 Article 5—Right to liberty and security

1. Everyone has the right to liberty and security of person. No one shall be deprived of his liberty save in the following cases and in accordance with a procedure prescribed by law:
   (a) the lawful detention of a person after conviction by a competent court;
   (b) the lawful arrest or detention of a person for non-compliance with the lawful order of a court in order to secure the fulfilment of any obligation prescribed by law;
   (c) the lawful arrest or detention of a person effected for the purpose of bringing him before the competent legal authority on reasonable suspicion of having committed an offence or when it is reasonably considered necessary to prevent his committing an offence or fleeing after having done so;
   (d) the detention of a minor by lawful order for the purpose of educational supervision or his lawful detention for the purpose of bringing him before the competent legal authority;
   (e) the lawful detention of persons for the spreading of infectious diseases, of persons of unsound mind, alcoholics or drug addicts or vagrants;

(f) the lawful arrest or detention of a person to prevent his effecting an unauthorised entry into the country or of a person against whom action is being taken with a view to deportation or extradition.

2. Everyone who is arrested shall be informed promptly, in a language which he understands, of the reasons for his arrest and of any charge against him.

3. Everyone arrested or detained in accordance with paragraph 1(c) of this Article shall be brought promptly before a judge or other officer authorised by law to exercise judicial power and shall be entitled to trial within a reasonable time or to release pending trial. Release may be conditioned by guarantees to appear for trial.

4. Everyone who is deprived of his liberty by arrest or detention shall be entitled to take proceedings by which the lawfulness of his detention shall be decided speedily by a court and his release ordered if the detention is not lawful.

5. Everyone who has been the victim of arrest or detention in contravention of the provisions of this Article shall have an exercisable right to compensation.

This is a limited right and will have most relevance in a magistrates' court, particularly in relation to the granting of bail. When a defendant is charged with a criminal offence he must appear before the magistrates who will decide whether or not there should be a release pending trial, with or without conditions, or a remand into custody. Article 5(3) states that he should be entitled to trial within a reasonable time or to release pending trial. The case of *Wemhoff v Germany* (1968) 1 EHRR 55 stated that the defendant was entitled to both things notwithstanding the wording and also that the defendant should be released pending trial unless there are *'relevant and sufficient'* reasons to justify continued detention. In the UK the Bail Act 1976 provides that the magistrates must be satisfied that there are substantial grounds for believing that a person should be deprived of his liberty and the exceptions to the prima facie right to bail are clearly set out in the Schedule to the Act.

Article 5(1)(c) has also been the subject of scrutiny in relation to the authorisation of the detention of claimants for over seven hours in Oxford Circus on May Day 2001. In *Austin and Saxby v Commissioner of Police of the Metropolis* [2005] HRLR 20,[2007] EWCA Civ 989 the question was whether it was capable of authorising the detention of individuals whom the police neither suspected of criminality nor intended to bring before a court on reasonable suspicion of having committed an offence or to prevent them doing so. The claims made were dismissed and a subsequent appeal in 2007 was unsuccessful. However, in the case of *R (Laporte) v Gloucestershire Chief Constable* (2006) UKHL 55, (2007) 2 WLR 46 anti-war protestors were prevented from reaching an anti-war demonstration at RAF Fairford. Their coaches were stopped before they reached the site and were searched. The coaches were then forcibly escorted back to London. The House of Lords held that this was a breach of Article 5 and in addition that there had been a breach of both Article 10 and 11 as they had prevented the protestors from reaching the demonstration when there was no imminent breach of the peace.

17.4.4.1 Disclosure and bail

Disclosure is an area which requires some consideration in relation to Article 6: the right to a fair trial and the equality of arms. However, disclosure will also be very relevant to bail applications where the prosecution is in possession of information which is not readily available to the defence. This may well prove to be a breach of the principle of equality of arms, placing the prosecution in breach of Article 5(4). Authority for this can be found in *Lamy v Belgium* (1989) 11 EHRR 529 where the applicant had been refused access to the prosecution file at both applications for bail and had bail refused. He merely had access to some information disclosed on the face of the warrant for his arrest. The European Court held that there had been a breach of Article 5(4) even though the national law at the time only allowed for disclosure 30 days after arrest. The Court then took the matter a stage further and said that not only should the information be disclosed but the applicant should have had sufficient time to consider and evaluate the material.

The recent case of *R (on the application of O) v Harrow Crown Court* [2006] UKHL 42; [2006] 3 WLR 195 (HL) dealt with this issue against the backdrop of the compatibility of s 25(1) of the Criminal Justice and Public Order Act 1994 with Article 5. O had been charged with rape, having previously been convicted of the same offence. An application to extend custody time-limits was refused, but he was not granted bail on the basis of s 25(1). He was in custody for 22 months, 16 of which followed the expiry of the custody time-limit. Whilst in custody, he had dispensed with his lawyers' services, and then had them reinstated, four times (twice, at least, causing delay). The indictment was eventually stayed as an abuse of process. The central issue on appeal here seemed to be the presumption in favour of custody indicated by s 25(1) and the presumption in favour of liberty favoured by Article 5. It is clear that the latter should take precedence. Strasbourg jurisprudence is quite clear that the decision to take away a person's liberty must be a judicial one and should take into account the presumption of innocence and the 'the rule of respect for the accused's liberty'. The presumption is in favour of liberty and it is for the prosecution to bear the burden of raising exceptional circumstances.

17.4.4.2 Right to review

Note the case of *T and V v United Kingdom*, Applications 24724/94 and 24888/94, 16 December 1999, which held that the two applicants had been denied the opportunity to have the lawfulness of detention reviewed by a judicial body.

17.4.5 Article 6—Right to a fair trial

1. In the determination of his civil rights and obligations or of any criminal charge against him, everyone is entitled to a fair and public hearing within a reasonable time by an independent and impartial tribunal established by law. Judgment shall be pronounced publicly but the press and public may be excluded from all or part of the trial in the interest of morals, public order or national security in a democratic society, where the interest of juveniles or the protection of the private life of the parties so require, or to the extent strictly necessary in the opinion of the court in special circumstances where publicity would prejudice the interests of justice.

2. Everyone charged with a criminal offence shall be presumed innocent until proved guilty according to law.

3. Everyone charged with a criminal offence has the following minimum rights:

    (a) to be informed promptly, in a language which he understands and in detail, of the nature and cause of the accusation against him

    (b) to have adequate time and facilities for the preparation of his defence

    (c) to defend himself in person or through legal assistance of his own choosing or, if he has not sufficient means to pay for legal assistance, to be given it free when the interests of justice so require

    (d) to examine or have examined witnesses against him and to obtain the attendance and examination of witnesses on his behalf under the same conditions as witnesses against him

(e) to have the free assistance of an interpreter if he cannot understand or speak the language used in court.

This Article will affect proceedings in both civil and criminal trials.

17.4.5.1 Criminal proceedings

Article 6(1) provides the right to a trial within a reasonable time and guarantees the expedition in the conduct of the proceedings themselves in order to prevent a defendant from remaining uncertain about the outcome of his fate for too long.

This has changed our approach to abuse of process proceedings. Under common law, the defence must show that the defendant has been prejudiced by the delay in order to make a successful application. However, since October 2000, there is no requirement to show prejudice as the delay, of itself, will be sufficient. In extreme circumstances the European Court may adjudge that a long delayed trial amounts to oppression.

17.4.5.2 Article 6(2)—Reverse burden of proof

The case of *Salabiaku v France* (1991) 13 EHRR 379 was notable in that it stated that:

> Article 6(2) does not therefore regard presumptions of fact or law provided for in criminal law with indifference. It requires states to confine them within reasonable limits which take into account the importance of what is at stake and maintain the rights of the defence.

Article 6(2) and the presumption of innocence has already been raised as an issue in UK proceedings, in particular the case of *R v Director of Public Prosecutions, ex parte Kebilene* [1999] 3 WLR 972. This case concerned ss 16A and 16B of the Prevention of Terrorism Act 1989 which carries with it a reverse burden of proof. The House of Lords held, in relation to the particular provision, that it was not clear that these sections were necessarily going to be contrary to Article 6(2). Two of their Lordships thought that the offence of possessing an article reasonably suspected of being possessed for terrorist purposes might well violate Article 6(2), since it required the accused to prove that the article was not in his possession for those purposes, and they proposed reinterpreting the burden on the accused as evidential only. Other members of the court disagreed and said it was sufficient that the prosecution has the burden of showing '*circumstances giving rise to a reasonable suspicion*' of terrorist purposes.

17.4.5.3 Article 6(3)(b)—Disclosure

Our present system of disclosure contains various anomalies which contravene a defendant's right to disclosure under the Convention. The main piece of legislation to be affected here is the Criminal Procedure and Investigations Act 1996 which deals with primary and secondary disclosure of unused material.

The Attorney-General's Guidelines: Disclosure of Information in Criminal Proceedings sought to deal with some of the unfairness that had been created by the 1996 Act and by disclosure provisions in general. Indeed, in its introduction it states that the guidelines are designed to:

> ensure that there is fair disclosure of material which may be relevant to an investigation and which does not form part of the prosecution case... Disclosure which does not meet these objectives risks preventing a fair trial taking place.

Some of the dissatisfaction with the disclosure system from both a defence and a prosecution point of view has been addressed in the Criminal Justice Act 2003 which has made significant amendments to the Criminal Procedure and Investigations Act 1996.

The 2003 Act amends the original two-stage test contained in the 1996 Act and replaces it with a new objective single test for the disclosure of unused prosecution material to the defence, requiring the prosecutor to disclose prosecution material that has not previously been disclosed and which might reasonably be considered capable of undermining the case for the prosecution against the accused, or of assisting the case for the accused. It replaces the present secondary disclosure material which meets the new test. The prosecutor is specifically required to review the prosecution material on receipt of the defence statement and to make further disclosure if required under the continuing duty.

The Act also extends the remit of the defence statement. The defence will now be required to set out the nature of the defence, including any particular defences on which the defendant intends to rely and indicate any points of law he wishes to take, including any points as to the admissibility of evidence or abuse of process.

17.4.5.4 Article 6(3)(c)—Public funding

Our present provisions in relation to the granting of public funding may result in minor cases being refused legal aid. However, even minor cases may result in a term of imprisonment being imposed and in these cases a refusal of public funding would lead to a breach of this part of Article 6.

17.4.5.5 Hearsay

Historically hearsay has also been considered inadmissible evidence unless either a common law or a statutory exception to the rule was made out. Sections 114 and 115 of the Criminal Justice Act 2003 have effectively abolished this rule and provide that such evidence will be admissible on behalf of the prosecution and the defence provided certain safeguards are met. There is also an additional statutory discretion to admit into evidence out of court statements where it would be in the interests of justice to do so. In addition, a witness's previous statement will be more widely admissible at trial as proof of the facts contained within it and in serious cases certain witnesses may use their video recorded statements in place of their main evidence.

These significant changes place a much greater reliance upon the discretionary decision-making process exercised by the judiciary. With their discretion to admit what would have been historically inadmissible evidence comes the potential for miscarriages of justice—the main principle behind the hearsay rule was that it was inherently unreliable evidence, the 'best evidence' being oral evidence from the percipient witness. With the abolition of these strict rules of evidence the right of an individual to a fair trial may well be jeopardised. In *R v Cole, R v Keet* [2007] EWCA Crim 1924 the two defendants challenged their convictions as the prosecution's case had been cased almost entirely on statements of absent witnesses which had been admitted into evidence. The Court of Appeal upheld the conviction stating that it would need to be decided on a case by case basis with the relevant factors set out in section 114(2) of the Criminal Justice Act 2003 taken in to account.

17.4.5.6 Article 6 and inferences from silence

The Criminal Justice and Public Order Act 1994 introduced various inroads into the right to silence which had hitherto been absolute. Under s 34, in particular, if an accused failed to mention when questioned, or charged, a fact which he later relied upon in court then such inferences as appeared proper could be drawn from that earlier silence, most notably the inference of recent fabrication. It is accepted that the mere fact of drawing inference from an accused's silence will not, of itself, involve a breach of

Article 6. However, the procedural safeguards involved in situations where inferences may be drawn have been subject to close scrutiny in our national courts and more recently have been challenged in the European Court (most notably in *Condron v United Kingdom*, Application 35718/97, 2 May 2000).

The Court held that there had in fact been a breach of Article 6 in that the direction given to the jury in respect of the s 34 inference had been incomplete. As a matter of fairness the judge should have directed them that if they were satisfied that the applicant's silence at the police interview could not sensibly have been attributed to their having no answer or none that would stand up to cross-examination it should not draw an adverse inference.

The problem in this case is that the Court of Appeal also accepted a defect in the summing up and also accepted that they could not know how much account the jury had taken of the defendant's silence when reaching their verdict. However, they were happy that, having looked at the other evidence before the court, the conviction of the defendant was not unsafe. This, in effect, seems to be suggesting that the Court of Appeal feels able to superimpose its own reasoning onto the trial process. It remains to be seen whether or not this attempt to override the jury's actual thought process in coming to a decision is in fact a breach of Article 6 itself.

The issue of maintaining silence upon legal advice has now advanced somewhat in the light of recent case law (see, eg, *R v Doldur* [2000] Crim LR 178 and the latest Judicial Studies Board's specimen direction). The jury must be reminded of all the relevant background considerations and directed that if it was satisfied that the applicant's silence at the police interview could not sensibly be attributed to his having no answer or none that would stand up to police questioning it should not draw an adverse inference. Therefore, cases such as *Beckles v United Kingdom* (44652/98) (2003) 36 EHRR 13 (ECHR), where the trial judge failed to emphasise the defendant's willingness to talk to the police prior to receiving legal advice and the fact that he had been prepared to provide details of the advice he had received from his solicitor at the police station should in the future receive more careful consideration in directions given to the jury.

Inferences under s 34 are clearly not going to invalidate a trial procedure but there are procedural issues involved which will need to be carefully scrutinised.

17.4.5.7 Article 6 and public interest immunity

Public interest immunity (PII) is an exclusionary rule of evidence which allows for material falling within the definition of public interest immunity to be withheld from the defence.

17.4.5.7.1 *Procedure*

The procedural requirements that govern the way in which the prosecution should claim such immunity have been quite vigorously challenged in Strasbourg in the case of *Rowe and Davis v United Kingdom* (2000) 30 EHRR 1. At trial, the prosecution decided, without informing the judge, to withhold relevant material on the grounds that it fell within the definition of PII. The court felt that:

> Such a procedure, whereby the prosecution itself attempts to assess the importance of concealed information to the defence and weigh this against the public interest in keeping the information secret, cannot comply with . . . Article 6(1).

The subsequent review of the material by the Court of Appeal could not cure the inherent unfairness arising from the initial trial. The trial judge had never seen the material and he would have been the person in the best possible position to assess the material in the light of the evidence being given as opposed to the Court of Appeal attempting artificially to manufacture the live trial situation from a set of lifeless manuscripts.

The later case of *Atlan v United Kingdom* (36533/97) [2001] Crim LR 819 (ECHR) unanimously found a breach of Article 6(1). The court applied the principle in *Rowe and Davis* that while Article 6(1) required in principle that the prosecution should disclose to the defence all material evidence in its possession for and against the defendant, it might be necessary to withhold certain evidence so as to preserve the fundamental rights of another individual or to safeguard an important public interest. The government, in this case, had conceded that the repeated denials of the existence of unused material and the prosecution's failure to notify the judge of its existence was inconsistent with the requirements of Article 56(1). The issue for the court was whether the *ex parte* procedure before the Court of Appeal was sufficient to remedy that unfairness at first instance. The evidence withheld was central to the applicant's defence and the trial judge was in the best position to decide whether the non-disclosure of the evidence was unfairly prejudicial. Therefore, the prosecution's failure to lay the evidence in question before the trial judge and to permit him to rule on the question of disclosure deprived the applicants of a fair trial.

The generic issue that the court was concerned with was the fact that in the UK the prosecution may make an *ex parte* application without notice to the judge in order to obtain PII status without the defence ever being involved in the decision-making process. This is as opposed to an *inter partes* hearing, or an *ex parte* hearing with notice, where the defence are allowed to make representation in writing or in person. Whilst the latter two options are clearly quite fair, the former *ex parte* without notice application has been severely criticised by Strasbourg and the position has yet to be clarified.

In *Fitt v United Kingdom* (2000) 30 EHRR 480 it was held that the procedures adopted with regards to disclosure, in this particular case, were Article 6(1) compliant. This was because, although the prosecution were heard *ex parte*, the defence were kept informed and permitted to make submissions and participate in those decisions as far as possible without disclosing the material the prosecution sought to withhold on PII grounds. The court also had regard to the judge's continuing duty to monitor the situation, which it felt was an important safeguard from a defence point of view. The court came to the same conclusion in similar terms in *Jasper v United Kingdom* (2000) 30 EHRR 441.

Consequently, care should always be taken to ensure that the trial judge is complying with the spirit of Article 6 by allowing the defence to have a role in the decision-making process, especially in cases where the prosecution adopt the *ex parte* method of application for claiming PII status. These representations can only be made, of course, where the defence is actually made aware of the fact of the application in the first place—a position that did clearly not exist in *Rowe and Davis*. Indeed, even where the defence are involved in some way in the decision-making process this will not always guarantee that the individual's rights are protected. In *R v Doubtfire* (2000) *The Times*, 28 December, the defence had been given the opportunity to explain its case to the judge, after a prosecution *ex parte* application, before he ruled, in the prosecution's favour, upon the issue of PII. Allowing the appeal, after a referral from the Criminal Cases Review Commission, the court held that it was sufficient to state that the trial had been materially unfair because there had been a failure in respect of disclosure in the context of submissions made at the *ex parte* PII application during trial, and the material in the confidential annex which the court had considered in private had not been available to the trial judge or at the earlier appeal hearing, confirming there had been unfairness.

In the *PG and JH v United Kingdom* (44787/98) *The Times,* 19 October 2001 (ECHR) further considered the issue of non-disclosure of prosecution material. However, in this case the court was satisfied that the defence were kept informed and allowed to participate 'as much as possible' in the judge's decision to withhold the evidence from them, and to allow the Inspector to give his oral evidence before the judge in chambers. The material that was withheld from the defence formed no part of the prosecution case and never went before the jury. The need for disclosure was at all times under assessment by the trial judge. Therefore, the domestic trial court applied standards that were in conformity with the relevant principles of a fair hearing embodied in Article 6(1).

The underlying theme of these decisions is clearly turning upon whether the extent to which the trial judge has or had not been able to view the material and continually review the decision to withhold during the trial itself.

17.4.5.8 Article 6—Unfairly obtained evidence

Traditionally, unfairly obtained evidence may be excluded under s 78 of the Police and Criminal Evidence Act 1984, and, following the implementation of the Human Rights Act 1998, it could also be held to be a violation of an individual's rights under Article 6 or Article 8, the latter sometimes resulting in the courts determining that there had consequently been a breach of Article 6.

Section 78(1) of the Police and Criminal Evidence Act 1984 provides that the court:

> may refuse to allow evidence on which the prosecution proposes to rely to be given if it appears to the court that, having regard to all the circumstances, *including the circumstances in which the evidence was obtained*, the admission of the evidence could have such an adverse effect on the fairness of the proceedings that the court ought not to admit it. (emphasis added)

Where the evidence was excluded under s 78 it did not automatically follow that the prosecution came to an end, or that conviction, upon appeal, was necessarily unsafe. Similarly, even where a breach of Article 6 and/or Article 8 was found, it was still possible for the Court of Appeal safely to uphold a conviction.

The case of *Teixera de Castro v Portugal* (1998) 28 EHRR 101, while notable for its decision regarding unfairly obtained evidence, also states:

> The Court reiterates that the admissibility of evidence is primarily a matter for regulation by national law and as a general rule it is for the courts to assess the evidence before them. The Court's task under the Convention is not to give rulings as to whether the statements of witnesses were properly admitted as evidence, but rather to ascertain whether the proceedings as a whole, including the way in which evidence was taken, were fair.

The practical consequences of evidence obtained primarily as a result of intelligence-led policing have been clarified in the House of Lords, in the *Attorney-General's Reference (No 3 of 2000)* [2002] 1 Cr App R 29 which dealt with the conjoined appeals of *R v G* and *R v Looseley*. What the House of Lords provides is a rationale for the courts to stay prosecutions based upon entrapment, described by Lord Hoffmann as a 'jurisdiction to prevent abuse of executive power' and which Lord Nicholls pronounced in greater detail as follows:

> It is not simply acceptable that the state through its agents should lure its citizens into committing acts forbidden by the law and then seek to prosecute them for doing so. That would be entrapment. That would be a misuse of state power, and an abuse of process for the courts. The unattractive consequences, frightening and sinister in extreme cases, which state conduct of this kind could have are obvious. The role of the courts is to stand between the state and its citizens and make sure this does not happen.

The House of Lords held that in *Looseley* the trial judge had been correct to refuse the application to stay the proceedings for abuse of process, as the police had reasonable grounds to suspect that the defendant was involved in the supply of Class A drugs and all the undercover officer had done was provide an opportunity for him to commit the offence; in contrast their Lordships found that the trial judge in the *Attorney-General's*

Reference had been correct in staying the proceedings because there were no reasonable grounds to suspect that the defendant was involved in the supply of Class A drugs and the officer had repeatedly phoned his mobile phone number offering cheap cigarettes in return for the supply of such drugs.

This approach has been confirmed more recently in the case of *R v Moon* [2004] EWCA Crim 2872 where the court held that the proceeding should have been stayed as an abuse of process. In this case more than mere opportunity had been provided. The appellant, charged with possession with intent to supply Class A drugs to an undercover police officer, had no predisposition to deal and had no previous history of dealing. The undercover officer had made the first approach and had been persistent. In addition, the undercover operation had not been properly authorised. However, the appellate court felt that that overall the operation had been bona fide and that this aberration of itself would not have been sufficient to justify a stay.

The approach adopted by the House of Lords is consistent with the reasoning of the European Court in *Teixera de Castro v Portugal*, which stated that where there was conduct amounting to entrapment, the defendant would be denied the right to a fair trial from the outset.

From a prosecution point of view, this is clearly the most serious consequence resulting from an abuse of state power; but it is not the only consequence. In cases where the court feels that a stay is inappropriate, it will still be open to the defence to make an application to exclude the evidence of the undercover officer under s 78 of the 1984 Act either because to admit it would have an adverse effect on the trial as a whole, or on grounds that could have been submitted to support an application for a stay. Even if the evidence remains, it may still be appropriate to refer to how it was obtained in the plea in mitigation.

How should the court determine what conduct should lead to the exclusion of evidence, or indeed the stay of proceedings for abuse of process? The case of *R v Smurthwaite and Gill* [1994] 1 All ER 898 has long since provided the courts with guidelines to apply in these cases in order to determine whether or not evidence ought to be excluded. Smurthwaite was convicted of soliciting to murder. The person solicited was in fact an undercover police officer who had posed as a contract killer. The prosecution's case relied upon covertly recorded conversations of meetings between the undercover officer and the defendant. The defendant appealed on the basis that this evidence should have been ruled inadmissible. The Court of Appeal held that the relevant factors to consider when applying s 78 to such circumstances included:

(a) whether the undercover officer was acting as an *agent provocateur*;

(b) the nature of any entrapment;

(c) whether the evidence consists of admissions to a completed offence, or relates to the actual commission of the offence;

(d) how active or passive the officer's role was in obtaining the evidence;

(e) whether there is an unassailable record of what occurred, or whether it is strongly corroborated; and

(f) whether the officer abused his (undercover) role to ask questions which ought properly to have been asked as a police officer in accordance with Code C of the Police and Criminal Evidence Act 1984.

In Smurthwaite's case, although there was an element of entrapment and trick, the officer had not acted as an *agent provocateur*. The tapes recorded the actual commission of the offence rather than an offence committed in the past, and they made it clear that it was the accused who was the instigator. The officer had very much taken a back seat and used no persuasion.

Both the *Attorney-General's Reference* and *Nottingham City Council v Amin* [2000] 1 WLR 1071 (see below) abandon the test of whether the officer's role is active or passive, in that they regard it as unhelpful. The basis of the distinction was not whether the officer had acted or not acted, but whether or not the extent of his involvement was acceptable to the court; but as Lord Bingham in *Amin* stated, 'there was nothing to suggest that without [the police officers'] intervention [the offence] would have been committed'.

The decision in *Nottingham City Council v Amin* [2000] 1 WLR 1071, where a driver was prosecuted for plying for hire without a licence, provides the modern approach to cases involving undercover officers. The defendant's cab was licensed for an adjoining area, but not the city centre where he was driving when stopped by two plain-clothes police officers. The light on his cab was not illuminated, but when the officers asked him to convey them to a specified destination he agreed, and did so for a fare. He argued that the evidence was obtained unfairly and should be excluded under s 78 of the 1984 Act. The Divisional Court held that the facts could not be construed as showing the defendant in any way being pressurised into committing the offence and that the evidence should be admitted. Confirming that it was the fairness of the proceedings as a whole that had to be looked at, the court identified two conflicting public interest points. On the one hand, it was recognised as deeply offensive to ordinary notions of fairness if a defendant were to be convicted and punished for committing a crime only because he had been incited, persuaded, or pressurised into doing so by a law enforcement officer. On the other hand, it had been recognised that law enforcement agencies had a general duty to the public to enforce the law, and it had been regarded as unobjectionable if such an officer gave a defendant an opportunity to break the law, of which he freely took advantage, in circumstances where it appeared that he would have behaved in the same way if the opportunity had been offered by anyone else. The court drew a distinction between creating an opportunity to commit an offence and inducing the commission of the offence. It would seem that positive action, beyond merely providing the opportunity to commit the offence, will be required before any breach of Article 6 becomes imminent.

17.4.5.8.1 *European perspective*

The use of participating informants was challenged in *Ludi v Switzerland* (1992) 15 EHRR 173 where the court refused to find that the use of an undercover agent infringed the applicant's Article 8 rights as he was a suspected member of a large group of drug traffickers in possession of five kilos of cocaine and 'must therefore have been aware from then on that he was engaged in a criminal act . . . and that consequently he was running the risk of encountering an undercover police officer whose task would in fact be to expose him'. In *Ludi* the drug trafficking was already under way when the undercover officer came on the scene and so the admission of evidence gathered in the course of the operation did not violate Article 6. Notable in this case was that the operation had been judicially sanctioned, and it is a weakness of our statutory scheme that certain types of covert activity do not require prior independent authorisation.

However, some cases are illustrative of the fact that covert human intelligence can be taken a stage too far, a classic example being found in the case of *Teixera de Castro v Portugal* (1998) 28 EHRR 101, where the Court ruled that the admissibility of evidence where there had been entrapment of a person not predisposed to that type of offence will not be left to regulation by national law. The applicant in this case, who had no record of drug dealing, was introduced to a third party by two police officers posing as drug addicts. They asked him to supply them with heroin. Initially he refused, but complied with a second request and supplied the officers with heroin at a profit. He maintained in his defence that he had been incited to commit an offence which, but for the intervention of the two officers, he would not have committed. The Court agreed, saying that 'the two police officers did not confine themselves to investigating criminal activities in an essentially passive manner, but exercised an influence such as to incite the commission of the offence'. The prosecution were unable to prove any predisposition to commit such a type of offence on the part of the applicant, and not even the public interest in fighting drug trafficking could justify relying on evidence obtained as a result of police incitement.

17.4.6 Article 7—No punishment without law (no retrospective criminal offences or penalties)

1. No one shall be held guilty of any criminal offence on account of any act or omission which did not constitute a criminal offence under national or international law at the time when it was committed. Nor shall a heavier penalty be imposed than the one that was applicable at the time the criminal offence was committed.

2. This Article shall not prejudice the trial and punishment of any person for any act or omission which, at the time it was committed, was criminal according to the general principles of law recognised by civilised nations.

There is the presumption in relation to criminal offences that there will be no retroactivity and that provisions of criminal law may be argued against if they are not clear. There are various changes in our domestic legislation which may cause a problem in relation to retroactivity which can be more clearly explained in relation to case law. In *SW and CR v United Kingdom* (1995) 21 EHRR 363 the defendant was charged with raping his wife. He argued that the change in the law making rape within marriage a crime was a violation of Article 7. It was held that there was no violation of Article 7 as it was sufficiently foreseeable.

Other changes to our legislation may give rise to an application under Article 7 as well. For example, the Criminal Evidence (Amendment) Act 1997 allows the police to take DNA samples from offenders convicted before the Act came into force. This could be viewed as retroactivity and in breach of Article 7.

17.4.7 Article 8—Right to respect for private and family life

1. Everyone has the right to respect for his private and family life, his home and his correspondence.

2. There shall be no interference by a public authority with the exercise of this right except such as is in accordance with the law and is necessary in a democratic society and in the interests of national security, public safety or the economic well being of the country, for the prevention of disorder or crime, for the protection of health and morals, or for the protection of the rights and freedoms of others.

Note that in the case of *X and Y v Netherlands* (1985) 8 EHRR 235 the European Court stated that Article 8:

does not merely compel the state to abstain from interference: in addition to this primarily negative undertaking, there may be positive obligations inherent in an effective respect for private and family life. These obligations may involve the adoption of measures designed to secure respect for private life even in the sphere of relations of individuals between themselves.

This imposes a secondary duty quite separate to the main function of the Article which refers to interference by a public authority. In *McVeigh, O'Neill and Evans v UK* Nos 8022/77, 8025/77 and 8027/77: D.R. 15 it was held that preventing the prisoners from communicating with their spouses was a breach of Article 8 even though they were held under anti-terrorist laws; if it was the case that such contact may facilitate an escape or the destruction or removal of evidence then the case may well be different.

17.4.7.1 Article 8—Intrusive surveillance

It is accepted that certain forms of intrusive surveillance adopted by the police prior to the implementation of the 1998 Act were incompatible with the rights conveyed under Article 8, not least because there was no legislative regulation of such conduct and therefore the requirement under Article 8(2) that the surveillance be legal could not be satisfied. However, following the implementation of the Police Act 1997, Pt III, and the Regulation of Investigatory Powers Act 2000, Pt II, such regulation is thought to exist. However, it is feared that the potential for challenge still exists, not perhaps in terms of the validity of the procedures as a compatible piece of legislation but in relation to the doctrine of proportionality, ie that that surveillance adopted is not a proportionate response to the actions complained of having regard to the legitimate aim under Article 8(2) of preventing crime.

Note that regard should be had to those undercover operations which do not fall under the umbrella of the Regulation of Investigatory Powers Act 2000 as they run the risk of being held to be prima facie unlawful.

The Regulation of Investigatory Powers Act 2000 is essentially a vehicle designed to ensure a valid legal basis is established for the use of covert human intelligence sources—be this a participating informant or an undercover police officer.

The position at common law is that the use of participating informants has always been recognised as a necessary evil by the courts. Indeed Lord Parker stated in *R v Birtles* [1969] 1 WLR 1047:

> whilst the police are entitled to make use of information concerning an offence already laid on, and while with a view to mitigating the consequences of the proposed offence, eg to protect the proposed witness, it may be perfectly proper for the police to encourage the informer to take part in the offence, or indeed for the police officer himself to do so, the police must never use an informer to encourage another to commit an offence he would not otherwise commit.

Clearly the source should not overstep the boundaries contained in *Smurthwaite and Gill*, and when applying the position at common law regard will now have to be had to relevant European case law (see **17.4.5.8**).

17.4.8 Article 9—Freedom of thought, conscience and religion

1. Everyone has the right to freedom of thought, conscience and religion; this right includes freedom to change his religion or belief and freedom, either alone or in community with others and in public or in private, to manifest his religion or belief, in worship, teaching, practice and observance.

2. Freedom to manifest one's religion or beliefs shall be subject only to such limitations as are prescribed by law and are necessary in a democratic society in the interests of public safety, for the protection of public order, health or morals, or for the protection of the rights and freedoms of others.

17.4.9 Article 10—Freedom of expression

1. Everyone has the right to freedom of expression. This right shall include freedom to hold opinions and to receive and impart information and ideas without interference by public authority and regardless of frontiers. This Article shall not prevent States from requiring the licensing of broadcasting, television or cinema enterprises.

2. The exercise of these freedoms, since it carries duties and responsibilities, may be subject to such formalities, conditions, restriction or penalties as are prescribed by law and are necessary in a democratic society, in the interests of national security, territorial integrity, or public safety, for the prevention of disorder or crime, for the protection of health and morals, for the protection of the reputation or rights of others, for preventing the disclosure of information received in confidence, or for maintaining the authority and impartiality of the judiciary.

This is a qualified Article which has dealt primarily with political and journalistic expression. In all cases the courts must look at the restriction on the freedom of expression, and decide whether or not there is a legitimate aim which has been prescribed by law and whether or not the restriction is proportionate to the legitimate aim.

Freedom of expression was defined in *Handyside v UK* (1976) 1 EHRR 737:

Freedom of expression constitutes one of the essential foundations of [a democratic] society, one of the basic conditions for its progress and for the development of every man. Subject to paragraph 2 of Article 10, it is applicable not only to 'information' or 'ideas' that are favourably received and regarded as inoffensive . . . but also to those that offend, shock or disturb that State or any sector of the population. Such are the demands of pluralism, tolerance and broadmindedness without which there is no 'democratic society'.

In *Observer and Guardian v United Kingdom* (1991) 14 EHRR 153, the government obtained an interlocutory injunction against two newspapers from publishing extracts from *Spycatcher* written by former MI5 agent Peter Wright. However, once the book had been published in the US and could therefore be transported to the UK, the European Court held that the injunctions could no longer be justified because from that time confidentiality of the material had been destroyed.

There is strong protection of journalistic sources, as evidenced by the case of *Goodwin v UK* (1996) 22 EHRR 123 where the European Court stated:

Protection of journalistic sources is one of the basic conditions for press freedom. Without such protection, sources may be deterred from assisting the press in informing the public on matters of public interest . . . [An order to disclose] cannot be compatible with Article 10 unless it is justified by an overriding requirement in the public interest.

Clearly issues of privacy arise here and may cause our courts some problems in the future. In the UK there has never been a right of privacy, but Article 8 quite clearly affords the individual some form of protection and the development of case law in this area will be quite drastic.

One of the most notable cases in relation to Article 8 is that of *Khan v UK* [2000] Crim LR 684. There, the court allowed evidence to be heard from a concealed listening device installed in the premises of another suspect in accordance with the Home Office guidelines on the use of equipment in police surveillance operations. K was convicted on the basis of this evidence. The court held that the tape-recording was an infringement of the right to private life guaranteed by Article 8(1) but that the interference could not be justified under Article 8(2). At the time there was no statutory framework to regulate the police. The court was not happy to accept the guidelines as they were not legally binding, neither were they directly accessible to the public. The comment was also made that they were of themselves insufficient to protect against arbitrary interference with an individual's rights under Article 8. The court was also concerned to point out that although there had been a breach of Article 8, this did not render the trial unfair under Article 6 as it was not the function of the European court to correct legal or factual errors made by national courts.

17.4.10 Article 11—Freedom of assembly and association

1. Everyone has the right to freedom of peaceful assembly and to freedom of association with others, including the right to form and to join trade unions for the protection of his interests.
2. No restrictions shall be placed on the exercise of these rights other than such as are prescribed by law and are necessary in a democratic society in the interest of national security or public safety, for the prevention of disorder or crime, for the protection of health or morals or for the protection of the rights and freedoms of others. This Article shall not prevent the imposition of lawful restrictions on the exercise of these rights by members of the armed forces, of the police or of the administration of the State.

17.4.11 Article 12—Right to marry

Men and women of marriageable age have the right to marry and to found a family, according to national laws governing the exercise of this right.

17.4.12 Article 14—Prohibition of discrimination (as regards the enjoyment of the rights and freedoms set out in the Convention)

The enjoyment of the rights and freedoms set forth in this Convention shall be secured without discrimination on any ground such as sex, race, colour, language, religion, political or other opinion, national or social origin, association with a national minority, property, birth or other status.

17.4.13 Article 16—Restrictions on political activity of aliens

Nothing in Articles 10, 11 and 14 shall be regarded as preventing the High Contracting Parties [the States] from imposing restrictions on the political activities of aliens.

17.4.14 Article 17—Prohibition of abuse of rights

Nothing in the Convention may be interpreted as implying for any State, group or person any right to engage in any activity or perform any act aimed at the destruction of any rights and freedoms set forth herein or at their limitation to a greater extent than is provided for in the Convention.

17.4.15 Article 18—Limitation on use of restriction on rights

The restrictions permitted under this Convention to the said rights and freedoms shall not be applied for any purpose other than those for which they have been prescribed.

The Human Rights Act 1998 also incorporates two existing Protocols in UK legislation, the First and the Sixth. They are set out as follows.

17.4.16 The First Protocol: Article 1—Protection of property

Every natural or legal person is entitled to the peaceful enjoyment of his possessions. No one shall be deprived of his possessions except in the public interest and subject to the conditions provided for by law and by general principles of international law.

The preceding provisions shall not, however, in any way impair the right of a State to enforce such laws as it deems necessary to control the use of property in accordance with the general interest or to secure the payment of taxes or other contributions or penalties.

17.4.17 The First Protocol: Article 2—Right to education

No person shall be denied the right to education. In the exercise of any functions which it assumes in relation to education and to teaching, the State shall respect the right of parents to ensure such education and teaching in conformity with their own religious and philosophical convictions.

17.4.18 The First Protocol: Article 3—Free elections

The High Contracting Parties [the States] undertake to hold free elections at reasonable intervals by secret ballot, under conditions which will ensure the free expression of the opinion of the people in the choice of the legislature.

17.4.19 The Sixth Protocol

This was ratified in 1999 and effectively outlaws the death penalty.

17.5 Judicial remedies

Section 8(1) of the Human Rights Act 1998 states that:

In relation to any act (or proposed act) of a public authority which the court finds is (or would be) unlawful, it may grant such relief or remedy, or make such order, within its powers as it considers to be just and appropriate.

But note that damages may be awarded only by a court which has powers to award damages, or to order the payment of compensation, in civil proceedings.

Where the court is required to remedy a Convention violation in relation to criminal proceedings it will be required to consider:

(a) directions in relation to the trial process;

(b) disclosure applications;

(c) an application for a stay of proceedings; and

(d) arguments in relation to the admissibility of evidence.

Where a court fails to take account of Convention provisions, individuals will be able to make use of judicial review and appeal mechanisms available under the Act and at common law. The Court of Appeal will have the right to quash a conviction in relation to an offence which of itself violates Convention rights, or where there has been a violation of an Article 6 right.

While a court may not strike down an Act of Parliament it may interpret it so as to give effect to Convention rights. Where it is not possible to construe a section to bring it within the Convention, the lower courts will have to apply the offending piece of legislation. The higher courts, including the High Court and Court of Appeal, will have the power to issue a 'declaration of incompatibility'. The government then has the power to either amend legislation or make a 'remedial order' under s 2 and Sch 2. Such a declaration would give rise to a ground for appeal against the conviction although it is only the Court of Appeal who has the power to quash a conviction.

17.6 Conclusion: checkpoints

You should now be able to:

- identify the background to the Convention and its subsequent incorporation into UK legislation;
- identify the general principles of European jurisprudence and its effect on case law interpretation;
- identify the Articles and the Protocols and where they may have an effect on UK legislation and procedure;
- correctly identify who has the right to invoke the protections afforded by the Convention;
- correctly identify potential causes of action; and
- correctly identify the procedural steps which need to be followed to enforce the rights of potential claimants under the Convention.

17.7 Bibliography

Ashcroft, P and others, *Human Rights and the Courts* (1999) Winchester: Waterside.
Starmer, K, *European Human Rights Law* (1999) London: Legal Action Group.
Wadham, J, Mountfield, H, and Edmundson, A, *Blackstone's Guide to the Human Rights Act 1998* (2006) Oxford: Oxford University Press.

Visit the Online Resource Centre for more information and useful weblinks.
www.oxfordtextbooks.co.uk/orc/foundations11_12/

APPENDIX 1
ANSWERS TO SELF-TEST QUESTIONS

Chapter 2

2.5 Answers to self-test questions

A.1 The Financial Services and Markets Act 2000 (FSMA 2000).

A.2 The Financial Services Authority.

A.3 (a) authorising
   (b) regulating
   (c) investigating
   (d) disciplining authorised persons.

A.4 (a) market confidence
   (b) financial stability
   (c) the protection of consumers
   (d) the reduction of financial crime.

A.5 It prohibits a person from carrying on a regulated activity unless that person is authorised under the Act (or is an exempt person).

A.6 (a) It is a criminal offence (FSMA 2000, s 23).
   (b) Any agreement made in contravention is unenforceable.
   (c) Action can be taken to recover money or property paid or transferred.
   (d) Action can be taken for compensation for any loss.

A.7 (a) authorised person, or
   (b) an exempt person.

A.8 An exemption to members of the professions.

A.9 s 22

A.10 (a) be an activity of a specified kind
   (b) be carried on by way of business, and
   (c) relate to a specified investment.

A.11 The Financial Services and Markets Act 2000 (Regulated Activities) Order 2001 (SI 2001 No. 544). The RAO.

A.12 (a) The Financial Services and Markets Act 2000 (Regulated Activities) Order 2001 (SI 2001 No 544); (b) Part III; (c) The RAO.

A.13 They are activities which arise out of a solicitor's main work as a solicitor; they are incidental to that work.

A.14 A designated professional body.

A.15 (a) The Solicitors' Financial Services (Scope) Rules 2001.
 (b) The Scope Rules.
 (c) The Solicitors' Financial Services (Conduct of Business) Rules 2001.
 (d) The Conduct of Business Rules.

A.16 A solicitor must account to the client for the commission.

A.17 (a) Dealing with or through authorised persons (RAO, Article 22).
 (b) Arranging deals with or through authorised persons (RAO, Article 29).
 (c) Funeral contract plans where the plan is covered by insurance or trust arrangements (RAO, Article 60).

A.18 Article 66.

A.19 The Scope Rules set out the conditions and restrictions with which solicitors' firms seeking to rely on the DPB regime must comply when carrying on regulated activities. Also the prohibitions which apply and the effect of a breach of the Rules. The Conduct of Business Rules set out the information clients must receive, how transactions should be effected, what records must be kept, and details of the safekeeping of clients' investments.

A.20 (a) A communication made in a face-to-face situation or in a telephone conversation.
 (b) One made in writing (a letter, a publication, an e-mail) or by e-mail.

APPENDIX 2
INVESTMENTS

INVESTMENT	Money invested for income or profit, for a return of income or capital
INCOME	Of a recurring nature
CAPITAL	One-off benefit
JARGON	
Gross interest	Taxable but not subject to taxation direct.
Variable rate	Rate of interest paid may change—usually in line with other interest rates.
Fixed rate	Rate of interest quoted at the outset does not change—even if other interest rates do.
Index-linked	Value of the capital invested is inflation proofed (its purchasing power remains the same from beginning to end of the investment period). The value of the capital changes in line with the retail prices index (RPI).
Base rate (official name—minimum lending rate)	Controlled by the Bank of England. It sets the general level of UK interest rates and is a valuable tool in managing the economy.
Tax-free	Excluded income for income tax purposes. No tax is charged either by direct assessment or deduction at source.
Tax-paid	Tax is deducted at source at the basic rate. There may be an additional liability if the taxpayer is a higher rate payer. Non-taxpayers or lower rate taxpayers can apply to the Inland Revenue for a tax refund.
Share	The proprietorship element in a company usually represented by transferable certificates, share certificates.
Equity/equities	A share or shares which do not bear fixed interest.
Quoted shares	Shares in companies listed on a stock market.
Unquoted shares	Shares in companies *not* listed on a stock market.
Warrant	Evidence that the holder has the right to subscribe for shares or stock.
Stock	A debt due for money loaned to a company or public body (government or local authority) usually with interest being paid from the company or public body to the investor.

Gilts 'Gilt-edged' Securities	Stocks issued by the government to finance its borrowing. They are issued on the National Savings Register or through the Bank of England and can be bought and sold on the Stock Market.
Investment trust	A company whose assets are solely shares in other companies.
Unit trust	Various banks and institutions offer unit trusts. The investor hands money to the institution and is issued with a number of units. The institution uses the money to invest in shares in other companies. The units can be sold back to the institution at any time.
Bid price	The price received if the investor sells his investment (usually units in a unit trust).
Offer price	The price an investor has to pay to buy units.
Bid/offer spread	The difference in the bid price and offer price.
Par	Nominal or face value.
Repayable at par	Nominal or face value is the amount paid to the investor on maturity.
Life-assured	Is the person on whose life a policy is taken out. The policy will be payable on the life-assured's death if it does not mature earlier.
Joint lives	Two lives are insured under one policy and the policy will pay out either on the death of the first to die or on the second death. It is agreed at the outset which is to occur.

Types of investments

WITHOUT RISK or LOW RISK:

Bank Accounts	Current:	money available immediately no interest or very little (due to immediate access) transactions recorded on statements.
	Deposit:	money available on specified period of notice differing rates of interest linked to notice period transactions recorded on statements.
Building Society Accounts	Deposit:	money available immediately priority on repayment if society faces difficulties low interest (due to security of investment) transactions recorded in pass books.
	Share:	money available on specified period of notice differing rates of interest linked to notice period and/or balance invested (tiered rates) transactions recorded in pass books.
National Savings		Schemes offered by the government. Security of the money invested is guaranteed by the government. Return is known at the outset.

Savings Certificates	Tax-free interest. Invested for a five-year term. Rate of interest increasing each year of the five-year term but rate fixed at outset. If Bank of England interest rate changes the government usually make available savings certificates on new terms (a new 'issue'). Existing 'issues' continue to the end of their five-year term. Can be index linked.
Income bonds	Repayable on three months' notice. Penalties if withdrawn before end of first year. Interest paid monthly. Rate of interest is variable.
Premium Bonds	Repayable on demand. No interest paid. Chance of winning a cash prize in the monthly draw.
Local Authority Bonds	Repayable only at end of term. Fixed rate of interest. Interest usually paid monthly.
GILTS	Repayable at par at end of term *but* can be sold before maturity. Fixed rate of interest. Interest usually paid half-yearly.

ISA	Individual Savings Account.
	    The risk depends on category invested in.
	    Tax-free investment income and capital gains.
	    Limit of £10,680 capital invested in any one tax year
	    maximum of £5,340 in cash, balance in stocks and shares
	    no minimum or maximum holding periods.
	Possibility of income—interest and dividends.
	Possibility of capital gain—on selling stocks or shares.
	Possibility of capital loss—on selling stocks or shares.

WITH RISK:	
Quoted Shares	With-risk investment. Money available on sale of the holding, delay in monies reaching investor. Possibility of income (dividends) and/or capital gain/loss on selling shares.
Investment Trusts	With-risk investment. Money available on sale of the holding, delay in monies reaching investor. Possibility of income (dividends) and/or capital gain/loss on selling shares.
Unit Trusts	With-risk investment. Money available on sale of the holding, delay in monies reaching investor. Possibility of income—dividends and/or capital gain/loss on selling shares.

LIFE ASSURANCE:

Whole life — No return until death of life-assured. Life-assured or policy holder pays regular premiums. Fixed sum is paid out on the death of the life-assured.

Term assurance — No return unless life-assured dies within specified period. Life-assured or policy holder pays regular premiums. Fixed sum is paid out if life-assured dies within a fixed period of time.

Endowment assurance — No return until specified date or death if earlier. Life-assured or policy holder pays regular premiums.
Sum is paid on a specified date or earlier if life-assured dies before that date.
If 'with profits' sum paid is greater of fixed sum assured or value of fund in which premiums are invested.

Annuities — No return of capital.
Capital sum is paid to the insurance company.
Guaranteed income will be paid to the investor for life or until agreed period ends.
Usually ceases on death but can be guaranteed for a fixed period notwithstanding death.

Stock market terminology

AIM — Alternative Investments Market.

Emerging markets — It is generally thought that the biggest stock market returns in the future will not be in the established markets but in cities such as Manila, Caracas, Lima, and Mexico City. Their economies are expected to grow faster than more mature economies.

Indices — **FT-SE 100:** An index jointly sponsored by the financial times, the London stock exchange and the Institute and Faculty of Actuaries. It contains shares of the top 100 UK companies ranked by market capitalisation. It is calculated every minute during the working day and shares enter and leave the index every quarter.
FT-SE Eurotrack 200: It contains the shares of 100 companies from Continental Europe and the constituents of the FT-SE 100 index. The weighting of the 100 shares from the UK are adjusted so as not to take up an inappropriate proportion of the index. It is calculated every minute.
DAX: This is the German share index and is published by the Frankfurt Stock Exchange. It contains 30 stocks from the main German markets. It is calculated every minute.
NIKKEI 225: This is the original Japanese share index published by Nihon Keizai Shimbun. It is calculated every minute and contains shares from 225 companies.

	DOW-JONES INDUSTRIAL AVERAGE: The grandfather of all indices. First calculated in January 1897. It contains 30 stocks chosen by Dow-Jones and Wall Street. It is also calculated every minute.
Insider dealing	When someone trades in a company's shares using specific information that has not been made public but which would seriously affect the company's share price if it were known. It can be done by a director or a receptionist.
Derivatives	High-risk investments. Can make or break an investor or a bank. They use futures and options. An option is a bet on the future price of anything—pork bellies to ordinary shares. An investor who takes an option retains the right to buy or sell a share within a set period with the price fixed at the outset. In a futures contract the investor has to exercise the option even if the market goes against him and, as Nick Leeson and Barings know, the losses can be unlimited.
Bulls & bears	Terms describing different types of investor. Bulls are optimists about market prices and believe that they will rise in a **bull** market. There was a bull market in the mid-1980s which ended in the crash on Black Monday, 19 October 1987. Bears are pessimists and believe that market prices will fall. There was a **bear** market after the 1929 Wall Street Crash.

INDEX

A

abatement of legacies 310
abuse of dominant position 362–5
abuse of process 387–8
abuse of rights 393
accounting
 administration of estate 286
 VAT 165–7
accounting basis
 assessment 171
acting for borrower and lender 29
actions to recover loss 320
additional personal representatives 249
ademption 213–14
administration of estates 11, 199–200, 248
 advertisements 295
 beneficiaries' right to compel 319
 corrective accounts 312
 diagrammatic representation of final stage 323
 diagrammatic representation of pre-grant procedure 257
 disclaimers 305–6
 estate accounts 314–17
 expense 312–13
 personal representatives 294–5
 post-death changes 305–7
 post-grant practice 285–323
 searches 295–6
 variations 306
administration expenses 304
administration proceedings 320
administration of tax *see under names of individual taxes*
administrators 249
 grants of representation 244
 renunciation 250
advertisements
 administration of estates 295
advice
 investment 45
Advocate-General 330–1
affidavits 256, 273–4
affirmations 256
age allowances 85
agent
 dealing in investments as 45
agreements between undertakings 356–7
 likely to breach Art.101 TFEU 358
agricultural property relief (APR) 114, 116
 additional rule for lifetime transfers 117
aircraft
 roll-over relief 103

aliens
 restrictions on political activity of 393
allowable expenditure
 capital gains tax 98–9
alterations
 wills 210–1
alternative business structures (ABSs) 4–5, 8
amount payable
 VAT 166–7
annual exempt amount 100
annual exemptions 122–3
annuities
 income tax 77
anti-competitive activity
 EU law 355–61
appeals
 income tax 88–9
 inheritance tax 110
apportionments
 statutory and equitable 287
appreciating assets 143
appropriation
 legacies 310
 matrimonial home 224
 personal representatives' power of 288
arm's length
 sale at 97
Article 101 TFEU 356–62
 sanctions for breach of 359
Article 101(1) TFEU
 exemptions to 359–61
Article 267 reference procedure 338–9
assembly
 freedom of 393
assents 317–18
 effect 317
 form 317–18
 power to 317
 protection of beneficiaries 318
 protection of personal representatives 318
 protection of purchasers 318
assessment
 basis of 171–2
assets
 chargeable 96–7
 collecting/realising 299–301
 disposals of pert 106
 duty to collect deceased's 285
 related property 113
 sales of 300–1
 transfer 317

association
   freedom of 393
attestation clauses 204–5
authorisation 56
   need for under FSMA 2000 44–7
authorised persons 319
   under FSMA 2000 44

B

back-duty cases 89
   inheritance tax 110
bail 381–2
bank interest
   income tax 74
bank loans
   for payment of inheritance tax 255
bankruptcy orders 304–5
bare trusts 193
beneficiaries
   contingent pecuniary legacies 320
   date for payment of entitlement under will or intestacy 319
   dying before testator 214
   with no right to trust income 195
   pecuniary legacies 320
   protection of 318
   remedies available to 320–1
   residuary gifts 320
   with right to trust income 194–5
   rights of 319–20
   settlements 193
   specific gifts 319
benefits in kind
   close companies 155–6
Benjamin Orders 296
bereaved minors
   trusts for 186, 188
bereaved young persons
   trusts for 1, 9, 186
bill delivered basis 171
blind person's allowance 83
block exemptions
   Art.101(1) TFEU 360–1
Board of HM Revenue & Customs
   role of 69–71
borrower
   acting for lender and 29
building society accounts
   risk 42
building society interest
   income tax 74
buildings
   roll-over relief 103
burden of proof
   reverse 383
business
   definition 163
   personal representatives' power to run deceased's 290–1
business assets 102
business ceasing
   closing-year rules 174
business incorporation
   carry-forward relief on 182
   roll-over relief 103

business property
   qualifying for BPR 115
business property relief (BPR) 114–15
   additional rule for lifetime transfers 115
business start-up
   opening-year rules 172–3

C

calculation
   capital gains tax 97–9
   chargeable gains 150–1
   corporation tax 156–8
   Form IHT 400 283
   income tax 75, 89–91
   lifetime chargeable transfer 119–22
   total income 76–7
   trading profits 170
capacity *see also* **mental capacity**
   grants of representation 272–3
   personal representatives 247–8
capital
   personal representatives' powers to advance 293–4
capital account 315–16
capital allowances 149, 170, 177–80
capital gains
   carry-across against 181
   carry-back against 181
capital gains tax (CGT) 68, 93–107, 306–7
   administration 69–70
   allowable expenditure 98–9
   basic structure 93
   calculations 97–9
   capital losses 99–100
   charities 95
   civil partners 104–5
   collection of 93
   companies 95
   consideration for disposal 97–8
   determining liability 95
   entrepreneur's relief 101
   exemptions 100–4
   gifts 98
   hold-over relief 101–2
   incidental cost of disposal 98
   individuals 94
   initial expenditure 98
   instalment option 105
   land 105
   legacies 311
   liability for 94–5
   non-chargeable persons 94–5
   partners 94
   payment of 94
   personal representatives 95, 105
   private dwelling house 100–1
   rates 104–5
   reliefs 100–4
   sales at arm's length 97
   sales at undervalue 97
   sales between connected persons 97–8
   settlements 191–3
   shareholdings 105
   sources of law 93
   spouses 104–5

subsequent expenditure 98
trustees 94, 105
capital loss relief 151
capital losses 99–100
capital profits 93
Capital Taxes Office
role of 70
carry-across
against capital gains 181
against other income 180–1
carry-across relief 149–50
carry-back
against capital gains 181
carry-back relief 149–50
carry-forward
against future profits 181
carry-forward relief 150
business incorporation 182
cartels
criminal offences for 368
cash
as chargeable assets 96
cash basis 171
Cassis de Dijon case 343–4
chargeable assets 96
chargeable gains
calculation 150–1
chargeable persons
capital gains tax 94
chargeable receipts 148, 170
chargeable transfers
excluded assets 111
inheritance tax 110–11
legislation governing 110–11
charges
VAT 162–3
charges on income 151–2
charging basis
immediate post-death interests trusts 189
charging clauses
wills 313–4
charitable trusts 190
charities
capital gains tax 95
children
definition 217
financial provision 234, 237–8
gifts to in wills 217–18
citizenship
EU 347
civil partner standard 234–5
civil partners
capital gains tax 104–5
disposals 96
financial provision 233
civil partnership exemption
inheritance tax 143
civil partnerships
gifts in consideration of 123
revocation of will by 208
termination of affecting rights of workers 349
civil service salaries 244
class gifts 217
class-closing rules 217–18
clearing off 271–2

client awareness 8
client care 16–17, 20–1
clients 16–18
complaints 18–19
identifying 29–30
instructions 19–20
publicly funded 18
resources 19–20
close companies
benefits in kind 155–6
corporation tax 154–6
gifts 155
participators 155
close investment holding companies
rates of tax 156
close trading companies
loans to invest in 81
closing-year rules 174
Code of Conduct 3, 5
structure 13–14
codicils
revocation of will by 209
wills 206
cohabitants
financial provision 233, 237
collection
capital gains tax 93
income tax 74
inheritance tax 110
collective investment schemes 46
collectors of taxes
role of 69
commercial awareness 8–9
commercial clients 30
commercial property
free movement of goods 345
Commission of Human Rights 374
Committee of the Regions 330
commorientes 214
companies
capital gains tax 95
corporation tax 147–58
as taxpayers 72
Competence Office for Finance and Administration
requirement to appoint 16
competition
legal profession 5
competition law
abuse of dominant position 362–4
agreements between undertakings 355–6
anti-competitive activity 356–62
Art.101 TFEU 355–61
concerted practice 356–7
De minimis Notice 358–9
differences between UK and EU 367–8
EU 355–66
limited immunity 368
preventing, restricting or distorting competition 358
prohibitions 367
UK or EU applicable 367
United Kingdom 366–8
complaints
clients 18–19
Compliance Officer for Legal Practice
requirement to appoint 16

408 Index

compulsory registration
    VAT 163–4
concerted practice 356–7
conditional fee agreements 18
conditional revocation
    wills 210
Conduct of Business Rules 52
confidentiality 23–5
    money laundering 62–3
conflicts of interest 22–4, 30–1
connected persons
    sales between 97–8
conscience
    freedom of 391
consumers
    legal services 3–4
contingent interest trust 186
contingent liabilities
    personal representatives 297
contingent pecuniary legacies
    beneficiaries 320
contracts of insurance 46, 51
Convention rights
    abuse of rights 393
    disclosure and bail 381–2
    European Convention on Human Rights 1950 379–94
    judicial remedies 394–5
    limitation on use of restriction on 394
    prohibition of slavery and forced labour 380
    prohibition of torture 380
    right to fair trial 382–90
    right to liberty and security 380–1
    right to life 379
    right to review 382
conversations
    written records 10–11
conveyancing
    undertakings 28–9
copyright
    free movement of goods 345
corporation tax 68, 147–58
    administration 69–70
    basic structure 147
    calculation 154, 156–8
    close companies 154–6
    payment 154
    rates 152–3
corrective accounts
    inheritance tax 312
costs
    client care 17
    conditional fee agreements 18
    publicly funded clients 18
    recording 8–9
Council of Ministers 328
Court of First Instance *see* General Court
courts
    as public bodies 373–4
covert intelligence 389
creditors
    statutory order 301–2
crime
    cash proceeds from 59–60
criminal offences
    cartels 368

criminal proceedings
    right to fair trial 383
Crown
    intestacy 225
cumulation
    principle of 117–18
currency 46
customer due diligence measures 61–2
customs duties
    free movement of goods 343

D

date
    disposals 97
date for payment
    income tax 87–8
    VAT 166
De minimis Notice 358–9
dealing
    investments 45
death
    disposals 96
    inheritance tax 110
    registration 253–4
    settlements created on 187, 192
    transfer of value on 112, 132–9
    value of estates immediately before 133
death certificate 253–4
death in service benefits 229
debenture interest 74
debts
    payment (insolvent estates) 303–5
    payment (solvent estates) 301–3
    statutory order of creditors 301–2
deceased's free estate 141
decisions
    direct effect 336
deductible expenditure 148–9, 170
deduction at source 74, 86–8
deductions
    personal reliefs treated as income tax 82–3
default surcharge
    VAT 167
delegation
    personal representatives 290
demonstrative legacies 213
dependants 231–2
    rights of workers 349
deposits 46
derogations
    human rights 377
designated professional bodies 47–8
destruction
    revocation of will by 209–10
devises 308–9
diary
    importance of 10
dictation 11
direct effect
    concept of 333–6
    decisions 336
    directives 334–5
    horizontal direct effect 335
    indirect effect 335–6

opinions 336
recommendations 336
regulations 336
treaty articles 334
directives
direct effect 334–5
EU 351–2
discharge
estate accounts 316–17
disclaimers
administration of estates 305–6
disclosure 24–6, 381–2
right to fair trial 383–4
Disclosure of Information in Criminal Proceedings 374, 383
discretionary trusts 185
discrimination
prohibition of 393
disposals
actual 192
capital allowances 178–9
chargeable 96–7
civil partners 96
consideration for 97–8
date 97
death 96
notional 192–3
part of asset 106
spouses 96
dispositions
for family maintenance 111
dissolution of civil partnership
revocation of will by 209
distorting competition 357–9
distribution account 315
distribution estates 308
distributions of profit 153–4
diversity 22
dividends
income tax 74, 77
divorce
affecting rights of workers 349
revocation of will by 208–9
dominant position
abuse of 362–4
affecting trade between Member States 364
definition 362
exemptions 365
factors relating to 364
relevant market 362–4
sanctions 365
donationes mortis causa 230, 302
donees 102
donors 102
duty of care
trustees and personal representatives 286

E

earnings basis 171
Economic and Social Committee 330
education
freedom to provide services 353–4
right to 394
elections

free 394
entitlement
estates 201–39
grant of letters of administration 245–6
intestacy 220
order of 225
surviving spouse/civil partner 221–4
entrapment 387–8
entrepreneur's relief 101
equality 21
equality of arms 374, 381
equitable apportionments 287
estate accounts 314–17
estates 132–3
definition 132
distribution 308
duty to administer 286
entitlement to 201–39, 273
issue 222
life interest 223
not forming part of succession estate but forming part of deceased's estate for IHT purposes 230
personal chattels 222–3
spouse/civil partner 221–2
whole blood relatives 223
excluded property 132
intestate 224
liabilities 132
payment of debts 301–3
related property 132
size and nature of 236
small sums due to 244
value immediately before death 133
value of 132
European Central Bank 331
European Commission 327–8
European Convention on Human Rights 1950
Convention rights 379–94
incorporation into UK law 374
limited rights under 375
as 'living instrument' 378–9
misconceptions regarding 375
Protocols 379
qualified rights under 375–6
state limitations 376
European Council 328–9
European Court of Auditors 330
European Court of Human Rights 374
European Court of Justice (ECJ) 329–30
European Investment Bank 330
European Ombudsman 330–1
European Parliament 329
European System of Central Banks 331
European Union (EU)
abuse of dominant position 362–5
Article 267 reference procedure 338–9
citizenship 347
competition law 355–66
direct effect 333–6
directives 351–2
enforcement of law against Member States 340
free movement of goods 342–7
free movement of persons 347–51
freedom of establishment 351–2
freedom to provide services 352–4

European Union (EU) *(cont.)*
  freedom to receive services 354
  fundamental rights 368–9
  harmonization 354
  institutions 327–31 *see also individual institutions*
  international agreements with non-Member States 352
  judicial review 339–40
  law of 327–70
  merger control 364–5
  regulations 351–2
  relationship between EU and national law 333–7
  remedies 338–41
  secondary legislation 351–2
  seeking remedy in national courts 340–1
  sources of law 351–3
  state liability 341
  supremacy of law 336–7
  treaties 351
  workers' rights 348–9
evidence
  inadmissible 384
  unfairly obtained 387–90
ewe and suckler cow quotas
  roll-over relief 103
excepted estates 264–5, 276–80
  claim to transfer unused nil rate band for 279–80
  definition 277–8
excluded activities
  SRA 50–1
  under FSMA 2000 46
excluded assets
  chargeable transfers 111
excluded property
  estates 132
executors 245, 249
  grants of representation 243–4
  oaths 258, 261, 263–4
  partners in firm 264
  powers reserved 250
  relationship with deceased 263
  renunciation 249
exempt persons
  under FSMA 2000 44
exempted suppliers
  VAT 174
exempted supplies
  VAT 161
exemptions
  Art.101(1) TFEU 359–61
  capital gains tax 100–4
  dominant position 365
  inheritance tax 122–6, 143
expenditure
  deductible 148–9
  out of income 123–4
expenses
  administration of estates 312–13
  personal representatives 290
expression
  freedom of 392–3
extra-statutory concessions
  HM Revenue & Customs statements 69

F

failure
  consequences of legacies 216

  gifts 212–17
  gifts to witnesses 215–16
  legacies 213–15
families
  rights of workers 349
family life
  right to respect for 390–1
family provision 231–2
family provision orders
  inheritance tax 238
  property available for 238–9
  types of 238
fees 18
financial instruments 46
financial promotions 49, 52
financial provision 231–2
  application for 232–3
  ascertaining whether grant of representation has been issued 232–3
  basis for claims 232
  categories of applicant 233–4
  children 234, 237–8
  civil partners 233
  cohabitants 233, 237
  evidence of testator's reasons 235–6
  former civil partners 233
  former spouses 233
  guidelines 235–8
  maintenance standard 235
  moral obligation 236
  physical or mental disability 236
  protection of personal representatives from personal liability 232–3
  reasonableness 234–6
  spouses 233
  stepchildren 234
  surviving civil partners 236–7
  surviving spouse 236–7
  test for 235–6
  time limit for applications 232
financial return 41
financial services 41–58, 298–9
  use of authorised person 319
Financial Services and Markets Act 2000
  authorisation 44
  background to 43–4
  effects of 43
  exemptions 44
  general prohibitions under 44
  regulatory objectives of 43–4
  relevance to solicitors 47–8
  sanctions under 44
firemen's pensions 244
forced labour
  prohibition of 380
Form IHT 400 280–3
  calculation 283
former civil partners
  financial provision 233
former spouses
  financial provision 233
fraud 9
free movement of goods 342–7
  copyright 345
  customs duties 343
  exceptions to Art.34 TFEU 344–7
  health 345

intellectual property 345
patents 345
protection of health and life of humans, animals and plants exception 345
protection of industrial and commercial property 345
protection of national treasures 345
public morality exception 344
public policy exception 344
public security exception 345
quantitative restrictions 343–4
rule of reason 346–7
trademarks 345
treaty provisions 342–3
free movement of persons 347–51
treaty provisions 347
free movement of workers
exceptions to Art.45 350–2
public health exceptions 351
public policy exceptions 350–1
public security exceptions 350–1
freedom of assembly and association 393
freedom of establishment
EU 352
freedom of expression 392–3
freedom of thought, conscience and religion 391
freedom to provide services
education and training 353–4
EU 352–3
professional conduct 354
freedom to receive services
EU 355
friendly societies
monies payable on death of member 244
fundamental rights (EU) 368–9
funeral expenses 304
funeral plan contracts 46
future 46
future liabilities
personal representatives 297
future profits
carry-forward against 181

G

gains
calculation 97–9
setting losses against 99
General Commissioners 88
General Court (formerly Court of First Instance) 329–30
general legacies 213
gifts 101–2
capital gains tax 98
close companies 155
failure 212–17
failure of, to witnesses 215–16
inheritance tax 123–4
subject to reservation 139–40
to children in wills 217–18
gifts with reservation of benefit
intestacy 230
goodwill
roll-over relief 103
government securities 46
grants of representation 232–3
administrators 244
application for 241–84
background 241–2

capacity in which sought 272–3
court's requirements 257
effect of issue 243–4
executors 243–4
limited grants 246
lodging papers 256
mental incapacity 248
minors 247
non-contentious business 242
obtaining grant 251, 253
preparing papers for 254
probate jurisdiction 241–2
registering 299–300
special grants 247
where not necessary 244
gratuitous benefit 111
grossing up 77–9
lifetime chargeable transfer 120–2
Guide to the Professional Conduct and Etiquette of Solicitors, A 5

H

Handbook
background to 13
mandatory parts 13–14
structure of 11–12
harmonization
EU 354
health
free movement of goods 345
hearsay 384
HM inspectors of taxes
role of 69
HM Revenue & Customs 159
statements 69
hold-over relief 101–2
horizontal direct effect 335
horizontality
human rights 374
hovercraft
roll-over relief 103
human rights 368–9, 373–95
background to legislation on 373–4
derogations 377
equality of arms 374
general principles 374
horizontality 374
proportionality 377
public policy 377
reservations 377
Human Rights Act 1998
effects of 374

I

immediate post-death interests trusts 186, 189
charging basis 189
termination 189–90
immunity
limited 368
inadmissible evidence 384
incidental cost of disposal
capital gains tax 98
income
calculation of profits 147–8
chargeable sources 77

income (*cont.*)
   charges on 151–2
   definition 73
   limit for age-related allowances 85–6
income account 315
income tax 68, 73–91
   administration 69–70
   appeals 88–9
   basic structure of 73
   blind person's allowance 83
   calculations 75, 89–91
   collection 74
   date for payment 87–8
   deduction at source 74
   grossing up 77–9
   legacies 311
   liability for 73–4
   liability of partnerships 169–70
   loans 80–2
   personal allowance (PA) 82–3
   personal reliefs treated as deductions 82–3
   personal representative 76
   rates 75–6
   reliefs 80–2
   savings income 76
   self assessment 74
   settlements 193–4
   sources of law 73
   trustees 76
incorporation by reference
   wills 211–12
indemnity
   personal representatives 296
indicative behaviour 14
indicative outcomes 11
indirect effect 335–6
individual exemptions
   Art.101(1) TFEU 361
individuals
   annual exempt amount 100
   capital gains tax 94, 104
   as taxpayers 71
industrial buildings
   capital allowances 179–80
industrial property
   free movement of goods 345
industrial societies
   monies payable on death of member 244
ineffective alterations
   wills 211
inferences from silence 384–5
inheritance tax (IHT) 68, 109–46, 306–7
   administration 70, 110
   appeals 110
   appreciating assets 143
   back duty cases 110
   basic structure 109–10
   chargeable transfers 110–11
   civil partnership exemption 143
   collection 110
   corrective accounts 312
   death 110
   exemptions 122–6, 143
   family provision orders 238
   funds for payment of 254–6
   gifts 123–4
   instalment option 141–2
   interest 142
   intestacy 225
   legacies 311–12
   liability 140–2
   life policies written in trust 124
   lifetime chargeable transfer 112–13
   loans to pay 81–2
   occasions to tax 112–19
   personal representatives 297–8
   rates 117
   sale of assets 300–1
   settlements 186–91
   sources of law 110
   spouse exemption 143
initial expenditure
   capital gains tax 98
input tax 161–2
insolvent estates 303–5
instalment option
   capital gains tax 105
   entitlement 142
   inheritance tax 141–2
instructions
   clients 19–20
insurance 289
   personal representatives 296
integration
   money laundering 60
intellectual property
   free movement of goods 345
intention
   wills 204
interest
   corporation tax 154
   income tax 74, 77
   inheritance tax 142
   unpaid VAT 168
interest in possession trust 185–6
interest in property
   potentially exempt transfers 141
interference
   public authorities 376, 391
international agreements with non-Member States
   EU 352
intestacy 219–39
   basic position 220–1
   Crown 225
   donationes mortis causa 230
   entitlement 220
   gifts with reservation of benefit 230
   inheritance tax 225
   issue 222, 224–5
   life assurance 229
   life interests in trust property 230
   order of entitlement 225
   pension scheme benefits 229
   personal chattels 222–3
   property not forming part of deceased's estate for succession or IHT purposes 230–1
   property not passing under rules of 226
   property passing outside rules of 226–8
   statutory nominations 229–30
   statutory provisions 220
   statutory trusts 220–1
   trust policies 228–9

whole blood relatives 223
Intestacy and Family Provision Claims on Death 219
intrusive surveillance 391
inventory 286
investment business 298–9
investments 41–3, 399–403
  advice 45
  dealing 45
    as agent 45
  definition 41
  managing 45
  powers of personal representatives 291–2
  statutory nominations 229
  types of 400–2
issue
  intestacy 222, 224–5

J

joint property 112, 114
judicial review
  EU law 339–40
jurat
  oaths 265

L

land
  assent 317–18
  capital gains tax 105
  investment in 46
  purchase by personal representatives 292
  roll-over relief 103
  sale within four years of death 133
lapse
  legacies 214–15
later will
  revocation of will by 209
Law Commission 219
  Consultation Paper No.191 244
law firms
  ownership and structure 5
Law Society 3, 5–6, 16, 51–3
  designated professional body 47
layering
  money laundering 60
lease
  personal representatives' powers to raise 287–8
legacies 213
  abatement 310
  appropriation 310
  ascertainment of residue 311–14
  consequences of failure of 216
  failure of 213–15
  payment of 308–11
  receipts 310–11
legal aid 384
legal ethics
  historical perspective 4–6
legal profession
  competition 5
legal services
  changes in market 3
  export of 5
Legal Services Board 52

lender
  acting for borrower and 29
letters of administration 243, 246
  with will annexed 243, 245–6
liberty
  right to 380–1
life assurance
  intestacy 228–9
life interest 223
  oaths 272
  residuary estates 223–4
life interests in trust property 230
life policies
  roll-over relief 104
  written in trust 124
lifetime chargeable transfers (LCTs) 112–13, 119–26, 130, 140
  additional tax due on death 140
  calculation 119–22
  date due for payment 140
  grossing up 120–2
  made seven years preceding date of death 137–9
  rates 119
  related property 120
lifetime gifts 142–3
lifetime settlements 191–2
lifetime transfers
  additional rule for 115, 117
limited grants
  grants of representation 246
limited immunity
  competition law 367
litigation 25, 29
'living instrument'
  European Convention on Human Rights 1950 as 378–9
loan from beneficiary
  for payment of inheritance tax 255
loans
  income tax 80–2
  to invest in close trading companies 81
  to invest in partnerships 80
  to pay inheritance tax 81–2
  to personal representatives to pay inheritance tax 81–2
lodging papers
  grants of representation 256
loss on sale reliefs 300
losses
  carrying forward 100
  setting against gains 99
lower rate
  VAT 160

M

machinery
  capital allowances 178
magistrates' courts 374
main rate
  corporation tax 152
maintenance
  dispositions for 111
maintenance payments
  withdrawal of tax relief on 86
maintenance standard
  financial provision 235

management
  investments 45
marginal rate
  corporation tax 153
market value 98
marriage
  gifts in consideration of 123
  revocation of will by 207–8
  right to 93
marshalling
  equitable doctrine of 303
matrimonial home
  appropriation of 224
  definition 224
Member States
  enforcement of EU law against 340
membership
  changes in partnerships 175–7
mental capacity
  common law test for 202
  lack of 203
  proof of 203
  statutory provisions 203
  wills 202–3
mental disability
  financial provision 236
mental incapacity
  grants of representation 248
merger control
  EU 364–5
migrant workers 348–9
  dependants 349–50
  divorce or termination of civil partnership affecting rights of 349
  exceptions to Art.45 350–2
  rights of families of 349–50
migration
  workers' rights 348
milk quotas
  roll-over relief 103
minority interests
  oaths 272
minors
  grants of representation 247
  maintenance by personal representatives 292–3
  property 288–9
money laundering 59–63
  confidentiality 62–3
  EU law pertaining to 59
  integration 60
  layering 60
  offences 60–1
  placement 59–60
  primary legislation pertaining to 60–1
  privilege 63
  professional conduct issues 62–3
  relevance to solicitors 61–3
Money Laundering Act 2007
  key requirements under 61–2
moral obligation
  financial provision 236
mortgage contracts 46
mortgages
  personal representatives' powers to raise 287–8
motor cars
  capital allowances 179
  as chargeable assets 96

moveable assets 96
moveable property
  exemptions from CGT 100
mutual recognition of qualifications 353–4
mutual wills
  revocation 207

N

name
  problems associated with 261
national courts
  correcting legal or factual errors made by 393
  seeking remedy against EU law in 340–1
National Savings Bank
  money held in 244
National Savings Certificates 244
national treasures
  free movement of goods 345
nil-rate band
  transfer of 135–6
nominated property 230
non-chargeable persons
  capital gains tax 94–5
non-contentious business
  grants of representation 242
non-investment services 50
non-real time communications 52
note taking 10–11
notification
  death 253–4
  late of liability for VAT registration 167
nullity of marriage
  revocation of will by 208–9

O

oaths 256–7, 261–5
  administrators with will annexed 265–8
  applicants 261–2
  clearing off 271–2
  court's requirements 274–5
  'customised' 258
  details of deceased 262–3
  entitlement to estate 273
  excepted estate 264–5
  executor's title 263–4
  form for administrators 269–70
  form for 59–60
  HMRC's requirements 275–6
  jurat 265
  minority and life interests 272
  order of applicants 271
  personal representatives 264
  settled land 263
  value of estate passing under grant 264–5
occupational pension schemes 229
Office of Fair Trading (OFT) 367–8
OFR Code 4, 8–12, 15–16
  application of 17–27
  scope of 6
  ten principles of 14–15
opening-year rules 172–3
opinions
  direct effect 336
options 46
output tax 161–2

overlap relief 175
ownership
  law firms 5

P

participators
  close companies 155
partners
  allocation of profits and losses between 180
  capital gains tax 94
  executors 264
  new 175–6
  retiring or deceased 177
partnerships
  allocation of profits and losses between partners 180
  capital allowances 177–80
  changes in membership 175–7
  income tax liability 169–70
  loans to invest in 80
  taxation of 169–81
  as taxpayers 71
patents
  free movement of goods 345
payment
  inheritance tax 254–6
payment into court
  personal representatives 296
pecuniary legacies 213, 309–10
  beneficiaries 320
penalties
  VAT 167–8
pension scheme benefits
  intestacy 229
pensions income
  income tax 77
persistent misdeclaration penalty
  VAT 167–8
personal allowance 82–3
personal chattels
  intestacy 222–3
personal reliefs
  treated as income tax deductions 82–3
  treated as income tax reductions 84–6
personal representatives 50
  administration of estates 294–5
  administrative powers 287–94
  annual exempt amount 100
  capacity 247–8
  capital gains tax 94, 105
  collecting/realising assets 299–301
  delegation by 290
  duties 264, 285–7
  duty of care 286
  executors 250
  financial services 298–9
  future and contingent liabilities 297
  income tax 76
  indemnity 296
  indemnity for expenses 290
  inheritance tax 297–8
  initial duties towards 242–3
  insurance 296
  investment powers 291–2
  liability 287
  loans to pay inheritance tax 81–2
  maintenance of minors 292–3
  marshalling 303
  not entitled to personal reliefs 82
  number 249
  payment into court 296
  personal action against 320–1
  power to advance capital 293–4
  power to appropriate 288
  power to run deceased's business 290–1
  powers to insure 289
  powers to sell, mortgage or lease 287–8
  protection from personal liability 232–3
  protection of 295–8, 305, 318
  purchase of land 292
  remuneration 313–14
  responsibilities of solicitors instructed by 242–3
  sale of assets 300–1
  several claimants 248
  as taxpayers 71
physical disability
  financial provision 236
placement
  money laundering 59–60
plant
  capital allowances 178
plant and machinery
  roll-over relief 103
police pensions 244
political activity
  restrictions on aliens 393
post-grant practice
  administration of estates 285–323
potato quotas
  roll-over relief 103
potentially exempt transfers (PETs) 111–12, 130–1
  death 141
  deceased's free estate 141
  due date for payment 141
  liability 141
  made in seven years preceding date of death 137–9
  property passing other than under deceased's will or intestacy 141
  settled property in which deceased had interest 141
powers reserved
  executors 250
Premium Savings Bonds 244
preventing competition 357–8
privacy 392
private dwelling house
  capital gains tax 100–1
private life
  right to respect for 390–1
privilege
  money laundering 63
probate 242, 245, 248
probate jurisdiction 241–2
professional bodies 48
professional conduct 11, 27–30
  freedom to provide services 354
  property 27
professional misconduct 5
professionalism 6–7, 12
profits
  apportionment on time basis between accounting periods 173–4
  calculation of 147–9
  distributions of 153–4
  income tax 77

property
  available for family provision orders 238–9
  conflicts of interest 27
  gift of 139–40
  minor's 288–9
  not forming part of deceased's estate for succession or IHT purposes 230–1
  not forming part of succession estate but forming part of deceased's estate for IHT purposes 230
  not passing under will or intestacy rules 226
  passing outside will or intestacy rules 226–8
  personal representatives' powers to sell, mortgage or lease 287–8
  professional conduct 27–8
  protection of 394
proportionality
  human rights 377
protection of health and life of humans, animals and plants exception
  free movement of goods 345
protection of property 394
Protocols
  European Convention on Human Rights 1950 379
provident societies
  monies payable on death of member 244
public authorities
  interference by 376, 391
public bodies
  courts and tribunals as 373–4
public funding 384
public health
  exceptions to free movement of workers 351
public interest immunity 385–7
public morality exception
  free movement of goods 344
public policy
  exceptions to free movement of workers 350–1
  human rights 377
public policy exception
  free movement of goods 344
public securities 46
public security
  exceptions to free movement of goods 345
  exceptions to free movement of workers 350–1
publicly funded clients 18
punctuality 10
punishment 390
purchasers
  protection of 318
pure personality
  assent 317

Q

qualifications
  mutual recognition of 353–4
qualifying business assets
  roll-over relief 103
  roll-over relief on replacement of 151
quantitative restrictions
  free movement of goods 343–4
quick succession relief 134
quotas 343

R

rates
  tax 75–6
  VAT 165
real-time communications 52
reasonableness
  financial provision 234–6
receipts
  legacies 310–11
recommendations
  direct effect 336
registration
  death 253–4
  VAT 163–4, 167
regulated activities
  under FSMA 2000 45
regulation
  changing 5
  diagrammatic representation 49
regulations
  direct effect 336
  EU 351–2
related property 113
  estates 132
  lifetime chargeable transfer 120
relationships 273–4
relevant market
  dominant position 362–4
reliefs 114–17
  capital gains tax 100–4
  income tax 80–2
  withdrawal from maintenance payments 87
religion
  freedom of 391
remedies
  available to beneficiaries 320–1
  EU law 338–41
remuneration
  personal representatives 313–14
rent
  income tax 77
renunciation
  administrators 250
representation
  grant of 232–3
reservation
  gifts subject to 139–40
reservations
  human rights 377
residents
  workers' rights 348
residuary beneficiaries 245
residuary estates
  life interest in 223–4
  trustees 245
residuary gifts
  beneficiaries 320
residuary legacies 213
residue
  legacies 311–14
resources
  clients 19–20
restricting competition 357–8
retired workers
  right to remain 348–9
revenue law 67–72
  case law 69
  EU dimension 68
  history of taxation 67
  main taxes 68

sources of 68
study of 67
reverse burden of proof
  right to fair trial 383
review
  right to 382
revocation
  mutual wills 207
  wills 207–10
right to education 394
right to fair trial 381–90
  hearsay 384
  inadmissible evidence 384
  inferences from silence 384–5
  legal aid 384
  public interest immunity 385–7
  unfairly obtained evidence 387–90
right to life 379
right to marry 393
right to respect for private and family life 390–1
risk
  investments 42–3
roll–over relief
  business incorporation 103
  life policies 104
  on replacement of qualifying business assets 103, 151
rule of law 376
rule of reason
  free movement of goods 346–7

S

salaries
  income tax 74
sale of assets 300–1
  inheritance tax 300–1
  for payment of inheritance tax 255
sale at arm's length 97
sale of land
  within four years of death 133
sales
  between connected persons 97–8
sales at undervalue 97, 101–2
sanctions
  dominant position 365
savings income
  income tax 76
searches
  administration of estates 295–6
secondary legislation
  EU 351–2
secured creditors 301, 303–4
security
  right to 380–1
self assessment
  income tax 74
serious misdeclaration penalty
  VAT 167
service pensions 244
settled land
  oaths 263
settled property 193
  definition 191
settlements
  background to creation of 185–6
  beneficiaries 193
  capital gains tax 191–3

created on death 192
creation of 187
definition 186–7
income tax 193–4
inheritance tax 186–91
liability of trustees 187–91
rates of tax 188
taxation of 185–96
settlors
  liability of 191–2
  settlement created during lifetime of 187
several claimants
  personal representatives 248
shareholdings
  capital gains tax 105
  death of holder 253–4
shares 46, 102
  risk 42
  sale of within 12 months of death 133
ships
  roll-over relief 103
signatures
  wills 205–6
silence
  inferences from 384–5
slavery
  prohibition of 380
small companies' rate
  corporation tax 153
small gifts exemption 123
social security
  income tax 77
sole proprietors
  capital allowances 177–80
  taxation of 169–81
Solicitors Financial Services Scope Rules 48, 51–2
Solicitors Regulation Authority (SRA) 3, 6, 48–55
  enrolling as student member 7–8
  excluded activities 50–1
Special Commissioners 88
  role of 70
special grants
  grants of representation 247
specialised courts 329–30
specific gifts
  beneficiaries 319
specific legacies 213, 308–9
spouse exemption
  inheritance tax 143
spouses
  capital gains tax 104–5
  disposals 96
  financial provision 233
standard rate
  VAT 160
standard of service 10
start-up loss relief 182
state liability 341
state limitations
  European Convention on Human Rights 1950 376
statements of practice
  HM Revenue & Customs statements 69
statutory apportionments 287
statutory income 182
  applying rates of tax to 83–4
statutory nominations 229
statutory substitutional clauses 215

statutory trusts
  intestacy 220–1
stepchildren
  financial provision 234
stock market
  terminology 402
student members
  SRA 7–8
subsequent expenditure
  capital gains tax 98
substitutional gifts 215
supply of goods
  definition 162
supply of goods and services
  categories of 160
  value of 163
  VAT chargeable on 162
  VAT rating 160
supply of services
  definition 162
surviving spouse
  financial provision 236–7
surveillance
  intrusive 391
surviving civil partners
  financial provision 236–7
surviving spouse standard 233–5
surviving spouse/civil partner
  entitlement 221–4
  special rules applying to 223–4
survivorship clauses 190–1

T

tangible assets 46
tangible moveable property 96
  exemptions from CGT 100
taper relief 127–8, 131, 142–3
tax avoidance 72
tax districts
  role of 69
tax evasion 72
tax invoices
  VAT 165–6
tax law *see* revenue law
tax planning 72, 106–7, 142–3
tax point
  VAT 164–5
tax reductions
  personal reliefs treated as 84–6
tax year 74
taxable income 183
taxable persons
  definition 162
  VAT registration 163
taxable profits
  corporation tax 147
taxation
  diagrammatic representation of administration 70
  evolving 67
  history of 67
taxation basis
  assessment 171–2
taxes
  types of 68
taxpayers 71–2

terminal loss relief 182
testamentary expenses 304
testator's reasons
  financial provision 235–6
third parties
  relations with 25–6
thought
  freedom of 391
time recording 9–10
torture
  prohibition of 380
total income
  calculating 76–7
tracing 321
trade unions
  monies payable on death of member 244
trademarks
  free movement of goods 345
trading loss relief 149–50, 180–1
trading profits 146–7
  calculation 170
training
  freedom to provide services 353–4
transfer of assets 317
transfers of value 111, 123–4, 132–9
  close companies 155
Treasury
  role of 69–70
treaties
  direct effect 334
  EU 351
Treaty of Lisbon 369
Treaty of Maastricht 369
tribunals
  as public bodies 373–4
trust income
  beneficiaries with no right to 195
  beneficiaries with right to 194–5
  income tax 74
trust policies
  intestacy 228–9
trust property
  life interests in 230
trustees 50
  annual exempt amount 100
  capital gains tax 94, 105
  duty of care 286
  income tax 76
  liabilities 187–95
  not entitled to personal reliefs 82
  residuary estate 245
  as taxpayers 71
trusts
  taxation of 185–96
  typing 10

U

undertakings 26
  agreements between 355–6
  conveyancing 28
  decision by association of 356
  definition 356
undervalue
  sales at 97
undue hardship 105

unfairly obtained evidence 387–90
unknown beneficiaries
   claims of 295
unsecured creditors 303–4

V

validity
   wills 202–6
value
   estates immediately before death 133
   estates 132
   transfers of 113–19, 123–4, 132–9, 155
value added tax (VAT) 68, 159–68
   accounting for 165–7
   administration of 70–1, 160
   amount payable 166–7
   charges 162–3
   date for payment 166
   default surcharge 167
   definition 159
   exempted supplies 161
   interest on unpaid 168
   late registration 167
   penalties 167–8
   persistent misdeclaration penalty 167–8
   rates 165
   registration 163–4
   serious misdeclaration penalty 167
   sources of law 159
   tax invoices 165–6
   tax point 164–5
   VAT records 166
value of estate passing under grant
   oaths 264–5
variations
   administration of estates 306
VAT Notices 159
VAT records 166
VAT tribunals
   role of 71
voluntary registration
   VAT 164

W

wasting assets 96
whole blood relatives
   intestacy 223

wills 199–200
   alterations 210–11
   attestation clauses 204–5
   basic requirements for 201
   capacity to make 202–3
   charging clauses 313–14
   checklist for 218–19
   class gifts 217
   codicils 206
   date effective 212–13
   failure of gifts by 212–17
   formalities 204–6
   gifts to children in 217–18
   incorporation by reference 211–12
   intention 204
   property not passing under 226
   property passing outside 226
   revocation 207–10
   sale of assets 300
   signature 205–6
   survivorship clauses 190–1
   validity 202–6
   witnesses 206
   written 205
witnesses
   failure of gifts to 215–16
   wills 206
woodlands relief 133–4
workers
   dependants 349
   divorce affecting rights of 349
   free movement of 348–9
   right to equal treatment 348
   right to migrate 348
   right to remain 348
   right to reside 348
   rights of families of 349
   termination of civil partnership affecting rights of 349
workers' rights 348–9
written records
   conversations 10
written wills 205

Z

zero rate
   VAT 160
zero-rated suppliers
   VAT 174

Taxation rates and allowances for 2011/12

Income Tax Thresholds

Basic rate	£0–£35,000
Higher rate	£35,001–£150,000
Additional rate	Over £150,000

Rates

Source of income	Basic rate	Higher rate	Additional rate
Non savings	20%	40%	50%
Savings	20%*	40%	50%
Dividends	10%	32.5%	42.5%

* Provided non-savings income does not exceed £2560, savings income up to £2,560 taxed at 10%

Trust Rate	50%
Personal Allowance	£7,475

Capital Gains Tax

Basic Rate	Highre and Additional Rate
18	28%
Rate for PRs and Trustees	28%
Annual Exempt Amount:	
Individuals:	£10,600
Trustees:	£5,300

Inheritance Tax

£0 - £325,000 (Nil Rate Band)	0%
Over £325,000	40%
Lifetime Transfers	20%

Corporation Tax

Small companies rate	£0 – £300,000	20%
Effective marginal rate	£300,001 – £1,500,000	27.5%
Standard rate	Over £1,500,000	26%

VAT

Registration threshold £73,000

Standard rate	20%
Lower rate	5%
Zero rate	0%